Management

A Skills Approach

SECOND EDITION

MANAGEMENT
A Skills Approach

Phillip L. Hunsaker

University of San Diego

PEARSON

Prentice Hall

Upper Saddle River, New Jersey 07458

Library of Congress Cataloging-in-Publication Data

Hunsaker, Phillip L.
    Management: a skills approach / Phillip L. Hunsaker.-- 2nd ed.
      p. cm.
    Rev. ed. of: Training in management skills. c2001.
    Includes bibliographical references and index.
    ISBN 0-13-144186-8
      1. Executives—Training of. 2. Management. 3. Interpersonal communication.
    4. Organization. I. Hunsaker, Phillip L. Training in management skills. II. Title.

    HD30.385.H869 2004
    658.4'07124--dc22

                                           2003064981

Acquisitions Editor: Michael Ablassmeir
Editorial Director: Jeff Shelstad
Editorial Assistant: Melissa Yu
Media Project Manager: Jessica Sabloff
Executive Marketing Manager: Shannon Moore
Marketing Assistant: Patrick Danzuso
Managing Editor: John Roberts
Production Editor: Kelly Warsak
Production Assistant: Joe DeProspero
Permissions Coordinator: Keri Jean Miksza
Manufacturing Buyer: Michelle Klein
Cover Design: Kiwi Design
Cover Illustration/Photo: Randy Faris/CORBIS
Composition: Laserwords
Full-Service Project Management: Heather Meledin/Progressive Publishing
Alternatives
Printer/Binder: Phoenix Color Corp.
Cover Printer: Phoenix Color Corp.

Credits and acknowledgments borrowed from other sources and reproduced, with
permission, in this textbook appear on appropriate page within text.

10 9 8 7 6 5 4
ISBN 0-13-144186-8

For my wife, Jo

Brief Contents

Contents

Contents

Preface

The need for training in managerial skills has been more pronounced over the last decade. Industry,[1] the media,[2] teaching faculty,[3] and the accrediting agencies of business school programs[4] have all noted the weakness in interpersonal skills among recent business graduates. A corporate recruiter succinctly summarized their concerns:

> Today's business graduates have an abundance of technical knowledge. They can do linear programming problems, calculate a discounted rate of return, develop a sophisticated marketing plan, and crunch numbers on a computer spreadsheet. They're technically solid, but most lack the interpersonal and social skills necessary to manage people. If there is an area where business schools need to improve, it's in developing the "people skills" of their graduates.[5]

Management is an applied topic, but if its classroom presentation traces the history of management research and theory development, it can leave students no better prepared to actually be a manager. Conceptual frameworks can provide business school graduates with needed information and ideas to understand management situations, but to become effective managers students need practice in behaving as managers and they need to receive feedback on their performance. The required shift today is from learning concepts for better understanding to learning skills for enhanced behaviors. As stated by one scholar of management education, "Management students need practice in motivating others to perform tasks and achieve goals, not just readings that compare and contrast six different theories of motivation."[6]

BACKGROUND OF THIS BOOK

Management faculty in colleges and universities have increasingly come to recognize the importance of developing managerial skill competencies in their students. To fulfill this need a number of skills books have been published over last 10 years, including *Training in Interpersonal Skills* (*TIPS*), the second edition of which I had the privilege of coauthoring with Steve Robbins.[7] *TIPS* is widely used in courses such as organizational behavior, management, human relations, supervision, organizational development, and interpersonal relations. It is also used in executive development programs where its action-oriented format favoring practicing and then receiving feedback, versus conceptual lectures, is especially effective. It particularly benefits practicing managers who have neither the time for long reading assignments, nor the patience to sit through hours of theoretical lectures. The growing need for management skills training coupled with the success of the *TIPS* learning formula generated the natural progression to create a comprehensive learning package covering the full gamut of managerial skills, as opposed to focusing on just "interpersonal" skills as *TIPS* and most of the other skills books do.

Another stimulus for creating a comprehensive management skills textbook came from the continual inquiries we receive from management professors for recommendations about supplemental readings they can put together with *TIPS* to form a complete management skills course. *TIPS* was created as a supplement to traditional management texts, which quite often do not provide opportunities for students to apply their conceptual learning. The role-plays in *TIPS* supply action-oriented exercises where students can receive feedback from their peers and develop action plans for real-world applications. Some professors were concerned, however, about the cost to the student of a comprehensive management text and another supplemental skills book.

Most often this problem is solved by combining *TIPS* with a smaller paperback "essentials" book, which summarizes the main management concepts from a complete hardback management text.[8] However, another problem remains: *TIPS* deals only with interpersonal skills, while management functions include additional conceptual and analytical skills. Consequently, professors wishing to provide practical training in the full range of skills considered essential for managerial success lack the exercises to do so. *Management: A Skills Approach* was a natural evolution to solve this problem. It combines the essential management concepts with training exercises for each of the critical skills required for students to improve their own personal management competencies.

Hence, *Management: A Skills Approach* provides a complete management skills training package. Additional textbooks or supplemental readings are not needed. In *Management: A Skills Approach*, the relevant concepts are presented as they apply to the specific behaviors necessary to successfully practice any given management skill. As one reviewer stated, "I feel that this material is super. This is the type of material that progressive schools are moving toward. This is the next step after the initial skills approaches to teaching management. You are to be commended in your insights and efforts to contributing to this progression."

ORGANIZATION OF THE BOOK

Each chapter of the book is organized around the learning model refined for *TIPS* from social learning theory, which combines relevant concepts with opportunities to practice and apply observable behaviors.[9] This learning model contains 10 components that ask students to do the following tasks:

- Assess their basic skill level.
- Review key concepts that are relevant to applying the skill.
- Test their conceptual knowledge.
- Identify on a checklist the specific behavioral dimensions that they need to learn for each skill.
- Observe how to apply the skill through watching others in a modeling exercise.
- Practice the skill in small groups.
- Use a summary checklist to identify their deficiencies.
- Answer application questions to cement practical understanding of the concepts.
- Complete reinforcement exercises outside the classroom.
- Develop an action plan for ongoing skill improvement in their own life.

The chapters and appendixes in this text each represent key skill areas essential for managerial success. After two introductory chapters explaining the field of management and general strategies to improve management skills, four integrative skills that are essential to effective management across a broad range of situations are presented so that they can be reinforced throughout the course. They include effective communication, time and stress management, diversity, and ethics. For instructors wishing to emphasize the critical communication skills of oral and written presentations, two skill-building appendixes are included at the end of the book. For the second edition, Appendix C on e-mail etiquette has been added.

The remainder of the book is organized around the traditional functions of management: planning, organizing, leading, and controlling. Part III presents the planning and control skills of goal setting, planning, evaluating performance, creative problem solving, and managing conflict. Part IV covers the organizing skills of designing work, identifying and hiring employees, creating high-performance teams, and diagnosing and modifying organizational culture. Part V explains the leadership skills of leading change management, building power bases, and motivating others.

SUPPLEMENTS

This book is accompanied by a user-friendly set of supplements, including the following:

Instructor's Manual

Each chapter includes learning objectives, an overview, a detailed lecture outline, and teaching notes to selected chapter exercises. Additional teaching suggestions also complement the chapters.

Test Item File

Each chapter contains multiple-choice, true-false, and essay questions. Together, the questions cover the content of each chapter in a variety of ways to test the students' knowledge of the text.

Computerized Test Bank

Containing all of the questions in the printed Test Item File, Computerized Test Bank is a comprehensive suite of tools for testing and assessment. The Test Bank allows educators to easily create and distribute tests for their courses, either by printing and distributing through traditional methods, or by online delivery via a local area network (LAN) server.

Instructor's Resource Center on CD-ROM

This CD-ROM contains the electronic Instructor's Manual, Test Manager, and Power-Point presentation. The PowerPoint slides, a comprehensive package of text outlines and figures corresponding to the text, are designed to aid the educator and supplement in-class lectures.

Companion Web Site

The Prentice Hall Companion Web Site, *<http://www.prenhall.com/hunsaker>*, features an interactive and exciting online Student Study Guide. Students can access multiple-choice, true/false, and Internet-based essay questions that accompany each chapter in the text. Objective questions are scored online, and incorrect answers are keyed to the text for student review. For more information, contact your local sales representative.

Skills Video

The Skills Video segments focus on a fictional video production company, Quick Takes Video. In these segments, professional actors address real business problems and the skills needed to manage them. Students receive questions throughout these segments and are asked to consider them. They then receive advice from experts in the field. The Skills Video offers a fun, hands-on way to view today's business world and learn the skills necessary to succeed within it.

Prentice Hall Self-Assessment Library CD-ROM

This library comprises 45 self-assessments, organized by individual, group, and organizational skills. Exercises are scored automatically and analyzed. It is also available in a printed format.

ACKNOWLEDGMENTS

The primary acknowledgment for this text goes to my friend and coauthor, Steve Robbins, who collaborated with me during the conceptual development and initial writing of the text. Steve's ideas, encouragement, and quality control are much appreciated.

The second, but no less significant, acknowledgment goes to my wife and colleague Jo Hunsaker, who endured the costs of my "grumpiness" and too frequent unavailability while I endeavored to complete trains of thought and book chapters. I am hopeful that my consistent underestimates of the time commitments required to complete this book will be understood as "enthusiastic optimism" and forgiven over time. I promise that I have learned to manage my time and priorities better as a result of this project.

I also want to share my gratitude to Dale Fetherling whose help in composing and editing some of the more technical chapters contributed immensely to the quality of this book. Without Dale's persistence, support, and contributions, this book would have been a lot longer reaching completion.

I am grateful to the members of the University of San Diego Research Committee for their confidence in me and for the support they provided to help me have the time to complete this manuscript. Thanks also to Curtis Cook, Dean of the School of Business Administration at the University of San Diego, for understanding and supporting my commitment to completing this book in lieu of other worthwhile university activities. Thank you Curtis, also, for agreeing to postpone for a time the third edition revision of our coauthored text, *Management and Organizational Behavior,* so that I could finish this one first.

Much appreciation also to the reviewers of both the book proposal and the reviews of the first chapter drafts. Your feedback, creative ideas, and helpful suggestions crested a much better learning package. People who formally reviewed the material and provided valuable feedback include:

- Forrest F. Aven, Jr.   University of Houston
- John D. Bigelow   Boise State University
- Joseph Garcia   Western Washington University
- Suzanne de Janasz   James Madison University
- Jay T. Knippen   University of South Florida
- Alison Konrad   Temple University
- Marian C. Schultz   University of West Florida
- Raymond C. Shea   Monroe Community College
- William Zachary   San Jose State University

Thanks also to the reviewers of the second edition who provided many valuable insights and suggestions. Significant contributions were made by:

- Josn Benek-Rivera   Bloomsburg University
- Penelope W. Brunner   University of North Carolina at Asheville
- Mildred Golden Pryor   Texas A&M University-Commerce

At Prentice Hall, a special thanks goes to my editor Mike Ablassmeir, whose confidence, understanding, and guidance were critical to this book's publication. I want to thank Melissa Yu whose coordinating skills guaranteed that all parts of this book were indeed organized and put together as required. I also want to thank Natalie Anderson without whose initial support and encouragement this book may never have even begun. Finally, my appreciation to Kelly Warsak and Shannon Moore, the people in production and marketing who made this book available in such an attractive and user-friendly form.

NOTES

1. American Assembly of Collegiate Schools of Business, "The Cultivation of Tomorrow's Leaders: Industry's Fundamental Challenge to Management Education," *Newsline* 23, no. 3 (Spring 1993): 1–3.
2. "The Battle of the B-Schools Is Getting Bloodier," *Business Week,* March 24, 1986, 61–70.
3. L. L. Cummings, "Reflections on Management Education and Development: Drift or Thrust Into the 21st Century?" *The Academy of Management Review* 15, no. 4 (October 1990): 694–96; M. Finney and C. Siehl, "The Current MBA: Why Are We Failing?" *The Organizational Behavior Teaching Review* X, no. 3 (1985–1986): 12–18.
4. L. W. Porter and L. E. Mckibbin, *Future of Management Education and Development: Drift or Thrust into the 21st Century?* (New York: McGraw-Hill, 1988).
5. S. P. Robbins and P. L. Hunsaker, *Training in Interpersonal Skills,* 2d ed. (Upper Saddle River, NJ: Prentice Hall, 1996) 1.
6. M. R. Blood, "The Role of Organizational Behavior in the Business School Curriculum," in J. Greenberg, ed., *Organizational Behavior: The State of the Science* (Hillsdale, NJ: Lawrence Erlbaum, 1994) 216.
7. Other management skills books include L. W. Mealiea and G. P. Latham, *Skills for Managerial Success: Theory, Experience, and Practice* (Burr Ridge, IL: Irwin, 1996); D. A. Whetten and D. S. Cameron, *Developing Management Skills,* 3rd ed. (New York: HarperCollins, 1995); R. N. Lussier, *Supervision: A Skill-Building Approach,* 2d ed. (Irwin, 1994); L. A. Mainiero and C. L. Tromley, *Developing Managerial Skills in Organizational Behavior: Exercises, Cases, and Readings,* 2d ed. (Upper Saddle River, NJ: Prentice Hall, 1994); C. T. Lewis, F. E. Garcia, and S. M. Jobs, *Managerial Skills in Organizations* (Allen & Bacon, 1990); R. E. Quinn, S. R. Faerman, M. P. Thompson, and M. R. McGrath, *Becoming a Master Manager* (New York: John Wiley & Sons, 1990); P. M. Fandt, *Management Skills: Practice and Experience* (St. Paul, MN: West, 1994).
8. For example, see S. P. Robbins, *Essentials of Management* (Upper Saddle River, NJ: Prentice Hall, 2001).
9. A. Bandura, *Social Learning Theory* (Upper Saddle River, NJ: Prentice Hall, 1977).

Management

A Skills Approach

PART I
Introduction

CHAPTER 1

Management Skills and Managerial Effectiveness

Learning Objectives

After completing this chapter, you should be able to:

■ Understand the nature of management.

■ Explain why skills are critical to management success.

■ Describe what skills are critical to management success.

■ Identify how this book will help you develop your skills.

CONCEPTS

Robert Allen is the chief executive officer (CEO) at AT&T. Michael Walsh is an elementary school principal in Tempe, Arizona. Mary Jean Giroux is a retirement-products supervisor at Canada's London Life Insurance Co. Theresa Gonzalez works as a regional director with the U.S. Internal Revenue Service. Yong Chang Chu is a construction foreman with Hong Kong-based Hutchison Whampoa. Even though these people have jobs with different titles and work in organizations that do different things, they all have one thing in common—they are **managers.** They all oversee the activities of other people with the purpose of accomplishing organizational goals.[1]

Most of you have reported to a boss at work, or a teacher in a classroom, who provided directions for what you were supposed to do. Now that you are preparing to

SOURCE: Dilbert © Distributed by United Features Syndicate. Reprinted by Permission.

become a manager, you may wonder what else managers do and what skills are required to do it. Management entails a big change and a much larger scope of responsibility. As a manager you become responsible for motivating others, for conveying or setting policies, and for relaying ideas between those above and below you on the organizational ladder. A new manager's success no longer is measured by how well he or she performs individually. It is tied to how well the new manager encourages and enables others to perform.

Managers give individuals, groups, and organizations direction. They provide formal leadership for people by clarifying what they are supposed to do. Managers coordinate the activities of those reporting to them with the activities of other units in an organization. They reduce ambiguity over performance outcomes by being accountable for achievement of performance goals. The success of organizations such as Microsoft, Southwest Airlines, Sony, General Electric, and the Dallas Cowboys football team is largely due to the quality of their management.

Management Functions

All of the previously listed activities can be broken down into four functions that all managers perform: planning, organizing, leading, and controlling. Although these activities provide a natural sequence for achieving a given goal, managers usually have many people working for them, striving for many different goals. Consequently, managers must be skilled at applying all of the four functions simultaneously. Each of these functions is described in the following paragraphs, along with the management skills necessary to effectively carry out the functions.

Because organizations exist to achieve some purpose, someone has to define that purpose and the means for its achievement. Management is that someone. The **planning** function encompasses defining an organization's goals, establishing an overall strategy for achieving those goals, and developing a comprehensive hierarchy of plans to integrate and coordinate activities.

Managers are also responsible for designing an organization's structure. This function is called **organizing.** It includes the determination of what tasks are to be done, who is to do them, how the tasks are to be grouped, who reports to whom, and where decisions are made in the organization.

Every organization contains people, and it is management's job to direct and coordinate those people through the **leading** function. When managers motivate employees, direct the activities of others, select the most effective communication channel, or resolve conflicts among members, they are engaging in leading.

The final function managers perform is **controlling.** After the goals are set, the plans formulated, the structural arrangements delineated, and the people hired, trained, and motivated, something may still go amiss. To ensure that things are operating as they should, management must monitor the organization's performance. Actual performance must be compared with the previously set goals. If any significant deviations are detected, it is management's job to get the organization back on track. This process of monitoring, comparing, and correcting constitutes the controlling function.

Management Skills

Twenty years ago, managers were valued primarily for their technical know-how. Most organizations identified outstanding people in the ranks, tapped them for promotions, and just trusted them to do well as managers. Today, increasing recognition is given to the importance of having managers and executives with strong interpersonal and communication skills.[2] In any line of work, the ability to be an outstanding technical performer does not always translate into the ability to be a good manager. Top salespeople

SOURCE: Dilbert © Distributed by United Features Syndicate. Reprinted by Permission.

do not necessarily make good sales managers. Top production workers do not necessarily make good supervisors. Top teachers do not necessarily make good principals. The list goes on.[3]

That is not to say that no skills are transferable. The work ethic that helps someone prosper in an entry-level job will continue to be a valuable tool in management. In addition, skills such as getting along with others are just as important for managers as they are for workers. Consequently, many new managers adapt and prosper. Success is less likely for a star performer who always relied on a skilled but solo route through the company. The performance of new managers today is rated as much on people skills as on measurable output.[4] Interviews by Price Waterhouse indicated that the trend reaches all the way up to CEOs who reported increased demands for sensitivity to human feelings because reshaping corporate culture and employee behavior was now equal in priority to monitoring financial information.[5]

In universities, instruction in management runs the gamut from highly theoretical research-based reviews of the literature, to hands-on courses where students learn about management by experiencing it in student-created and -run organizations. Skill building through experiential learning techniques such as interactive case discussions, role-playing, structured exercises, and work simulations have become an accepted added dimension to many college and university courses in human behavior.[6]

The premise of this book is that it's not enough just to *know about* managing organizations and people. You need to also be prepared to *do it!* Today's business organizations expect college graduates to possess skill competencies beyond content knowledge that enable them to effectively solve the problems inherent in a diverse and rapidly changing global environment.[7] **Management skills** identify those abilities or behaviors that are crucial to success in a managerial position. This chapter begins by elaborating on why skills are so important to managerial effectiveness. Then the general and specific skills you'll need to acquire to successfully manage others are identified.

The Importance of Management Skills

Would you want to submit yourself to an appendectomy if your surgeon had read everything available on the appendix and its removal but had never actually removed one before? You'd also be apprehensive if your surgeon had years of experience operating but had never studied the sciences of physiology and anatomy. Just as competent surgeons need both a sound understanding of how the body works and surgical skills finely honed through practice and experience, competent managers need a sound understanding of management functions and the opportunity to hone their behavioral skills through practice and experience.

Increasing amounts of evidence indicate that training programs focusing on management skills such as leadership, cultural awareness, communication, and self-awareness produce improvements in managerial performance.[8] This research has convinced business and public-sector organizations to cumulatively spend billions of dollars each year on development programs to improve their managers' skills. While it is true that nothing in the research suggests that skills training can magically transform every very incompetent manager into a highly effective leader, the evidence strongly demonstrates that these skills can be learned.[9] Although people differ in their baseline abilities, the research shows that skills training can result in better results for most people who want to improve their managerial effectiveness.

Recent articles have questioned whether business schools are adequately preparing students to cope successfully with the real challenges in organizations. The prevailing opinion is that academicians may be too interested in the theoretical knowledge of functional specialties such as marketing and finance, at the expense of turning out students with insufficient pragmatic people skills in such areas as creative problem solving, teamwork, and interpersonal communications. Based on these studies, the American Assembly of Collegiate Schools of Business, which accredits business schools, recommends the following:

> Business curricula should begin to address [interpersonal skills and personal characteristics] in a manner more nearly approximating the same explicit and systematic approach that characterizes the cognitive category if students are to be comprehensively prepared at the point of graduation for the managerial challenges ahead.[10]

Research had established four general skill areas[11] and six specific skill areas[12] that influence managerial effectiveness. Seventeen functional skills vital to success in management can be derived from these general and specific skill areas.

General Skills

Management scholars generally agree that effective managers must be proficient in four general skill areas.[13] *Conceptual skills* refer to the mental ability to analyze and diagnose complex situations. These skills allow managers to see how things fit together and facilitate making good decisions. *Interpersonal skills* encompass the ability to work with, understand, and motivate other people, both individually and in groups. Because managers rely on others to get things done, they must have good interpersonal skills in order to communicate, motivate, delegate, and resolve conflicts. Managers also need *technical skills*, which provide them with the ability to apply specialized knowledge or expertise. For top-level managers these abilities tend to be related to knowledge of the industry and a general understanding of the organization's processes and products. For middle and lower-level managers, they are related to the specialized knowledge required in the areas with which they work, such as finance, human resources, manufacturing, computer systems, law, and marketing. Finally, managers need *political skills*. This area is related to the ability to enhance one's position, build a power base, and establish the right connections. Organizations are political arenas in which people compete for resources. Managers with good political skills tend to be better at getting resources for their group than are managers with poor political skills. They also receive higher evaluations and get more promotions.[14]

Specific Skills

Research has identified six sets of behaviors that explain more than half of a manager's effectiveness.[15] They can be classified into the following general skill categories:

1. *Controlling the organization's environment and its resources.* The ability to be proactive and stay ahead of environmental changes is vital for planning and allocating resources, as well as for on-the-spot decision making. To achieve the

organization's objectives, resource decisions need to be based on clear, up-to-date, accurate knowledge.

2. ***Organizing and coordinating.***   In this skill, managers organize around tasks and then coordinate interdependent relationships among tasks wherever they exist.

3. ***Handling information.***   This set of behaviors comprises using information and communication channels for identifying problems, understanding a changing environment, and making effective decisions.

4. ***Providing for growth and development.***   Managers provide for their own personal growth and development, as well as for the personal growth and development of their employees, through continual learning on the job.

5. ***Motivating employees and handling conflicts.***   Managers enhance the positive aspects of motivation so that employees feel compelled to perform their work, while eliminating those conflicts that may inhibit employees' motivation.

6. ***Strategic problem solving.***   Managers take responsibility for their own decisions and ensure that subordinates effectively use their decision-making skills.

Required Skills for Managerial Competence

By integrating these specific skills and the previously discussed general skills into the functions of management, 17 skills that are vital to managerial success can be identified. These 17 skills also match up with the primary categories of the 41 skills, tasks, and attributes that literature searches have determined are needed for managers to successfully do their jobs.[16] They include the five skill sets of self-awareness, general/integrative, planning and control, organizing, and leading.

Self-Awareness Skills

It is difficult to improve ourselves unless we know our strengths and weaknesses. But because we all seek to protect, maintain, and enhance our self-concepts, we don't often focus on negative information about ourselves, much less seek it out. Sometimes we even avoid awareness of certain personal strengths if that knowledge would entail responsibilities we are not willing to undertake. Nevertheless, "know thyself" has been the cornerstone of advice of intellectuals to leaders for centuries. To manage others well, you must be able to manage yourself. To manage yourself well, you must know yourself well. Knowing yourself is certainly the first step in a skills development program.

Knowing Yourself   To know yourself better requires new knowledge about what you do, how you do it, and the consequences of your actions. Sometimes these insights can be acquired by self-observation of the consequences of your actions, but usually they are provided by others who share feedback about the their reactions to your behavior. Another way to learn about yourself is by taking self-assessment inventories that reveal certain attitudes, values, and knowledge bases. In the next chapter, you will take a set of self-assessment inventories to establish a baseline for your important values, attitudes, motives, and styles as they apply to effective management. Then at the beginning of each following chapter you will test your starting knowledge of each skill. Then, after completing each chapter, you will assess your acquired conceptual knowledge through a quiz, and receive performance feedback from peers, to determine what you have learned and whether still more is needed to increase your competence in the specific skill.

Developing Yourself   Self-knowledge isn't enough for skill development. You also have to want to improve. First, you have to be open to the possibility that you are not perfect and that you can become better. Next, you must be open to acquiring knowledge about yourself, which the majority of the time means listening nondefensively to feedback from others. Finally, you must be willing to risk and be assertive enough to try out new behaviors, which may not work perfectly the first time, and to keep practicing them until you become skilled in their application. Skill development requires a high degree of psychological investment. If you are unable or unwilling to make this kind of commitment, you may not even want to know the skills you could improve, let alone put the work into developing them.

Self-Directed Career Planning

Another aspect of self-development is career planning. In today's rapidly changing world, organizations no longer accept the responsibility for career development. So, to remain a valuable human resource, it is imperative that managers keep current and constantly upgrade needed skills. In the past, a skill learned in youth could provide a living for life. Now, technology changes so rapidly that as soon as you have learned something, that "something" may become obsolete. In this climate, employees are increasingly recognizing that "if you snooze, you lose." Learning is a lifelong process. Other people out there are keeping current, preparing themselves to assume your work responsibilities if you show signs of falling behind.

Some analysts say that workers can expect to change careers—not just jobs, but careers—three or four times during their working lives.[17] If they are right, today's worker must be prepared to go back to school and learn new skills at a minimum of every 5 to 10 years. Because fewer and fewer employers are providing this retraining, most employees will be balancing current work responsibilities with taking courses during their off hours. Self-directed careers require continuous training and learning.

General Integrative Skills

Managers need to have certain personal skills in order to behave competently across a broad range of organizational situations. They are interrelated to the functional area skills described in this book and need to be integrated into them in order to perform the functional skills most effectively. Regardless of whether managers are solving problems, working with teams, or creating change, they need to be able to communicate effectively, cope with diversity, uphold ethical principles, and effectively manage their time and stress.

Interpersonal Communicating You can have the greatest vision, plans, work designs, and performance teams, but if you cannot effectively communicate what is required, you will not succeed as a manager. Communication is the glue that holds an organization together and allows a manager to coordinate all the activities of many different people to accomplish organizational objectives. A successful manager is skilled in both formal and informal communications.

Managers are frequently required to address various groups of employees, customers, other managers, and the general public. Unfortunately, oral communication skills are often lacking in new managers as well as the majority of today's college graduates.[18] It is better to get over problems like stage fright and gain self-confidence through learning and practicing in a classroom setting, than it is to be thrown into a stressful situation on the job where you are unprepared to deliver an effective oral presentation.

Valuing Diversity The values, needs, interests, and expectations of workers have never been homogeneous, but the increased diversity in today's workforce requires managers to be on constant alert for differences. Managers need to understand that it is difficult for some employees to put in overtime hours without substantial notice, to work weekends, to be gone overnight on business, or to accept a transfer to a new location. Similarly, physical barriers such as narrow doorways or stairs can be troublesome for some employees. Managers cannot assume that all employees share a common mastery of English. In addition, managers have to be sure that employees are sensitive to coworkers who are different. That means being observant of overt expressions of sexism, racism, ageism, and more subtle biases within the work group.

Organizational environments are also filled with change and diversity. In his best-selling book *Thriving on Chaos: Handbook for a Management Revolution*,[19] management guru Tom Peters argued that successful managers in today's unpredictable environment must be able to thrive on change and uncertainty. The manager's job is increasingly one of juggling a dozen balls at once, in the dark, on the deck of a boat, during a typhoon! It requires turning an environment of chaotic change into an opportunity—the chance for well-managed organizations to gain a competitive advantage over rivals by being smarter, more flexible, quicker, more efficient, and better at responding to customer needs. Consequently, flexibility is required for a manager to cope successfully with temporariness and adapt successfully to change.

Developing Ethical Guideposts   Today's public has high standards for the behaviors of companies. Laws and lawsuits more frequently follow violations of formalized ethical standards, and competitors are quick to market how they are more ethical than other companies. Also, the behavior of managers is under greater scrutiny than ever before. Because the public has easier and greater access to information, misdeeds can almost instantly become widely known, damaging an organization's reputation and a manager's career.

Managing Time and Stress   Reports of high stress levels and job burnout among managers have risen as the work climate has become more chaotic and ambiguous.[20] Downsizing, reengineering, cost reductions, reduced job security, pressures to learn new skills, and heightened workloads all work to create a workplace that is increasingly stressful.[21]

When managers experience high stress levels, their performance is impeded as they become more dogmatic, less tolerant of ambiguity, less able to generate creative thoughts, and more prone to see events in a short-term, crisis mentality.[22] Considering that incompetent management is the largest cause of workplace stress for subordinates,[23] it is imperative that managers cope effectively with stress not only for their own well-being, but also for the survival of their employees and the entire organization.

One good way to reduce stress level is to effectively manage one's time. Management guru Peter Drucker has said that time is a manager's scarcest resource. Of course, we all have exactly the same amount of time, so time management really refers to managing yourself in such a way that you get the most from your time. If you can't manage yourself, you certainly can't manage anyone else.

Planning and Control Skills

If you don't much care where you want to get to, then it doesn't matter which way you go, as the Cheshire cat explained to Alice in Wonderland. Organizations exist to achieve some purpose; therefore, someone has to define that purpose and the means for its achievement. A manager is that someone. The planning function encompasses defining an organization's goals, establishing an overall strategy for achieving those goals, and developing a comprehensive hierarchy of plans to integrate and coordinate activities. Even if the best structural arrangements have been determined, and the best people have been hired, trained, and motivated, plenty of things can still go amiss. To ensure that things are going as they should, a manager must monitor the organization's performance. Actual performance must be compared with the previously set goals. If there are any significant deviations, it is the manager's responsibility to get the organization back on track. This process of monitoring, comparing, and correcting is the control function.

Planning and Goal Setting   One element of planning that permeates just about every manager's job—from CEOs to project managers and first-line supervisors—is setting objectives. Objectives, or goals, refer to desired outcomes for individuals, groups, or entire organizations. Setting goals keeps employees properly focused on the work to be done and helps organizational members keep their attention on what is most important.

Creating strategy is the process of identifying and pursuing an organization's mission by aligning the organization's internal capacities with the external environmental demands. This alignment is accomplished by developing a long-range plan that will obtain stated organizational goals.

In order to anticipate and interpret changes in their environments, managers in both small and large organizations need to scan their environments continually for information relevant to their present or future situations. Information needs to be obtained from all possible sources about all institutions outside the organization that might affect the organization's performance. Although every specific organization is different, its environment usually includes suppliers, customers, competitors, unions, government regulatory agencies, and public pressure groups.

Evaluating Performance   Control is the process of monitoring activities to ensure that they are being accomplished as planned and correcting any significant deviations. Managers can't really know whether their units are performing properly until they've compared the actual performance with the desired standard.[24]

Creative Problem Solving   Almost everything a manager does involves making decisions to solve problems. Selecting the organization's objectives requires making decisions to solve the problem of how we get from where we are now to where we want to be. Time management requires decisions on how to solve the problem of what is the best use of our time right now to achieve our most important objectives. Other typical managerial problems include how to design the best organization structure, select among alternative technologies, choose among job candidates, or motivate low-performing employees. Effective managers identify critical problems, assimilate the appropriate data, make sense of the information, and decide the best course of action to take for resolving the problem.

Managing Conflict   Every relationship, including those in organizations, experiences conflicts where incompatible differences emerge. It's true that conflict has the potential to destroy relationships and organizations. On the other hand, the lack of conflict can make an organization static, apathetic, and nonresponsive to the needs for change and innovation. Managers need skills to maintain an optimum level of conflict and guide employees in productive problem-solving efforts to learn and profit from it.

Organizing Skills

Managers have to divide work into manageable components and coordinate results to achieve objectives. Organizing includes determining what tasks are to be done, who is to do them, how the tasks are to be grouped, who reports to whom, and where decisions are to be made. To organize effectively, managers need skills in designing work, identifying and hiring employees, creating work teams, and modifying organizational culture.

Designing Work   The design of a person's job has significant motivational impact on behavior and goal achievement.[25] As a manager, you want to design jobs that maximize your employees' performance. Designing work is the process of incorporating tasks and responsibilities that utilize your employees' important talents into jobs that are meaningful, productive, and satisfying.

Diagnosing and Modifying Organizational Culture Managers need to understand their own organization's culture and those of other organizations they interact with because these cultures consist of the shared meanings, values, and accepted behaviors commonly agreed upon by members of the organizations. As such, cultures determine the attitudes of organization members toward how things are done and the ways members are supposed to behave. Managerial suggestions that are out of sync with the organizational culture face a formidable barrier. Fortunately, the manager's own behavior is one of the primary factors that modifies the culture of an organization.

Selecting and Developing People If the people working for you lack skills, experience, or motivation, their work performance is sure to reflect it. Managers need to know how to identify and attract qualified people and develop them into high-performing employees.

Today's manager is increasingly more like a coach than a boss.[26] Coaches don't play the game. They create a climate in which their players can excel. They define the overall objectives, set expectations, define the boundaries of each player's role, ensure that players are properly trained and have the resources they need to perform their roles, attempt to enlarge each player's capabilities, offer inspiration and motivation, and evaluate results. As coaches, managers help employees develop as they guide, listen to, encourage, and motivate them. Managers also need the skills to act as mentors and counselors when appropriate.

Creating High-Performance Teams Because work in organizations is increasingly organized around teams, employees have had to become team players.[27] This means developing the kind of skills necessary to contribute to high-performance teams. These skills include problem solving, group decision making, active listening, feedback, conflict resolution, and other interpersonal skills.

Being a team player is especially challenging for people who have grown up in cultures that encourage and reward individual achievement. They typically find it difficult to think like a team player and to sublimate their personal ambitions for the good of the team. Consequently, teams benefit when managers model cooperative team behaviors and instill them in their subordinates.

Leading Skills

The leading function of management involves creating a vision of what organizational members are working for and then directing and coordinating them so that they achieve their objectives. Managers are leading whenever they clarify what is to be accomplished, provide desired rewards for goal achievement, communicate needed information, initiate changes, empower people to be more independent, or resolve conflicts among team members. To be an effective leader, managers must have skills in building power bases, promoting change, motivating others, developing subordinates, and managing conflict.

Building Power Bases To accomplish your organizational goals, you need to have a power base that allows you to influence others to do what you need done. Managers need politicking skills to develop powerful images, form alliances, gain control of resources, and develop relationships with subordinates that allow them to be influential and function as leaders.

Leading Leadership is the process of providing direction, energizing others, and obtaining their voluntary commitment to the leader's vision. To maximize effectiveness, leaders need to know how to differentiate between management and leadership requirements, act in both transactional and transformational capacities, adapt their styles to follower needs, facilitate followers in finding paths to goals, use charisma to influence others, and act as stewards and servants of all stakeholders.

Motivating Others   You can't do it all yourself. In fact, the manager's job is to get things done through the efforts of others. Therefore, effective managers are skilled at determining what their employees want from work and showing them how to get it by working hard to achieve organizational objectives. They also need to be skilled in identifying and eliminating demotivators.[28]

Managing Change

Managers are on both the receiving and the giving ends of change. They have to adjust to change, and they also are the catalyst for initiating change within their organizations. Managers design and execute planned change programs to improve interpersonal interactions within organizations, change work processes and methods, and redesign organization structures.[29] They also continuously look for changes that will improve performance quality.[30] If confronted with dramatic environmental changes, managers must be willing to implement radical changes that completely reinvent their organizations.[31] Because people often resist change, managers are required to help employees deal with the uncertainty and anxiety that the changes may bring.

The Learning of Skills

How can management skills be taught? What teaching methods should be used? Universities attempt to teach management in a wide variety of ways, ranging from reviews of research-based literature, to having students experience management in student-created and -run organizations.[32] This section summarizes the current knowledge about how to best teach skills and describes how you will learn management skills from this book.

How Can Interpersonal Skills Be Taught?

"I hear and I forget. I see and I remember. I do and I understand." This famous quote, attributed to Confucius, is frequently used to support the value of learning through experience. The saying has some truth to it, but contemporary research on learning suggests that a more accurate rephrasing would be "I understand best when I hear, see, and do!"

University faculty members in business schools have explored the role of various techniques in teaching the skill sets that are needed by their students.[33] The lecture format is a proven, effective means for increasing student awareness and understanding of concepts.[34] As such, it probably should be part of any comprehensive system for learning skills—but it should be only a part! A skill, by definition, is "the ability to demonstrate a system and sequence of behavior that is functionally related to attaining a performance goal."[35]

Management skills are learned through *conditioning:* the ability of the human mind to create programs in the subconscious that automate behavior. For example, driving a car requires coordination of a number of activities when we manipulate the clutch, transmission, steering, accelerator, brakes, and so forth. But, after we learn how to do these things, they become automatic as we subconsciously hook into our "car driving program." A major implication of this notion of programming is that managerial skills can be learned only through experience. One must experiment with behavior, observe results, and learn from experience. As behaviors work, we are rewarded and we become "programmed" to do the same thing again. If we try something and it is not effective, that behavior is "extinguished." Eventually, if this learning by trial and error results in a set of behaviors that provide effective results, they become programmed into our subconscious skill repertoire.[36]

The Experiential Learning Model

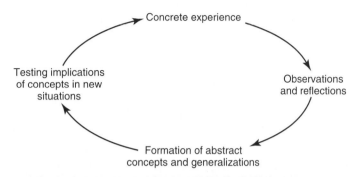

EXHIBIT 1-1 The Experiential Learning Model

SOURCE: D. A. Kolb, I. M. Rubin, and J. M. McIntyre, *Organizational Psychology: Readings on Human Behavior in Organizations*, 4th ed. (Upper Saddle River, NJ: Prentice Hall, 1984) 128. Reprinted with permission.

The Experiential Learning Model

Countless studies show that people learn faster and retain more information if they have to exert some kind of active effort. An example is the current trend of employing executive coaching, that is, bringing managers out from behind their desks and involving them in interactions and behavioral counseling that mimic real encounters.[37] To become competent at any skill, a person needs to understand it both conceptually and behaviorally; have opportunities to practice it; get feedback on how well he or she is performing the skill; and use the skill often enough so that it becomes integrated into his or her behavioral repertoire.[38] One model that encompasses most of these learning dimensions is presented in Exhibit 1-1.

Consistent with social-learning theory,[39] this experiential learning model emphasizes that the development of behavioral skills comes from observation and practice. According to the model, comprehensive learning encompasses four elements: active participation in a new experience *(concrete experience);* examination of that experience *(reflective observation);* integration of conclusions based on the new experience into workable theories *(abstract conceptualization);* and application of the theories to new situations *(active experimentation).*[40] The learning of skills is maximized, according to this model, when students get the opportunity to combine watching, thinking, and doing.[41]

Using the experiential learning model and well-known learning principles, the following 10-step learning model was created for acquiring managerial skills.[42]

Management Skills Learning Model

1. Self-assessment
2. Learn skill concepts
3. Check concept learning: Quiz
4. Identify behaviors that make up skill: Checklist
5. Modeling the skill in a demonstration exercise
6. Practice the skill in group exercises
7. Assess skill competency level in summary checklist
8. Questions to assist in the application of the skill
9. Exercises to reinforce the application of the skill
10. Action planning for continued skill development

To help individuals appreciate the need for improvement, they first need to assess their baseline skill competency. Each skill chapter in this book begins with a self-assessment questionnaire, followed by a scoring key and an interpretation to facilitate "self-discovery."[43] The majority of the self-assessment quizzes are highly valid measurement devices that are intended to give readers insights into how much they already know about the skill in question. Second, a person needs to learn the basic concepts underlying the skill. This learning is achieved by reviewing the published materials available on the skill. The third step is providing feedback to ensure that the basic concepts are understood, which in this model is accomplished by a short quiz.

The fourth step is the identification of specific behaviors that the individual desires to learn to master the skill. This behavioral checklist, derived from the skill concepts, clarifies what specific behaviors the individual needs to acquire. It is limited to approximately seven behaviors because the research has established that people have difficulty working with more than about seven pieces of information at one time.[44] The behavioral checklist is also used by others to evaluate how well the individual has learned the behaviors in question. The importance of this behavioral checklist can't be overstated. It contains the sole criteria by which actual behavioral performance will be judged. By keeping evaluation focused only on the behaviors identified in the checklist, we reduce the likelihood that appraisals will veer off to include personality variables, personal styles, or similar extraneous factors.

The fifth step is a modeling exercise that allows the learner to observe others exhibiting the desired skill behaviors. In the sixth step, students form small groups and practice their newly acquired skills in a series of role-plays or exercises where they must apply the targeted skill behaviors. Individuals not actively involved in a group exercise learn and contribute through observation and evaluation. The seventh step—completing a summary checklist—requires the learners to identify behaviors, if any, in which they have deficiencies. This appraisal comes from self-assessment and evaluations made by others. Deficiency feedback should be used to focus on where further practice is needed. Application questions provide opportunities to check understanding of how skill behaviors relate, and reinforcement exercises facilitate the transfer of classroom learning to real-life situations. Finally, the action plan provides the development of specific changes to implement.

Some Guidelines for Effective Skill Performance[45]

Keep in mind that whenever we apply behavioral skills with someone else, we are attempting to motivate some specific behavior in them. You will learn more about how to motivate others in a later chapter, but for now, just think of people's basic motivation as an effort to improve, or at least maintain, their quality of life. Skill application is more effective when we convince others that by acting as we suggest, they will gain something that they value positively. If, on the other hand, you attempt to influence someone by threatening a negative outcome for noncompliance, a block is immediately created in the relationship and the other focuses on figuring out how to avoid the negative outcome. Because people always have freedom of choice about how they are going to respond to us, successful skill application consists of being able to inspire people to want to cooperate with us. When applying behavioral skills, we want something positive to happen for ourselves, but the other person also wants a positive outcome for him- or herself. Knowing how to create win-win encounters where both parties gain something positive is crucial to obtaining cooperation and lasting outcomes.[46]

Another thing to keep in mind is that we tend to mirror the emotional feelings and behaviors of others. Have you ever noticed, for example, that if you are talking with someone and you get angry, then he or she will quite frequently get angry also? If you smile at someone, he or she will tend to smile too. When we present negative feelings, we invariably get mirrored back to us a negative reaction; on the other hand, when we put out something positive, we invariably get mirrored back something positive. The skill guideline derived from this mirroring phenomena is that doing things in a positive way is usually far more effective than doing them in a negative way. Managers who are most effective in applying people skills are usually perceived as a consistently positive force in relationships with others, in the context of getting work done.

Although they will vary in different skill applications—goal setting, delegation, conflict resolution, and so on—some specific actions will increase the likelihood of effective skill application by being positive and creating win-win outcomes in each situation. These guidelines are described as follows:

1. ***Be prepared.*** When you anticipate an encounter with someone else, know ahead of time what you want the outcome of your skill application to be. Unless you know where you want things to go, you won't know how to conduct yourself to get there.

2. ***Listen.*** Often, the key to the resolution of a situation is offered by someone else, but the manager is so intent on forcing a preconceived solution that he or she fails to hear it. Managers can learn much from their employees, but people must feel that they are being heard to keep the communication lines open. Listening indicates to others that their opinions are important to us, which increases contributions and builds mutual respect. This important skill will be discussed in greater detail in Chapter 3.

3. ***Use questions to respect freedom of choice.*** Asking instead of telling will usually get better reactions from another whom you are trying to influence. People almost always respond negatively to any attempt to invade their freedom of choice. If you are delegating, for example, and you order an employee to be responsible for achieving a task, quite often he or she will resent you by either avoiding the responsibility or shoving it back. But if you present alternatives and their consequences, and then ask others if they will accept responsibility, you show respect by allowing them to make the decision.

4. ***Be affirmative.*** Effective skill application involves being a consistently positive force. For example, you can correct employee mistakes in a way that puts people down and makes them feel worthless and inferior, or you can motivate them to improve by giving implicit positive messages such as, "I can see that you want to do well and I think that I can help you learn to do better."

5. ***Be honest and up-front.*** People will be more willing to accept your requests if they trust and respect you because they believe that you are honest and forthright. This includes being clear about what is really required and why it is important.

6. ***Be assertive.*** Assertiveness is being able to take a stand while treating another person with care and respect. Whatever the skill you are applying, you should indicate the acceptable level of performance you expect from other people so they will know what to strive for. You should then consistently hold them to that standard. In the long run, they will respect you more for it, and they will know the praise they receive for success is sincere and deserved.

A Final Note About Skills Learning

As you progress through the different skill applications in the following pages, you will experience and observe both successful and unsuccessful behaviors. You will see what works and what does not work, and then you can choose what you want to do when you are in a similar situation in the future. Consequently, since different people will find different things more or less valuable, the majority of responsibility for your own learning rests with you. Past students who seem to get the most out of this type of learning are the ones that really want to improve their managerial skills and are willing to help others do the same.

SUMMARY AND COMING ATTRACTIONS

This text has been developed to help college and university students learn the managerial skills necessary for successful careers in management and supervision. Behavioral science knowledge about how people learn interpersonal skills provides a solid basis for designing each chapter's learning modules. After reviewing the importance of management and management skills in Chapter 1, Chapter 2 provides a battery of self-assessment tests to provide a realistic evaluation of your own management skills, both your assets *and* liabilities. These address your social intelligence, values, needs, and interpersonal style in dealing with others. Most skill development programs stress the importance of such self-objectivity as an essential starting point for an individual's interpersonal skills development.

The remaining chapters cover the skills necessary to be proficient in the four managerial competency areas of general integrative competence, planning and control, organizing, and leading. These chapters generally follow the 10-step skill development model described in Chapter 1. Part II of the text addresses general integrative skills that are essential across a broad range of managerial situations: communicating, valuing diversity, developing ethical guideposts, and managing stress and time.

Parts III through V cover the skills necessary to perform the functions of management effectively. Part III covers the skills of planning, goal setting, evaluating and controlling performance, creative problem solving, and managing conflict. Part IV addresses the organizing skills of designing work, diagnosing, modifying organization culture, selecting and developing people, and creating high-performance teams. Part V explores the skills of building a power base, leading, motivating others, and managing change.

CONCEPT QUIZ

Complete the following true-false quiz by circling the correct answers. Answers are at the end of the quiz. After marking your answers, remember to go back and check your understanding of any answers you missed.

True or False	1. Organizing is the act of establishing an overall strategy for achieving goals.
True or False	2. When managers motivate employees and direct their activities, they are leading.
True or False	3. Technical skills refer to the ability to enhance one's position and build a power base.
True or False	4. To manage others well you must know yourself.
True or False	5. The overriding characteristic of effective skill application is acting positively.
True or False	6. Listening is critically important to creating a positive attitude in others.
True or False	7. Telling, instead of asking, contributes to the development of mutual respect.
True or False	8. Being assertive and saying no to poor performance is an important key to success as a manager.

True or False   9. The real source of managerial authority comes from their position, rather than their subordinates' willingness to follow.

True or False   10. The majority of responsibility for successfully acquiring effective skills rests with the learner.

Answers.   (1) False; (2) True; (3) False; (4) True; (5) True; (6) True; (7) False; (8) True; (9) False; (10) True

MODELING EXERCISE

Getting to Know the Class and Each Other

One of the more unnerving aspects of beginning a new semester is gaining an understanding of what is expected in each class.[47] Most of us feel anxiety about course requirements, getting to know new classmates, and about how to carve out our roles in the class. By now, you have read the course syllabus and the introductory material in this chapter. They have provided some necessary information about how the instructor wants the class to function. It is also important to give your instructor some indication of what you want or expect from the class. Specifically, some data can be useful for providing insights into why you are taking this class. To collect these data, you will need to answer some questions.

Directions.   First, take out a piece of paper and place your name at the top; then answer the following questions:

1. What do I want from this course?
2. Why is this class important to me?
3. How does this course fit into my career plans?
4. How do I want the instructor to guide the class?
5. What is my greatest challenge in taking this class?

When you have finished answering these questions, pair up with another class member (preferably someone you do not already know) and exchange papers. Get to know one another (using the information on these sheets as a starting point). Prepare an introduction of your partner, and share your partner's responses to the five questions with the class and your instructor.

Time.   Allow 5 minutes to individually answer the questions, 10 minutes to form dyads and share information, and 2 minutes per student for introductions.

NOTES

1. S. P. Robbins, *Managing Today!* (Upper Saddle River, NJ: Prentice Hall, 1997) 32–33.
2. R. D. Fowler, "Psychologists as Managers," *Monitor* (March 1999): 3.
3. D. Stafford, "For Managers, People Skills Are Paramount," *San Diego Union-Tribune,* October 5, 1998, E-3.
4. Ibid.
5. G. W. Dauphinalis and C. Price, "The CEO as Psychologist," *Management Review* (September 1998): 3–9.
6. J. A. Waters, "Managerial Skill Development," *Academy of Management Review* 5, no. 3 (1980): 449–53; American Assembly of Collegiate Schools of Business, "The Cultivation of Tomorrow's Leaders: Industry's Fundamental Challenge to Management Education," *Newsline* 23, no. 3 (Spring 1993): 1–3.
7. K. L. Fowler and D. M. Scott, "Experiential Learning in the Capstone Strategic Management Course: Collaborative Problem Solving, the Student Live Case, and Modeling," *Journal of Business and Management* (Spring 1996): 103–20.
8. M. J. Burke and R. R. Day, "A Cumulative Study of the Effectiveness of Management Training," *Journal of Applied Psychology* (May 1986): 232–45; L. Cummings, "Reflections on Management Education

and Development: Drift or Thrust Into the 21st Century?" *The Academy of Management Review* 15, no. 4 (October 1990): 694–96.

9. Ibid.

10. AACSB, "Outcome Measurement Project of the Accreditation Research Committee, Phase II: An Interim Report," American Assembly of Collegiate Schools of Business (December 1984), 3.

11. The first of three were originally proposed in R. L. Katz, "Skills of an Effective Administrator," *Harvard Business Review* (September–October 1974): 90–102. The fourth was added by C. M. Pavett and A. W. Lau, "Managerial Work: The Influence of Hierarchical Level and Functional Specialty," *Academy of Management Journal* (March 1983): 170–77.

12. J. J. Morse and F. R. Wagner, "Measuring the Process of Managerial Effectiveness," *Academy of Management Journal* (March 1978): 23–35.

13. The first of three were originally proposed in R. L. Katz, "Skills of an Effective Administrator," *Harvard Business Review* (September–October 1974): 90–102. The fourth was added by C. M. Pavett and A. W. Lau, "Managerial Work: The Influence of Hierarchical Level and Functional Specialty," *Academy of Management Journal* (March 1983): 170–77.

14. F. Luthans, R. M. Hodgetts, and S. A. Rosenkrantz, *Real Managers* (Cambridge, MA: Ballinger Publishing, 1988); and D. A. Gioia and C. O. Longnecker, "Delving into the Dark Side: The Politics of Executive Appraisal," *Organizational Dynamics* (Winter 1994): 47–58.

15. J. J. Morse and F. R. Wagner, "Measuring the Process of Managerial Effectiveness," *Academy of Management Journal* (March 1978): 23–35.

16. See R. D. Teach and G. Govahi, "The Role of Classroom Techniques in Teaching Management Skills," *Simulation & Gaming* 24, no. 4 (December 1993): 429–45; J. A. Waters, "Managerial Skill Development," *Academy of Management Review* 5, no. 3 (1980): 449–53; H. Mintzberg, "Some Distinguishing Characteristics of Managerial Work," *The Nature of Managerial Work* (New York: Harper & Row, 1973).

17. Cited in M. Calabresi, J. Van Tassel, M. Riley, and J. R. Szczesny, "Jobs in an Age of Insecurity," *Time*, November 22, 1993, 38.

18. *Endicott Report* (Baton Rouge: Louisiana State University Press, 1992).

19. T. Peters, *Thriving on Chaos: Handbook for a Management Revolution* (New York: Knopf, 1988). See also J. Huey, "Managing in the Midst of Chaos," *Fortune*, April 5, 1993, 38–48.

20. L. Smith, "Burned-Out Bosses," *Fortune*, July 25, 1994, 44.

21. R. C. Barnett and R. T. Brennan, "The Relationship Between Job Experiences and Psychological Distress: A Structural Equation Approach," *Journal of Organizational Behavior* (May 1995): 250–76; Hammonds, "The New World of Work"; B. Baumohl, E. W. Desmond, W. McWhirter, R. Woodbury, and S. Ratan, "We're #1 and It Hurts," *Time*, October 24, 1994, 48–56; and J. Connelly, "Have We Become Mad Dogs in the Office?" *Fortune*, November 28, 1994, 197–79.

22. K. Weick, "The Collapse of Sensemaking in Organizations," *Administrative Science Quarterly* 38 (1993): 628–52.

23. T. D. Wall, P. R. Jackson, S. Mullarkey, and S. K. Parker, "The Demands-Control Model of Job Strain: A More Specific Test," *Journal of Occupational and Organizational Psychology* (June 1996): 153–66.

24. For a thorough review of control systems, see R. Simmons *Levers of Control* (Boston, MA: Harvard Business School Press, 1995).

25. J. R. Hackman "Work Design," in J. R. Hackman and J. L. Suttle, eds., *Improving Life at Work* (Glenview, IL: Scott Foresman, 1977) 136–40.

26. See, for instance, C. D. Orth, H. E. Wilkinson, and R. C. Benfari, "The Manager's Role as Coach and Mentor," *Organizational Dynamics* (Spring 1987): 67–74; R. D. Evered and J. C. Selman, "Coaching and the Art of Management," *Organizational Dynamics* (Autumn 1989): 16–31.

27. This section is based on J. R. Katzenbach and D. K. Smith, *The Wisdom of Teams* (Boston: Harvard Business School Press, 1993) 43–64; and T. D. Schellhardt, "To Be a Star Among Equals, Be a Team Player," *Wall Street Journal*, April 20, 1994, B1.

28. D. R. Spitzeer, *Supermotivation* (New York: AMACON Books, 1995) 2.

29. See, for example, K. Lewin, *Field Theory in Social Science* (New York: Harper & Row, 1951); N. Margulies and J. Wallce, *Organizational Change: Techniques and Applications* (Glenview, IL: Scott Foresman, 1973); and W. L. French and C. H. Bell, Jr., *Organization Development*, 4th ed. (Upper Saddle River, NJ: Prentice Hall, 1990).

30. See, for example, M. Walton, *The Deming Management Method* (New York: Putnam/Perigee, 1986).

31. M. Hammer and J. Champy, *Reengineering the Corporation: A Manifesto for Business Revolution* (New York: Harper Business, 1993).

32. J. A. Waters, "Managerial Skill Development," *Academy of Management Review* 5, no. 3 (1980): 449–53; American Assembly of Collegiate Schools of Business, "The Cultivation of Tomorrow's Leaders: Industry's Fundamental Challenge to Management Education," *Newsline* 23, no. 3 (Spring 1993): 1–3.

33. R. D. Teach and G. Govahi, "The Role of Classroom Techniques in Teaching Management Skills," *Simulation & Gaming* 24, no. 4 (December 1993): 429.

34. D. L. Bradford, "Learning in Groups," in C. Vance, ed., *Mastering Management Education* (Newbury Park, CA: Sage, 1993) 173–78.

35. R. E. Boyatzis, *The Competent Manager: A Model for Effective Performance* (New York: John Wiley & Sons, 1982) 33.

36. D. D. Bowen, "Developing a Personal Theory of Experiential Learning," *Simulation & Games* 18, no. 2 (June 1987): 192–206.

37. D. Stafford, "Profiting from Active Learning," *The San Diego Union-Tribune*, November 3, 1997, C-2.

38. D. W. Johnson, and F. P. Johnson, *Joining Together: Group Theory and Group Skills* (Upper Saddle River, NJ: Prentice Hall, 1975) 8–10.

39. A. Bandura, *Social Learning Theory* (Upper Saddle River, NJ: Prentice Hall, 1977).

40. D. A. Kolb, I. M. Rubin, and J. M. McIntyre, *Organizational Psychology: Readings on Human Behavior in Organizations*, 4th ed. (Upper Saddle River, NJ: Prentice Hall, 1984) 29–31.

41. H. B. Clark, R. Wood, T. Kuchnel, S. Flanagan, M. Mosk, and J. T. Northrup, "Preliminary Validation and Training of Supervisory Interactional Skills," *Journal of Organizational Behavior Management* (Spring–Summer 1985): 95–115.

42. S. R. Robbins, and P. L. Hunsaker, *Training in Interpersonal Skills*, 2d ed. (Upper Saddle River, NJ: Prentice Hall, 1977).

43. C. R. Rogers, *On Becoming a Person* (Boston: Houghton Mifflin, 1961) 12.

44. G. A. Miller, "The Magical Number Seven, Plus or Minus Two: Some Limits on Our Capacity for Processing Information," *The Psychological Review* (March 1956): 81–97.

45. This section is adapted from M. R. McKnight, "The Nature of People Skills," *Journal of Management Education* 10, no. 2 (May 1995): 193–98.

46. S. R. Covey, *The 7 Habits of Highly Effective People* (New York: Simon & Schuster, 1989) 204–34.

47. The idea for this exercise came from B. Goza, "Graffiti Needs Assessment: Involving Students in the First Class Session," *Journal of Management Education* 17, no. 1 (February 1993): 99–106.

CHAPTER 2

Self-Awareness: Understanding and Developing Yourself

> Success in the knowledge economy comes to those who know themselves—their strengths, their values, and how they best perform.
> —PETER DRUCKER

Learning Objectives

After completing this chapter, you should be able to:

- Understand yourself better.

- Know how to continually learn about yourself.

- Improve existing skills and build new ones.

- Use the remaining chapters of this book to improve your management skills.

- Self-direct your career in management.

CONCEPTS

Recruits rise at dawn at the leadership boot camp run by the Center for Creative Leadership at Colorado Springs. After a continental breakfast, they are subjected to a *60 Minutes*–style interview in front of television cameras, and snooped on by note-taking psychologists peering through one-way windows. But the toughest ordeal takes place in dead silence around a seminar table. That's when they see the results of questionnaires filled out by colleagues back home rating their character and job skills. "At least 15–20 percent will learn dismaying things, and everyone will feel a twinge," says David Campbell, who runs the five-day, $7,400 course for top executives. It is part of the "360-degree feedback," in which a manager's strengths and weaknesses are evaluated in lengthy questionnaires by bosses, subordinates, and peers.[1]

Why Increase Your Self-Awareness?

The biggest payoff for attendees of the Center for Creative Leadership's boot camp is the self-knowledge they gain from peers attending the training and colleagues back home. Feedback from peers tends to correlate with the results from the surveys of colleagues back home. This dual feedback causes an extensive self-examination and creates the motivation to become more effective managers.[2]

Unfortunately, many of us have a tendency to avoid exposure to this type of self-awareness. Opening ourselves up to honest self-appraisal may result in exposing things we do not want to see. But the more you know about your unique, personal characteristics, the more insight you will have concerning your basic behavioral tendencies and inclinations for dealing with others. According to Peter Drucker, "Success in the knowledge economy comes to those who know themselves—their strengths, their values, and how they best perform."[3] The more you know about yourself, the better you will be able to understand how you are perceived by others and why they respond to you the way they do. Then you can choose to decrease ineffective behaviors and try out new ones to enhance your managerial effectiveness.

This chapter's contents are designed to help you gain insights into your aptitude for managing other people: your attitudes about motivating people, preferences to manage or lead, level of emotional intelligence, and styles of making decisions and working with others. You will also gain insights into the consequences of your predispositions for a successful managerial career. In addition, because self-assessment is the primary step in skills development,[4] you will learn how to assess your behavioral strengths and weaknesses both by yourself and with the help of others. This chapter's objectives are threefold: (1) to establish an understanding of your existing aptitude to manage, (2) to enhance your skills in conducting ongoing self-assessments so that you can continually improve your skills, and (3) to learn how to self-direct your managerial career.

How to Increase Your Self-Awareness

We all want to protect, maintain, and enhance our self-concepts and the images others have of us. But, we also have fears, inadequacies, self-doubts, and insecurities that we do not want to reveal to others. Many of these we may not even want to admit to ourselves. So the first step in increasing our self-awareness is taking some risks by emphasizing our need to know a little more than our fear of knowing. None of us is perfect, and knowledge about our strengths and weaknesses can help us gain insights into what areas we want to change and improve.

The good news is that most of us are less defensive about deficits in skills, which can be improved through practice, than about deficits in personality, which are usually thought of as relatively permanent.[5] If we can reduce our fear of knowing about skills deficits enough to satisfy our need to grow and improve them, what are some of the ways that we can gain insights about our behaviors? Two general ways allow us to do self-assessments: individual data gathering and obtaining feedback from others.

Individual Data Gathering

Although you can obtain personal insights with the aid of professional coaches or therapists, this section will focus on things you can do yourself to gather and analyze information that will enhance your self-awareness. One thing you can do to gather data for self-assessment is learning from your experiences. Another is taking and interpreting self-assessment questionnaires. The first part of this section will show you how to learn from experience. The second section will provide some key self-assessment questionnaires for you to take and interpret.

Learning from Experience   A number of self-evaluation techniques will facilitate data collection and self-analysis. We will describe three in this section: (1) experience-goal matching, (2) keeping a journal, or (3) finding solitude to reflect. Exhibit 2-1 summarizes a number of additional techniques often used to collect and organize personal information and gain greater self-awareness.

EXHIBIT 2-1   Individual Control Self-Assessment Techniques

- *Self-written interviews, life events, autobiographical story.*   This technique requires an individual to write an autobiography that describes his or her life. It is a written narrative of personal history. Specific content statements would describe life events, education, hobbies, major changes that have occurred in the past, consequences of the described events, and the individual's feelings about these events. Also included is a description of turning points in one's life and the pros and cons of past career decisions.

- *Written daydreams.*   The individual first develops a fantasy or vision about the future or a currently preferred surrounding. Individuals then record what they have visualized for future analysis.

- *Written future obituaries or retirement speeches.*   Individuals write personal obituaries or retirement speeches that might be given at the time of their death or retirement. The individual describes what he or she will be remembered for and the comments made by coworkers and acquaintances.

- *Ranking of significant work values.*   The individual lists what he or she believes are important or relevant values and then ranks them in terms of appropriateness or desirability. Listed values may relate to the following general categories: money, financial security, material gain; helping people, social contribution; power over self, self-improvement; security, stability, predictability; mental challenge and mental stimulation.

- *Assets and liabilities balance sheet.*   The individual makes two lists. The first list articulates assets or strengths, the second articulates liabilities or weaknesses. When using this technique, it is desirable to have individuals describe specific situations and behaviors to help ensure accurate and complete assessment of personal assets and liabilities.

- *Lifestyle representation.*   Individuals describe their current lifestyle in either written or pictorial form. When using this technique, individuals are encouraged to be as behaviorally specific as possible.

SOURCE: L. W. Mealiea and G. P. Latham, *Skills for Managerial Success* (Chicago: Irwin, 1996) 34.

Experience-Goal Matching.   Peter Drucker suggests that one way to learn about your strengths is by analyzing your experiences in goal achievement. It works this way: Whenever you make a key decision or take a key action, write down what you expect will happen. Nine or 12 months later, compare the actual results with your expectations. If you practice this method consistently for several years, Drucker believes that it will show you what your strengths and weaknesses are. It will also indicate what you are doing, or failing to do, that deprives you of the full benefits of your strengths. Finally, it will demonstrate areas in which you are not particularly competent or where you have no strengths at all and cannot perform adequately.[6]

Several useful implications for action typically follow from experience-goal matching analysis. First, you will know what you are good at so you can concentrate on your strengths to do what you do best to produce important results. Second, you will know where you need to work on improving your strengths and what skills you need to acquire. Third, you will discover areas of "disabling ignorance" where you need to acquire additional knowledge to fully realize your strengths. Fourth, you will discover your bad habits—the things you do or fail to do that inhibit your effectiveness and performance, for example, being a great planner but being lax at implementation. Or, your bad habit may be failing to practice good manners and common courtesies that are the "lubricating oil" of an organization. Finally, you will be confronted with areas in which you have no talent or interest whatsoever. Drucker suggests that you should not waste effort on improving areas of low competence because it takes far more energy to improve from incompetence to mediocrity than it takes to improve an area of strength from good to excellent performance.[7]

Keeping a Journal.   Another way to learn from experiences is by keeping a journal. Journals are similar to diaries, but they are not just accounts of a day's events. A journal should include entries that address critical aspects of your managerial experience. Journal entries might include comments about insightful or interesting quotes, anecdotes, newspaper articles, or even humorous cartoons about management. They might also include reflections on personal events, such as interactions with bosses, coaches, teachers, students, employees, players, teammates, roommates, and so on. Such entries can emphasize a good (or bad) way somebody handled something, a problem in the making, the differences between people in their reactions to situations, or people in the news, a book, or a film. Managers should also use their journals to "think on paper" about management readings from textbooks or formal management programs or to describe examples from their own experience of a concept presented in a reading.[8]

At least three good reasons support keeping a journal. First, the very process of writing increases the likelihood that you will be able to look at an event from a different perspective or learn something from it. Putting an experience into words can be a step toward taking a more objective look at it. Second, you can (and should) reread earlier entries. Earlier entries provide an interesting and valuable autobiography of your evolving thinking about management and about particular events in your life. Third, as seen in Exhibit 2-2, good journal entries can provide a repository of ideas that you may later want to use more formally for papers, pep talks, or speeches.

Finding Solitude to Reflect.   The third way to learn from experience is to seek out solitude to reflect on your experiences and learn from them. Solitude means being out of human contact, being alone, and being so for lengthy periods of time. Silence is an essential part of solitude. Silence means to escape from sounds and noises, other than

---

EXHIBIT 2-2   Sample Journal Entries

- I went skiing this weekend and saw the perfect example of a leader adapting her leadership style to her followers and situation. While putting on my skis I saw a ski instructor teaching little kids to ski. She did it using the game "red light, green light." The kids loved it and seemed to be doing very well. Later that same day, as I was going to the lodge for lunch, she was teaching adults, and she did more demonstrating than talking. But when she talked she was always sure to encourage them so they did not feel intimidated when some little kid whizzed by. She would say to the adults that it's easier for children, or that smaller skis are easier. She made the children laugh and learn, and made the adults less self-conscious to help them learn too....

- Today may not exactly be a topic on leadership, but I thought it would be interesting to discuss. I attended the football game this afternoon and could not help but notice our cheerleaders. I was just thinking of their name in general, and found them to be a good example (of leadership). Everyone gets rowdy at a football game, but without the direction of the cheerleaders there would be mayhem. They do a good job of getting the crowd organized and the adrenaline pumping (though of course the game is most important in that too!). It's just amazing to see them generate so much interest that all of the crowd gets into the cheering. We even chant their stupid-sounding cheers! You might not know any of them personally, but their enthusiasm invites you to try to be even louder than them. I must give the cheerleaders a round of applause....

- I've been thinking about how I used to view/understand leadership, trying to find out how my present attitudes were developed. It's hard to remember past freshman year, even harder to go past high school. Overall, I think my father has been the single most important influence on my leadership development—long before I even realized it. Dad is a strong "Type A" person. He drives himself hard and demands a great deal from everyone around him, especially his family and especially his only son and oldest child. He was always pushing me to study, practice whatever sport I was involved in at the time, get ahead of everybody else in every way possible.

SOURCE: R. L. Hughes, R. C. Ginnett, and G. J. Curphy, *Leadership: Enhancing the Lessons of Experience*, 3d ed. (Burr Ridge, IL: Irwin McGraw-Hill, 1999) 490.

the ones of nature. Solitude is especially important for managers with heavy demands on their attention and social skills who tend not to have much time alone.

What you do during time alone—walking, meditating, or just relaxing—really does not matter as long as you are achieving solitude. The amount of solitude you need for rejuvenation and reflection will vary with the demands of your environment. The benefits of solitude are many, including a chance to contemplate who you are, what your relationships are to other people, and what your goals will be. Solitude also fosters creativity because it gives you a chance to speculate without the censorship and evaluation that comes with putting forth new ideas in public.[9]

So how do you engage in solitude? What do you do in solitude or silence? Well as far as things to "get done," nothing at all. As long as you are doing "things to get done," you have not broken human contact. So do not go into solitude and silence with a list of things to accomplish. Just be there. Enjoy it. See what happens.[10]

Self-Assessment Inventories   A second method of individual data gathering is taking and interpreting self-assessment questionnaires. They have the advantage of being private and under the control of the individual using them. These same advantages are disadvantages because self-assessments are subject only to individual perspectives, which can at times be biased or defensive. Consequently, the results of self-assessments should always be checked out by soliciting feedback from relevant others to verify their validity from multiple perspectives.

Each of the following chapters in this book starts off with a self-assessment inventory to establish your baseline ability in the skills that are the focus of that specific chapter. Each chapter concludes with feedback from peers and self-evaluation to assess your level of skill development after reading the concepts and completion of the exercises in that skill chapter. The self-assessment inventories presented in this section were chosen because they provide feedback on general skills that influence your overall managerial style and application of the specific skills presented in the other chapters of this book.

The five self-assessment questionnaires that follow provide feedback on characteristics found to be associated with managerial success and offer important insights to you.[11] You may want to check out other characteristics as well to get a more complete understanding of yourself. One source of additional information is the *Prentice Hall Self-Assessment Library CD-Rom*. Other sources of self-assessment instruments are campus counseling centers, professional counselors, and career search organizations.

The following five self-assessment questionnaires (SAQs) will provide you with information regarding your aptitude for management, whether you prefer managing or leading, your degree of emotional intelligence, your cognitive style for processing information and making decisions, and your assumptions about what motivates people at work. Take the time now to complete these SAQs. When you are finished, read the directions for scoring the questionnaires and the discussions of what the results say about you. You will have the opportunity to compare your scores to those of other students and discuss what you can do to improve your scores in the closing exercise of this chapter.

SAQ 1: Is Management for You?[12]

Although many want to manage because of the excitement, status, power, or rewards, knowing how to manage is not automatic; it requires specific skills and competencies as well as a desire to manage.

Directions.   The following 20 questions are designed to provide insight into your aptitude for management. Rate each question according to the following scale:

ML = Most like me SU = Somewhat unlike me	SL = Somewhat like me MU = Most unlike me	NS = Not sure				
1. I can get others to do what I want them to do.		ML	SL	NS	SU	MU
2. I frequently evaluate my job performance.		ML	SL	NS	SU	MU
3. I prefer not to get involved in office politics.		ML	SL	NS	SU	MU
4. I like the freedom that open-ended goals provide me.		ML	SL	NS	SU	MU
5. I work best when things are orderly and calm.		ML	SL	NS	SU	MU
6. I enjoy making oral presentations to groups of people.		ML	SL	NS	SU	MU
7. I am confident in my abilities to accomplish difficult tasks.		ML	SL	NS	SU	MU
8. I do not like to write.		ML	SL	NS	SU	MU
9. I like solving difficult puzzles.		ML	SL	NS	SU	MU
10. I am an organized person.		ML	SL	NS	SU	MU
11. I have difficulty telling others they made a mistake.		ML	SL	NS	SU	MU
12. I like to work set hours each day.		ML	SL	NS	SU	MU
13. I view paperwork as a trivial task.		ML	SL	NS	SU	MU
14. I like to help others learn new things.		ML	SL	NS	SU	MU
15. I prefer to work alone.		ML	SL	NS	SU	MU
16. I believe it is who you know, not what you know, that counts.		ML	SL	NS	SU	MU
17. I enjoy doing several things at once.		ML	SL	NS	SU	MU
18. I am good at managing money.		ML	SL	NS	SU	MU
19. I would rather back down from an argument than let it get out of hand.		ML	SL	NS	SU	MU
20. I am computer literate.		ML	SL	NS	SU	MU

Scoring. For statements 1, 2, 4, 6, 7, 9, 10, 11, 13, 14, 16, 17, 18, and 20, give yourself 5 points for every ML; 4 points for SL; 3 points for NS; 2 points for SU; and 1 point for MU. For statements 3, 5, 8, 12, 15, and 19, reverse the scoring. That is, give yourself 1 point for each ML, 2 points for SL, and so on. Total your score: _____.

Interpretation. In this assessment, a total of 100 points is possible. A score ranging between 80 and 100 demonstrates high management potential. You possess the desire and many of the skills, attitudes, and competencies that successful managers need. A score between 40 and 79 indicates moderate potential. You have some of the skills and competencies to manage successfully, but you need some fine-tuning. Learning new management skills and experiencing "managing" techniques may serve you well. A score below 40 indicates low management potential. Your management skills are dormant or you have previously had a low desire to manage others. People in this category who now want to manage should pay particular attention to the management skills, competencies, and techniques in this book that are related to the questions they scored lowest on.

SAQ 2: What's Your Preference: Leadership or Management?[13]

Directions. Questions 1 to 6 are about you right now. Questions 7 to 22 are about how you would like to be if you were the head of a major department at a corporation. Answer yes or no to indicate whether the item describes you accurately, or whether you would strive to perform each activity.

Me Right Now

1. When I have a number of tasks or homework to do, I set priorities and organize the work to meet the deadlines.
2. When I am involved in a serious disagreement, I hang in there and talk it out until it is completely resolved.
3. I would rather sit in front of my computer than spend a lot of time with people.
4. I reach out to include other people in activities or during discussions.
5. I know my long-term vision for career, family, and other activities.
6. When solving problems, I prefer analyzing things to working through a group of people.

As Head of a Major Department

7. I would help subordinates clarify goals and how to achieve those goals.
8. I would give people a sense of mission and higher purpose.
9. I would make sure jobs get out on time.
10. I would scout for new product or service opportunities.
11. I would use policies and procedures as guides for problem solving.
12. I would promote unconventional beliefs and values.
13. I would give monetary rewards in exchange for high performance levels from subordinates.
14. I would inspire trust from everyone in the department.
15. I would work alone to accomplish important tasks.
16. I would suggest new and unique ways of doing things.
17. I would give credit to people who do their jobs well.
18. I would verbalize the higher values that I and the organization stand for.
19. I would establish procedures to help the department operate smoothly.
20. I would question the "why" of things to motivate others.
21. I would set reasonable limits on new approaches.
22. I would demonstrate social nonconformity as a way to facilitate change.

Scoring. Count the number of yes answers to even-numbered questions. Count the number of yes answers to odd-number questions. Compare the two scores.

Interpretation. The even-numbered items represent behaviors and activities typical of leadership. Leaders are personally involved in shaping ideas, values, vision, and change. They often use an intuitive approach to develop fresh ideas and seek new directions for the department or organization. The odd-numbered items are considered more traditional management activities. Managers respond to organizational problems in an impersonal way, make rational decisions, and work for stability and efficiency.

If you answered yes to more even-numbered than odd-numbered items, you may have potential leadership qualities. If you answered yes to more odd-numbered items, you may have management qualities. Leadership and management qualities can be developed or improved with awareness and experience.

SAQ 3: What's Your Emotional Intelligence at Work?[14]

Directions. For each of the following items, rate how well you are able to display the ability described. Before responding, try to think of actual situations in which you have had the opportunity to use the ability.

Very Slight Ability		*Moderate Ability*		*Very Much Ability*
1	*2*	*3*	*4*	*5*

_____ **1.** Associate different internal physiological cues with different emotions.

_____ **2.** Relax when under pressure in situations.

_____ **3.** "Gear up" at will for a task.

_____ **4.** Know the impact that your behavior has on others.

_____ **5.** Initiate successful resolution of conflict with others.

_____ **6.** Calm yourself quickly when angry.

_____ **7.** Know when you are becoming angry.

_____ **8.** Regroup quickly after a setback.

_____ **9.** Recognize when others are distressed.

_____ **10.** Build consensus with others.

_____ **11.** Know what senses you are currently using.

_____ **12.** Use internal "talk" to change your emotional state.

_____ **13.** Produce motivation when doing uninteresting work.

_____ **14.** Help others manage their emotions.

_____ **15.** Make others feel good.

_____ **16.** Identify when you experience mood shifts.

_____ **17.** Stay calm when you are the target of anger from others.

_____ **18.** Stop or change an ineffective habit.

_____ **19.** Show empathy for others.

_____ **20.** Provide advice and emotional support to others as needed.

_____ **21.** Know when you become defensive.

_____ **22.** Know when you are thinking negatively and head it off.

_____ **23.** Follow your words with actions.

_____ **24.** Engage in intimate conversations with others.

_____ **25.** Accurately reflect people's feelings back to them.

Scoring. Sum your responses to the 25 questions to obtain your overall emotional intelligence score. Your score for *self-awareness* is the total of questions 1, 6, 11, 16, and 21. Your score for *managing emotions* is the total of questions 2, 7, 12, 17, and 22. Your score for *motivating yourself* is the sum of questions 3, 8, 13, 18, and 23. Your score for *empathy* is the sum of questions 4, 9, 14, 19, and 24. Your score for *social skills* is the sum of questions 5, 10, 15, 20, and 25. Enter you scores in Exhibit 2-3 and compare them to the norms.

Interpretation. This questionnaire provides an indication of your emotional intelligence. If you received a total score of 100 or more, you have a high level of emotional intelligence. A score from 50 to 100 means you have a good platform of

EXHIBIT 2-3 Emotional Intelligence—Scores and Norms

Emotional Intelligence Questions		*Your Scores*	*Norms*		
Component	*Questions*	*Sum*	*High*	*Medium*	*Low*
Overall EIQ	all		100+	50–100	25–50
Self-awareness	1, 6, 11, 16, 21		20+	10–20	below 10
Manage emotions	2, 7, 12, 17, 22		20+	10–20	below 10
Motivating self	3, 8, 13, 18, 23		20+	10–20	below 10
Empathy	4, 9, 14, 19, 24		20+	10–20	below 10
Social skills	5, 10, 15, 20, 25		20+	10–20	below 10

emotional intelligence from which to develop your managerial capability. A score below 50 indicates that you realize that you are probably below average in emotional intelligence. For each of the five components of emotional intelligence—self-awareness, managing emotions, motivating one's self, empathy, and social skill—a score above 20 is considered high, while a score below 10 would be considered low.

Managers who are attuned to their own feelings and the feelings of others can use their understanding to enhance the performance of themselves and others in their organizations. The five basic components of emotional intelligence most important for managers are discussed here.[15] Review the following discussion of the five components of emotional intelligence and think about what you might do to develop those areas in which you scored low.

- *Self-awareness.* This component provides the basis for all the other components of emotional intelligence. Self-awareness means being aware of what you are feeling, being conscious of the emotions within yourself. People who are in touch with their emotions are better able to guide their own lives. Managers need to be in touch with their emotions in order to interact effectively and appreciate emotions in others. Managers with high levels of self-awareness learn to trust their "gut feelings" and realize that these feelings can provide useful information about difficult decisions. Answers are not always clear about who is at fault when problems arise, or when to let an employee go, reorganize a business, or revise job responsibilities. In these situations, managers have to rely on their own feelings and intuition.

- *Managing emotions.* The second key component of emotional intelligence is managing emotions. Operationally it means the manager is able to balance his or her own moods so that worry, anxiety, fear, or anger do not get in the way of what needs to be done. Managers who can manage their emotions perform better because they are able to think clearly. Managing emotions does not mean suppressing or denying them, but instead understanding them and using that understanding to deal with situations productively.[16] Managers should first recognize a mood or feeling, think about what it means and how it affects them, and then choose how to act.

- *Motivating oneself.* This ability to be hopeful and optimistic despite obstacles, setbacks, or even outright failure is crucial for pursuing long-term goals in life or in business. A classic example of self-motivation occurred when the MetLife insurance company hired a special group of job applicants who tested high on optimism but failed the normal sales aptitude test. Compared to salespeople who passed the regular aptitude test but scored high on pessimism, the optimistic group made 21 percent more sales in their first year and 57 percent more in their second.[17]

- *Empathy.* The fourth component is empathy, which means being able to put yourself in someone else's shoes—to recognize what others are feeling without them needing to tell you. Most of the time, people don't tell us what they feel in words but rather in tone of voice, body language, and facial expression. Empathy is built from self-awareness; being attuned to one's own emotions makes it easier to read and understand the feelings of others.

- *Social skills.* The ability to connect to others, build positive relationships, respond to the emotions of others, and influence others is the final component of emotional intelligence. Managers need social skills to understand interpersonal relationships, handle disagreements, resolve conflicts, and pull people together for a common purpose.

SAQ 4: Cognitive Style Self-Assessment[18]

Cognitive style refers to the general way you approach and attempt to solve problems. You have similarities and differences from other people. The differences measured here are not better or worse, merely different. Complete and score the inventory below to find out your cognitive style. Then read the interpretation to learn what it means.

COGNITIVE STYLE SELF-ASSESSMENT

This is a set of questions designed to indicate your cognitive style. The answer you choose to any question is neither "right" nor "wrong." It simply helps to point out where your cognitive preferences lie.

Below you will find a number of paired statements and words. Please give every one a score so that each pair will add up to 5. For example:

"In describing my work, I would say it is:"

a. Challenging and exciting   4
b. Routine and dull   +1
       = 5

Clearly, work can sometimes be challenging and sometimes dull. In the above example we have weighted four parts challenging and one part dull. The score could, in your case, be 3 + 2 or 5 + 0 or another combination.

Please choose your scores, one against another, from the following scale:

Minimum ————————————————————— Maximum
0   1   2   3   4   5

1. Are you influenced more by:

   a. Values   _____
   b. Logic   + _____
     =   5

2. When you have to meet strangers, do you find it:

   a. Something that takes a good deal of effort   _____
   b. Pleasant, or at least easy   + _____
     =   5

3. Does following a plan:

   a. Appeal to you   _____
   b. Constrain you   + _____
     =   5

4. Do you get along better with people who are:

   a. Creative and speculative   _____
   b. Realistic and "down to earth"   + _____
     =   5

5. Are you naturally:

   a. Somewhat quiet and reticent around others   _____
   b. Talkative and easy to approach   + _____
     =   5

6. Is it harder for you to adjust to:
   a. Standard procedures
   b. Frequent changes   + _____
                                                   = _____ 5

7. Is it better to be:
   a. A person of compassion
   b. A person who is always fair   + _____
                                                   = _____ 5

8. At a party, do you usually:
   a. Try to meet many new people
   b. Stick with the people you know   + _____
                                                   = _____ 5

9. When you learn something new, do you:
   a. Try to do it like everyone else does
   b. Try to devise a way of your own   + _____
                                                   = _____ 5

10. Are you at your best:
   a. When following a carefully worked out plan
   b. When dealing with the unexpected   + _____
                                                   = _____ 5

11. Do you get more annoyed at:
   a. Fancy theories
   b. People who don't like theories   + _____
                                                   = _____ 5

12. Is it better to be regarded by others as a person with a:
   a. Visionary outlook
   b. Practical outlook   + _____
                                                   = _____ 5

13. Are you more often:
   a. Soft-hearted
   b. Hard-headed   + _____
                                                   = _____ 5

14. When you buy a gift, are you:
   a. Spontaneous and impulsive
   b. Deliberate and careful   + _____
                                                   = _____ 5

15. Do you find talking to people you don't know:
   a. Usually easy
   b. Often taxing   + _____
                                                   = _____ 5

16. Do you think it is a worse mistake to:
   a. Show too much emotion
   b. Try to be too rational   + _____
                                                   = _____ 5

17. Do you prefer people who have:
   a. Vivid imaginations
   b. Good common sense   + _____
                                                   = _____ 5

18. Do you usually:
   a. Organize and plan things in advance
   b. Allow things to just happen and then adapt   + _____
                                                          = _____ 5

19. Do people get to know you:
   a. Quickly
   b. Slowly   + _____
                                                          = _____ 5

20. At work, would you rather:
   a. Encounter an unscheduled problem that must be solved right away   _____
   b. Try to schedule your work so you won't be up against the clock   + _____
                                                          = _____ 5

21. When you are with people you don't know, do you usually:
   a. Start conversations on your own
   b. Wait to be introduced by others   + _____
                                                          = _____ 5

Please allocate scores on the same basis to the following choice of words and phrases so as to indicate your preferences.

22. a. Personal
      b. Objective   + _____
                                                          = _____ 5

23. a. Timely
      b. Casual   + _____
                                                          = _____ 5

24. a. Reason
      b. Feeling   + _____
                                                          = _____ 5

25. a. Make
      b. Design   + _____
                                                          = _____ 5

26. a. Easy
      b. Hard   + _____
                                                          = _____ 5

27. a. Nonjudgmental
      b. Judgmental   + _____
                                                          = _____ 5

28. a. Composed
      b. Lively   + _____
                                                          = _____ 5

29. a. Facts
      b. Theories   + _____
                                                          = _____ 5

30. a. Imaginative
      b. Practical   + _____
                                                          = _____ 5

Scoring Scheme

Look back at the scores you allocated to each of the questions. Those scores should now be added up as shown below.

Dimension E

Question	Score Given
2b	_____
5b	_____
8a	_____
15a	_____
19a	_____
21a	_____
28b	_____
Total:	_____

Dimension I

Question	Score Given
2a	_____
5a	_____
8b	_____
15b	_____
19b	_____
21b	_____
28a	_____
Total:	_____

Dimension S

Question	Score Given
4b	_____
9a	_____
11a	_____
12b	_____
17b	_____
25a	_____
29a	_____
30b	_____
Total:	_____

Dimension N

Question	Score Given
4a	_____
9b	_____
11b	_____
12a	_____
17a	_____
25b	_____
29b	_____
30a	_____
Total:	_____

Dimension T

Question	Score Given
1b	_____
7b	_____
13b	_____
16a	_____
22b	_____
24a	_____
26b	_____
27b	_____
Total:	_____

Dimension F

Question	Score Given
1a	_____
7a	_____
13a	_____
16b	_____
22a	_____
24b	_____
26a	_____
27a	_____
Total:	_____

Dimension J

Question	Score Given
3a	_____
6b	_____
10a	_____
14b	_____
18a	_____
20b	_____
23a	_____
Total:	_____

Dimension P

Question	Score Given
3b	_____
6a	_____
10b	_____
14a	_____
18b	_____
20a	_____
23b	_____
Total:	_____

Now transfer each of the Total Scores to the columns below. Thus, your total score under Dimension E should be placed next to the E, the total score under Dimension I should be placed next to the I, and so on.

	Total		*Total*
E	_____	I	_____
S	_____	N	_____
T	_____	F	_____
J	_____	P	_____

Your Score Is

Write in the letter with the most points for each of the four combinations below.

I or E _____   S or N _____   T or F _____   J or P _____

Interpretation: Cognitive Style Self-Assessment[19]

Jung's personality typology was operationalized in the Myers-Briggs Type Indicator, which was the basis of the Cognitive Style Self-Assessment inventory you just completed. Jung observed that people's behavior, rather than being unique, fit into patterns, and that much of the seemingly random differences in human behavior are actually orderly and consistent, being explained by differences in psychological attitudes and functions.

Theory of Personality

These differences were termed *preferences*, because people actually prefer one type of functioning over another.[20] Two of these preferences concern the person's attitude toward the world. Jung believed that people tend to approach the world through either extraversion—focus on the outer world—or introversion—focus on their inner world.

The *introvert* is interested in exploring and analyzing their own inner world. An introvert is introspective and preoccupied with personal thoughts and reflections.[21] What is happening inside the introvert's head is much more interesting than what is outside. Therefore, the introvert seems to be in continuous retreat from the outer world, holding aloof from external happenings and feeling lonely and lost in large gatherings. This type may often appear awkward and inhibited because their best qualities are shared with only a few close people. Mistrust and self-will characterize the introvert; however, this apprehensiveness of the objective world is not due to fear but because the outer world seems negative, demanding, and overpowering. The introvert's best work is done by self-initiative without interference from others and not influenced by majority views or public opinion. In work situations, introverted managers tend to "like quiet for concentration, be careful with details, like to think a lot before they act, and work contentedly alone."[22]

The *extrovert*, on the other hand, is characterized by an interest in the outer world, by responsiveness to and a willing and ready acceptance of external events, by desire to influence and be influenced by events, a need to join in, the actual enjoyment of all kinds of noise and bustle, by a constant attention to environment, the cultivation of friends and acquaintances (none too carefully selected), and, finally, by the great importance associated with the image one projects and therefore a strong tendency to make a show of oneself. At work, extraverted managers "like variety and action, tend to be faster"; "dislike complicated procedures"; are often impatient with long, slow jobs; are interested in the results of their job; often act quickly (sometimes without thinking); and usually "communicate well."[23]

No one is a "pure" type. We are all in a state of balance between extraversion (E) and introversion (I), but we use one type more naturally and more frequently. Earlier research indicates a disproportionate number of extraverted managers. Since a manager is often required to work with and through other people, some extraversion would be useful. But too much can be counterproductive, with the real threat of getting "sucked" into external demands and becoming completely lost in them as well as losing identify and becoming submerged in conformist herd psychology.

Psychological Functions

Jung described four psychological functions that exist along two continua: the perception dimension, with sensing at one end and intuition at the other; and the judgment dimension, with thinking at one end and feeling at the other. According to Jung, one of these four functions will tend to dominate the personality of the individual. For example, a person may be a sensation-thinking, an intuition-thinking, a sensation-feeling, or an intuition-feeling type. No one is a "pure" type, but we all strive to achieve a state of balance.

Perceiving   The *perception dimension* of sensation versus intuition relates to the ways in which a person becomes aware of ideas, facts, and occurrences. When using *sensing*, perception occurs literally through the use of the five senses.[24] As a result, this type is very much present-oriented, interested in practical matters, and prefers things to be orderly, precise, and unambiguous. They typically work steadily, like established routine, seldom make errors of fact, and rarely trust their inspirations.[25]

Perceiving by *intuition*, alternatively, cannot be traced back to a conscious sensory experience but rather it is a subconscious process, with ideas or hunches coming "out of the blue," yielding the hidden possibilities of a situation. The intuitive is future-oriented,[26] always looking ahead and inspiring others with innovations. By the time everyone else catches up, the intuitive is off on another idea. In fact, the intuitive finds it difficult to tolerate performance of routine tasks; as soon as one is mastered, another is started. Intuitives also "like solving new problems, work in bursts of energy, frequently jump to conclusions, are impatient with complicated situations, dislike taking time for precision, and follow their inspirations, good or bad."[27]

Judging   Just as there are two ways of perceiving the world, there are two ways of making judgments about one's perceptions; namely, by thinking or by feeling. *Thinking* is a logical and analytical process, searching for the impersonal, true versus false, correct versus incorrect. Principles are more important to the thinker than are people,[28] and the thinker often has a difficult time adapting to situations which cannot be understood intellectually.[29] Other characteristics of this type can be described in the following way: They "are relatively unemotional and uninterested in people's feelings, may hurt people's feelings without knowing it, like analysis and putting things into logical order, can get along without harmony, need to be treated fairly, are able to reprimand people or fire them when necessary, and may seem hard-hearted."[30]

Alternatively, *feeling* is a personal, subjective process, seeking a good versus bad or like versus dislike judgment. Whereas thinking occurs using objective criteria, feeling occurs on the basis of personal values and, in this sense, is different from emotion since feeling judgments are mental evaluations and not emotional reactions. The feeling type lives according to such subjective judgments based on a value system that is either related to society's values, as in the case of the extrovert, or personal values, as in the introvert.

Dominant Process

The remaining preference determines which function is the principal or dominant one (i.e., whether perceiving or judging is the primary mode). For instance, when a person follows explanations open-mindedly, then perception (P) is being used; if, on the other hand, one's mind is rather quickly made up as to agreement or disagreement, then judgment (J) is preferred.

A fundamental difference in these two preferences is manifested in terms of which process is turned off or ignored. In order for judging to take place, perception must stop; all the facts are in, so a decision can be made. On the other hand, in order for perception to continue, judgments are put off for the time being as there are not enough data, and new developments may occur.

Basically, the preference shows the difference between the perceptive types who live their lives, as opposed to the judging types who run theirs. Each type is useful, but works better if the person can switch to the other mode when necessary. A pure perceptive type is like a ship with all sail and no rudder, while a pure judging type is all form and no content.[31]

The perception-judgment (P-J) preference determines the principal function. For instance, an ST who prefers perceiving would have sensation, that is, the perceiving function, as his or her principal function. The principal function of an NF who prefers judging would be feeling, the judging function.

However, in the case of the introvert, the dominant process is turned inward and the auxiliary or secondary function is shown to the world. Hence, the best side is kept for self or very close friends. The inventory you just completed measures the principal function that is used on the outside world; in the case of the introvert, it is actually the auxiliary function.

Perception-Judgment Combinations

The four functional types are a means to comprehend the world. Sensation tells us something exists, thinking tells us what that something is, feeling enables us to make value judgments on this object, and intuition gives us the ability to see the inherent possibilities.[32]

In each person, one of the perception dimensions and one of the judgment dimensions are favored, so that we all prefer one of the following: (1) sensation with thinking, (2) intuition with thinking, (3) sensation with feeling, or (4) intuition with feeling. Jung's personality typology is summarized in Exhibit 2-4.

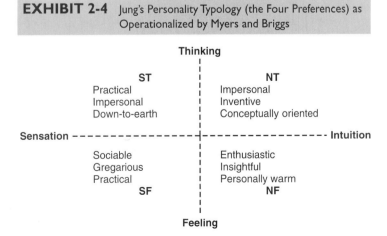

EXHIBIT 2-4 Jung's Personality Typology (the Four Preferences) as Operationalized by Myers and Briggs

Thinking

ST
Practical
Impersonal
Down-to-earth

NT
Impersonal
Inventive
Conceptually oriented

Sensation – **Intuition**

Sociable
Gregarious
Practical
SF

Enthusiastic
Insightful
Personally warm
NF

Feeling

Sensation with Thinking (ST)   This type is usually practical, impersonal, and down-to-earth, being interested in facts, data, and statistics and wanting everything to be orderly, precise, and unambiguous. The STs tend to value efficiency, production, and clear lines of authority. In problem solving, the ST analyzes the facts through step-by-step logic, focusing on short-term problems and using standard procedures to find solutions.[33]

Intuition with Thinking (NT)   NTs are inventive and concept-oriented and are likely to see the possibilities in a situation through impersonal analysis, though sometimes their conceptualizations confuse the other types. Flowcharts, graphs, PERT, and so on all are tools that NTs feel comfortable with. These people are innovators of new ideas, frequently spark enthusiasm in others, and, when solving problems, will often rely on hunches that they attempt to analyze later.

Sensation with Feeling (SF)   Individuals who are SFs tend to be practical, yet also sociable and gregarious. Like the STs, they are interested in facts, but SFs are more interested in facts about people; and they too, dislike ambiguity. SFs would strive to create an open, trusting environment where people care for one another and communicate well.[34] Although concerned with people's welfare, SFs have no time or inclination for global reflections on problems, but rather look at small aspects of problems and try to solve these.[35]

Intuition with Feeling (NF)   Creativity, imagination, and personal warmth are valued by the NF, who is enthusiastic and insightful, generally seeing possibilities in and for people. Their goals are proud and general, often encompassing world problems. Their ideal organization is a decentralized one that has no strict hierarchy, few rules, policies and procedures, and encourages flexibility and open communication.[36] It is very important to NFs to be committed to organizational goals. They may seem to be "dreamers" when solving problems, because theirs is, at times, an idealistic view of the world and its difficulties; but they are persistent and committed.[37]

Exhibit 2-5 provides a summary of your overall profile as a basis for self-understanding. It also provides a look at the profiles of senior and middle managers to help you assess your similarity with successful managers.

EXHIBIT 2-5   Overall Profile Comparisons as a Basis for Self-Understanding

Each person has a personal way of working and living that is influenced considerably by a number of important factors. These, of course, are not by any means the only factors. However, they are very influential in the way a person organizes his or her work. We can summarize these preferences in the following way:

E = Extrovert Preference	or	**I = Introvert Preference**
Prefers to live in contact with others and things		Prefers to be more self-contained and work things out personally
S = Sensing Preference	or	**N = Intuition Preference**
Puts emphasis on fact, details, and concrete knowledge		Puts emphasis on possibilities, imagination, creativity, and seeing things as a whole
T = Thinking Preference	or	**F = Feeling Preference**
Puts emphasis on analysis using logic and rationality		Puts emphasis on human values, establishing personal friendships; decisions mainly on beliefs and dislikes
J = Judging Preference	or	**P = Perceiving Preference**
Puts emphasis on order through reaching decisions and resolving issues		Puts emphasis on gathering information and obtaining as much data as possible

As indicated in the above comparisons, the initial letter of each preference provides a short-hand reference to the factor for understanding and discussion, except for intuition, which is coded *N*, so that it does not conflict with *I* for introvert. These letters are used below to describe the combinations of preference alternatives and present the data on managerial style types.

There are 16 combinations from the alternatives outlined. These can be seen from the following model, which builds upon the shorthand letters that have been adopted for each factor.

Combinations of Preference Alternatives

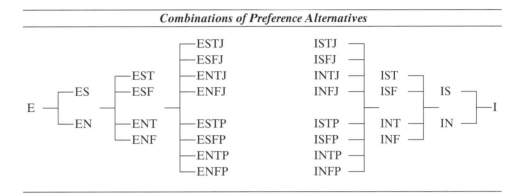

The individual descriptions, while valuable for self-understanding, are insufficient for predicting managerial effectiveness. It is the combination of the various preferences that gives us a better indication of how a person will manage. Research, based on 849 managers attending business school short courses, showed the following breakdown:

	Percentages			
	Extrovert	*Total*	*Introvert*	
ESTJ	20.7	44.5	23.8	ISTJ
ESFJ	5.9	12.4	6.5	ISFJ
BNTJ	8.8	15.3	6.5	INTJ
ENFJ	1.6	4.0	2.4	INFJ
ESTP	3.9	8.2	4.4	ISTP
ESFP	1.2	2.4	1.2	ISFP
ENTP	4.2	7.1	2.9	INTP
ENFP	2.9	6.0	3.1	INFP

It can be seen that the STJs form by far the largest chunk of the senior and middle managerial ranks. This suggests that not only are there certain types of people who are attracted to managerial roles, but also that they are selected more often than not. Also of interest is the low proportion of SFPs—the most "sociable" of the types. This may mean that managers are not "sociable" or at least that they find it difficult to maintain relationships with others. Some implications for managers can be gleaned by examining the percentage breakdown for the four basic conceptual types that were outlined earlier.

	Total	*ST*	*SF*	*NF*	*NT*
Managers	848	53%	15%	10%	22%

Managers are predominantly the ST type. Consequently, they will be concerned first and foremost with practical and logical problems. They will also prefer problems that are concrete and specific rather than ambiguous and abstract; hence, their impatience and distrust of issues that to them seem nebulous and not based on tangible factors. This is not to say that some managers do not prefer problem exploration and definition. As can be seen from the table, all the basic types are represented. However, it is also of interest to note that the types most concerned with people problems are outnumbered three to one by those most concerned with technical problems. Perhaps this explains the need for "interpersonal" skills courses for managers. The SFs are a low proportion—these are the types who act as "lubricant" to the social mechanism of management—and again perhaps their low proportion explains some of the industrial relations problems that occur in organizations.

SOURCE: Adapted from C. Margerison and R. Lewis, "Mapping Managerial Style," *International Journal of Manpower*, Special Issue 2, no. 1 (1981): 2–20.

SAQ 5: Leadership Assumptions Questionnaire[38]

This instrument is designed to help you better understand the assumptions you make about people and human nature. For each of the 10 pairs of statements, assign a weight from 0 to 10 to each statement to show the relative strength of your belief in the statements in each pair. The points assigned for each pair must total 10 in each case. Be as honest with yourself as you can and resist the natural tendency to respond as you would like to think things are. This instrument is not a test. It has no right or wrong answers, but rather is designed to be a stimulus for personal reflection and discussion.

1. It is only human nature for people to do as little work as they can get away with. _____ (a)

   When people avoid work, it is usually because their work has been deprived of its meaning. _____ (b)

   10

2. If employees have access to any information they want, they tend to have better attitudes and behave more responsibly. _____ (c)

   If employees have access to more information than they need to do their immediate tasks, they will usually misuse it. _____ (d)

   10

3. One problem in asking for the ideas of employees is that their perspective is too limited for their suggestions to be of much practical value. _____ (e)

   Asking employees for their ideas broadens their perspective and results in the development of useful suggestions. _____ (f)

   10

4. If people do not use much imagination and ingenuity on the job, it is probably because relatively few people have much of either. _____ (g)

   Most people are imaginative and creative but may not show it because of limitations imposed by supervision and the job. _____ (h)

   10

5. People tend to raise their standards if they are accountable for their own behavior and for correcting their own mistakes. —————— (i)

   People tend to lower their standards if they are not punished for their misbehavior and mistakes. —————— (j)

   10

6. It is better to give people both good and bad news because most employees want the whole story, no matter how painful. —————— (k)

   It is better to withhold unfavorable news about business because most employees really want to hear only the good news. —————— (l)

   10

7. Because a supervisor is entitled to more respect than subordinates in the organization, it weakens a supervisor's prestige to admit that a subordinate was right and the supervisor was wrong. —————— (m)

   Because people at all levels are entitled to equal respect, a supervisor's prestige is increased when that supervisor supports this principle by admitting that a subordinate was right and the supervisor was wrong. —————— (n)

   10

8. If you give people enough money, they are less likely to be concerned with such intangibles as responsibility and recognition. —————— (o)

   If you give people interesting and challenging work, they are less likely to complain about such things as pay and supplemental benefits. —————— (p)

   10

9. If people are allowed to set their own goals and standards of performance, they tend to set them higher than the boss would. —————— (q)

   If people are allowed to set their own goals and standards of performance, they tend to set them lower than the boss would. —————— (r)

   10

10. The more knowledge and freedom a person has regarding a job, the more controls are needed to keep that employee in line. —————— (s)

    The more knowledge and freedom a person has regarding a job, the fewer controls are needed to ensure satisfactory job performance. —————— (t)

    10

Scoring. Record the number you assign to each of the following letters in the space provided and then total each column.

Theory X	*Theory Y*
a _____	b _____
d _____	c _____
e _____	f _____
g _____	h _____
j _____	i _____
l _____	k _____
m _____	n _____
o _____	p _____
r _____	q _____
s _____	t _____
_____ (Total)	_____ (Total)
Theory X Score	Theory Y Score

Interpretation. McGregor proposed that a manager's view of the nature of human beings tends to fall into one of two sets.[39] In the first, which is called Theory X, managers assume that:

1. Employees inherently dislike work and, whenever possible, will attempt to avoid it.
2. Because employees dislike work, they must be coerced, controlled, or threatened with punishment to achieve goals.
3. Employees will shirk responsibility and seek formal direction whenever possible.
4. Most workers place security above all other factors associated with work and will display little ambition.

In contrast to these negative views about the nature of human beings, McGregor listed four other assumptions that constituted what he called Theory Y:

1. Employees can view work as natural as rest or play.
2. People will exercise self-direction and self-control if they are committed to the objectives.
3. The average person can learn to accept, and even seek, responsibility.
4. The ability to make innovative decisions is widely dispersed throughout the population and is not necessarily the sole province of those in management positions.

Do you see people as basically lazy and irresponsible or as industrious and trustworthy? Look at your Theory X and Theory Y scores. In which box did you score highest? Now, subtract your low score from your highest. The larger this number is, the more strongly you hold to the assumptions of the higher category. Conversely, the lower the number, the more flexibility you show. That is, the closer each of your Theory X and Theory Y scores is to 50, the less intensity you have about the fixed nature of human behavior. You regard some people as hard-working and trustworthy, but see others as irresponsible and needing direction.

If you scored high only on Theory X assumptions (above 65 points), you do not have much confidence in others—an attitude that is likely to show itself in behaviors such as unwillingness to delegate, authoritarian leadership, and excessive concern with closely monitoring and controlling the people who work for you. A similar high score on Theory Y assumptions indicates a great deal of confidence in other people and may lead, at the extreme, to insufficient managerial attention. How? Excessive delegation of authority, inadequate coordination of subordinates' activities, and unawareness of problems that need attention are some of the possible dysfunctional outcomes of an unrealistic confidence in one's employees.

Soliciting Feedback from Others

In order to really know ourselves, it is of paramount importance to solicit feedback from others.[40] No matter how much self-examination we engage in through reflecting in solitude about our goal achievements, journal entries about life experiences, or results of self-assessment inventories, to get a true picture of our interpersonal effectiveness we need to understand how others perceive and react to us.

Before we receive meaningful feedback from others, it is beneficial to self-disclose our assumptions, frames of reference, paradigms, and motives about the behaviors they observe. When we self-disclose, we force ourselves to assess who we are and why we do things, allow others to better understand our behavior, and facilitate trust by demonstrating a willingness to share.[41]

Next, we need to actively solicit feedback from others about their reactions and the consequences of our behaviors. Then we can judge whether we are being effective or need to modify what we do to achieve our goals. The monitoring and truthful evaluation of feedback facilitates behavior changes necessary to improve managerial behavior.[42] It should be emphasized that to receive honest feedback, we need to actively solicit it, because others, especially subordinates, are often reluctant to share reactions to our behaviors, especially those that they think may be perceived in an unfavorable light.[43] Our initial self-disclosures and request for feedback to improve our behaviors for the benefit of ourselves and others is a good place to set the tone for receiving honest reactions.

A Model for Self-Disclosing and Soliciting Feedback

The Johari Window[44] (see Exhibit 2-6) is a model of the different degrees of self-disclosure and solicitation of feedback utilized when someone is interacting with another person. The model presents four "windowpanes" of potential self-awareness resulting from the information flow between ourselves and others. A description of these four cells follows.

Open Area   In this high-balanced area, the manager openly self-discloses and solicits feedback from others. Consequently, others know what the manager's perceptions and intentions are, and the manager's self-awareness is high because of the feedback received from others. Managers using this style know and understand themselves

EXHIBIT 2-6   Johari Window

	Solicit Feedback	
	High Known	*Low* Not Known
High Known	Open Area	Blind Area
Low Not Known	Hidden Area	Unknown Area

SOURCE: J. Luft, *Group Processes,* 3d ed. (Palo Alto, CA: Mayfield Publishing Company, 1984) 11–20.

because of the timely and accurate feedback they receive. They can make appropriate changes when necessary. Their open sharing increases the comfort level of others and thereby increases the likelihood that they will establish open channels of communication, which can lead to full sharing of information, mutual understanding, and mutual trust. The resulting open and positive relationship maintains a source of continued feedback for ongoing self-assessment.[45]

Hidden Area Managers with relatively large hidden areas ask a lot of questions to solicit feedback but do not self-disclose much to others. Consequently, others have a difficult time knowing how the manager feels or what he or she wants. After a while, people can become irritated at continually being asked to open up and share things without any reciprocation from the manager. They may become suspicious about how the information will be used, and may begin to shut down on the quantity and quality of information they are willing to share, thereby decreasing the chances of a manager increasing self-awareness.

Managers using this conservative-probing style have an aversion to self-disclosure, but still seek to maintain open channels of communication with others by seeking feedback. This reluctance to self-disclose may reflect a manager's own insecurity or a mistrust of others. Or the manager may be afraid that if others knew all the information, then they would think less of him or her, use the information to their advantage, or be angry because it hurt their feelings. Whatever the reason, conservative-probing managers are likely to create personal facades designed to mislead others. Unfortunately, once such behavior is recognized, others are likely to withdraw their willingness to provide meaningful and candid feedback about the situation or themselves. The result may ultimately be isolation and mistrust on the part of relevant others, which closes off opportunities for receiving information relevant to self-assessment.

Blind Area The blind area encompasses certain things about a manager that are apparent to others but not to the manager. These blind spots occur either because no one has ever told the manager about them or because the manager defensively blocks them out. Managers with large blind areas frequently tell others how they feel and where they stand on issues, but they are insensitive to feedback from others. Because they don't "hear" what others say to and about them, these managers do not know how they come across and what impact their behavior has on others. Because they limit self-awareness, blind spots make a manager less effective in interactions with others. A manager may be terrible at running meetings, for example, but may not know it because no one has given him or her any feedback.

In many cases, managers with large blind spots rate their own skills highly and become egoistically involved in the correctness and importance of their actions. These types of managers tend to dominate and seek compliance from others without seeking their feelings or perceptions. Because ego-dominant managers overuse self-disclosure and fail to balance disclosure with feedback-seeking behaviors, they are not aware of their impact on others. They miss opportunities to allow others to participate in the decision-making process and are unaware of the perceptions and feelings of others. When relevant others believe that managers are not interested in their feelings and perceptions, they not only quit trying to provide meaningful feedback, but also are likely to feel disenfranchised and withdraw their support for the relationship.[46]

Unknown Area Finally, in the unknown area lie repressed fears and needs or beneficial potentials that neither the manager nor subordinates are aware of. Managers using this last style minimize the use of both self-disclosure and feedback-seeking behaviors. They tend to be perceived as impersonal and closed in their relationships with relevant others who are unaware of how these managers feel, and what information they (relevant others) might have to contribute to the situation. While such managers minimize their risks during interpersonal exchanges, they create an environment characterized by withdrawal, detachment, and a reliance on rules as the basis for control. The result of such a style is an environment characterized by closed impersonal relationships and a minimum level of interaction and creativity within the system. Others are also likely to experience frustrations because they do not know where they stand with the manager and may begin to perceive the manager's behavior as an obstacle to their own need for achievement.

Maximizing Self-Awareness In a supportive environment, an open, "high-balanced," interpersonal style would produce the maximum self-awareness for the manager because he or she would be fully understood by others, and would fully understand them in return. Decisions would be based on complete information and involved subordinates would be committed to their effective implementation. Unfortunately, not all environments are mutually supportive. In competitive situations, or situations with sufficient reasons not to trust others, open self-disclosure may not be in the manager's best interest. Consequently, an appropriate style is a function of differences in situational characteristics as well as differences in the participants themselves. To be most effective, managers should develop a strategy for determining the appropriate level of self-disclosure and feedback-seeking behavior when interacting with others. If open communication is not justified, managers may want to use some of the techniques described in later chapters of this book to resolve conflicts, develop open cultures, and build supportive teams.

Guidelines for Soliciting Feedback

Managers can use two general strategies for collecting feedback information. First, they can actively monitor their environment by observing the behavior of others. In this case, managers make no attempt to directly interact with others. Information is obtained by vicariously observing how others respond to their behavior. Second, they can be direct by specifically asking others how they feel about or would evaluate the manager's behavior. The seven steps in Exhibit 2-7 provide guidelines about how to obtain feedback in a productive manner.

After the feedback has been received and accepted, the best type of reinforcement for the manager is to make appropriate changes or to maintain behaviors where feedback is positive. Where necessary, the manager may want to point out changed or maintained behaviors to the individual who provided the feedback.

Who Should Feedback Be Solicited From?

Insights from others can be obtained by soliciting feedback about your skill performance from those around you who are immediately effected. If the manager is having difficulty obtaining the feedback needed by soliciting it during daily interactions, more formal interventions such as 360 degree feedback or personal coaches may work.

360 Degree Feedback Companies such as Alcoa, Pitney Bowes, AT&T, Nestle's Perrier division, Chase Manhattan Corp., DuPont, Levi Strauss, and UPS are using this innovative approach for career coaching and helping managers recognize their strengths and weaknesses.[47] The 360 degree feedback approach utilizes feedback from supervisors, subordinates, and coworkers to provide multiple perspectives from the full circle of people with whom the manager interacts. With proper training, managers who use formal periodic surveys or questionnaires have a greater chance of obtaining valid feedback from all sources rather than those who randomly request it,[48] although some incidents may be especially ripe for immediate learning.

EXHIBIT 2-7	Guidelines for Soliciting Feedback

Step 1: Identify areas in which feedback would be of most value to goal achievement and growth. The question is, would additional information improve the manager's skill capabilities?

Step 2: Assess the relative value of monitoring versus inquiring behaviors. Monitoring behaviors are less visible than inquiring behaviors, and as a result minimize the potential loss of credibility by not making it appear that managers lack knowledge or understanding. Unfortunately, monitoring behavior takes longer as managers wait for desired behaviors or activities to take place. Monitoring also requires the manager to rely on inferential skills to interpret each situation. Inquiring behaviors allow the manager to take direct control of the situation and ask specific questions of specific individuals. Although managers can increase personal control, there are accompanying costs in time and effort to track down relevant others, finding free time to discuss target areas, and having to explain why the information is needed. If the manager chooses the direct inquiry alternative, the following steps can be taken.

Step 3: Inform others of the specific areas in which you desire feedback. Be specific and provide as much guidance and information to the target individual(s) as possible. Also take the time to educate others about the characteristics of effective feedback, which can be accomplished by explaining the guidelines for effective feedback in Chapter 3 of this book or through example, that is, the manager acts as a model when giving feedback to others. You should ask for feedback only in areas where you really want or need feedback. Individuals who take the time to provide feedback are likely to be turned off if they see their efforts discarded because the information provided relates to an area of little interest to the manager.

Step 4: To facilitate the feedback process, managers should make themselves accessible to relevant others. This can be accomplished by setting aside time for feedback encounters, walking through one's department, and allowing sufficient time at the end of planned meetings for receiving feedback.

Step 5: Managers should monitor their own behavior to ensure that verbal and nonverbal behaviors are not in conflict. The flow of feedback will be quickly turned off if you give nonverbal cues that indicate indifference, impatience, or even anger. Managers who ask for feedback and arrange to meet with a subordinate are facilitating the feedback process. However, if during the feedback session they continue to look at their watches or shake their heads back and forth in disapproval of comments made, it is likely that subordinates will limit the amount of feedback given as well as its content.

Step 6: During the feedback exchange, managers should ensure that they have understood the sender's message. Active listening techniques such as questioning, summarizing, and reflecting will be described in Chapter 3.

Step 7: Provide positive reinforcement for feedback provided by others. During the feedback exchange, maintain good eye contact, smile when good points are made, nod the head, etc. It would also be desirable to thank the individuals giving the feedback for their efforts. The manager should never attack or personally criticize the feedback given. If the feedback is inappropriate, attempt to explain why. Similarly, if nothing can be done in response to the feedback received, also explain why it is the case.

SOURCE: Adapted from L. W. Mealiea and G. P. Latham, *Skills for Managerial Success* (Chicago: Irwin, 1996) 52–54.

What are the benefits and drawbacks of these full-circle reviews?[49] The obvious advantage is the comprehensive perspective provided by soliciting information from all the individuals a manager interacts with during normal activities. It also allows the manager to compare his or her own perceptions with the perceptions that others have of the manager's skills, styles, and performance. The main drawback to the process is that formal questionnaires are time-consuming and complex to administer. Collecting and compiling information from a number of sources takes more time than having only one person provide feedback.

Personal Coaches[50] Companies in trouble have long looked to outside experts for advice on market strategy, quality control, and other straight-ahead business topics. But when the problems turn out to be interpersonal, an executive coach may be called to the rescue. The small but growing practice has been embraced by companies like Texaco, AT&T, Citibank, and Sun Microsystems. So how do personal coaches provide relevant feedback for effective self-assessment?

Let us take the example of a 40-something CEO of a blue-chip entertainment company, who, although smart and self-assured, had acquired some blind spots on his way up. Key vice presidents were on the verge of mass resignation when the directors got wind of the crisis. They made a call to Howard J. Morgan, a human resources consultant who specializes in executive coaching. For five days Morgan attached himself to the executive, sitting through his meetings, eavesdropping on his phone calls, and tagging along on business lunches. One thing he observed was that the executive micromanaged, signing off on every small decision. Another was that his meetings were disasters: people wandered in every few minutes, with the boss doing nothing to fend off distractions. So, Morgan provided this feedback and came up with practical solutions. Then he continued shadowing the executive to make sure he followed through. If it was a time management problem, Morgan became the boss's gate-keeper. When subordinates knocked on the door, he told them, politely but firmly, to take a hike. If the boss was hurrying to a meeting and stopped to chat, Morgan demanded, "Couldn't that have waited?"

Personal coaches are expensive, and some managers may object to having people like Morgan following them around at all times. But they provide 100 percent individual attention and comprehensive feedback regarding a manager's behaviors. Plus, they can be perfectly honest because the coaches do not work for the manager and are not affected by organizational politics. Coaching is aimed not only at faltering managers, but for companies like Texaco and Avon, coaching is provided as a tool for continued self-development under the assumption that everyone has blind spots and can benefit from the comments of a detached observer.[51]

Not everyone has access to a personal coach to provide them with feedback for self-awareness. But most of us are able to utilize the other methods of generating relevant data about ourselves so that we can do meaningful self-assessments. After we know ourselves—our values, strengths, preferences, and ways of working—we can make informed decisions about where we belong and what we can contribute in our careers.

Self-Directed Career Management

Self-assessment is an ongoing process for successful managers. In order to keep abreast of rapid change in today's work world and to determine where and how they can best contribute, managers have to know themselves, continually develop themselves, and be able to ascertain when and how to change the work they do. According to Peter Drucker, successful careers are not planned. Rather, they develop when people are prepared for opportunities because they know their strengths, their methods of work, and their values. People who have done this type of self-assessment know themselves and are ready to decide where they belong, or, just as important, where they do *not* belong. Knowing where one belongs can transform a hard-working and competent person into an outstanding performer.[52]

The Self-Directed Career Management Process

Self-directed career management is a process by which individuals guide, direct, and influence the course of their careers.[53] Exploration and awareness of not only oneself, but also one's environment are necessary conditions to self-direct your career.[54] Individuals who are proactive and collect relevant information about personal needs, values, interests, talents, and lifestyle preferences are more likely to (1) be more satisfied and productive when searching for job opportunities, (2) develop successful career plans, and (3) be productive in their jobs and careers.[55]

Exhibit 2-8 describes a self-directed career management process.[56] The organization, of course, has a big stake in you and will usually actively support your career development, but in this one area effective self-management is the key. Some organizations, like Amoco, provide career development programs for all employees, which include benefits such as self-assessment and self-development sessions, web sites for job postings, and a network of career advisers.[57] Although programs like Amoco's help employees reflect on their marketability both inside and outside Amoco, they are still designed around employee self-reliance. Most of us in today's rapidly changing workplace know how important it is to keep skills current and to develop new ones that are needed now or anticipated to be needed in the near future. This need will only increase in the future. So self-directed career management is a continuing lifelong process of learning and relearning.[58] And, to maximize our potential contribution and satisfaction, each of us must accept the ultimate responsibility for our own career development.

As exhibited in Level 1 of Exhibit 2-8, the first step in self-directed career management is planning. After you have assessed yourself so you know your strengths, weaknesses, and values, you are prepared to search the environment for matching opportunities. Then you can establish realistic career goals and develop a strategy to

EXHIBIT 2-8 A Model for Self-Directed Career Planning

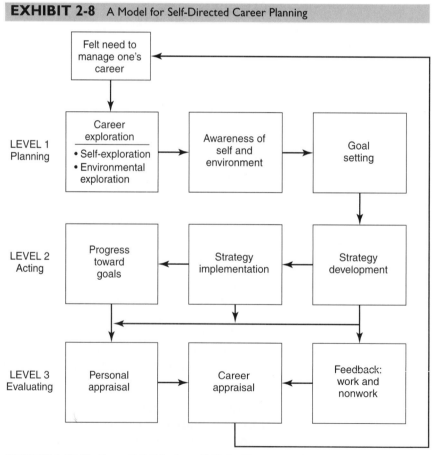

SOURCE: L. W. Mealiea and G. P. Latham, *Skills for Managerial Success* (Chicago: Irwin, 1996) 31.

achieve them.[59] Level 2 is the implementation stage where you put your career plan into action, and Level 3 entails performance appraisal to make sure that you keep on track.[60]

Although the model of career management holds at all stages, individuals just beginning their careers are usually more concerned with identifying organizations that have the potential to satisfy their care goals and match their values. After settling into a job, their focus shifts to achieving initial successes, gaining credibility, learning to get along with their boss, and managing image. Managers in the middle of their careers are more likely to be concerned with career reappraisal, overcoming obsolescence due to technological advances, and becoming more of a generalist. In the later stages of their careers, managers focus more on teaching others and leaving a contribution before retirement.[61]

It has been predicted that most people starting work today can expect to change careers at least three or four times during their working lives.[62] Continual self-assessment and exploration of the environment are necessary conditions for effectively self-managing your career.[63] These activities are also necessary for all employees, however, and managers do have responsibilities to help develop subordinate potential also.

Helping Subordinates Manage Their Careers

What responsibilities do managers have for their subordinates' career development and what can they do to contribute? Today, the key is for managers to instill in all subordinates the need to take responsibility for managing their own careers. Then the manager can provide support for employees to continually add to their skills, abilities, and knowledge, in order to maintain their employability within the organization. So what are some of the key forms of support that a manager can provide to help subordinates develop their careers?[64]

First of all, managers should inform employees about the organization's goals and future strategies so that they will know where the organization is headed and be better able to develop a personal career development plan to share in that future. Next, managers should create growth opportunities for subordinates to get new, interesting, and professionally challenging work experiences. Also, managers can offer financial assistance, like tuition reimbursement for college courses or skills training to help employees keep current. Finally, managers can provide time for employees to learn from these opportunities by allowing paid time off from work for off-the-job training, and managers can assure reasonable workloads so that employees are not precluded from having time to develop new skills, abilities, and knowledge.[65]

CONCEPT QUIZ

Take the following 10-question, true-false quiz concerning self-awareness and personal development. Answers are at the end of the quiz. If you miss any, go back and find out why you got them wrong.

Circle the right answer.

True or False   1. You can only learn about yourself by comparing your experiences with your goals.

True or False   2. Self-awareness is the basis for all the other components of emotional intelligence.

True or False   3. Introverts are more interested in what is happening inside their heads than what is going on outside in the world.

True or False   4. Because managers work with and through other people, the more extroversion they possess, the better.

True or False	5. To get a true picture of our interpersonal effectiveness, we need to understand how others perceive and react to us.
True or False	6. In a supportive environment, high degrees of both self-disclosure and soliciting feedback would produce the maximum self-awareness for a manager.
True or False	7. After the feedback has been received, the best type of reinforcement is for the manager to make appropriate changes or to maintain behaviors where feedback is positive.
True or False	8. Because of their biases, you should not solicit feedback from those who are immediately affected by your actions.
True or False	9. Knowing where one belongs can transform a hard-working and competent person into an outstanding performer.
True or False	10. Self-directed career management is a lifelong process of learning and relearning.

Answers.   (1) False; (2) True; (3) True; (4) False; (5) True; (6) True; (7) True; (8) False; (9) True; (10) True

BEHAVIORAL CHECKLIST

The following behaviors are important for enhancing self-awareness and managing yourself. Refer to them when evaluating your own and other's skills in these areas.

Managers Skilled at Self-Awareness and Self-Management:

- Compare actual experiences with previously set goals.
  - Reflect on what went right and why.
  - Reflect on what went wrong and why.
- Keep a journal.
  - Address critical aspects of their managerial experience.
  - Reflect on personal events.
  - Store ideas for later use in speeches, reports, or papers.
- Create time to find solitude and reflect.
  - Reflect on their experiences and learn from them during uninterrupted time.
  - Create new ideas.
- Solicit feedback from others.
  - Self-disclose so that others know their needs and intentions.
  - Use 360 degree feedback.
  - Contract with significant others to provide specific feedback.
- Take responsibility for self-directing their careers.
  - Assess their strengths, weaknesses, and values.
  - Search the environment for matching opportunities.
  - Establish realistic career goals.
  - Develop a strategy to achieve goals.
  - Implement their career plan.
  - Ask for performance appraisals to keep on track.

SUMMARY SHEET

Summarize your self-assessment profile in the spaces provided on this page. Then tear out the page and turn it in to your instructor. Do not put your name on the sheet. Your instructor will aggregate your class's scores and summarize your interpersonal profiles. Then you can see how you compare to others in the class.

From page 24, **SAQ 1: Is Management for You?** _____

From page 25, **SAQ 2: Preference: Leadership or Management?**

Leadership Score (Sum of even numbered items): _____

Management Score (Sum of odd numbered items): _____

From page 26, **SAQ 3: What's Your Emotional Intelligence at Work?**

Overall emotional intelligence score _____

   Self-awareness _____

   Managing emotions _____

   Motivating yourself _____

   Empathy _____

   Social skill _____

From page 29, **SAQ 4: Cognitive Style Self-Assessment** _____

From page 38, **SAQ 5: Leadership Assumptions**

Theory X _____

Theory Y _____

GROUP EXERCISE

Self-Disclosure and Solicitation of Feedback to Know Yourself Better

Form small groups with five to seven class members you do not know well. The following activities take approximately 40 minutes to complete and should be conducted within these groups.

1. Each group member spends five minutes developing two lists: first, a list of his or her five most valuable personal strengths; second, a list of his or her five most valuable accomplishments.

2. Then each group member has three to five minutes to introduce himself or herself: Highlight your background, career goals, and most important accomplishments to date, and briefly describe what you believe are your interpersonal strengths and limitations.

3. Instigate a round-robin of self-disclosure and receiving feedback: One person volunteers to be the focus and shares his or her scores from the self-assessment questionnaires and feelings about their accuracy. Then, group members each give that person feedback about how closely they see assessment profile scores aligning with each person's behaviors exhibited in steps 1 and 2 of this exercise and their thoughts about the consequences.

4. After the first volunteer clarifies the feedback received, another person volunteers to be the focus, and the process continues until all group members have shared and received feedback.

APPLICATION QUESTIONS

1. How would you describe to a prospective employer the kind of person you are?
2. What is your current career plan?
3. To whom do you feel most comfortable self-disclosing your intentions and feelings? Why? To whom do you feel least comfortable self-disclosing your intentions and feelings? Why?
4. Who are your best resources for providing you with meaningful feedback? Why did you pick these people?
5. Do you really know yourself? What can you do to know yourself even better?
6. What are the implications of your self-assessment scores for your career planning?

REINFORCEMENT EXERCISES

The following suggestions are activities you can do to reinforce the self-assessment and self-management techniques in this chapter. You may want to adapt them to the Action Plan you will develop next, or try them independently.

1. Review the section on journals earlier in this chapter. Keep a daily journal for the remainder of this semester. Record significant events and insights that will enhance your self-awareness. At the beginning of each new week, study your journal entries from the previous week to see what you can learn about yourself.
2. Share your self-assessment inventory scores with a significant other. Explain their meaning. Discuss their implications and see what you can learn from the other person's reactions and experiences with you.
3. Visit your campus counseling center. Ask what self-assessment inventories are available.
4. Visit your campus counseling center or placement office. Ask what career development services are provided.
5. Ask a good friend to share with you his or her perceptions of your strengths and weaknesses as a friend.
6. Practice finding solitude for 30 minutes each day for a week.

ACTION PLAN

1. In what areas do I most need to improve my self-awareness?
2. Why? What will be my payoff?
3. What potential obstacles stand in my way?
4. What are the specific things I will do to enhance my self-awareness? (For examples, see the Reinforcement Exercises.)
5. When will I do them?
6. How and when will I measure my success?

NOTES

1. T. Gabriel, "Away at Management Camp and Feeling Alone," *New York Times*, April 28, 1996, 10.
2. Ibid.
3. P. F. Drucker, "Managing Oneself," *Harvard Business Review* (March–April 1999): 65.
4. B. Van Buskirk and J. Seltzer, "LaSalle University's Model of Teaching Management Skills," Paper presented at the Symposium for Management Education and Development, Academy of Management 1995 Meeting, San Diego, CA, 11.
5. R. L. Hughes, R. C. Ginnett, and G. J. Curphy, *Leadership: Enhancing the Lessons of Experience*, 3d ed. (Burr Ridge, IL: Irwin McGraw-Hill, 1999) 487.
6. P. F. Drucker, "Managing Oneself," *Harvard Business Review* (March–April 1999): 66.
7. Ibid., 66–67.
8. Ideas about how to keep and apply a journal for optimal results can be found in M. Csikszentmihalyi, *Flow: The Psychology of Optimal Experience* (New York: Harper & Row, 1990).
9. H. McIntosh, "Solitude Provides an Emotional Tuneup," *The APA Monitor* 27, no. 3 (March 1996): 9–10.
10. K. Blanchard, "A Call to Solitude," Handout for the Master of Science in Executive Leadership seminar, University of San Diego, San Diego, California, November 10, 1999.

11. It should be noted that these assessment instruments have all been validated in North American cultures and that the implications drawn are predominately oriented for North American business organizations. Different implications may be drawn for managers in other countries.

12. The idea for this assessment came from J. B. Miner and N. R. Smith, "Decline and Stabilization of Managerial Motivation over a 20-Year Period," *Journal of Applied Psychology* (June 1982): 298.

13. Adapted from R. Daft, *Leadership: Theory and Practice* (Fort Worth: Dryden Press, 1999) 55–6.

14. Adapted from H. Weisinger, *Emotional Intelligence at Work* (San Francisco: Jossey-Bass, 1998) 214–15.

15. This discussion is based on B. Murray, "Does Emotional Intelligence Matter in the Workpace?" *APA Monitor* (July 1998): 21; A. Fisher, "Success Secret: A High Emotional IQ," *Fortune,* October 26, 1998, 293–98; D. Goleman, *Working with Emotional Intelligence* (New York: Bantam Books, 1998); R. Daft, *Leadership: Theory and Practice* (Fort Worth: Dryden Press, 1999) 346–47.

16. H. Weisinger, *Emotional Intelligence at Work* (San Francisco: Jossey-Bass, 1998) 214–15.

17. N. Gibbs, "The EQ Factor," *Time,* October 2, 1995, 65.

18. D. Ancona, T. Kochan, M. Scully, J. Van Maanen, and D. E. Westney, *Managing for the Future: Organizational Behavior and Process,* 2d ed. (Cincinnati: South-Western College Publishing, 1999) C5–C15.

19. Adapted from D. Maric, *Organizational Behavior: Experiences and Cases,* 3d ed. (New York: West Publishing Company (1992) 376–79. Copyright 1985 by Dorothy Marcic. All rights reserved.

20. I. B. Myers, *The Myers-Briggs Type Indicator Manual* (Princeton, NJ: Education Testing Service, 1962).

21. C. Jung, *Psychological Types* (Princeton, NJ: Princeton University Press, 1971).

22. Myers, 1962.

23. Myers, 1962.

24. Jung, 1971.

25. Myers, 1962.

26. Myers, 1962.

27. Myers, 1962, 50.

28. Myers, 1962.

29. Jung, 1971.

30. Myers, 1962, 80.

31. Myers, 1962.

32. H. Mann, M. Siegler, and H. Osmond, "The Many Worlds of Time," *Journal of Analytical Psychology* 13, no. 1 (1968): 33–56.

33. D. Hellriegel and J. W. Slocum, Jr., "Managerial Problem-Solving Styles," *Business Horizons,* December 1975, 29–37.

34. R. Kilmann, "Stories Managers Tell: A New Tool for Organizational Problem Solving," *Management Review* (July 1975): 18–28.

35. Hellriegel and Slocum, 1975.

36. R. Kilmann, "Stories Managers Tell: A New Tool for Organizational Problem Solving," *Management Review* (July 1975): 18–28.

37. Hellriegel and Slocum, 1975.

38. Adapted from S. P. Robbins and P. L. Hunsaker, *Training in Interpersonal Skills,* 2d ed. (Upper Saddle River, NJ: Prentice Hall, 1996) 12–14.

39. D. McGregor, *The Human Side of Enterprise* (New York: McGraw-Hill, 1960).

40. J. Powell, *Why Am I Afraid to Tell You Who I Am?* (Chicago: Argus Communications, 1969); W. J. A. Marshall, "The Importance of Being Earnest: A Primer for Leaders," *Management Quarterly* 27, no. 2, (Summer 1986): 7–12; J. Luft, *Group Processes,* 3d ed. (Palo Alto, CA: Mayfield Publishing Company, 1984) 11–20.

41. R. L. Weaver II, *Understanding Interpersonal Communications* (New York: HarperCollins College Publishers, 1993).

42. S. Ashford, "Feedback-Seeking in Individual Adaptation: A Resource Perspective," *Academy of Management Journal* (September 1986): 465–87; P. L. McLeod, J. K. Liker, and S. A. Lobel, "Process Feedback in Task Groups: An Application of Goal Setting," *Journal of Applied Behavioral Science* 28, no. 1 (March 1992): 15–41.

43. G. B. Northcraft, and S. J. Ashford, "The Preservation of Self in Everyday Life: The Effects of Performance Expectations and Feedback Context on Feedback Inquiry," *Organizational Behavior & Human Decision Processes* 47, no. 1 (October 1990): 42–64.

44. For a comprehensive discussion of the Johari Window, see J. Luft, *Group Processes,* 3d ed. (Palo Alto, CA: Mayfield Publishing Company, 1984) 11–20; J. Hall, "Communication Revisited," *California Management Review* 15, no. 3 (Spring 1973).

45. R. L. Weaver II, *Understanding Interpersonal Communications* (New York: HarperCollins College Publishers, 1993).

46. L. W. Mealiea and G. P. Latham, *Skills for Managerial Success* (Chicago: Irwin, 1996) 50.

47. J. F. Milliman, R. A. Zawacki, C. Norman, L. Powell, and J. Kirksey, "Companies Evaluate Employees from All Perspectives," *Personnel Journal* (November 1994): 99–100.

48. C. Cherniss and D. Goleman, *Bringing Emotional Intelligence to the Workplace,* Technical Report Issued by the Consortium for Research on Emotional Intelligence in Organizons (Piscataway, NJ: Rutgers University, 1998) 4.

49. Ibid.

50. This section is based on T. Gabriel, "Personal Trainers to Buff the Boss's People Skills," *New York Times,* April 28, 1996, Section 3, 1, 10.

51. Ibid., 10.

52. P. F. Drucker, "Managing Oneself," *Harvard Business Review* (March–April 1999): 70–71.

53. J. H. Greenhaus, *Career Management* (Chicago: Dryden Press, 1987).

54. J. G. Clawson, J. P. Kotter, V. A. Faux, and C. C. McArthur, *Self-Assessment and Career Development* (Upper Saddle River, NJ: Prentice-Hall, 1985).

55. O. C. Brenner, "The Impact of Career Exploration on the Career Decision-Making Process," *Journal of College Student Personnel* 24 (1983): 495–502; Greenhaus, 1987.

56. J. H. Greenhaus, *Career Management* (Chicago: Dryden Press, 1987) 18.

57. M. Hequet, "Flat and Happy?" *Training* (April 1995): 29–34.

58. B. Filipczak, "You're On Your Own: Training, Employability, and the New Employment Contract," *Training* (January 1995): 29–36.

59. See Chapter 7 for skills on planning, goal setting, and strategy development.

60. See Chapter 8 for a review of the skills necessary for effectively evaluating performance.

61. K. Labich, "Taking Control of Your Career," *Fortune* 124, part 2 (November 18, 1991): 87; J. E. A. Russell, "Career Development Interventions in Organizations," *Journal of Occupational Behavior* 38 (1991): 237–87.

62. M. Calabresi, J. Van Tasel, M. Riley, and J. R. Szczesny, "Jobs in an Age of Insecurity," *Time*, November 22, 1993, 38.

63. J. G. Clawson, J. P. Kotter, V. A. Faux, and C. C. McArthur, *Self-Assessment and Career Development* (Upper Saddle River, NJ: Prentice Hall, 1985).

64. These ideas are based on D. T. Hall and Associates, eds. *The Career Is Dead—Long Live the Career* (San Francisco: Jossey Bass, 1996); M. Cianni and D. Wnuck, "Individual Growth and Team Enhancement: Moving Toward a New Model of Career Development," *Academy of Management Executive* (February 1997): 105–15; D. T. Hall, "Protean Careers of the 21st Century," *Academy of Management Executive* (November 1996): 8–16.

65. S. P. Robbins, *Managing Today!* 2d ed. (Upper Saddle River, NJ: Prentice Hall, 2000) 295–96.

SELF-AWARENESS

All of us have doubts, fears, and insecurities, some we can admit to, and others we cannot. Self-awareness—recognizing our own feelings and the ways they guide our behavior—is a skill that can be sharpened with practice. It is the first step to overcoming the weaknesses we acknowledge *and* the weaknesses we do not.

Learning from experience is one way to enhance self-awareness. There are three techniques for learning from experience: experience-goal matching, keeping a journal, and finding solitude to reflect. Asking others for feedback about our interpersonal effectiveness is another way to increase awareness of our own feelings; it shows us how our actions affect others. As a manager, you should ask for such feedback, since subordinates may otherwise be reluctant to say what they think.

This video segment introduces Quicktakes Video, a small television production company started by Hal Boylston and Karen Jarvis. Quicktakes produces short films and videos for various corporate and entrepreneurial clients and is based on a real company.

We first meet Hal Boylston in a stressful moment as a problem at home follows him to the office. Then we see him confront a crisis at work that calls for a management decision. Hal fills an emergency need for a producer to do a video shoot in San Francisco by going himself, a choice that leaves his staff concerned and dissatisfied.

See whether you can spot the reasons why Hal's staff is unhappy with his decision to go on location. Decide whether you think they are justified. If Hal had another option, why do you think he did not take it?

Explain exactly how Hal's lack of self-awareness leads him to make his decision and why he chose to ignore its possible consequences. Be alert to the behavior of his subordinates too. Are there ways they could be supporting Hal more effectively? ∎

QUESTIONS

1. What feelings does Hal ignore as he starts his workday? What is an appropriate way for him to acknowledge those feelings?

2. Hal does not realize that his production techniques are somewhat rusty and cause extra work for the post-production crew, yet he recognizes the same weakness in Jim, a Quicktakes producer about whom he complains. Why do you think this situation occurs?

3. What opportunities did you see for people to give Hal feedback about his performance? How well do you think his employees handled these opportunities?

4. What unacknowledged feelings strengthen Hal's rash decision to make the trip? How might greater self-awareness have helped him in this situation?

PART II
General Integrative Skills

CHAPTER 3

Interpersonal Communication

Learning Objectives

After completing this chapter, you should be able to:

■ Identify and avoid the barriers to effective communication.

■ Send clear, understandable messages.

■ Listen actively to others.

■ Utilize nonverbal signals.

■ Solicit meaningful feedback.

■ Adapt to style, gender, and cultural diversity.

■ Give appropriate feedback.

SELF-ASSESSMENT EXERCISE

What Is Your Communication Style?

Think of how you usually communicate with others in everyday situations. For each of the following 18 *pairs* of statements, distribute three points between the two alternatives depending upon which is most characteristic of your style. The point range is from 0–3: 0 = Never; 1 = Rarely; 2 = Sometimes; 3 = Always. *The numbers you assign to each pair of statements should add up to 3.*

1A _____ I am open to getting to know people personally and establishing relationships with them.

1B _____ I am not open to getting to know people personally and establishing relationships with them.

2A _____ I react slowly and deliberately.

2B _____ I react quickly and spontaneously.

3A _____ I am open to other people's use of my time.

3B _____ I am not open to other people's use of my time.

4A _____ I introduce myself at social gatherings.

4B _____ I wait for others to introduce themselves to me at social gatherings.

5A _____ I focus my conversations on the interests of the parties involved, even if it means that the conversations stray from the business or subject at hand.

5B _____ I focus my conversations on the tasks, issues, business, or subject at hand.

6A _____ I am not assertive, and I can be patient with a slow pace.

6B _____ I am assertive, and at times I can be impatient with a slow pace.

7A _____ I make decisions based on facts or evidence.

7B _____ I make decisions based on feelings, experiences, or relationships.

8A _____ I contribute frequently to group conversations.

8B _____ I contribute infrequently to group conversations.

9A _____ I prefer to work with and through others, providing support when possible.

9B _____ I prefer to work independently or dictate the conditions in terms of how others are involved.

10A _____ I ask questions or speak more tentatively and indirectly.

10B _____ I make emphatic statements or directly express opinions.

11A _____ I focus primarily on the idea, concept, or results.

11B _____ I focus primarily on the person, interaction, and feelings.

12A _____ I use gestures, facial expressions, and voice intonation to emphasize points.

12B _____ I do not use gestures, facial expressions, and voice intonation to emphasize points.

13A _____ I accept others' points of view (ideas, feelings, and concerns).

13B _____ I do not accept others' point of view (ideas, feelings, and concerns).

14A _____ I respond to risk and change in a cautious or predictable manner.

14B _____ I respond to risk and change in a dynamic or unpredictable manner.

15A _____ I prefer to keep my personal feelings and thoughts to myself, sharing only when I wish to do so.

15B _____ I find it natural and easy to share and discuss my feelings with others.

16A _____ I seek out new or different experiences and situations.

16B _____ I choose known or similar situations and relationships.

17A _____ I am responsive to others' agendas, interests, and concerns.

17B _____ I am directed toward my own agendas, interests, and concerns.

18A _____ I respond to conflict slowly and indirectly.

18B _____ I respond to conflict quickly and directly.

SOURCE: Adapted from T. Alessandra and M. J. O'Connor, *Behavioral Profiles: Self-Assessment* (San Diego: Pfeiffer & Company, 1994).

Scoring and Interpretation

People develop habitual ways of communicating with others based on behaviors that were reinforced when growing up. Your communication style can be understood by looking at how open or self-contained you are, and how direct or indirect you are.

To determine your degrees of openness and directness, transfer your scores from the questionnaire to the table below. Then, total each column to get your Open (O), Self-Contained (S), Direct (D), and Indirect (I) scores.

Communication Style Scoring Sheet			
O	*S*	*D*	*I*
1A	1B	2B	2A
3B	3A	4A	4B
5A	5B	6B	6A
7B	7A	8A	8B
9A	9B	10B	10A
11B	11A	12A	12B
13A	13B	14B	14A
15B	15A	16A	16B
17A	17B	18B	18A
O	S	D	I
Total _____	Total _____	Total _____	Total _____

Compare the O and S scores. Which is higher? Write the higher score in the following blank and circle the corresponding letter: _____   **O   S**
Compare the D and I scores. Which is higher? Write the higher score in the following blank and circle the corresponding letter: _____   **D   I**

Are you more **Open** [higher **O** score] or **Self-Contained** [higher **S** score] when you communicate? When an Open person communicates, he or she is relationship oriented, supportive of others' needs, and shares feelings readily. A Self-Contained person is task oriented, aloof, and not prone to sharing feelings.

Are you more **Direct** [higher **D** score] or **Indirect** [higher **I** score] when you communicate with others? Direct people are extroverted and express their thoughts and feelings quite forcefully. Indirect people hold back and appear more introverted. Direct communicators range from highly assertive to aggressive, while indirect communicators go the other way from moderately assertive to passive.

As illustrated in Exhibit 3-1, the four different communication styles can be discerned by how direct and open you are. If your scores are highest on open and direct, you are an assertive and relationship-oriented *Socializer.* If your scores are highest on self-contained and direct, you are an assertive and task-oriented *Director.* If your scores are highest on indirect and self-contained you are a task-oriented and low assertive *Thinker.* If your scores are highest on indirect and open, you are a low assertive and relationship-oriented *Relater.*

Your communication style affects all other aspects of communication discussed in this chapter: what specific communication barriers you face, how you send messages, how you listen to others, how you use nonverbal signals, how you react to diversity of communication styles, and how you approach making formal oral presentations. We will talk more about the ramifications of your communication style later in this chapter.

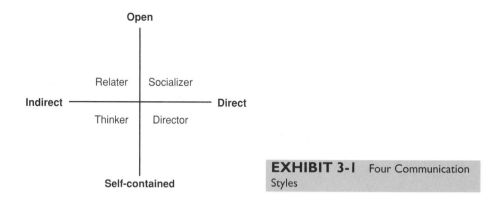

EXHIBIT 3-1 Four Communication Styles

CONCEPTS

Read about the following events that all occurred the same day at a large hotel in Atlanta, Georgia, to learn how miscommunication can cause myriads of problems in daily business operations.[1] Think about what common communication problems were operating in these situations and what the probable consequences were.

Episode 1 The manager of convention sales, Jan Decker, was reviewing last quarter's sales report in preparation for a performance review with each of her three employees. Concerned particularly about Kim Wong's performance, Jan called Kim into her office.

"Kim, I just saw your last quarter's sales numbers. I thought we had agreed upon a goal of six major conventions [1,000 or more room nights] for the quarter. The data state that you booked only four conventions. What happened?"

"I don't understand the problem," Kim responded. "Six was our goal, a target. It was something we were trying to reach."

Clearly upset, Jan was trying to control her frustration. "Kim, six was our goal all right, but it wasn't some 'pie-in-the-sky' number. It was the minimum number of bookings we were counting on. You're responsible for getting us the big conventions. Ted and Dawn handle the smaller ones, but you know we rely on the big conventions to keep our occupancy rates up. I told Dave [the hotel's general manager and Jan's immediate boss] we'd book at least six big conventions in the second quarter. Now I've got to explain why we missed our goal!"

Episode 2 Several months earlier, the hotel's director of human resources had sent a memo to all managers. The topic of the memo was a change in the hotel's leave-without-pay policy. The director of human resources just received a complaint from a buyer in the food and beverage department. The employee's request for a two-week leave without pay to handle personal and financial problems related to the death of his mother had been denied by his manager. He felt his request was reasonable and should have been approved. Interestingly, the memo in question specifically stated that leaves of up to three weeks because of a death in the family were to be uniformly approved. When the human resources director called the beverage manager to follow up on the employee complaint, she was told by the manager, "I never knew there was a change in the policy on leaves without pay."

Episode 3 The following conversation took place between two accounts payable clerks in the accounting department. "Did you hear the latest? The general manager's daughter is marrying some guy from Pittsburgh who's serving a five-year sentence for stealing."

"You're kidding?"

"No, I'm not kidding! I heard it this morning from Chuck in purchasing. Can you imagine the heartache the family must feel?"

This rumor had some basis in fact but was far from accurate. The previous week, the general manager had announced the engagement of his daughter to a Pittsburgh Steelers' football player who had just signed a new five-year contract.

Why Is Communication Important?

In extreme cases, the effectiveness of communication can make the difference between life and death. Examples of miscommunication occur all too frequently on the operating table, in aircraft emergencies, and in fatal industrial accidents. In addition, daily communication breakdowns contribute to numerous organizational problems ranging from minor irritations and conflicts, low productivity and quality due, to employee injuries and deaths (particularly in industries where workers operate heavy machinery or handle hazardous materials).[2]

The events described in the opening hotel vignette demonstrate three common communication problems. First, words mean different things to different people. In the first situation, for Jan Decker a goal meant a minimum level of attainment, while to Kim Wong it meant a maximum target that one tried to reach. Second, the initiation of a message provides no assurance that it has been received or correctly understood. Third, communications often become distorted as they are transmitted from person to person. As the marriage rumor illustrates, "facts" in messages can lose much of their accuracy as they are transmitted and translated.

These episodes illustrate the potential for communication problems and how easily they can plague managers. The importance of effective communication for managers can't be overemphasized because almost everything a manager does involves communicating.[3] For example, managers can't make an informed decision without getting all the relevant information. Once a decision is made, it must be communicated to those charged with implementing it. The best idea, the most creative suggestion, or the finest plan will not make any difference unless effectively communicated.

Managers work with their employees, peers, immediate supervisors, people in other departments, customers, and others to get their own department's objectives accomplished. Interactions with these various individuals all require communication of some type. We are not suggesting that good communication skills alone make a successful manager. However, ineffective communication skills can lead to a continuous stream of problems for the manager.

What Is the Interpersonal Communication Process?

Communication begins when one person sends a message to another with the intent of evoking a response. Often, for a variety of reasons, however, the response that occurs is not what the sender desired. *Effective* communication occurs when the sender transmits ideas and feelings completely and accurately, and the receiver interprets the message exactly as the sender intended. Communication is *efficient* when it uses less time and fewer resources. Communicating with each subordinate individually, for example, is less efficient than addressing all subordinates as a group. Effectiveness, however, means the accurate conveyance of information, which is more important than the speed of transmission. Explaining a new operating procedure to each staff member individually, for example, might be less efficient than calling a meeting where everyone can hear about it together, but if staff members have unique sets of problems, they may require individual coaching. It may be more effective to meet with each one individually. What a manager wants to achieve is effective communication in the most efficient way.

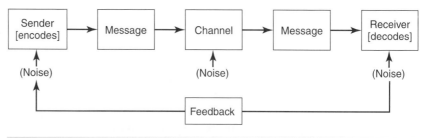

EXHIBIT 3-2 The Communication Process Model

Exhibit 3-2 depicts the interpersonal communication process.[4] The main components of this model are the sender, the receiver, the message, and the channel. The communication process includes the sequential steps of encoding, transmitting, and decoding.

Steps of the Communication Process

First, the sender **encodes** an idea into a message. Then the message is **transmitted** through various channels *orally* (e.g., speeches, meetings, phone calls, or informal discussions), *nonverbally* (e.g., touch, facial expression, and tone of voice), *in writing* (e.g., letters, memoranda, reports, and manuals), or *electronically* (e.g., e-mail, voice mail, facsimiles).

No matter how effectively an idea is encoded in a message and transmitted, communication will not be effective if the receivers fail to perceive and understand the sender's message. **Decoding** is the receiver function of perceiving the communication and interpreting its meaning. It is often more than half the equation.

Noise is anything that interferes, at any stage, with the communication process. The success of the communications process depends to a large degree on overcoming various sources of noise. **Feedback** is the manager's primary tool for determining how clearly a message was understood and what effect it had on the receiver.

Basic Interpersonal Communication Skills

Most communication problems can be avoided by applying six essential skills for effectively sending and receiving interpersonal messages. They include avoiding barriers to communication, sending understandable messages, actively listening, utilizing nonverbal signals appropriately, giving and soliciting meaningful feedback, and adapting appropriately to diversity of communication styles. After reading about the main barriers to communication, methods to overcome them will be presented and you will have opportunities to practice them in later exercises.

What Are the Barriers to Communication?

Barriers to communication, such as semantics, mistrust, or different frames of reference, are often responsible for confusion and misunderstanding. Misinterpretation occurs when the receiver understands the message differently from the way in which the sender intended. A deadly example of misinterpretation occurred in 1990 when a Colombian Avianca pilot told controllers that the plane was "running low on fuel," as it approached New York's Kennedy Airport.[5] Because the controllers heard this phrase all the time, they took no special action. Unfortunately, this time the pilot intended a different meaning. Consequently, the jet ran out of fuel and crashed 16 miles from the airport killing 73 people. Had the pilots used the phrase "fuel emergency," the controllers would have been obligated to clear the Avianca flight to land immediately. The next section describes some of the primary sources of misunderstanding and then techniques to overcome these barriers.

Frames of Reference

As illustrated in the Avianca incident, a combination of past experience and current expectations often leads two people to perceive the same communication differently. Even if two individuals hear the actual words accurately, they may assign different meanings to them, depending on their different frames of reference.

Semantics

Semantics pertains to the meaning and use of words. A common example of semantic noise is evident when people from different cultures try to communicate. In another airline tragedy, Chinese pilots flying a U.S.–built airliner crashed in a fog in 1993 in Urumqu, China, killing 12 people. The cockpit recording of the pilot's last words as they tried to figure out the meaning of the message on the jet's ground proximity warning system were, "What does 'pull up' mean?"[6]

Many professional and social groups adopt a specialized technical language called *jargon* that simplifies communication within the in-group. But sophisticated technical or financial terms can intimidate and confuse outsiders, especially when members of a specialized group use them to project a professional mystique. The military and aerospace companies are examples of organizations that actually produce telephone-sized dictionaries to define all of their acronyms.

Value Judgments

Value judgments are a source of noise when a receiver evaluates the worth of a sender's message before the sender has finished transmitting it. Often such value judgments are based on the receiver's previous experience either with the sender or with similar types of communications. A manager may tune out when a subordinate begins to describe a scheduling problem because "workers are always complaining about something." In businesses where union leaders are perceived as political exploiters, managers will rarely hear their messages without making some inference as to the speaker's intent. When listeners form value judgments, speakers are usually aware of them because nonverbal signals, like frowns or smiles, give them away. Subsequently, the senders become guarded and defensive, which often inhibits transmission of their real concerns.

Selective Listening

Value judgments, needs, and expectations cause us to hear what we want to hear. When a message conflicts with what a receiver believes or expects, *selective listening* may cause the receiver to block out the information or distort it to match preconceived notions. Feedback to an employee about poor performance, for example, may not be "heard" because it doesn't fit the employee's self-concept or expectations.

Filtering

Filtering is selective listening in reverse; in fact, we might call it "selective sending." When senders convey only certain parts of the relevant information to receivers, they are said to be *filtering* their message. Filtering often occurs in upward communication when subordinates suppress negative information and relay only the data that will be perceived by superiors as positive. Filtering is common when people are being evaluated for promotions, salary increases, or performance appraisals.

Distrust

A lack of trust on the part of either communicator is likely to evoke one or more of the barriers we've just examined. Senders may filter out important information if they distrust receivers, and receivers may form value judgments, make inferences, and listen only selectively to distrusted senders.

How Do You Send Clear, Understandable Messages?

Many times these barriers to effective communication can be neutralized or avoided altogether if communicators are simply aware of them and guard against their negative effects. Barriers can also be eliminated by applying effective sending and receiving behaviors. First let's examine behaviors that help send messages more effectively.[7]

Use Multiple Channels

The impact of a message can be increased by using more than one channel or mode of transmission. For example, matching facial and body gestures to a message and diagramming it on a piece of paper uses three channels. This kind of multiple-mode communication ensures that the receiver has the opportunity to receive the message through more than one sense.

Be Complete and Specific

The sender can make the message complete and specific by providing sufficient background information and details. Once the receiver understands the sender's frame of reference, he or she is more likely to interpret the message accurately. By referring to concrete deadlines and examples, like 4:00 P.M. on Friday instead of "as soon as possible," a sender can decrease the probability of misinterpretation.

Claim Your Own Message

To claim a message as your own, use personal pronouns such as "I" and "mine." These labels indicate to the receiver that you take responsibility for the ideas and feelings expressed in the message. General statements like "everyone feels this way" leave room for doubt (someone might not feel that way, which could damage your credibility). But an "I message" such as "I feel strongly about this" is an unambiguous personal opinion. It is probably more effective to say "I think improvement is necessary," rather than, "Don't you think you can do better?" which could put the receiver on the defensive.

Be Congruent

Make sure your messages are congruent with your actions. Being incongruent by saying one thing and doing another confuses receivers. If, for example, managers tell subordinates that they are "always available" to help them but then act condescending and preoccupied when people come to them with problems, they are communicating something quite different from the verbal message.

Simplify Your Language

Complex rhetoric and technical jargon confuse individuals who do not use such language themselves. You should also refrain from using *lingo* (i.e., the company's own words and phrases for people, situations, events, and things). If during a financial negotiation at Walt Disney, for example, the Disney representative referred to a proposal as a "good Mickey," the banker might not realize it was an indication of approval.

Maintain Credibility

Sender credibility is reflected in the receiver's belief that the sender is trustworthy (i.e., what he or she says is accurate). Things you can do to maintain credibility include only trying to influence others when you have sufficient *expertise* on the topic, being *reliable* by providing all relevant information accurately, and being *supportive* of others' concerns. President Clinton's credibility, and consequently his communication effectiveness, was damaged when his lack of reliability and truthfulness became evident during testimonies under oath during the Monica Lewinsky affair.

Obtain Feedback

Effective communication means both top-down and bottom-up communication. All too often managers concentrate on communicating messages to employees without providing a mechanism for the subordinates to respond and give feedback.[8] Without feedback, you have no immediate way to know whether your message has been understood as you intended. When you ask for feedback, on the other hand, the receiver's response will indicate the degree of understanding. You can then modify the original message if necessary. Some rules for giving and receiving feedback effectively are summarized in Exhibit 3-3.

How Do You Receive and Understand Messages Accurately?

The final step to ascertain whether you understand another's message accurately is to provide feedback by sharing your understanding of what has been communicated and to ask for feedback to confirm your interpretation. This and other skills necessary for understanding messages accurately are contained in the technique of active listening.

Listening is an intellectual and emotional process in which a receiver processes physical, emotional, and intellectual messages from a sender in search of meaning. Listening to others is our most important means of gaining the information we need to understand people and assess situations. Poor listeners miss important messages and emerging problems. Disinterest makes listening effectively difficult. To listen well, you have to *care* about the speaker and the message. Then you need to put energy into the process.[9] This process is called active listening.

Active listening means refraining from evaluating other people's words, trying to see things from their point of view, and demonstrating that you are trying to truly understand.[10] Active listeners search for the intent and feeling of the message and indicate their understanding both verbally and nonverbally. Active listeners do not interrupt. They look for verbal and visual cues that the other person would like to say something more.

The three main skills in active listening are sensing, attending, and reflecting. *Sensing* is the ability to recognize the silent messages that the speaker is sending through nonverbal clues such as vocal intonation, body language, and facial expression. *Attending* refers to the verbal, vocal, and visual messages that an active listener sends to the speaker to

---

EXHIBIT 3-3   Guides for Giving and Receiving Feedback

Criteria for Giving Feedback

1. Make sure your comments are intended to help the recipient.
2. Speak directly and with feeling.
3. Describe what the person is doing and the effect the person is having.
4. Don't be threatening or judgmental.
5. Be specific, not general (use clear and recent examples).
6. Give feedback when the recipient is open to accepting it.
7. Check to ensure the validity of your statements.
8. Include only things the receiver can do something about.
9. Don't overwhelm the person with more than can be handled.

Criteria for Receiving Feedback

1. Don't be defensive.
2. Seek specific examples.
3. Be sure you understand (summarize).
4. Share your feelings about the comments.
5. Ask for definitions.
6. Check out underlying assumptions.
7. Be sensitive to the sender's nonverbal messages.
8. Ask questions to clarify.

SOURCE: Summarized from P. L. Hunsaker and A. J. Alessandra, *The Art of Managing People* (New York: Simon & Schuster, 1986) 209–13.

indicate full attention. These cues include direct eye contact, open posture, affirmative head nods, and appropriate facial and verbal expressions.

When *reflecting,* the active listener summarizes and gives feedback on the content and feeling of the sender's message. These actions encourage the speaker to elaborate, make the speaker feel understood, and can even improve the speaker's own understanding of the problem or concern. Reflecting also includes asking questions to obtain additional information, motivate additional communication, and explore the sender's feelings.

How Can You Utilize Nonverbal Cues?

As much as 93 percent of the meaning that is transmitted in face-to-face communication can come from nonverbal channels.[11] Nonverbal communications are more reliable than verbal communications when they contradict each other. Nonverbal communications function as a lie detector to aid a watchful listener in interpreting another's words. Most people choose to believe the nonverbal meaning instead of the verbal one when contradictions are present.

People also judge books and other people by their covers. Managers who look and act like executives, for example, communicate an *image* that makes them more successful than those who do not.[12] Furthermore, by "reading" a person's *facial expressions,* we can detect unexpressed feelings[13] of anger, fear, sadness, disgust, surprise, and happiness.[14] *Eye contact* can communicate things such as honesty, interest, openness, and confidence.[15] *Posture* provides clues about the attitude of the bearer,[16] and *gestures* can signify entire meanings all by themselves.

To the sender of a message, a receiver's visual nonverbal cues serve as feedback. For example, disagreement can be indicated in a side-to-side head shake, while a smile and nod will signal agreement. Caution in reading nonverbal movements is always advisable, however, especially when communicating with people from different cultures where the same gesture can mean entirely different things. The American "V" for "victory" or "peace," for example, means "up yours!" in England when the palm faces inward.[17]

Visual, tactile, and vocal aspects of communication, plus the use of time and space, make up the nonverbal dimensions.[18] The components, consequences, and examples of each of these are illustrated in Exhibit 3-4.

EXHIBIT 3-4   Means of Nonverbal Communication[19]

Components	Examples	Meanings Communicated
Visual		
Image	Clothing; hygiene	Values; competence
Facial expressions	Frown; smile; sneer	Unexpressed feelings
Eye movements	Looking away; staring	Intentions; state of mind
Posture	Leaning in; slumped	Attitude
Gestures	Handshake; wave	Intentions, feelings
Tactile		
Touch	Pat on the back	Approval
	Gentle touch on an arm	Support and concern
Vocal		
How things are said	Loudness, pitch, rate, vocal intonations, rhythm, pitch, clarity	Different meanings (e.g., sarcasm, disapproval, agreement, surprise)
Spacial[20]		
Body closeness	0–2 feet	Feelings of intimacy
Furniture arrangement	Large pieces far apart	Formal and serious

How Can You Make Communication More Productive?[21]

According to Pryor et al. (1998), "productive communication is the process of identifying the desired result, streamlining the message, and communicating with finesse." Productive communication is important in personal and professional, work-related situations. This is because communication is the enabling force that links situations and people. If this linking or networking force is too weak, negative, or nonproductive, then families, work teams, and other groups of people (even armies and governments) are less effective and take steps toward disintegration of mutual efforts. Someone must then become the facilitator who helps resolve conflicts, uncovers unhealthy agreement, and encourages positive, productive communication. The following are examples of productive and nonproductive communication.

Scenario One: Nonproductive Communication

LOAN OFFICER:	Mr. Smith is coming in today to talk to us about a loan.
ASSISTANT (JACK):	Oh?
LOAN OFFICER:	Yes, I'm sure he will take two hours and tell me everything I do wrong as a banker. I could live without seeing him today. [The Loan Officer wants his Assistant to volunteer to handle this customer.]
JACK:	He sure can be a pain sometimes. [The Assistant knows the Loan Officer wants him to volunteer but avoids it.]
LOAN OFFICER:	Say, Jack, you need to learn how to handle customers like this. [The Loan Officer is making a request but pretends he isn't.]
JACK:	You sure are lucky Mr. Smith asked for you. [Jack does not have to acknowledge the message that was sent if there was no specific request.]
LOAN OFFICER:	"Look, I don't need any help. I handle 90 percent of the loans anyway. I really don't care what you do." [Not true, but....]
JACK:	I would have offered to help, but you typically handle the tough cases anyway.
LOAN OFFICER:	Well, somebody has to!

The Loan Officer and the Assistant are now both frustrated because of poor (nonproductive) communication. More efficient communication occurs as a result of applying the productive communication process. Communication from a productivity perspective would have conveyed the message "I want you to do this." A better, more productive way to communicate is demonstrated in Scenario Two.

Scenario Two: Productive Communication

LOAN OFFICER:	Jack, I want you to handle Mr. Smith's loan application at 1 P.M. today. Use a little extra finesse on this one.
JACK:	Mr. Smith can be difficult, but I'll take care of it.
LOAN OFFICER:	Thanks, Jack.

How Can You Adapt to Diversity of Communication Styles?

Effective communication is a challenge even when the workforce is culturally homogeneous, but when participants possess a variety of languages and cultural backgrounds, it becomes even more difficult. First, we'll examine how to cope with differences in communication styles. Then we'll look at cultural and gender differences.

Differences in Communication Styles

Have you ever wondered why it seems so difficult to talk with some people, and so easy to talk with others? Can you remember immediately liking or disliking people the first time you met them? The chances are that your reactions were caused by differences in communication styles.

One frequently occurring communication barrier is the tendency to favor one, usually one's own, communication style, often at the cost to being insensitive to other styles. Ideally managers should be conscious of their own stylistic preferences and dislikes, be able to quickly detect such preferences and dislikes in other people, and be able to adjust their own styles to match those of other people. If managers attempt to achieve this ideal, a surprising number of payoffs result, both in personal insights and in interpersonal skills.[22]

Review your scores on the *"What Is Your Communication Style"* self-assessment exercise at the beginning of this chapter. Although you probably have a number of style variations you can utilize, the predominate style you use most easily and skillfully was indicated at the end of the communication style scoring sheet. Let's review the four dominant communication styles and then explore how managers can practice "style flexing" to get on the same wave length as their conversational partners.

The Socializer Style   Socializers communicate in an open and direct manner. The animated and lively Socializers speak quickly and are less concerned than other styles about facts and details. They are emotional and are relatively comfortable sharing their own feelings and hearing about the feelings of others. To communicate productively with Socializers, don't hurry a discussion and be entertaining.

The Director Style   Directors keep feelings self-contained but are direct about what results are expected. Their communications are oriented toward immediate productivity so Directors can be stubborn, impatient, and strong willed. They strive to dominate and control people to achieve their tasks. Directors like expressing and reacting to tough emotions, but are uncomfortable either receiving or expressing tender feelings. You can maintain productive communications with a Director if you are precise, efficient, and well organized. You should keep communications businesslike.

The Thinker Style   Thinkers also keep feelings self-contained but are indirect about concerns for task accomplishment. Thinkers sometimes appear aloof, picky, and critical mainly because of their need to be right and their constant search for perfection. Thinkers avoid being confrontational and think before they speak.

Thinkers suppress their feelings because they are uncomfortable with any type of emotion. To get on the same communication wavelength with Thinkers, try to be systematic, organized, and prepared. Thinkers require solid, tangible, and factual evidence. Take time to explain the alternatives and the advantages and disadvantages of your point of view.

The Relater Style   Relaters are indirect about what is desired but open about feelings. Relaters are supportive and acquiescent when they talk with others. They want to know how other people feel about a decision before they commit themselves. Because they dislike interpersonal conflict, Relaters often tell others what they think others want to hear rather than what is really on their minds.

Relaters like expressing and receiving tender feelings of warmth and support, but abhor tough emotions like anger or hostility. To communicate effectively with Relaters, support their feelings and show personal interest in them. Move along in an informal manner and show that you are "actively listening."

Cultural Differences

Differences in backgrounds create differences in meanings attached to particular words and behaviors, regardless of whether communicators are different sexes, or are from different countries or different subcultures in the same country. Even if two communicators are speaking the same language, the same words and phrases may mean different things to people from different cultures. For example, the phrase "that would be very hard to do" to a Norwegian or American means that some adjustments or extra contributions may be necessary, but the deal is still possible. To a Japanese, the phrase clearly means, "No, it won't be possible." For a nonverbal example, Americans think that maintaining eye contact is important and others who don't are dishonest or rude. Japanese, on the other hand, lower their eyes as a gesture of respect when speaking with a superior.[23]

Gender Differences

Gender can create subculture communication barriers within the same country. In the United States, for example, men frequently use talk to emphasize status differences because of their need for independence, while women more often use it to create interpersonal connections based on common ground because of their greater need for intimacy. Men frequently complain that women talk a lot about their problems, and women criticize men for not listening. What men are doing is asserting their independence and desire for control by providing solutions, which women do not necessarily want in their quest for support, understanding, and connection.[24]

Because of these differences, most people interact differently with same-sex than with different-sex communicators. Male managers' communication behaviors are often characterized by task orientation, dominance, challenges to others, and attempts to control the conversation. For example, males talk more and interrupt more often than do females. Females are usually more informative, receptive to ideas, focused on interpersonal relations, and concerned for others. They are more reactive and show more emotional support.[25]

Women are more precise in their pronunciation than men, who, for example, tend to shorten the ends of words (e.g., using "in" instead of "ing").[26] Men and women also differ in word choice. Women tend to select more intense adverbs, such as "awfully friendly," whereas men use words that are more descriptive and defining.

Women more often use qualifying terms, which are phrases that soften or qualify the intent of our communication. They make language less absolute and less powerful. Examples include "maybe," "you know what I mean," "it's only my opinion," and so on.[27]

Women also frequently use tag questions, which are qualifying words at the end of a sentence that ask the other for confirmation of the statement presented. When using these tags, they automatically defer to others: "It's time for a break now, right?" "We did a great job, didn't we?" By adding the tag question, the speaker gives the impression of being unsure and surrenders decision-making power.[28]

Women learn to listen with empathy and to be responsive and sensitive to others' emotions. Men, on the other hand, are encouraged to be rational and strong, and to deny feelings in order to maintain rationality and control. Women's stronger empathy is thought to be valuable in maintaining collaborative, growth-enhancing relationships.

How Can You Facilitate Communication with Diversity?

Even with the best of intentions, the unknowing manager can get into deep trouble when communicating with people with different gender or cultural backgrounds. Some specific guidelines, however, can help facilitate communications when diversity is present.[29]

1. *Assume differences until similarity is proven.*   Effective cross-cultural communicators know that they don't know how people with different backgrounds perceive a situation or interpret certain forms of communication. They do not assume that a person from another culture interprets a word or behavior the same way that they do.
2. *Emphasize description rather than interpretation or evaluation.*   Effective cross-cultural communicators delay judgment until they have observed and interpreted the situation from the perspectives of all cultures involved.
3. *Empathize.*   When trying to understand the words, motives, and actions of a person from another culture, try to interpret them from the perspective of that culture rather than your own. When you view behaviors from your own perspective, you can completely misinterpret the other's actions if he or she has different values, experiences, and objectives.
4. *Treat your interpretations as guesses until you can confirm them.*   Check with others from other cultures to make sure that your evaluation of a behavior is accurate if you are in doubt.

CONCEPT QUIZ

Complete the following true-false quiz by circling the correct answers. Answers are at the end of the quiz. After marking your answers, remember to go back and check your understanding of any answers you missed.

True or False   1. Efficient communication is almost always better than effective communication.

True or False   2. Communication takes more time than any other managerial activity.

True or False   3. People develop habitual ways of communicating with others based on behaviors that were reinforced when growing up.

True or False   4. Feedback is the receiver function of perceiving communication and interpreting its meaning.

True or False   5. An army colonel should avoid using technical military jargon when addressing the general public.

True or False   6. Sally is filtering when she tells her supervisors only about sales successes but not about setbacks.

True or False   7. Active listening involves sensing, attending, and reflecting.

True or False   8. You should not ask questions in order to avoid confusing a sender.

True or False   9. In the United States, direct eye contact is usually a sign of honesty, interest, openness, and confidence.

True or False   10. Interpret the meaning of a foreign speaker's statements from your own point of view.

Answers. (1) False; (2) True; (3) True; (4) False; (5) True; (6) True; (7) True; (8) False; (9) True; (10) False

BEHAVIORAL CHECKLIST

The following skills are important to effective communication. Use them when evaluating your communication skills and those of others.

The Effective Communicator

- Avoids barriers to communication.
- Sends clear, understandable messages.
- Actively listens to others.
- Utilizes nonverbal signals.
- Gives appropriate feedback.
- Adapts to diversity of other communicators.
- Solicits meaningful feedback.

MODELING EXERCISE

Controversial Issue Debate

Purpose. To practice all the interpersonal communication skills in a highly charged situation and receive feedback on your effectiveness.

Directions. Two class members volunteer to participate in a debate in front of the class. The debaters can choose any contemporary issue they disagree on. Or they can role-play their differences by debater A selecting one position on the issue and debater B taking the counterposition. Some examples: business ethics, value of unions, stiffer college grading policies, gun control, and money as a motivator. The debate is to proceed, with only one catch. Before each debater speaks, he or she must first summarize, in his or her *own* words and without notes, what the other has said. If the summary isn't what the first debater meant, it must be corrected and restated until it does. Then the second debater says his or her piece, and the first debater restates the second debater's position satisfactorily before responding.

Observer's Role. In addition to rating both debaters' interpersonal communication skills on the rating sheet, the observers should remind each debater to paraphrase the other's statements until acknowledged as correct, before stating their own points.

Time. 15 minutes.

OBSERVER'S RATING SHEET

On completion of the exercise, class members rate each debater's application of interpersonal communication skills. Use the following scale to rate each role-player between 1 and 5. Write concrete examples in the space below each criteria to use in explaining your feedback.

1	2	3	4	5
Unsatisfactory	*Weak*	*Adequate*	*Good*	*Outstanding*

Communication Behaviors	*Debater A Rating*	*Debater B Rating*
Avoids communication barriers	_____	_____
Sends understandable messages	_____	_____
Actively listens (attends, reflects, follows)	_____	_____
Utilizes nonverbal signals well	_____	_____
Gives effective feedback	_____	_____
Adapts to diversity (style, gender, culture)	_____	_____
Solicits meaningful feedback	_____	_____

GROUP EXERCISES

Three different types of group exercises follow. First is a business case to apply your conceptual understanding of effective communication. Second is an active listening exercise applied to solving personal problems where you have an opportunity to practice your behavioral skills. Third is an experiential exercise to practice your nonverbal communication skills.

Group Exercise 1: A Case of Deadly Communication Problems[30]

Directions. Individually read the following case and answer the questions at the end. Then form groups of five or six and discuss your answers, or discuss your answers in the class as a whole.

Deadly Communication Problems At 7:40 P.M. on January 25, 1990, Avianca Flight 52 was cruising at 37,000 feet above the southern New Jersey coast. The aircraft had enough fuel to last nearly two hours—a healthy cushion considering the plane was less than half an hour from touchdown at New York's Kennedy Airport. At this point, a series of delays began. First, at 8:00, the air traffic controllers at Kennedy told the pilots on Flight 52 that they would have to circle in a holding pattern because of heavy traffic. At 8:45, the Avianca copilot advised Kennedy that they were "running low on fuel." The controller at Kennedy acknowledged the message, but the plane was not cleared to land until 9:24. In the interim, the Avianca crew relayed no information to Kennedy that an emergency was imminent, yet the cockpit crew spoke worriedly among themselves about their dwindling fuel supplies.

Flight 52's first attempt to land at 9:24 was aborted. The plane had come in too low and poor visibility made a safe landing uncertain. When the Kennedy controllers gave Flight 52's pilot new instructions for a second attempt, the crew again mentioned that they were running low on fuel, but the pilot told the controllers that the newly assigned flight path was okay. At 9:32, two of Flight 52's engines lost power. A minute later; the other two cut off. The plane, out of fuel, crashed on Long Island at 9:34. All 73 people on board were killed.

When investigators reviewed the cockpit tapes and talked with the controllers involved, they learned that a communication breakdown caused this tragedy. A closer look at the events of that evening help to explain why a simple message was neither clearly transmitted nor adequately received. First, the pilots kept saying they were "running low on fuel." Traffic controllers told investigators that it is fairly common for pilots to use this phrase. In times of delay, controllers assume that everyone has a fuel problem. However, had the pilots uttered the words "fuel emergency," the controllers would have been obligated to direct the jet ahead of all others and clear it to land as soon as possible. As one controller put it, if a pilot "declares an emergency, all rules go out the window and we get the guy to the airport as quickly as possible." Unfortunately, the pilots of Flight 52 never used the word "emergency," so the people at Kennedy never understood the true nature of the pilots' problem.

Second, the vocal tone of the pilots on Flight 52 didn't convey the severity or urgency of the fuel problem to the air traffic controllers. These controllers are trained to pick up subtle tones in a pilot's voice in such situations. Although the crew of Flight 52 expressed considerable concern among themselves about the fuel problem, their voice tones in communicating to Kennedy were cool and professional. Finally, the culture and traditions of pilots and airport authorities may have made the pilot of Flight 52 reluctant to declare an emergency. A pilot's expertise and pride can be at stake in such a situation. Declaration of a formal emergency requires the pilot to complete a wealth of paperwork. Moreover, if a pilot has been found to be negligent in calculating how much fuel was needed for a flight, the Federal Aviation Administration can suspend his or her license. These negative consequences strongly discourage pilots from calling an emergency.

QUESTIONS FOR DISCUSSION

1. Analyze the communications between pilots on Flight 52 and the air traffic controllers at Kennedy Airport using the concepts in this chapter.
2. Could active listening skills have prevented this crash? Cite examples.
3. Avianca is a Colombian airline. A large number of planes that fly into major world airports are international carriers. How is it possible for world air traffic controllers to be effective when they and many pilots do not share the same native language?
4. Could the guidelines for communicating with diversity have helped?

Group Exercise 2: Listening to Understand Problems

Purpose.   To practice the skills of active listening when trying to be compassionate and understand another's problem.

Directions.   Form triads. Each person will play the role of listener, speaker, and observer. Decide who will play each role for the first round.

1. If you are the *speaker,* choose an unresolved interpersonal problem and explain it and your feeling about it to the listener. Continue to share and expand until you feel certain the listener completely understands both the problem and your feelings about it. (Take no more than 10 minutes.)
2. The *listener* should use as many of the active listening skills as possible to understand (not solve) the speaker's problem (e.g., attending, reflecting, concentrating, and so on). Your goal is to have the speaker say, "Yes, you understand my problem and how I feel about it perfectly."
3. The *observer* should remain totally silent during the exercise and take notes on the listener's effective and ineffective listening behaviors.
4. At the conclusion of the exercise, first the observer and then the speaker should give the listener feedback on points they felt indicated effective or ineffective listening skills. (Take no more than 5 minutes for this feedback.)
5. Steps 1 through 4 should be repeated two more times so that each person in the triad has a chance to play each role once.

Time.   15 to 20 minutes per session.

OBSERVER'S RATING SHEET

On completion of the exercise, rate each actor's application of interpersonal communication skills. Use the following scale to rate each role player between 1 and 5. Write concrete examples in the spaces between behaviors to use when explaining your feedback.

1	*2*	*3*	*4*	*5*
Unsatisfactory	*Weak*	*Adequate*	*Good*	*Outstanding*

Communication Behaviors	*Sender Rating*	*Listener Rating*
Avoids communication barriers	_____	_____
Sends understandable messages	_____	_____
Actively listens (attends, paraphrases, questions)	_____	_____
Utilizes nonverbal signals	_____	_____
Gives effective feedback	_____	_____
Adapts to diversity (styles, gender, cultural)	_____	_____
Solicits meaningful feedback	_____	_____

APPLICATION QUESTIONS

1. What does your professor do in class to ensure sending clear messages? What could he or she do to improve the clarity of the messages?
2. What do the students in your class do in terms of active listening to improve the communication process? How could they improve?
3. Describe some common nonverbal gestures that are widely known in your country but would be misunderstood in other parts of the world.
4. Describe how you feel when a person whom you just met is standing in your intimate zone. What do you do about it? What are your options?

REINFORCEMENT EXERCISES

The following suggestions are activities you can do to reinforce the interpersonal communication techniques in this chapter. You may want to adapt them to the Action Plan you will develop next, or try them independently.

1. Watch a talk show on television and observe how the host and guests are communicating. Is the host actively listening to the guest's problems? Are the guests actively listening? Is anyone attempting to clarify their messages using the clarity-enhancing techniques outlined in the chapter?
2. The next time a friend shares a problem with you, apply your active listening skills. Attend, ask open-ended questions, and paraphrase without trying to provide a solution or talk about one of your own experiences. When you think you really understand how your friend perceives and feels about the problem, paraphrase your understanding and ask whether you have a complete understanding. When you receive an affirmative response, go ahead and share your own reactions or advice, but not before. Afterwards think about what you learned about your interpersonal communication skills from this exercise.

ACTION PLAN

1. Which interpersonal communication behavior do I want to improve the most?
2. Why? What will be my payoff?
3. What potential obstacles stand in my way?
4. What are the specific things I will do to improve? (For examples, see the Reinforcement Exercises.)
5. When will I do them?
6. How and when will I measure my success?

NOTES

1. Adapted from S. P. Robbins and D. A. De Cenzo, *Supervision Today,* 2d ed. (Upper Saddle River, NJ: Prentice Hall, 1998) 388–89.
2. B. L. Reece and R. Brandt, *Effective Human Relations in Business,* 5th ed. (Boston: Houghton Mifflin, 1993) 97.
3. Ibid., 27.
4. D. K. Berlo, *The Process of Communication* (New York: Holt, Rinehart & Winston, 1960) 30–2.
5. E. Weiner, "Right Word Is Crucial in Air Control," *New York Times,* February 29, 1990, B-5.
6. J. Ritter, "Poor Fluency in English Means Mixed Signals," *USA Today,* January 18, 1996, 1A.
7. L. L. Tobias, "Twenty-Three Ways to Improve Communication," *Training and Development Journal* (1989): 75–77.
8. E. Lewis and B. K. Spiker, "Tell Me What You Want Me to Do," *Manufacturing Systems* (December 1991): 46–49.
9. R. McGarvey, "Now Hear This," *Entrepreneur* (June 1996): 87–89.
10. T. Alessandra and P. Hunsaker, *Communicating at Work* (New York: Simon & Schuster, 1993) 54–68.
11. A. Mehrabian, *Nonverbal Communication* (Chicago: Aldine/Atherton, 1972) 25–30.
12. Alessandra and Hunsaker, 1993, pp. 111–19.

OBSERVER'S RATING SHEET

On completion of the exercise, rate each actor's application of interpersonal communication skills. Use the following scale to rate each role player between 1 and 5. Write concrete examples in the spaces between behaviors to use when explaining your feedback.

1	*2*	*3*	*4*	*5*
Unsatisfactory	*Weak*	*Adequate*	*Good*	*Outstanding*

Communication Behaviors	*Sender Rating*	*Listener Rating*
Avoids communication barriers	_____	_____
Sends understandable messages	_____	_____
Actively listens (attends, paraphrases, questions)	_____	_____
Utilizes nonverbal signals	_____	_____
Gives effective feedback	_____	_____
Adapts to diversity (styles, gender, cultural)	_____	_____
Solicits meaningful feedback	_____	_____

Group Exercise 3: Getting to Know You: Connecting By Rubber Bands

Purpose. To practice nonverbal communication skills to send messages about yourself and learn about another person.

Preparation. Requires a room with space to move about freely.

Directions. Class members stand up and move all furniture out of the way if possible to allow open space in the classroom to move about in. The instructor then reads the instructions for the following nonverbal activities for students to engage in. At the end of the exercise, first dyads and then the entire class debriefs the experience.

Activity 1. All members of the class stand up and silently mill around greeting each other nonverbally. After you have greeted everyone (about 2 minutes), *nonverbally* choose a partner for Activity 2. Remember, at no times are participants allowed to speak to each other.

Activity 2. Stand about two feet apart facing your partner. Put your hands out in front of you, almost touching the hands of your partner. Pretend that your hands are connected by rubber bands and that your are facing your partner in a mirror. Nonverbally move your hands around in creative ways while they are "connected" to your partner's. (3 minutes)

Activity 3. Stay in your hand-mirroring position. Now pretend that your feet are also connected by rubber bands, about two inches away from your partner's feet. Again, nonverbally, move both your hands and feet around. Be creative: See if you can move around the room, encounter other dyads, etc. (3 minutes)

Activity 4. With your partner, nonverbally choose another dyad. Sit down together and share what you learned about your partner from participating in Activities 1, 2, and 3 to the other dyad. Rotate sharing until all are finished (10 minutes), then discuss the following questions in your small group:

Debriefing. At the end of the exercise, first dyads and then the entire class debriefs the experience. The purpose of the debriefing is to analyze what you learned about yourself and your partner during the nonverbal exercise. The following questions will help get you started. (10 minutes)

1. What were the main mechanisms you and your partner used for communicating nonverbally in this exercise?
2. How did you feel about interacting in this close interpersonal space with your partner? Why? Would it have been different with another partner?
3. What were the primary ways you influenced each other nonverbally? For example, who invited the other to be his or her partner and how did it happen nonverbally? How did you nonverbally decide to choose another dyad?
4. What else did you learn about yourself, your partner, or others in the nonverbal exercise? For example, how comfortable were you during the nonverbal milling? Why? How did other dyads respect your personal space and how did you feel about it?

Time. 25 minutes for the exercise. 10 minutes for debriefing.

SUMMARY CHECKLIST

Take a few minutes to reflect on your performance and look over others' ratings of your skill. Assess yourself on each of the key learning behaviors. Make a check (✓) next to those behaviors on which you need improvement.

_____ **Identify and avoid communication barriers.**
1. Different frames of reference.
2. Not recognizing semantic differences.
3. Value judgments.
4. Selective listening.
5. Inappropriate filtering.
6. Distrust.

_____ **Send clear, understandable messages.**
1. Use multiple channels.
2. Be complete and specific.
3. Claim messages as your own.
4. Be congruent.
5. Simplify language.

_____ **Develop credibility.**
1. Demonstrate expertise.
2. Be reliable.
3. Be supportive of others.

_____ **Actively listen.**
1. Attend.
2. Paraphrase.
3. Follow.

_____ **Utilize nonverbal signals.**
1. Be aware of visual components like eye movements, gestures, and facial expressions.
2. Listen for vocal intonations.
3. Observe spacial arrangements.

_____ **Give appropriate feedback.**
1. Specifically describe actions.
2. Avoid being judgmental or threatening.
3. Include only things receiver can do something about.

_____ **Adapt to style, gender, and cultural diversity.**
1. Assume differences.
2. Empathize.
3. Treat interpretations as guesses.

_____ **Solicit meaningful feedback.**
1. Seek examples.
2. Avoid being defensive.
3. Ask for definitions.
4. Check out assumptions.
5. Ask clarifying questions.

APPLICATION QUESTIONS

1. What does your professor do in class to ensure sending clear messages? What could he or she do to improve the clarity of the messages?
2. What do the students in your class do in terms of active listening to improve the communication process? How could they improve?
3. Describe some common nonverbal gestures that are widely known in your country but would be misunderstood in other parts of the world.
4. Describe how you feel when a person whom you just met is standing in your intimate zone. What do you do about it? What are your options?

REINFORCEMENT EXERCISES

The following suggestions are activities you can do to reinforce the interpersonal communication techniques in this chapter. You may want to adapt them to the Action Plan you will develop next, or try them independently.

1. Watch a talk show on television and observe how the host and guests are communicating. Is the host actively listening to the guest's problems? Are the guests actively listening? Is anyone attempting to clarify their messages using the clarity-enhancing techniques outlined in the chapter?
2. The next time a friend shares a problem with you, apply your active listening skills. Attend, ask open-ended questions, and paraphrase without trying to provide a solution or talk about one of your own experiences. When you think you really understand how your friend perceives and feels about the problem, paraphrase your understanding and ask whether you have a complete understanding. When you receive an affirmative response, go ahead and share your own reactions or advice, but not before. Afterwards think about what you learned about your interpersonal communication skills from this exercise.

ACTION PLAN

1. Which interpersonal communication behavior do I want to improve the most?
2. Why? What will be my payoff?
3. What potential obstacles stand in my way?
4. What are the specific things I will do to improve? (For examples, see the Reinforcement Exercises.)
5. When will I do them?
6. How and when will I measure my success?

NOTES

1. Adapted from S. P. Robbins and D. A. De Cenzo, *Supervision Today,* 2d ed. (Upper Saddle River, NJ: Prentice Hall, 1998) 388–89.
2. B. L. Reece and R. Brandt, *Effective Human Relations in Business,* 5th ed. (Boston: Houghton Mifflin, 1993) 97.
3. Ibid., 27.
4. D. K. Berlo, *The Process of Communication* (New York: Holt, Rinehart & Winston, 1960) 30–2.
5. E. Weiner, "Right Word Is Crucial in Air Control," *New York Times,* February 29, 1990, B-5.
6. J. Ritter, "Poor Fluency in English Means Mixed Signals," *USA Today,* January 18, 1996, 1A.
7. L. L. Tobias, "Twenty-Three Ways to Improve Communication," *Training and Development Journal* (1989): 75–77.
8. E. Lewis and B. K. Spiker, "Tell Me What You Want Me to Do," *Manufacturing Systems* (December 1991): 46–49.
9. R. McGarvey, "Now Hear This," *Entrepreneur* (June 1996): 87–89.
10. T. Alessandra and P. Hunsaker, *Communicating at Work* (New York: Simon & Schuster, 1993) 54–68.
11. A. Mehrabian, *Nonverbal Communication* (Chicago: Aldine/Atherton, 1972) 25–30.
12. Alessandra and Hunsaker, 1993, pp. 111–19.

13. P. Ekman, "Facial Expression and Emotion," *American Psychologist* (April 1993): 384–92.

14. D. Blum, "Face It," *Psychology Today* (September–October 1998): 32–9, 66–70.

15. F. Williams, *The New Communications* (Belmont, CA: Wadsworth, 1989) 45.

16. J. W. Gibson and R. M. Hodgetts, *Organizational Communication: A Managerial Perspective* (Orlando, FL: Academic Press, 1986) 95.

17. "What's A-O-K in the U.S.A. Is Lewd and Worthless Beyond," *New York Times,* August 18, 1996, E7.

18. M. Henricks, "More Than Words," *Entrepreneur* (August 1995): 54–57.

19. See O. P. Kharbanda and E. A. Stallworthy, "Verbal and Non-Verbal Communication," *Journal of Managerial Psychology* 6, no. 4 (1991): 10–13, 49–52, for an expansion of these ideas.

20. For elaboration see R. T. Barker and C. G. Pearce, "The Importance of Proxemics at Work," *Supervisory Management* 35 (1990): 10–11.

21. Mildred Golden Pryor, J. Chris White, and Leslie A. Toombs, *Strategic Quality Management: A Strategic Systems Approach to Continuous Improvement* (Cincinnati: Thomson Learning, 1998) 12:27.

22. T. Carney, "The Four-Communication-Styles Approach," *The 1980 Handbook for Group Facilitators* (San Diego: University Associates, 1980) 127–32.

23. P. Harris and R. Moran, *Managing Cultural Differences,* 3d ed. (Houston: Gulf Publishing, 1991) 13.

24. D. Tannen, *You Just Don't Understand: Women and Men in Conversation* (New York: Ballantine Books, 1991) 24–25.

25. J. Bard and P. Bradley, "Styles of Management and Communication: A Comparative Study of Men and Women," *Communication Monographs* 46 (1979): 101–11.

26. J. Hunsaker and P. Hunsaker, *Strategies and Skills for Managerial Women* (Cincinnati: South-Western Publishing, 1991) 252–53.

27. B. Eakins and R. Eakins, *Sex Differences in Human Communication* (Boston: Houghton Mifflin Company, 1978) 117–19.

28. J. Hunsaker and P. Hunsaker, 1991, p. 139.

29. N. J. Adler, *International Dimensions of Organizational Behavior,* 2d ed. (Boston: Kent Publishing, 1991) 83–84.

30. Case based on J. Cushman, "Avianca Flight 52: The Delays That Ended in Disaster," *New York Times,* February 5, 1990, B-1; and E. Weiner, "Right Word Is Crucial in Air Control," *New York Times,* February 29, 1990, B-5.

CHAPTER 4

Valuing Diversity

Learning Objectives

After completing this chapter, you should be able to:

■ Explain how diversity strengthens organizations.

■ Encourage and support diversity to meet organizational needs.

■ Be creative and flexible in dealing with difficulties faced by diverse employees.

■ Be accountable by recruiting broadly and selecting employees fairly.

■ Assist diverse employees through training and orientation.

■ Break down barriers standing in the way of appreciating diversity.

SELF-ASSESSMENT EXERCISE[1]

Circle the response that most closely correlates with each item below.

Always	*Frequently*	*Sometimes*	*Infrequently*			*Never*
1	*2*	*3*	*4*			*5*

		Always	Freq	Some	Infreq	Never
1.	I recognize that diversity exists and I am learning to value differences.	1	2	3	4	5
2.	I know what prejudices I have and am committed to reducing them.	1	2	3	4	5
3.	I have developed plans for changing my biases.	1	2	3	4	5
4.	I vocally dispel myths about diverse others when I am in groups of friends or colleagues.	1	2	3	4	5
5.	I have broadened my experience base.	1	2	3	4	5
6.	I am consciously practicing enhanced communication skills.	1	2	3	4	5
7.	I use words that are inclusive rather than exclusive.	1	2	3	4	5
8.	I avoid adjectives that spotlight certain groups.	1	2	3	4	5
9.	I avoid terms that demean or devalue others.	1	2	3	4	5
10.	I seek opportunities to interact with a wide variety of peers and associates.	1	2	3	4	5
11.	I seek feedback from others about how I communicate with them.	1	2	3	4	5

	Always	Frequently	Sometimes	Infrequently		Never
	1	*2*	*3*	*4*		*5*

12.	I try to incorporate the positive elements of both "female" and "male" types of communication.	1	2	3	4	5
13.	I try to be well-read in subjects of interest to both women and men.	1	2	3	4	5
14.	I avoid situations with coworkers that could be construed as intimate.	1	2	3	4	5
15.	I encourage others to speak before I share my point of view.	1	2	3	4	5
16.	I avoid using humor that could be viewed as insensitive to members of certain groups.	1	2	3	4	5
17.	I know or am learning a language other than my primary language.	1	2	3	4	5
18.	I have traveled, lived, or worked (or have plans to do so) in a country other than my own.	1	2	3	4	5
19.	When I travel, I try to immerse myself in local life.	1	2	3	4	5
20.	I have developed friendships with people from nationalities, ethnicities, or cultures other than my own.	1	2	3	4	5
21.	I have developed nonsexual friendships with members of the opposite sex.	1	2	3	4	5
22.	I do not impose my religious views on others and am accepting of people with religious views that differ from my own.	1	2	3	4	5
23.	I learn about the business and social customs and practices of any new country before I visit it for the first time.	1	2	3	4	5

Scoring and interpretation. Add up the numbers you have circled. The lower your score, the more you accept diversity. If your score is 69 or greater, it may be helpful to create a plan to improve your skills in working with others who differ from you.

CONCEPTS

• Miyako, a Japanese-American, performed well as part of a team that assembled semiconductors. She was quick, attentive to detail, and got along well with group members, but when rewarded with a supervisory job, she seemed almost to change personalities. She became withdrawn and reluctant to take responsibility. You wonder: *What did I do wrong?*

• Charles was the firm's premier drill-press operator for 20 years. He knew his job and did it masterfully, coming and going on a schedule he largely devised and asking for nothing more than a paycheck and a yearly raise. Mildred, an equally skilled drill-press operator, replaced him, but she complained of "isolation," "lack of feedback," and "not feeling like an integral part of the operation." You want women and minorities to get ahead, but you find yourself asking: *Why can't they be like the old-timers?*

• You appointed two teams to come up with ways to sell more bread products. The first team—consisting of exceptionally able supervisors and favorite rank-and-filers—came up with warmed-over versions of old ideas, such as trying to break into the school market, special holiday breads, and a line of "natural," whole-grain products. The other group, however, comprised of more recent hires who had complained generally about lack of input, blew you away when it suggested *tortillas, bollilos,* and *buneolos* for the growing Hispanic population that is not really served in your area. You scratched your head and pondered: *Do my best people have a blind spot? How can I give more responsibility to the newcomers without alienating my most trusted associates?*

Understanding and managing people who are similar to us are challenges—but understanding and managing those *who are dissimilar from us and from each other* can be even tougher. As the workplace becomes more diverse and as business becomes more global, managers can no longer assume that all employees want the same thing, will act in the same manner, and can be managed the same way. Instead, managers must understand how cultural diversity affects the expectations and behavior of everyone in the organization.

What Is Diversity?

Diversity is not a synonym for equal employment opportunity, nor is it another word for affirmative action, though either or both of those may aid diversity. Instead, diversity refers to the vast array of physical and cultural differences that constitute the spectrum of human differences.

Achieving workforce diversity means hiring and including people with different human qualities, such as age, ethnicity, gender, and race from various cultural groups. It is important to remember that diversity includes everyone, not just racial or ethnic minorities.[2]

Six core dimensions of diversity form the inside wheel of Exhibit 4-1. The inherent differences of age, ethnic heritage, gender, mental/physical abilities, race, and sexual orientation have impact throughout a person's life. These fixed dimensions shape individuals' self-image and perspective of the world.

The outside wheel in Exhibit 4-1 represents secondary dimensions that can be acquired or changed throughout one's lifetime. They have less impact than the core dimensions but still influence how people think of themselves and how others perceive them. Secondary dimensions such as work style, communication style, and educational or skill level are particularly relevant in the organizational setting. The challenge for managers is to recognize that each person can bring value and strengths to the workplace based on his or her own unique combination of diversity characteristics.[3]

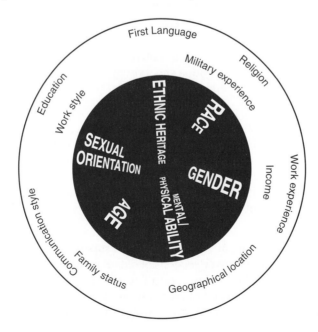

EXHIBIT 4-1   The Diversity Wheel

SOURCE: M. Loden, *Implementing Diversity* (Homewood, IL: Irwin, 1996) 14. Used with permission. © Irwin Co. Reprinted by permission of the McGraw-Hill Companies.

Due to an aging workforce, an influx of immigrants, and a rapid increase in the number of working women, the preponderance of white males in the U.S. labor market is shrinking. In the year 2000, white males made up less than half of the North American workforce. In the twenty-first century, white males are estimated to contribute only 15 percent of new workforce entrants, while Asians, Africans, and Hispanics will add 85 percent of the U.S. population growth and 30 percent of the workforce.[4]

The challenge of managing this increasingly diverse workforce is to provide a workplace where differences are recognized and valued—and where, as a result, productivity is fostered. That's easier said than done. And diversity, if it's not managed well, can cause distrust, communication problems, and even resistance to authority.

Changing Workforce

Less than 25 years ago, North American organizations were made up of a clear majority of male Euro-Americans. Since then, the percentage of males and of employees with European origins has shrunk and will continue to shrink. By 2050, the average U.S. resident will have a non-European background, and the workforce will be shaped accordingly.[5]

For instance, by the year 2005, black and Hispanic employees are expected to make up more than 25 percent of the North American workforce, and the percentage of white males is expected to decrease from 51 percent to 44 percent.[6] In addition, as one study[7] reported, the United States is facing the following issues:

- A shrinking labor pool, due mainly to slower population growth
- An aging workforce, as the baby boom generation grows older and fewer young workers enter the pool
- More women in the workforce
- Increasing numbers of immigrants

The historical approach to managing diversity was to expect minorities to adapt so they blended into the organization's dominant culture. But now few minority employees feel as though they have to "play it safe" by hiding their differences. Although many managers haven't felt much pressure to adapt to diversity in the past, they certainly are challenged to do so today. If managers fail to accept and promote diversity as a valuable corporate asset, they will pay the price of decreased work effort and low performance levels.[8]

The globalization of business also is bringing a cross-cultural mandate. With more businesses selling and/or manufacturing more products and services abroad, managers increasingly see the need to relate to their foreign customers, including the need to have managers and salespeople who can understand overseas customers. "We are in a war for talent," is the way Rich McGinn, CEO of Lucent Technologies, put it in 1999. "The only way you can meet your business imperatives is to have all people as part of your talent pool—here in the United States and around the world."[9]

Workers who believe their differences are not merely tolerated but valued by their employer are likely to be more loyal, productive, and committed. Further, a firm with a reputation for providing opportunities will have a competitive advantage in the labor market and will be sought out by the most qualified employees. FedEx, for instance, made it a point to show in its television ads the diversity of its workforce, after they were prescreened on an in-house cable television system by it's 90,000 employees.[10]

What's more, just as women and minorities may prefer to work for an employer who values diversity, so may they prefer to patronize such organizations. Minorities now control billions of consumer dollars, and a multicultural workforce can provide a company with greater knowledge of the preference of shoppers.

Because people with different backgrounds often come with different perspectives, work-team diversity promotes creativity and innovation.[11] Effectively managed, such teams come up with more options and create more solutions than homogeneous groups. Recall the third example at the beginning of this chapter about the new, more diverse group that came up with more creative ideas to sell more bread products to the expanding Hispanic population.

A diverse workforce also enhances organizational flexibility. Successfully managing diversity requires a corporate culture that tolerates many different styles and approaches. Such a culture tends to enable organizations to become more free-ranging in other areas such as manufacturing or marketing.

So the goal of diversity is not diversity for its own sake. Nor do diversity programs want to reinforce employee differences. Rather, it's to bring in new points of view and ideas, in all aspects of the organization, from developing the vision and mission statement to improving products, services, and processes. For example, a culturally diverse group that designs a marketing campaign for a new product can more likely help develop better plans for reaching different cultural market segments.

From Affirmative Action to Promoting Diversity[12]

Traditionally in the United States, managers did not make concerted efforts to recruit members of minority groups, resulting today in a dearth of women, minorities, and disabled at senior levels of management in many organizations. Now, affirmative action laws encourage hiring members of underrepresented groups over members of majority groups when all things are equal. Affirmative action has been met with resistance by some organizations for several reasons. Some believe that affirmative action results in reverse discrimination where individuals from majority groups were overlooked in favor of less-qualified applicants from underrepresented groups. This is often the case where managers try to comply by simply filling quotas.

Managers who focus on hiring good people through affirmative action programs are not promoting diversity in its fullest. They are only managing representation by filling quotas rather than promoting diversity by creating environments that allow diverse individuals to be themselves, be accepted for who they are, and be promoted. This problem is evidenced by the high number of women and minorities who leave corporate America to start their own businesses, citing as a primary motivation the lack of advancement opportunities and a lack of acceptance by their bosses and coworkers.[13]

Promoting diversity is broader than simply bringing in diverse people. It is creating an environment that will enable all employees to reach their full potential.[14] More progressive organizations have used the concept of managing diversity rather than affirmative action as a means to making their work environment more inclusive for all employees. Their motivation is voluntary because they realize that diversity will enhance productivity, as opposed to government-mandated affirmative action that was often complied with because of concern for complying with the law.[15] Exhibit 4-2 describes the differences between approaches for affirmative action and managing diversity.

EXHIBIT 4-2   Differences Between Affirmative Action and Managing Diversity[16]

Affirmative Action	*Managing Diversity*
Government mandated	Voluntary—company driven
Legally driven	Productivity driven
Quantitative	Qualitative
Problem focused	Opportunity focused
Assumes assimilation	Assumes integration
Internally focused	Internally and externally focused
Reactive	Proactive

How Organizations Promote Diversity

Organizations have taken two major approaches to getting rid of prejudicial attitudes. The first is affirmative action. Derived from the civil rights initiatives of the 1960s, affirmative action involves special efforts to hire and promote disadvantaged groups. Implicit in this approach was the idea that if an organization was proactive, it might avoid government strictures. Further, as women and minorities get better positions in the workforce, others will see that their negative stereotypes were misguided. As those stereotypes crumble, prejudice and discrimination wither. Although prejudice continues to exist, affirmative action has contributed to major gains in opportunities available to women and minorities.

The second approach, and the focus of this chapter, is the use of diversity management programs. They go beyond affirmative action and entail not just hiring a broader group of workers but creating an atmosphere in which minorities can flourish.

A company often lauded for its diversity efforts is Microsoft, which states, "A diverse company is better able to sell to a diverse world." Although high-tech firms generally have lagged in hiring and retaining minorities, Microsoft places a premium on diversity. For example, it recruits minorities with the aid of black, Hispanic, Native American, and women's groups; donates money and goods to encourage minority education and professional development as well as minority businesses; supports 13 employee-run diversity groups, including employees with disabilities, women, gays and lesbians, blacks, Hispanics, Native Americans, and Jewish Americans.[17]

Such diversity management programs recognize that diversity is a business issue, not just a legal one—and the goal of such programs is not to treat all people the same but to treat each person as an individual. As a Hewlett-Packard CEO put it, "At HP, we don't just value diversity because it's the right thing to do, but also because it's the smart thing to do."[18] Evidence shows that efforts to make the workforce more diverse pays big dividends, including more contented employees, lower costs (gained by improving retention), improved recruiting, increased sales and market share, heightened creativity and innovation, and possibly added productivity and problem-solving ability.[19]

About two-thirds of all U.S. organizations today have adopted diversity management programs.[20] However, not all companies are equally proactive. In fact, some implement diversity programs only after top officials have been accused of being insensitive to racial differences. For example, at Texaco in the mid-1990s company officials were caught on tape making racially indiscreet remarks.[21] Following that incident, and on top of a history of allegedly passing over black employees for the best promotions, Texaco settled a discrimination lawsuit by agreeing to spend $35 million on diversity management training.

As the Texaco case illustrates, workplace diversity presents three challenges for organizations and their managers: a fairness and justice challenge, a decision-making and performance challenge, and a flexibility challenge. Let us explore the nature of these challenges in greater depth. Then we will look at how managers can meet those challenges.

Fairness and Justice

How can you allocate jobs, promotions, and rewards in a way that honors diversity without making white males feel cheated? This challenge is difficult because seniority plays a large role in promotions and rewards—and many minorities are recent hires. On the other hand, rectifying this imbalance by actively recruiting and promoting women and minorities reduces the prospects for white males, who still compose a large part of the workforce. That practice, in turn, could adversely affect performance.

Decision Making and Performance

Many organizations have found that tapping into diversity reveals new ways of viewing traditional problems. The tapping-in process, however, is not automatic. Research has shown that many supervisors do not know how to manage and lead diverse work groups. Further, supervisors are often unsure how to communicate with employees with different cultural backgrounds and sometimes even different languages.[22]

Flexibility

Being sensitive to the needs of different kinds of employees is the first step to flexibility. The second step is developing flexible employment approaches. Such approaches can include benefit packages customized to fit needs of different groups, such as single workers with no children, homosexuals in long-term committed relationships, and workers caring for aged parents. Flexibility may entail flextime and other scheduling options, such as job sharing, that give workers input into the length and scheduling of their work weeks. Further, it could mean designing jobs and buildings to be sensitive to the special needs of disabled workers (and customers), establishing informal networks among minority employees to provide social support, and creating programs to encourage feedback to employees about their personal styles of dealing with minorities.

Diversity's Importance to Managers

If the percentage of women and minority workers is increasing and the skills and talents of such workers aren't being fully utilized, the organization will suffer a clear loss of potential productivity. Thus, managing a diverse workforce has quickly become a core competency for effective managers. The overall challenge is to harness the wealth of differences, but that is a sensitive, potentially volatile, and sometimes uncomfortable task.

For example, one recent study of 1,800 American working women concluded that "communication in today's workplace is often difficult and that mistrust is rampant between the sexes and the races."[23] Many women feel their bosses don't support them, and many African-American workers expect their white bosses to treat them unfairly. What's more, many white males share a fear factor that should they lose their job, another one would be hard to find because white males are not in demand.[24]

Simply sending employees to diversity training does not guarantee that diversity will be valued. In fact, one study of 785 human resources professionals revealed that both the adoption and success of diversity training was strongly related to top management's support for the program.[25] Also affecting the success of diversity training was whether attendance was mandatory for all managers, whether a long-term evaluation of results was conducted, and whether managers were rewarded for increasing diversity.

Another landmark study in this decade examined the diversity practices of 16 organizations that successfully managed diversity.[26] The researcher found 52 practices and grouped them into three main types: accountability, development, and recruitment. The top 10 practices in each type are shown in Exhibit 4-3.

Accountability means practices relating to a manager's responsibility to treat diverse employees fairly. Such procedures and policies are aimed at integrating diverse employees into the ranks. *Development* practices focus on preparing diverse employees for greater responsibility and advancement. *Recruitment* aims at attracting diverse job applicants.

What Can the Individual Manager Do?

Diversity issues for managers are many. They include issues such as coping with employees' unfamiliarity with English; learning which rewards are valued by different ethnic groups; developing career development programs that fit the skills, needs, and values of the ethnic group; and rewarding subordinate managers for effectively recruiting, hiring,

EXHIBIT 4-3 Common Diversity Practices

Accountability Practices

1. Top management's personal intervention
2. Internal advocacy groups
3. Emphasis on equal employment opportunity (EEO) statistics, profiles
4. Inclusion of diversity in performance evaluation goals, ratings
5. Inclusion of diversity in promotion decision, criteria
6. Inclusion of diversity in management succession planning
7. Work and family policies
8. Policies against racism, sexism
9. Internal audit or attitude survey
10. Active affirmative action (AA)/EEO committee, office

Development Practices

1. Diversity training programs
2. Networks and support groups
3. Development programs for all high-potential managers
4. Informal networking activities
5. Job rotation
6. Formal mentoring program
7. Informal mentoring program
8. Early development programs for all high-potential new hires
9. Internal training (such as personal safety or language)
10. Recognition events, awards

Recruitment Practices

1. Targeted recruitment of nonmanagers
2. Key outside hires
3. Extensive public exposure on diversity
4. Corporate image as liberal, progressive, or benevolent
5. Partnerships with educational institutions
6. Recruitment incentives such as cash supplements
7. Internships
8. Publications or public relations products that highlight diversity
9. Targeted recruitment of managers
10. Partnerships with nontraditional groups

SOURCE: A. M. Morrison, *The New Leaders: Guidelines on Leadership Diversity in America* (San Francisco: Jossey-Bass, 1992).

and training a diverse workforce. However, some positive steps are available to managers at every level to improve their handling of diversity issues.

Demonstrate Acceptance of Diversity

Yes, it is true that diversity management probably won't be effective unless top management, by word and action, endorses it, but it's also true that acceptance of the principle of multiculturalism starts with the individual.

Managers should look into their hearts and minds to root out prejudice, even if it's latent. They must accept the value of diversity for its own sake—not just because diversity will increase employee creativity, make workers more contented, and maybe even cut costs, and not just because to do so will accredit the manager as a "team player." Valuing diversity is important because it is the right thing to do. Equally important, managers must reflect this acceptance in what they say and do.

Managers who truly want to promote diversity must shape organizational culture to allow diversity to flourish. As you will learn more about in Chapter 12, the behavior of managers is a key determinant of organizational culture. A manager who is committed to the advantages that diversity can bring to the organization and the world at large cannot just go through the motions, but needs to truly believe as well as act.

Communicate Diversity Goals

Communicate your objectives and expectations about diversity to employees through a variety of means. These can include formal vision, mission, and value statements, as well as slogans, creeds, newsletters, speeches, e-mails, memos, and everyday conversations. Diversity awareness training programs can also be set up to formally communicate diversity goals and processes. Whatever means you use, make sure to spell out the benefits of promoting diversity for each individual as well as for the organization itself.[27]

Sensitize Employees to Diversity Issues

Because diversity means two-way understanding, many organizations provide special workshops to raise diversity awareness among current employees as well as offering programs for new employees. The Marriott Marquis Hotel in New York, for example, serves a diverse customer base with 1,700 highly diverse employees. One thing the top hotel managers have done is require *all* its managers to take diversity classes, during which they are introduced to cross-cultural norms such as body language, eye contact, touching, and religious customs.[28] At a Kraft cheese plant in Missouri, managers started a program to reward "diversity champions," individual employees who supported and promoted the benefits of diversity. Further, they added diversity goals to employee evaluations, encouraged nontraditional promotions, sponsored six "ethnic meals days," and trained more than half the plant's workers in diversity issues.[29]

Another example is Digital Equipment Corporation (DEC), whose "Valuing Differences" program includes training sessions designed to get employees to understand the diversity in their workplace by examining the cultural norms of the different people who work there. DEC also celebrates these differences by sponsoring a calendar of events (e.g., "Black History Month," "Gay and Lesbian Pride Week," and "International Women's Month") and supporting an information network on ongoing discussion groups of seven to nine members who meet monthly to discuss stereotypes and ways of improving relationships with those regarded as different.[30]

This training can take many forms apart from the traditional "classroom" structure. For instance, some organizations use diversity board games to help participants answer questions about gender, age, race, cultural differences, sexual orientation, and disabilities. Here is an example from a training game:[31]

> In Hispanic families, which one of the following values is probably most important?
>
> a. Achievement
> b. Money
> c. Being on time
> d. Respect for elders

The answer is *d*, but the larger point is that as participants play the game, they gain an understanding of the values and beliefs of other cultures.

Recruit Broadly and Select Fairly

Managers need to cast their nets wide to capture a diverse applicant pool. It's easier to rely on current employee referrals as a source of job applicants. But that tends to produce candidates who are similar to the present staff, as will be explained in greater detail in Chapter 13. Some nontraditional sources are women's job networks, over-50 clubs, urban job banks, training centers for the disabled, ethnic newspapers, and gay-rights organizations.

Once a manager has a diverse group of applicants, he or she must ensure that the selection process doesn't discriminate. As you will see in Chapter 13, tests used for selection are often culturally biased. As a result, people from different cultures, minorities, or even those who are functionally illiterate may not understand the meaning of test questions, causing them to be rejected as candidates for jobs they actually could perform well.

One way to make tests more valid for diverse employees is to use job-specific tests rather than general aptitude or knowledge tests. A firm that is hiring word-processing people, for instance, may give applicants a timed test to measure their typing speed and accuracy. Such tests would measure the specific skills, not subjective personal characteristics.

Provide Orientation and Training

Making the transition from an outsider to an insider is often more difficult for women and minorities than for white males. Thus, many organizations have programs to create opportunities for diverse groups and train them to succeed. They may have support groups within the organization to give emotional support and/or career guidance. Others may encourage mentoring in which a trusted coach or advisor is teamed up with minority employees, teaching them the cultural values of the organizations, and coaching them on how to make the most of their chances for advancement. Many firms now require their managers to serve as mentors. Among those are Bell Laboratories, NCR, Hughes Aircraft, Johnson & Johnson, and Merrill Lynch.

Be Flexible and Creative When Dealing with Diversity Problems

With dual-career households now so common, work/family programs seek to give employees flexibility in balancing their home and work demands. Some of the most common forms of these include flextime, the compressed work week, job sharing, and telecommuting. Other types of work/family programs could include child-care facilities at the work site, transportation of aging parents to a senior citizens center, and life-cycle accounts, which are savings accounts designed to pay for specific life events such as a college education.

Motivate According to Individual Needs

Motivating is one of a manager's key tasks, and motivating a diverse workforce requires special efforts because not everyone has the same needs and goals. For instance, studies tell us that men generally place more importance on having autonomy in their jobs than women do.[32] On the other hand, women are more likely to value the opportunity to learn, good interpersonal relations, and convenient work hours. Thus, managers need to recognize that what motivates a single mother with two young children and who is working full-time to support her family may be different from the needs of a young, single, part-time employee, or an older employee who's only working to supplement his or her retirement income.

Most of our knowledge of motivation is based on studies by North American researchers on North American workers. Consequently, the underlying belief that most people work to help promote their own well-being and get ahead may be at odds with people in more collectivist countries, such as Venezuela, Singapore, Japan, and Mexico, where the link to the organization is the individual's loyalty to the organization or to society rather than to his or her self-interest.[33] Thus, employees in or from collectivist cultures may be more receptive to team-based job design, group goals, and group performance evaluations. Reliance on the fear of being fired in such cultures is also likely to be less effective because of the belief that the fired person will be taken care of by extended family, friends, or community.

One study, for example, showed that Japanese-owned *maquiladoras* (foreign-owned businesses in Mexican border towns) were better able to motivate and retain employees than the U.S.-owned *maquiladoras*.[34] Researchers credited the Japanese success to the similarity between the Japanese and Mexican cultures. U.S. firms expected their Mexican workers to take individual initiative and get the job done at all costs. The Japanese culture, however, with its emphasis on teamwork and avoiding uncertainty, was a better fit with the Mexican workers, who were easier to train in the structured Japanese ways.

As differences in the employee pool continue, managers will need to study socialization much more closely. Studying the ethnic background and national cultures of workers will be necessary.

Reinforce Positive and Minimize Negative Employee Differences

Managers should encourage individuals to value and promote diverse views, creating traditions and ceremonies that celebrate diversity. For example, at Ortho Biotech, president Dennis Longstreet meets regularly with "affinity groups," such as white males; single people; gay, lesbian, and bisexual men and women; secretaries; black males; and others. "It's about listening to people, their problems, and their aspirations," Longstreet says. "It's amazing how unaware you can be of the impact you have on people different from you."[35]

In these ways and others, a manager may accentuate the positives of diversity. However, it's misleading to claim that having employees from different backgrounds only provides benefits.

Diversity also can create a lack of cohesiveness. Because of the lack of similarity in language, culture, and/or experience, diverse groups are often less tightly knit than homogeneous groups. Mistrust, miscommunication, stress, and attitudinal differences reduce cohesiveness, which in turn can lessen productivity.

Perhaps the most common negative effect is communication problems, including misunderstanding, inaccuracies, inefficiencies, and slowness. Group members may assume they interpret things similarly when actually they do not, or they may disagree because of their different frames of reference.[36] Managers need to accept the likelihood of these side effects while working hard to keep them at a minimum.

CONCEPT QUIZ

Complete the following true-false quiz by circling the correct answers. Answers are at the end of the quiz. After marking your answers, remember to go back and check your understanding of any answers you missed.

True or False   1. If an organization complies with government affirmative action guidelines, then it's doing all it needs to do on diversity.

True or False   2. Six core dimensions of diversity are age, ethnic heritage, gender, mental/physical abilities, race, and sexual orientation.

True or False   3. The percentages of males and of employees with European origins in the workplace are growing and will continue to grow.

True or False   4. The old approach to managing diversity was to expect people who were different to hide their differences or adapt to the dominant culture.

True or False   5. Workers whose differences are not merely tolerated but valued are likely to become more loyal and productive employees.

True or False	6. A diverse workforce enhances an organization's flexibility.
True or False	7. Affirmative action programs have eliminated prejudice from the workplace.
True or False	8. The success of a diversity training program depends strongly on the degree of support from top management.
True or False	9. One way to make tests more valid for diverse employees is to make them job-specific rather than general aptitude or knowledge tests.
True or False	10. Most of our knowledge of motivation is based on studies by North American researchers on North American workers, and thus may not be valid for those from other cultures.

Answers. (1) False; (2) True; (3) False; (4) True; (5) True; (6) True; (7) False; (8) True; (9) True; (10) True

BEHAVIORAL CHECKLIST

The following behaviors are important to managing a diverse workforce. Use them when evaluating your skills and those of others.

Effective Managers of Diversity

- Demonstrate acceptance of diversity.
- Communicate diversity goals and expectations.
- Sensitize employees to diversity issues.
- Encourage and support diversity.
- Recruit broadly and select fairly.
- Provide orientation and training.
- Be flexible and creative when responding to diversity problems.
- Motivate people based on their unique individual needs.
- Reinforce positive and minimize negative differences.

> **Attention!**
> Do not read the following until assigned to do so by your instructor.

MODELING EXERCISE

A Problematic Promotion

Directions. The entire class should read the descriptions of the four actors and the following situation. Four students should be selected to play the roles of Sam, Charlotte, Harry, and Edgar. Role-players should then read their assigned roles. They should not read the other roles. The rest of the class should read all four roles and review the Observer's Rating Sheet in preparation for observing and critiquing them.

Time. 30 minutes

Actors.

Sam, an experienced, able technician, who has been with Acme Medical Products for three years. He's one of the few persons of color working for this company in a technical position. He was a manager at his previous place of employment.

Edgar, a well-regarded white technician who has been with the company for 10 years and aspires to management.

Charlotte, the division vice president, who is white and is committed to seeing more women and minorities progress at the firm.

Harry, the department head, also white, who must choose between Sam and Edgar.

Situation.   Sam was hired three years ago at the behest of Charlotte, who thinks, with some justification, that Acme's record of hiring and promoting minorities is poor. In fact, the company was the object of a federal Department of Labor action several years ago, though it was settled by the higher-ups before it garnered too much publicity. Due to a reorganization, a new manager's spot has been created. The question is, who should get it? Charlotte and Harry have a meeting set to discuss the candidates, who at this point have been narrowed to Sam and Edgar. After the meeting, Charlotte and Harry will jointly interview the two contenders, then discuss the results between themselves and try to pick the new manager.

Sam's Role   You left your previous employer, where you where a manager, in hopes that you could achieve a similar position with Acme, a larger, more prestigious, and better-paying firm. You were not promised a managerial spot, but certainly you made your aims known in the job interviews and those who hired you didn't discourage you from thinking you had a good shot. It has been three years now, and you had hoped you would have been promoted before now. You hope this firm is not the "whites-only boy's club" that it is sometimes made out to be in water-cooler talk around the industry. This new spot ought to have your name on it. If it does not, you will be forced to conclude that you made a mistake in joining Acme. You will probably leave if that is the case, though you are not sure whether you should make that threat at today's interview.

Charlotte's Role   Being a company officer, you know a lot about Acme. You know that the company historically has not done much to attract and reward minorities, but the Department of Labor threat a few years back did put the fear of God into the top ranks of the firm. Maybe they are not pursuing minorities for the right reason, but at least they are pursuing them. For example, improving the numbers and positions of minorities is a key element of your management by objectives (MBO). So, if Sam and others like him get ahead, you will get more money. That is good, but that is not your primary motivation. You genuinely want to see a multiethnic, multicultural workforce because, well, the world is multiethnic and multicultural. You feel the firm must approximate the makeup of its customers if it is going to effectively sell to them. What is more, it is the *right* thing to do. You were in college during the civil rights movement of the 1960s. You thought that it was a just and righteous cause, and you think fully integrating the workplace is a logical extension of that struggle. Sam is a good man, respected by nearly everyone. We are unlikely to get a better minority candidate. You have always tried to empower Harry and let him make decisions in his department. In this case, however, he may not understand the "big picture" the way you do, and you may have to overrule him.

Edgar's Role   You have been with the company for 10 years. You are the senior technician in this department, and you are long overdue for a promotion. This manager's slot rightfully ought to be yours. Sam is a good man, but he is a johnny-come-lately compared to you. You have worked hard for a decade, enduring sometimes cruel and capricious bosses. You gave up your vacation plans one year to meet a pressing deadline. You have taken special courses to improve your skills. You have made a point of getting along with everyone. You cannot think of a single enemy in the department, remarkable in a company known for the intensity of its infighting.

You hope it does not come down to a racial decision. Because if it does, you will lose; word is the company wants and needs more minority managers. What's more, if it is clearly a racial decision, you will probably leave because you will otherwise be doomed: You can work hard, you can gain others' respect, you can play by the rules . . . but you cannot change your skin color. If the executives turn you down because you are white, you'll have no choice but to go elsewhere—and you think a lot of the other technicians will follow you out the door. In today's interview you hope to show Charlotte and Harry how promoting you is a no-risk move that not only is the right thing to do but will help morale throughout the department.

Harry's Role   You feel caught in the middle. You are not racist, but you do have an investment in making this department the best it can be. Sam is probably every bit the technician that Edgar is, but Edgar has paid his dues; Sam has not. You suspect Charlotte favors Sam because of some things she has said. But if she forces the issue and orders you to promote Sam, you feel sure there will be a rank-and-file rebellion. She does not realize how tenuous morale is. Edgar is highly competent and well liked, and he has earned his stripes. How can anyone beat those credentials?

OBSERVER'S RATING SHEET

During the dialogue, observers should note closely how Charlotte and Harry discuss the issues. What points do they make and what questions do they pose? Be prepared to suggest additional queries and draw conclusions about what arguments the pair makes. Notice what questions they ask of the two candidates and how the candidates respond.

Using the following scale, rate Charlotte's and Harry's application of techniques discussed in this chapter. Also write in comments that will help explain your feedback.

1	*2*	*3*	*4*	*5*
Unsatisfactory	*Weak*	*Adequate*	*Good*	*Outstanding*

Overall, how well did Charlotte:	*Rating*	*Comments*
• Demonstrate acceptance of diversity	_____	
• Sensitize employees to diversity issues	_____	
• Encourage and support diversity	_____	
• Communicate diversity goals and expectations	_____	
• Recruit broadly and select fairly	_____	
• Provide orientation and training	_____	
• Flexible and creative when responding to diversity difficulties	_____	
• Motivate people based on unique needs	_____	
• Reinforce the positive and minimize the negative	_____	

Overall, how well did Harry:	*Rating*	*Comments*
• Demonstrate acceptance of diversity	_____	
• Sensitize employees to diversity issues	_____	
• Encourage and support diversity	_____	
• Communicate diversity goals and expectations	_____	
• Recruit broadly and select fairly	_____	
• Provide orientation and training	_____	
• Flexible and creative when responding to diversity difficulties	_____	
• Motivate people based on unique needs	_____	
• Reinforce the positive and minimize the negative	_____	

Debriefing. At the completion of the exercise, provide the role-players with feedback from your observations. Then discuss the following questions as a total class:

1. What appeared to be the motivations of each of the four players based on the behaviors you observed?
2. How did those motivations reveal themselves in the discussions?
3. What was not discussed?
4. Whom would you pick for manager? Why?
5. What are the possible repercussions of your decision? How would you deal with them?

GROUP EXERCISES

In the following three exercises, you will be asked to show an understanding of diversity issues. The first exercise involves looking at how prejudices are formed, the second concerns being flexible about employees' needs, and the third helps you become more aware of your own stereotypes and prejudices.

Group Exercise 1: Choosing Music[37]

Step 1. Imagine that you are traveling in a rental car in a city you have never visited before. You face an hour-long drive on an uncrowded highway before you reach your destination. You decide that you would like to listen to the car radio while making the trip.

The rental car has four radio-selection buttons, each with a preset station. Each button plays a different type of music. Button A plays country music, B plays rock, C plays classical, and D plays jazz.

Which type would you choose to listen to for the duration of the trip? (Assume you want to relax and stick with one station. You don't want to bother with switching around among stations.)

Step 2. Form four groups, depending on the type of music chosen. In each group, debate the following questions and appoint a spokesperson from within the group to report your answers to the class.

Questions

- What are your feelings about each of the other three sorts of music?
- What words would you use to describe people who like to listen to each of the other three forms of music? Specify for each type.
- Have you listened to enough of the other three types of music to form a valid conclusion about the kinds of people they attract? Why or why not?

Step 3. Have each spokesperson report the responses of his/her group to the questions in Step 2.

Step 4. Reconvene as a class and discuss the following questions.

1. What was the purpose of this exercise?
2. What did you notice about the words used to describe the other groups?
3. Upon what sorts of data do you think these images were based?
4. What terms do we normally use to describe such generalized perceptions of other groups?
5. What could be some of the consequences of these perceptions?

6. What parallels are there to other kinds of group differences, such as race, gender, culture, ethnicity, nationality, age, and so on?
7. If an organization was interested in helping employees to value music lovers in the other three genres, what might it do?

Group Exercise 2: Motivation in Action[38]

Consider the following descriptions of three employees working in the same organization. Then individually write down your answers to the questions that follow.

Marvin   He is 55 years old, a college graduate, and a vice president of the firm. He is a second-generation Polish-American and a practicing Roman Catholic. His two children are married, and Marvin is a grandfather. He lives in a condo with his wife who does volunteer work and is active in their church. Marvin is healthy and likes to play golf and handball.

Maria   Thirty years old, she is a Mexican-American clerical worker. She is active in a Mexican civil rights group and is a single parent with two children under the age of 10. She completed high school after moving to the United States, and she has begun to attend evening classes at a local community college. She is a practicing Roman Catholic in excellent health. One of Maria's children suffers from a severe learning disability.

Yuri   A recent immigrant from one of the former Soviet republics, he is 42 and speaks halting, heavily accented English. He earned an engineering degree overseas but being unlicensed in the United States, he is employed as a parts clerk. He is unmarried and has no children but sends much of his paycheck to relatives back in Eastern Europe. A few others from his country also work at your firm or in your city.

Based on this information, answer the following questions:

1. What do you expect the goals and priorities of each of those employees to be?

   Marvin: _____

   _____

   Maria: _____

   _____

   Yuri: _____

   _____

2. Indicate which employee(s) you think would be motivated by the following additional benefits:

   a. On-site day care _____

   b. fitness center _____

   c. tuition reimbursement _____

   d. executive bonus plan _____

   e. rigorous affirmative-action plan _____

   f. enhanced retirement benefits _____

   g. supervisory training _____

   h. financial aid for special education _____

   i. corporate country club membership _____

   j. having a mentor _____

   k. being a mentor _____

   l. English classes _____

      m. more time off _____

      n. flextime _____

      o. job sharing _____

3. Form groups of five to six members and share your answers. Discuss your differences and their implications for managing diversity.

4. Groups share with the entire class what they learned from their discussions.

Group Exercise 3: Diversity Squares

Instructions.   The entire class participates in the exercise. Pass out the Diversity Squares matrix. This is like BINGO in that you try to complete all five boxes in a row. However, your objective is to complete as many rows as you can in the 30 minutes allotted. Move about the room and try to find people who can answer yes to your questions. Once you have found someone to answer yes to the question, you can cross off the square, placing that person's name or initials in the box. Each person who answers yes to one of your questions can only be used once. Continue to find others until you are able to complete a row.

Time.   Thirty minutes to complete rows. Thirty minutes for discussion questions. The instructor may vary the timing of either the exercise or discussion.[39]

Have you ever worked with anyone who is 20 or more years older than you?	Have you ever worked on a farm?	Do you speak more than one language?	Have you ever worked with anyone with a physical disability?	Have you ever worked with anyone who is a non-Christian?
Have you ever had a female boss?	Are you of Hispanic or Latin American heritage?	Do you have a family member or friend on welfare?	Have you ever had an African-American boss?	Do you have a best friend of a different race?
Do you have a friend who is gay, lesbian, or bisexual?	Have you ever been discriminated against because of race or ethnicity?	Have you ever lived outside of your home country?	Have you ever known a convicted felon?	Did a single parent raise you?
Have you ever been sexually harassed at work?	Has either of your parents been in the military?	Are you of Asian heritage?	Are you a vegetarian?	Have you ever had a doctor whose race or ethnicity differs from yours?
Do you know someone with a chronic disease such as Cancer or AIDS?	Have you ever dated someone who was less educated than you?	Have you ever been discriminated against because of gender?	Were your parents or grandparents immigrants?	Have you ever had a boss who was younger than you?

QUESTIONS FOR DISCUSSION

1. How did you feel asking individuals certain questions? What approach did you use to ask the questions?
2. Were some questions more difficult to ask than others? Why?
3. Why did you approach certain individuals for certain questions? Provide some examples.
4. Were you approached by several people about the same question. If so, how did it make you feel? Why did they select you for certain questions?
5. Would some of the questions be more difficult to ask or more likely to offend others if worded in the first person? For example, "Are you gay, lesbian, or bisexual?"
6. What did this exercise make you realize about your own stereotypes and prejudices?
7. What did this exercise make you realize about stereotypes and prejudice in general?

SUMMARY CHECKLIST

Take a few minutes to reflect on your performance in the preceding exercises. Assess yourself as to how your analysis compared to other students (and if you were an actor in the role-play, how others rated your skill). Make a check (✓) next to those behaviors you may need to improve.

_____ **Demonstrate acceptance of diversity.**
1. Reflect on your own level of acceptance of diversity.
2. Commit to the advantages of diversity.
3. Walk your talk.

_____ **Communicate diversity goals and expectations.**
1. Communicate through a variety of means.
2. Use formal vision, mission, and value statements.
3. Use informal newsletters, speeches, and everyday conversations.
4. Spell out the benefits of promoting diversity individual and the organization.

_____ **Sensitize employees to diversity issues.**
1. Offer diversity awareness training.
2. Hold meetings to resolve diversity issues.

_____ **Encourage and support diversity.**
1. Publicize the advantages of diversity.
2. Reward those who promote diversity.

_____ **Recruit broadly and select fairly.**
1. Seek applicants from nontraditional sources.
2. Build relationships with minority organizations.
3. Use performance-related tests.
4. Focus on specific skills, not personal characteristics.

_____ **Provide orientation and training.**
1. Encourage support groups.
2. Set up mentoring.
3. Meet regularly with minority groups or representatives.

_____ **Flexibility and creativity when responding to diversity difficulties.**
1. Be open to alternative work schedules.
2. Establish work/family programs.

_____ **Motivate people based on their unique individual needs.**
1. Learn about ethnic backgrounds and national cultures.
2. Talk to workers about their goals.
3. Consider differences when making assignments.

_____ **Reinforce positive and minimize negative differences.**
1. Encourage employees to value and promote diverse views.
2. Create traditions and ceremonies that honor diversity.

APPLICATION QUESTIONS

1. Does your organization (employer or school) show signs of bias against certain groups of people? What is your first "gut" response to that question? _____ Yes _____ No. Why do you feel this way?
2. How might a manager's role for promoting diversity change as the organization changes by becoming more diverse?
3. How can more diversity contribute to greater creativity and better problem solving?
4. What diversity programs have you observed at school or work? Were they effective? Why or why not?
5. What steps could be taken to change these practices? Do you think your organization would be willing to do so?

REINFORCEMENT EXERCISE

The following are suggested activities for enhancing your awareness and reinforcing the techniques described in this chapter for valuing diversity. You may want to adapt them to the Action Plan you will develop next, or try them independently.

1. Ask your minority friends what kinds of biases they perceive in school or in the workplace. Do you agree with their assessments? Even if you think they are wrong or are exaggerating the problem, try to imagine yourself in their role.
2. Think of places where you have worked. Were minorities expected to adapt to that culture? Did the employer make any concessions to diversity? If so, what were those efforts? Were the minority employees content? If not, could their discontent have been reduced by more sensitivity by management?
3. Use the following checklist to gather the information indicated.[40] Use either your existing knowledge of the organization or ask someone who might know. (If you do ask others, explain to them that it is for a class project.)

Does your organization . . .

_____ Have signs and manuals in English only, although several employees are more comfortable in other languages?
_____ Ignore important holidays celebrated by people of certain cultures, such as Yom Kippur, Cinco de Mayo, or Chinese New Year?
_____ Limit social events to married people?
_____ Restrict training opportunities available to women and minorities?
_____ Emphasize male-oriented sporting events, such as football?
_____ Limit its recruitment efforts to colleges and universities with predominantly white students?
_____ Hire predominantly females for secretarial and clerical positions?
_____ Discourage styles of dress that express varied cultural and ethnic backgrounds?

4. What items in the preceding checklist, if any, did you find that may represent bias?
5. What steps could be taken to change the practices you cite in question 4? Do you think your organization would be willing to do so?
6. Go by yourself to a culturally different place that you have never been to before. Examples are a church service for a different religion, a school for the deaf or blind, etc. Report your experiences and feelings to others in your group.

ACTION PLAN

1. How can I improve my sensitivity to diversity issues?
2. What will be the payoff for doing so?
3. What potential obstacles stand in my way?
4. What are the specific things I will do to improve my sensitivity?
5. When will I do them?
6. How will I measure my improvement?

NOTES

1. Suzanne C. de Janasz, Karen O. Dowd, and Beth Z. Schneider, *Interpersonal Skills in Organizations* (Boston: McGraw-Hill, 2002) 159–60.
2. R. L. Daft, *Leadership: Theory and Practice* (Fort Worth: Dryden Press, 1999) 302.
3. F. Milliken and L. I. Martins, "Searching for Common Threads: Understanding the Multiple Effects of Diversity in Organizational Groups," *Academy of Management Review* 21, no. 2 (1996): 402–33.
4. G. W. Fairholm, *Leadership and the Culture Trust* (Westport, CT: Prager, 1994) 184.
5. P. C. Early and M. Erez, *Managing Across Cultures and Countries: Inside Understanding* (New York: Oxford University, 1996); D. C. Limirick, "Managers of Meaning: From Bob Geldorf's Band Aid to Australian CEOs," *Organizational Dynamics* (Spring 1990): 22–23; A. Nahavandi and E. Aranda, "Restructuring Terms for the Re-Engineered Organization," *Academy of Management Executive* 8, no. 4 (1994): 56–58.
6. W. B. Johnson and A. H. Packer, *Workforce 2000: Work and Workers in the 21st Century* (Indianapolis: Hudson Institute, 1987); M. Galen and A. T. Palmer, "White, Male and Worried," *Newsweek,* January 31, 1994, 50–55.
7. *Opportunity 2000: Creative Affirmative Action Strategies for a Changing Workforce.* Prepared for the U.S. Department of Labor by Hudson Institute, Indianapolis, IN, (September 1988) 3–14.
8. Daft, 1991, p. 318.
9. G. Colvin, "The 50 Best Companies for Asians, Blacks, and Hispanics," *Fortune,* July 19, 1999, 53.
10. L. E. Wynter, "Minorities Play the Hero in More TV Ads as Clients Discover Multicultural Sells," *Wall Street Journal,* November 24, 1993, B6.
11. C. Hall, "Hoechst Celanese Diversifying Its Ranks," *Dallas Morning News,* September 27, 1992, 1H, 7H.
12. This section was adapted from Suzanne C. de Janasz, Karen O. Dowd, and Beth Z. Schneider, *Interpersonal Skills in Organizations* (Boston: McGraw-Hill, 2002), 155.
13. Dayle M. Smith, *Women at Work: Leadership for the Next Century* (Upper Saddle River, NJ: Prentice Hall, 2000), 18

14. R. Roosevelt Thomas Jr., "The Concept of Managing Diversity," *The Public Manager: The New Bureaucrat* (Winter 1996): 41.
15. Dinesh D'Souza, "Beyond Affirmative Action: The Perils of Managing Diversity," *Chief Executive* (U.S.) (December 1996): 42.
16. Adapted from Marilyn Loden and Judy B. Rosener, *Workforce America: Managing Employee Diversity as a Vital Resource* (Burr Ridge, IL: Irwin Professional Publishing, 1991).
17. R. D. Jager and R. Ortez, *In the Company of Giants* (New York: McGraw-Hill, 1997); *http://www.microsoft.com/diversity*.
18. Hewlett-Packard's Web site, *http://www.hp.com*.
19. See, for example, J. C. McCune, "Diversity Training: A Competitive Weapon," *Management Review* (June 1996): 25–28; A. A. Johnson, "The Business Case for Work-Family Programs," *Journal of Accountancy* (August 1995): 55–56; J. T. Ferguson and W. R. Johnston, "Managing Diversity," *Mortgage Banking* (September 1995): 36; M. Fleschner, "Universally Diverse: Expert Advice for Turning Your Organization into a Totally Integrated Selling Dynamo," *Selling Power* (July–August 1996): 20–24; R. Moss-Kanter, *The Change Masters* (New York: Simon and Schuster, 1983); R. R. Mai-Dalton, "Managing Cultural Diversity on the Individual, Group, and Organizational Levels" in M. M. Chemers and R. Ayman, eds., *Leadership Theory and Research: Perspectives and Directions* (New York: Academic Press, 1993); and R. T. Mowday and R. J. Sutton, "Organizational Behavior: Linking Individuals and Groups to Organizational Contexts" in L. W. Patton and M. R Rosenzweig, eds., *Annual Review of Psychology* 44 (Palo Alto, CA: Annual Reviews, Inc., 1993) 195–289.
20. N. L. Mueller, "Wisconsin Power and Light's Model Diversity Program," *Training and Development* (March 1996): 57–60.
21. *http://www.texaco.com*.
22. S. Jackson and Associates, *Diversity in the Workplace: Human Resource Initiatives* (New York: Guildford Press, 1992).

23. H. Collingwood, "Who Handles a Diverse Work Force Best?" *Working Woman* (February 1996): 23.

24. J. Kaufman, "How Workplaces May Look Without Affirmative Action," *Wall Street Journal,* March 20, 1995, B7.

25. S. Rynes and B. Rosen, "A Field Survey of Factors Affecting the Adoption and Perceived Success of Diversity Training," *Personnel Psychology* (Summer 1995): 247–70.

26. A. M. Morrison, *The New Leaders: Guidelines on Leadership Diversity in America* (San Francisco: Jossey-Bass, 1992).

27. Charlene M. Solomon, "Communicating in a Global Environment," *Workforce* (November 1999): 50.

28. A. Markels, "How One Hotel Manages Staff's Diversity," *Wall Street Journal,* November 20, 1996, B1.

29. R. Leger, "Linked by Differences," *Springfield (Mo.) News Leader,* December 31, 1993, B6.

30. J. Greenberg, *Managing Behavior in Organizations: Science in Service to Practice,* 2d ed. (Upper Saddle River, NJ: Prentice Hall, 1999) 98.

31. F. Luthans, *Organizational Behavior,* 8th ed. (Burr Ridge, IL: Irwin McGraw-Hill, 1998) 69.

32. I. Harpaz, "The Importance of Work Goals: An International Perspective," *Journal of International Business Studies* (First Quarter 1990): 75–93.

33. G. Hofstede, "Motivation, Leadership and Organizations: Do American Theories Apply Abroad?" *Organizational Dynamics* (Summer 1980): 55.

34. T. McDermott, "TQM: The Total Quality Maquiladora," *Business Mexico* 4, no. 11 (1994): 42–45.

35. S. P. Robbins and M. Coulter, *Management,* 6th ed. (Upper Saddle River, NJ: Prentice Hall, 1999) 89.

36. N. Adler, *International Dimensions of Organizational Behavior,* 3d ed. (Boston: PWS—Kent, 1997); and T. Cox and S. Blake, "Managing Cultural Diversity: Implications for Organizational Competitiveness," *Academy of Management Executives 5* (August 1991): 45–66.

37. Adapted from D. Bowen, et al. *Experiences in Management and Organizational Behavior,* 4th ed. (New York: Wiley, 1996) 329.

38. Adapted from A. J. Kinicki, *Valuing Diversity* (Chandler, AZ: Angelo Kinicki, 1994) 1–5.

39. This exercise was adapted from J. William Pfeiffer and Leonard D. Goodstein (Eds.), *The 1994 Annual: Developing Human Resources*, Pfeiffer & Company, 1994.

40. Adapted from Greenberg, 99.

CHAPTER 5

Developing Ethical Guideposts

Learning Objectives

After completing this chapter, you should be able to:

■ Develop your own ethical parameters.

■ Analyze your organization's ethics policy.

■ Evaluate business situations to determine ethical courses of action.

■ Create a positive ethical environment for subordinates.

SELF-ASSESSMENT EXERCISE

How Important Are Ethics to You?[1]

Everyone likes to think of themselves as honest, moral, and ethical, especially on "big" matters. Few of us would likely cheat, steal, or lie if we perceived the stakes (or perhaps the chances of being caught) as extraordinarily high.

But how principled would you be—or *should* you be—when faced with routine business situations involving ethical choices? If your self-interest were on a collision course with your principles, how would you act?

Respond as candidly as possible to the following self-assessment situations involving potential business conflicts. Describe your level of agreement with each of the statements by circling the number in the appropriate column.

		Strongly Agree				*Strongly Disagree*
1.	I would speak my mind if the boss asked my view of the new ad campaign, which he conceived and adores but which I think is dreadful.	5	4	3	2	1
2.	I would not copy software without getting permission from the publisher.	5	4	3	2	1
3.	If it meant making a sale that I needed for my monthly quota, I would give the customer an overly optimistic delivery date.	1	2	3	4	5
4.	In applying for a job, I would omit a prior experience if I was fired or left under a cloud.	1	2	3	4	5

		Strongly Agree				Strongly Disagree
5.	I would pad my expense account just a bit if I thought I was being shortchanged by the company in other ways.	1	2	3	4	5
6.	If I saw a coworker make false statements to a customer or a supervisor, I would tell the boss.	5	4	3	2	1
7.	I would flirt with my superior if I thought it could win me a bigger raise.	1	2	3	4	5
8.	I would use my office phone to make a long-distance call on personal matters if no easy alternative was available.	1	2	3	4	5
9.	I would never take home paper clips, stationery, or other office supplies.	5	4	3	2	1
10.	I would accept a permanent, full-time job even if I knew I could stay for only a few months.	1	2	3	4	5
11.	I would never call in sick when I just needed some time off.	5	4	3	2	1
12.	If a supplier gave me an expensive gift that I really liked, I'd return it only if keeping it would be obvious to my boss.	1	2	3	4	5
13.	If I felt sexually attracted to a job candidate with lesser qualifications than the others, I wouldn't let that influence my hiring decision.	5	4	3	2	1
14.	If I didn't win the promotion, I would be inclined to slack off when working for the guy who did.	1	2	3	4	5
15.	If my secretary weren't busy, I would ask her to type some personal correspondence for me.	1	2	3	4	5

Scoring and Interpretation.   Add the numbers you have circled to obtain your total score.

70–75   You are a strongly ethical person whom some may accuse of being too rigid.

50–69   You show average ethical awareness and thus may need to sharpen your ethical focus.

40–50   Although you show some awareness of ethical issues, your actions may not be consistently ethical.

0–40   Your ethical values appear to be below contemporary standards and could become a negative factor in your career.

CONCEPTS

What Is Ethics? Why Is It Important?

•   You are the founder and president of a small electronics company. Your whole financial future is wrapped up in the success of your firm. An engineer at a competing company makes an important scientific breakthrough that promises big profits for the rival firm at your expense. You ponder whether you should hire that engineer away in an attempt to learn the details of his discovery.[2]

•   A foreign worker is seriously hurt in an accident in one of your overseas plants. Your facility there meets local standards, but the plant manager tells you the accident wouldn't have occurred in the United States because U.S. safety laws would have mandated the installation of protective equipment. Your company is under no legal requirement to install the expensive devices in foreign countries, but does it have a *moral* obligation?[3]

• Your assistant controller, after some not-too-subtle hints from you, is starting to look for a new job at another firm. You are relieved because you will not have to fire him; his work has been substandard for quite some time. But your relief turns to dismay when he asks you to write a strong letter of recommendation for him. Do you say no and run the risk that he will not leave? Or do you write the letter, knowing that you're influencing someone else to take on the problem you are finding so troublesome?[4]

In the workplace, acting ethically is not just an abstraction. Especially for managers, making the right choices in ethics-laden situations, big and small, is an almost-everyday occurrence. Read about Enron, Arther Andersen, and Martha Stewart, among others, daily on the front page of your newspaper's business section.

Ethics is commonly thought of as the rules or principles that define right and wrong conduct.[5] In this chapter, however, you will encounter many examples in which the task isn't as simple as just choosing the "correct" answer. Rather, the decision may involve the many shades of gray in between "right" and "wrong."

In this chapter, you will be encouraged to develop your own ethical decision-making process. You also will learn how managers as well as organizations can help or hinder the development of a moral climate.

Why Study Ethics?

Ethics is important for everyone, but it is particularly crucial for the manager for a number of reasons. One obvious reason is that his or her decisions set the standard for subordinates and help create a tone for the organization as a whole.

Second, the behavior of managers is under increasing scrutiny. Because people have more access to information, misdeeds may become quickly and widely known. The reputation of an organization or individual, which may have taken many years to build, can be destroyed in minutes. In addition, today's public has high standards for the behavior of managers and their companies. Customers are no longer forced to tolerate an unethical company; competition allows them to choose the company that best suits their expectations.

Behaving ethically also improves the quality of work life. If employees believe all are held to similar high standards, they likely will feel better about themselves, their colleagues, and their organization.

Further, many businesses want employees to behave ethically because such a reputation is good for business (which, in turn, can mean larger profits). Similarly, encouraging employees to act ethically can save money by reducing employee theft, downtime, and lawsuits. Because many unethical acts are also illegal, a firm that allows workers to engage in unfair practices might be prosecuted.

However, the law itself is not an adequate guide to ethics. Some unethical acts—lying under oath, for example, or embezzling—are illegal. But many legal acts are potentially unethical, and it is those situations that often pose the toughest choices. For instance, charging a higher price to a naïve customer than to a savvy one is not illegal. In fact, it may be seen by some as a smart business practice. But is it *ethical?* Dismissing an employee for cause is not illegal, but if the poor performance has been tolerated for years and the problem employee will qualify for his pension in a few more months, is firing him ethical?

How Strong Are Our Business Ethics?

Perhaps all behavior contains a potential conflict between doing what is morally right and what is in our own self-interest. But in business—where our self-interest also constitutes our economic well-being—the dividing line between these two motives is especially blurred. Indeed, a cynic would say business ethics is an oxymoron, that making money and advancing one's career are so essential that observing moral niceties is a luxury few can afford.

However, interest in ethics is on the rise. Ethics education, for example, is being widely expanded in college curriculums and in the workplace. Such attempts to codify business ethics are not new. As far back as 1750 B.C., the Babylonian ruler Hammurabi etched in an eight-foot-high stone an elaborate code of conduct, including some provisions aimed at curtailing unfair business practices.[6]

Although many companies are setting up ethics codes, ethics training, and ethics officers to help instill proper values, many observers believe that we are currently suffering an ethics crisis. Behaviors that were once thought of as reprehensible—lying, cheating, misrepresenting, and covering up mistakes—have become, in many people's eyes, acceptable or necessary practices. Some managers have profited from illegal use of insider information. Others have covered up information about the safety of their products. Some government contractors overcharge for their work. Price fixing, polluting the environment, and industrial espionage are further illustrations of ethical lapses.

Pundits and pollsters often try to gauge the state of business ethics. According to a Yankelovich Partners survey, three-quarters of working Americans say they have never been asked or told to do something on the job that they thought was unethical. However, of those who *were* asked, 4 in 10 did the unethical act.[7]

Most Americans believe they can balance the demands of the job with their own conscience. When that same Yankelovich survey asked what workers would do if they found out an employer was up to no good, only a small minority said they would look the other way (9 percent) or quit (5 percent.) Most (78 percent) said they would talk to the boss and try to resolve the situation short of losing their jobs, suggesting most feel they have some scope to affect ethical behavior in their workplaces. (The remaining 8 percent were uncertain or unclear in their answers.) Interestingly, responses from people who said they regularly attend religious services were no different from others' responses.

College students studying to be future business leaders seem also to have become caught up in the wave of questionable behavior. A Rutgers University study of more than 6,000 students found that, among those preparing for careers in business, 76 percent admitted to having cheated on at least one test and 19 percent acknowledged having cheated on four or more tests.[8]

Yet, the study and practice of ethics are not as precise as, say, accounting or engineering. As you will see, the variables are many and the absolutes few. Often the decision is not between good and bad or between fair and unfair alternatives as much as it is a choice among competing goods or lesser evils.

Why Ethics Questions Are Often Tougher Than They Seem

It is easy to *say* you want to do the right thing, but figuring out the proper action can be difficult because often no single "correct" answer is available.

For example, some years ago when South Africa's apartheid policies were earning global scorn, many U.S. firms were urged by their stockholders to pull out of that segregated country. Doing so, it was reasoned, would apply economic pressure on the racist government to change its policies. More than 100 universities—whose endowments controlled vast stockholdings—did sever ties with companies operating in South Africa.

The University of Notre Dame, in contrast, decided to invest in U.S. firms there that were helping South African blacks. Believing that apartheid would eventually crumble and that withdrawal of Western companies would only make conditions worse, Notre Dame leaders took a course that was neither obvious nor popular. Some

U.S. firms did stay and work for reforms, training blacks for supervisory positions, help-ing them buy homes, and even taking out ads to challenge the government to disman-tle apartheid.[9]

Who was right? The companies that pulled out to signify their disgust with the racist government? Or those who stayed to helped blacks prepare for a heightened role?

On a much smaller scale, most of us would agree that lying is wrong. Yet most of us also would say that at times it may be better to disguise or embellish the truth than to be totally candid. In one survey of middle managers, for example, 9 percent admitted that they had lied to customers, 5 percent said they had lied to a superior, and 3 percent acknowledged lying to subordinates.[10]

What would you do, for example, if a company vice president, whose support is critical to your success as a human resources officer, asked for your help to get one of his managers transferred to another division? You know the manager in question is a marginal performer. Furthermore, you know that the VP hasn't mentioned this inade-quate performance in the manager's performance appraisals. Do you support the VP by not saying anything about the manager's poor, but unrecorded, performance to the heads of the other divisions? Or, do you risk your own career success and share a note about the manager's questionable performance? Put another way, is not telling the whole truth the moral equivalent of lying?

That dilemma, and many others, have no easy answers. And opinions differ on the key questions to ask oneself when faced with an ethical dilemma. We will give you our own ethical-screening recommendations later in this chapter. Meanwhile, see Exhibit 5-1 for a simple "ethics check" suggested by a prominent business consultant and a well-known clergyman.

Taking the time to think through ethical quandaries and debating them with trusted associates is often wise because many situations are more complex than they may seem at first. For example, is it ethical for a salesperson to offer an expensive gift to a purchasing agent as an inducement to buy? Instinctively, you might say "no." But what if the gift comes out of the salesperson's commission? In other words, the sales-person, trying to get ahead, is willing to make a personal investment in his clients. Does that make it any different?

Similarly, is it ethical for an employee to "blow the whistle" by complaining to authorities about an improper company practice? Sure, you might say. But what if the whistleblower does so without first consulting company officials or exhausting in-house remedies? Or, what if he is going public with his revelation because there is a financial reward? Or because he will be on the television news? Or because he mistak-enly believes he was mistreated by the company? Would your view of the whistle-blower's ethics change if you knew more about his motivation and what procedures he followed?

EXHIBIT 5-1   How Will You Feel?

In their book, *The Power of Ethical Management*, clergyman Norman Vincent Peale and business consultant Ken Blanchard suggest the following ethics check:

- ***Is it legal?***   Will I be violating either civil law or company policy?
- ***Is it balanced?***   Is it fair to all concerned in the short term as well as the long term? Does it promote win-win relationships?
- ***How will it make me feel about myself?***   Will it make me proud? Would I feel good if my decision were published in the newspaper? Would I feel good if my family knew about it?

SOURCE: K. Blanchard and N.V. Peale, *The Power of Ethical Management* (New York: William Morrow, 1988) 27.

Organizations and individuals can do a number of things to encourage ethical behavior. Next, we will look at what influences a person's choices and ways to improve the ethical climate.

Factors Affecting Managerial Ethics

Whether a manager acts ethically or unethically depends on several factors, including his or her personal characteristics; the organization's culture and structure; the issue that is being called into question; and the national culture in which the manager operates.[11]

The Individual's Characteristics

People who lack a strong moral sense are much less likely to do the wrong things if they are constrained by rules, policies, job descriptions, or strong cultural norms that discourage such behaviors. Conversely, moral people can be corrupted by an organizational structure and culture that permits or encourages unethical practices. How strong is your personal moral sense?

For example, if someone in your class were selling a copy of the final exam, would you have the strength not to buy it? Would you have that resolve even if you suspected the department faculty knew a copy was floating around but had done little to discourage cheating? Would a decision not to buy the exam be easier to reach if you knew that automatic expulsion was the outcome if you were caught?

The Organization's Culture

Unwittingly perhaps, organizations often reward unethical behavior. In fact, they may develop "counternorms" that are contrary to prevailing ethical standards. For example, although government regulations may require full disclosure of certain information, some organizations send out the tacit message to their employees that being secretive and deceitful is not only acceptable, but also desirable. In those organizations, employees who are too open and honest may even be punished.[12]

In addition, some managerial values can undermine integrity. Although the vast majority of managers appears to recognize that "good ethics is good business," some managers have developed ways of thinking that can encourage unethical decisions. Such thinking patterns include the following:

Bottom-line mentality.   People who think like this believe that financial success is the only criterion for decision making. Any ethical concerns are ignored or given a lesser priority.

Exploitive mentality.   This perspective sacrifices concern for others in favor of benefits to oneself. Such managers "use" people to achieve their goals.

"Madison Avenue" mentality.   This reasoning suggests that anything is right if the public can be made to see it as right. Appearances are valued more than reality, and, thus, executives are less concerned with doing the right thing than with what looks good.[13]

The Organization's Structure

Some structures provide for strong guidance while other companies are organized in ways that create ambiguity for managers. Lax supervision is one example, or no clear code of conduct may be in place. Or perhaps a code does exist, but it's often only paid lip service. Structures also differ in the amount of time, competition, cost, and other pressures put on employees. In short, the more pressure and the less guidance, the more likely it is that managers will compromise their ethical standards.

A good structure, on the other hand, is one that constantly reminds managers about what is ethical and uniformly disciplines those who use bad judgment. Formal rules and regulations as well as clear job descriptions and written codes of ethics help reduce ambiguity.

The performance appraisal system also may weaken or reinforce ethical standards. If the appraisals focus exclusively on outcomes and ignore what means are used to reach the ends, then employees feel increased pressure to do "whatever is necessary" to reach the goals.

The Intensity of the Issue

We tend to give more thought to ethical questions when the stakes are higher—when potential for harm is great, or if a lot of money or the chance of a big career gain is involved. An executive who would think nothing of taking home a few office supplies, for example, would be highly concerned about embezzlement of company funds. The distinction is made because actual pilfering of money, in addition to being prosecutable, is an act with greater consequences for both the individual and the firm.

However, deciding what is a major and what is a minor ethical issue can be a slippery slope. For example, almost everyone would consider taking a monetary bribe as unethical; it also may well be illegal. But what if the "bribe" is not monetary? What if you are a purchasing officer and several vendors are pitching similar products to you? Vendor A makes an attractive price offer. Vendor B makes a comparable offer but also invites you, a known football fanatic, to a big game that you otherwise would not be able to go to because of a scarcity of tickets. If you go and you choose Vendor B as your supplier, have you been bribed, even though the prices are comparable and the company incurs no loss?

The National Culture

Some of the most difficult global business decisions involve ethical considerations because the basis of what is "right" and "wrong" is culturally determined. How rigid can you be in applying only your country's ethical and legal templates while operating in foreign lands?

For instance, using child labor in the United States is neither legal nor ethically acceptable, but in many foreign countries, the practice is routine. Which cultural norm should prevail in the foreign plants of U.S. companies?

Similarly, the issue of bribery is one of the toughest to resolve in the international context. It regularly occurs in business overseas even though most Americans would condemn it as unethical. But can or should U.S. firms resist joining in this universally illegal act if their competitors are doing it in response to local custom?[14]

Consider this scenario, based on an actual situation.[15] You are marketing director for a construction firm in the Middle East. Your company bids on a substantial and much-needed project, but the cousin of the government minister who will award the contract contacts you. He suggests that in exchange for a $20,000 fee to the government minister, your chances of getting the contract will greatly improve. If you do not pay, you are sure the award will be to your competitor, which routinely makes these kinds of payments and routinely wins the contracts, too.

Your company has no code of conduct yet, although it has formed a committee to consider one. The government of your country recently passed an Ethical Business Practices Act. The pertinent paragraph is somewhat vague but implies that this kind of payment would probably be in violation of the act. Your boss, and those above him, do not want to become involved. What do you do?

How Can Organizations Encourage Ethical Behavior?

Ethics, as we have seen, is an organizational issue, a personal issue, or a cultural issue. Management, however, can take a number of actions that, in aggregate, may help to reduce unethical practices.[16]

Make Better Personnel Selections

An organization's employee-selection process—interviews, tests, and background checks—should be used to eliminate ethically undesirable applicants. The selection process should be seen as an opportunity to learn not only about the candidate's job skills but also his or her personal values.[17] Who is hired, promoted, and rewarded (or punished) sends a strong signal to employees about valued moral standards in the organization. Chapter 13 will elaborate on how to identify and hire the right kinds of employees.

Develop a Code of Ethics

Codes of ethics are an increasingly popular tool for reducing ethical ambiguity. Nearly 90 percent of *Fortune* 1000 firms now have a formal code of ethics stating the organization's ethical rules.[18] One study of 83 corporate codes found the content of the codes falls in three general areas: (1) be a dependable organizational citizen, (2) do not do anything unlawful or improper that could harm the organization, and (3) be good to customers.[19] Exhibit 5-2 lists the variables in each of those three clusters in order of their frequency of mention.

Obviously, no code can cover every possible situation. Ideally, the codes should be specific enough to show employees the spirit in which they are supposed to act but loose enough to allow freedom of judgment in unique situations.

Probably as important as the content of the code is how seriously it is taken by top management. In isolation, the code is not likely to be much more than window dressing. However, if the codes are communicated often and well, if they are vigorously

---

EXHIBIT 5-2   Variables Found in 83 Corporate Codes of Business Ethics

Cluster 1: Be a Dependable Organizational Citizen

1. Comply with safety, health, and security regulations.
2. Demonstrate courtesy, respect, honesty, and fairness.
3. Do not compromise your performance through illegal drugs or alcohol.
4. Manage personal finances well.
5. Exhibit good attendance and punctuality.
6. Follow directives of supervisors.
7. Do not use abusive language.
8. Dress in business attire.
9. Do not violate laws prohibiting firearms.

Cluster 2: Do Not Do Anything Unlawful or Improper That Will Harm the Organization

1. Conduct business in compliance with all laws.
2. Payments for unlawful purposes are prohibited.
3. Bribes are prohibited.
4. Avoid outside activities that impair duties.
5. Maintain confidentiality of records.
6. Comply with all antitrust and trade regulations.
7. Comply with all accounting rules and controls.
8. Do not use company property for personal benefit.
9. Employees are personally accountable for company funds.
10. Do not propagate false or misleading information.
11. Make decisions without regard for personal gain.

Cluster 3: Be Good to Customers

1. Convey true claims in product advertisements.
2. Perform assigned duties to the best of your ability.
3. Provide products and services of the highest quality.

SOURCE: F. R. David, "An Empirical Study of Codes of Business Ethics: A Strategic Perspective," paper presented at the 48th Annual Academy of Management Conference, Anaheim, CA (August 1988).

endorsed by higher-ups, and if employees who violate the codes are treated firmly and publicly, a code can provide a strong foundation for an ethics program.[20]

Lead by Example

Top management sets the cultural tone through words and action. In fact, research continues to show that the behavior of superiors is *the strongest single influence* on an individual's ethical or unethical behavior.[21] Because employees use their higher-ups' behavior as a benchmark for what is expected, how the executives act is probably more important than what they say. The four chapters in Part V of this text will help you hone your leadership skills.

Set Realistic Job Goals

Employees should have tangible, realistic goals. If goals are ambiguous or make unrealistic demands, they can encourage employees to take an "anything goes" attitude, but clear, realistic goals help reduce ambiguity and motivate rather than punish. Goal-setting skills will be elaborated on in Chapter 7.

Provide Ethics Training

More than 40 percent of U.S. companies provide some form of ethics training.[22] Though debate continues over the value of these seminars, workshops, and similar programs, ethics training, at its best, can provide a number of benefits. It reinforces the organization's standards. It reminds employees that top managers put a priority on ethics. It clarifies what practices are or are not permissible. And, when managers discuss such common concerns, they may be reassured that they aren't alone in facing ethical dilemmas. Such reassurance can strengthen their resolve when they need to take an ethically correct, but unpopular, stance.[23]

Use Comprehensive Performance Appraisals

If performance appraisals focus only on economic outcomes, employees will infer that the ends justify the means. Thus, if an organization wants managers to uphold high ethical standards, it should include this dimension in the appraisal process. For instance, a manager's annual review might include a point-by-point evaluation of his or her decisions on an ethical scale as well as by more traditional economic criteria. Skills for effective performance evaluation are explained in Chapter 8.

Do Independent Social Audits

Having an outsider evaluate decisions and practices in terms of the organization's code of ethics can increase the likelihood of an unethical practice being detected. Such audits should probably be done on a regular basis and at random and be conducted by auditors responsible to the company's board of directors, which would hear the findings directly. Such autonomy not only gives the auditors clout but lessens the opportunity for retaliation by those being audited.

Create Ethics Officers

More than 500 companies have created ethics officers, up from 200 just a few years ago.[24] These ombudspersons hear from employees, anonymously or by name, with a view toward counseling them on matters of fairness and working to improve the firm's ethical climate. Thus, such ethics officers can act as both a sounding board and a possible advocate for the "right" alternative.[25]

Again, this trend appears to be a welcome one, but it is not a panacea. For instance, cynics point out that one of the factors behind the sudden popularity of ethics officers was the creation in 1991 of sentencing guidelines that reduce fines for white-collar crimes committed by corporations with comprehensive ethics programs. Second, critics contend that the job too often is reserved for long-time company loyalists who are unlikely to challenge higher executives and/or who wield little real power. Third, the ethics officers themselves often complain that they can recommend but have little clout with which to create real change.[26]

What You as an Individual Can Do

The organization can do much to foster ethical behavior. But in the final analysis it is the individual manager who must make the decisions, and quite often individuals make poor choices on ethical issues. See Exhibit 5-3 for some of the reasons. Thus, it is important that you develop your own ethical guideposts and decision-making processes to apply for yourself.

What guideposts can you use, especially in those "gray" areas, where right and wrong are not easily defined? What processes can you follow to enhance your ethical thinking and decisions?

We offer some guidelines, then a step-by-step template for individual decision making.

Skill Guidelines for Developing and Applying Ethical Guideposts

1. ***Know and understand your organization's policy on ethics.*** A Company policies on ethics, if they exist, describe what the organization perceives as ethical behavior and what it expects you to do. Knowing and understanding this policy will clarify what is permissible and what discretion you may have.

2. ***Anticipate unethical conflict.*** Managers should be alert to situations that may promote unethical behavior. Under unusual circumstances, even an otherwise ethical employee may be tempted to act out of character. The manager needs to anticipate those unusual situations and be proactive.

For example, a manager may know that an important client has a reputation for cutting corners. He or she may also know that this quarter's sales goals are high, putting added pressure on the salespeople. If so, the manager could seek to blunt any temptation by meeting with the customer to tactfully restate the company's ethical credo.

Further, the manager probably will want to give the sales staff helpful advice on how to rebuff questionable overtures and meet goals through ethical means.

3. ***Think before you act.*** Ask yourself, "Why am I doing what I'm about to do? What led up to the problem? What is my true intention in taking this action? Is my reason valid? Or are there ulterior motives behind it—such as proving myself to my peers or superiors? Will my action injure someone?"

Also ask yourself, "Would I disclose to my boss or family what I am about to do?" Remember, it is *your* behavior and *your* actions. You need to make sure that you are not doing something that will jeopardize your reputation or your organization.

EXHIBIT 5-3 Why Do Individuals Make Poor Choices on Ethical Issues?

1. The individual and/or the organization is immature.
2. Economic self-interest is overwhelming.
3. Special circumstances outweigh ethical concerns.
4. People are uneducated in ethical decision making.
5. Possible rewards outweigh possible punishments for unethical behavior.
6. The prevailing attitude is "All's fair in love, war, and business."
7. There is powerful organizational pressure to commit unethical acts.

SOURCE: O. C. Ferrell and G. Gardiner, *In Pursuit of Ethics: Tough Choices in the World of Work* (Springfield, IL: Smith Collins Co., 1991) 9–13.

4. ***Ask yourself what-if questions.***   As you ponder your decision, you should also be asking what-if questions. For example: "What if I make the wrong decision? What will happen to me? To my job?" "What if my actions were described, in detail, on a local TV news show or in the newspaper? Would that public notice bother or embarrass me or those around me?" "What if I get caught doing something unethical? Am I prepared to deal with the consequences?"

5. ***Seek opinions from others.***   Asking for advice from other managers is often wise. Maybe they have been in a similar situation and can give you the benefit of their experience. Or maybe they can just listen and act as a sounding board for you.

6. ***Do not allow yourself to become isolated.***   Managers can easily become isolated from what is occurring in the office. But it is the manager's responsibility to be aware of all activities. You can combat isolation by promoting an open-door policy and continually looking for ways to improve ethical behavior.

7. ***Do what you truly believe is right.***   You have a conscience, and you are responsible for your behavior. Whatever you do, if you truly believe it is the right action to take, then what others will say is immaterial. You need to be true to your own internal ethical standards. Ask yourself, "Can I live with what I have done?"

Ethical Screening

Ethical screening refers to running a contemplated decision through an ethics test. This screening makes the most sense when, as is often the case, the contemplated action is in that gray area between clearly right or clearly wrong.

The following formula contains nothing magical.[27] Other authors will offer other litmus tests. What is important is that you are familiar with the basic steps you should take when faced with an ethical dilemma.

Step 1:   ***Gather the facts.***   You should find out the answers to pertinent questions: Does the situation present any legal questions? What are the precedents for this kind of decision? What do our rules and regulations say?

Step 2:   ***Define the ethical issues.***   It may be helpful to talk the situation over with someone to clarify these issues. Such issues might include conflicts of interest, dealing with confidential information, proper use of company resources, or more intangible questions concerning kindness, respect, or fairness.

Step 3:   ***Identify the affected parties.***   Major corporate decisions, such as shutting down a plant, can affect thousands of people. Even a much more modest action—hiring or not hiring a handicapped worker, for example—can involve many more people than you might initially think.

Step 4:   ***Identify the consequences.***   Try to predict the consequences for each party. Concentrate on those outcomes with the highest probability of occurring and especially those with negative outcomes. Both the short- and long-term results should be considered. Closing down the plant, for example, might create short-term harm but in the long-term the firm may be financially healthier.

Do not neglect the symbolic consequences, either. Every action sends a message, good or bad. If you hire the handicapped worker, that act may send a message that is larger and more meaningful than all your words about equal opportunity. It is not just what you say, it is what you *do* that your subordinates will pick up on.

Step 5: *Consider your character and integrity.* It is fair to ask yourself the following questions:

- What would my family, friends, superiors, and coworkers think of my actions?
- How would I feel if my decision was publicly disclosed in the newspaper or via e-mail?
- Does this decision or action agree with my religious teachings and beliefs (or with my personal principles and sense of responsibility)?
- Would I want everyone to make the same decision and take the same action if faced with these same circumstances?
- How would I feel if I were on the other side of this decision?

Step 6: *Think creatively about alternatives.* More alternatives can often be identified than just the choice between doing or not doing something. Try to be imaginative when considering options. For example, what could you do if a grateful client sends you a rare and expensive bottle of wine that you cannot ethically accept? To keep it would be wrong. But if you returned it, you may appear ungrateful and make the client feel foolish.

So, another possibility might be giving the gift to a charity auction, then penning the client a thank-you note mentioning that you passed the wine along to a good cause. You would not have violated your policy or set a bad example for your staff. Meanwhile, you also would have graciously informed the client about your policy and probably discouraged future gift giving.

Step 7: *Check your intuition.* Quite apart from the rational decision-making process, you should also ask yourself, "How does this feel in my gut? Will I be proud of myself?"

Step 8: *Prepare to defend your action.* Will you be able to explain adequately to others what you are about to do? Will they also likely feel it is ethical or moral?

CONCEPT QUIZ

Complete the following true-false quiz by circling the correct answer. Answers are at the end of the quiz. After marking your answers, remember to go back and check your understanding of any answers you missed.

True or False   1. An explicitly written code of conduct is an increasingly common tool for reducing ethical ambiguity.

True or False   2. Management's actions, both verbal and physical, have little to do with how employees behave.

True or False   3. Tasks that are unrealistic and highly stressful may cause an employee to resort to unethical measures.

True or False   4. Managers should take into consideration an employee's values only after they are hired and can be observed in a work environment.

True or False   5. An ethically sound corporate culture can lead to long-term success for the company.

True or False   6. A manager's ethics are especially important because the manager sets the standard for subordinates.

True or False	7. Some unethical acts are legal.
True or False	8. An organization's culture and structure influence how ethical its employees act.
True or False	9. Business operations in foreign lands often present difficult ethical choices because of differences in cultural norms.
True or False	10. Because an individual facing an ethical dilemma needs to rely on his or her reasoning skills and moral compass, rarely can anything be gained by discussing the circumstances with others.

Answers. (1) True; (2) False; (3) True; (4) False; (5) True; (6) True; (7) True; (8) True; (9) True; (10) False

BEHAVIORAL CHECKLIST

The following behaviors are important to ethical management. Use them when evaluating your ethical management skills and those of others.

The Ethical Manager

- Disseminates the organization's policy on ethics.
- Hires and promotes individuals with high ethical standards.
- Leads by ethical example.
- Sets job goals that are realistic.
- Provides ethical training.
- Anticipates unethical conflict.
- Avoids isolation and seeks opinions from others.
- Applies the ethical-screening process to ethical dilemmas.

Attention!
Do not read the following until assigned to do so by your instructor.

MODELING EXERCISE

Competing Ethical Criteria[28]

Directions. The entire class should read the following situation. Then two class members volunteer to act out the roles of John Higgins, director of research, and Mary Fernandez, who heads his design team. The role-players read only their assigned role and prepare to explain their position at the forthcoming meeting. Do NOT read the other person's role. The remainder of the class reads both roles and reviews the Observer's Rating Sheet. Upon completion of the dialogue, class members rate Higgins's application of ethical management skills.

Observers should also note what points Higgins and Fernandez make and be prepared to suggest additional arguments and alternatives.

Time. 20 minutes.

Actors.

> John Higgins, director of research for Radartec, a major electronics firm
>
> Mary Fernandez, leader of design team charged with developing a critical component for a new radar system

Situation.   John Higgins appointed Mary Fernandez about three months ago to head the design team for a new radar tracking system. The success of the new radar system is crucial to the firm's profitability. The new component has a tight development deadline of 18 months. In fact, the CEO issued a statement indicating that the company's financial future may hinge on the timely development of the new radar.

The CEO's statement also applauded the promotion of Mary Fernandez to a key role. She is Hispanic, and the first woman in company history to lead such a unit. The company has traditionally lagged in the hiring and promotion of minorities.

Now, more than halfway through the project, certain members of the otherwise all-male team have been complaining about Fernandez. The project is on schedule, and no one has faulted Fernandez's technical knowledge. But general criticisms ("She does not know how to lead men" and "She does not understand teamwork") have been made and discussed publicly. The grousing has started to snowball, and recently the pace of work has slowed. Higgins suspects some team members are quietly sabotaging the project.

Higgins's Role.   You respect and admire Fernandez as an employee as well as a human being. You are sure she has a lot to offer the company as she grows professionally. You do not want to crush her hopes—or stymie her potential—by reneging on this big chance you gave her.

On the other hand, neither you nor the firm can risk having this radar project fail for any reason, so you are considering removing her as team leader. You and Fernandez have always gotten along well in the past, but now you fear that if you take her off the project, she will become embittered and perhaps even file a gender-discrimination lawsuit against you and the company. Furthermore, you feel sure some will see her removal as symbolic of the traditional shortchanging of minorities by the firm.

You feel torn between your responsibility to the company and to a valued employee. You want to explain to Fernandez the ethical quandary you find yourself in and how the economic considerations are at war with the moral ones. Your goal is to try to understand the other person's view and perhaps to try to reach an ethical solution that is satisfactory to both parties and the company. You have asked Fernandez to meet with you to discuss "a critical question" relating to her work role.

Fernandez's Role.   The men on the design team have been difficult, almost mutinous, but you think they would be that way with any woman or minority in charge. You are qualified for this job. You have earned it. You want it. You are prepared to endure insults and whatever other hurdles are placed in your way; those challenges are the price pioneers must pay. You owe it not only to yourself but also to other women and minorities to persevere and not let Higgins cave into pressure from the men who are upset because their "white males only" club has been disrupted.

If this question is one of ethics, it is a clear issue of fairness and equity, one that can only be resolved by allowing you to complete the job assigned to you.

OBSERVER'S RATING SHEET

Upon completion of the dialogue, class members, using the following scale, rate Higgins's application of ethical management skills. Write concrete examples in the space for comments below each criteria skill to use in explaining your feedback.

1	*2*	*3*	*4*	*5*
Unsatisfactory	*Weak*	*Adequate*	*Good*	*Outstanding*

_____ Disseminated the organization's policy on ethics

_____ Hired and promoted individuals with high ethical standards

_____ Led by ethical example

_____ Set job goals that are realistic

_____ Provided ethical training

_____ Anticipated unethical conflict

_____ Avoided isolation and sought opinions from others

_____ Applied the ethical-screening process to ethical dilemmas

> **Attention!**
> Do not read the following until assigned to do so by your instructor.

GROUP EXERCISES

In the three exercises that follow you will be asked to practice ethical management skills, sharpen your ethical sensitivity, and stretch and expand your moral reasoning and ethical judgment capability.

Group Exercise 1: West Oceans Bank Role-Play

Directions.   Upon completion of the dialogue, class members rate Carrie's application of ethical guideposts. Also note other options the role-players may have missed.

Time.   20 minutes.

Actors.

Carrie Makson, vice president of West Oceans Bank

Pat Jergen, corporate account executive manager

Situation.   Pat Jergen, a 20-year banking veteran, is reputed to be the best account executive at West Oceans Bank. Carrie Makson, the bank's vice president, has come across an opportunity to get an enormous new corporate account with Acme Chemical, the world's largest chemical company. This account, if landed and handled properly, could mean an entirely new scope and size of business for the bank. Over the past five years, however, Acme has been widely accused of dumping hazardous waste and polluting the environment; it is even on the "most wanted" list at the Environmental Protection Agency (EPA).

Carrie Makson's Role   You have been a vice president at West Oceans Bank for 10 years and a friend and admirer of Pat Jergen almost as long. You have recently felt pressure from the board of directors to increase your corporate business, and the Acme account would more than remedy the problem. In addition, you feel your present job has put you on a plateau. Thus, you desperately want this new account not only for the bank's sake but also for the good of your career and also Pat's.

You want Pat to personally handle the Acme effort, but you know that he is likely to have major reservations about taking the new account because of Acme's environmental record. You know that Pat feels strongly about the environment; in fact, you once bailed him out of jail after he was arrested in a pro-environment demonstration. Pat almost got fired because his arrest was filmed by a local television station. But you intervened with the CEO and saved Pat's job, arguing that what he did on his own time was not the company's concern. You still believe that, but you wonder, Where do we draw the line? Can an employee legitimately refuse to take an important assignment because of his or her beliefs?

If the Acme Chemical account is not landed because of Pat's personal feelings, the boss will not be so easily placated as he was when Pat was arrested. Meanwhile, you don't quite know how Pat will react. He may be outraged that you would even consider assigning the Acme account to him. Whatever his feelings, you need Pat to complete and manage the deal. But you don't want to order him to do so because he might quit, which would leave you and the company in a pickle. Pat could easily move to another bank, and you are concerned that he might because the environmental issue is so important to him. In any event, the time has come to talk to him.

Pat Jergen's Role You rose quickly at the bank, from teller to corporate account manager. You know the banking business inside out and have many contacts in the industry. You have been courted by other banks but you believe in loyalty and you like your job and you like West Oceans. You love the people there and are friendly with Carrie Makson, who helped smooth the waters some time back when you were arrested in an environmental protest. Carrie knows the depth of your commitment to the environment, knows how you ride a bicycle to work, recycle everything, and stay active in environmental politics.

You feel strongly that people need to make sacrifices for that which they believe in. Not to do so is hypocrisy. In your mind, the environment must come first. Believing that, you know that you sometimes need to take a stand or no one else will.

You've heard some rumors about Acme Chemical being wooed by West Oceans. You hope that doesn't happen, or if it does, that you aren't involved. That would surely put your principles to the test. But, meanwhile, Carrie has asked to see you. Could it be about *that?*

DISCUSSION QUESTIONS

1. Did Carrie handle this situation in an ethical way? What were some examples?
2. What could Carrie have done to better deal with the situation?

OBSERVER'S RATING SHEET

Use the following scale to rate each role-player on what arguments he/she comes up with. Also write specific examples in the space for comments to use in explaining your feedback.

1	2	3	4	5
Unsatisfactory	*Weak*	*Adequate*	*Good*	*Outstanding*

_____ Disseminated the organization's policy on ethics

_____ Hired and promoted individuals with high ethical standards

_____ Led by ethical example

_____ Set job goals that are realistic

_____ Provided ethical training

_____ Anticipated unethical conflict

_____ Avoided isolation and sought opinions from others

_____ Applied the ethical-screening process to ethical dilemmas

Additional points:

Group Exercise 2: Minicases[29]

Directions.   Form groups of four to six people and select a leader. Discuss each of the following minicases and arrive at a consensus on the best ethical courses of action.

Limit yourself to the options presented. Note that some cases have more than one satisfactory solution, and others may have no good solutions. So it's important to decide on the *one best solution* of those offered.

Allot no more than five minutes per case before moving on to the next one. The group leader should be prepared to present and defend the group's decision to the class.

Time.   40 minutes.

Minicase 1   You work for a defense contractor that has apparently made a successful bid for a big project. Final approval has gotten bogged down in the government bureaucracy, though it is likely the funds will be allocated; the question is *when*. You feel you need to get started in order to meet the tight deadline. You start negotiating with a supplier. You decide to tell the supplier:

a. "Approval is imminent. It is an important deal that will benefit us both in the long run. So, like us, you need to shoulder your share of the startup costs between now and when the contract is okayed. So let's get going on preliminary work without a contract."
b. "The program is a 'go.' I'll spare you the details."
c. "Start work now and we will cover your costs when we get the contract."
d. "The program is almost certain to be approved. Let's quickly put together an interim contract to cover us on the first, tentative phase of the work."

Minicase 2   Office supplies are disappearing from the stockroom almost as soon as they're brought in. You're told unofficially that two subordinates, who are well paid and should know better, are taking them for their children's school. Should you:

a. Lock up the supplies and issue them only as needed and signed for?
b. Tell the two suspected pilferers that supplies are for office use only?
c. Install video cameras to monitor the stockroom to get proof?
d. Send a reminder to all employees that supplies are for office use only and that disregard for this rule could result in disciplinary action?

Minicase 3   Your operation is being relocated. The personnel regulations governing moving expenses, mileage reimbursement, and storage of personal goods are so complex that you fear they may dissuade your team from making the move. Relocating without your experienced staff would be difficult for you. Do you:

a. Tell the staff the regulations are so complex that you can't go into them now but assure them that everything will work out all right in the end?
b. Not mention the regulations but instead stress the excitement of the move and the importance of the team remaining intact?
c. Present them with a highly simplified version of the regulations and encourage them to come along?
d. Give them a complete copy of the regulations and promise to work with them to get the answers they need?

Minicase 4   You make the low bid on an electronics system for the U.S. Army. However, because of staffing problems, you believe it will take you several months longer than your competitor to build the system. When the Army asks for further details on the schedule before deciding to whom to award the contract, you:

a. Say your schedule will be "essentially the same" as what you believe your competitor's would be?
b. Predict you will complete the job as quickly as your competitor, then tell your engineers they must do it faster than they say it can be done?
c. Sidestep the time issue and instead stress the quality of your firm's work?
d. Admit that your people say you won't meet the competitor's schedule even though you suspect this revelation may cause you to lose points on the evaluation?

Minicase 5 A friend of yours wants to transfer to your division. He is a loyal and hardworking, if not exceptionally talented, employee. You have an opening, and one other candidate, whom you do not know, has applied. Do you:

a. Select the friend in whom you have confidence?
b. Select the other person, who you are told is qualified?
c. Request a qualifications comparison from human resources?
d. Ask human resources to extend the search for additional candidates before choosing?

Minicase 6 Your newest employee is a niece of a company vice president. Her performance is poor, and she doesn't get along with her coworkers. Do you:

a. Call her in and discuss her inadequacies?
b. Ask human resources to counsel her and put her on a performance improvement plan?
c. Go see her uncle?
d. Because she is new, do nothing for now in the hope she will improve?

Minicase 7 You discover that an employee hired four months ago—and who appears to be competent—falsified his employment application by claiming to have a college degree when he did not. Do you:

a. Do nothing because you are happy with his work and a degree is not a job prerequisite?
b. Recommend he be fired for lying?
c. Point out the discrepancy to him and tell him that he is on probation?
d. Refer the matter to human resources?

Minicase 8 A current supplier offers you a chance to be a paid consultant on matters not pertaining to your company's business. He assures that you would work only on weekends and that the arrangement could remain confidential if you so chose. Should you:

a. Accept the job?
b. Turn down the position?
c. Accept the job if the legal department poses no objection?
d. Report the offer to your supervisor?

Group Exercise 3: Anticipating Ethical Conflict

Directions. Break into groups of four to five students and study the following situation. Your goal is to come up with as many relevant questions and options as possible for the meeting between Anna and Jessica. Then compare results with the other groups.

Time.   20 minutes.

Situation.   Jessica has filled an entry-level sales position at Myers Equipment for about 18 months. Her performance has been exceptional. Anna, the inside sales manager and Jessica's supervisor, knows that Jessica is ambitious, a hard worker, and a widowed mother of three who is devoted to her children and gives all her off-hours attention to her family. Anna knows that Jessica not only needs more money but also deserves a promotion.

But the only job opening on the horizon is in outside sales in another unit, which Anna does not supervise. If Anna talked to the outside sales manager about Jessica's work, Jessica would probably get the job. That would be just. It would also make Jessica happy and help her to better provide for her family.

That outside sales slot normally is filled by a more experienced salesperson, although Anna thinks Jessica would grow into the job. However, Anna has other concerns. For one, the new job would put Jessica in with a group of other experienced and extremely competitive salespeople. Anna believes that unit is productive but not well supervised, and she has heard rumors that some outside salespeople use dubious methods to meet their goals. Reportedly, there have been complaints from customers to the company about the outside sales crew, but nothing has been done because the outside salesforce is highly regarded by upper management because of its sales volume. But Anna feels Jessica, who is young and somewhat naïve, would find her peers there to be poor role models with questionable ethics. In turn, Jessica's ethics might be affected.

Anna also fears Jessica would feel under intense pressure because of the highly competitive nature of outside sales. Sales goals there are high, and so is the peer pressure as well as management pressure to do whatever it takes to meet those goals.

Jessica has been ethical in all her actions so far. But Anna is worried that in any major conflicts in the new job, Jessica may be tempted to act unethically because of what she observes in her colleagues, the pressure to produce, and the needs of her family.

Jessica, for her part, does not yet know about the opening in outside sales. She knows only that she deserves a break and desperately needs more money. When Anna summons Jessica to her office to talk about this promotion possibility, Jessica hopes that her big chance has come at last.

QUESTIONS FOR DISCUSSION

1. What questions should Anna ask of Jessica?
2. What questions should Jessica ask of Anna?
3. What safeguards could Anna insist on as a way of protecting Jessica from acting unethically?
4. What could Jessica ask for to reduce the likelihood that time and competitive pressures would be too intense?
5. Does Anna have any options besides promoting Jessica to outside sales or not doing so?
6. In what ways could others help?

SUMMARY CHECKLIST

Take a few minutes to reflect on your performance in the preceding exercises. Assess how your analysis compared to other students (and if you were a presenter, how others

rated your skill). Make a check (✓) next to those behaviors on which you may need improvement. Ethical managers:

_____ **Anticipate ethical conflicts.**
1. Ask what-if questions.
2. Be alert to situations that promote unethical behavior.
3. Unusual circumstances may tempt otherwise ethical employees.

_____ **Consider all points of view.**
1. Identify all affected parties.
2. Consider actual and symbolic consequences to everyone concerned.

_____ **Provide creative alternatives.**
1. Always look for more than one choice.
2. Consider all possibilities before deciding what to do.

_____ **Defend the morality of their decisions.**
1. Be able to explain the rational for actions to others.
2. Will others feel those actions are ethical?

_____ **Think before acting.**
1. Ask, "Why am I doing what I'm about to do?"
2. Consider all the consequences.
3. "Would you disclose to your boss or family what you are about to do?"

_____ **Have a good inner sense of right and wrong.**
1. Develop your own personal code of ethics.
2. Know your organization's policy on ethics.
3. Do what you truly believe is right.

_____ **Lead by example.**
1. The superior's behavior is the strongest influence on subordinates' behavior.
2. Actions speak louder than words.

_____ **Seek opinions from others before deciding.**
1. Avoid becoming isolated.
2. Others in similar situations may have sound advice.
3. Others can act as a sounding board.

APPLICATION QUESTIONS

1. Describe an ethical situation you've faced recently. How did you handle it? Would you handle it any differently now? How? Why?
2. What questions will you ask yourself when you next encounter an ethical dilemma?
3. Think about managers for whom you worked. Which did you think were highly ethical and which were not? What makes you say this? Did they act differently in similar situations? Why or why not?

REINFORCEMENT EXERCISES

The following are suggested activities for reinforcing the application of ethical guideposts described in this chapter. You may want to adapt them to the Action Plan you will develop next, or try them independently.

1. Check the newspapers and business periodicals for news of a controversial business decision—closing a plant, for example, or disciplining an employee for some infraction. List the various alternatives that might have been available and the ethical guideposts that should apply.

2. When your class or school has a speaker or guest lecturer from the business community, ask him/her to describe the kinds of ethical dilemmas faced in his/her business and how they are resolved.
3. When you interview with a corporate recruiter, ask if the firm has a code of ethics and/or ethics training and, if appropriate, to see a copy of the code or a training syllabus.
4. Ask your friends and/or relatives what kinds of ethical situations they run into in their jobs and how they handle them.
5. Search the Internet for company Web sites of interest to you. See whether you can find a published code of ethics for the company. What does that tell you?

ACTION PLAN

1. Which ethical behaviors do I want to improve the most?
2. Why? What will be my payoff?
3. What potential obstacles stand in my way?
4. What are the specific things I will do to improve? (For examples, see the Reinforcement Exercises.)
5. When will I do them?
6. How and when will I measure my success?

NOTES

1. Adapted from numerous sources, including A. J. DuBrin, *Human Relations: Interpersonal, Job-Oriented Skills*, 6th ed. (Upper Saddle River, NJ: Prentice Hall, 1997) 249–50; S. P. Robbins and D. A. De Cenzo, *Supervision Today!* 2d ed. (Upper Saddle River, NJ: Prentice Hall, 1998) 65.
2. Adapted from G. Dessler, *Management: Leading People and Organizations in the 21st Century* (Upper Saddle River, NJ: Prentice Hall, 1998) 78.
3. Adapted from T. Kelly, "Ethics Officers Guide Workers to Right Choices," *New York Times News Service* report in *San Diego Union-Tribune*, March 3, 1998, C2.
4. K. Ireland, "The Ethics Game," *Personnel Journal*, no. 5 (1979): 171–81.
5. K. Davis and W. C. Frederick, *Business and Society: Management, Public Policy, Ethics*, 5th ed. (New York: McGraw-Hill, 1984) 76.
6. K. Durham, "Right and Wrong: What's Ethical in Business? It Depends on When You Ask," *Wall Street Journal*, January 11, 1999, R48.
7. "You're Asked to Cheat. What to Do?" *New York Times*, October 11, 1998, Business, 5.
8. R. Tetzeli, "Business Students Cheat Most," *Fortune* (July 1, 1991): 14.
9. R. Gunther, "What We Stand For," *Notre Dame Business* (November 1998): 9.
10. "Ethics and Middle Managers in the U.S.," *Manpower Argus*, no. 350 (November 1997): 11.
11. B. Domaine, "Exporting Jobs and Ethics," *Fortune* (October 5, 1992): 10.
12. E. Jansen and M. A. Von Glinow, "Ethical Ambivalence and Organizational Rewards Systems," *Academy of Management Review*, no. 10 (1985): 814–22.
13. D. M. Wolfe, "Is There Integrity in the Bottom Line? Managing Obstacles to Executive Integrity," in S. Srirastava, ed., *Executive Integrity: The Search for High Values in Organizational Life* (San Francisco: Jossey-Bass, 1988) 140–71.
14. In the case of payments to influence foreign officials or politicians, the law to guide U.S. managers is the Foreign Corrupt Practices Act, passed in 1997, which makes it illegal for U.S. firms to knowingly corrupt a foreign official. However, the statute does not expressly prohibit small payoffs to foreign government employees whose duties are primarily ministerial or clerical *when* such payoffs are an accepted part of a country's business practices. See S. P. Robbins and M. Coulter, *Management*, 6th ed. (Upper Saddle River, NJ: Prentice Hall, 1999) 165.
15. N. J. Adler, *International Dimensions of Organizational Behavior*, 3d ed. (Cincinnati: South-Western College Publishing, 1997) 174.
16. Kelly, *New York Times News Service* report in *San Diego Union-Tribune*, March 3, 1998, C2.
17. L. K. Trevino and S. A. Youngblood, "Bad Apples in Bad Barrels: A Causal Analysis of Ethical Decision-Making Behavior," *Journal of Applied Psychology* (August 1990) 378–85.
18. Cited in C. Fredman, "Nationwide Examination of Corporate Consciences," *Working Woman* (December 1991): 39.
19. F. R. David, "An Empirical Study of Codes of Business Ethics: A Strategic Perspective," paper presented at the 48th Annual Academy of Management Conference; Anaheim, CA (August 1988).
20. R. Sweeney and H. Siers, "Survey: Ethics in Corporate America." *Management Accounting* (June 1990): 34–40.

21. B. Z. Posner and W. H. Schmidt, "Values and the American Manager: An Update," *California Management Review* (Spring 1984): 202–16; R. B. Morgan, "Self- and Co-Workers Perceptions of Ethics and Their Relationships to Leadership and Salary," *Academy of Management Journal* (February 1993): 200–14.

22. "Cheating Rampant in the Workplace, Study Says," Associated Press report in *Springfield News Leader*, April 5, 1997, A5.

23. P. F. Miller and W. T. Coady, "Teaching Work Ethics," *Education Digest* (February 1990): 54–55; Robbins and Coulter, 170.

24. Kelley, *New York Times News Service* report in *San Diego Union-Tribune*, March 2, 1998, C2.

25. Ibid.; Robbins and Coulter, 171.

26. Kelley, *New York Times News Service* report in *San Diego Union-Tribune*, March 2, 1998, C2.

27. Adapted from L. K. Trevino and K. A. Nelson, *Managing Business Ethics: Straight Talk About How to Do It Right* (New York: John Wiley, 1995) 71–75.

28. Adapted from J. R. Boatright, *Ethics and the Conduct of Business* (Upper Saddle River, NJ: Prentice Hall, 1993) 1.

29. Adapted from G. Sammet, Jr., *Gray Matters: The Ethics Game* (Orlando: Martin Marietta Corporation, 1992).

CHAPTER 6

Managing Stress and Time

Learning Objectives

After completing this chapter, you should be able to:

- Perceive symptoms of stress.
- Identify causes of stress.
- Reduce causes of stress.
- Develop resiliency to stress.
- Reduce stress symptoms.
- Focus activities to achieve priority goals.
- Help subordinates manage their stress.

SELF-ASSESSMENT EXERCISE

For each of the following questions, select the answer that best describes your behavior when you are experiencing stress.

When I feel anxious and stressful:		*Usually*	*Sometimes*	*Seldom*
1.	I try to determine the sources.	_____	_____	_____
2.	I do not want to bother my friends by talking about it.	_____	_____	_____
3.	I check my priorities and organize my activities.	_____	_____	_____
4.	I refrain from seeking help so I will not appear weak.	_____	_____	_____
5.	I try to relax or meditate to gain composure.	_____	_____	_____
6.	I have a couple of drinks to feel better.	_____	_____	_____
7.	I exercise to work it off.	_____	_____	_____
8.	I drink plenty of coffee to keep my energy level up.	_____	_____	_____
9.	I confront the stressor directly.	_____	_____	_____
10.	I take time for recreation in order to relax.	_____	_____	_____

Scoring and Interpretation.   For questions 1, 3, 5, 7, 9 and 10, give yourself 3 points for "Usually," 2 points for "Sometimes," and 1 point for "Seldom." For questions 2, 4, 6, and 8, give yourself 3 points for "Seldom," 2 points for "Sometimes," and 1 point for "Usually." Sum up your total points.

27 or higher	You're good at managing stress.
22–26	You have some room for improvement.
Below 22	You need to find a more effective way to manage your stress.

Carla could not get her mind off work. During weekend hikes in the hills north of San Francisco with her husband, this marketing professional tried to concentrate on the beautiful landscape. Instead, her mind drifted back to the office and how much work was piled in her "in" box. "I reached a stage where I was thinking about work 24 hours a day," she said. "I couldn't sleep. I would go into work feeling like a zombie." She became short-tempered and irritable. Some days, thinking about work made her so stressed that she had difficulty breathing. She didn't realize it at the time, but she was suffering from burnout.

In today's fast-paced society, burnout runs rampant as people increasingly cram more into their already packed schedules. And with pagers, e-mail, voice-mail, and cell phones, today's workers are tethered to their jobs more than ever. Certainly, some people feel energized by the crisis, surprise, and excitement that are inherent in many of today's jobs. To them, long hours and tons of work are a way of life. For others, they spell burnout—a state of fatigue and frustration brought about by devotion to a cause, way of life, or relationship that fails to produce the expected reward.[1]

CONCEPTS

Many of you may feel like Carla in the preceding vignette, and wish you had read this chapter about stress management skills earlier. As you well know, you don't need to wait until you are a manager to feel overwhelmed with the amount of stress in your life. The list of stress-causing elements for students never seems to end: monster reading assignments, difficult homework problems, simultaneous exams, papers, multiple group projects, boring subjects, balancing school with work, relentless parents, fickle friends, difficult roommates, unreliable automobiles, not enough money. Any of these sound familiar?

The list of stressors is even greater for those of you who are already managers. Today's work environment is increasingly characterized by heavier work loads, longer hours, fewer resources, more ambiguities, and less job security. Almost half of the workers in the United States characterize their jobs as highly stressful, and more than a third think the stress is bad enough to warrant quitting.[2]

What Is Stress?

Think of how you would react to seeing an automobile speeding straight at you as you were crossing an intersection. How do you feel when you are faced with nonphysical stressors such as giving a speech, making a deadline, or resolving a disagreement? **Stress** is the body's psychological, emotional, and physiological response to any demand that is perceived as threatening to a person's well-being. These changes prepare a person to cope with threatening environmental conditions called *stressors* either by confronting them (fight) or by avoiding them (flight).[3] Stress is created by a multitude of overlapping factors that threaten the achievement of our goals at work, in relationships, in school, and in life in general. Although stress sometimes stimulates and challenges us to perform at higher levels, too much stress for too long a time has negative effects on both our work quality and personal life. The reality is that work stress will not go away, but it can be managed to lessen its negative consequences.

Why Is Stress Management Important?

Work stress is an equal opportunity dilemma. It affects men and women from all cultures and job situations. Stress affects employees ranging from executives to secretaries, student interns to retiring veterans. The vast majority of U.S. workers say that work is their primary source of stress and that their jobs are continually becoming more stressful. Managers also believe that stress is a significant and growing problem in the workplace.[4]

Organizational Costs

According to the American Institute of Stress in Yonkers, New York, the cost of stress-related consequences, such as absenteeism, attrition, deficient productivity, compensation claims, lawsuits, medical insurance, and direct medical expenses, is estimated to be $200 billion to $300 billion per year.[5] Stress-related incidents account for 12 percent of all workers' compensation claims nationwide. In fact, in the 1990s, stress-related claims were the fastest-growing segment of the workers' compensation system.[6]

Another harmful employee response to stress is the use of alcohol and other drugs, leading to more accidents, costly errors, and decreases in task performance levels. Compared to their nonuser coworkers, employees who use drugs and alcohol are far less productive, miss 10 or more times as many workdays, and are three times as likely to injure themselves or someone else.[7]

Frustration and stress can also result in aggression and sabotage. If employees blame the organization for the stress-induced symptoms, they may adopt aggressive behaviors in an effort to "get even." This aggression can take the forms of verbal or physical abuse, intentional slowdowns, and acts of sabotage such as making intentional mistakes, damaging products, and starting negative rumors. Left unchecked, such reactions to stress can cause irreparable harm to an organization.[8] An all-too-frequent example is a fired employee returning to the former workplace and killing the former boss and several coworkers. Another is a sales representative insulting the president of a company of a key account during a business dinner because he or she has overindulged on alcohol or didn't understand important cultural differences.

Individual Costs

Workers experiencing high job stress typically have increased job dissatisfaction, reduced productivity, and more illnesses than those with low stress.[9] People with inadequate stress coping skills often become ineffective and may exhibit physical symptoms such as headaches, elevated blood pressure, fatigue, and depression.[10]

Health Impairment   Chronic stress is often accompanied by increased cholesterol levels and elevated blood pressure, two conditions that precipitate a number of serious health impairments.[11] Medical experts attribute between 50 and 75 percent of all illness to stress-related sources. Perhaps the most significant stress-related illness in industrialized countries is coronary heart disease, which kills about 25 percent of male workers. In fact, significant correlations between job dissatisfaction and heart disease have been discovered among workers from more than 40 different occupations.[12]

Chronic high stress contributes to a variety of other physical ailments, including ulcers, arthritis, and allergies. Its potential to cause depression and anxiety is widely recognized. While attempting to cope with the ailments and discomforts brought on by stress, some individuals compound their problems by turning to alcohol or drugs.

Job Burnout When prolonged exposure to stress uses up available adaptive energy, exhaustion can take the forms of depression, mental breakdown, or what is termed *burnout*.[13] Job burnout is a feeling of exhaustion that develops when an individual simultaneously experiences too much pressure and too few sources of satisfaction.[14] Business owners, managers, professionals, and technical personnel have especially high probabilities of suffering from burnout.[15] When we confront continual role ambiguity, performance pressures, interpersonal conflicts, or economic problems while trying to fulfill personal and organizational expectations, the most likely effects are fatigue, frustration, helplessness, and literal exhaustion.[16]

A recent Northwestern National Life Insurance study found that one in three Americans seriously thought about quitting work because they were afraid they would burn out if they did not. It is interesting to note that about one-third more women than men felt "constantly under pressure for trying to accomplish more than they can handle."[17] One interesting real-life example of a woman confronting burnout was provided by Nancy Bauer.[18]

"A lot of people think I'm completely nuts," said Nancy Bauer two years after walking away from a successful five-year career in marketing communications. Why leave a prestigious client list, a healthy income, and a midtown Manhattan office at age 38? In a single word, stress. The harder Bauer tried to be a corporate superwoman, the more her stress level increased. "I was handling 15 accounts, had 12 people working for me, and at a minimum was dealing with 30 people at a time." On top of all the work stress, Bauer wanted to get pregnant. "I was 38 years old and didn't have any children." Bauer said she was a product of "male-held perceptions" that rule the corporate world—"the value system of produce, produce, produce and work, work, work."

As the grip of stress tightened, her weight fluctuated. She began to lose strands and then clumps of hair. She spent her weekends sleeping. "I would come home and sleep all weekend as a way to replenish myself. I was that drained." Her doctor told her she needed a break. But in her company, "people who take pit stops are looked at as if they are not cut out to be this superperson. And New York tends to glorify people who live on just four hours' sleep a night … always doing, doing, doing. It's a sense of being invincible, rather than being vulnerable, yet strong," Bauer said.

"I forgot my own definition of success," she recalls, "and started living according to one that fit the circumstances, no matter how disagreeable." Other people in the company had ulcers and cholesterol problems, and they were still working at outrageous levels. However, her doctor told her, "You've got to take a leave from your job, to save your life. Go away. Get out of New York. Reflect for a while."

With her hair falling out, her physiology a wreck, her professional life in turmoil, and still childless, Bauer actually flew to India for several weeks of meditation, where she successfully got back on track. She no longer works 90 hours a week, but instead resigned from her corporate position to start her own freelance business and again have time for her husband and even herself. Meditation was responsible for allowing her to find appropriate balance in her life.

Performance Decline The relationship between stress and performance resembles an inverted U-curve, as shown in Exhibit 6-1. Stress is like a violin string: The optimal degree of tension is essential to obtaining the proper performance. A string that is too tight or too loose will not produce the desired effect. Insufficient stress leads to boredom, apathy, and decreased motivation. Increasing stress from insufficient levels enhances performance by increasing arousal and concentration. Group leaders and members, for example, become

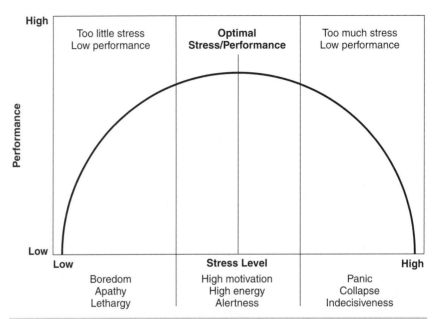

EXHIBIT 6-1   Inverted-U Relationship Between Stress and Job Performance

more receptive to problem-solving information provided by others when the group is under increased stress.[19] After an optimal level of stress is attained, however, further increases in stress for long periods of time overload our ability to cope, create anxiety, and deplete energy. As a result, our ability to perform effectively decreases.[20]

Although managers can't eliminate all stressors that negatively affect employees, they can do things to modify stressors and help employees manage stress more productively. But, before they help their employees, managers need to develop better stress coping skills themselves. Managers who are overwhelmed by personal stress often underperform themselves and are consequently unable to help others. So it's important for managers to be competent in the skills of personal stress management. Then they can model and teach these important skills to subordinates.

What Skills Are Needed to Cope with Stress?

Both individual and organizational stress management consist of three general skills. First, is becoming *aware* of negative stress symptoms. Second, is to *determine the sources*. Third, is *doing something constructive* to cope with the stress. The last step includes developing your resiliency to stress, dealing directly with the stressor, and alleviating the immediate stress that you are experiencing.

The stress management process illustrated in Exhibit 6-2 demonstrates that potential stressors can originate from personal, organizational, job, or environmental sources. The arrows indicate the direction of influence of the factors in Exhibit 6-2. Personal awareness of experiencing stress comes from recognizing symptoms like those listed in Exhibit 6-3. If nothing is done to constructively cope with the stress or symptoms, negative psychological, emotional, and behavioral consequences occur. However, constructive stress management techniques can be applied either to prevent potential factors from causing stress in the first place, or after stress is experienced, to prevent its negative consequences.

How Can Awareness of Stress Symptoms Be Enhanced?

According to Lisa McNee, a career counselor for Careers in Transition in San Jose, California, if you can learn to recognize the signs of stress sooner, you can take some

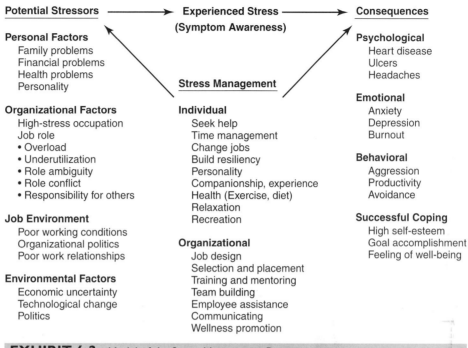

EXHIBIT 6-2 Model of the Stress Management Process

form of action quickly. If you do not take care of it up front, it will filter into all other areas of your life.[21]

Individuals experiencing unhealthy levels of stress often exhibit *physical symptoms* such as headaches, elevated blood pressure, and fatigue.[22] If they are unable to escape from their stressors, people may resort to common *psychological substitutes* such as negativism, boredom, dissatisfaction, irritability, anger, feelings of persecution, criticism, apathy, hopelessness, depression, withdrawal, forgetfulness, procrastination, or inability to decide.[23]

Intermittent checking of your own stress symptoms may aid self-diagnosis and provide insights into the nature of personal stress. Warning signs include constant fatigue, recurring headaches, bad breath, inability to sleep, moodiness, compulsive eating, and chronic worrying. Complete the questionnaire in Exhibit 6-3 to check your own stress symptoms.

Managers should be on the lookout for similar symptoms in their employees. Any continuing negative change in employees' work behavior may also be a warning signal. For example, when employees who are usually reliable, industrious, and friendly start missing numerous work days, coming in late, exhibiting irritable and noncooperative behaviors, appearing absent-minded, making unusual errors, or decreasing their performance, they are likely to be experiencing too much stress.

How Can Stressors Be Identified?

Karen Richards, a 37-year-old vice president who supervises bond trading and under-writing at First Eastern Bank Corp. of Wilkes-Barre, Pennsylvania, has to sell twice as many municipal bonds as she did five years ago to make the same profit. Because of the recent trend of mergers in the banking industry, she is also concerned about just keeping her job if her bank is acquired by a bigger rival. In addition, shopping, meal preparation, helping her kids with homework, and other family demands leave her little free time for any stress-alleviating activities, such as exercise or a night out with her husband.[24]

EXHIBIT 6-3   Checklist of Stress Symptoms

Check the box that most closely describes how often you have experienced each symptom during the past month.

	Never	*Rarely*	*Sometimes*	*Often*	*Always*
Constant fatigue	[ ]	[ ]	[ ]	[ ]	[ ]
Low energy level	[ ]	[ ]	[ ]	[ ]	[ ]
Recurring headaches	[ ]	[ ]	[ ]	[ ]	[ ]
Gastrointestinal disorders	[ ]	[ ]	[ ]	[ ]	[ ]
Bad breath	[ ]	[ ]	[ ]	[ ]	[ ]
Sweaty hands or feet	[ ]	[ ]	[ ]	[ ]	[ ]
Dizziness	[ ]	[ ]	[ ]	[ ]	[ ]
High blood pressure	[ ]	[ ]	[ ]	[ ]	[ ]
Pounding heart	[ ]	[ ]	[ ]	[ ]	[ ]
Constant inner tension	[ ]	[ ]	[ ]	[ ]	[ ]
Inability to sleep	[ ]	[ ]	[ ]	[ ]	[ ]
Temper outbursts	[ ]	[ ]	[ ]	[ ]	[ ]
Hyperventilation	[ ]	[ ]	[ ]	[ ]	[ ]
Moodiness	[ ]	[ ]	[ ]	[ ]	[ ]
Irritability	[ ]	[ ]	[ ]	[ ]	[ ]
Inability to concentrate	[ ]	[ ]	[ ]	[ ]	[ ]
Increased aggression	[ ]	[ ]	[ ]	[ ]	[ ]
Compulsive eating	[ ]	[ ]	[ ]	[ ]	[ ]
Chronic worrying	[ ]	[ ]	[ ]	[ ]	[ ]
Anxiety	[ ]	[ ]	[ ]	[ ]	[ ]
Inability to relax	[ ]	[ ]	[ ]	[ ]	[ ]
Feeling inadequate	[ ]	[ ]	[ ]	[ ]	[ ]
Increase in defensiveness	[ ]	[ ]	[ ]	[ ]	[ ]
Dependence on tranquilizers	[ ]	[ ]	[ ]	[ ]	[ ]
Excessive use of alcohol	[ ]	[ ]	[ ]	[ ]	[ ]
Excessive smoking	[ ]	[ ]	[ ]	[ ]	[ ]

Totals __ × 0   __ × 1   __ × 2   __ × 3   __ × 4

0   +   [ ]   +   [ ]   +   [ ]   +   [ ] = ____

Scoring and Interpretation.   Tally the number of responses you checked in each column. Next, multiply the column totals by the factor indicated. Finally, add the products to get your stress symptoms score. Check your total score against the following scale to determine how well you are reacting to the stress you are currently experiencing.

Score	*Stress State*
Below 20	= Bored
20–30	= Relaxed
31–40	= Alert
41–50	= Tense
51–60	= Stressed
Over 60	= Panicked

Many factors contribute to the stress experienced by people such as Karen Richards. The organizational environment can certainly provide many stressors, but so can a number of personal and environmental factors. Let's take a look at each of these.

Major Organizational Stressors

Although things like time pressures and work overload have been cited as sources of stress for years, others of particular concern for managers today include the nature of occupations, job roles, and interpersonal relationships.[25]

High-Stress Occupations   Certain occupations cause more stress than others. They are the ones that allow incumbents little control over their jobs, impose relentless time pressures, carry weighty responsibilities, or have threatening or unpleasant physical conditions, such as extreme heat, cold, noise, crowding, or lack of privacy.[26] Occupations such as manager, secretary, and air traffic controller possess these high-stress characteristics, while jobs such as stock handler, actuary, and artisan do not.[27]

Job Role   Whatever the occupation, certain negative characteristics of a person's role at work can increase the likelihood of experiencing stress. You may have already experienced the number one job role stressor: work *overload*. Overload occurs when people are expected to accomplish more than their ability or time permit.[28] Students often encounter overload at the end of each semester. On the other hand, *underutilization* of time or abilities causes stress for unskilled workers who often feel anxiety about wasting their lives doing unimportant things.[29]

Stress also occurs when people are expected to work without a clear understanding of their job definition, performance expectations, preferred methods of meeting those expectations, or consequences of their behaviors. This type of *role ambiguity* often occurs in class projects or research assignments. If it is a group project, *role conflicts* can also occur when duties or responsibilities conflict with one another. If you are put in a supervisory position with responsibility for the group's task performance, you may experience even more stress.

Interpersonal Relationships   Poor work relationships with other coworkers is another frequent source of stress. Working for a boss you do not like is the most stressful relationship aspect of a job for the majority of workers.[30] Of course, disciplining and giving poor performance reviews are stressful for managers. Difficult peers can be stressful, especially for women who may experience sexual harassment or gender discrimination.[31] It can also be stressful to be assigned to a team where members do not get along. Finally, when people compete for power and play politics, stress levels rise.

Major Personal Stressors

Of the 168 hours each week, most people only spend about 40 of them at work. The challenges individuals face during their nonwork hours also create stress that spills over into the work environment. The primary sources of nonwork stress are family, financial, and health problems, and personality.

Family Problems   These problems can be a major stressor in North America.[32] A growing stressor is the dilemma of two-career families that must balance the conflicting demands of child care, career moves, time conflicts, priorities, and expectations. Other common family stressors are marital difficulties, discipline troubles with children, relative conflicts, and caring for elderly parents.

Financial Problems   Regardless of income level, many people are poor money managers or have wants that exceed their earning capacity. All too frequently individuals overextend their financial resources, which causes stress, which distracts from work effectiveness.

Health Problems   Diseases, injuries, or psychological problems, either your own or those affecting family members and close friends, exact a toll in anxiety and stress. Stress caused by poor health creates a circular dilemma because stress itself is a major cause of health problems.

One of the contributors to stress-related health problems occurs when a person experiences too much change in too short a period of time.[33] To determine whether the rate of change in your life has the potential to contribute to stress-related illness, complete the Life Units Change Scale in Exhibit 6-4.

Stress occurs each time a person experiences a change, and those changes add up in a cumulative fashion. Too much change eventually overloads the endocrine system,

EXHIBIT 6-4 Life Change Unit Scale

Fill in the mean values for the life events you have experienced in the past 12 months, then total your personal points.

Rank	Life Event	Mean Value	Personal Points
1.	Death of spouse	100	_____
2.	Divorce	73	_____
3.	Separation from mate	65	_____
4.	Detention in jail or other institution	63	_____
5.	Death of close family member	63	_____
6.	Major personal injury or illness	53	_____
7.	Marriage	50	_____
8.	Fired at work	47	_____
9.	Reconciliation with mate	45	_____
10.	Retirement from work	45	_____
11.	Major change in health of family member	44	_____
12.	Pregnancy	40	_____
13.	Sex difficulties	39	_____
14.	Gain new family member (birth, roommate)	39	_____
15.	Business readjustment (bankruptcy, reorganization)	39	_____
16.	Major change in financial state (better or worse)	38	_____
17.	Death of a close friend	37	_____
18.	Change to different line of work	36	_____
19.	Major change in number of arguments with spouse (or significant other)	35	_____
20.	Mortgage or loan for major purchase (home, business, etc.)	31	_____
21.	Foreclosure of mortgage or loan	30	_____
22.	Major change in responsibilities at work (e.g., promotion, demotion, transfer)	29	_____
23.	Son or daughter leaving home	29	_____
24.	Trouble with in-laws	29	_____
25.	Outstanding personal achievement	28	_____
26.	Wife/husband begins or stops work	26	_____
27.	Begin or end formal education	26	_____
28.	Major change in living conditions	25	_____
29.	Revision of personal habits (e.g., eating, schedule)	24	_____
30.	Trouble with boss	23	_____
31.	Major change in work hours or conditions	20	_____
32.	Change in residence	20	_____
33.	Change in schools	20	_____
34.	Major change in recreation (type, amount)	19	_____
35.	Major change in church activities (more, less)	19	_____
36.	Major change in social activities	18	_____
37.	Mortgage or loan for moderate purchase (e.g., car, TV, appliance, etc.)	17	_____
38.	Major change in sleeping habits	16	_____
39.	Major change in number of family get-togethers	15	_____
40.	Major change in eating habits	15	_____
41.	Vacation	13	_____
42.	Christmas	12	_____
43.	Minor violations of the law (e.g, traffic ticket)	11	_____
	TOTAL POINTS		_____

Interpretation. People with a score totaling less than 150 generally have good health the following year. Those with scores between 150 and 200 have a 37% chance of developing health problems, while those with scores between 200 and 300 have a 51% chance. People scoring more than 300 have an 80% chance of having a major illness.

SOURCE: This scale was first published as "The Social Readjustment Rating Scale" by T. H. Holmes and R. H. Rahe, *Journal of Psychosomatic Research* 11 (1967): 213–18.

thereby depleting the stress-coping resources and suppressing the immune system. This reaction makes the body more susceptible to certain types of disease.

Personality   People with what is called the Type A personality have a chronic sense of time urgency and excessive competitive drive to achieve more and more in less and less time. To determine whether you are a Type A personality take the self-assessment inventory in Exhibit 6-5.

Type As were originally thought to be more likely to experience stress on or off the job and have a much higher chance of having a heart attack as a result.[34] More recent research has found that it is only the hostility and anger characteristics of the Type A personality that are contributors to coronary heart disease.[35]

So, if you are a workaholic but still get along well with others, you probably are not unduly susceptible to heart disease because of this aspect of your personality. People who are quick to anger, have a persistently hostile outlook, and a cynical mistrust of others are at risk.

Major Environmental Stressors

Most of what goes on outside of our personal and work environments is beyond our control. Because economic, political, and technological factors do affect our well-being, however, they are sources of worry and concern.

Economic Uncertainty   An abundance of economic uncertainty in society today has the potential to cause anxiety. The constant possibility of downsizing can generate fear of being terminated and forced to find other means of income. Stock market declines affect where our pension funds are invested and increase fears of insecurity in old age.

Political Uncertainties   Although North Americans do not experience the political uncertainties of prior communist countries, such as Russia, the indiscretions of elected officials can create an underlying anxiety about the future well-being of the

---

EXHIBIT 6-5   Type A Personality Self-Assessment

Circle the number on the scale that best characterizes your behavior for each trait.

1. Casual about appointments	1	2	3	4	5	6	7	8	Never late
2. Not competitive	1	2	3	4	5	6	7	8	Very competitive
3. Never feel rushed	1	2	3	4	5	6	7	8	Always feel rushed
4. Take things one at a time	1	2	3	4	5	6	7	8	Try to do many things at once
5. Slow doing things	1	2	3	4	5	6	7	8	Fast (e.g., eating, walking)
6. Express feelings	1	2	3	4	5	6	7	8	"Sit on" feelings
7. Many interests	1	2	3	4	5	6	7	8	Few interests outside work

SOURCE: Adapted from R. W. Bortner, "Short Rating Scale as a Potential Measure of Pattern A Behavior," *Journal of Chronic Diseases* (June 1969): 87–91.

Scoring.   Total your score on the seven questions. Now multiply the total by 3. A total of 120 or more indicates that you are a hard-core Type A. Scores below 90 indicate that you are a hard-core Type B. The following gives you more specifics:

Points	*Personality Type*
120 or more	A+
106–119	A+
100–105	A–
90–99	B+
Less than 90	B+

government. At a more personal level, jobs for many government employees, and contracts for some companies working for the government, depend directly upon whom and which party is in political office.

Technological Change   Most of us experience constant pressure just trying to keep up with continual upgrades for personal computers and Internet enhancements. More serious stress can be created by automation, computerized systems, and robotics, which displace workers and force them to relearn skills for different occupations.

What Constructive Things Can Be Done to Reduce Stress?

There are two main categories of stress management strategies. The first are *problem-focused strategies*, which deal directly with stressors by either removing or changing them. Problem-focused strategies are applicable where the manager believes that it is possible to eliminate or alter the stressor.

When changing the stressor does not appear to be possible, the use of techniques from the second category of stress management strategies, or *emotion-focused* strategies, may be helpful. Emotion-focused strategies are ways of modifying our negative reactions to stressful situations so that we feel more optimistic and self confident.[36] If you are experiencing negative emotions and reacting in nonproductive ways to a stressor (e.g., denying your problem or attacking others), it is important to get your emotions under control so that you more accurately assess underlying problems and determine the most appropriate coping strategy.[37]

Individual Coping Strategies

The ultimate responsibility for stress management rests with you as an individual. A number of proven methods can help you to cope with stress or modify stressors directly. Some of the most effective techniques can help you do both simultaneously. Let's look at these techniques in reverse order because applying them in this fashion will lead to the most effective management of stress.

Seeking Help   Soliciting ideas from colleagues, advice from your boss, or training from the human resources department can provide knowledge and skills to deal productively with stressors. If you have a mentor, he or she may be able to coach you about how to relieve stress caused by high performance demands, pressures for change, and low job challenge.[38] Most companies also have Employee Assistance Programs for counseling and other assistance. In addition, simply sharing your dilemmas with an understanding coworker can release anxiety.

Numerous people can assist you in your personal environment, ranging from friends and family members to professional trainers and doctors. These people can help you apply some of the individual stress-coping strategies we will discuss in the following sections. For example, they can help you decrease the negative aspects of a Type A personality. Because it is hostility and anger that contribute to coronary heart disease, you need to solicit and be open to feedback from others to determine whether you exhibit hostile and angry behavior at inappropriate times. If so, you need to make a positive change, such as reducing cynical mistrust of others or learning to treat others with kindness and consideration.[39] Use others' feedback to help monitor your progress.

Managing Time   Losing control of our time can generate serious anxiety, frustration, and even panic for most of us. This feeling is common for people with Type A personalities who suffer from a chronic sense of time urgency and excessive competitive drive to achieve more and more in less and less time. Time management consists of applying the principles of management to yourself; in other words, planning, organizing, directing, and controlling the use of your time. Time management strategies entail deciding what goal is to be accomplished and by what deadline. All tasks necessary to accomplish the goals need to be listed and prioritized. Estimates of how long it will take to accomplish the tasks need to be computed. Activities then should be planned starting with the most important task first. Finally, the prioritized tasks are implemented until the goal is accomplished.[40] Let's take a closer look at each component of this vital skill and some of the techniques that facilitate them.

Planning   Just as an organization needs to have a mission statement, identify its values, and determine its objectives, so does an individual. If you don't know what kind of person you are and what you want out of life, how can you rationally decide what to do with your time at any given moment? You can reduce your stress dramatically if you know what your values are, what you want to accomplish, and how you prefer to behave as you strive to achieve your goals.

Determine Your Values.   Values are enduring beliefs about what is worthwhile. They determine what behaviors and objectives are desirable to you and which are not. Once you clarify what is important to you, you can determine your mission in life, that is, what kind of person you want to be and what things you want to accomplish.

Determine Your Goals and Objectives.   You can't be sure whether you are spending your time wisely unless you know what tasks contribute to your **lifetime goals.** Once you know the kind of person you want to be, your overriding mission in life, and the values that will guide your behavior, you can determine your lifetime goals in other important areas such as career, family, religion, recreation, and relationships. You can determine what you have to do to achieve the goals that will contribute to your mission in life.

Next, determine what **intermediate goals** you need to achieve to accomplish your long-term, lifetime goals. For example, to become a physician, you need to graduate from college, graduate from medical school, serve an internship, and so on. To raise a family successfully, you need to find a suitable partner and acquire the means for supporting family members. A statement of intermediate goals that follow from these long-term ones could be as follows: "In the next four years I will graduate from college with a 4.0 grade point average and date people suitable for potentially sustaining a permanent relationship."

Now you can look at **short-term goals** for one year, one semester, a month, a week, and finally for a day. As you probably have already surmised, if we reverse the order, each short-term goal should be compatible and contribute to the next longer-term goal. Otherwise, you are not getting the best use of your time. If what you are doing right now does not contribute to your goals for today, why are you doing it? The same analysis should be done for who you are dating, what courses you are taking, where you are working, and so on.

Prioritize Your Objectives.   Some goals are more important than others in contributing to your mission in life. Therefore, the next step is to prioritize your objectives in each time frame from most to least important. The most stress-resilient individuals maintain a balance of life activities.[41] At any given time, however, you will find that certain goals are clearly more important than others. During exam time, for example, developing friendships may be less important than learning a certain subject matter.

Once you know what you want to accomplish, you are ready to determine what you have to do to achieve your goals. Now you can organize and schedule your time and resources to achieve your goals. The next step is determining what tasks are required to achieve your objectives, how to do them, and when to do them.

Organizing   The goal of organizing is to work smarter, not harder. You want to be both efficient and effective, but in reverse order. Remember that effectiveness is doing the right things to achieve the results you desire. Efficiency is a high input-output ratio; it means being fast and doing things right. However, you can be efficient at doing the wrong things, which will not result in the outcomes you desire. Consequently, you need both to determine the necessary tasks to be undertaken, and to prioritize them in order of importance.

List Activities.   You need to identify the specific actions necessary to achieve your goals. Record these activities on a sheet of paper, an index card, or a computer-generated schedule. This record should be made for each time frame—long, intermediate, and short term.

Prioritize Activities.   This step involves imposing a second set of priorities. Here, you need to emphasize both importance and urgency. If the activity is not important, you should consider delegating it to someone else. If it is not urgent, it can usually wait. Completing this step helps you identify activities you *must* do, activities you *should* do, those you will do *when you can*, and those you can *get others* to do *for you*. See Exhibit 6-6 for examples of urgent and important activities.

Perhaps the most widely used prioritizing approach is the **ABC system** developed by time management guru Alan Lakein.[42] To apply it, give tasks an A, B, or C value depending upon their urgency and importance (see Exhibit 6-6). *A tasks* are urgent and important. They can yield extraordinary results or disastrous consequences if they are not attended to immediately. *B tasks* are those that should be done as soon as possible. They have important consequences but are not pressing emergencies. *C tasks* can be put off indefinitely without creating dire consequences. They should only be attended to if you have extra time.

Schedule Activities.   After prioritizing your activities, the next step is to plan *when* you will do each of them. Time spent scheduling *when you will do things* can save you hours of anxiety, confusion, and making up for things you forgot to do. It can also provide you with a feeling of being in control of yourself and how you are spending your time. You need to schedule both immediate and future activities.

Horizontal scheduling consists of determining what you will be doing over the longer term, e.g., the next month or next week. A number of planning aids such as "Week at a Glance" or "Month at a Glance" calendars or electronic organizers are available to help you. Remember to schedule your activities well in advance. For a week, do it Friday or Sunday before the action actually begins. Do not block activities in so tightly that you have no flexibility for unexpected emergencies. Also, schedule according to your personal biological clock; some of us are morning people and some of us are not.

Vertical scheduling consists of developing a *daily plan* for what you will do and when you will do it. Each morning (or the night before) identify what you want to accomplish during the day. This to-do list should identify five to seven things you want to do during the day. It will allow you to spend time actually doing tasks versus trying to remember them.

First complete the most important urgent activity, then tackle other important tasks. Follow with those you should do, and so forth. Be realistic about what you can really accomplish in your schedule. Given the nature of your activities, you may be

EXHIBIT 6-6	Urgent and Important Activities	
	Not Important	*Important*
Urgent	Subordinates desire to know who will attend a luncheon tomorrow *C task*	Preparation for key client presentation tomorrow *A task*
Not Urgent	Review junk mail for ideas *C task to delegate*	Plan next year's objectives *B task*

unable to complete everything. The key, however, is to concentrate on the A tasks, or must-do items, making sure they do get done. Fifteen minutes here, a half-hour there, add up in getting a must-do done. Do not make the mistake of working on C tasks, or "when you can" activities, just because they are easier to accomplish. You will be spending time on activities that really won't add to your effectiveness.

This to-do list will help you avoid the *reaction mentality* of putting out fires for other people when they approach you about help with their problems. Now you are in control because you know what you need to do when. Of course you have to be able to say "no" when you have something more important and urgent to accomplish. To get the most out of your *to-do list*, check your horizontal planning calendar and focus on high-priority tasks you have scheduled for the current day. Then list all activities you want to accomplish, prioritize them, plan your day, and stick with your plan.

Directing and Controlling   The preceding steps ensure that you have (1) established goals, (2) listed activities, (3) prioritized them based on urgency and importance, and (4) established schedules for their completion. The following techniques can help you make sure you get the right things done on time.[43]

Constantly Ask: What Is the Most Effective Use of My Time Right Now?   To do this apply the **80/20 Rule** (sometimes referred to as the Pareto Principle), which states that 80 percent of our activities are trivial and only provide 20 percent of the results that we desire, while 20 percent of what we do is really vital and contributes to 80 percent of our desired results. The 80/20 rule is presented in Exhibit 6-7.

To apply this principle, first determine which activities give you the most payoff—the vital 20 percent—versus the trivial 80 percent, which really are time wasters. Then expand the time allocated to the high payoff activities. Next, constantly check to make sure that what you are doing is the most effective use of your time at the moment.

Capitalize on Your Productivity Cycle.   Some people are most productive in the mornings, others at midday or in the evening. Once you know your productivity cycle, you should schedule your larger and most important activities when you are able to give them the most effort.

Avoid Procrastinating.   None of us consciously want to procrastinate, but all of us do it at one time or another, some more than others. The first thing to do is to figure out why you do it. Be honest with yourself about what you are doing, why, what it costs you, and what benefits you derive from it. Unpleasant or overwhelming tasks and unclear goals or ambiguous task flow are enough to make most of us want to postpone doing things. On the other hand, a number of psychological reasons, like fear of failure, fear of change, tendency to overcommit, and addiction to cramming, can contribute to the tendency to procrastinate.

Next, do something about it. Suggestions for overcoming procrastination for each of the external and internal reasons are provided in Exhibit 6-8.

Minimize Disruptions.[44]   Disruptions are time wasters that can steal your time before you know it. These include interruptions such as phone calls and unscheduled visitors. During your most productive time, you need to insulate yourself from the time

EXHIBIT 6-7   80/20 Rule

	Activities	Time Spent	Results
	Trivial	80%	20%
	Vital	20%	80%

EXHIBIT 6-8   Methods for Dealing with Procrastination

Environmental Reasons	Potential Solutions
Unpleasant task	Do it first thing.
	Find someone else to do it.
Overwhelming task	Divide and conquer by breaking it into smaller pieces.
	Ride the momentum. Once you get going, keep at it.
Unclear goal	Ask for clarification.
	Clarify yourself, if it is your own goal.
Unclear task flow	Ask for clarification.
	Plan how to do it yourself.
Psychological Reasons	
Fear of failure	Realize that fear is natural and can actually provide added energy.
Fear of change	Accept that change is an opportunity for growth.
Tendency to overcommit	Just say no, but explain.
Addiction to cramming	Admit that cramming is dangerous because it does not allow time to correct mistakes or attend to urgent tasks that may arise.

SOURCE: Adapted from M. Mancini, *Time Management* (Burr Ridge, IL: Irwin/Mirror Press, 1994) 41–53.

wasters. Go somewhere, if possible, where you won't be disturbed. Have calls screened, or let them roll over to voice mail. Close your door to keep interruptions to a minimum. Obviously, the degree of insulating yourself will depend on your job, your organization's policies, your boss, and your employees. However, you must attempt to protect your productive time at all costs. But if you are disturbed, take it in stride, deal with the issue, then return to your task as soon as you can.

Meeting Management.   As a manager, you will be attending many meetings. If it is your meeting, have a good reason for it. Meeting just to meet is often a waste of time. Set an agenda for the meeting, describing its purpose and what you want to accomplish. Distribute it ahead of time so participants can be prepared, and then stick to it during the meeting. If it is not your meeting, ask for an agenda if one has not been sent. If you can, find out why you need to attend. Maybe someone on your staff could represent you. If that is not possible, try to attend only the part of the meeting that requires your presence. If that fails, don't waste more time worrying about it. Just go, but leave immediately afterward and avoid wasting time chit-chatting after the meeting. Do what you need to do, then return to your priority tasks!

Delegate.   One of the best ways to save time is to assign tasks to someone else to do. However, before you do, three important questions need to be addressed: What types of tasks should I delegate? To whom should I delegate? How should I delegate?

Appropriate types of tasks to delegate are those (1) you do not want but others might or (2) you are not qualified to do but someone else is. It is possible to delegate in three directions: downward when subordinates have responsibility in the area or need to learn and you have formal authority; sideways when others are more interested or have more expertise; and upward recommendations when you do not have the necessary authority or contacts.

After you thoroughly understand the task and have decided the right person to delegate it to, the next consideration is how to do it to achieve acceptance and effective implementation. Start by thoroughly explaining the assignment from beginning to end. Then, explain the benefits for the person taking on the task, the quality standards required, the deadline, and encourage questions. After clarifying questions and obtaining agreement on all expectations and procedures, establish a reporting method to provide timely feedback. You may also want to conduct unscheduled status checks to evaluate results. Finally, remember to recognize achievements and even reward effort if things do not turn out as well as you expected to help turn the process into a learning experience for you and the person to whom you delegated.

Changing Jobs   Sometimes renegotiating your job role can eliminate the stress caused by role ambiguity, conflict, overload, or underutilization.[45] If job-related stress is still not reduced to a satisfactory level, and you cannot get on top of it through better time management, changing jobs or even leaving the organization may be the answer. No job is worth the sacrifice of physical and mental health if burnout occurs.[46]

However, you should not jump ship immediately. First, determine exactly what it is about your job that is causing the stress. Is it your immediate boss, coworkers, the profession? Draw up a well-thought-out exit plan that will leave you on good terms in your old organization and secure you a better position in a new one. Making a haphazard change and ending up in a similar situation does not make sense.[47]

Developing Resiliency   The same stressors do not cause the same reactions in all people. Some people seem to fall apart at the slightest problem, while others apparently thrive when confronted with a stressor. Those who don't experience stress in a negative way and cope better with stressors have *resiliency*. Factors that moderate reactions to stressors include differences in personality hardiness, social support, and good health.

Personality Hardiness.   Hardiness is a combined personality characteristic of people who believe that they are in control of their lives, have the ability to respond to and transform potentially negative situations, and actively seek out novelty and challenge. Hardy people welcome change and have a high tolerance for ambiguity. Consequently, "hardy" individuals experience far lower than average rates of illness in high-stress environments.[48]

Some of the most important characteristics of hardy individuals include high self-esteem, internal locus of control, and extroversion. First, we will explain how these factors affect stress; then, we will share some ideas for developing them to make you more resilient to stress.

High Self-Esteem.   High self-esteem causes people to feel good about themselves and have high confidence levels in their abilities to cope effectively. Consequently, people with high self-esteem experience less stress when experiencing threatening situations than do those with low self-esteem.[49] People with high self-esteem often exhibit a "self-serving bias," where they take credit for success and blame external factors for failure. Those with low self-esteem do the opposite by exhibiting the "imposter syndrome," when they attribute their successes to factors outside their control and take personal blame for all of their failures or unpleasant experiences. The imposter syndrome leads to greater stress because people cannot benefit from past successes to feel more confident in a recurring situation.

Psychotherapist Nathaniel Branden, acknowledged pioneer of the self-esteem movement, described six essential practices to building self-esteem.[50] The first is *living consciously*, which means keeping yourself aware of what you are doing, for example, really listening to a salesperson who is talking to you. Second is *self-acceptance:* the willingness to take responsibility for your own actions and thoughts without evaluating them. Third is *self-responsibility:* realizing that you are the author of your choices and responsible for attaining goals in your life. Fourth is *self-assertiveness:* being willing to stand up for your ideals in appropriate ways. Fifth is *living purposefully*, which is identifying the things you want out of life and the actions needed to obtain them, then applying yourself and monitoring your results to stay on track as opposed to just drifting through life. Finally, Branden advises that you should practice *personal integrity:* living with congruence between what you profess and what you do. Examples are telling the truth, honoring commitments, exemplifying in action the values you profess, and dealing with others fairly and benevolently.

Internal Locus of Control. People with an *external locus of control* believe that whatever happens is either a matter of chance or determined by forces external to them. Externals are more likely to feel helpless to deal with stressors, so they experience more stress.[51] People with an *internal locus of control*, on the other hand, believe that they make a difference and that their destinies are primarily under their own control.

One way to shift your locus of control is by **reframing,** which in this case means changing your perception from being helpless to being in control of altering the situation to cope with stressors yourself. Instead of assuming that you must passively accept an overtime assignment, for example, you could reframe it as an opportunity to negotiate with your boss to delegate other tasks that you do not like to do.

After you reframe, confidence in your self-efficacy can be built through the **small-wins strategy.** Instead of perceiving a large, perhaps overwhelming situation, look at a smaller part of it that you can tackle immediately. As you work for small, concrete outcomes that are more likely to be attained, you have a better chance for visible success and heightened confidence.

Another way to demonstrate your internal locus of control is to get *proper training* to perform more effectively on the job. You will then have a higher probability of experiencing small wins, which in turn can increase self-esteem and confidence. The more *experience* you get, the more confidence you will have dealing with recurring situations that originally were threatening because of their novelty.[52] New hires who have never given a sales presentation before, know little about the product, and doubt their ability to make presentations in an articulate manner, may feel much more pressure on a sales call than more experienced salespeople who already know the client and product well.

Extroversion. *Introverts* are inner-directed, private, reserved people who spend time in their inner world of thoughts. Consequently, introverts experience stress when attempting to cope with the interpersonal aspects of role conflict.[53] *Extroverts* are more outer-directed, friendly, and expressive. They are more comfortable dealing with, and even initiating, conflict resolution with others.

To become more extroverted, the practices of reframing and small wins can help again. Begin by refocusing personal encounters in a positive frame of mind. You might, for example, eliminate your fear of rejection by the new product team you have just been assigned to by reframing your introduction as a chance to meet some interesting new people. When the meeting begins, you could initiate an encounter with one relatively safe person whom you already get along with pretty well. Because you will probably have positive results through a small win, this experience will help you continue with others, which can snowball into another pillar of resiliency: social support.

Social Support. Positive relationships with colleagues, family members, and friends can lessen the impact of stress.[54] Social support provides comfort and assistance that can buffer people from negative stressors.[55] Consequently, it is important to spend time nurturing and building relationships with supportive others. The natural place to start is with people who already support you at work, home, or social groups. Other ways to build additional social support range from professional help to joining interest groups.

Health Maintenance. Appropriate exercise, diet, and rest are three keys to maintaining a healthy mind and body to cope with stressors. Regular physical exercise improves self-esteem as well as physical capacity to cope with stressors. Exercisers experience lower degrees of anxiety, depression, and hostility than nonexercisers.[56] A balanced diet can help you maintain optimal weight, avoid anxiety from too much sugar or caffeine, and keep from depleting stress fighters, like vitamin B, which can be diminished by too much alcohol consumption. Finally, getting enough sleep can help you keep an alert mind for rationally coping with stressors.

Short-Term, Emotion-Focused Strategies   If the stressor can't be reduced or eliminated through problem-focused strategies such as those already discussed, emotion-focused strategies are called for. Anything that works to reduce stress in a healthy, productive manner should be used. Common emotion-focused strategies are relaxation and recreation.

Relaxation.   Stress can be reduced by concentrating on relaxing all your muscles while you listen intently to your own breathing for 20 minutes, two times a day.[57] This exercise decreases muscle tension, which in turn decreases heart rate, breathing rate, and blood pressure.[58] Long-term payoffs include increases in coping effectiveness, work performance, and sociability, as well as decreases in blood pressure, sick days, anxiety, depression, and hostility.[59]

   You can sample the relaxation technique in the exercise at the end of this chapter. You can also learn to relax by getting formal training in self-hypnosis or meditation. Meditating twice a day, for example, can relax you by reducing your heart rate, oxygen consumption, and blood pressure.[60]

Recreation.   If all you do is work, you're bound to experience stress, no matter how much you love your job. Everyone needs hobbies and recreational interests that have no purpose beyond the relaxation and pleasure they bring. It is especially important that Type A personalities take their minds off work and relax with some sport or hobby that forces them to forget their job-related troubles.

Organizational Coping Strategies

Organizations have plenty of incentive to decrease stress at work. In addition to ethical and humanitarian reasons, work-related stress costs organizations billions of dollars each year through sickness, accidents, turnover, and absenteeism. *Problem-focused strategies* include job redesign, selection and placement, training, team building, and work/family programs.

Job Redesign   Careful job analysis can reveal role ambiguity, overload, underutilization, and conflict, as well as poor working conditions. Then jobs can be redesigned to eliminate these problems and reduce the distress they cause.[61] You might find through job analysis, for example, that the tedium of performing one simple operation repeatedly on an automobile assembly line—such as installing weather stripping for doors—can be eliminated by having work teams rotate tasks (e.g., attaching antennas, installing floor mats, etc.) every hour throughout the work shift.

Selection and Placement   Selection and placement procedures can prevent role overload by ensuring that employees' education level, abilities, and experience match the requirements of the job.[62] Personality factors can also be assessed to ensure a good person-job fit. Putting introverted people in sales positions or extroverted people in isolated research jobs can cause stress because of mismatches in job demands and personality preferences.

Training   When employees have been trained properly, a major source of stress is eliminated. Training should include role clarification that specifies job duties in order to reduce the likelihood of role ambiguity and conflict.

Team Building   When jobs require group interaction, their design should include incentives to cooperate rather than compete. Team spirit and a supportive climate can prevent many common stressors from occurring. Chapter 14 will elaborate on this important skill. On the other hand, when jobs require silence for individual concentration, companies can institute "quiet time" an hour or two a day when people are not to be disturbed from their work.

Work/Family Programs   The "three o'clock syndrome" refers to the productivity drop, increase in errors, and rise in accidents that occur to working parents as thoughts turn to their children at the end of the school day. Companies can provide on-site facilities for emergencies and encourage employees to check on their children in other locations. They can also offer on-site after-school programs or help finance improvements in after-school care in communities where their employees live.[63]

Organizations can offer facilities and training to help employees cope with the negative emotional states caused by stressors that cannot be prevented, eliminated, or modified. Things that organizations can do include providing open communication, employee assistance programs, mentoring, wellness programs, and time off.

Open Communication   Stress levels run high when rumors or newspaper articles hint of an impending layoff but employees are not given clues as to who may be affected or when the event will occur. Because trust is based on communication clarity[64] we are not suggesting that managers share every conceivable potential problem. Sharing to this extent could create unfounded anxieties unnecessarily and reduce a manager's credibility. However, when employees are kept informed about what is actually going on, trust increases, ambiguity decreases, and so does the general level of anxiety.

Employee Assistance Programs   By providing and encouraging the use of free counseling, in-house or by referral, an organization acknowledges the existence of stress-related problems among personnel and demonstrates its support of those who suffer from them. Because nonwork-related stress often carries over into the job, assistance can also be offered for health, financial, and family problems.

Mentoring   Mentoring programs assign senior employees to show junior employees the ropes and provide emotional support. Mentors reduce stress caused by uncertainty about how to do things and are a source of comfort when newer employees need to let off steam.

Wellness Promotion   Wellness programs focus on employees' total physical and mental condition.[65] Organizations offer a variety of opportunities including physical exams, counseling, and workshops on how to quit smoking, control alcohol use, lose weight, eat better, reduce stress, and develop a regular exercise program, often in the organization's own gym. Some provide employees with "personal days," and sabbaticals of several months for higher-level administrators and professionals.

CONCEPT QUIZ

Complete the following true-false quiz by circling the correct answer. Answers are at the end of the quiz. After marking your answers, remember to go back and check your understanding of any answers you missed.

True or False   1. The first step in stress management is determination of the sources.

True or False   2. Work overload, when people are expected to accomplish more than their ability or time permits, is the number one *job role* stressor.

True or False   3. Personality characteristics are stress moderators.

True or False   4. *Emotion-focused strategies* deal directly with stressors.

True or False	5. *Time management* is a problem-focused coping strategy.
True or False	6. The stress response prepares a person to cope with threatening environmental conditions.
True or False	7. One thing that helps productivity is that people leave the stress from personal sources at home.
True or False	8. Underutilization of time or abilities causes stress for white-collar workers.
True or False	9. Positive relationships lessen the impact of stress.
True or False	10. Keeping employees uninformed about what is going on or is about to happen decreases stress levels.

Answers. (1) False; (2) True; (3) True; (4) False; (5) True; (6) True; (7) False; (8) False; (9) True; (10) False

BEHAVIORAL CHECKLIST

The following skills are important to effective stress and time management. Use them when evaluating your skills and those of others.

The Effective Stress and Time Manager

- Is aware of stress symptoms.
- Identifies stressors.
- Reduces causes of stress.
- Develops stress resiliency.
- Reduces stress symptoms.
- Focuses activities to achieve priority goals.
- Helps subordinates manage stress.

> **Attention!**
> Do not read the following until assigned to do so by your instructor.

MODELING EXERCISE

The Stress of Success Role-Play

Directions. After the class reads the situation, pick two role-players. The role-players then read their own role, *but not the other role*, and prepare for the role-play. The class reads both roles, and reviews the observer's rating form to prepare for providing meaningful feedback at the end of the role-play.

Time. 20 minutes

Actors.

Terry Peterson, account executive at Sellit, Inc., a marketing communications firm

Cory Smith, the firm's president

Situation. Terry Peterson handles more accounts than any other representative and is acknowledged as one of the best account executives at Sellit. This reputation is quite an honor in the New York business environment, which tends to glorify people who live on just four hours of sleep, always doing, doing, doing. Many people in the company have stress-related health problems but continue to work at outrageous levels.

The firm's president, Cory Smith, has just received two of the most lucrative accounts the firm has ever had. Of course Cory wants to assign the new accounts to the best performers, and Terry is one of them. The accounts are important to the firm, especially in light of the poor financial results so far this year. The executive overseeing the accounts will be well rewarded financially if everything goes smoothly, and maybe even be nominated for a vice presidency. The accounts will require a lot of extra attention and effort.

Terry Peterson's Role   You are one of the top producers at Sellit, handling 15 accounts and a minimum of 30 crisis calls from clients every day. While you enjoy success, having a prestigious client list, a healthy income, and a midtown Manhattan office, you are concerned about your increasing stress level. You also feel that at 38, it is time to develop a serious relationship and think about having a family. Unfortunately, the only thing anyone at the company cares about is "produce, produce, produce, and work, work, work."

Your stressful situation is beginning to have adverse effects on your health. You're gaining a lot of weight and you spend your entire weekends working with little sleep. Although your doctor said that you need a break, you know that people in your company who take pit stops are soon derailed from the fast track.

Yesterday, your boss, Cory Smith, asked you to consider taking on two new accounts that are vital to the company. The financial rewards and promotion opportunities are attractive, but you are already on overload with your current accounts. You agree with your doctor's recommendation to take a break and get away for a while before you have a breakdown.

You are asking yourself, "What kind of life do I want, and what do I need to do to get it?" when you hear your boss knock on your door. How do you want to handle the situation?

Cory Smith's Role   It has not been a great year for Sellit. The company is facing a loss after two break-even years. You have had to cut back on personnel and you know that all account executives are under a tremendous amount of pressure, but Sellit compensates them accordingly.

These conditions motivated you to put on a major push to acquire some new clients. After an incredible amount of hours, meetings, and negotiations, you landed two spectacular new accounts that could save your firm. These accounts are crucial to the firm's future and you want special attention and extra effort given to them.

You do not want anything to go wrong with these new accounts so you asked your best account executive, Terry Peterson, to look them over yesterday. You are a little apprehensive about the situation because Terry really seems to be stressed out lately and does not look well. Terry has consistently been your highest performer and your father always told you that "if you want something done right, and on time, give it to a busy person."

You decide to go over to Terry's office to see whether the new assignments are acceptable. You know what you want, and who you want to do it.

OBSERVER'S RATING SHEET

On completion of the exercise, class members rate each role-player's application of stress management skills. Use the following scale to rate each role-player between 1 and 5. Write concrete examples in the space under each factor for comments to use in explaining your feedback.

1	2	3	4	5
Unsatisfactory	*Weak*	*Adequate*	*Good*	*Outstanding*

Stress Management Behaviors	*Rating* *Terry*
Points out stress symptoms	_____
Identifies stressors	_____
Modifies stressors	_____
Develops resiliency	_____
Reduces stress symptoms	_____
Focuses on priority goals	_____
Helps subordinates (protects self against superiors)	_____

	Rating *Cory*
Points out stress symptoms	_____
Identifies stressors	_____
Modifies stressors	_____
Develops resiliency	_____
Reduces stress symptoms	_____
Focuses on priority goals	_____
Helps subordinates (protects self against superiors)	_____

GROUP EXERCISES

Three different types of group exercises are presented here. First is a case for you to practice your awareness, analysis, and action planning skills. Second is a role-play to practice your skills. Finally, you will learn the relaxation response technique to apply whenever you need to reduce your stress level.

Group Exercise 1: Case Analysis: A Hectic Day at Alcala Savings and Loan Association[66]

Tad Kadet awoke to the ring of the telephone next to his bed. It was after midnight. Tad thought instantly of his aging parents in Minneapolis and reached for the receiver with a feeling of dread. Instead, it was the sergeant at police headquarters downtown, making what was to him a routine call.

"Mr. Kadet. The back door down here at Alcala Savings and Loan is unlocked. You're gonna have to come down and check the place out with our officer and lock up the building."

Tad was both relieved and agitated. "So what else can go wrong at work?" he asked himself as he grappled in the dark for jeans and a sweatshirt.

Tad was vice president of Alcala Savings and Loan Association, a small financial institution that had come into its own in the 10 years since Tad had started to work there. At that time it had only two employees: the managing officer, Mario Piconni, and Tad. Now it had 18.

As Tad drove toward town, he began to recall the events of the preceding day at work. It had been one of those days that were becoming increasingly common. Such days left him exhausted—so much so that at home he had begun to argue with his wife and to scold his three children for minor things that had once left him unruffled.

Yesterday the turmoil had started early in the morning when the chairperson of the board burst into his office and created a disturbance because she had not yet received last month's statistical data. She had to review them prior to that afternoon's board of directors' meeting. Tad had intended to get the statistical information together, but in what little spare time he could find between customers he had made out the monthly report for the Federal Home Loan Bank instead. That deadline could not be ignored.

After the board chair departed, Tad went to tell Piconni that he needed another clerical person to help relieve his work load. Piconni asserted that the association was currently overstaffed and that more efficient use of the personnel on board would solve the problem. Tad agreed with him that the present number of personnel should be adequate, but their efficiency was poor. Piconni took this comment as a direct criticism of his niece and two cousins he had hired, and a heated argument developed. Eventually their tempers cooled, and Tad returned to his office and resumed his work.

About two o'clock in the afternoon, Tad stepped out of his office and spotted two customers waiting at the counter. Not a single teller was in evidence. His quick investigation disclosed three tellers downstairs having coffee. Another had gone out for cigarettes, and the fifth was in the supply room stocking up on forms for his window. Tad called Piconni out of his office and quickly pointed out the situation. Piconni snapped, "You take care of it!" Then he ducked back into his office and slammed the door. Tad herded the tellers out of the lunchroom with a sharp reprimand and then went to see Anita Farelli, who was supposed to supervise them.

Anita was in her middle twenties and had worked for Alcala Savings and Loan for nearly five years. At first she had shown marginal interest in her work, but after she got married and her husband entered law school, her interest picked up; now she was progressing quite rapidly.

Tad asked Anita for an explanation of the teller situation. Anita advised him that she had no real control over the tellers. She told Tad that she had asked Piconni for help but got none, and that on occasions when she had attempted to discipline certain tellers, Piconni had reprimanded her for doing so. By this time Tad was sorely frustrated, but he managed to keep himself under control.

Just before five o'clock, Tad's secretary (a Piconni cousin) brought him the typed letters that he had dictated earlier that day. As Tad prepared to sign them, he noted that two contained so many errors that he needed to stay late and retype them himself.

Now, as the steeple clock in the center of town struck a single gong, Tad Kadet drove into the parking lot pondering why the back door was unlocked. Hadn't Piconni been the last person to leave? "But Mario always checks both doors before he leaves the building … could I myself have forgotten?"

QUESTIONS FOR DISCUSSION

1. What symptoms of stress is Tad exhibiting in this case?
2. What are the sources of Tad's stress? Which is he responsible for?
3. What could Tad do to improve his management of stress in this situation?
4. How could Tad apply time management techniques?

Group Exercise 2: Role-Play: Time Management at Dewey, Cheatum, & Howe, Inc.

Directions. After the class reads the situation, pick three role-players. The role-players then read their own role, *but not the other roles*, and prepare for the role-play. The class reads all roles, and reviews the observer's rating form to prepare for providing meaningful feedback at the end of the role-play.

Actors.

Pat Pool, director of sales

Chris Criley, sales representative

Lorin Lipper, Chris's assistant

Situation. Dewey, Cheatum, & Howe, Inc., is a high velocity investment company with heavy quotas and deadlines to meet on a daily basis. Pat Pool is a 20-year veteran with the company and has worked up to the position of director of sales. Pat has been successful in this industry and has high expectations for all people in the company. It is well known that Pat doesn't have a problem bombarding them with heavy workloads. Chris Criley is a recent MBA graduate who was hired last year as a sales representative. Chris was characterized by most people as an extremely nice person who always gives maximum effort, and would do anything required for a respected person. Lorin Lipper has been with the company for 10 years and is the assistant for five sales representatives, including the company's newest hire, Chris Criley.

At the moment, Pat is starting to leave Chris's office after dropping off a second set of portfolios Pat just delegated to Chris to analyze for tomorrow. Lorin is just entering the office with a list of urgent messages that arrived for Chris earlier this morning. As Chris asks Pat about the necessity of completing the portfolios by tomorrow, a impromptu meeting begins between the three of them.

Pat Pool's Role   You feel that you have earned your stripes the hard way and you want your subordinates, including Chris Criley, the new hotshot MBA, to work hard for the money you pay. You also feel that you shouldn't have to do a lot of the busywork because of your seniority, so you delegate most of it to Chris, the new kid on the block.

As a matter of fact, you want to see how much work Chris will do for you, even if it means taking advantage of your seniority. Chris has the utmost respect for you and wants to excel within this company.

At 8:00 A.M. you realize that you have five large portfolios to analyze today, but you also have some work left from yesterday, a golf game at 10:00 A.M., and a corporate lunch at the club following the game. After the usual martinis, you would just as soon knock off after lunch and beat the traffic home, because the club is closer to your home than the office.

In order to carry out your plans, you decide to delegate the portfolios to Chris. Because you know that Chris already has a heavy workload, and that the analysis will be quite involved, you do not want to give them all to Chris at the same time. You decide to drop the work off in parts so that this huge downloading won't be so obvious. You are aware that the analyses will take a significant amount of time but you're going to tell Chris that you need them first thing tomorrow morning.

Chris Criley's Role This morning you woke up late, took a quick shower, grabbed a cup of coffee, and ran out the door. Halfway to work you realized you forgot your briefcase, which contained some important notes for a meeting with your attorney today and it was necessary that you return home and get them. Traffic was awful and the freeway was bumper to bumper, which made you a little late for work. At the moment you are going through an ugly divorce and custody battle and you have a difficult time staying focused on any one thing at any one time.

Your job is important to you because money is tight and you are using your savings for your mortgage and lawyer fees. You have been working as a sales rep for Dewey, Cheatum, & Howe since obtaining your MBA a year ago. You are really looking forward to the early promotion to associate, which Pat mentioned to you a couple of months ago because of your record production figures. You feel Pat is somewhat demanding at times, but you want to make a positive impression, because Pat is the one who determines who gets what in the company. At times, Pat gives you more work than you can handle, but you don't have much of a choice. You make the best of the situation and complete your work no matter how unhappy you may be. Today you have a long list of important personal things you need to do, so you are hoping for a light day at work, so you can knock off a little early. Your *to do list* includes the following A priority tasks:

1. Meet with three regular clients for one-hour financial planning sessions each, starting at 9:00 A.M.
2. Make your hair appointment during your lunch hour because of court appearance tomorrow.
3. Meet with lawyer to discuss tomorrow's court appearance at 5:00 P.M.
4. Determine who to cold-call from a list of 30 potential clients to inform about a new IPO [initial public offering of a new stock], because you need to replace two clients who passed away last month in order to keep your profits to DC&H up to Pat's expectations.
5. Pick up your daughter from school and drop her off at ballet class at 4:00 P.M.

You have a great assistant who has been with the company for 10 years. Lorin is aware of your personal dilemmas and has been almost like a mother helping you learn the ropes at DC&H and lending an ear when you need to unload about problems on the home front. She is at your disposal if you need her, but you know that she also reports to four other busy reps, and you do not want to take advantage of her generosity or interfere with her other responsibilities.

Your goal for today is to accomplish all that you can at work before your personal agenda takes over. You think that you will have just enough time to get everything done as long as Pat does not surprise you with more work.

Lorin Lipper's Role   You are assistant to five sales reps, including the nice, bright, new MBA, Chris Criley. You have been with DC&H for 10 years and know all there is to know about it. You also know about Chris's pending divorce and legal dilemmas. Chris is a nice young man who is always polite and considerate to you. You have gone out of your way when you could to help Chris learn the ropes at DC&H and lend an ear when Chris needed to unload about problems on the home front. You are more than willing to help Chris out if you can, but you do not want to embarrass anyone, so you will do so only if you are asked.

You've noticed that Chris has been running behind for the past few days with all the legal hassles, the daughter's summer visitation with him, and the loss of two major clients. You've actually had to cover a couple of times when Chris had to be out of the office to deal with personal crises. You are aware that Pat asks more than necessary from Chris, and you would like to confront Pat about these unrealistic expectations. Even though you know that confronting Pat would be inappropriate, you also know that Chris will never say anything, even if the stress is substantial. You are actually concerned about Chris's health and mental well-being if the current situation continues much longer.

Before Chris arrived late for work this morning, you received four messages you need to pass on:

1. Chris's daughter is sick and needs to be picked up at school.
2. Chris's lawyer needs to meet at 4:00 P.M. instead of 5:00 P.M. today.
3. Chris's father has been admitted to the hospital for tests and observations due to chest pains last night, but is currently experiencing no problems.
4. A request from the president's assistant for Chris to make a presentation at the board of directors meeting tomorrow about trends in the Asian financial markets. The scheduled speaker canceled and the president thought that a recent MBA would be a perfect substitute.

OBSERVER'S RATING SHEET

On completion of the exercise, observers rate the person role-playing Chris Criley on application of time management skills using the following rating scale:

1 = Unsatisfactory   2 = Weak   3 = Adequate   4 = Good   5 = Outstanding

Write in concrete examples in the space below each skill component for comments to use in explaining your feedback.

Rating	*Skill Component*
_____	Determines priorities and sticks with high ones.
_____	Plans and organizes tasks to achieve daily and longer-term goals.
_____	Schedules activities according to top priorities.
_____	Delegates.
_____	Avoids interruptions.
_____	Says no to unimportant tasks.
_____	Schedules most important activities during peak productivity cycle.

Group Exercise 3: Relaxation Response

Purpose. To learn the relaxation-response technique to reduce stress.

Time. Fifteen minutes for the exercise. Five minutes for debriefing.

Instructions. The instructor will slowly read the following guidelines to class members while they relax with their eyes closed.

1. Select a comfortable sitting or reclining position.
2. Close your eyes.
3. Direct your attention to your own breathing process. Think about nothing but your breath as it flows *in* and *out* of your body.
4. Continue to focus on your breathing while you follow the next steps for tensing and relaxing your body.
5. Tense your toes and feet (curl the toes, turn feet in and out). Hold and study the tension. Relax.
6. Now tense your lower legs, knees, and thighs. Hold the tension, study the tension, then relax your legs.
7. Now tense your buttocks. Hold and study the tension. Relax.
8. Tense your fingers and hands. Hold and study the tension. Relax.
9. Tense your lower arms, elbows, and upper arms. Hold and study the tension. Relax.
10. Tense your abdomen. Hold and study the tension. Relax.
11. Now tense your chest. Hold and study the tension. Relax. Take a deep breath and exhale slowly.
12. Tense your lower back. Hold and study the tension. Relax.
13. Now tense your shoulders. Hold and study the tension. Relax.
14. Now tense your neck. Hold and study the tension. Relax.
15. Finally, check and relax every part of your body. Concentrate on your breathing and the relaxed feeling for a couple of minutes.
16. (Wait a couple of minutes.) When you are ready, open your eyes and check how you feel.

Debriefing. Participants now share how they feel, their general reactions to the exercise, which parts of the exercise were most difficult, and how they can practice relaxation on their own. Participants may also share other relaxation techniques they have experienced, such as visualization and meditation.

SUMMARY CHECKLIST

Take a few minutes to reflect on your performance and look over others' ratings of your skill. Now assess yourself on each of the key learning behaviors. Make a check (✓) next to those behaviors on which you need improvement.

_____ **I am aware of stress symptoms.**
　　1. Physical problems (e.g., fatigue, headaches, dizziness)
　　2. Psychological problems (e.g., inability to sleep, compulsive eating)
　　3. Emotional problems (e.g., moodiness, irritability, aggression)

_____ **I identify stressors.**
　　1. Personal
　　2. Work-related
　　3. Environmental

_____ **I develop resiliency to stressors.**
1. Work on increasing self-esteem.
2. Maintain social support.
3. Maintain my health through diet, exercise, and sleep.

_____ **I reduce my stress symptoms by:**
1. Seeking help.
2. Managing my time productively.
3. Managing my job stress.
4. Exercising regularly.
5. Relaxing.

_____ **I directly eliminate stressors by:**
1. Changing jobs or tasks.
2. Avoiding stressful people.
3. Planning ahead.

_____ **I focus on priority goals.**
1. Determine my values.
2. Determine my life goals and priorities.
3. Practice good time management.

_____ **I help subordinates cope with stress.**
1. Watching for stress symptoms.
2. Make them aware of employee assistance programs.
3. Appropriate selection and placement.
4. Provide proper training.
5. Wellness promotion.

APPLICATION QUESTIONS

1. What are your most common stress symptoms? How do these symptoms affect your performance in school, your relations with friends, and your happiness?
2. What are your major stressors? If you are not currently experiencing stress symptoms, how do you account for this state of affairs?
3. How do you and other students you know cope with end-of-the-semester stressors such as term papers and final examinations? What are the short-term and long-term consequences of these various methods?
4. How do you react to the stress of giving a speech? Check out how five of your friends feel about public speaking. Why is it considered stressful? Why do some people perceive it as more stressful than do others?
5. What are your major time wasters? What can you do to overcome them?

REINFORCEMENT EXERCISES

The following suggestions are activities you can do to reinforce the stress management techniques in this chapter. You may want to adapt them to the Action Plan you will develop next, or try them independently.

1. Interview a practicing manager to determine the most stressful parts of his or her job and how he or she manages the resulting stress.
2. Attend a stress management seminar. Many are available free of charge through universities, hospitals, and community education programs.

3. Make a to-do list for tomorrow. List eight things you would like to do tomorrow. Now decide which things are A tasks (really must be done to achieve important goals), which are B tasks (can probably be put off without dire consequences if you don't get to them), and which are C tasks (would be nice to do but really do not have to be done at all). Now try it out by starting with your top A and sticking with it until completed.

ACTION PLAN

Diagnosing Stress and Managing It Effectively

1. Describe a stressful situation you are experiencing.
2. What symptoms of stress do you experience?
3. What causes the stress (what are the stressors)?
4. What are the consequences of the stress?
5. What can you do to eliminate or reduce the stressor?
6. What can you do to better cope with the stress you are experiencing?
7. When will you do the things listed in numbers 5 and 6?
8. What will be your payoff?
9. What potential obstacles stand in your way?
10. How and when will you measure your success?

NOTES

1. S. Eng, "Time Out," *The San Diego Union-Tribune*, September 14, 1998, C1–C2.
2. A. Farnham, "Who Beats Stress Best—and How," *Fortune*, October 7, 1991, 71.
3. C. W. Cook, P. L. Hunsaker, and R. E. Coffey, *Management and Organizational Behavior*, 2d ed. (Burr Ridge, IL: Irwin, 1997) 498.
4. J. Bales, "Work Stress Grows, but Services Decline," *The APA Monitor* 22, no. 11 (November 1991): 32.
5. Eng, 1998.
6. R. S. DeFrank, and J. M. Ivancevich, "Stress on the Job: An Executive Update," *Academy of Management Executive* (August 1998): 55–66.
7. The basis of this discussion is R. L. Kahn and P. Byosiere, "Stress in Organizations," in M. D. Dunnette, and L. M. Hough, *Handbook of Industrial and Organizational Psychology*, 2d ed., vol. 3 (Palo Alto, CA: Consulting Psychologists Press, 1992): 573–80.
8. B. Fletcher, "The Epidemiology of Occupational Stress," in C. L. Cooper and R. Payne, *Causes, Coping and Consequences of Stress at Work* (New York: John Wiley & Sons, 1988) 3–52.
9. J. W. Jones, "A Cost Evaluation for Stress Management," *EAP Digest* 1 (1984): 34–39.
10. D. Schwimer, "Managing Stress to Boost Productivity," *Employee Relations Today* (Spring 1991): 23–27.
11. K. Matthews, E. Cottington, E. Talbott, L. Kuller, and J. Siegel, "Stressful Work Conditions and Diastolic Blood Pressure Among Blue-Collar Factory Workers," *American Journal of Epidemiology* (1987): 280–91.
12. Fletcher, 1988.
13. *Employee Burnout: America's Newest Epidemic*, (Milwaukee: Northwestern Life Insurance Company, 1991).
14. R. R. Golembiewski and R. F. Munzenrider, *Phases of Burnout: Developments in Concepts and Application* (New York: Praeger, 1988) 6–10.
15. D. P. Rogers, "Helping Employees Cope with Burnout," *Business* (October–December 1984): 3–7.
16. S. E. Jackson, R. L. Schwab, and R. S. Schuler, "Toward an Understanding of the Burnout Phenomenon," *Journal of Applied Psychology* 71 (1986): 630–40.
17. R. Zemke, "Workplace Stress Revisited," *Training* (November 1991): 35–39.
18. H. Schlossberg, "Meditation Uplifts Her Life on the Fast Track," *Marketing News* (October 1, 1990): 10–11.
19. Schwimer, 1991.
20. M. Jamal, "Relationship of Job Stress to Job Performance: A Study of Managers and Blue-Collar Workers," *Human Relations* (May 1985): 409–24.
21. Eng, 1998.
22. Schwimer, 1991.
23. Fletcher, 1988.
24. "Fear and Stress in the Office Take Toll," *Wall Street Journal*, November 6, 1990, B1.
25. For a review of recent organization stressors see DeFrank and Ivancevich, August 1998.
26. Ibid., 56–57.
27. T. D. Schellhardt, "The Pressure's On," *Wall Street Journal*, February 26, 1996, B4.
28. Zemke, 1991.
29. *Employee Burnout: America's Newest Epidemic*, 1991.

30. R. Hogan, and J. Morrison, "Work and Well-Being: An Agenda for the '90s," paper presented at the American Psychological Association and National Institute for Occupational Safety and Health Conference, Washington, DC (November 1990).

31. B. Gutek, "Women's Fight for Equality in the Workplace," paper presented at the American Psychological Association and National Institute for Occupational Safety and Health Conference, Washington, DC (November 1990).

32. A. L. Delbecq and F. Friedlander, "Strategies for Personal and Family Renewal: How a High-Survivor Group of Executives Cope with Stress and Avoid Burnout," *Journal of Management Inquiry* (September 1995): 262–69.

33. T. H. Holmes and R. H. Rahe, "The Social Readjustment Rating Scale," *Journal of Psychosomatic Research* 11 (1967), 213–18.

34. M. Friedman and R. Rosenman, *Type A Behavior and Your Heart* (New York: Knopf, 1974).

35. R. B. Williams, Jr., "Type A Behavior and Coronary Heart Disease: Something Old, Something New," *Behavior Medicine Update* 6 (1984): 29–33.

36. S. Folkman and R. S. Lazarus, "Coping as a Mediator of Emotion," *Journal of Personality and Social Psychology* 54 (1988): 466–75.

37. S. Folkman, "Personal Control and Stress Coping Processes: A Theoretical Analysis," *Journal of Personality and Social Psychology* 46, no. 4 (1984): 839–52.

38. K. E. Kram, and D. T. Hall, "Mentoring as an Antidote to Stress During Corporate Trauma," *Human Resource Management* (Winter 1989): 493–511.

39. R. Williams, "The Trusting Heart," *Psychology Today* (January–February 1989): 35–42.

40. A. Lakein, *How to Get Control of Your Time and Your Life* (New York: Peter H. Wyden, 1973).

41. S. R. Covey, *The 7 Habits of Highly Effective People* (New York: Simon & Schuster, 1990) 95–144.

42. Lakein, 1973, pp. 25–27.

43. These principles are commonly found in most time management books, such as those listed in these references. Please consult them for further elaboration.

44. R. Garters, *Time to Manage Time* (Christchurch, New Zealand: New Zealand Institute of Management, 1990) 47–55.

45. W. L. French and C. H. Bell, Jr., *Organizational Development: Behavioral Science Interventions for Organization Improvement* (Upper Saddle River, NJ: Prentice Hall, 1990).

46. Schlossberg, 1990.

47. Eng, 1998.

48. M. T. Matteson, and J. M. Ivancevich, *Controlling Work Stress* (San Francisco: Jossey-Bass, 1987) 88–91.

49. D. A. Girdano, G. S. Everly, Jr., and D. E. Dussek, *Controlling Stress and Tension: A Holistic Approach*, 3d ed. (Upper Saddle River, NJ: Prentice Hall, 1990) 114–15.

50. N. Branden, *Self-Esteem at Work* (San Francisco, Jossey-Bass, 1998) 33–36.

51. L. R. Murphy, "A Review of Organizational Stress Management Research," *Journal of Organizational Behavior Management* (Fall–Winter 1986): 215–27.

52. S. J. Motowidlo, J. S. Packard, and M. R. Manning, "Occupational Stress: Its Causes and Consequences for Job Performance," *Journal of Applied Psychology* (November 1987): 619–20.

53. R. W. Kahn, D. M. Wolfe, R. P. Quinn, J. D. Snoek, and R. A. Rosenthal, *Organizational Stress* (New York: Wiley, 1964) 72–95.

54. R. C. Cummings, "Job Stress and the Buffering Effect of Supervisory Support," *Group & Organization Studies* (March 1990): 92–104; J. J. House, *Work Stress and Social Support* (Reading, MA: Addison-Wesley, 1981).

55. J. G. Anderson, "Stress and Burnout Among Nurses: A Social Network Approach," *Journal of Social Behavior and Personality* 6, no. 7 (1991): 251–72.

56. K. Mobily, "Using Physical Activity and Recreation to Cope with Stress and Anxiety: A Review," *American Corrective Therapy Journal* (May–June 1982): 62–68.

57. H. Benson, *The Relaxation Response* (New York: William Morrow, 1975).

58. J. C. Smith, *Cognitive-Behavioral Relaxation Training* (New York: Springer Publishing Company, 1990).

59. K. E. Hart, "Managing Stress in Occupational Settings: A Selective Review of Current Research and Theory," in C. L. Cooper, *Stress Management Interventions at Work* (Rochester, England: MCB University Press Limited, 1987) 11–17.

60. R. L. Woolfold, R. Lehrer, B. McCann, and A. Ronney, "The Effects of Progressive Relaxation and Meditation on Cognitive and Somatic Manifestations of Daily Stress," *Behavior Research and Therapy* 20 (1982): 325–38.

61. "Workplace Flexibility Is Seen as Key to Business Success," *Wall Street Journal*, November 23, 1993, A1.

62. R. S. Schuler and S. E. Jackson, "Managing Stress Through PHRM Practices: An Uncertainty Interpretation," in K. Rowland and G. Ferris, eds, *Research in Personnel and Human Resources Management*, vol. 4 (Greenwich, CT: JAI Press, 1986): 183–224.

63. "Helping Parents Cope with Latchkey Anxiety," *Wall Street Journal*, November 1, 1991, B1.

64. Delbecq and Friedlander, 1995.

65. C. E. Beadle, "And Let's Save 'Wellness.' It Works," *New York Times*, July 24, 1994, F9.

66. Cook, et. al., 1997, 526.

MANAGING STRESS

Few of us are able to compartmentalize every aspect of our lives. In addition to the sources of stress we find in the workplace, such as deadlines, quotas, workloads, relationships, changes, and poorly defined job roles, we all bring our own individual stressors such as financial, family, and health problems. When work and family pressures collide, for example, there is often an increase in stress in both areas.

The first step to developing coping skills is to recognize what factors or situations create stress for us. Once we have done that, there are a number of effective strategies for coping with stress. Changing the situation, for instance, includes relying on such stress relievers as better planning, time management, to-do lists, schedules, and prioritizing. An extreme but sometimes necessary response to stress is to change jobs or even careers. Changing ourselves to handle stress better can include making such efforts as increasing self-esteem, developing an inner locus of control, working toward smaller and more manageable goals, keeping healthy through diet and exercise, and enjoying recreation and relaxation regularly.

You may recognize in Susan's day some familiar sources of stress: Susan's son calls her at work with a school problem that seems to have no solution and leaves her feeling guilty. Ray is worried about Susan's use of recording equipment on a shoot and their conversation does not go well. In her chance meeting with Andrew, Susan begins to acknowledge some of the sources of stress she feels and admits that it is not all about Ray.

Try to pinpoint what it is about Ray's approach to Susan that adds stress to their interaction. Does she contribute to the strain on their relationship? What other factors are working on Susan as her day draws to a close? Does she have control over any of these? ■

QUESTIONS

1. How could Susan have avoided the stressful conversation with her son?

2. Specifically how is Ray a source of stress for Susan? Is he responsible in any way for their difficulties communicating? How could Susan improve her interpersonal relationship with Ray?

3. How can Susan relieve some of the stress she feels? Do you think Andrew's suggestion that she take a vacation will help? Why or why not?

PART III
Planning and Control Skills

CHAPTER 7

Planning and Goal Setting

Learning Objectives

After completing this chapter, you should be able to:

■ Create strategic and operational goals.

■ Perform SWOT analyses.

■ Create plans to achieve goals.

■ Determine distinctive competencies.

■ Formulate competitive strategies.

■ Obtain employee commitment to goals.

SELF-ASSESSMENT EXERCISE

How Well Do I Plan and Set Goals?

In this two-part assessment, the first part explores how well you plan. The second part helps you assess your goal-setting skills.

Part I: Am I a Good Planner?[1]

The following assessment is designed to help you understand your planning skills. Answer either Yes or No to each of the following questions.

	Yes	No
1. My personal objectives are clearly spelled out in writing.	_____	_____
2. Most of my days are hectic and disorderly.	_____	_____
3. I seldom make any snap decisions and usually study a problem carefully before acting.	_____	_____
4. I keep a desk calendar or appointment book as an aid.	_____	_____
5. I use "action" and "deferred action" files.	_____	_____
6. I generally establish starting dates and deadlines for all my projects.	_____	_____
7. I often ask others for advice.	_____	_____
8. I believe that all problems have to be solved immediately.	_____	_____

Part II: How Well Do I Set Goals?[2]

For each of the following questions, select the answer that best describes how you set goals for yourself. Respond as you have behaved or *would* behave, not as you think you *should* behave. Indicate how much you agree or disagree with each statement. When you finish, review the items that received the lowest scores.

	Strongly Disagree	Disagree	Neutral	Agree	Strongly Agree
Scale	1	2	3	4	5

_____ **1.** I am proactive rather than reactive.

_____ **2.** I set aside enough time and resources to study and complete projects.

_____ **3.** I am able to budget money to buy the things I really want without going broke.

_____ **4.** I have thought through what I want to accomplish in my education.

_____ **5.** I have a plan for completing my education.

_____ **6.** My goals for the future are realistic.

Scoring and Interpretation

Part I: Am I a Good Planner?

The perfect planner would have answered as follows. If you answered differently, look for reasons that the alternative is more desirable as you read the following concepts.

(1) Yes (2) No (3) Yes (4) Yes (5) Yes (6) Yes (7) Yes (8) No

Part II: How Well Do I Set Goals?

This assessment helps you focus on basic aspects of the goal-setting processes in your personal life. Several keys help in making *any* goal-setting process effective, and we discuss those throughout the Concepts section that follows. Our intent with this brief assessment is to get you thinking about goal setting as it relates to your school, personal, and work settings.

In the first part of the assessment, we focus on whether your personal goal setting is *passive* or *active*. Question 1 queries your general tendency around "action," and questions 4 and 5 select a specific example of proaction versus reaction (i.e., having a plan for completing your education). Allocating "resources" for the completion of goals is queried in questions 2 and 3. Question 6 focuses on a cornerstone of effective goal setting: creating goals that are attainable, yet challenging. If your score on any of these questions is "3" or less, you should pay particular attention to the corresponding material that follows.

CONCEPTS

"Cheshire Puss," she [Alice] began, "would you tell me, please, which way I ought to walk from here?" "That depends a good deal on where you want to get to," said the Cat. "I don't much care where," said Alice. "Then it doesn't matter which way you walk," said the Cat.[3]

Unlike Alice, most of us have goals we want to achieve. As managers, we also have organizational goals we are charged to accomplish through the efforts of those who work for us. Consequently, we should make sure employees have a clear idea of what they are trying to accomplish in their jobs. Then, we need to help employees determine how to best achieve their objectives.

Planning

Planning involves defining the organization's objectives, establishing an overall strategy for achieving those goals, and developing the means to integrate and coordinate necessary activities. Planning is concerned with both ends (what needs to be done) and means (how it is to be done). Depending on their level in the organization, managers are concerned with different types of planning.

Strategic plans apply to the entire organization. They establish the organization's overall objectives, and seek to position the organization in terms of its environment. Strategic planning is done by top-level managers to determine the long-term focus and direction of the entire organization. Wal-Mart's strategy, for example, is to build large stores in rural areas, offer an extensive selection of merchandise, provide the lowest prices, and then draw consumers from the many surrounding small towns. All other shorter-term and specific plans for lower-level managers are linked and coordinated so that they contribute to the organization's strategic plan.

Operational plans specify the details of how the overall objectives in the strategic plan are to be achieved. Operational plans are of a short-term nature, usually one year or less. They are formulated to achieve specific objectives assigned to lower-level managers regarding their contribution to the organization's strategic plan. The Wal-Mart store manager in Fargo, North Dakota, for example, would be doing operational planning when making out a quarterly expense budget or weekly employee work schedules.

The planning process is essentially the same for managers at all levels of the organization. The breadth, time frames, specificity, and frequency vary, however, becoming smaller as managerial level decreases. Top-level strategic planning is also unique because of the environmental scanning and analysis of overall organizational resources that are required. Because the majority of managers are at supervisory or mid-level positions, we will summarize the strategic aspects of planning but focus on the operational applications.

How the Planning Process Works

The nine-step planning process is illustrated in Exhibit 7-1. The steps include identifying the overall goal, analyzing the environment for opportunities and threats, analyzing your own resources for strengths and weaknesses, formulating specific objectives, deciding how to implement the plan, and determining how to evaluate results.

EXHIBIT 7-1 The Planning Process

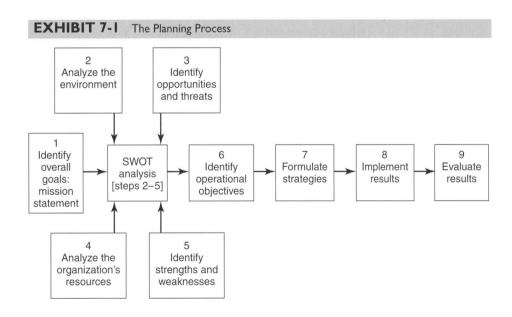

Step 1: Identify Overall Goals   In order to create a plan, managers must first identify what the organization is trying to achieve. Goals are the foundation of all other planning activities. They refer to the desired outcomes for the entire organization, groups, and individuals. Goals provide the direction for all management decisions and form the criteria against which actual accomplishments can be measured.

Goals differ in breadth, time frame, specificity, and frequency of change just as plans do. At the highest level, every organization should have a **mission statement** that defines its purpose and answers the questions: Why do we exist? What do we do? What business are we in? Defining the organization's mission forces management to identify the scope of its products or services carefully. For example, Rubbermaid's mission statement gives direction to managers and employees alike when it states that the company seeks "to be the leading world-class creator and marketer of brand-name, primarily plastic products which are creatively responsive to global trends and capable of earning a leading market share position."[4]

The organization's mission establishes the overreaching goal or basis on which objectives and strategies are formulated, providing guidance for all managers. Every unit in an organization needs to have an overriding goal, or mission statement, of its own that indicates its major contribution to the overall organization mission. Mission statements help managers focus on their units' strengths, which give the organization a competitive advantage. Rubbermaid's management, for instance, understands that its company's strength lies in producing plastic products, marketed under their brand name, where they can be the market leader. Even if management saw opportunities in steel products, or in selling to large retailers who would sell Rubbermaid products under the retailer's house brand, Rubbermaid's mission statement would deter pursuing those opportunities. Although some companies can make money by following those strategies, they do not play to Rubbermaid's mission and strengths.

Once managers know the purpose for their organization, they can perform a **SWOT analysis** to examine the fit between their organization's **S**trengths and **W**eaknesses, and the environmental **O**pportunities and **T**hreats. The first step is environmental scanning to determine what is taking place in the organization's environment. Then they can begin the essence of strategic planning, the SWOT analysis to identify a niche that the organization can exploit to achieve its mission. Because an organizations's environment largely defines management's options, a successful strategy will be one that aligns well with the environment.

Step 2: Analyze the Environment   Once the mission has been identified, managers should look outside their organization to ensure that their goals align well with current and future environments.[5] This *environmental scanning* can be challenging for managers because of their numerous day-to-day responsibilities. Some companies, such as Southwest Airlines and Frito-Lay, have special departments with primary responsibility for helping managers keep track of environmental forces.[6] Nevertheless, because all decisions about what plans and strategies to pursue in obtaining goals need to be grounded in a thorough assessment of the external situation, all managers must constantly evaluate environmental forces as they diagnose issues and weigh decisions.

The most general, or macro, environment includes those external factors that usually affect all or most organizations. General environmental forces include the condition of the economic system, political system events, ecosystem changes, demographic trends, technological developments, and the general business culture. Second are specific environmental factors that directly affect the organization. These organization-specific factors include changes in competitors (e.g., new entrants, substitute goods and services), customers, laws and regulations, and suppliers.[7]

Understanding and being aware of developments in all these factors will give a manager a solid foundation for knowing where to look and for analyzing the data retrieved about the business environment. Several behaviors can facilitate the environmental scanning process.[8]

Make Scanning a Priority.   To combat the problem of being too busy to keep up with the latest developments, managers should shift the priority given to environmental scanning from something they do if time permits, to something that is a vital part of their job. It can be implemented by ongoing activities ranging from attending relevant seminars and college courses to learn the latest innovations in the field; to daily reading of trade publications and newspapers; or "surfing the Net" to stay current with political, economic, demographic, and competitor developments.

Anticipate Change.   Any environmental factor can change without warning. You can adapt easier and more effectively if you have anticipated and planned for possible changes than if you are caught by surprise and have to catch up in a crisis mode. Anticipation means never taking the present environment for granted and always being proactive by continually scanning the environment for clues about potential developments. A classic example of what happens if you do not occurred when IBM entered the computer industry. Apple Computer was so focused on its own success that it dismissed IBM as a serious competitor.[9]

Flexible Thinking.   Forming strong opinions about the future and preparing for them to occur in the predicted manner is a risky means of dealing with the environment. The intent of environmental scanning is to keep one step ahead of changes and thus outperform the competition. Successful environmental scanning entails constantly thinking ahead and staying open to all change possibilities. The key to successful anticipation and effective adaptation is flexibility of opinions about how to best prepare for environmental changes.

Consult with Colleagues.   You need to get as many different takes on as many environmental factors as possible to be best informed and develop a comprehensive analysis. You can get help by consulting colleagues who are specialists from different business functions such as finance, marketing, and purchasing. Some managers even obtain data from their counterparts at competing companies when chatting at professional conventions or business club meetings.[10] Students intuitively do the same thing when they seek out others who have completed the final exam in earlier sections of an instructor's course to get guidance on what to expect and how to prepare.

Be Patient with Ambiguity.   The causes of environmental change are often ambiguous and a culmination of many uncertain events. When scanning the environment, expect to find a lot of ambiguous information that may not make sense at first. But keep at it and try to determine ways in which certain environmental factors affect others. As you mull over potential alternative outcomes, trust your intuition to provide needed insights and hunches that can be checked out.

Step 3: Identify Opportunities and Threats   After thoroughly analyzing the environment, managers can determine and evaluate **opportunities** that the organization can exploit and **threats** that the organization faces.[11] Keep in mind, however, the same environment can present opportunities to one organization and pose threats to another in the same or a similar industry because of their different resources. For example, telecommuting technologies have enabled organizations that sell computer modems, fax machines, and the like to prosper. On the other hand, organizations such as the U.S. Post Office and even FedEx, a major part of whose business it is to get written material from one person to another, have been adversely affected by this environmental change.

Step 4: Analyze the Organization's Resources   Next, we move from looking outside the organization to looking inside in order to evaluate the organization's internal resources. What skills and abilities do the organization's employees have? What is the organization's cash flow? Has it been successful at developing new and innovative products? How do customers perceive the image of the organization and the quality of its products or services?

Every organization is constrained to some degree by the resources and skills it has available. A small six-person computer software design firm with annual sales of less than $2 million might see a huge market for online services, but their minimal resources limit their ability to act on this opportunity. In contrast, Microsoft's management was able to create the Microsoft Network because it had the access, people skills, name recognition, and financial resources to pursue this market.

Step 5: Identify Strengths and Weaknesses   The analysis in Step 4 should lead to a clear assessment of the organization's internal resources, such as capital, worker skills, patents, and the like. It should also indicate organizational abilities such as training and development, marketing, accounting, human resources, research and development, and management information systems. An organization's **strengths** refer to the internal resources that are available or things that it does well. **Weaknesses** are activities that the organization does not do well, or resources it needs but does not possess. Strengths that represent unique skills or resources and give the organization a competitive edge are called its **distinctive competence.** For example, Black & Decker bought General Electric's small appliance division—which made coffeemakers, toasters, irons, and the like—renamed them, and capitalized on Black & Decker's reputation for quality and durability to make these appliances far more profitable than they had been under the GE name.

Step 6: Identify Operational Objectives   The results of the SWOT analysis provide a clear understanding of environmental opportunities and threats and the organization's internal strengths and weaknesses. It can then lead to the identification of a unique set of opportunities, or *niche*, where the organization has a competitive advantage. Using this information, managers can formulate more specific operational objectives that will contribute to its mission.

The purpose of setting operational objectives is to convert managerial statements of business mission and company direction into specific performance targets. Objectives create a standard that organization progress can be measured against.[12] The objectives established should include both short-range and long-range performance targets. Short-range objectives spell out the immediate improvements and outcomes management desires. Long-range objectives prompt managers to consider what to do now to position the company to perform well over the long term.

To achieve one of Wal-Mart's visions of maintaining consistent growth, founder Sam Walton gave employees their goal for the 1990s of doubling the number of stores and increasing dollar volume per square foot 60 percent by the year 2000. It was a tangible and meaningful goal. It only took five years for Wal-Mart to increase dollar volume per square foot by 45 percent and be two-thirds of the way toward doubling the number of stores.[13] At this rate, Wal-Mart was able to achieve the goal years earlier than projected.

Step 7: Create Strategies   According to Michael Porter at Harvard's Business School, no firm can successfully perform at an above-average profitability level by trying to be all things to all people. Porter proposed that management must select a **competitive strategy** that will give its unit a distinct advantage by capitalizing on the strengths of the organization and the industry it is in.[14]

Porter recommends that managers can choose among three generic competitive strategies. These three strategies are (1) **cost-leadership,** where the organization strives to be the low-cost producer in the industry, like Costco or Southwest Airlines; (2) **differentiation,** where an organization seeks to be unique in its industry in ways that are widely valued by buyers, like Porsche (high performance) or L.L. Bean (service); and (3) **focus,** where an organization seeks uniqueness in a narrow market segment, like Stouffer's Lean Cuisine for calorie-conscious consumers, or the University of Phoenix's online degree program that appeals to working adults.

The strategies management chooses depend on the organization's strengths and competing organizations' weaknesses. Management should avoid a position in which it has to "slug it out" with everybody in the industry. Rather, the organization should work on its area of strength in which the competition is lacking. Success depends on selecting the right strategy that fits the complete picture of the organization and the industry of which it is a part in order to gain the most favorable competitive advantage.

The selection of a grand strategy sets the stage for the entire organization. Subsequently, each unit within the organization has to translate this strategy into a set of operational plans that will give the organization a competitive advantage. That is, to fulfill the overall strategy, managers will seek to position their units so that they can gain a relative advantage over the company's rivals. This positioning requires careful evaluation of the competitive forces that dictate the rules of competition within the industry in which the organization operates.

Step 8: Implement Strategies   No matter how effectively an organization has planned its strategies, it cannot succeed if the strategies are not implemented properly. Other chapters in this book address a number of issues related to strategy implementation. For instance, Chapter 11 explores work design as a means of achieving strategic goals, and shows that many of the new organization structural designs are ways for organizations to cope with environmental and strategic changes. Chapter 13 looks at how developing employees can contribute to competitive advantage. Chapter 14 shows how creating high performance teams is an important part of implementing strategy. Chapter 17 discusses ways to motivate people, and Chapter 16 offers suggestions for improving leadership effectiveness.

Step 9: Evaluating Results   The final step in the strategic management process is evaluating results. How effective have our strategies been? What adjustments, if any, are necessary? Chapter 8 shows how the concepts and techniques of performance evaluation can be used to assess the results of strategies and to correct significant deviations. Chapter 16 explains how a leader can function as a change agent when corrections are called for.

Progress toward goals needs to be constantly evaluated and strategies must be adjusted to ensure that the desired results are being achieved. Environmental scanning should be an ongoing process: competitors introduce new products, technological innovations make production process obsolete, and societal trends reduce demands for some products or services, while boosting demand for others. As a result, planning is an evolutionary process requiring the need to be alert to opportunities and threats that might demand modifying or in some cases totally abandoning the original goals and/or plans to achieve them.[15]

Nevertheless, at any point in time, employees need to know what they are supposed to do; otherwise, they become like Alice and don't know "which way to walk from here." If managers don't know specific employee goals, they become like the Cheshire Cat and are unable to provide appropriate guidance because it "depends a good deal on where you want to get to." If employees don't know and managers don't help, it is easy to see why employees may feel that "it doesn't matter which way you walk." With clearly understood plans, however, managers and employees can get on with the goal-setting process so that energy can be directed toward achieving organizational objectives.

Goal Setting

One of the most basic skills in planning is goal setting. Goals are the foundation of all other planning activities. They provide the direction for management decisions as well as the criteria against which actual accomplishments can be measured. The following section can help you learn how to effectively set goals for yourself and your subordinates.

Goal setting serves four main purposes.[16] First, it provides a clear, documented statement of what you intend to accomplish. When written, objectives are a form of acknowledgment and reminder of commitment. Second, setting objectives establishes a basis for measuring performance. Third, knowing what is expected and desired provides positive motivation to achieve goals. And fourth, knowing exactly where you're going is much more likely to get you there than trying different solutions in a haphazard way.

Characteristics of Effective Goals

Five attributes of effective goals can be remembered by the acronym SMART. These characteristics can guide you in defining and setting goals that employees can understand and implement with confidence. SMART goals are specific, measurable, aligned, reachable, and time bound.

1. *Specific.*   If a goal is vague (e.g., "do the best you can"), people interpret it in many different ways, depending on their own personal experience, ability, and ambition. In contrast, if a goal is specific (e.g., "increase sales by 20 percent"), ambiguity and idiosyncratic interpretations are eliminated.[17] When confusion over the desired result is eliminated, the likelihood of a goal being achieved is increased.

2. *Measurable.*   Goals are only meaningful for those who will implement them when they are specific enough to be verified and measured. Measurable goals have a clear outcome that can be objectively assessed. They also have clear benchmarks that can be checked along the way.

3. *Aligned.*   Goals should contribute to the mission, vision, and strategic plan of the organization. They should also be congruent with the objectives and values of the employees implementing them. Employee participation can facilitate personal and organizational goal matching.

4. *Reachable.*   Goals that are set unrealistically high create frustration and are likely to be abandoned. On the other hand, goals should not be so easily achieved that they offer no challenge. The best motivators are stretch goals that are perceived as challenging yet reachable.[18] An example of a stretch goal is Hewlett-Packard's 50 percent performance improvement per year.[19] Keep in mind that stretch goals are a matter of perception: One person's "challenging" is another person's "impossible," and a third person's "easy." Stretch goals are more likely to be perceived as challenging rather than impossible if the person has high degrees of self-confidence, ability, ambition, and has previously had more success in goal attainment than in failure.[20] For people without these qualities, the same goal might be broken down into less challenging steps, or subgoals, which add up to the same outcome over time when all have been completed.

5. *Time bound.*   Open-ended goals with no specified ending point are likely to be neglected because no sense of urgency is associated with them. Goals should include a specific time limit for accomplishment.[21] So, instead of stating, "I'm going to complete the bank management training program, with a score higher than 85," a time-specific goal would state, "I'm going to complete the bank management training program, with a score of 85 or more, by February 1 of next year."

The Goal Setting Process

The elements of effective goal setting are exemplified in management by objectives (MBO) systems. In MBO systems, employees and their supervisors jointly determine specific performance goals. Progress toward objectives is periodically reviewed, and rewards are allocated on the basis of this progress.

The MBO process starts from the top down by converting organizational objectives into specific objectives for organizational units and individual members. Then MBO works from the bottom up as lower-unit managers jointly participate in setting their own goals. The result is a hierarchy that links objectives at one level to those at the next level. For the individual employee, MBO provides specific personal performance objectives.

The results of MBO programs are SMART goals that are specific, measurable, aligned, reachable, and time bound. The MBO process also generates commitment and provides control because it uses participative decision making and performance feedback.[22] Elements of effective goal setting can be drawn from the MBO process. They are spelled out in the following sequential steps that are necessary to obtain the optimal results from goal setting.[23]

1. *Clarify alignment to organizational objectives.*   Goals for every person in every area should be supported and be integrated with overall company objectives and strategy. Consequently, goal setting for any specific person or group starts with asking, "How do this unit's performance outcomes contribute to the entire organization's overall goals?"[24]

The objectives for any particular person or group should also mesh with the objectives of all others who might be affected by them. If goals are not coordinated, a potential for conflict arises. Failure to coordinate interdependent goals can lead to territorial fights, abdication of responsibility, and overlapping of effort.

2. *Set specific objectives with employees.*   Goal setting begins by defining what it is that employees need to accomplish and the specific tasks required to meet their objectives. This information is contained in job descriptions that outline what tasks employees are expected to perform, how these tasks are to be accomplished, and what outcomes employees are responsible for achieving.[25]

The level of performance expected also needs to be defined.[26] If the criteria by which a salesperson will be judged is the number of repeat customer purchases, a specific target needs to be determined, for example, 30 percent of last month's customers will make repeat purchases in the current month. The standard needs to meet the requirements of being both specific and challenging for the employee. How difficult should you make these standards? The standard must be perceived as difficult, but still attainable by those who are trying to reach it.

How do you determine if employees perceived their goals as difficult, but attainable? Have them participate in the process. Although most people will accept reasonable goals from managers,[27] participation increases people's goal aspiration levels and leads to setting more difficult goals.[28] People are more likely to accept and be committed to obtaining goals that are participative than unilaterally imposed, which makes them more likely to be achieved.[29]

3. *Obtain commitment to goals.*   The existence of goals is no assurance that employees accept and are committed to them. Commitment to pursue a goal independently must be self-motivated. So, the best way to persuade others to pursue specific goals is to appeal to their values and needs. To obtain commitment from employees, managers need to explain how achieving organizational objectives can support each employee's

SOURCE: Dilbert © Distributed by United Features Syndicate. Reprinted by permission.

personal goals.[30] Explain how the results should be meaningful to employees and make a difference to them.[31]

Managers can also exhibit support by encouraging initiative, expressing confidence, and helping employees reduce barriers that stand in the way of goal attainment. This includes making sure employees have the necessary equipment, supplies, time, training, and other resources to complete their tasks. Support can also entail removing organizational roadblocks such as bureaucratic rules that impede rather than help goal attainment.

As already discussed, employee participation in goal setting is a key to getting these goals accepted. To be effective, participation must be authentic—employees must perceive managers are truly seeking and utilizing their input. If a manager attempts to co-opt employees by pretending to want their participation when, in fact, specific goals, levels of performance, or target dates are already established, they will be quick to label it as phony.

People must believe that they are capable of attaining a goal before they will commit serious energy to it. When a person's abilities aren't adequate to meet satisfactory goals, this matching effort may signal the need for additional skill training. Benchmarks, based on what other companies have achieved, are useful in showing that a certain level of achievement is possible, as are role models within the company. Finally, helping employees develop suitable strategies for approaching the task and explicit expressions of support can boost their confidence.

Offering money, promotions, recognition, time off, or similar rewards to employees contingent on goal achievement is a powerful means to increase goal commitment. Recognition for goal attainment or goal progress is extremely important because everyone values credit and appreciation for their work. When the going gets tough on the road toward meeting a goal, people are prone to ask themselves, "What's in it for me?" Linking rewards to the achievement of goals helps employees to answer that question.

4. *Prioritize goals according to their importance.*   When employees are given several goals, they need to be ranked in order of importance so that those with the biggest payoffs are given priority in terms of time and effort expended. If goals are not prioritized, people tend to choose easy goals in order to ensure success, especially if they are rewarded only for the number of goals attained. Difficult, but more important goals can be awarded lower priorities by employees unless they are emphasized and rewarded appropriately. Employees who reach only low-priority goals and neglect

those with high priorities should be evaluated lower than those who try for important goals even if they only partially achieve them.

5. *Specify the time span involved.* After targets are set, deadlines for each goal need to be established. For example, the goal of "install the new customer service information system" needs to be accompanied by a deadline; for example, "complete project within six months." Putting a time target on each goal is important because it reduces ambiguity and sets priorities. Deadlines should be kept as short as possible. The reason is that people tend to focus on whatever time span is attached to any given goal. If daily goals are assigned, the time focus will be one day. If quarterly goals are set, actions will be directed accordingly. To paraphrase Parkinson's Law, effort toward a goal will be expended to fill the time available for its completion. Give people a month to complete a task that requires a week, and they'll typically take the full month. Also keep in mind that overemphasis on short-term goals can undermine long-term performance. Short-range time targets encourage people to do whatever is necessary to get immediate results, even if it's at the expense of achieving long-term goals.

6. *Specify how the performance will be measured.* An old management adage says it all: "What gets measured gets done." The converse is that what isn't measured won't get done. If a professor places 30 percent of a course grade on student participation, for example, but doesn't even take roll or know the students' names, attendance may be low while people prepare papers and read assignments for tests that receive concrete marks.

Typically, work outcomes are measured in physical units (i.e., quantity of production, number of errors), time (i.e., meeting deadlines, coming to work each day), or money (i.e., profits, sales, costs). Some areas are difficult to measure, such as customer satisfaction, but even the subjective can be quantified. Examples are questionnaires that ask customers to rate their satisfaction with specific employees, amount of their repeat business, or how often they recommend the company to others. Measurements can be made of employee actions that are assumed to lead to desired outcomes (e.g., smiling at customers, or asking if the customers need help as soon as they enter a specific department). Quantitative measurements can even be obtained, for example, by having "mystery shoppers" (paid individuals posing as customers) complete a checklist to show how many of the required employee actions were shown.

7. *Provide performance feedback.* After progress is measured, it is essential that the results be provided to employees so that they know whether they are on track and whether their level of effort is sufficient or it needs to be increased. Feedback can also induce employees to raise their goal level and to inform them of ways in which to improve their performance. Because of these factors, a higher performance level is more likely if individuals are given feedback while they are striving to achieve goals.[32]

Feedback can be provided in many ways—memos, charts, printouts, reports, computer displays, or personal interaction. The ideal frequency of feedback depends on how often it is required to keep organizational processes on target. On-time delivery goals need to be tracked daily. Cost management, however, might only require monthly information.

Ideally, feedback should be requested and sought after rather than inflicted by managers on subordinates.[33] Encouraging employees to solicit frequent feedback from internal and external customers on their own, and dropping by the manager's office when they have questions, are examples. When employees are able to monitor their own progress, the feedback is less threatening and less likely to be perceived as part of a management control system. This self-generated feedback can be supplemented by periodic managerial evaluations, when progress is reviewed.

OBSERVER'S RATING SHEET

The class is to evaluate R. J. Simpson's goal-setting skills on a scale of 1 to 5 (5 being highest). Write in concrete examples in the space provided after each skill component to use in explaining your feedback.

Skill Component	Rating
• Formulates goals that contribute to the organization's mission	_____
• Conducts SWOT analyses	_____
• Formulates competitive strategies based on distinctive competencies	_____
• Sets specific and challenging goals	_____
• Relates goals to personal needs and values	_____
• Sets deadlines for each goal	_____
• Provides for subordinate participation	_____
• Prioritizes goal difficulty and importance	_____
• Builds in feedback mechanisms	_____
• Commits rewards based on performance	_____

those with high priorities should be evaluated lower than those who try for important goals even if they only partially achieve them.

5. *Specify the time span involved.* After targets are set, deadlines for each goal need to be established. For example, the goal of "install the new customer service information system" needs to be accompanied by a deadline; for example, "complete project within six months." Putting a time target on each goal is important because it reduces ambiguity and sets priorities. Deadlines should be kept as short as possible. The reason is that people tend to focus on whatever time span is attached to any given goal. If daily goals are assigned, the time focus will be one day. If quarterly goals are set, actions will be directed accordingly. To paraphrase Parkinson's Law, effort toward a goal will be expended to fill the time available for its completion. Give people a month to complete a task that requires a week, and they'll typically take the full month. Also keep in mind that overemphasis on short-term goals can undermine long-term performance. Short-range time targets encourage people to do whatever is necessary to get immediate results, even if it's at the expense of achieving long-term goals.

6. *Specify how the performance will be measured.* An old management adage says it all: "What gets measured gets done." The converse is that what isn't measured won't get done. If a professor places 30 percent of a course grade on student participation, for example, but doesn't even take roll or know the students' names, attendance may be low while people prepare papers and read assignments for tests that receive concrete marks.

Typically, work outcomes are measured in physical units (i.e., quantity of production, number of errors), time (i.e., meeting deadlines, coming to work each day), or money (i.e., profits, sales, costs). Some areas are difficult to measure, such as customer satisfaction, but even the subjective can be quantified. Examples are questionnaires that ask customers to rate their satisfaction with specific employees, amount of their repeat business, or how often they recommend the company to others. Measurements can be made of employee actions that are assumed to lead to desired outcomes (e.g., smiling at customers, or asking if the customers need help as soon as they enter a specific department). Quantitative measurements can even be obtained, for example, by having "mystery shoppers" (paid individuals posing as customers) complete a checklist to show how many of the required employee actions were shown.

7. *Provide performance feedback.* After progress is measured, it is essential that the results be provided to employees so that they know whether they are on track and whether their level of effort is sufficient or it needs to be increased. Feedback can also induce employees to raise their goal level and to inform them of ways in which to improve their performance. Because of these factors, a higher performance level is more likely if individuals are given feedback while they are striving to achieve goals.[32]

Feedback can be provided in many ways—memos, charts, printouts, reports, computer displays, or personal interaction. The ideal frequency of feedback depends on how often it is required to keep organizational processes on target. On-time delivery goals need to be tracked daily. Cost management, however, might only require monthly information.

Ideally, feedback should be requested and sought after rather than inflicted by managers on subordinates.[33] Encouraging employees to solicit frequent feedback from internal and external customers on their own, and dropping by the manager's office when they have questions, are examples. When employees are able to monitor their own progress, the feedback is less threatening and less likely to be perceived as part of a management control system. This self-generated feedback can be supplemented by periodic managerial evaluations, when progress is reviewed.

CONCEPT QUIZ

Goal setting is a vital skill for planning, motivating, and measuring performance. It is necessary at the personal, supervisory, and organizational levels. To see how well you understand goal-setting skills, complete the following true-false quiz by circling the correct answer. Answers are at the end of the quiz. After marking your answers, remember to go back and check your understanding of any answers you missed.

True or False   1. Specific goals reduce ambiguity about what an employee is expected to do.

True or False   2. Goals should be set beyond what a person can realistically achieve to maximize motivation.

True or False   3. To avoid confusing employees, managers should never deviate from original plans.

True or False   4. Participation reduces employee commitment to goals.

True or False   5. Feedback on goal progress is best if self-generated.

True or False   6. Everything an employee does on his or her job can and should be quantified and have a goal set for it.

True or False   7. Because of their immediacy, short-term goals should take priority over long-term goals.

True or False   8. Achieving an easy goal should be evaluated more positively than coming up short on a difficult goal.

True or False   9. Competitive strategy that provides a distinct advantage should be used to achieve goals.

True or False   10. People accept goals more readily when the goals are tied to rewards they desire.

Answers.   (1) True; (2) False; (3) False; (4) False; (5) True; (6) False; (7) False; (8) False; (9) True; (10) True

BEHAVIORAL CHECKLIST

Look for these specific behaviors when evaluating your planning and goal-setting skills and those of others.

The Effective Planner and Goal-Setter

- Formulates goals that contribute to the organization's mission.
- Conducts SWOT analysis.
- Determines distinctive competencies to formulate competitive strategies.
- Establishes specific and challenging goals for each key task.
- Explains how task goals contribute to individual needs and values.
- Encourages participation in goal setting.
- Prioritizes goals according to difficulty and importance.
- Specifies deadlines for each goal.
- Builds in feedback mechanisms to assess goal progress.
- Commits rewards contingent on goal attainment.

Attention!
Do not read the following until assigned to do so by your instructor.

MODELING EXERCISE

Role-Play: Goal Setting for Women's Basketball

Directions.   The class should read the following information about the actors and the situation, but do *NOT* read the roles. Then two students volunteer to play the roles of R. J. Simpson and Pat Bell. Volunteers then read their own role (not the other person's role) and prepare for the role-play. The remainder of the class reads both roles and reviews the Observer's Rating Sheet. When the role-play begins, the observers rate R. J. Simpson's goal-setting effectiveness and note examples they can use to provide specific feedback at the end of the role-play.

Time.   Not to exceed 20 minutes for the role-play. About 15 minutes for feedback.

Actors.

R. J. Simpson, athletic director at State College
Pat Bell, new women's basketball coach at State College

Situation.   R. J. Simpson made a recent offer to Pat Bell to join State College as the college's new women's basketball coach at a salary of $65,000 a year. Pat has accepted. Pat will replace the previous coach, who held the job for three years and had a combined record of 20 wins and 42 losses. Pat previously was head women's basketball coach at a junior college where she won 92 percent of her games and two national JC championships.

State College has 12,000 students and is a member of the 10-school Northwest Athletic Conference. During the past three years, State College has finished no higher than sixth in the conference and has not been in any postseason tournaments. The team averages 1,500 fans for its home games in the college's arena, which has a capacity of 9,000. The women's basketball program, which last year had a budget of $150,000, was responsible for a loss of $60,000 to the college's overall athletic program.

This meeting is to set goals for the women's basketball program's coming season. These goals will be used to judge Pat's performance and as a basis for allocating performance-based bonuses, provided by alums and athletic boosters, of up to $20,000 annually.

R. J. Simpson's Role   You are delighted to have hired Pat Bell with such an excellent record from a competitive JC league. State College is at a crucial juncture with its women's basketball program this year after losing $60,000 last year. If you can't at least break even this year, the Board of Governors is insisting that the program be dropped, which means you will face women's rights protests, possible discrimination lawsuits, and problems in meeting NCAA requirements that universities spend equally (excluding football) on men's and women's intercollegiate sports programs. You want to make sure that Pat has extremely clear-cut goals and is motivated to achieve them.

Pat Bell's Role   You feel that you are at the right place at the right time. You were fortunate over the last two years at JC to have some extraordinary talent playing for you. Nevertheless, you have to pat yourself on the back because you were able to capitalize on your team's skills by implementing some creative strategies during the national championship playoffs. You have enjoyed complete independence and freedom to do as you choose as a coach. If you can get the right recruits and do things your way, you feel that you can turn State's record around, improve the school's prestige, and boost your career.

OBSERVER'S RATING SHEET

The class is to evaluate R. J. Simpson's goal-setting skills on a scale of 1 to 5 (5 being highest). Write in concrete examples in the space provided after each skill component to use in explaining your feedback.

Skill Component	*Rating*
• Formulates goals that contribute to the organization's mission	_____
• Conducts SWOT analyses	_____
• Formulates competitive strategies based on distinctive competencies	_____
• Sets specific and challenging goals	_____
• Relates goals to personal needs and values	_____
• Sets deadlines for each goal	_____
• Provides for subordinate participation	_____
• Prioritizes goal difficulty and importance	_____
• Builds in feedback mechanisms	_____
• Commits rewards based on performance	_____

GROUP EXERCISES

The following three exercises are designed to give you a chance to practice your planning and goal-setting skills in small groups and receive feedback from others about your strengths and weaknesses. The first exercise is a case describing the planning and goal-setting approach of a practicing manager for you to analyze. Next is a role-play in which you can practice participative goal setting with a surrogate subordinate. Last is an exercise that gives you a chance to set goals for a relevant person in this class, your instructor.

Group Exercise 1: Case: I Can See Clearly Now[34]

"The most important thing for any organization is to have everyone focused on the same objectives and to have the objectives clearly defined." So says Kathleen Cote, chief executive officer of Computervision Corporation of Bedford, Massachusetts. Computervision Corporation *http://www.cv.com*, is a leading supplier of desktop and enterprise-wide product design and development software and services. Its vision is to be the partner of choice for the most important thing its customers do—product development. The company pioneered CAD/CAM (computer-aided design/computer-aided manufacturing) hardware and software years ago. It was flying high for the subsequent 10 years as revenues and profits soared. Then, as patents expired and competitors entered the market, the once-profitable company started posting losses, which accumulated over the next three years to nearly $1.3 million. Cote headed the operating committee that developed the strategic plan for Computervision's turnaround and ultimate survival. Her work in that area led to her being named president and chief operating officer of the company. The following year she was appointed to the top management job.

Cote's management style happens to be people oriented, and she knew how she wanted to run the company. What the company had to do to become successful again and what she had to do as CEO to make that happen were crystal clear in her mind: The company had to clearly define its objectives, and she had to make sure that everyone was focused on those objectives. Cote stated, "The top three things I am working on have to be the top three things everyone is working on. We are only going to be successful together." How did she go about creating a focused environment?

The first thing Cote did was to have her senior managers identify where Computervision was winning business and where it was losing business. On the basis of that analysis, they decided to shift the company's focus to providing product development solutions through software and services and putting less of an emphasis on hardware. The top managers then established corporate objectives and communicated them down through the organization. Those objectives were then used to clearly define individual performance objectives. In addition, Cote was firmly committed to sticking to the objectives. She said, "I'm a firm believer that if you stay on course and never get off, you will have great success. There really is no surprise if you have a plan in place."

Cote isn't just focused on establishing and communicating common objectives for organizational employees. She is also strongly committed to making sure objectives are met. Managers (and all organizational employees) are held accountable for meeting their respective objectives and doing what they say they are going to do. Says Cote, "I don't like surprises. If something isn't going right, let me know what you can do about it to work through the issues and the problem." According to Cote, achieving the objectives entails showing employees how they are a part of making the plans happen and making them feel that they play an important role in helping the company meet its goals.

How has Computervision performed under Cote's leadership? The company posted a net income of $9.8 billion, a profit of $22.8 million, during her first year as chief operating officer, and a profit of $26 million in Cote's next three quarters as CEO. But, Computervision did suffer a loss of $5.9 million in the fourth quarter of that year. That loss abruptly ended the company's string of 11 consecutive profitable quarters. But, despite the unexpected fourth-quarter loss, industry and financial analysts expect Computervision to continue its history of solid profits.

QUESTIONS FOR DISCUSSION

1. What is your reaction to Cote's philosophy that the most important plan for any organization is to have everyone focused on the same objectives and to have the objectives clearly defined? Do you agree? Why or why not? What would be the drawbacks of such a philosophy?
2. What role did strategic plans play in Computervision's turnaround? What role should they play in the company's future? What role should operational plans play?
3. One of the major criticisms of formal planning is that planning may create rigidity, particularly in a dynamic environment. How do you think Kathleen Cote would respond to that criticism?
4. How might the commitment concept affect planning at Computervision?
5. Would you call Computervision's approach to setting objectives a more traditional approach or more of an MBO approach? Explain your choice.

Group Exercise 2: Role Play: Prioritizing Goals for Juvenile Probation Officers[35]

Directions.   The class should read the following information about the actors and the situation, but do *NOT* read the roles. Then two students volunteer to play the roles of Terry Donahue and Chris Espo. Volunteers then read their own role (not the other person's role) and prepare for the role-play. The remainder of the class reads both roles and reviews the Observer's Rating Sheet. When the role-play begins, the observers rate Terry Donahue's goal-setting effectiveness and note examples they can use to provide specific feedback at the end of the role-play.

Time.   Not to exceed 20 minutes for the role-play. About 15 minutes for feedback.

Situation.   Terry Donahue is a probation supervisor. Chris Espo is a newly hired juvenile probation officer. A description of the job of juvenile probation officer and Chris's qualifications follow. Both are currently in Terry's office.

Juvenile Probation Officer

TASKS

1. *Meets with parolees weekly to assess their current behavior.*

   Conditions:

   - Caseload of not more than 40 appointments per week will be scheduled by receptionist.
   - Supervisor will help with difficult cases.
   - Use procedures stated in rules and regulations.

   Standards:

   - All parolees must be seen weekly.
   - Those showing evidence of continued criminal activity or lack of a job will be reported to supervisor.

2. *Prepares presentence reports on clients.*

Conditions:

- Prepared when requested by the judge.
- There will be an average of five per week, per instructions issued by judge.
- Supervisor will review and approve.

Standards:

- Your reports will be complete and accurate as determined by the judge.
- Judge will accept 75 percent of presentence recommendations.

SKILLS, KNOWLEDGE, AND ABILITIES REQUIRED

- Knowledge of the factors contributing to criminal behavior
- Ability to counsel parolees
- Ability to write clear and concise probation reports
- Knowledge of judge's sentencing habits for particular types of offenders and offenses
- Knowledge of law concerning probation

CHRIS ESPO'S QUALIFICATIONS:

- B.S. in business administration from State University
- Four years' part-time experience running recreation programs for juvenile offenders in halfway homes
- 3.5 GPA in all college work
- Golf team captain and amateur state golf champion two years in a row

Terry Donahue's Role   You are happy to have been allocated a new juvenile probation officer because your department is understaffed and has a heavy caseload. Chris Espo seems like a bright and capable addition to your staff who desires to learn the job quickly. You are concerned that his recent business degree has not provided some of the essential knowledge and skills desired for the job, but with some extra classes and training, that can be upgraded. Everyone in your agency has read about Chris's golf championships and he is quite a hero in your small town. You want to set goals for Chris's job and professional development.

Chris Espo's Role   You are happy to have the juvenile probation officer job because, next to golf, you really like working with kids. It was a tough decision to stay off of the pro golf tour but you married your high school sweetheart two years ago and just had a new baby. Both of your families still live in the small town you've grown up in, and you feel okay about your trade-offs, as long as you can use your spare time to practice and to compete in amateur golf tournaments.

OBSERVER'S RATING SHEET

The class is to evaluate Terry Donahue's goal-setting skills on a scale of 1 to 5 (5 being highest). Write concrete examples in the space provided after each skill component to use in explaining your feedback.

Skill Component	*Rating*
• Formulates goals that contribute to the organization's mission	_____
• Conducts SWOT analyses	_____
• Formulates competitive strategies based on distinctive competencies	_____
• Sets specific and challenging goals	_____
• Relates goals to personal needs and values	_____
• Sets deadlines for each goal	_____
• Provides for subordinate participation	_____
• Prioritizes goal difficulty and importance	_____
• Builds in feedback mechanisms	_____
• Commits rewards based on performance	_____

Group Exercise 3: Goal Setting for Your Instructor

Purpose.   This exercise will help you learn how to write tangible, verifiable, measurable, and relevant goals as might evolve from an MBO program.

Time.   Approximately 20 to 30 minutes.

Instructions.

1. Break into groups of three to five students.
2. Spend a few minutes discussing your class instructor's job. What does he or she do? What defines good performance? What behaviors will lead to good performance?
3. Each group is to develop a list of five goals that, although not established participatively with your instructor, you believe might be developed into an MBO program at your college. Try to select goals that seem most critical to the effective performance of your instructor's job.
4. Each group selects a leader who will share his or her group's goals with the entire class.
5. The class then discusses the goals presented by the groups focusing on their (a) specificity, (b) ease of measurement, (c) importance, and (d) motivational properties.
6. Continue until all groups have shared their goals and the class has discussed them. Then find out your instructor's reactions.

SUMMARY CHECKLIST

Review your performance and look over others' ratings of your planning and goal-setting skills. Now assess yourself on each of the key learning behaviors. Put a check (✓) next to those behaviors on which you need improvement.

_____   **I formulate goals that contribute to the organization's mission.**
1. Determine the organization's purpose for existing.
2. Create a vision.
3. Create a mission statement.

_____   **I conduct SWOT analyses.**
1. Assess organizational strengths.
2. Assess organizational weaknesses.
3. Assess environmental opportunities.
4. Assess environmental threats.

_____   **I formulate strategies based on distinctive competencies.**
1. Determine the organization's unique skills and resources.
2. Determine the niche where the organization has competitive advantage.
3. Develop objectives and plans to take advantage of the niche.

_____   **I establish specific and challenging goals for each key task.**
1. Identify operational objectives that provide specific performance targets.
2. Develop achievable goals that stretch capabilities.

_____   **I relate task goals to personal needs and values.**
1. Assess individual differences in skills, values, and needs.
2. Develop commitment to goals by adjusting to individual differences.

_____ **I set deadlines for each goal.**
1. Balance required quality with time requirements.
2. Determine a specific time limit for realistic accomplishment.

_____ **I have subordinates actively participate in setting their goals.**
1. Determine coordination requirements.
2. Get ideas from all people collaborating in goal implementation.
3. Sincerely seek and utilize subordinates' inputs.

_____ **I prioritize goals based on difficulty and importance.**
1. Determine which goals will contribute most to the organization mission.
2. Determine the difficulty and time required to achieve each goal.
3. Determine the time urgency for completion of each goal.
4. Determine which goals should be completed first and by when.

_____ **I build in feedback mechanisms to assess goal progress.**
1. Determine how performance will be measured quantitatively and qualitatively.
2. Specify standards and targets to be reached.
3. Set up time frames for providing feedback.

_____ **I commit rewards based on performance toward goal attainment.**
1. Explain goal relevance to personal needs and values.
2. Link rewards to achievement of goals.

APPLICATION QUESTIONS

1. Does goal setting emphasize short-term results at the expense of long-term effectiveness?
2. How does goal setting deal with employees who have multiple goals, some of which are conflicting?
3. What barriers in an organization can you identify that may limit the effectiveness of a goal-setting program? How can these barriers be overcome?
4. Explain what an instructor can do to use goal setting with students in a classroom.
5. How can an organization develop and sustain a competitive advantage? How can you do the same for your career?

REINFORCEMENT EXERCISES

The following suggestions are activities you can do to reinforce the planning techniques and goal-setting skills in this chapter. You may want to adapt them to your Action Plan or try them independently.

1. Visit the Web sites for companies that you are interested in and see what they say about their missions, objectives, and strategies, for example, go to *http://www.llbean.com*, *http://www.mercedes-benz.com/*, etc. The same can be done by looking through companies' annual reports.
2. Perform a SWOT analysis on a local business you feel you know well. What, if any, competitive advantage has this organization staked out?
3. Locate and read the strategic plan for your university. Does it cover all the necessary steps effectively? Is it current? Does it provide a good fit with the most relevant environment to provide a competitive niche?
4. Set specific and challenging goals for yourself in this class. Do the same for your other classes. Prioritize and rate them for difficulty.

ACTION PLAN

Planning Your Career

The following questions can help you formulate a strategic plan for achieving your career goals. Periodically rethinking them can also help you keep your career from drifting.

1. What is your mission statement? What business are you in? What is your product (the service or value you create for others)? Who is your market (what type of employer or client is willing to buy your service)?
2. What are your strengths and weaknesses as an employee or self-employed provider of services? What are your core skills and competencies?
3. What external opportunities and threats do you anticipate? Where could you best use your competencies following graduation? What could go wrong in controlling your career?
4. Where would you like your career to be in 5 or 10 years? What is your vision?
5. How do you plan to get there? What actions do you need to undertake now to reach your career vision?
   a. What added education/training do you need?
   b. What organizational experiences do you need?
   c. What people are critical to your progress?
6. How do you know you are still on the right course? What milestones do you have for periodically checking up on your career progress?

NOTES

1. Copyright 1994 by National Research Bureau, P.O. Box 1, Burlington, IA 52601–0001. Reprinted by permission.
2. Adapted from R. E. Quinn, S. R. Faerman, M. P. Thompson, and M. R. McGrath, *Becoming a Master Manager* (New York: Wiley, 1990) 33–34.
3. L. Carroll, *Alice's Adventures in Wonderland* (New York: The Platt & Peck Co., 1900) 62–63.
4. Cited in Rubbermaid's "Philosophy, Management Principles, Mission, and Objectives," April 1993.
5. N. Venkatraman and J. E. Prescott, "Environment-Strategy Coalignment: An Empirical Test of Its Performance Implications," *Strategic Management Journal* (January 1990): 1–23.
6. A. A. Thompson and A. J. Strickland, III, *Crafting and Implementing Strategy* (Burr Ridge, IL: Richard D. Irwin, 1995) 85.
7. A. A. Thompson and A. J. Strickland, III, *Strategic Management: Concepts and Cases*, 9th ed. (Burr Ridge, IL: Irwin, 1996) 78–89.
8. Ibid., 90–104.
9. Ibid., 103.
10. H. G. DeYong, "Thieves Among Us," *Industry Week* (June 17, 1996): 12–16.
11. S. E. Jackson and J. E. Dutton, "Discerning Threats and Opportunities," *Administrative Science Quarterly* (September 1988): 370–87.
12. J. C. Collins and J. I. Porras, "Building a Visionary Company," *California Management Review* 37 (Winter 1995): 80–100.
13. Wal-Mart, *1995 Annual Report.*

14. M. E. Porter, *Competitive Advantage: Creating and Sustaining Superior Performance* (New York, Free Press, 1985).
15. C. C. Miller and L. B. Cardinal, "Strategic Planning and Firm Performance: A Synthesis of More Than Two Decades of Research," *Academy of Management Journal* (March 1994): 16–61.
16. G. L. Morrisey, *Management by Objectives and Results for Business and Industry*, 2d ed. (Reading, MA: Addison-Wesley, 1977).
17. E. A. Locke, "Motivation Through Goal Setting," in R. T. Golembiewski, ed., *Handbook of Organizational Behavior* (New York: M. Dekker, 1999) 4.
18. P. F. Drucker, "Managing Oneself," *Harvard Business Review* (March–April, 1999): 71.
19. J. Quinn, P. Anderson, and S. Finkelstein, "Managing Professional Intellect: Making the Most of the Best" *Harvard Business Review* (March–April 1996): 71–80.
20. E. A. Locke, "Motivation Through Goal Setting," in R. T. Golembiewski, ed., *Handbook of Organizational Behavior* (New York: M. Dekker, 1999) 14–15; G. P. Latham and G. A. Yukl, "A Review of Research on the Application of Goal Setting in Organizations," *Academy of Management Journal* (December 1975): 824–45.
21. G. P. Latham and E. A. Locke, "Goal Setting—A Motivational Technique That Works," *Organizational Dynamics* (Autumn 1979): 68–80.
22. P. F. Drucker, *The Practice of Management* (New York: Harper & Row, 1954).

23. E. Locke and G. Latham, *A Theory of Goal Setting and Task Performance* (Upper Saddle River, NJ: Prentice Hall, 1990).

24. R. Kaplan and D. Norton, "Using the Balances Scorecard as a Strategic Management System," *Harvard Business Review* (January–February 1996): 75–85.

25. S. Nelton, "Put Your Purpose in Writing," *Nations's Business* (February 1994): 61–64.

26. Locke, 1999, pp. 11–12.

27. Locke, 1999; G. P. Latham and L. M. Saari, "The Effects of Holding Goal Difficulty Constant on Assigned and Participatively Set Goals," *Academy of Management Journal* (March 1979): 163–68.

28. G. P. Latham, T. R. Mitchell, and D. L. Dossett, "Importance of Participative Goal Setting and Anticipated Rewards on Goal Difficulty and Job Performance," *Journal of Applied Psychology* (April 1978): 163–71.

29. E. A. Locke, and D. M. Schweiger, "Participation in Decision Making: One More Look," in B. M. Staw, ed., *Research in Organizational Behavior,* vol. 1 (Greenwich, CT: JAI Press, 1979) 265–339.

30. G. P. Latham, and E. A. Locke, "Goal Setting—A Motivational Technique That Works," *Organizational Dynamics* (Autumn 1979): 68–80; E. A. Locke, "Motivation Through Goal Setting," in R. T. Golembiewski, ed., *Handbook of Organizational Behavior* (New York: M. Dekker, 1999) 6–7.

31. P. F. Drucker, "Managing Oneself," *Harvard Business Review* (March–April 1999): 71.

32. P. C. Early, G. C. Northcraft, and T. R. Litucy, "The Impact of Process and Outcome Feedback on the Relation of Goal Setting to Task Performance," *Academy of Management Journal* 33 (1990): 87–105.

33. J. M. Ivancevich and J. T. McMahon, "The Effects of Goal Setting, External Feedback, and Self-Generated Feedback on Outcome Variables: A Field Experiment," *Academy of Management Journal* (June 1982): 359–72.

34. M. A. Verespej, "Future Vision," *IW*, February 17, 1997, 50–55.

35. Adapted from D. E. Klingner, "When the Traditional Job Description Is Not Enough." Reprinted with the permission of *Personnel Journal*, Inc., Costa Mesa, CA, all rights reserved, 1979.

CHAPTER 8

Evaluating and Controlling Performance

Learning Objectives

After completing this chapter, you should be able to:

■ Conduct performance appraisal interviews.

■ Create appraisal criteria from stated goals.

■ Determine what best to appraise in a given situation.

■ Apply the most effective methods to measure performance.

■ Utilize performance appraisals as control devices.

■ Provide meaningful feedback for development.

■ Avoid rating errors.

■ Appraise team effectiveness.

SELF-ASSESSMENT EXERCISE

For each of the following questions, select the answer that best describes how you would prefer to conduct a performance appraisal.

	Usually	*Sometimes*	*Seldom*
1. Compare results to original objectives as a control process.			
2. Make sure the person knows what others do not like about his or her personality.			
3. Keep my comments descriptive rather than evaluative.			
4. Ask the recipient to summarize what I have said to ensure that my feedback is clearly understood.			
5. Focus my comments on generalities rather than specific job-related behaviors.			
6. Use objectives previously set with the employee as a basis for measuring performance.			

	Usually	*Sometimes*	*Seldom*
7. Be sure to use only control criteria applicable to any management situation.	_____	_____	_____
8. Use multiple sources of information for measuring actual performance.	_____	_____	_____
9. Sometimes revise the standard of measurement rather than correct the employee.	_____	_____	_____
10. Conduct the performance feedback interview whenever a convenient opportunity arises, rather than scheduling it in advance.	_____	_____	_____

Scoring.   For questions 1, 2, 4, 6, 8, and 9, give yourself 3 points for "Usually," 2 points for "Sometimes," and 1 point for "Seldom." For questions 3, 5, 7, and 10, give yourself 3 points for "Seldom," 2 points for "Sometimes," and 1 point for "Usually."

Interpretation.   Sum up your total points. A score of 27 or higher means you're good at conducting performance appraisal interviews. A score of 22 to 26 suggests you have some room for improvement. A score below 22 indicates that you are probably not effective at this skill and should concentrate on improving it.

CONCEPTS

The following individual quotes were reportedly taken from actual employee performance evaluations in a large U.S. corporation.[1]

"Since my last report, this employee has reached rock bottom . . . and has started to dig."

"This employee is really not so much of a 'has-been,' but more of a definite 'won't-be.'"

"This young lady has delusions of adequacy."

"He sets low personal standards and then consistently fails to achieve them."

"This employee is depriving a village somewhere of an idiot."

"This employee should go far . . . and the sooner he starts, the better."

The preceding quotes are not the ones that will help an employee's career. They are not things managers want to hear about their employees, either, because in today's competitive environment highly qualified employees are the primary source of sustained competitive advantage for most organizations.[2] In fact, these types of comments about employees' performance won't help anyone. Instead they are an indication of the degree of frustration that can occur if the performance evaluation process is not carried out effectively. They are indicative of the importance *and* difficulty of managers' responsibilities in assessing the work of their employees through performance appraisals.[3]

So, why is performance appraisal so critical? In addition to being a daily function at which managers spend about 10 percent of their time,[4] several key reasons explain its importance.[5] In Chapter 7, you learned how to plan and set goals with your subordinates using management by objectives. Performance appraisal is the process of periodically measuring employees' progress toward agreed-upon objectives, providing constructive feedback, reinforcing successes with rewards, and taking corrective action if goals are not being achieved. Appraisals are important to managers to help develop and obtain the best performance from their employees. According to former General Electric CEO Jack Welch, "If we get the right people in the right job, and keep them there, we've won the game."[6] Appraisals are important to employees because they often serve as the basis for promotions, terminations, training opportunities, and pay adjustments. When conducted effectively, performance appraisals can increase productivity and morale and decrease absenteeism and turnover. But when handled poorly, they can have the opposite effects.[7] Performance appraisal is one of the primary tools for helping managers meet organizational goals and compete effectively internationally.

This chapter is designed to help you develop the skills to ensure that objectives are obtained and that employees learn how to enhance their performance through the performance appraisal process. These skills include applying a number of control processes to aid the attainment of objectives and providing effective feedback to enhance employee performance and development.

As you learned in Chapter 7, setting goals is a prerequisite to performance appraisal. The goal-setting process provides a documented statement of what you intend for the subordinate to accomplish, a form of acknowledgment, and a reminder of commitment. Setting objectives also establishes a basis for measuring performance and provides positive motivation to achieve goals.[8] In this chapter you will learn about how to measure progress toward goals and provide feedback to enhance employee performance and goal achievement.

Performance appraisals become control devices because employees tend to behave in ways to look good in light of the criteria on which they will be appraised. If performance is positive, the employee's behavior can be rewarded with praise, pay increases, or promotions. If performance is below standard, managers can seek to correct it or, depending on the nature of the deviation, discipline the employee. Let us look a little more closely at the control aspect of performance appraisal.

Performance Appraisal as a Control Process

Control is the process of monitoring activities to ensure that they are accomplishing planned goals and of correcting any significant deviations. Managers can't really know whether their employees are performing properly until they have evaluated what activities are being undertaken and have compared the actual performance with desired standards.[9] It might help to think of the **control process** as consisting of three separate and distinct steps: (1) *measuring* actual performance, (2) *comparing* actual performance against a standard, and (3) taking *managerial action* to correct deviations or inadequate standards.

Focus on Objectives

If the manager has utilized management by objectives (MBO) described in Chapter 7, the standards of performance already exist and have been agreed upon by both the manager and employee. These standards are the specific objectives against which progress can be measured. MBO objectives are, by definition, tangible, verifiable, and measurable, so they are the standards by which progress is measured and against which it is compared. If MBO isn't practiced, then standards are the specific performance indicators that management uses. In either case, keep in mind that planning must precede the setting of controls because it is in planning that the standards are established.

What Performance Should Be Measured?

To determine what actual performance is, managers need to acquire information about it. This process is known as *measuring*, a key step in the control process. Two important questions here are *how* to measure and *what* to measure.

The most frequently used sources of information for measuring actual performance are personal observation, statistical reports, oral reports, written reports, and computer-accessed databases. The effective manager tends to use multiple sources, recognizing that different sources provide different types of information. Personal observations obtained by walking around and talking with employees, for instance, can be a rich source of detailed performance data. A manager can pick up important clues about potential problems from an employee's facial expression or casual comment that might never be evident from reviewing a statistical report. On the other hand, statistical reports typically contain more comprehensive and objective data.

What we measure is probably more critical to the control process than how we measure it. Selecting the wrong criteria can have serious dysfunctional consequences. Besides, what we measure determines, to a great extent, in what areas people in the organization will attempt to excel.[10]

Some control criteria are applicable to any management situation. For instance, because all managers, by definition, direct the activities of others, criteria such as employee attendance or turnover rates can be measured. Keeping costs within budget is a common control measure for monetary costs. Any comprehensive control system, however, needs to recognize the diversity of activities among managers. A production manager in a manufacturing plant might use measures of the quantity of units produced per day, number of units produced per labor-hour, or percent of units rejected by customers because of inferior quality. The manager of an administrative department in a government agency might use number of orders processed per hour or average time required to process service calls. Marketing executives often use such criteria as percent of market captured, average dollar value per sale, or number of customer visits per salesperson.

The performance of some activities is difficult to quantify, however. It is more difficult, for instance, for an administrator to measure the performance of a research chemist or an elementary school teacher than of a person who sells life insurance. But most activities can be broken down into objective segments that allow for measurement. A manager needs to determine what value a person contributes to the organization and then convert the contribution into standards. When a performance indicator cannot be stated in quantifiable terms, subjective measures are always preferable to having no standards at all. However, when moving into subjective areas, managers need to be careful to follow government laws against discrimination.

EEOC Guidelines   The Equal Employment Opportunity Commission (EEOC) is the government agency charged with enforcing federal laws against discrimination. The EEOC published the Uniform Guidelines on Employee Selection Procedures, which include guidelines for designing and implementing performance appraisals. In general, the behaviors or characteristics measured by a performance appraisal should be related to the job and to succeeding on the job. For example, if the appraisal measures "grooming," then good grooming should be important for success in the job. Because of this requirement, a supervisor and others responsible for the content of performance appraisals should make sure that what they measure is relevant to a particular job.

Just as hiring should be based on a candidate's ability to perform the essential tasks of a particular job, so appraisals should be based on the employee's success in carrying out those tasks. The ratings in a performance appraisal should not be discriminatory; they should not be based on an employee's race, sex, or other protected category but on an employee's ability to meet standards of performance. Employees should know in advance what those standards are and the organization should have a system in place for employees to ask questions about their ratings.[11]

It is especially important that managers make certain that their performance appraisals do not result in adverse effects on minorities, women, or older employees. If they do, the results could be judged illegal.[12] Suggestions to make performance appraisal systems more legally acceptable include (1) deriving the content of the appraisal system from job analyses; (2) emphasizing work behaviors rather than personal traits; (3) ensuring that the results of the appraisals are communicated to employees; (4) ensuring that employees are allowed to give feedback during the appraisal interview; (5) training managers in conducting proper evaluations; (6) ensuring that appraisals are written, documented, and retained; and (7) ensuring that personnel decisions are consistent with the performance appraisals.[13]

Performance Appraisal Criteria The three most popular sets of criteria used in appraising performance are individual task outcomes, behaviors, and traits.[14] **Individual task outcomes** measure ends, rather than means. A salesperson, for example, might be assessed on overall sales volume, dollar increase in sales, or number of new accounts established. When specific outcomes are difficult to attribute directly to one employee's actions, behaviors that contribute to these goals might be all you can measure. If the employee being appraised is part of a team, for example, the team's task outcome can be measured, but the contribution of each individual on the team may be difficult to identify. In this case, example **behaviors** you could measure would be things such as attendance, number of contact calls made per week, or number of deadlines achieved. Although individual **traits** are weaker than other task outcomes or behavior because they are more difficult to correlate with goal achievement, characteristics such as "good attitude," "highly motivated," and "dependable" are still prevalent on performance appraisal forms in many organizations.[15]

Measuring Performance: Rating Methods for Comparing Performance to Standards

The comparison step determines the degree of variation between actual performance and the standard. Because some variation in performance can be expected in all activities, it is critical to determine the acceptable range of variation. Deviations in excess of this range merit corrective action. In the comparison stage, managers should be particularly concerned with the size and direction of the variation. But, how should these comparisons be made and documented? Six popular long-standing methods and a newer computer-based approach are described next.[16]

Checklists On a checklist appraisal, the manager simply answers yes or no to a series of questions about an employee's performance. Examples of checklist questions are provided in Exhibit 8-1. Items on the list can then be scored or reviewed to determine

---

EXHIBIT 8-1 Example Checklist Appraisal Questions

	Yes	No
1. Does the employee willingly cooperate with others in completing work assignments?	_____	_____
2. Does the employee have adequate job knowledge to perform duties in a satisfactory manner?	_____	_____
3. In terms of quality, is the employee's work acceptable?	_____	_____
4. Does the employee meet deadlines for the completion of work assignments?	_____	_____
5. Does the employee's record indicate unexcused absences?	_____	_____
6. Does the employee follow safety rules and regulations?	_____	_____

SOURCE: S. E. Catt and D. S. Miller, *Supervision: Working with People*, 2d ed. (Homewood, IL: Richard D. Irwin, 1991) 374. © Irwin Co. Reprinted by permission of the McGraw-Hill Companies.

a rating for the employee's appraisal. Although checklists are easy to complete, they require a great deal of thought and analysis to be sure that meaningful questions are included for each job. They usually do not provide ways to adjust the answers for special circumstances that may affect performance.[17] To make up for this weakness, checklists are sometimes combined with essays.

Written Essays   The written essay requires no complex forms or extensive training to complete. Based on remembered observations, the appraiser writes a narrative describing an employee's past performance, strengths, weaknesses, potential, and suggestions for improvement—but the results often reflect the ability of the writer. The quality of the appraisal may be determined as much by the evaluator's memory, perception, and writing skill as by the employee's actual level of performance. Essay appraisals are often used to supplement checklist questionnaire appraisals to allow for a description and explanation of ratings.

Critical Incidents   With this method, the appraiser writes down anecdotes that describe what the employee did that was especially effective or ineffective. A list of critical incidents provides a set of examples to show the employee specific behaviors that are desirable and those that call for improvement. The key here is that only specific behaviors, not personality traits, are cited. A drawback is that the definition of a critical incident is unclear and may be interpreted differently by different managers. Also, managers need to keep a log of incidents, which is a lot of work, for incidents that may occur at inconvenient times.

Graphic Rating Scales   In this commonly used method, a set of performance factors, such as quantity and quality of work, depth of knowledge, cooperation, loyalty, attendance, honesty, and initiative, are listed. The appraiser then goes down the list and rates each on incremental scales. The scales typically specify five levels, so a factor such as *job knowledge* might be rated from 1 ("poorly informed about work duties") to 5 ("has complete mastery of all phases of the job").

Though they don't provide the depth of information that essays or critical incidents do, graphic rating scales are easy to use and less time-consuming to develop and administer. They also allow for quantitative analysis and comparison. On the other hand, the ratings are subjective so that what one manager deems "excellent" may be only "average" to another. Some of these problems can be overcome by providing descriptions of excellent or poor behaviors in each area. An example of a graphic rating scale is provided in Exhibit 8-2.

Behaviorally Anchored Rating Scales   This approach combines major elements from the critical incident and graphic rating scale approaches. The appraiser rates the employees on items along a continuum, but the points are examples of actual behavior on the given job rather than general descriptions or traits. Examples of job-related behavior and performance dimensions are found by asking participants to give specific illustrations of effective and ineffective behavior regarding each performance dimension. These behavioral examples are then translated into a set of performance dimensions, each dimension having varying levels of performance. The results of this process are behavioral descriptions, such as "anticipates, plans, executes, solves immediate problems," "carries out orders," and "handles emergency situations." An example of a behaviorally anchored rating scale is illustrated in Exhibit 8-3.

Multiperson Comparisons   With this method, a specific individual's performance is evaluated against the performance of one or more others. It is a relative rather than an absolute measuring device. The three most popular comparisons are group order ranking, individual ranking, and paired comparisons.

EXHIBIT 8-2 Sample Graphic Rating Scale

Name _____ Dept. _____ Date _____

		Outstanding	Good	Satisfactory	Fair	Unsatisfactory
Quantity of work	Volume of acceptable work under normal conditions Comments:	[ ]	[ ]	[ ]	[ ]	[ ]
Quality of work	Thoroughness, neatness, and accuracy of work Comments:	[ ]	[ ]	[ ]	[ ]	[ ]
Knowledge of job	Clear understanding of the facts or factors pertinent to the job Comments:	[ ]	[ ]	[ ]	[ ]	[ ]
Personal qualities	Personality, appearance, sociability, leadership, integrity Comments:	[ ]	[ ]	[ ]	[ ]	[ ]
Cooperation	Ability and willingness to work with associates, supervisors, and subordinates toward common goals Comments:	[ ]	[ ]	[ ]	[ ]	[ ]
Dependability	Conscientious, thorough, accurate, reliable with respect to attendance, lunch periods, reliefs, etc. Comments:	[ ]	[ ]	[ ]	[ ]	[ ]
Initiative	Earnestness in seeking increased responsibilities, self-starting, unafraid to proceed alone Comments:	[ ]	[ ]	[ ]	[ ]	[ ]

SOURCE: J. M. Ivancevich, *Human Resource Management: Foundations of Personnel*, 7th ed. (New York: Irwin/McGraw-Hill, 1998) 272. © Irwin Co. Reprinted by permission of the McGraw-Hill Companies.

EXHIBIT 8-3   Sample Behaviorally Anchored Rating Scale (BARS)

Engineer's Name: _____

9 _____   This engineer applies a full range of technical skills and can be expected to perform all assignments in an excellent manner.

8 _____

7 _____   This engineer is able to apply in most situations a good range of technical skills and can be expected to perform most assignments well.

6 _____

5 _____   This engineer is able to apply some technical skills and can be expected to adequately complete most assignments.

4 _____

3 _____   This engineer has difficulty applying technical skills and can be expected to bring in most projects late.

2 _____

1 _____   This engineer is confused about using technical skills and can be expected to disrupt the completion of work because of this deficiency.

SOURCE: J. M. Ivancevich, *Human Resource Management: Foundations of Personnel,* 7th ed. (New York: Irwin/McGraw-Hill, 1998) 277. © Irwin Co. Reprinted by permission of the McGraw-Hill Companies.

The **group order ranking** requires the appraiser to place employees into a particular classification, such as top one-fifth or second one-fifth. This method is often used in recommending students to graduate schools. Appraisers are asked whether the student ranks in the top 5 percent of the class, the next 5 percent, the next 15 percent, and so forth. When managers use this method to appraise employees, they deal with all their employees. Therefore, a forced distribution will be created that does not consider the degree of difference between employees in each category. For example, if a rater has 20 employees, only 4 can be in the top fifth and, of course, 4 must also be relegated to the bottom fifth.

The **individual ranking** approach rank-orders employees from best to worst. If the manager is required to appraise 30 employees, this approach assumes that the difference between the first and second employee is the same as that between the twenty-first and twenty-second. Even though some of the employees may be closely grouped, this approach allows for no ties. The result is a clear ordering of employees, from the highest performer down to the lowest, but no indication of the degree of difference is provided.

The **paired comparison** approach compares each employee with every other employee and rates each as either the superior or the weaker member of the pair. After all paired comparisons are made, each employee is assigned a summary ranking based on the number of superior scores he or she achieved. This approach ensures that each employee is compared against every other, but it can obviously become unwieldy when many employees are being compared.

Multiperson comparisons can be combined with one of the other methods to blend the best from both absolute and relative standards. For example, a college might use the graphic rating scale and the individual ranking method to provide more accurate information about its students' performance. Each student's relative rank in the class could be noted next to an absolute grade of A, B, C, D, or F. A prospective employer or graduate school could then look at two students who each got a B in their different financial accounting courses and draw considerably different conclusions about each because next to one grade it says "ranked fourth out of 26," whereas next to the other it says "ranked seventeenth out of 30." Obviously, the latter instructor gives out a lot more high grades!

Computer-Managed Appraisals   If you are not comfortable applying one of the rating methods already described, you might want to look into using a computer program to assist you. One program, called *Performance Now!*, features a series of 30 categories for rating employees ranging from such things as job quality to overall cleanliness. If rating an employee on a category such as job quality, for example, the manager would simply click the appropriate icon and various headings, such as "Strives to Achieve Goals" and "Meets Deadlines," appear. Employees can then be rated in each subcategory on a scale of 1 to 5. The program automatically summarizes the ratings in a descriptive paragraph, which can be edited further by the manager. A sample summary generated by the program might read, "Bob produces more work than expected. He always meets his deadlines and demonstrates a strong commitment to increasing productivity and achieving his goals." An added bonus is that if managers write something inappropriate, the program alerts them to their mistake, making them aware of important policy distinctions. For example, if a manager writes, "The employee is too young for the position," a box appears on the screen with a warning not to confuse experience with age. When managers aren't clear about what a term means, they can click on an advice section and get additional information.[18]

Things to Watch Out for When Rating Performance[19]

Several common potential errors can occur when rating performance and they can invalidate the accuracy of an appraisal. They include rushing, bias, leniency, central tendency, recency emphasis, focusing on activities, and the halo effect. **Bias** occurs when managers develop feelings about employees based on work-related interactions that may have little to do with their performance. These feelings can be negative, positive, or neutral, and they may be related to personality, race, religion, or other nonwork-related factors. Feelings should be separated from objective assessments when rating work performance.

Managers with positive feelings (bias) toward certain employees tend to be lenient when rating their performance. **Leniency** is the grouping of ratings at the positive end of the performance scale instead of spreading them throughout the scale. Consequently, employees are rated higher than actual performance warrants.[20]

When managers have neutral feelings about employees, they exhibit a central tendency when rating their performance. **Central tendency** occurs when performance appraisal statistics indicate that most employees are evaluated as doing average or above-average work, even though in actuality a distribution is present because all employees do not perform the same all the time on specific tasks.[21]

The **recency emphasis** occurs when performance evaluations are based on most recent work performed. It sometimes occurs because of the difficulty in remembering things that happened six months to a year ago versus work performed one or two months before evaluation. It also can occur when a manager is **rushing** the appraisal process because of a heavy workload or lack of sufficient time. Rushing also can make managers susceptible to **focusing on activities,** which occurs when employees are rated on how busy they appear versus how well they perform in achieving results.

The next rating error occurs when managers allow a single prominent characteristic of an employee to influence their judgment on all other items in the performance appraisal. This problem often results in the employee receiving approximately the same rating on every item.[22] It can go either way, however. The **halo effect** often occurs when a manager has positive feelings about an employee, causing him or her to rate the employee positively on all criteria because of outstanding performance in one specific area, which has impressed the manager.[23] On the other hand, if the manager feels negative about an employee, the **horns effect** may occur. In this case, a manager rates an employee low on all criteria, based on unfavorable performance on only one.[24]

Bias, leniency, central tendency, recency, and activity errors make it difficult to separate superior from inferior performers. These errors also make it difficult to compare ratings from different managers. For example, it is possible for a good performer who is evaluated by a manager with a negative bias, or who is committing central tendency errors, to receive a lower rating than a poor performer who is rated by a manager with a positive bias or one who is committing leniency errors.[25]

Rushing, recency emphasis, personal biases, and halo or horns effects can also cause errors in performance appraisals. Rushed managers with biases tend to look for employee behaviors that conform to their halo or horns first impressions of employees, and they do not take the time to seriously consider contradictory evidence. Also, as we all know, appearance, social status, dress, race, and sex influence many performance appraisals, even though these factors are not relevant.[26]

Taking Managerial Action

Managers can choose among three courses of action in this final step of the control process: (1) They can do nothing; (2) they can correct the actual performance; or (3) they can revise the standard. Doing nothing is not really a feasible alternative if performance is not acceptable, so let's look more closely at the latter two options.

Correct Actual Performance   If the source of variation from anticipated results is deficient performance, managers will want to take corrective action. Examples of such corrective action include a change in work methods, reorganization of work groups, or providing employees with training. First you will want to determine how and why performance has deviated. This analysis will take more time, but it will increase the chances that you can permanently correct significant variances between standard and actual performance, rather than just provide a Band-Aid for a problem what will reemerge later.

Revise the Standard   Sometimes, the variance is a result of an unrealistic standard—that is, the goal may be too high or too low. In such cases, it is the standard that needs corrective attention, not the performance. A more troublesome problem is the revising of a performance standard downward. If an employee falls significantly short of reaching the target, the natural response is to shift the blame for the variance to the standard. Students, for example, who make a low grade on a test often attack the grade cutoff points as too high. Rather than accept the fact that their performance was inadequate, students argue that the standards are unreasonable. Similarly, salespeople who fail to meet their monthly quota may attribute the failure to an unrealistic quota. It may be true that standards are too high, resulting in a significant variance and acting to demotivate those employees being assessed against it. Keep in mind, however, that if employees or managers do not meet the standard, the first thing they are likely to attack is the standard itself. If you believe the standard is realistic, hold your ground. Explain your position, reaffirm to the employee that you expect future performance to improve, and then take the necessary corrective action to turn that expectation into reality.

Performance Appraisal as a Means of Providing Constructive Feedback

Many managers are reluctant to give performance feedback. In fact, unless pressured by organizational policies and controls, a large number of managers are likely to ignore this responsibility.[27] At least three reasons can be cited for this avoidance behavior.[28] First, managers are often uncomfortable discussing performance weaknesses with employees. Given that almost every employee could stand to improve in some areas, managers fear a confrontation when presenting negative feedback. Second, many employees tend to become defensive when their weaknesses are pointed out. Instead of accepting the feedback as constructive and a basis for improving performance, some employees challenge the evaluation by criticizing the manager or redirecting blame to someone else. Finally, employees tend to have an inflated assessment of their own performance. Statistically speaking, half of all employees must be below-average performers, but the evidence indicates that the average employee's estimate of his or her own performance level generally falls around the 75th percentile.[29] Even when managers are providing "good news," employees are likely to perceive it as "not good enough!"

In spite of managers' reluctance to give performance feedback, their employees still need it, so the solution is to train managers in how to conduct constructive feedback sessions. An effective review—one in which the employee perceives the appraisal as fair, the manager as sincere, and the climate as constructive—can result in the employee's leaving the interview with a positive attitude, with knowledge about the performance areas in which he or she needs to improve, and motivated to correct the deficiencies.[30] These things are more likely to happen if the performance review is designed more as a counseling activity than a judgment process. How do you conduct an effective performance appraisal feedback interview?

The Value of Feedback in a Performance Appraisal

An important reason to be skilled at giving feedback in a performance interview is because it can increase employee performance in a number of ways.[31]

First, feedback can induce a person who previously had no goals to set some. And, as was demonstrated in the previous chapter, goals act as motivators to higher performance. Second, where goals exist, feedback tells people how well they are progressing toward those goals. To the degree that the feedback is favorable, it acts as a positive reinforcer. Third, if the feedback indicates inadequate performance, this knowledge may result in increased effort. Further, the content of the feedback can suggest ways—other than exerting more effort—to improve performance. Fourth, feedback often induces people to raise their goal sights after attaining a previous goal. Finally, providing feedback to employees conveys that others care how they are doing. So feedback is an indirect form of recognition that can motivate people to higher levels of performance.[32]

Positive Versus Negative Feedback

Just as managers treat positive and negative feedback differently, so too, do recipients. Positive feedback is more readily and accurately perceived than negative feedback. Further, while positive feedback is almost always accepted, the negative variety often meets resistance.[33] Why? The logical answer seems to be that people want to hear good news and block out the bad. Positive feedback fits what most people wish to hear and already believe about themselves. As a result, you may need to adjust your style accordingly.

Does this tendency mean you should avoid giving negative feedback? No! What it means is that you need to be aware of potential resistance and learn to use negative feedback in situations where it is most likely to be accepted.[34] What are those situations? Research indicates that negative feedback is most likely to be accepted when it comes from a credible source or if it is objective in form. Subjective impressions carry weight only when they come from a person with high status and credibility.[35] Negative feedback that is supported by hard data or specific examples has a better chance of being accepted than subjective evaluations.

The Performance Appraisal Feedback Interview Process

As a counseling activity, the performance appraisal identifies areas where employee growth and development are needed.[36] The feedback interview is the last step in the performance appraisal process. It follows the establishment of performance standards, the gathering of performance data, and actually rating performance. During the performance interview, the ratings are shared with the employee in an effort to clarify any personnel decisions that have been made based upon them, and to help the employee learn and develop. Following are some guidelines for conducting a successful performance appraisal interview.

The performance appraisal interview can be broken down into four stages. It begins with *preparation*, followed by the *opening*, a period of *questioning and discussion*, and a *conclusion*. During the last three stages of the performance review interview, a problem-solving approach where the manager acts as a partner and works jointly with the subordinate to develop the employee's performance is recommended.[37] To use this format, you need to practice your communication skills, especially effective listening, during these stages of the performance review interview.

Preparation   Schedule the appraisal interview in advance and be prepared. Simply calling in an employee and giving feedback that is not well organized serves little purpose for you or your employee. For a performance review interview to be effective, you should plan ahead.[38] Review the employee's job description. Go over your rating sheet. Identify the issues you wish to address and have specific examples to reinforce what you are saying. Have you carefully considered the employee's strengths as well as weaknesses? Can you substantiate, with specific examples, all points of praise and criticism? Given your past experiences with the employee, what problems, if any, do you anticipate popping up in the review? How do you plan to react to these problems? Once you have worked out these kinds of issues, you should schedule a specific time and place for the review and give the employee ample advance notice. Make sure that what you do is done in private and can be completed without interruptions. You may need to close your office door, have your phone calls held, and so on.

Opening   Put the employee at ease. The performance review can be a traumatic experience for the best of employees. People don't like to hear their work criticized. Add the fact that people tend to overrate themselves—approximately 60 percent place their own performance in the top 10 percent[39]—and you have the ingredients for tension and confrontation. Because the employee is apt to be nervous, be supportive and understanding.

Be sure that the employee understands the purpose of the appraisal interview. Employees are often concerned about whether the results of the appraisal interview will be used for personnel decisions or to promote their growth and development.[40] In the problem-solving approach, the interview provides recognition for things the employee is doing well and an opportunity to discuss any job-related problems. Any uncertainty the employee may have about what will transpire during the review and the resulting consequences should be clarified at the start.[41]

Questioning and Discussion   Keep it goal-oriented. Feedback should not be given primarily to "dump" or "unload" pent up feelings on the recipient.[42] If you have to say something negative, make sure it is directed toward the *recipient's* goals. Keep in mind who your feedback is designed to help. If it is you, just to get something off your chest, for example, it is probably a good idea just to keep these statements to yourself. This kind of "feedback" undermines your credibility and lessens the credibility and influence of future feedback.

Make it well-timed. Feedback is most meaningful to a recipient if the interval between his or her behavior and the receipt of feedback about that behavior is short. To illustrate, a football player who makes a mistake during a game is more likely to respond to his coach's suggestions for improvement right after the mistake, immediately following the game, or during the review of that game's films a few days later, rather than feedback provided by the coach several months later. If you have to spend time recreating a situation and refreshing someone's memory of it, the feedback you are providing is likely to be ineffective.[43] Moreover, if you are particularly concerned with changing behavior, delays providing feedback on the undesirable actions lessen the likelihood that the feedback will be effective in bringing about the desired change.[44] Of course, making feedback prompt merely for the sake of promptness can backfire if you have insufficient information, if you are angry, or if you are otherwise emotionally upset. In such instances, *well-timed* may mean "somewhat delayed."

Minimize threats. Create a helpful and constructive climate.[45] Try to maximize encouragement and support, while minimizing threats.[46] Little value comes from reminding a person of some shortcoming over which he or she has no control. Negative feedback should be directed toward work-related behavior that the employee can do something about.[47] For example, to criticize an employee who is late because he forgot to set his alarm is valid. To criticize the same employee for being late when the subway he takes to work every day had a power failure, trapping him underground for half an hour, is not valid. He could do nothing to correct what happened. Additionally, when negative feedback is given concerning something that is controllable by the recipient, it may be a good idea to indicate specifically what can be done to improve the situation. This tactic takes some of the sting out of the criticism and offers guidance to recipients who understand the problem but do not know how to resolve it.

Obtain employee participation. The more employees talk, the more satisfied they will be with the appraisal.[48] So, let employees do the majority of the talking. Get the employee's perceptions of what you are saying, especially if you are addressing a problem. Of course, you are not looking for excuses. But you need to be empathetic to the employee. Get his or her side. Maybe something has contributed to the issue. Letting the employee speak involves the individual and just might add information you were unaware of.

Encourage the employee to engage in self-evaluation. If the climate is supportive, employees may openly acknowledge performance problems you have identified, thus eliminating your need to raise them. They may even offer viable solutions to these problems.

Criticize performance but not the person. Feedback, particularly the negative kind, should be descriptive rather than judgmental or evaluative.[49] If something needs to be criticized, direct the criticism at specific job-related behaviors that negatively affect the employee's performance.[50] It is the person's performance that is unsatisfactory, not the individual person. No matter how upset you are, keep the feedback job-related and never criticize someone personally because of an inappropriate action. Telling people they are "stupid," "incompetent," or the like is almost always counterproductive. It provokes such an emotional reaction that the performance deviation itself is apt to be overlooked. When you are criticizing, remember that you are censuring a job-related behavior, not the person. You may be tempted to tell someone he or she is "rude and insensitive" (which may well be true); however, such a comment is hardly impersonal. Better to say something like, "You interrupted me three times with questions that were not urgent when you knew I was talking long distance to a customer in Scotland."

Focus on specific behaviors. Feedback should be specific rather than general.[51] General statements are vague and provide little useful information, especially if you are attempting to "correct" a problem. Document your employee's performance ratings with specific examples.[52] Avoid statements such as "You have a bad attitude" or "I'm really impressed with the good job you did." They are vague, and while they provide information, they don't tell the recipient enough to correct the "bad attitude" or on *what basis* you concluded that a "good job" had been done. You can generate more positive results from saying something like, "Jack, you called yesterday to say that you would have to miss the project proposal meeting because you did not have time to read the preliminary report, and today you are leaving work three hours early for your daughter's soccer game. I am concerned about your commitment and involvement to completing the new project proposal on time. Is there anything we need to discuss about it?"

Statements that focus on specific behaviors tell the recipient *why* you are being critical or complimentary. These supporting statements add credibility to your ratings and help employees to better understand what you mean by "good" and "bad." Tell your employee how you came to your "conclusion" on his or her performance. Hard data help your employees to identify with specific behaviors.

When criticizing, soften the tone but not the message. If criticism is necessary, do not water down the message, do not dance around the issue, and certainly do not avoid discussing a problem in the hope that it will just go away. State your criticism thoughtfully and show concern for the employee's feelings, but do not soften the message. Criticism is criticism, even if it is constructive. When you try to sell it as something else, you are liable to create ambiguity and misunderstanding.

Do not exaggerate. Don't make extreme statements in order to make a point. If an employee has been late for four out of five recent meetings, do not say, "You are *always* late to meetings." Avoid absolutes such as *always* or *never*. Such terms encourage defensiveness and undermine your credibility. An employee only has to introduce one exception to your "always" or "never" statement to destroy the entire statement's validity.

Give positive as well as negative feedback. Avoid turning the performance review into a totally negative feedback session.[53] Also, identify the things that were done correctly and reinforce them. State what was done well and why it deserves recognition.

Tailor the feedback to fit the person. Take into consideration the person to whom the feedback is directed. You should consider the recipient's past performance and your estimate of his or her future potential in designing the frequency, amount, and content of performance feedback.[54] For high performers with potential for growth, feedback should be frequent enough to prod them into taking corrective action, but not so frequent that it is experienced as controlling and saps their initiative. For adequate performers who have settled into their jobs and have limited potential for advancement, little feedback is needed because they have displayed reliable and steady behavior in the past, know their tasks, and realize what needs to be done. For poor performers—that is, people who will need to be removed from their jobs if their performance doesn't improve—feedback should be frequent and specific, and the connection between acting on the feedback and negative sanctions such as being laid off or fired should be made explicit.

Conclusion   Ensure understanding. To be effective your feedback should be concise and complete enough so that the recipient clearly and fully understands it.[55] Consistent with the discussion of listening techniques in Chapter 3, you should have the recipient rephrase the content of your feedback to see whether it fully captures the meaning you intended. As the review nears its conclusion, encourage the employee to summarize the discussion that has taken place.[56] This process gives your subordinate an opportunity to put the entire review into perspective. It will also tell you whether you have succeeded in clearly communicating your evaluation.

Detail a future plan of action. In areas of performance inadequacies, the final part of the review should be devoted to helping the employee draft a detailed, step-by-step plan to improve the situation.[57] This plan includes what has to be done, when, and how you will monitor the activities. Offer whatever assistance you can to help the employee.

Your role should be supportive: "What can I do to provide assistance?" Do you need to make yourself more available to answer questions? Do you need to give the employee more freedom or responsibility? Would securing funds to send the employee to professional meetings or training programs help?[58] It must be made clear that it is the employee, not you, who has to make the corrections. On the other hand, do not forget that good performance should be reinforced, and that new performance goals need to be set even for exceptional employees. Some additional guidelines for improving performance appraisal interviews are provided in Exhibit 8-4.

Team Performance Appraisals

Performance appraisal concepts have been almost exclusively developed with only individual employees in mind. This fact reflects the historical belief that individuals are the core building blocks on which organizations are built. But more and more organizations are restructuring themselves around teams. How should organizations using teams appraise performance? Four suggestions are provided for designing a system that supports and improves the performance of teams.[59]

EXHIBIT 8-4   Guidelines for Improving Performance Appraisal Interviews

The following guidelines can provide a framework for improving employee performance review feedback evaluations.

- Review evaluations written by other experienced supervisors to see what works and what doesn't.
- Keep notes throughout the evaluation period. Do not rely on recall at the end of the session.
- Seek input from other observers when appropriate.
- Base written evaluations on multiple, firsthand observations.
- Know what you are looking for. Evaluate the right things. Concentrate exclusively on factors directly related to job performance.
- Don't include rumors, allegations, or guesswork as part of your written evaluations.
- Be complete. Include the good, the bad, and the ugly.
- Do not be afraid to criticize. Do not forget to praise.
- Focus on improvement. Use the evaluation to set goals for better performance.
- Never use an evaluation as a threat or as punishment.
- Supplement periodic written evaluations with frequent verbal feedback. Negative written evaluation should not come as a surprise.
- Do not put anything in writing that you would not say to the employee in person.
- Do not beat around the bush or sugarcoat needed criticism. Say what has to be said and move on.
- If checklists are part of the evaluation, be sure written comments are consistent with the items checked.
- Be as specific as possible. Use examples. Glittering generalities don't help much in targeting action or improvement plans.
- Relate evaluations to previous reviews. Are things better? Worse? The same?
- Allow plenty of time to prepare evaluations properly. Do not work under pressure.
- Avoid completing an evaluation when you are angry or frustrated.
- Choose words carefully. The goal is clarity.
- Let the evaluation "cool" overnight before distributing it.
- Be willing to change an evaluation if new information becomes available.

SOURCE: R. D. Ramsey, "How to Write Better Employee Evaluations," *Supervision* (June 1998): 5ff. Reprinted by permission. © National Research Bureau, P.O. Box 1, Burlington, IA 52601–0001.

1. ***Tie the team's results to the organization's goals.***   It is important to find measurements that apply to important goals that the team is supposed to accomplish.
2. ***Begin with the team's customers and the work process the team follows to satisfy its needs.***   The final product the customer receives can be appraised in terms of the customer's requirements. The transactions between teams can be appraised on the basis of delivery and quality, and the process steps on the basis of waste and cycle time.
3. ***Measure both team and individual performance.***   Define the roles of each team member in terms of accomplishments that support the team's work process. Then assess each member's contribution and the team's overall performance.
4. ***Train the team to create its own measures.***   Having the team define its objectives and those of each member ensures that every member understands his or her role on the team and helps the team develop into a more cohesive unit.

Another approach to team performance evaluation is to have teams evaluate themselves. At Con-Way Transportation Services, teams engage in a process called the team improvement review, where members ask themselves questions such as, "What are we doing that is working? What are we doing that is not working? How can we change that?" As in an individual performance appraisal process, teams start by creating an agreement about how to do things, which includes a definition of excellent performance against which to measure team results. The appraisal process itself has three parts. First, it separates feedback sessions from salary reviews, to take the pressure off employees reluctant to affect coworkers' salaries. Second, feedback is given in a safe environment, with a professional facilitator, but no management personnel present. Finally, the team undergoes a formal feedback process.

Team reviews take place about every three months, with preparation starting a week before when the members rate the team's performance on 31 criteria, using a scale of 1 to 5. During the review, team performance is discussed and individual performance is covered in the context of the team. Each person writes down his or her own strengths and "things to work on," which are passed around the room so everyone can comment on everyone else's list.[60] More information on team performance will be covered in Chapter 14, Creating High-Performance Teams.

CONCEPT QUIZ

Complete the following true-false quiz by circling the correct answer. Answers are at the end of the quiz. After marking your answers, remember to go back and check your understanding of any answers you missed.

True or False   1. One of the most important parts of performance appraisal starts before the interview begins.

True or False   2. Performance appraisals become control devices because employees tend to behave in ways to look good on the criteria by which they will be appraised.

True or False   3. Specific objectives previously set with employees should be used as standards against which to measure progress.

True or False   4. Graphic rating scales use a list of critical incidents to provide examples to show the employee specific behaviors that are desirable and those that call for improvement.

True or False   5. Sometimes it is the standard that needs corrective attention, not the performance.

True or False	6. Most employees estimate their own performance level considerably higher than managers do.
True or False	7. Feedback is an indirect form of recognition that can motivate people to higher levels of performance.
True or False	8. Negative feedback is most likely to be accepted when it comes from a distant source such as the human resource department and is in subjective form.
True or False	9. Feedback is most meaningful if a short interval separates the behavior and the receipt of feedback about that behavior.
True or False	10. The most productive feedback is judgmental and evaluative.

Answers.   (1) True; (2) True; (3) True; (4) False; (5) True; (6) True; (7) True; (8) False; (9) True; (10) False

BEHAVIORAL CHECKLIST

The following skills are important to effective performance evaluation. Use them when evaluating your performance evaluation skills and those of others.

The Effective Performance Appraiser

- Uses specific objectives previously set with employees as standards to measure progress against.
- Puts the employee at ease and explains the purpose of the feedback interview.
- Encourages and supports while minimizing threats.
- Criticizes performance, not the person, when giving negative feedback.
- Obtains employee participation and encourages self-evaluation.
- Uses specific examples to support ratings.
- Has the employee summarize the feedback to ensure understanding.
- Creates a future plan of development with the person receiving the feedback.

> **Attention!**
> Do not read the following until assigned to do so by your instructor.

MODELING EXERCISE

Research has identified seven performance dimensions to the college instructor's job: instructor knowledge, testing procedures, student-teacher relations, organizational skills, communication skills, subject relevance, and utility of assignments.[61] These dimensions are included on the performance appraisal rating sheet at the end of this exercise.

Instructions.   A class leader is to be selected (either a volunteer or someone chosen by the instructor). The class leader will preside over a performance appraisal feedback session for the instructor.

The instructor will leave the room for 15 minutes. During this time the class members develop constructive feedback for the class leader to provide to the instructor on each performance dimension. The class leader should take notes from the class input to prepare his or her feedback. (No written documentation is required, however.)

After the 15-minute period is up, the class leader should invite the instructor back into the classroom and begin the feedback session. The class leader role-plays the performance feedback provider and the instructor plays him or herself.

Important Note:
Your instructor understands that this session is only an exercise and is prepared to accept criticism (and, of course, any praise you may want to convey). Your instructor also recognizes that the class leader's feedback is actually a composite of many students' input. So be open and honest in your feedback and make the session valuable for the instructor's development.

Time. Not to exceed 15 minutes.

Instructor Performance Appraisal Rating Form

Rate your instructor for this course for each of the following performance dimensions by entering the appropriate grade. (You can use plus and minus.) Provide explanatory feedback after your rating.

A	B	C	D
Way above average	*Average*	*Passing but below average*	*Way below average, not passing*

_____ Instructor knowledge

_____ Testing procedures

_____ Student-teacher relations

_____ Organizational skills

_____ Communication skills

_____ Subject relevance

_____ Utility of assignments

OBSERVER'S RATING SHEET

On completion of the exercise, evaluate the performance appraisal feedback skills of the class member providing the feedback to the professor. Rate the feedback provider between 1 and 5 using the following scale. Write concrete examples in the space for comments below each criteria skill to use in explaining your feedback.

1	*2*	*3*	*4*	*5*
Unsatisfactory	*Weak*	*Adequate*	*Good*	*Outstanding*

_____ Used specific objectives previously set with employees as standards to measure progress against.

_____ Put the employee at ease and explained the purpose of the feedback interview.

_____ Encouraged and supported while minimizing threats.

_____ Criticized performance, not the person, when giving negative feedback.

_____ Obtained employee participation and encouraged self-evaluation.

_____ Used specific examples to support ratings.

_____ Had the professor summarize the feedback to ensure understanding.

_____ Created a future plan of development with the person receiving the feedback.

GROUP EXERCISES

Three different types of group exercises are presented here. First is a performance appraisal case for you to practice your analysis and action planning skills. Second is an opportunity to practice, observe, and receive feedback in a performance appraisal role-play. Third is a peer review where you will both give and receive feedback on your own and your classmates' actual performance in this class.

Group Exercise 1: Case Analysis: Conducting a Performance Appraisal[62]

Plant manager Paul Dorn wondered why his boss, Leonard Hech, had sent for him. Paul thought Leonard had been tough on him lately; he was slightly uneasy at being asked to come to Leonard's office at a time when such meetings were unusual. "Close the door and sit down, Paul," invited Leonard. "I've been wanting to talk to you." After preliminary conversation, Leonard said that because Paul's latest project had been finished, he would receive the raise he had been promised on its completion.

Leonard went on to say that because it was time for Paul's performance appraisal, they might as well do that now. Leonard explained that the performance appraisal was based on four criteria: (1) the amount of high-quality merchandise manufactured and shipped on time, (2) the quality of relationships with plant employees and peers, (3) progress in maintaining employee safety and health, and (4) reaction to demands of top management. The first criterion had a relative importance of 40 percent; the rest had a weight of 20 percent each.

On the first item, Paul received an excellent rating. Shipments were at an all-time high, quality was good, and few shipments had arrived late. On the second item, Paul also was rated as excellent. Leonard said plant employees and peers related well to Paul, labor relations were excellent, and no major grievances had arisen since Paul had become plant manager.

However, on attention to matters of employee safety and health, the evaluation was below average. His boss stated that no matter how much he bugged Paul about improving housekeeping in the plant, he never seemed to produce results. Leonard also rated Paul below average on meeting demands from top management. He explained that Paul always answered yes to any request and then disregarded it, going about his business as if nothing had happened.

Seemingly surprised at the comments, Paul agreed that perhaps Leonard was right and that he should do a better job on these matters. Smiling as he left, he thanked Leonard for the raise and the frank appraisal.

As weeks went by, Leonard noticed little change in Paul. He reviewed the situation with an associate. "It's frustrating. In this time of rapid growth, we must make constant changes in work methods. Paul agrees but can't seem to make people break their habits and adopt more efficient ones. I find myself riding him hard these days, but he just calmly takes it. He's well liked by everyone. But somehow, he's got to care about safety and housekeeping in the plant. And when higher management makes demands he can't meet, he's got to say, 'I can't do that and do all the other things you want, too.' Now he has dozens of unfinished jobs because he refuses to say no."

As he talked, Leonard remembered something Paul had told him in confidence once. "I take Valium for a physical condition I have. When I don't take it, I get symptoms similar to a heart attack—but I only take half as much as the doctor prescribed." Now, Leonard thought, I'm really in a spot. If the Valium is what is making him so lackadaisical, I can't endanger his health by asking him to quit taking it. And I certainly can't fire him. Yet, as things stand, he really can't implement all the changes we need to fulfill our goals for the next two years.

QUESTIONS FOR DISCUSSION

1. Do you think a raise was justified in Paul's situation? Explain.
2. What could have been done differently in the performance appraisal session?
3. What can be done now to change the situation?

Group Exercise 2: Role-Play: A Difficult Performance Appraisal[63]

You have two responsibilities as a participant in a role-play. First, read *only* the background information on the exercise and *your own* role. Reading your counterpart's role will lessen the effectiveness of the exercise. Second, get into the character. Role-playing is acting. The role description establishes your character. Follow the guidelines it establishes. Do not change or omit the facts you are given. If you are an observer in an exercise, you should read everything pertaining to the role-play and review the Observer's Rating Sheet.

Actors.

Dana (head of personnel)

Blair (employee relations manager)

Dana's Role   You are head of personnel for a manufacturing firm. You are well thought of in the firm and have excellent rapport with your boss, the vice president for administration. Blair is your employee relations manager. You know that Blair is reasonably good at her job, but you also know that Blair believes herself to be "outstanding," which is not true. Blair is scheduled to have a meeting with you in five minutes, and you would like to establish clearer communication, as well as convince Blair to adopt a less grandiose self-image.

You believe that Blair is on the right track, but it will take her about two years to reach the stage at which she can be promoted. As to Blair's performance, you have received some good reports, as well as *three* letters of complaint. Blair prepared four research reports that you considered to be above average, but to keep her motivated and happy, you exaggerated and said they were "excellent." Maybe that was a mistake.

You are worried about the impact on other employees, whose performance is nearly as good as Blair's, if Blair is promoted. So you plan to set meaningful targets for Blair this year, evaluate her performance one or two years from now, and then give the promotion if it is deserved.

Blair's Role   You are the employee relations manager in a manufacturing firm. Dana is your boss and her title is head of personnel. You know that you are one of the best performers in your department, and may even be the best. However, you were not promoted last year, even though you expected to be, so you would like to be promoted this year.

You expect your boss to raise some obstacles to your promotion. Dana is bound to mention three letters of complaint against you, for instance. Dana seems to point out only your errors. Up front, you plan to remind Dana that you wrote four research reports that Dana herself said were *excellent*. If Dana tries to delay your promotion unnecessarily, you plan to confront her and, if necessary, take the issue to Dana's boss, the vice president for administration. You think that in many instances you were rated better on performance than your colleagues in the department. You have decided that you will press your point of view firmly, but also rationally, in a professional manner.

Time.   Not to exceed 15 minutes.

OBSERVER'S RATING SHEET

On completion of the exercise, evaluate the performance appraisal feedback skills of the class member playing Dana, head of personnel. Rate Dana's skills as a performance appraisal feedback provider between 1 and 5 using the following scale. Write concrete examples in the space for comments below each criteria skill to use in explaining your feedback.

1	2	3	4	5
Unsatisfactory	*Weak*	*Adequate*	*Good*	*Outstanding*

_____ Used specific objectives previously set with employees as standards to measure progress against.

_____ Put the employee at ease and explained the purpose of the feedback interview.

_____ Encouraged and supported while minimizing threats.

_____ Criticized performance, not the person, when giving negative feedback.

_____ Obtained employee participation and encouraged self-evaluation.

_____ Used specific examples to support ratings.

_____ Had the employee summarize the feedback to ensure understanding.

_____ Created a future plan of development with the person receiving the feedback.

Group Exercise 3: Peer Review of Class Members' Performance

Purpose.   To practice giving and receiving performance feedback.

Instructions.

Step 1:   Form groups of five to seven students who have worked together in several class exercises. If permanent learning groups have already been formed, use them.

Step 2:   Put your name, followed by the words *Self-Appraisal*, on a piece of paper and draw a vertical line down the center to form two columns. Write and underline the word *Strengths* at the top of the left column. Write and underline the words *Things to Work On* at the top of the right column. Then turn the paper over and do the same thing, except put the word *Others' Appraisal* after your name. These forms are illustrated in Exhibit 8-5, which you may want to tear out of the book and use for the exercise, or photocopy.

Step 3:   On the side of the paper titled *Self Appraisal*, do a self-appraisal of your class performance. In the left column of this side write a list of the strengths that you contribute to the class learning. Example strengths are things such as always prepared for class, ask relevant questions, encourage others to participate, and so on. In the right column of the same side, *Things to Work On*, write a list of things to work on to be a better contributor to the class.

Step 4:   When you are finished with your self-evaluation, turn your paper over. Be sure that your name followed by the word *other* is at the top and two columns are labeled *Strengths* and *Things to Work On*. Pass your blank form to the person on your left.

Step 5:   When you receive another student's *Others' Appraisal* form, fill in the strengths and things you think they could improve on in the appropriate columns. If others have previously written the same comments you were going to put down, just put a check mark after the comment. When you are finished writing your feedback, pass the form on the next student to your left. Continue the process until you receive your own form.

Step 6:   Compare your own evaluation of your strengths and things to work on to those listed by your classmates. Make notes of things you would like to clarify.

Step 7:   One at a time, take about five minutes to ask others in your group to clarify and elaborate on the comments that you want to understand better. When receiving feedback, your goal is listening to understand, not to rationalize or explain your behavior. When providing feedback, follow the Behavioral Checklist summary of the skills for providing effective performance appraisal feedback.

Step 8:   After all group members have clarified their performance appraisal feedback, the group should discuss the outstanding examples of skills exhibited by group members in providing effective performance appraisal feedback.

Time.   Plan about 10 minutes for self-appraisal, two to three minutes per student for writing feedback, approximately five to seven minutes per student for feedback clarification, and 10 minutes to examine examples of effective skills for providing effective performance appraisal feedback. So, if groups of five students participate, the time estimate would be 55 to 65 minutes. Experience suggests that you should be prepared for the longer times.

EXHIBIT 8-5   Class Performance Appraisal Feedback Form

Name: _____

Self-Appraisal

Strengths	*Things to Work On*

EXHIBIT 8-5 (Continued)

Name _____

Others' Appraisal

Strengths	*Things to Work On*

SUMMARY CHECKLIST

Take a few minutes to reflect on your performance and look over others' ratings of your performance evaluation skills. Now assess yourself on each of the key learning behaviors. Make a check (✓) next to those behaviors on which you need improvement.

_____ **Use specific objectives previously set with employees as standards to measure progress against.**
1. Make sure these objectives are tangible, verifiable, and measurable.
2. Use multiple sources to gather data for measurement: personal observation, statistical reports, oral reports, written reports, and computer-accessed databases.
3. Decide on appropriate measures for aspects such as individual task outcomes, behaviors, and traits.

_____ **Put the employee at ease and explain the purpose of the feedback interview.**
1. Explain what will transpire during the review and the resulting consequences.
2. Be supportive and understanding.

_____ **Encourage and support while minimizing threats.**
1. Create a helpful and constructive climate.
2. Direct negative feedback toward work-related behavior that the employee can do something about.

_____ **When giving negative feedback, criticize performance, not the person.**
1. Be sure feedback is descriptive rather than judgmental or evaluative.
2. Direct any criticism at specific job-related behaviors that negatively affect the employee's performance.

_____ **Obtain employee participation and encourage self-evaluation.**
1. Let employees do the majority of the talking.
2. Get the employee's perceptions of what you are saying, especially if you are addressing a problem.

_____ **Use specific examples to support ratings through methods such as:**
1. Written essays.
2. Critical incidents.
3. Graphic rating scales.
4. Behaviorally anchored rating scales.
5. Multiperson comparisons.
6. Group order ranking.
7. Individual ranking.
8. Paired comparison.
9. Combined methods.

_____ **Have the employee summarize the feedback to ensure understanding.**
1. Have the recipient rephrase the content of your feedback to see whether it fully captures the meaning you intended.
2. Encourage the employee to summarize the discussion that has taken place.

_____ **Create a future plan of development with the person receiving the feedback.**
1. Help the employee draft a detailed, step-by-step plan to improve the situation.
2. Be sure this plan includes what has to be done, when, and how you will monitor the activities.
3. Offer whatever assistance you can to help the employee.

APPLICATION QUESTIONS

1. Examine the performance appraisal rating methods presented in this chapter. Pick the best one for each of the following situations: college classroom; football team; production line; research lab; sales team; middle management; top management.
2. Which of the performance appraisal rating methods would you prefer to be evaluated by and why? Which method would you prefer if you were a manager and were required to evaluate employees and why? If there are differences between the methods, why do you think that the differences have occurred?
3. What are the benefits of performance appraisal for the organization? For the individual?
4. How do your teachers rate your performance? How is feedback provided? Are these methods effective? How could they be made more effective?
5. Which of the performance rating methods do you think is the fairest? Why?

REINFORCEMENT EXERCISES

The following suggestions are activities you can do to reinforce your performance appraisal skills discussed in this chapter. You may want to adapt them to the Action Plan you will develop next, or try them independently.

1. Visit a local company and interview a manager or human resource staff member about how they conduct performance appraisals. Ask questions about their methods, the results that they obtain, their confidence in the method, and how they interpret the law with respect to appraisals. After the interview, critique the appraisal method that you researched.
2. Interview five students who have worked and ask them about how they feel about performance evaluations. Ask them to describe the problems, fairness, or legal situations that might have occurred. Now, consider what the dangers would be if you only listened to one side of the story when it comes to reviewing cases dealing with performance evaluation.
3. Find someone who is trying to accomplish a difficult goal within the next year. Help this person create a plan of development by applying the performance appraisal steps.

   - Help the person set specific objectives against which progress can be measured and which are tangible, verifiable, and measurable.
   - Help the employee draft a detailed step-by-step plan to achieve these objectives.
   - Be sure this plan includes what has to be done and when.
   - Determine how the person will use the previously set objectives as the standards to measure progress.
   - Offer whatever assistance you can as a coach or monitor to help the person.

4. Design a performance appraisal to evaluate your own performance in one of your main lines of endeavor. Examples could be your success as a student, your performance on a job, or your contribution to your family.

ACTION PLAN

1. Which performance appraisal behavior do I want to improve the most?
2. Why? What will be my payoff?
3. What potential obstacles stand in my way?

4. What are the specific things I will do to improve? (For examples, see the Reinforcement Exercises.)
5. When will I do them?
6. How and when will I measure my success?

NOTES

1. D. Hirshberg, "Quotes taken from employee evaluations," PACE (Policy Analysis for California Education), School of Education University of California, Berkeley, CA 94720-1670, November 5, 1999.

2. M. A. Huselid, S. E. Jackson, and R. S. Schuler, "Technical and Strategic Human Resource Management Effectiveness as Determinants of Firm Performance," *Academy of Management Journal* (February 1997): 171–88.

3. T. Pollock, "Are You Ready to Conduct That Appraisal?" *Supervision* (January 1986): 24.

4. C. MacDonald, *Performance Based Supervisory Development* (Amherst, MA: Human Resources Development, 1982) 20.

5. J. N. Cleveland, K. R. Murphy, and R. E. Williams, "Multiple Uses of Performance Appraisal: Prevalence and Correlates," *Journal of Applied Psychology* (February 1989): 130–35.

6. T. Smart and J. H. Dobrzynski, "Jack Welch on the Art of Thinking Small," *Business Week/Enterprise,* 1993, 212–26.

7. L. Bonifant, "The 423–Minute Manager," *Personnel Administrator* (July 1986): 25.

8. G. L. Morrisey, *Management by Objectives and Results for Business and Industry,* 2d ed. (Reading, MA: Addison-Wesley, 1977).

9. For a thorough review of control systems, see W. H. Newman, *Constructive Control: Design and Use of Control Systems* (Upper Saddle River, NJ: Prentice Hall, 1975). See also A. Globerson, S. Globerson, and J. Frampton, *You Can't Manage What You Don't Measure: Control and Evaluation in Organizations* (Brookfield, VT: Gower Publishing, 1991); and R. Simons, *Levers of Controls* (Boston: Harvard Business School Press, 1995).

10. See, for instance, E. E. Lawler III and J. G. Rhode, *Information and Control in Organizations* (Pacific Palisades, CA: Goodyear, 1976).

11. S. Nelton, "Nurturing Diversity," *Nation's Business* (June 1995): 25–27.

12. D. C. Martin, and K. M. Bartol, "The Legal Ramifications of Performance Appraisals: An Update,"*Employee Relations Law Journal* (Autumn 1991): 257–86.

13. G. C. Reed, "Employers' New Burden of Proof in Discrimination Cases," *Employment Relations Today* (Summer 1989): 112.

14. A. H. Locher and K. S. Teel, "Appraisal Trends," *Personnel Journal* (September 1988): 139–45.

15. Ibid.

16. Adapted from S. P. Robbins, *Managing Today!* 2d ed. (Upper Saddle River, NJ: Prentice Hall, 2000) 289–91.

17. S. E. Catt and D. S. Miller, *Supervision: Working with People* 2d ed. (Homewood, IL: Richard D. Irwin, 1991) 373–74.

18. A. Field, *Inc. Technology #1* (Boston, MA: Goldhirsh Group, Inc., 1977) 55f.

19. For further discussion about problems in conducting performance appraisals see K. Phillips, "Red Flags in Performance Appraisal," *Training and Development Journal* (March 1987): 80–85; "The Trouble with Performance Appraisal," *Training* (April 1984): 91–94; A. Tsui and B. Barry, "Interpersonal Affect and Rating Errors," *Academy of Management Journal* (September 1986): 595–612.

20. "Performance Appraisals—Reappraised," *Management Review* (November 1983): 5.

21. A. Tsui and B. Barry, "Interpersonal Affect and Rating Errors," *Academy of Management Journal* (September 1986): 595.

22. W. K. Blazer and L. M. Sulsky, "Halo and Performance Appraisal Research: A Critical Examination," *Journal of Applied Psychology* (December 1992): 976–85.

23. Ibid.

24. Ibid.

25. Phillips, 1987.

26. Tsui and Barry, 1986.

27. C. Lee, "Performance Appraisal: Can We 'Manage' Away the Curse?" *Training* (May 1996): 44–59.

28. H. H. Meyer, "A Solution to the Performance Appraisal Feedback Enigma," *The Executive* (February 1991): 68–76.

29. R. J. Burke, "Why Performance Appraisal Systems Fail," *Personnel Administration* (June 1972): 32–40.

30. B. R. Nathan, A. M. Mohrman Jr., and J. Milliman, "Interpersonal Relations as a Context for the Effects of Appraisal Interviews on Performance and Satisfaction: A Longitudinal Study," *Academy of Management Journal* (June 1991): 352–69.

31. J. L. Komaki, R. L. Collins, and P. Penn, "The Role of Performance Antecedents and Consequences in Work Motivation," *Journal of Applied Psychology* (June 1982): 334–40; E. A. Locke, and G. P. Latham, *Goal-Setting: A Motivational Technique That Works!* (Upper Saddle River, NJ: Prentice Hall, 1984).

32. C. W. Cook, R. E. Coffey, and P. L. Hunsaker, *Management and Organizational Behavior,* 2d ed. (Burr Ridge, IL: Austin Press/Irwin, 1997) 271–73.

33. D. Ilgen, C. D. Fisher, and M. S. Taylor, "Consequences of Individual Feedback on Behavior in Organizations," *Journal of Applied Psychology* (August 1979): 349–71.

34. F. Bartolome, "Teaching About Whether to Give Negative Feedback," *The Organizational Behavior Teaching Review,* XI, no. 2 (1986–1987): 95–104.

35. K. Halperin, C. R. Snyder, R. J. Shenkel, and B. K. Houston, "Effect of Source Status and Message Favorability on Acceptance of Personality Feedback," *Journal of Applied Psychology* (February 1976): 85–88.

36. M. J. Kavanagh, "Evaluating Performance," in K. M. Rowland and G. R. Ferris, eds., *Personnel Management* (Boston: Allyn & Bacon, 1982) 187–226.

37. N. R. F. Maier, *The Appraisal Interview: Three Basic Approaches* (La Jolla, CA: University Associates, 1976).

38. M. Beer, "Performance Appraisal," in J. W. Lorsch, ed., *Handbook of Organizational Behavior* (Upper Saddle River, NJ: Prentice Hall, 1987) 286–300.

39. "How Do I Love Me? Let Me Count the Ways," *Psychology Today* (May 1980): 16.

40. D. L. Kirkpatrick, "Performance Appraisal: Your Questions Answered," *Training and Development Journal* (May 1986): 68–71.

41. Beer, 1987.

42. C. R. Mill, "Feedback: The Art of Giving and Receiving Help," in L. Porter and C. R. Mill, eds., *The Reading Book for Human Relations Training* (Bethel, ME: NTL Institute for Applied Behavioral Science, 1976) 18–19.

43. K. S. Verderber and R. F. Verderber, *Inter-Act: Using Intepersonal Communication Skills,* 4th ed. (Belmont, CA: Wadsworth, 1986).

44. L. E. Bourne, Jr. and C. V. Bunderson, "Effects of Delay of Information Feedback and Length of Post-Feedback Interval on Concept Identification," *Journal of Experimental Psychology* (January 1963): 1–5.

45. P. W. Dorfman, W. G. Stephan, and J. Loveland, "Performance Appraisal Behaviors: Supervisor Perceptions and Subordinate Reactions," *Personnel Psychology* (Autumn 1986): 579–97.

46. H. K. Baker and P. L. Morgan, "Two Goals in Every Performance Appraisal," *Personnel Journal* (September 1984): 74–78.

47. Verderber and Verderber, 1986.

48. Ibid.

49. T. Alessandra and P. Hunsaker, *Communicating at Work* (New York: Simon & Schuster, 1993) 86–90.

50. C. Fletcher, "The Effects of Performance Review in Appraisal: Evidence and Implications," *Journal of Management Development* 5, no. 3, (1986): 3–12.

51. Cook, Hunsaker, and Coffee, 1997, 271–73.

52. Beer, 1987.

53. Fletcher, 1986.

54. L. L. Cummings, "Appraisal Purpose and the Nature, Amount, and Frequency of Feedback," paper presented at the American Psychological Association meeting, Washington, DC, September 1976.

55. C. R. Mill, "Feedback: The Art of Giving and Receiving Help," in L. Porter and C. R. Mill, eds., *The Reading Book for Human Relations Training.* (Bethel: NTL Institute for Applied Behavioral Science, 1976) 18–19.

56. R. Brett and A. J. Fredian, "Performance Appraisal: The System Is Not the Solution," *Personnel Administrator* (December 1981): 62.

57. Beer, 1987.

58. Dorfman, Stephan, and Loveland, 1986.

59. J. Zigon, "Making Performance Appraisal Work for Teams," *Training* (June 1994): 58–63.

60. G. Imperato, "How Con-Way Reviews Teams," *Fast Company* (September 1998): 152.

61. H. J. Bernardin and C. S. Walter, "Effects of Rater Training and Diary-Keeping on Psychometric Error in Ratings," *Journal of Applied Psychology* (February 1977): 64–69.

62. R. W. Rue and L. L. Byars, *Management: Skills and Applications*, 9th ed. (Burr Ridge, IL: Irwin McGraw-Hill, 2000) 418–9.

63. Based on S. Umapathy, "Teaching Behavioral Aspects of Performance Evaluation: An Experiential Approach," *The Accounting Review* (January 1985): 107–08.

CHAPTER 9

Creative Problem Solving

Learning Objectives

After completing this chapter, you should be able to:

■ Stimulate creativity and innovation.

■ Apply the five steps of the rational problem-solving process.

■ Appreciate the value of ethics in decision making.

■ Utilize the strengths and avoid the weaknesses of groups in solving problems.

■ Apply quality management tools for problem solving.

SELF-ASSESSMENT EXERCISE

How Creative Are You?

Directions. Place a check mark by the 10 words in the following list that best characterize you.

___ energetic	___ persuasive	___ observant	___ fashionable	___ self-confident
___ persevering	___ original	___ cautious	___ habit-bound	___ resourceful
___ egotistical	___ independent	___ stern	___ predictable	___ formal
___ informal	___ dedicated	___ factual	___ open-minded	___ forward-looking
___ tactful	___ inhibited	___ enthusiastic	___ innovative	___ poised
___ acquisitive	___ practical	___ alert	___ curious	___ organized
___ unemotional	___ dynamic	___ polished	___ courageous	___ clear-thinking
___ helpful	___ efficient	___ perceptive	___ quick	___ self-demanding
___ good-natured	___ thorough	___ impulsive	___ determined	___ understanding
___ realistic	___ modest	___ involved	___ flexible	___ absentminded
___ sociable	___ well-liked	___ restless	___ retiring	

Scoring. For each of the following adjectives that you checked, give yourself 2 points:

energetic	resourceful	original	enthusiastic	dynamic
flexible	observant	independent	perceptive	innovative
persevering	dedicated	courageous	curious	self-demanding involved

For each of the following adjectives that you checked, give yourself 1 point:

thorough	determined	restless	informal
alert	open-minded	forward-looking	self-confident

The rest of the adjectives receive no points.

Add Up Your Total Number of Points: _____

Interpretation.

16–20	Very creative
11–15	Above average
6–10	Average
1–5	Below average
0	Noncreative

SOURCE: Copyright © 1981 Adapted from E. Raudsepp, *How Creative Are You?* (New York: Putnam, 1981) 22–24.

CONCEPTS

The economic boom in the early 1980s fueled Porsche sales to more than 50,000 vehicles a year. Then the recession of the early 1990s hit, and sales plummeted to 14,000 units in 1993, including a paltry 3,000 in the United States, its largest market. Porsche teetered on the brink of bankruptcy in 1992. Recession had crippled sales, and costs were out of control. That was when the company's family owners called in 43-year-old Wendelin Wiedeking to be Porsche's chief executive and solve its problems.

Wiedeking brought the Shin-Gijutsu group, a cadre of former Toyota engineers, to the Porsche plant and gave them carte blanche to revitalize the system. With help from the Japanese engineers, assembly time for a car was reduced from 120 hours to 72. The number of errors per car fell 50 percent, to an average of 3. The workforce has shrunk 19 percent, to about 6,800 employees from more than 8,400 in 1992. The line itself has been shortened and inventories have been cut back so much that factory space has been reduced by 30 percent. All of these changes mean Porsche is making more cars at lower cost, and the company recently reported its first profit in four years, after $300 million in losses.[1]

So how did the Japanese problem solvers pull off such a turnaround? In general a diverse task team applied the scientific problem-solving process to analyze the situation, generate a creative action plan for improvement, and implement that plan through the quality control process. You will learn how to apply the problem-solving process to generate creative solutions to problems in the remainder of this chapter. Then you will have opportunities to apply and improve your problem-solving skills in the exercises that follow.

The Importance of Effective Problem Solving

Managerial success depends on making the right decisions at the right times.[2] However, decision making is just one component of the problem-solving process. Unless a problem has been defined and its root causes identified, managers are unlikely to be able to make an appropriate decision about how to solve it. Effective managers, like Porsche's Wiedeking, know how to gather and evaluate information that clarifies a problem. They know the value of generating more than one action alternative and weighing all the implications of a plan before deciding to implement it. They acknowledge the importance of following through to make sure that changes are effective. This chapter explains how to be an effective problem solver and decision maker by using the scientific problem-solving process, tapping into individual and group creativity, and applying quality control techniques.

What Are the Steps for Rational Problem Solving?

Problem solving is the process of eliminating the discrepancy between actual and desired outcomes. Although sometimes subconsciously, most people confront problems by first acknowledging that they exist. Next, the problem needs to be defined and analyzed. Then, alternative solutions need to be generated. **Decision making**—selecting the best solution from among feasible alternatives—comes next. Finally, the solution needs to be implemented. For optimal problem solving, social scientists advocate the use of the rational problem-solving approach (see Exhibit 9-1).[3]

A problem exists when the actual situation is not what is needed or desired. For example, when a work project needs to be completed by a certain deadline, and information needed to complete the assignment has not been supplied, a problem exists.

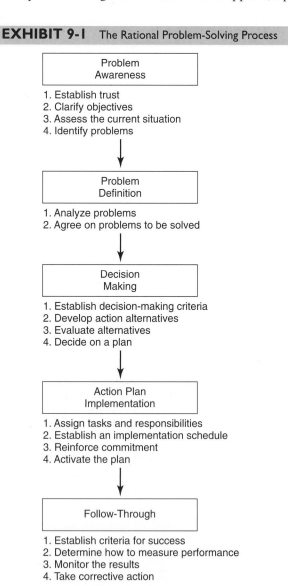

EXHIBIT 9-1 The Rational Problem-Solving Process

Problem
Awareness

1. Establish trust
2. Clarify objectives
3. Assess the current situation
4. Identify problems

Problem
Definition

1. Analyze problems
2. Agree on problems to be solved

Decision
Making

1. Establish decision-making criteria
2. Develop action alternatives
3. Evaluate alternatives
4. Decide on a plan

Action Plan
Implementation

1. Assign tasks and responsibilities
2. Establish an implementation schedule
3. Reinforce commitment
4. Activate the plan

Follow-Through

1. Establish criteria for success
2. Determine how to measure performance
3. Monitor the results
4. Take corrective action

Problem Awareness

A major responsibility for all managers is to maintain a constant lookout for actual or potential problems. Managers fulfill this responsibility by keeping channels of communication open, monitoring employees' current performance, and examining deviations from present plans as well as from past experience.[4] Four situations usually alert managers to possible problems: (1) a deviation from past experience, (2) a deviation from a set plan, (3) when other people communicate problems to the manager, and (4) when competitors outperform the overall organization.[5]

Being aware that problems exist is not always easy, however. People may be genuinely unaware of a problem's source or reluctant to acknowledge that a negative situation actually exists. The problem may appear threatening to them, they may fear reprisal from a supervisor for their share of the responsibility, or they may not want to be considered inept.

Establish Trust   When a problem involves several people, they need to feel understood and accepted. They need to have confidence that the problem can be resolved, and they need to trust management to see the problem as a learning experience, not as an excuse to punish someone.[6] People need to feel secure enough to acknowledge that a problem exists and to acknowledge their own contributions to it.

Clarify Objectives   If you do not know what your objectives are, it is difficult to know what your problems are, let alone what to do about them. Therefore, objectives must be set and clarified before a current situation can be assessed. As described in Chapter 7, objectives provide documented statements of what you intend to accomplish and the basis for measuring performance.

Assess the Current Situation   The immediate need is to determine whether goals are met by the current situation. Do actual conditions match desired ones? If not, what are the differences? Mismatches usually show up clearly, but sometimes an inadequate current situation is taken for granted because it is how things have been for so long. If the matching process reveals discrepancies, the next step is to determine why.

Identify Problems   Serious mistakes can be made if managers act before they accurately identify all of the sources of a problem. To identify a problem accurately, it must be understood from all points of view.

The full determination of how a particular problem prevents people from accomplishing desired goals can be made only when all parties are free to participate in its identification without fear of being blamed or criticized. If problem solving is perceived as a joint learning experience, people will be much more likely to contribute needed information than if they fear punishment for disclosing information that may indicate they have made mistakes.

Routine Problems.   Problem identification and solution are much easier in routine than nonroutine situations. Routine problems are those that arise on a regular basis and can be solved through *programmed decisions*—standard responses based on procedures that have been effective in the past. One example of a programmed decision is the reordering of supplies as soon as inventory on hand falls below a certain quantity. Most routine problems are anticipated, which allows managers to plan in advance how to deal with them and sometimes to delegate problem solving to their subordinates.

Nonroutine Problems.   These situations are not anticipated by managers. They are unique. These types of problems require *nonprogrammed decisions*—innovative solutions tailored to fit specific dilemmas. Innovative solutions are required in the case of multinational mergers like the one between Daimler and Chrysler in 1998, where neither company had experienced anything like the new multinational management situation that was created.

Flowcharts.   One way to be prepared for potential problems and to be able to identify their causes quickly is to have a thorough understanding of the process involved. A **flowchart** is a pictorial representation of all the steps of a process. Flowcharts document a process and help demonstrate how the various steps relate to each other. See Exhibit 9-2 for a sample flowchart involving quality inspection of incoming parts.

The flowchart is widely used in problem identification. The people with the most knowledge about the process meet to draw a flowchart of what steps the process actually

EXHIBIT 9-2   Example Flowchart for Receiving Inspection

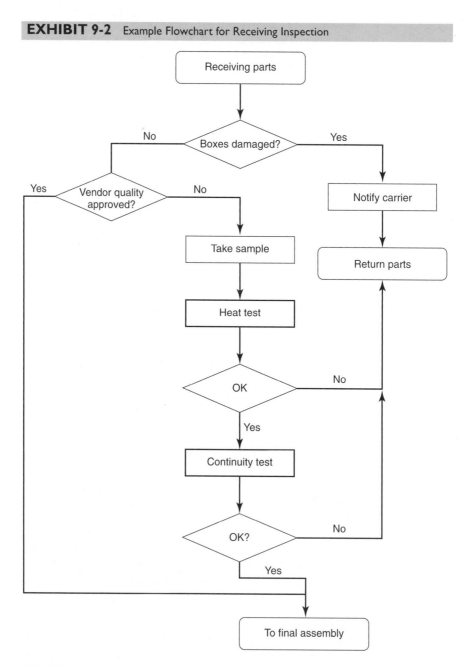

SOURCE: M. Brassard, *The Memory Jogger: A Pocket Guide of Tools for Continuous Improvement* (Methuen, MA: GOAL/QPC, 1988) 26.

follows. Then they draw a flowchart of what steps the process should ideally follow. By comparing the two charts they find differences that can point to where problems arise.[7]

Problem Definition

If the problem is not defined clearly, any attempt at solving it will be doomed to fail because the parties involved will not know what they are working on. All the remaining steps will be distorted because they will be based on insufficient or erroneous information. Lack of information often inhibits the generation of adequate alternatives and exploration of potentially negative consequences.

All necessary information should be gathered so that all relevant factors can be analyzed to determine the exact problem that must be solved. The goal is to determine the root causes of the problem. If instruction forms are constantly misinterpreted, for example, are the forms incomplete, or is the required information poorly supplied? Causes should not be assumed; instead, all plausible alternatives should be investigated before settling on the most probable cause(s).

Hasty assumptions can also result in symptoms being mistaken for sources of problems. When symptoms are eliminated, it is often erroneously assumed that the problem has also been eliminated. For example, you receive medication from your doctor to control a skin rash, which is only a symptom that something is wrong. The medication clears the rash, but the actual cause of the problem is not identified until you or the physican looks for clues. When you discover that the onset of the rash coincided with the arrival of a new plant in your living room, you have identified the problem: an allergy to that plant.

Analyze Problems   Checking to make sure that the problem is defined accurately and analyzed completely provides a safeguard against incorrect assumptions, treatment of symptoms only, and incomplete understanding. The way a problem is actually defined has a major impact on what alternatives are considered, what decision is reached, and how the action plan is implemented. Failure to define an identified problem accurately can impede consideration and eventual application of the best solution.

Failure to diagnose a problem thoroughly can result from inadequate time and energy available to review all the possible causes and implications. Other times, underlying psychological reasons come into play, such as not wanting to know what the real problems are, fearing that we are to blame, being concerned that a close associate will be hurt, or anticipating that the problem will prove too enormous for us.

One technique for facilitating a thorough problem analysis is the cause-and-effect diagram.[8] A **cause-and-effect diagram,** or fishbone chart, is constructed to represent the relationship between some effect and all possible causes influencing it. As illustrated in Exhibit 9-3, the effect or problem is stated on the right side of the chart and the major influences or causes are listed on the left. Although a problem may have various sources, the major causes can usually be summarized under the four *M* categories of *manpower, methods, machines*, and *material.* Data can then be gathered and shared to determine the relative frequencies and magnitudes of contribution of the different potential causes.

Agree on Problems to Be Solved   If more than one problem has been identified and defined, the next step is to set priorities regarding which problem will be worked on first and which ones will be put aside temporarily or indefinitely. One criterion for rank ordering multiple problems is how much their solutions will contribute to desired objectives. The most important problems should be dealt with first, even if their solutions seem more difficult.

Decision Making

After information has been gathered, goals have been clarified, situations assessed, and problems identified, the next step is to develop a particular course of action that will

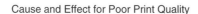

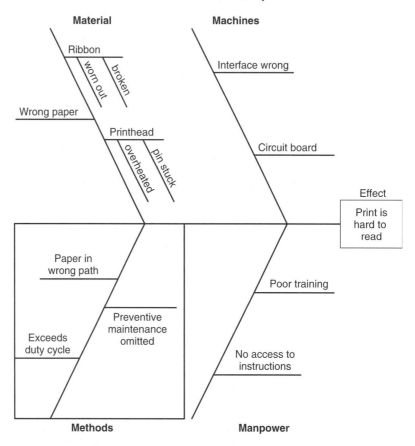

EXHIBIT 9-3 Cause-and-Effect Diagram (Fishbone Analysis)

SOURCE: M. Brassard, *The Memory Jogger: A Pocket Guide of Tools for Continuous Improvement* (Methuen, MA: GOAL/QPC, 1988) 26.

either restore formerly acceptable conditions or improve the situation in a significant way. Because more than one way can usually be found to solve a problem, it is critical to consider all possible solutions and arrive at several alternatives from which to choose.

Establish Decision-Making Criteria   Decision-making **criteria** are statements of objectives that need to be met for a problem to be solved. Effective criteria should be specific, measurable, attainable, complementary, ethical, and acceptable to those who will implement the decision.

Specific, Measurable, and Attainable.   "I need to reduce scrap material waste by 10 percent, avoid a reduction in product quality, and increase production by 5 percent," is an example of a concise decision-making criteria statement. Decision-making criteria should be *specific:* "I will increase productivity by 5 percent," not just "I want to increase productivity." Second, they should be *measurable:* Saying you want to increase employee morale is not as good a criterion statement as saying that you will increase employee morale as indicated by a 4 percent reduction in absenteeism over the next three months. Third, to gain commitment to meeting criteria, there should be sufficient time, resources, and expertise available to make them *attainable.*

Complementary. The criteria must also complement one another. The achievement of one should not reduce the likelihood of achieving another. For example, you would not improve the quality and detail of your written reports at the expense of spending the necessary time with those who must interact with you.

Ethical. Decision criteria should conform to what is considered morally right by society. Criteria should be legal, fair, and observant of human rights. As discussed in Chapter 5, organizations need to establish a commonly agreed-upon set of ethical standards to guide decisions when individuals are confronted with conflicting obligations, cost-benefit trade-offs, and competing value choices.[10]

A large majority of American managers agree that unethical practices occur in business, and a substantial portion (about 65 percent) report that they have been pressured to compromise their own ethical standards when making organizational decisions.[9] Some of the underlying causes for individuals and organizations making poor choices when considering ethical issues are the following:[11]

- Economic self-interest is overwhelming.
- Special circumstances outweigh ethical concerns.
- Education is lacking in the areas of morality and ethics.
- Potential rewards outweigh possible punishments for unethical behavior.
- The culture or mindset is that "All's fair in love, war, and business."
- Organizational pressures make individuals commit unethical acts.

One way managers can prevent the occurrence of ethical dilemmas is by prioritizing all competing values and standards of behavior in advance. When thinking through particular dilemmas, the following questions can sharpen ethical sensitivity and moral awareness.[12]

- Does this decision or action meet the highest societal standards about how people should interact with each other?
- Does this decision or action agree with my religious teachings and beliefs (or with my personal principles and sense of responsibility)?
- How will I feel about myself if I take this action?
- Do we (or I) have a rule or policy for cases like this one?
- Would I want everyone to make the same decision and take the same action if faced with these circumstances?
- What are my true motives for considering this action?
- How would I feel (or how will I feel) if (or when) this action becomes public knowledge?
- Will I be able to explain adequately to others why I have taken this action?
- Would others feel that my action or decision is ethical or moral?

Acceptable. Even the best technical decision will not be workable if it is unacceptable to the parties involved. You may be convinced, for example, that the best solution for meeting a production deadline without increasing costs is to have the department work weekends for the next month without additional compensation. However, this action plan may not be viable if it is not acceptable to those on whom its implementation depends. Negative reactions to changes can create more problems than are solved. Sensitivity to emotional factors, personal values, family issues, and individual objectives is vital in choosing a successful action plan.

Develop Action Alternatives The value, acceptance, and implementation of an action plan are enhanced by involving all affected parties in the generation and analysis of alternatives. Acceptance can be tested by soliciting feedback to determine whether those involved understand the potential benefits and to assess their readiness to make the necessary commitment. As many solutions as possible should be generated to avoid picking a premature solution that does not meet all long-run criteria. Techniques to facilitate this step are provided in the following section on how problems can be solved more effectively.

Evaluate Benefits and Risks of Alternatives It is important to look at all the long-run consequences of the alternatives being considered. This step is sometimes overlooked because of our tendency to avoid spending extra time and energy and our fear of discovering negative consequences in preferred solutions. Important criteria to consider in evaluating action alternatives are each alternative's *probability of success* and the associated *degree of risk* that negative consequences will occur. If the chance of failure is high and the related costs for an alternative are great, the benefits of it may not justify its use. Risk can be personal as well as economic—just ask the person whose reputation is on the line or who is soon to undergo a performance review.

The degree of risk can range from none to potential catastrophy. **Certainty** exists when the exact results of implementing a problem solution are known in advance, like when you put your money in a savings account for one year. **Known risk** is present when the probability that a given alternative will produce specific outcomes can be predicted. For example, an executive may know that by taking a commercial airline flight tonight, he or she has a 99.5 percent probability of arriving on time for a business meeting in New York tomorrow morning. **Uncertainty** exists when decision makers are unable to assign any probabilities to the consequences associated with an alternative. **Turbulence** occurs when the environment is rapidly changing and decision makers are not clear about relevant variables, available solution options, or potential consequences of decisions. In times of recession, economic reforms, or military conflict, turbulence usually prevails.[13]

Decide on a Plan As alternatives are evaluated according to these criteria, many will be clearly unsatisfactory and can be eliminated. Sometimes the evaluation will reveal that one alternative is decidedly superior to all others. At other times none of the proposed action plans will be acceptable, signaling a need to develop additional alternatives. Most often, however, several alternatives will appear feasible, and the best one must be selected. Exhibit 9-4 illustrates a decision-making grid that summarizes the preceding criteria for evaluating alternatives. Such a grid can help to visualize which alternative offers the maximum benefits with minimal risks and costs. The decision-making goal is to select the best solution alternative for solving the entire problem without creating additional negative consequences for anyone else in the organization.

EXHIBIT 9-4 Decision Making Grid

Alternatives	*Criteria*					
	Benefits	*Probability of Success*	*Costs*	*Risks*	*Associated Consequences*	*Timing*
Alternative A						
Alternative B						
Alternative C						

Perfect Rationality.   In a world of perfect rationality, all problems can be clearly defined, all information and alternatives are known, the consequences of implementing each alternative are certain, and the decision maker is a completely rational being who is concerned only about economic gain. These conditions allow for an optimal solution to every problem and provide the basics for ideal management decision making. The real world, however, is made up of real people with real problems, and it rarely conforms to these ideal conditions.

Bounded Rationality.   Usually, real-world limitations prevent obtaining and processing all relevant information that might optimize decision making. Consequently, most managers exhibit bounded rationality when they reach satisfactory rather than "perfect" decisions. Bounded rationality is necessary in the face of constraints on time, money, and intellectual resources.[14] Even though the goal of the decision model presented here is to optimize decision outcomes, **satisficing**—choosing the first satisfactory alternative that meets minimal requirements—probably describes the majority of daily managerial decision making.

Action Plan Implementation

A decision and action plan are of little value unless they are implemented effectively. How the action plan is to be accomplished connects the decision with reality. Implementation includes assigning tasks and responsibilities, and establishing an implementation schedule.

Assign Tasks and Responsibilities   It is important to clarify both verbally and in writing what each person involved will do to make the new action plan work. To avoid misunderstandings, it is essential to specify who is to do what, by when, and how.

Establish an Implementation Schedule   To be implemented effectively, all necessary tasks need a specified time schedule for completion. One way to approach scheduling is to start at an end point (the date by which the objective should be completed) and work backward. Action implementation steps can be listed in order of priority and assigned reasonable time periods for completion, starting with the last step before the objective is accomplished.

A **Gantt chart** is a graphic planning and control method that breaks down a project into separate tasks and estimates the time needed for their completion. The chart has a space for planned starting and completion dates and actual dates filled in as implementation occurs. A sample Gantt chart appears in Exhibit 9-5.

Gantt charts help to make certain that all implementation tasks are considered in relation to each other and appropriate people are assigned to each task. They provide checkpoints for all tasks to ensure that they are finished on time. Gantt charts are developed by defining goals and setting completion dates, then bracketing time blocks based on the time required and completion date of each task.

Once an action plan is implemented, managers often move on to another task. It is of key importance, however, to follow through to be sure that the solution is working effectively and that no additional problems have been created. Follow-through is the final stage of the problem-solving process.

Follow-Through

Following-through entails the development and maintenance of positive attitudes in everyone involved in the implementation process. Several guidelines help establish the positive climate necessary for the implementation steps.

- Visualize yourself in the position of those doing the implementing so that you understand their feelings and perspectives.
- Establish sincere respect and concern.
- Make sure necessary resources are available.

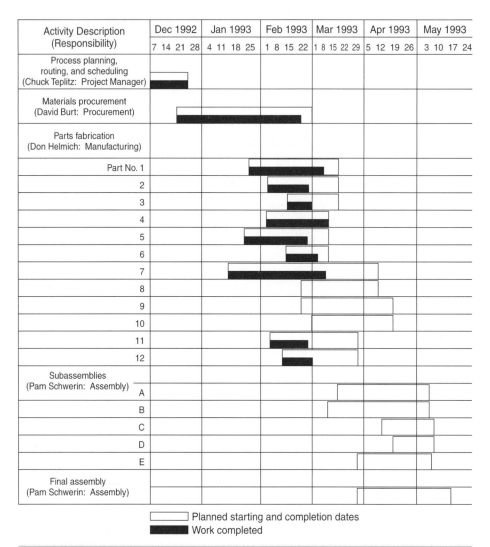

Activity Description (Responsibility)	Dec 1992	Jan 1993	Feb 1993	Mar 1993	Apr 1993	May 1993
	7 14 21 28	4 11 18 25	1 8 15 22	1 8 15 22 29	5 12 19 26	3 10 17 24
Process planning, routing, and scheduling (Chuck Teplitz: Project Manager)						
Materials procurement (David Burt: Procurement)						
Parts fabrication (Don Helmich: Manufacturing)						
Part No. 1						
2						
3						
4						
5						
6						
7						
8						
9						
10						
11						
12						
Subassemblies (Pam Schwerin: Assembly) A						
B						
C						
D						
E						
Final assembly (Pam Schwerin: Assembly)						

☐ Planned starting and completion dates
■ Work completed

EXHIBIT 9-5 Gantt Chart

SOURCE: L. W. Rue and L. L. Byars, *Management Skills and Applications*, 6th ed. (Homewood, IL: Richard D. Irwin, 1992) 210. Adapted from E. S. Buffa. *Modern Production Management*, 4th ed. (New York: John Wiley & Sons, 1973) 576.

With this kind of positive climate set up, several sequential steps in the follow-through process are necessary for implementation. They include establishing the criteria for measuring success, monitoring the results obtained, and taking corrective action when necessary.

Establish Criteria for Measuring Success Unless circumstances change, the criteria for measuring problem-solving success are the time, quality, and quantity goals already developed in the action planning stage. These criteria serve as *benchmarks* for measuring and comparing the actual results.

Monitor the Results The data on the results can be compared with the established criteria. If the new performance meets the criteria, no further action is necessary other than continued monitoring. If the new results do not measure up, the next step is to determine why. Each implementation step may alter the problem situation in unanticipated ways.

Take Corrective Action   The problem-solving process is a *closed-loop system*. If performance fails to match the success criteria, the problem needs to be identified by again applying the problem-solving process. For any new corrective action plan, new measures and schedules need to be determined and new data need to be gathered and tested against the criteria.

When Is Participation Appropriate for Decision Making?

Who should be involved in the problem-solving process? Just the manager? A committee? A coalition of key individuals? The entire department? In 1992, General Motors was losing $2.5 million a day. To turn this negative trend around, employees were encouraged to participate wholeheartedly with GM management in a $3 billion gamble to build a tight, light, high-quality, peppy subcompact in competition with Tercel, Civic, and the rest of Japan's best cars. GM's approach was to merge management and labor into a team where they would make decisions and share the pains, gains, and profits. The result was a lean production facility, a familial management-labor structure, and an obsession with quality control. The product was the Saturn, which during its first nine months sold at twice the rate of Toyotas or Hondas.[15]

Degrees of Decision Participation

Evidence indicates that participation can enhance morale, satisfaction, and productivity, but in emergencies or when others do not have sufficient information, an autocratic decision may be more appropriate.[16] Degrees of decision participation can be grouped into the following three broad levels.[17]

- *Autocratic.*   The manager solves the problem alone using only information personally available or solicited from subordinates. Subordinates are not involved in analyzing the problem or generating solutions.
- *Consultative.*   The manager shares the problem with subordinates, either individually or as a group, and solicits their ideas and suggestions. The manager then makes an independent decision, which may or may not reflect subordinates' inputs.
- *Group.*   The manager shares the problem with subordinates as a group. Together with subordinates, the manager generates and evaluates alternatives and attempts to reach a consensus agreement on a solution, which the manager then accepts and implements.

Victor Vroom and Phillip Yetton have developed a diagnostic framework for matching the amount of participation in decision making with situational requirements.[18] Their five possible decision-making processes, described in Exhibit 9-6, vary in the degrees of participation they allow.

Criteria for Participation

When deciding how much participation to use when making a decision, several factors need to be considered. Three of the most important are the quality requirements, the degree necessary for subordinates to accept the decision, and the time required to make the decision.

Quality Requirements   Whether a decision is best made by an individual or a group depends on the nature and importance of the problem. Important decisions that have large impacts on organizational goal achievement need to be the highest quality possible. In complex situations, it is unlikely that any one individual will have all the necessary information to make a top-quality decision. Therefore, the decision maker should at least consult with others who are either closer to the problem or more

---

EXHIBIT 9-6   Types of Participation in Decisions

Key: A = Autocratic, C = Consultant, G = Group: I and II denote variations of a process.

AI   You solve the problem or make the decision yourself, using information available at the time.

AII   You obtain the necessary information from your subordinate(s), then decide on the solution to the problem yourself. You may or may not tell your subordinates what the problem is when getting information from them. The role played by your subordinates in making the decision is clearly one of providing the necessary information to you, rather than generating or evaluating alternative solutions.

CI   You share the problem with relevant subordinates individually, getting their ideas and suggestions without bringing them together as a group. Then you make the decision that may or may not reflect your subordinates' influence.

CII   You share the problem with your subordinates as a group, collectively obtaining their ideas and suggestions. Then you make the decision that may or may not reflect your subordinates' influence.

GII   You share the problem with your subordinates as a group. Together you generate and evaluate alternatives and attempt to reach agreement (consensus) on a solution. Your role is much like that of chairman. You do not try to influence the group to adopt "your" solution, and you are willing to accept and implement any solution that has the support of the entire group.

SOURCE: Adapted from V. H. Vroom and A. G. Jago, *The New Leadership* (Upper Saddle River, NJ: Prentice Hall, 1988) 35.

"expert" in dealing with it. One person with appropriate knowledge and experience, on the other hand, can decide what to do to solve simple routine problems.

Acceptance Requirements   The effectiveness of the action plan decided upon is a combination of its quality and the effort put into implementing it. A top-quality decision, if not implemented appropriately, will not be effective. A lower-quality decision that receives enthusiastic support from all involved may be more effective than a higher-quality alternative that implementers do not buy into.

Those affected by a decision are usually more highly motivated to implement the action plan if they have had an opportunity to influence it. Being involved usually increases participants' understanding and generates a feeling of commitment to make "our" decision work, whereas an arbitrary, autocratic decision that is handed down often results in passive acceptance or even active resistance to implementation. This response to plans and changes will be discussed further in Chapter 16.

Time Requirements   Allocating problem solving and decision making to a group requires a greater investment of time in meetings, which is unavailable for usual tasks. But the level of acceptance and probability of efficient execution is greater for participative decisions than autocratic methods. Also, a higher-quality decision may result from the inclusion of a variety of perspectives and approaches. It is important to determine whether additional time investment produces significantly higher degrees of quality, acceptance, and commitment.

Choosing the Appropriate Degree of Participation

The specific needs for quality, acceptance, and time provide the impetus for choosing among the five degrees of participation in any given decision situation. The answers to seven questions about decision quality and acceptance can indicate the most appropriate degree of participation in any given decision situation.[19] Exhibit 9-7 illustrates the appropriate sequence of these three questions regarding quality and four questions regarding acceptance in a decision-tree format.

It is possible that more than one style may be appropriate for a problem situation. In that case, the optimal style indicated by this model is the more autocratic one

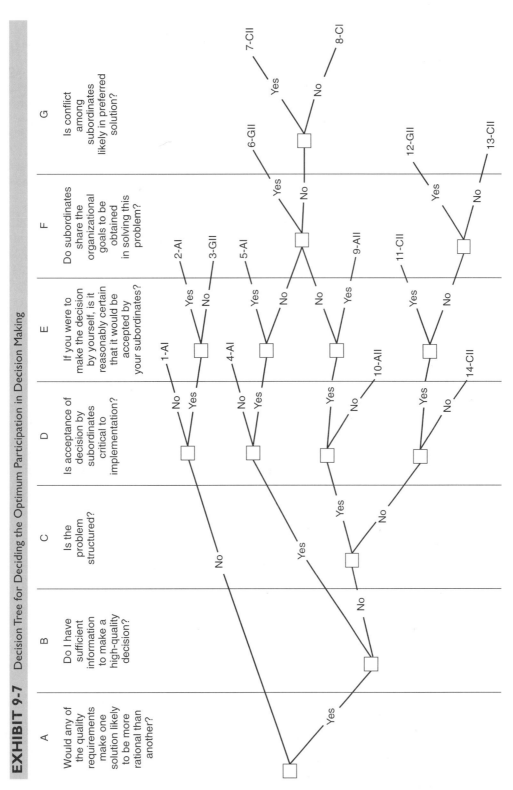

EXHIBIT 9-7 Decision Tree for Deciding the Optimum Participation in Decision Making

A	B	C	D	E	F	G
Would any of the quality requirements make one solution likely to be more rational than another?	Do I have sufficient information to make a high-quality decision?	Is the problem structured?	Is acceptance of decision by subordinates critical to implementation?	If you were to make the decision by yourself, is it reasonably certain that it would be accepted by your subordinates?	Do subordinates share the organizational goals to be obtained in solving this problem?	Is conflict among subordinates likely in preferred solution?

1-AI
2-AI
3-GII
4-AI
5-AI
6-GII
7-CII
8-CI
9-AII
10-AII
11-CII
12-GII
13-CII
14-CII

SOURCE: Adapted from V. H. Vroom and A. G. Jago, *The New Leadership* (Upper Saddle River, NJ: Prentice Hall, 1988) 62.

because it will require the least amount of time to implement. Therefore, the decision tree is most useful in situations where time is a critical factor. In situations where it is important to increase things such as morale, employee development, or group cohesiveness, it may be more appropriate to choose a more time-consuming decision style that emphasizes team development.

Advantages and Disadvantages of Group Decision Making

As we have just discussed, groups usually take more time than individuals to make decisions, but groups are often more creative and group involvement is essential for gaining acceptance of decisions that members must implement. Although groups are often able to produce more and better solutions to problems than are individuals[20] and more commitment to higher-quality decisions,[21] extensive research demonstrated that groups have both strengths and weaknesses in reaching decisions.[22] These aspects are summarized in Exhibit 9-8.

Advantages of Making Decisions in Groups   When a number of people meet in a group to solve a problem, one advantage is that they usually have greater amounts of knowledge available than does one individual working alone. They have more diverse viewpoints, which lead to more options and creative solutions. More people also means more approaches to solving the problem, which can eliminate constantly trying to approach a problem in a way that will not work. By participating in the discussion and problem-solving process, group members have a better understanding of the decision and why it was made. Being a part of the decision process contributes to an increased probability of acceptance and implementation of the decision because of the group ownership of "our decision" versus one by some authority figure. Chapter 14, on creating high performing teams, will expand on ways to capitalize on group strengths.

Disadvantages of Making Decisions in Groups   Although groups have the potential for making more creative and effective decisions, the increased number of individuals involved and group dynamics often create barriers. Some of the main problems that occur in group decision making will be described next. Then ways for overcoming these potential problems will be explained.

More Time Investment.   Group decisions are usually more time consuming than individual ones because of the interaction required. Individuals in groups need to get to know each other, build rapport, satisfy social needs, and clarify communications. Groups also spend time organizing, resolving conflicts, and developing operating procedures. In addition, the time group members spend solving problems is time away from other work responsibilities.

Individual Agendas.   Individual group members may have competing goals or prior commitments that lead to disagreements about alternative solutions and destructive conflict. Groups may also be subject to domination by a few strong individuals who may not have the best ideas. At times even the best group decision may be blocked by an individual who stands to lose personally if it occurs.

Shared Responsibility.   Ambiguous responsibility regarding who is actually accountable for the final decision and implementation of a group decision can be an issue. At times this shared responsibility can lead to more risky decisions than are appropriate because individuals feel less personally responsible for negative consequences because the group made the decision.

Pressure to Conform.   One of the main disadvantages of making decisions in groups is the potential social pressure to conform to premature decisions before all the

EXHIBIT 9-8 Advantages and Disadvantages of Group Problem Solving

Advantages Groups Have over Individuals	Disadvantages Groups Have Compared to Individuals
• *More knowledge and information.* A group of people meeting together to solve a problem has more breadth and, quite often, more depth of experience and knowledge than does any one individual. This is especially true if members come from diverse backgrounds.	• *Competing goals.* Group members often have prior commitments to other reference groups or have personal agendas that conflict. These differences can lead to disagreement about alternative solutions and destructive conflict.
• *Diversity of viewpoints.* A number of people with different experiences can generate more options and creative alternatives. They also bring a greater number of approaches to solving the problem.	• *Time consuming.* People have to plan and coordinate group meetings and then wait for everyone to arrive. The processes of being understood, resolving interpersonal conflicts, and listening to irrelevant side conversations also detract from group problem-solving efficiency.
• *Increased understanding.* By participating in the problem-solving process, group members have a better understanding of the decision and why it was made.	• *Social pressure to conform.* Especially in highly cohesive groups, members often conform to majority opinions that are not optimal in order to gain group acceptance.
• *Increased acceptance.* Group members are also more likely to accept a decision they understand. Also, a participative decision, in North American democratic societies, is often perceived as more legitimate than an autocratic decision by a single manager, which might be considered arbitrary.	• *Domination by a few.* High status, power, or just an assertive personality can cause certain members to dominate group discussions and influence decisions that they prefer. If the dominating people do not have the best ideas and those who do are kept silent, the quality of the group decision will suffer.
• *Better implementation.* Participation in a decision creates a feeling of ownership of "our decision" versus one made by some unapproachable authority figure. People want to show that their decision is the right one, and consequently will work hard to implement it themselves as well as encouraging others to do the same.	• *Ambiguous responsibility.* Since no one individual is held responsible for a group's decision, there is often uncertainty about who is accountable for implementing decisions and who gets the credit or blame for outcomes. Often this can lead to decisions that are more risky than appropriate for the organization, because no one in particular will be held accountable if the decision fails.

SOURCE: Adapted from N. R. F. Maier, "Assets and Liabilities in Group Problem Solving," *Psychological Review 74* (July 1967): 239–49.

information has been processed thoroughly. In highly cohesive groups this pressure to conform can lead to the groupthink phenomenon.[23]

Groupthink exists when members' desire to agree is so great that it tends to override the concern for realistic appraisal of alternative courses of action.[24] One disastrous example of groupthink was the decision made by NASA in 1986 to launch the *Challenger* space shuttle, which exploded, killing all seven crew members. The technical cause of the explosion was determined to be a faulty O-ring seal that broke down in the previous night's freezing temperatures. Investigation by a government commission, however, concluded that the primary cause of this tragedy was a faulty decision-making process. Further analysis illustrated that NASA decision makers were victims of the classic symptoms of groupthink. The group was under intense pressure to launch, due to promises of success confounded by time delays. Consequently, decision makers failed to voice dissenting opinions, avoided disagreements, and were reluctant to explore unsettling information. Engineers raising concerns about O-ring problems before the launch, for example, were chastised and ignored, causing the decision-making group to reject valuable criticism that could have avoided the whole disaster. Exhibit 9-9 highlights symptoms to look for to determine whether groupthink exists.

The Manager's Role in Making Group Decision Making Effective   Whether a group will be effective or ineffective depends primarily on the skills of its members and its leader. For example, lower-status group members usually defer to those with higher status, even though they may be the ones with the best ideas.[25] Group leaders need to ensure that all participants feel free to contribute by not trying to persuade others in the problem-solving group to adopt the leader's own preference. The leader's role is to establish a cooperative environment in which all opinions are heard and evaluated before a solution is reached.[26] If the leader is not aware of the dynamics of group process or is not effective in the role of facilitator, a cohesive group may fall into the pattern of groupthink.

Groupthink can be avoided if a leader remains neutral, encourages criticism, asks for new ideas, and brings in outside consultants to present alternative views. When solving the Cuban missile crisis, Kennedy's top aids avoided groupthink by applying the following strategies.[27] One is to assign a critical evaluator role to each member and emphasize the need to air doubts like those Schlesinger outlined in the Bay of Pigs decision. Another is for the leader to remain impartial and refrain from stating preferences. The third option is to encourage members to discuss their deliberations with people outside the group and relay these opinions to the group. Outside experts can even be invited to meetings for the express purpose of challenging prevailing views. A devil's advocate can be assigned to raise deliberate opposition to the proposals being considered. Finally, after a tentative decision has been reached, a second-chance meeting can be called, in which members air every possible doubt.

EXHIBIT 9-9   Symptoms of Groupthink

- *Illusions of group invulnerability.*   Members of the group feel they are invincible, resulting in risk taking (e.g., Pearl Harbor).
- *Collective rationalization.*   Refusal to consider contradictory data or to consider unpleasant alternatives thoroughly (e.g., failure to consider engineers' warnings about the O-rings in the *Challenger* disaster).
- *Illusion of group morality.*   Members of the group feel it is "right" and morally correct (e.g., religious or ethnic wars like the Arabs and Jews, or Serbs, Croats, and Muslims).
- *Stereotypes of competitors.*   Shared negative opinions of treating groups as weak, evil, and stupid (e.g., communists versus capitalists, Muslims versus Christians).
- *Pressure to conform.*   Direct pressure to conform is applied to a member who suggests other alternatives or that the group may be wrong (e.g., L.A. police officer hitting Rodney King because the others expected him to, even though the officer thought it was wrong).
- *Self-censorship.*   Members do not share personal concerns if contrary to overall group opinion (e.g., President Kennedy's cabinet members with doubts about the Bay of Pigs invasion remaining silent).
- *Illusions of unanimity.*   Erroneously believing that all are in agreement and accepting consensus prematurely (e.g., if one person had opposed the Bay of Pigs invasion, Kennedy would have canceled it, but no one did and consensus was assumed).
- *Mind guarding.*   Members protect the group as a whole from hearing disturbing ideas or viewpoints from outsiders (e.g., keeping new conflicting test results suppressed just before the FDA approves a new drug).

SOURCE: I. L. Janis, *Groupthink: Psychological Studies of Policy Decision and Fiascoes*, 2d ed. (Boston: Houghton Mifflin Company, 1982). © by Houghton Mifflin Company. Adapted with permission.

Another thing a manager can do to enhance group decision-making effectiveness is to encourage creativity. A number of strategies and techniques for encouraging creativity are described next.

Encouraging Creativity

For organizations to solve problems creatively, managers have to demonstrate that they value it and know how to deal with innovations when they are suggested. The Center for Creative Leadership has determined some characteristics of managers who generate creativity in their organizations.

Characteristics of Managers Who Generate Creativity[28]

Managers who encourage creativity are willing to *absorb risks* taken by subordinates. They allow their people freedom, expect some errors, and are willing to learn from inevitable failures. Managers who are afraid of mistakes, on the other hand, restrict the freedom of their subordinates to experiment and be creative.

Productive managers of creativity can live with *half-developed ideas*. They do not insist that an idea be 100 percent proven before supporting its development. They are willing to listen to and encourage subordinates to press on with "half-baked" proposals that hold promise. They know that criticism can kill an innovation.

Creative managers have a feel for the times when the company rule book needs to be ignored and will *stretch normal policies* for the greater long-term good. Managers who permit no deviation from standard operating procedures will make predictable progress and avoid mistakes, but will not realize giant breakthroughs that calculated risk taking can promote.

Productive managers are *good listeners*. They listen to their staff, try to pull out good ideas, and build on suggestions. They do not try to impose new policies or procedures on people without listening to the other side first.

Creative managers *do not dwell on mistakes*. They are more future oriented than past oriented. They do not hold the mistakes of others against them indefinitely. They are willing to begin with the world as it is today and work for a better future. They learn from experience, but they do not wallow in the past.

When good ideas are presented, productive managers are willing to decide on the spot to try them without waiting for further studies. They are courageous enough to *trust their intuition* and commit resources to implementing promising innovations.

Finally, productive managers are *enthusiastic and invigorating*. They encourage and energize others. They enjoy using the resources and power of their position to push projects forward and make improvements.

Promoting Creative Thinking in Organizations

To encourage creativity, a manager needs to provide a bureaucracy-free environment that tolerates diverse behavior. When a wealthy patron once asked Pablo Picasso what he could do to help him, Picasso looked at him and said succinctly, "Stand out of my light."[29] Several examples of how universities and businesses have promoted creativity by eliminating organizational barriers follow.

In a course at the University of Houston, nicknamed Failure 101, students are requested to build the tallest structure possible out of ice-cream-bar sticks, then look for "the insight in every failure. Those who end up with the highest projects went through the most failures. Whoever followed a fixed idea from the outset never finished first."[30]

Training students to learn from mistakes and to try, try again may be good groundwork for future careers in business. But "you can't just order up a good idea or spend money to find one," points out Jon Henderson, director of Hallmark's Creative Resources Center. "You have to build a supportive climate and give people the freedom to create things."[31]

One famous example of how a creative climate can pay off is Minnesota Mining & Manufacturing Company (3M) in Minneapolis, where employees are encouraged to devote about 15 percent of their work time to non-job-related creative thinking. Doing "Skunkworks duty," as it is known at 3M, has resulted in such creative products as Post-It notes, three-dimensional magnetic recording tape, and disposable medical masks. 3M estimates that in the 1990s, nearly 70 percent of its annual $12 billion in sales, and 30 percent of its total revenues, came from new products derived from creative ideas that originated with the workforce.[32]

At W. L. Gore & Associates, the company that brought us Teflon products, employees are urged to take risks. The feeling is that if they are not making mistakes, they are doing something wrong. This philosophy has propelled W. L. Gore from a glorified mom-and-pop operation to a company with 37 plants worldwide, turning out everything from electronics to dental products.[33]

For those managers who see the necessity of creativity but are still apprehensive, several structured alternatives to promoting problem-solving creativity exist that do not entail giving up control in the work environment.[34] Among them are brainstorming, the nominal group technique, the Delphi technique, and group decision support systems.

Brainstorming **Brainstorming** is a demonstrated approach for achieving high participation and increasing the number of action alternatives.[35] To engage in brainstorming sessions, people meet in small groups and feed off one another's ideas, which provide stimuli for more creative solutions. Rules for effective brainstorming promote the goal of provoking lots of ideas, no matter how far fetched; allow no criticism or evaluation of ideas as they are generated; allow only one idea at a time from each person; and encourage people to build on each other's ideas.

Brainstorming groups are encouraged to be freewheeling and radical. Through the use of a nonevaluative environment that is intentionally fun, brainstorming ensures involvement, enthusiasm, and generation of a large number of solution alternatives.

Brainstorming generally works well in a participative, team-oriented climate where people are comfortable with each other and are committed to pulling together toward a common goal. In some situations, it may not be effective, however. One example occurred in Paris, France, where the expatriate general manager from the United States attempted a brainstorming session with department managers and instead of a number of exciting ideas was met with a room full of frowns and complete silence. When he inquired why no responses were made, he was told very seriously that he was the director general, and it was his job to tell them what to do. The staff's job was to follow orders and accept his suggestions, not to do his job for him.

At other times, a hostile or political climate might inhibit the free flow of ideas. In restrictive interpersonal climates, more structured techniques such as the nominal group or Delphi group technique may be more effective. The recent development of computer-supported data-processing tools, such as electronic brainstorming, can also circumvent the need for face-to-face brainstorming meetings. These tools will be discussed next.

Nominal Group Technique In the **nominal group technique,** participants meet together in a highly structured format that governs the decision-making process.[36] First, participants independently write down their ideas about the problem. Second, each presents one idea to the group in a round-robin fashion without discussion. These ideas are summarized and written on a flip chart or chalkboard so all can see them. After a group discussion to clarify and evaluate the ideas, an independent ranking of the proposals takes place. These rankings are pooled to determine the proposal with the highest aggregate ranking, which is the group's decision.

The nominal group technique offers the advantages of multiple idea generation, balanced participation, and participant satisfaction. It is time consuming and does require participants to meet together at one location. In any group decision-making situation, the advantages and disadvantages of a proposed technique should be weighed with respect to the nature of the participants and the specific decision being made.

Delphi Technique   In the **Delphi technique,** participants do not meet together but interact through a series of written judgments and suggestions.[37] After each participant has been presented with the problem, he or she writes down comments and possible solutions and sends them to a central location for recording and reproduction. Each participant then receives a copy of all other comments and solutions to use as a springboard for additional ideas or comments, which are also returned to the central location for compilation and reproduction, after which an independent vote on solution priority is taken.

The Delphi technique allows for the pooling of a variety of ideas, viewpoints, independent feedback, and criticism at minimal expense, because participants do not have to congregate at a common meeting place. It does, however, take an extended period of time and offers really no control over the decision-making process. Depending on the nature of the decision group, participants' lack of face-to-face interaction can be either an asset or a liability.

Group Decision Support Systems   **Group decision support systems** are electronic and computer-supported data-processing tools that can facilitate group decision making in certain situations. "Same time—same place" interactions among team members can be facilitated by software tools such as mathematical models, spreadsheets, graphics packages, and electronic brainstorming activities. "Same place—different time" interactions are supported by such tools as retrieval systems for information sharing and display software. "Same time—different place" group interactions can be accomplished through video conferencing, which combines audio and video communications. "Different time—different place" decision making can be helped by such mechanisms as electronic mail and groupware. Group decision support system tools have been shown to increase the efficiency of group problem solving, better document it, and produce higher-quality decisions.[38]

Electronic brainstorming, for example, is similar to the nominal group technique, except that group members exchange ideas on interactive computer terminals instead of writing their ideas on paper. It is especially effective in groups with more than five members, where experiments have demonstrated that more unique and high-quality ideas are generated and members are more satisfied than when they use verbal brainstorming. Electronic brainstorming is not a face-to-face medium, which reduces the negative effects of ideas being blocked due to apprehension about their rejection.

Electronic brainstorming also enables widely dispersed group members to generate ideas interactively. In this application, electronic brainstorming is a sophisticated form of computer conferencing, wherein group members' ideas are automatically sent to each other's screens during the idea generation session. This process may be particularly helpful when people's schedules differ markedly because of time zones and workloads. It may offer an attractive alternative to conference calls that require everyone to be available to interact at the same time.

Finally, the simultaneity of input in electronic brainstorming also prevents one individual from dominating the idea generation process. Inputs tend to be evenly distributed over group members, which helps increase not only the number of ideas generated but also people's satisfaction with the process.[39]

CONCEPT QUIZ

Decide whether the following 10 statements are true or false, and circle the right answer. Answers are at the end of the quiz. After marking your answers, remember to go back and check your understanding of any answers you missed.

True or False	1. A problem exists whenever the actual situation is not what is desired.
True or False	2. It is more important to analyze a problem thoroughly than it is to generate many solutions.
True or False	3. Flowcharts are most useful for deciding which alternative to implement.
True or False	4. Pareto charts indicate which causes of problems should be solved first.
True or False	5. Acceptance and implementation of action plans are enhanced by involving all affected parties in the generation and analysis of alternatives.
True or False	6. The last step in problem solving is deciding on the best solution to the problem.
True or False	7. Autocratic decisions often result in passive acceptance or even active resistance to implementation.
True or False	8. Groupthink facilitates realistic appraisals of alternative courses of action.
True or False	9. Shared responsibility is a strength for identifying who is actually accountable for the implementation of a group decision.
True or False	10. Brainstorming promotes a higher quantity of far-fetched ideas.

Answers. (1) True; (2) True; (3) False; (4) True; (5) True; (6) False; (7) True; (8) False; (9) False; (10) True

BEHAVIORAL CHECKLIST

The following skills are important to creative problem solving. Use them when evaluating your own problem solving skills and those of others.

The Creative Problem Solver

- Identifies problems by establishing trust, clarifying objectives, assessing the situation.
- Analyzes problems by separating symptoms from sources and determining all causes.
- Decides on an action plan by establishing criteria, developing alternatives, and choosing the best one.
- Implements the action plan by assigning responsibilities and establishing a schedule.
- Follows through by measuring performance and taking corrective actions.
- Decides who should participate in decision making based on quality, acceptance, and time.
- Avoids the problems in group decision making by remaining neutral, encouraging critical evaluation, asking for new ideas, and allowing second-chance decision meetings.
- Encourages creativity by absorbing risks, listening, and committing resources.
- Applies techniques to promote group problem solving.

Attention!
Do not read the following until assigned to do so by your instructor.

MODELING EXERCISE[40]

Instructions. One person volunteers to play Jan, the manager of personnel for Beacon Lights. Another person volunteers to play the role of Sean, Jan's secretary. Everyone, including the person playing Sean, should read Jan's role, but the person playing Jan is not to read Sean's role. Class members not playing one of the roles should also review the Observer's Rating Sheet on page 235, which they will use to rate Jan's performance in creatively solving the problem and providing feedback at the end of the exercise.

Jan's Role   You have been director of personnel for Beacon Lights for 10 years. Just when you thought you had your job "down pat," the sky fell in. A strong labor union has been trying to organize your plant, the federal government recently filed a claim against your company for discriminatory hiring practices, the president and vice president of sales were forced to resign last month because of the company's poor performance, and on top of all that, your long-time secretary just died of an unexpected heart attack.

A month ago you hired Sean to replace your secretary. Sean has only two years of secretarial experience so you could save some salary money and you think that Sean should have no difficulty picking up the pieces. Sean asked for some temporary help recently, but you really cannot afford it right now and said you would keep Sean informed about the more urgent items you wanted to concentrate on first. Your former secretary had no problems getting the job done and you do not expect that Sean will, either.

You have been asked to give a talk at a national convention on a new productivity program your company has pioneered, and you are looking forward to getting away from the office for a few days to catch your breath. You gave your talk to Sean a couple of days ago so there would be plenty of time to get it typed and reproduced.

This morning you have come into the office to proofread and rehearse your talk prior to catching a plane this evening and you are shocked to find a note saying your secretary called in ill this morning. You rush over to Sean's desk and frantically begin searching for your paper. You find it mixed in with some material for the quarterly report that should have been sent in two weeks ago, a stack of overdue correspondence, and two days' worth of unopened mail.

As you dial your secretary's home phone number, you realize that you are perspiring heavily and your face is flushed. This foul-up is the worst one you can remember in years.

Sean's Role   You hear the phone ring and it is all you can do to get out of bed and limp into the kitchen to answer it. You really feel rotten. On the way up your driveway last night, you slipped on your kid's skateboard and sprained your knee. You can hardly move today and the pain is excruciating. You are also a bit hesitant to answer the phone because you figure it is probably your boss, Jan, calling to chew you out for getting behind in your work. You know you deserve some blame, but it was not all your fault. Since you began working for Jan a month ago, you have asked several times for a thorough job description. You feel you do not really understand Jan's priorities or your specific job responsibilities. You are replacing a secretary who died suddenly after working for Jan for 10 years. You were hired to pick up the pieces, but you have found working with Jan extremely frustrating. Jan has been too busy to train you properly and assumes you know as much about the job as your predecessor. This assumption is particularly a problem because you have not worked as a secretary for three years, and you feel a bit "rusty."

Jan's talk is a good example of the difficulties you have experienced. Jan gave you the talk a couple of days ago and said it was urgent—but that was on top of a quarterly report that was already overdue and a backlog of correspondence, filing, and so on.

You never filled out a report like this before, and every time you asked Jan a question you were told that you would have to discuss it later as Jan ran off to a meeting. When you asked if it would be possible to get some additional help to catch up on the overdue work, Jan said the company could not afford it because of poor sales. This response irked you because you knew you were being paid far less than your predecessor. You knew Jan faced some urgent deadlines so you had planned to return to the office last night to type Jan's speech and try to complete the report, but two hours in the emergency room at the hospital put an end to that plan. You tried calling Jan to explain the problem, only to find out Jan has an unlisted number.

You sit down and prop up your leg, and wince with pain as you pick up the phone.

Time.   Not to exceed 15 minutes.

OBSERVER'S RATING SHEET

On completion of the exercise, evaluate Jan's creative problem-solving skills. Rate the problem-solving skills between 1 and 5 using the following scale. Write concrete examples in the space for comments below each criteria skill to use in explaining your feedback.

1 *Unsatisfactory*	*2* *Weak*	*3* *Adequate*	*4* *Good*	*5* *Outstanding*

_____ Identified problems by establishing trust, clarifying objectives, and assessing the situation.

_____ Analyzed the problem by separating symptoms from sources and determining all causes.

_____ Decided on an action plan by establishing criteria, developing alternatives, and choosing the best one.

_____ Implemented the action plan by assigning responsibilities and establishing a schedule.

_____ Followed through by measuring performance and taking corrective actions.

_____ Decided who should participate in decision making based on quality, acceptance, and time.

_____ Avoided the problems in group decision making by remaining neutral, encouraging critical evaluation, asking for new ideas, and allowing second-chance decision meetings.

_____ Encouraged creativity by absorbing risks, listening, and committing resources.

_____ Applied techniques to promote group problem solving.

GROUP EXERCISES

Three different types of group exercises are presented here. First is a short case for you to practice your conceptual problem-solving skills. Second is an opportunity to apply the decision tree to determine the appropriate degree of participation in several different problem situations, according to the criteria of quality, acceptance, and time restraints. Third is an exercise demonstrating the advantages of group versus individual problem solving.

Group Exercise 1: Dealing with Academic Dishonesty Case Discussion[41]

Purpose. To apply the creative problem-solving process to a current situation familiar to participants.

Directions. All steps in this exercise can be conducted by the instructor with the entire class, or autonomous groups can apply the process themselves.

Step 1: Read the following description of academic dishonesty.

Step 2: Form groups of five or six members and discuss the case questions in your groups.

Step 3: Groups share their solutions with the entire class.

Step 4: Groups analyze their application of the creative problem solving process using the Observer's Rating Sheet on page 000.

Time. 55 to 85 minutes. Allocate 30 minutes for group problem solving, 30 minutes for class discussions, and 25 minutes for groups to analyze their problem-solving process. If time is limited, eliminate the 30-minute class discussion, leaving 55 minutes for group problem solving and debriefing.

The Problem of Academic Dishonesty At some point it happens to every professor. A student will turn in such an excellent, well-written paper that its authenticity is in serious doubt. Or, during a test, the professor looks up and sees one student copying from another or from crib notes lying on the floor. Studies show that about 40 percent of students cheat in a given term, and it is not only the lazy student looking for a shortcut. In fact, overachievers are more likely to cheat than underachievers when a professor springs a test on them and they feel they are losing control of their ability to prepare for class. For example, a student who is taking 16 course-hours, working 30 hours a week, and still trying to squeeze in a social life may not feel adequately prepared for a test and feel pressured to cheat. The question for professors is what to do about it.

It seems unthinkable that a professor would ignore students' whispering answers to one another during a test, or obviously copying from crib notes, yet some admit that they frequently overlook such dishonesty. Although cheating rates are rising nationwide, many professors turn a blind eye to it because it puts them in the uncomfortable role of police officer instead of educator. Most universities' academic dishonesty policies scare professors with their onerous, ambiguous regulations. Professors typically do not know what to expect of the policies and often avoid dealing with them. Many fear that complex legal proceedings will hurt their reputations and feel that it is their word against the student's. Others have trouble with the penalties. Some believe that lowering students' grades is unlikely to stop them from cheating again, but having them expelled from the university is too severe.

University administrators are worried about these faculty attitudes toward cheating, and some feel that "academic dishonesty is one of the most serious problems facing higher education today." They know that many professors are anxiety-ridden about it and believe that it is reducing the validity of the education students are receiving.

Students at universities with honor codes are much less likely to cheat than those at schools without such codes. Many students report a confusing lack of set rules about what professors define as cheating, which makes cheating seem unimportant. Others, however, report that they rely on faculty to stop their classmates from cheating and express disappointment in the professors who let them get away with it.

QUESTIONS FOR DISCUSSION

1. What types of student cheating behavior have you observed?
   a. How did you detect the cheating?
   b. Whose responsibility was it to control the cheating?
   c. Was the cheating dealt with? If so, how? If not, why not?
2. Apply the creative problem-solving process to develop an action plan to prevent the problem of academic cheating. Be prepared to present your plan to the class.

Group Exercise 2: Choosing a Decision Style[42]

Objective.   To learn how to apply the Vroom and Yetton decision participation model.

Preparation.   Review the earlier section in this chapter, When Is Participation Appropriate for Decision Making? Make sure you understand the five decision participation styles (Exhibit 9-6) and the decision participation tree (Exhibit 9-7). **(10 minutes)**

Step 1: Individual Case Analyses.   Individually read each of the three hypothetical cases that follow. Decide which of the five decision participation styles from Exhibit 9-7 on page 225 you would use in each situation. Record your decisions. **(10–15 minutes)**

Case A   You are manufacturing manager in the northeastern division of a large electronics plant. Upper management is always searching for ways to increase efficiency.

Recently management installed new machines and introduced a simplified work system, but to everyone's surprise (including your own) the expected increase in productivity has not been realized. In fact, production has begun to drop, quality has fallen, and the number of employee resignations has risen.

You do not believe anything is wrong with the machines. You have requested reports from other companies that are using them, and their responses confirm this opinion. You have also called in representatives from the firm that built the machines. These technicians have examined the machines thoroughly and report that they are operating at peak efficiency.

You suspect that some elements of the new work system may be responsible for the decreased output and quality, but this view is not shared by your five immediate subordinates—the four first-line supervisors who head your four production sections and your supply manager. They have attributed the drop in production to various factors: poor operators, insufficient training, lack of adequate financial incentives, and poor worker morale. Clearly, it is an issue surrounded by considerable depth of individual feeling. A high potential for discord exists among your five key subordinates, and this development may be just the tip of the iceberg.

This morning you received a phone call from your division manager, who had just reviewed your production figures for the last six months and was clearly concerned. The division manager has indicated that the problem is yours to solve in any way that you think best but has requested that you report within a week what steps you plan to take.

Certainly you share your manager's concern and you know that, despite their differing views, your subordinates share it as well. Your problem is to decide what steps must be taken by whom in the effort to reverse the decline.

Case B You are the general supervisor in charge of a large work gang that is laying an oil pipeline. It is now necessary to estimate your expected rate of progress in order to schedule material deliveries to the next field site.

You know the nature of the terrain you will be traveling and have the historical data you need to compute the mean and variance in the rate of speed over that type of terrain. Given these two variables, it is a simple matter to calculate the earliest and the latest times at which materials and support facilities will be needed at the next site. It is important that your estimate be reasonably accurate. Underestimates result in idle workers, and overestimates result in securing materials for a period of time before they are to be used.

Up to this point, progress has been good. Your five group supervisors and other members of the gang stand to receive substantial bonuses if the project is completed ahead of schedule.

Case C You are supervising the work of 12 engineers. All 12 have similar levels of formal training and work experience, a condition that enables you to use them interchangeably on most projects. Yesterday your manager informed you that a request had come in from an overseas affiliate for four engineers to go abroad on extended loan for a period of six to eight months. For a number of reasons, he argued (and you agreed) that this request should be met from your group.

All your engineers are capable of handling this assignment and, from the standpoint of present and future projects, no particular reason dictates why anyone should be retained over any other. The major problem is that the location of the overseas assignment is considered undesirable by most members of the organization.

Step 2: Group Discussion. After individuals have recorded their opinions of the most appropriate decision participation style in each of these cases, proceed with the following steps:

1. Divide the class into groups of five to six people.
2. Each person shares with others in the group why he or she chose a particular decision style for each of the three cases. Focus on determining all the reasons why people chose different decision styles. One person should write down the styles chosen for each case and note briefly the associated reasons. The group should not try to reach a consensus; you merely want to discover how many different approaches were taken and why. **(20 minutes)**
3. Using the decision-making tree in Exhibit 9-7 on page 000, individually answer the questions at the top and work through the decision tree until you reach the recommended decision style for each of the three cases. **(10 minutes)**
4. Repeat step 4 as a group. Now establish consensus as to the appropriate decision style prescribed by this model. **(10 minutes)**
5. Check your answers with the authors' recommendations, which your instructor will provide. Discuss any variations and reread the chapter explanation if misunderstandings persist. Speculate as to why differences occurred. The recorder should note the outcome of this group discussion. **(10 minutes)**

Step 3: Class Discussion. Reconvene as a class. The recorders report group outcomes, including discrepancies between the original (individual) analyses and the decision tree's solutions. Note any sharp disparities among the groups' responses, and try to determine why they occurred.

Participate in a class discussion based on the following questions:

1. To what extent do you agree with the model? What are its strengths and weaknesses in application?
2. Do you have a preferred decision style (AI, AII, CI, CII, GII)? Why or why not? Will knowledge of this model make any difference in your decision-style flexibility?
3. How closely does your decision behavior match that prescribed by the model? What evidence do you have that you are concerned more with time (efficiency) or with participation in choosing a decision style? **(15 minutes)**

Time. Count on approximately 75 minutes for the entire exercise. If the total class discussion is left out, the exercise takes about 55 to 60 minutes.

Group Exercise 3: Winter Survival Exercise[43]

Purpose. This exercise is designed to demonstrate the potential advantages of participative group decision making compared to individual decision making.

Time. 85 minutes for the complete exercise. If less time is available, skip step 7 or shorten steps 6 and 7 by the time needed. For example, leaving out step 7 saves 20 minutes, and if 5 minutes are taken off of step 6, the exercise can be completed in 55–60 minutes.

Directions. All class members read the Winter Survival Situation. **(5 minutes)**

Step 1: *Individually rank* the 12 items shown in the following Winter Survival Tally Chart according to their importance to your survival in the Winter Survival Situation. In the "Individual Ranking" column, indicate the most important item from 1 to 12, most to least important. Keep in mind the reasons why each item is or is not important. **(5 minutes)**

Step 2: Form groups of five or six members. Reach a *group consensus* of the best rank-order for the 12 items and record it in the second column of the Winter Survival Tally Chart. Remember, a consensus means that everyone agrees it is the best ranking the group can agree on; it is not simply an average of the individual rankings. **(30 minutes)**

Step 3: Enter the *expert's ranking,* which will be provided by the instructor, in the third column.

Step 4: Compute the absolute difference (i.e., ignore minus signs) between the *individual ranking* and the *expert's ranking* for each item and record this information in column four. Put the sum of the absolute differences for each item at the bottom of column 4.

Step 5: Compute the absolute difference for each item between the *team's ranking* and the expert's ranking. Sum these absolute scores at the bottom of column 5. **(5 minutes for steps 3 through 5)**

Step 6: Compare the differences between your absolute difference score and your group's absolute difference score. Based on these results, discuss the merits of individual versus team decision making. **(20 minutes)**

Step 7: Share your group's absolute difference scores and conclusions with the class. The class discusses common conclusions about the merits of individual versus team decision making. **(20 minutes)**

The Winter Survival Situation

You are somewhere in the woods of southern Manitoba or northern Minnesota. It is 11:32 A.M. in mid-January. The small plane in which you were traveling crashed on a small lake. The pilot and co-pilot were killed. Shortly after the crash, the plane sank completely into the lake, taking the pilot's and co-pilot's bodies with it. Everyone else on the flight escaped to land without getting wet and without serious injury.

The crash was so sudden that the pilot had no time to radio for help or to inform anyone of the plane's position. Because the pilot was trying to avoid the storm, you know the plane was considerably off course. The pilot announced shortly before the crash that you were 45 miles northwest of the nearest small town.

You are in a wilderness area made up of thick woods broken by many lakes and rivers. The snow depth varies from ankle-deep in windswept areas to more than knee-deep where it has drifted. The last weather report indicated that the temperature would reach 5°F in the daytime and −15°F at night. Plenty of dead wood and twigs can be found in the area around the lake. You and the other surviving passengers are dressed in winter clothing appropriate for city wear—suits, pantsuits, street shoes, and overcoats. While escaping from the plane, your group salvaged the 12 items listed in the "Items" column on the Winter Survival Tally Chart. You may assume that the number of persons in the group is the same as the number in your group, and that you have agreed to stay together.

Winter Survival Tally Chart

	Step	1	2	3	Individual 4	Team 5
Items		Your Individual Ranking	Group Consensus Ranking	Survival Expert's Ranking	Difference Between 1 and 3 Values	Difference Between 2 and 3 Values
Ball of steel wool						
Newspapers (one per person)						
Compass						
Hand ax						
Cigarette lighter (without fluid)						
Loaded .45-caliber pistol						
Sectional air map made of plastic						
20' × 20' piece of heavy-duty canvas						
Extra shirt and pants for each survivor						
Can of shortening						
Quart of 100-proof whiskey						
Family-size chocolate bar (one per person)						
			Difference	Totals		

SUMMARY CHECKLIST

Take a few minutes to reflect on your performance and look over others' ratings of your creative problem-solving skills. Now assess yourself on each of the key learning behaviors. Make a check (✓) next to those behaviors on which you need improvement.

_____ **Proactively identify problems.**
1. Establish trust with people involved in the situation.
2. Clarify objectives.
3. Assess the current situation.
4. Identify problems.

_____ **Analyze the problem identified.**
1. Separate symptoms from sources.
2. Determine all causes.

_____ **Make decisions.**
1. Establish decision-making criteria.
2. Develop action alternatives.
3. Evaluate alternatives.
4. Choose the best alternative.
5. Develop a plan of action.

_____ **Implement action plans.**
1. Assign tasks and responsibilities.
2. Establish an implementation schedule.
3. Reinforce commitment.
4. Activate the plan.

_____ **Follow through.**
1. Establish criteria for success.
2. Determine how to measure performance.
3. Monitor the results.
4. Take corrective action.

_____ **Decide who should participate in the decision process based on:**
1. Quality requirements.
2. Acceptance requirements.
3. Time availability.

_____ **Avoid group decision-making problems.**
1. Remain neutral.
2. Encourage critical evaluation and devil's advocates.
3. Ask for new ideas.
4. Bring in outside experts.
5. Allow second-chance meetings to reconsider decisions.

APPLICATION QUESTIONS

1. Explain why it is so important to establish an atmosphere of trust in situations of group problem solving. Can you cite situations in which you have not trusted others with whom you were involved in solving a problem? Compare them with situations in which you have felt trust. Have you ever felt that others in a group distrusted you? Why?
2. What four purposes are served by clarifying objectives early in the problem-solving process? Whose objectives should be considered?
3. Explain this statement: "No problem solution can be better than the quality of diagnosis on which it is built."

4. With regard to selecting an action plan, indicate whether you agree or disagree with each of the following statements and why: (a) Experience is the best teacher (b) Intuition is a helpful force (c) Advice from others is always beneficial (d) Experiment with several alternatives.
5. What difficulties might you anticipate when using the rational problem-solving process? Why? What additional difficulties might arise because of personal attributes? Which of these have you experienced? Explain. What were the consequences? How can these difficulties be avoided?
6. Explain under what circumstances you would want to use participation to solve a problem. When would you rather solve the problem individually?
7. How can a manager encourage creative problem solving by department members?

REINFORCEMENT EXERCISES

1. Interview several managers about how they make decisions. Compare the answers you receive to the steps in the rational problem-solving model. Also, check the degree of participation that these managers used against those recommended by the participation decision tree.
2. Ask some other people to help you solve a problem that you are concerned with. Get their ideas by applying the rational problem-solving model and techniques for enhancing creativity, such as brainstorming.
3. Help a group you are involved with such as your family, roommates, church group, or sport team creatively solve a problem it is having difficulty with by applying the creative problem-solving skills you have acquired from this chapter.
4. Watch a movie or television show where the objective is to solve a crime. Note the problem-solving process that the actors apply and compare it to the creative problem-solving techniques you have learned about in this chapter. What did you learn from this comparison?

ACTION PLAN

1. Which creative problem-solving behavior do I most want to improve?
2. Why? What will be my payoff?
3. What potential obstacles stand in my way?
4. What are the specific things I will do to improve? (For examples, see the Reinforcement Exercises.)
5. When will I do them?
6. How and when will I measure my success?

NOTES

1. N. C. Nash, "Putting Porsche in the Pink: German Craftsmanship Gets Japanese Fine-Tuning," *New York Times,* January 20, 1996, 17–18.
2. B. M. Bass, *Organizational Decision Making* (Homewood, IL: Richard D. Irwin, 1983).
3. E. R. Archer, "How to Make a Business Decision: An Analysis of Theory and Practice," *Management Review* (February 1980): 289–99.
4. W. F. Pounds, "The Process of Problem Finding," *Industrial Management Review II* (Fall 1969): 1–19.
5. Ibid.
6. P. L. Hunsaker and A. J. Alessandra, *The Art of Managing People* (New York: Simon & Schuster, 1986) 224–26.
7. M. Brassard, *The Memory Jogger: A Pocket Guide of Tools for Continuous Improvement* (Methuen, MA: GOAL/QPC, 1988) 9–13.
8. Ibid., 24–29.
9. J. Tsalikis and D. J. Fritzsche, "Business Ethics; A Literature Review with a Focus on Marketing Ethics," *Journal of Business Ethics* 8 (1989): 695–743.
10. L. S. Klein, "Ethical Decision Making in a Business Environment," *Review of Business* 13, no. 3 (Winter 1991–1992): 27–29.
11. O. C. Ferrell and G. Gardiner, *In Pursuit of Ethics: Tough Choices in the World of Work* (Springfield, IL: Smith Collins Company, 1991) 9–13.
12. S. Baker, "Ethical Judgment," *Executive Excellence* (March 1992): 7–8.
13. S. M. Natale, C. F. O'Donnell, and W. R. C. Osborne, Jr., "Decision Making: Managerial Perspectives," *Thought* 63, no. 248 (1990): 32–51.
14. H. A. Simon, *Administrative Behavior,* 2d ed. (New York: Free Press, 1957).

15. P. Dean, "Open-and-Shut for Value," *Los Angeles Times,* October 30, 1992, E1, E6.

16. J. L. Cotton, D. A. Vollrath, and K. L. Froggatt, "Employee Participation: Diverse Forms and Different Outcomes," *Academy of Management Review* (January 1988): 8–22.

17. V. H. Vroom and A. J. Jago, *The New Leadership: Managing Participation in Organizations* (Upper Saddle River, NJ: Prentice Hall, 1988).

18. Ibid.

19. Ibid.

20. M. E. Shaw, *Group Dynamics,* 3d ed. (New York: McGraw-Hill, 1981) 78.

21. R. G. Fulmer, C. P. Koelling, A. R. Doss, and H. A. Kurstedt, Jr., "The Effects of Information Availability on the Group Consensus Process," *Computers & Industrial Engineering* 19, nos. 1–4 (1990): 510–13.

22. N. R. F. Maier, "Assets and Liabilities in Group Problem Solving," *Psychological Review* 74 (July 1967): 239–49.

23. I. Janis, *Victims of Groupthink* (Boston: Houghton Mifflin, 1972); and "Groupthink" *Psychology Today* (November 1971): 43–46.

24. I. Janis, *Groupthink: Psychological Studies of Policy Decisions and Fiascoes,* 2d ed. (Boston: Houghton Mifflin, 1982).

25. J. E. Driskell and E. Salas, "Group Decision Making Under Stress," *Journal of Applied Psychology* (June 1991): 473–8.

26. A. E. Schwartz and J. Levin, "Better Group Decision Making," *Supervisory Management* (June 1990): 319–42.

27. Janis, "Groupthink," 43–45.

28. D. Campbell, "Some Characteristics of Creative Managers," *Center for Creative Leadership Newsletter,* no. 1 (February 1978): 6–7.

29. Ibid., 7.

30. The company examples in this section are from J. Cocks, "Let's Get Crazy," *Time,* June 11, 1990, 40–41.

31. Ibid.

32. A. Stewart, "3M Fights Back," *Fortune,* February 5, 1996, 94–99.

33. *Time,* 1990.

34. M. Alari, "Group Decision Support Systems: A Key to Business Team Productivity," *Journal of Information Systems Management* 8, no. 3 (Summer 1991): 36–41.

35. A. F. Osborn, *Applied Imagination* (New York: Scribner, 1957).

36. A. H. Van de Ven and A. Delbecq, "The Effectiveness of Nominal, Delphi, and Interacting Group Decision-Making Processes," *Academy of Management Journal* 17 (1974): 605–21.

37. N. C. Dalkey and O. Helmer, "An Experimental Application of the Delphi Method to the Use of Experts," *Management Science* 9 (1963): 458–67.

38. Alari, "Group Decision Support Systems," 36–41.

39. R. B. Gallupe, et al., "Electronic Brainstorming and Group Size," *Academy of Management Journal* 35, no. 2 (1992): 350–69.

40. Adapted from D. A. Whetton and K. S. Cameron,*Developing Management Skills,* 2d ed. (New York: Harper Collins, 1991) 438–39.

41. The case was prepared based on material appearing in B. Murray, "Are Professors Turning a Blind Eye To Cheating?" *The APA Monitor* (January 1996): 1, 42; D. McBurney, "Cheating: Preventing and Dealing With Academic Dishonesty," *APS Observer* (January 1996): 32–35.

42. The three cases cited in this exercise are from V. H. Vroom and A. G. Jago, "Decision Making as a Social Process," *Decision Sciences* 5, no. 4 (October 1974): 734–69.

43. Adapted from D. Johnson and F. Johnson, *Joining Together,* 5th ed. (Boston: Allyn and Bacon, 1994) 261–66.

PLANNING

In this episode, we find out that John got the production manager job at Quicktakes. We meet up with John on his first day on the job. We join him at his first meeting at Quicktakes and are reintroduced to Hal and Karen, the owners of the company. We also meet Alexandra, the company's general manager. It seems that the purpose of this meeting is to give John an idea of how the company is organized, what its goals are, and how things are run.

What can you learn from this meeting that relates to what you have learned about planning? Before considering this question, we might want to make some assumptions about the management of the company. Given that this meeting is set up to introduce John to the company, we assume that the people invited are those that the owners believe are important in setting the direction and focus of the company, or are those most responsible for keeping it running. This may not be a correct assumption, but it is logical that John might get this idea. He will only know for sure after he has been at Quicktakes for a while.

This meeting is John's first real chance to learn about who is really running Quicktakes and about how the people interact. In this meeting he gets some idea about how Hal and Karen operate and interact on the job. It is likely that someday, maybe soon, you will be in a meeting like this and you will be in John's shoes. Think about the kinds of information you would hope to get, the expectations you might have of new employers, and the kinds of things you would hope your new employer thinks are important. With these things in mind, you might now consider how you think John feels after this meeting.

There are a couple of important areas covered in this orientation meeting. First, we get some idea about the culture at Quicktakes. This comes across in the comments Hal makes to John about a dress code and the degree of formality that you observe in the meeting. You also get some hints about what Hal and Karen, and to some degree Alexandra, think Quicktakes' main product focus is. They tell John about things they think make them different from their competitors and things that they seem to think are important.

It is interesting that John asks about plans and goals more than once. This gives us an idea about what is important to John. He does not necessarily get the answer he is looking for and seems to think that there might be more to planning than what is currently considered at Quicktakes. ∎

QUESTIONS

1. Hal and Karen talk about their ideas for the company. Do you think they are both moving in the same direction and aiming at the same target? If not, how do you think this affects the ongoing operation of the company?

2. It was explained to John that it is difficult to plan because of changes in economic conditions and areas of public interest. What areas of Quicktakes' operation might economic and market factors affect the most? Do you think that these issues make it impossible to develop a general plan and goal for the company? What areas might be important to consider anyway?

3. There was discussion of things that Quicktakes does other than video production. Why do you think they do these other things? To what degree should a small company like Quicktakes spread itself across multiple products?

CHAPTER 10

Managing Conflict

Learning Objectives

After completing this chapter, you should be able to:

- Assess sources of a conflict.
- Modify your conflict management style appropriately.
- Empathize with positions of others in conflicts.
- Deal with emotions.
- Negotiate conflict resolution.
- Stimulate appropriate conflict.
- Implement procedures to manage conflict.

SELF-ASSESSMENT EXERCISE

Indicate how often you do the following when you differ with someone by inserting the appropriate number after the statements. Answer as you actually do behave, not as you would like to behave.

5 Usually	4 Quite a bit	3 Sometimes	2 Occasionally	1 Seldom

When I differ with someone: | | | | Points

Set A:

1. I explore our differences, not backing down, but not imposing my view either. _____
2. I disagree openly, then invite more discussion about our differences. _____
3. I look for a mutually satisfactory solution. _____
4. Rather than let the other person make a decision without my input, I make sure I am heard and also that I hear the other out. _____

Sum the points for questions 1 through 4 to get your **Set A score** = _____ _____

Set B:

5. I agree to a middle ground rather than look for a completely satisfying solution. _____
6. I admit I am half wrong rather than explore our differences. _____

7. I have a reputation for meeting a person halfway.   _____

8. I expect to get out about half of what I really want to say.   _____

Sum the points for questions 5 through 8 to get your **Set B score** =   _____

Set C:

9. I give in totally rather than try to change another's opinion.   _____

10. I put aside any controversial aspects of an issue.   _____

11. I agree early on, rather than argue about a point.   _____

12. I give in as soon as the other party gets emotional about an issue. _____

Sum the points for questions 9 through 12 to get your **Set C score** =   _____

Set D:

13. I try to win the other person over.   _____

14. I work to come out victorious, no matter what.   _____

15. I never back away from a good argument.   _____

16. I would rather win than end up compromising.   _____

Sum the points for questions 13 through 16 to get your **Set D score** =   _____

Set E:

17. I prefer to avoid the other person until the problem is solved.   _____

18. I would rather we both lose than risk an emotional confrontation.   _____

19. I feel that most differences are not worth worrying about.   _____

20. I try to postpone discussing the issue until I can think it through
thoroughly.   _____

Sum the points for questions 17 through 20 to get your **Set E score** =   _____

Scoring and Interpretation

• Total your choices for each set of statements, grouped as follows:

Set A (items 1–4):   _____
Set B (items 5–8):   _____
Set C (items 9–12):   _____
Set D (items 13–16):   _____
Set E (items 17–20):   _____

• Sets A, B, C, D, and E represent the following different conflict-resolution strategies:

A = Collaborating	I win, you win.
B = Compromising	Both win some, lose some.
C = Accommodating	I lose, you win.
D = Competing/Forcing	I win, you lose.
E = Avoiding	I lose, you lose.

• Treat each set separately to determine your relative frequency of use.

• A score of **17 or above** on any set is **high.** When you differ with someone you do these things more often than most people.

• Scores of **8 to 16** are **moderate.** When you differ with someone you behave in these ways the same as most people.

• Scores of **7 or less** are considered **low.** When you differ with someone you behave in these ways less often than most people.

Everyone has a preferred or habitual conflict-handling style. High scores in a set indicate the strategies you rely upon or use most often. Scores do not indicate proficiency at using a strategy. The key thing to consider when analyzing your style is whether it is appropriate for the conflict situations you usually encounter with respect to the outcomes you desire. The five styles and their appropriated uses will be explained in the following section on knowing the basic styles of handling conflicts.

SOURCE: Adapted from T. J. Von der Embse, *Supervision: Managerial Skills for a New Era* (New York: Macmillian Publishing Co., 1987); and K. W. Thomas, "Conflict and Negotiation Processes in Organizations," in M. D. Dunnette and L. M. Hough (eds.), *Handbook of Industrial and Organizational Psychology*, 2nd ed., vol. 3 (Palo Alto, CA: Consulting Psychologist Press, 1992), pp. 651–717.

CONCEPTS

It is difficult, if not impossible, to think of a relationship of any type that does not encounter disagreements at one time or another. Unless relationships are able to withstand the stress involved in their inevitable conflicts, and manage them productively, those relationships are not likely to endure.[1] Because of inherent characteristics such as scarce resources, interdependence, different goals, and the need for coordination, conflict is a natural phenomenon in organizational life. Consequently, it is not surprising that some organization researchers have concluded that "no skill is more important for organizational effectiveness than the constructive management and resolution of conflict."[2] This chapter provides concepts for understanding and skills for managing conflict productively in both personal and organizational situations.

What Is Conflict?

Conflict is a disagreement between two or more parties (individuals, groups, departments, organizations, countries, etc.) who perceive that they have incompatible concerns. Conflicts exist whenever an action by one party is perceived as preventing or interfering with the goals, needs, or actions of another party. Conflicts can arise due to a variety of organizational experiences, such as incompatible goals, differences in the interpretation of facts, negative feelings, differences of values and philosophies, or disputes over shared resources.[3]

Conflict is natural to organizations and can never be completely eliminated. If not managed properly, however, conflict can be dysfunctional and lead to undesirable consequences such as hostility, lack of cooperation, violence, destroyed relationships, and even company failure. But, when managed effectively, conflict has many beneficial properties. It stimulates creativity, innovation, change, and can even result in better relationships. If organizations were completely devoid of conflict, they would become apathetic, stagnant, and unresponsive to change. Given this reality, comprehensive conflict management should encompass both conflict stimulation and conflict-resolution techniques.[4] Typically when managers talk about conflict problems they are referring to conflict's dysfunctional effects and they are seeking ways to eliminate them.

What Are the Main Sources of Conflict?

Conflicts do not just magically appear out of thin air. They have causes. Research indicates that while conflicts have varying causes, they can generally be separated into three categories: communication problems, structural design, and personal differences.[5]

Communication Problems

Disagreements frequently arise from semantic difficulties, misunderstandings, poor listening, and noise in the communication channels. People are often quick to assume that most conflicts are caused by lack of communication. In reality, plenty of communication is usually going on during a conflict. The mistake many people make is equating good communication with having others agree with their views; they assume that if others do not accept their position, a communication problem must be at fault.[6] After a closer analysis, what might look like an interpersonal conflict based on poor communication is quite often determined to be a disagreement caused by things such as different role requirements, incompatible goals, or different value systems.

Structural Design

When performing the organizing function, management divides up tasks, groups common tasks into departments, sets up a hierarchy of authority to coordinate departments, and establishes rules and regulations to facilitate standardized practices between departments. Exhibit 10-1 illustrates a functional organization chart. This structural differentiation creates interdependence between units and the need to coordinate activities. Unfortunately, integration efforts frequently result in conflict when various units disagree over goal priorities, decision alternatives, performance criteria, and resource allocations. The "goodies" that people want—budgets, promotions, pay increases, additions to staff, office space, influence over decisions, and the like—are scarce resources that must be divvied up. The creation of horizontal units (departments) and vertical levels (the management hierarchy) brings about efficiencies through specialization and coordination, but at the same time produces the potential for structural conflicts.

Personal Differences

Conflicts can evolve out of individual idiosyncrasies and personal value systems. The chemistry between some people makes it hard for them to work together. Factors such as cultural background, education, experience, and training mold each individual into a unique personality with a particular set of values and different behavioral styles. The result is people who may be perceived by others as abrasive, untrustworthy, or strange by individuals with different backgrounds. The conflicts created by these types of personal differences are exacerbated when people from different countries or subcultures interact with each other. Stereotypes and prejudice are often the culprits, but ignorance and misunderstanding also create confusing conflicts.

What Are the Key Conflict Management Skills?

If conflict is dysfunctional, what skills and knowledge does a manager need to manage it successfully? Although many of the skills discussed earlier in this book can help—for

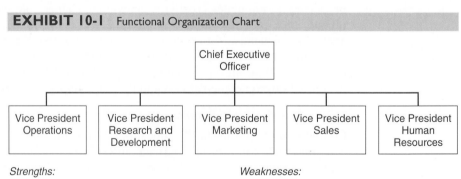

EXHIBIT 10-1 Functional Organization Chart

Chief Executive Officer

- Vice President Operations
- Vice President Research and Development
- Vice President Marketing
- Vice President Sales
- Vice President Human Resources

Strengths:

- Lowers headquarters–subsidiary conflicts
- Increases international orientation of all managers
- Facilitates coordination within function
- Effective when market demands are similar

Weaknesses:

- Often creates problems in cross-functional coordination
- Slower response to specific market changes
- Ineffective when international market demands differ

SOURCE: Adapted from J. S. Blac and L. W. Porter, *Management* (Upper Saddle River, NJ: Prentice Hall, 1999) 271.

example, listening, goal setting, and problem solving—you need to be able to do a number of specific things to deal effectively with conflicts. The following skills are discussed in the order that they are usually applied in a conflict situation. First, you need to assess the nature of the conflict: what created it, who is involved, what the consequences are, and so on. Second, you need to decide which conflicts to take on and which to avoid. Third, you need to understand the different conflict-handling styles, including your own preferred style. Fourth, it helps to determine the other party's preferred conflict style and empathize with that position. Fifth, you are now ready to determine your objectives, assess your options, and decide on a game plan to achieve the preferred one. Sixth, it is often necessary, however, to deal effectively with the emotional aspects of conflict before a rational solution can be worked out. Seventh, at times you will determine that it is appropriate to negotiate a satisfactory outcome, or eighth, even stimulate conflict to provide optimal long-term results for all involved.

Assess the Nature of the Conflict

The best approach to resolving a conflict can quite often be determined by understanding its causes. Consequently, the first, and perhaps most important, thing you need to do is to identify the source of the conflict (e.g., cultural differences, communication problems, structural differences, personal style incompatibilities, and so on).

Next, examine the long-term and short-term consequences of the conflict. Is the conflict dysfunctional, hindering the achievement of personal and organizational goals? Is there hostility, decreased communication, negative stereotypes, lack of cooperation? Are any functional consequences of value, which you may want to maintain, such as increased problem awareness, clarification of priorities, personal or organizational learning, or improvements in operating practices? Sometimes you may want to just let the conflict play out. Other times, immediate intervention will be required.

Judiciously Select the Conflicts You Try to Manage

Not every conflict justifies your attention. Some might not be worth the effort; others might be unmanageable. Although avoidance might appear to be a cop-out, it can sometimes be the most appropriate response. You can improve your overall managerial effectiveness, and your conflict management skills in particular, by avoiding trivial conflicts. Choose your battles judiciously, saving your efforts for the ones that have serious consequences. Regardless of our desires, reality tells us that some conflicts are unmanageable.[7] When antagonisms are deeply rooted, when one or both parties wish to prolong a conflict, or when emotions run so high that constructive interaction is impossible, your efforts to manage the conflict are unlikely to meet with much success. Do not be lured into the naive belief that a good manager can resolve every conflict effectively. Some are not worth the effort. Some are outside your realm of influence. Still others may be functional and, as such, are best left alone.

Know the Basic Styles of Handling Conflicts

Even though most of us have the ability to vary our conflict response according to the situation, each of us has a preferred style for handling conflicts.[8] The Self-Assessment Exercise at the beginning of this chapter can help you identify the conflict-handling style you use the most. You might be able to change your preferred style to suit the context in which a certain conflict exists; however, your basic style indicates how you are *most likely* to behave in most conflict situations.

Managers can draw upon five basic conflict resolution approaches when attempting to resolve dysfunctional conflicts: avoidance, accommodation, forcing, compromise, and collaboration.[9] The five basic conflict-handling style options are presented graphically in Exhibit 10-2. Each has particular strengths and weaknesses, and no one option is ideal for every situation. You should consider each one a tool in your conflict-management toolbox. Even though you might be better at using some tools than others, the skilled manager understands the potential of each tool and knows when each is most effective.

Not every conflict requires an assertive action. Sometimes **avoidance**—withdrawing from or postponing the conflict—is the best solution. When is avoidance a desirable strategy? It is most appropriate when the conflict is trivial, when emotions are running high and time is needed for the conflicting parties to cool down, or when the potential disruption from a more assertive action outweighs the benefits of resolution.

The goal of **accommodation** is to maintain harmonious relationships by placing another's needs and concerns above your own. You might, for example, yield to another person's position on an issue because it is much more important to him or her. This option is most viable when the issue under dispute is not that important to you or when you want to "build up credits" for later issues.

When **competing,** you attempt to satisfy your own needs at the expense of the other party. In organizations, this style is most often illustrated by a manager using his or her formal authority to resolve a dispute. Competing works well when you need a quick resolution on important issues where unpopular actions must be taken, and when commitment by others to your solution isn't crucial.

A **compromise** requires each party to give up something of value. Typically, this approach is taken by management and labor in negotiating a new labor contract. Compromise can be an optimal strategy when conflicting parties are about equal in power, when it is desirable to achieve a temporary solution to a complex issue, or when time pressures demand an expedient solution.

Finally, **collaboration** is the ultimate win-win solution. All parties to the conflict seek to satisfy their interests. It is typically characterized by open and honest discussion among the parties, active listening to understand differences, and careful deliberation over a full range of alternatives to find a solution that is advantageous to all. When is collaboration the best conflict option? When time pressures are minimal, when all parties seriously want a win-win solution, and when the issue is too important to be compromised.

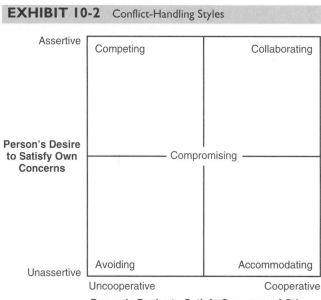

EXHIBIT 10-2   Conflict-Handling Styles

Empathize with the Other Parties in the Conflict

If you choose to manage a conflict situation, it is important that you take the time to get to know the players. Who is involved in the conflict? What interests does each party represent? What are each player's values, personality, feelings, and resources? Your chances of success in managing a conflict will be greatly enhanced if you can view the conflict situation through the eyes of the conflicting parties.

Empathizing is more difficult for most of us when the other conflict parties are from another country and culture. As international trade increases, so does the frequency of business negotiations among people from different countries and cultures regarding joint ventures, acquisitions, mergers, licensing, distribution agreements, and sales of products and services. To successfully manage such negotiations, businesspeople need to know how to influence and communicate with members of cultures other than their own.[10]

Do North Americans negotiate with the same expectations and approaches as Arabs? Are Japanese negotiation styles similar to Russian styles? Do Brazilian negotiators possess the same characteristics as those from China? The answers to all of these questions is no. A growing literature exists documenting that people from different countries negotiate in widely different ways.[11] Exhibit 10-3 illustrates how negotiation styles of people from three different countries differ.

When preparing for negotiations with people from different cultures it is especially important to imagine what the situation looks like through their eyes. This ability may require some research on your part if you are not familiar with the country's culture. The fact of international negotiations is that no formula guarantees success. You should address specific questions about the other culture such as the following:

- What is important to them?
- Who has power?
- What is at stake?

EXHIBIT 10-3   National Styles of Persuasion

	North Americans	*Arabs*	*Russians*
Primary negotiating style and process	*Factual:* Appeals made to logic	*Affective:* Appeals made to emotions	*Axiomatic:* Appeals made to ideals
Conflict: Counterparts' arguments countered with …	Objective facts	Subjective feelings	Asserted ideals
Making concessions	Small concessions made early to establish a relationship	Concessions made throughout as a part of the bargaining process	Few if any concessions made
Response to counterparts' concessions	Usually reciprocate counterparts' concessions	Almost always reciprocate counterparts' concessions	Counterparts' concessions viewed as weakness and almost never reciprocated
Relationship	Short term	Long term	No continuing relationship
Authority	Broad	Broad	Limited
Initial position	Moderate	Extreme	Extreme
Deadline	Very important	Casual	Ignored

SOURCE: E. S. Glenn, D. Witmeyer, and K. A. Stevenson, "Cultural Styles of Persuasion," *International Journal of Intercultural Relations* 1, no. 3 (Fall 1977). Reprinted with permission from Elsevier Science.

- What is their time frame?
- Where do they draw their personal and organizational bottom line?[12]

Deal with the Emotional Aspects of Conflict

When feelings such as anger, fear, or resentment are strong, it is usually better to deal with the emotional aspects of conflict first before trying to settle substantive issues. Why? When we are highly emotional, our ability to think through all the consequences of our actions is not optimal. The following three steps are designed to help alleviate negative emotions for both parties, which better prepares them to deal with the substantive issues in a more constructive manner.

1. ***Treat the other person with respect.*** During emotional disagreements, words of disrespect are often spoken carelessly, but they can block communication and create wounds that may never fully heal. We all have made or endured disrespectful statements like "That's the dumbest idea I've heard in years," or "You're such an idiot," or much worse. Nonverbal behaviors, such as the way you look at the other, not listening, or sarcasm in your voice, can also convey disrespect.

After such an outburst, you often apologize and explain that you were just mad and did not really mean what you said. But the other person has heard and reacted to what you said, and may think that it took a burst of anger for you to speak the truth and that your apology is just a feeble attempt to backpeddle out of the situation. Consequently, the receiving party is on the defensive and less likely to trust what you say next.

To avoid slipping into a disrespectful conversation, you need to check your own emotions. It helps to get the end in mind, which usually means understanding how the other sees the situation, getting what you need, and maintaining the relationship. It frequently requires an act of willpower, but it is worth it to keep the situation rational and respectful.

2. ***Listen and restate to the other's satisfaction.*** The goal here is to understand the other person's point of view and feelings, and to make that person feel understood. Your job is to understand, not necessarily to agree. When you indicate that you understand the other's feelings, it is amazing how quickly any bad feelings subside. This acknowledgment opens the way for you to share your point of view with a much higher probability of being understood.

3. ***Briefly state your views, needs, and feelings.*** After demonstrating respect for the other person and conveying your understanding of his or her feelings and point of view, it is your turn to share your position. During a conflict you will usually communicate better if you keep your message short and to the point, avoid loaded words that might upset the other party, do not exaggerate or leave out things, and disclose your feelings about the issue and what has transpired.

Determine Your Objectives

The next thing you should look at is your goals. The best solution is closely intertwined with your definition of "best." Three goals seemed to dominate our discussion of strategies: (1) the importance of the conflict issue, (2) concern over maintaining long-term interpersonal relations, and (3) the speed with which you need to resolve the conflict. All other things held constant, if the issue is critical to the organization's or relationship's success, collaboration is preferred. If sustaining supportive relationships is most important to you, the best strategies, in order of preference, are accommodation, collaboration, compromise, and avoidance. If it is crucial to resolve the conflict as quickly as possible, forcing, accommodation, and compromise, in that order, are preferred.

Implement the Optimal Long-Term Strategy for All Involved

Start by looking at your preferred conflict-handling style (see the Self-Assessment Exercise), and gaining an awareness of the styles with which you feel most comfortable. Next consider the source of the conflict. What works best depends, to a large degree, on the cause of the conflict.[13] Communication-based conflicts revolve around misinformation and misunderstandings. Such conflicts lend themselves to collaboration. In contrast, conflicts based on personal differences arise out of disparities between the parties' values and personalities. Such conflicts are most susceptible to avoidance because these differences are often deeply entrenched. When managers have to resolve conflicts rooted in personal differences, they frequently rely on forcing—not so much because it placates the parties, but because it works! The third category, or structural conflicts, seems to be amenable to most of the conflict strategies depending on other variables in the situation. Exhibit 10-4 illustrates when you should and should not use each conflict management strategy.

This process of blending your personal style, your goals, and the source of the conflict should result in identifying the strategy or set of strategies most likely to be effective for you in any specific conflict situation. Keep in mind, however, that most conflict situations involve interdependent parties that need each other over the long term to achieve joint objectives. Overall, over the long run, interdependent relationships can only endure when collaborative solutions are reached and both parties feel that they have achieved what they need. Otherwise, one party may win a battle but lose the war when the losing party, whom the winner needs, leaves for a more beneficial relationship. So, in the long run, either both sides win, or both parties lose.

EXHIBIT 10-4   When to Use the Different Conflict Management Styles

Conflict Management Style	When to Use	When Not to Use
Collaborating	When issues are complex and require input and information from others When commitment is needed When dealing with strategic issues When long-term solutions are needed	When time is critical When others are not interested or do not have the skills When conflict occurs because of different value systems
Accommodating	When the issues are unimportant to you When your knowledge is limited When there is long-term give and take When you have no power	When others are unethical or wrong When you are certain you are correct
Competing	When time is critical When issues are trivial When any solution is unpopular When others lack expertise When issues are important to you	When issues are complex and require input and information from others When working with powerful competent others When long-term solutions and commitment are needed
Avoiding	When issues are trivial When conflict is too high and parties need to cool off	When a long-term solution is needed When you are responsible for resolving the conflict
Compromising	When goals are clearly incompatible When parties have equal power When a quick solution is needed	When an imbalance in power is present When the problem is complex When long-term solutions are needed When conflict is rooted in different value systems

SOURCE: Based on M. A. Rahim, "A Measure of Styles of Handling Interpersonal Conflict," *Academy of Management Journal* (June 1983): 368–76; M. A. Rahim, *Managing Conflict in Organizations,* 2d ed. (Westport, CT: Praeger, 1992).

You can do a few things to facilitate win/win outcomes.[14] First, do your homework so that you are prepared, know the facts, and understand the other's situation. Second, do not underestimate the others' knowledge about the situation or the importance of their commitment to their position. Third, always share the credit for solutions, even if it means just letting the other person save face and win something. After all, the real goal in interdependent relationships is more than just getting your own way; it is making sure that both parties feel that they win and are on the same side.

Option of Last Resort[15]

When interdependent parties try for collaborative solutions and fail, they can sometimes agree to disagree, and still cooperate in their joint endeavors. Often putting aside disagreements is necessary in value conflicts where each party is strongly committed, but agreement is not necessary to continue the relationship. If agreement is required, a positive relationship can still be maintained by agreeing to no deal: If the two parties cannot find a collaborative solution, they agree not to continue their relationship, because it is not right for both of them, and they part friends, open to future collaborative possibilities.

Before moving to this option of last resort, however, the parties should attempt to negotiate a solution that will allow both to achieve satisfactory, although not optimal, outcomes. A subset of skills can contribute to successful negotiating, which we will discuss next.

Negotiation

Negotiation is a process in which two or more parties exchange goods or services and attempt to agree upon the exchange rate for them.[16] For our purposes, we will also use the term interchangeably with *bargaining*.

We know that lawyers and car salespeople spend a lot of time negotiating. Actually the managers do also. They have to negotiate salaries for incoming employees, cut deals with superiors, bargain over budgets, work out differences with associates, and resolve conflicts with subordinates. First, two broad bargaining strategies will be discussed, then specific negotiation tactics will be summarized.

Bargaining Strategies

The two general approaches to negotiation are distributive bargaining and integrative bargaining. It is important to know the distinction between the two and when each is appropriate. A graphic comparison of the two is shown in Exhibit 10-5.

Distributive Bargaining

You see a used car advertised for sale in the newspaper. It appears to be just what you have been looking for. You go out to see the car. It is great and you want it. The owner tells you the asking price, which is more than you want to pay. The two of you then negotiate over the price. The negotiating process you are engaging in is called

EXHIBIT 10-5 Distributive Versus Integrative Bargaining

Bargaining Characteristic	Distributive Bargaining	Integrative Bargaining
Available resources	Fixed amount of resources to be divided	Variable amount of resources to be divided
Primary motivations	I win, you lose	I win, you win
Primary interests	Opposed to each other	Convergent or congruent with each other
Focus of relationships	Short-term	Long-term

SOURCE: Based on R. J. Lewicki and J. A. Litterer, *Negotiation* (Homewood, IL: Irwin, 1985) 280.

distributive bargaining. Its most identifying feature is that it operates under zero-sum conditions. That is, any gain I make is at your expense, and vice versa. Referring back to the used-car example, every dollar you can get the seller to cut from the car's price is a dollar you save. Conversely, every dollar more he or she can get from you comes at your expense. Thus, the essence of distributive bargaining is negotiating over who gets what share of a fixed pie.

One of the most widely cited examples of distributive bargaining is labor-management wage negotiations. Typically, labor's representatives come to the bargaining table determined to get as much money as possible out of management. Because every cent more that labor negotiates increases management's costs by the same amount, each party bargains aggressively and treats the other as an opponent who must be defeated. Exhibit 10-6 depicts the distributive bargaining strategy. Parties A and B represent the two negotiators. Each has a target point that defines what he or she would like to achieve. Each also has a resistance point, which marks the lowest outcome that is acceptable—the point below which he or she would break off negotiations rather than accept a less favorable settlement. The area between their resistance points is the settlement range. As long as their aspiration ranges overlap somewhat, a settlement area exists where each one's aspirations can be met.

When engaged in distributive bargaining, your tactics should focus on trying to get your opponent to agree to your specific target point or to get as close to it as possible. Examples of such tactics are persuading your opponent of the impossibility of getting to his or her target point and the advisability of accepting a settlement near yours; arguing that your target is fair, while your opponent's is not; and attempting to get your opponent to feel emotionally generous toward you and thus accept an outcome close to your target point.

Integrative Bargaining

Assume a sales representative for a women's sportswear manufacturer has just closed a $15,000 order from a small clothing retailer. The sales rep calls in the order to her firm's credit department. She is told that the firm cannot approve credit to this customer because of a past slow-pay record. The next day, the sales rep and the firm's credit supervisor meet to discuss the problem. The sales rep does not want to lose the business; neither does the credit supervisor, but he also doesn't want to get stuck with an uncollectible debt. The two openly review their options. After considerable discussion, they agree on

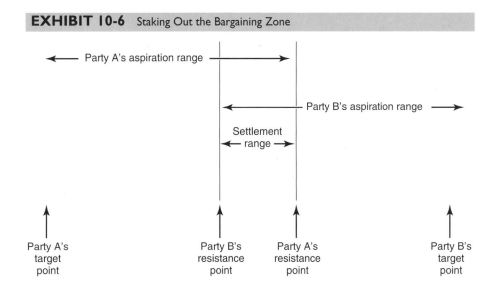

EXHIBIT 10-6   Staking Out the Bargaining Zone

a solution that meets both their needs: The credit supervisor will approve the sale, but the clothing store's owner will provide a bank guarantee that will assure payment if the bill is not paid within 60 days.

The sales-credit negotiation is an example of **integrative bargaining.** In contrast to distributive bargaining, integrative problem solving operates under the assumption that at least one settlement exists that can create a win-win solution.

In general, integrative bargaining is preferable to distributive bargaining. Why? Because the former builds long-term relationships and facilitates working together in the future. It bonds negotiators and allows each to leave the bargaining table feeling that he or she has achieved a victory. Distributive bargaining, on the other hand, leaves one party a loser. It tends to build animosities and deepen divisions between people who have to work together on an ongoing basis.

Why, then, do we not see more integrative bargaining in organizations? The answer lies in the conditions necessary for this type of negotiation to succeed. These conditions include openness with information and frankness between parties, sensitivity on the part of each party to the other's needs, the ability to trust one another, and a willingness by both parties to maintain flexibility. Because many organizational cultures and interpersonal relationships are not characterized by openness, trust, and flexibility, it is not surprising that negotiations often take on a win-at-any-cost dynamic.

Guidelines for Effective Negotiating

The essence of effective negotiation can be summarized in the following 10 guidelines. Careful attention to them can increase your odds of successful negotiation outcomes.

1. ***Consider the other party's situation.***   Acquire as much information as you can about your opponent's interests and goals. What are his or her real needs versus wants? What constituencies must he or she appease? What is his or her strategy? Jerry Anderson, president of the Minneapolis-based architectural-glass fabricator, Apogee Enterprises, is consistently successful at reaching consensus in negotiations between architects, engineers, and building contractors. He attributes a large amount of his success to forethought. "Always try to figure out where the other guy is coming from," he says. "If you think enough about it, you can usually come up with a reading."[17] This information will help you understand your opponent's behavior, predict his or her responses to your offers, and frame solutions in terms of his or her interests. Additionally, when you can anticipate your opponent's position, you are better equipped to counter his or her arguments with the facts and figures that support your position.

2. ***Have a concrete strategy***.   Treat negotiation like a chess match. Expert chess players have a strategy. They know ahead of time how they will respond to any given situation. How strong is your situation and how important is the issue? Are you willing to split differences to achieve an early solution? If the issue is important to you, is your position strong enough to let you play hardball and show little or no willingness to compromise? These questions should be addressed before you begin bargaining.

3. ***Begin with a positive overture.***   Establish rapport and mutual interests before starting the negotiation. Then begin bargaining with a positive overture, perhaps a small concession. Studies show that concessions tend to be reciprocated and lead to agreements. A positive climate can be further developed by reciprocating your opponent's concessions.

4. ***Address problems, not personalities.***   Concentrate on the negotiation issues, not on the personal characteristics of your opponent. When negotiations get tough, avoid the tendency to attack your opponent. If other people feel threatened, they concentrate on

defending their self-esteem, as opposed to solving the problem. It is your opponent's ideas or position that you disagree with, not him or her as a person. Separate the people from the problem, and avoid personalizing differences.

5. ***Maintain a rational, goal-oriented frame of mind.***   Use the previous guideline in reverse if your opponent attacks or gets emotional with you. Do not get hooked by emotional outbursts. Let the other person blow off steam without taking it personally while you try to understand the problem or strategy behind the aggression.

6. ***Insist on using objective criteria.***   Make your negotiated decisions based on principles and results, not emotions or pressure.[18] Agree upon objective criteria that can help both parties to assess the reasonableness of an alternative. Avoid emotional pleas, assertiveness, or stubbornness if their underlying rationale does not meet these criteria.

7. ***Pay little attention to initial offers.***   Treat an initial offer as merely a point of departure. Everyone has to have an initial position. These initial offers tend to be extreme and idealistic. Treat them as such. Focus on the other person's interests and your own goals and principles, while you generate other possibilities.

8. ***Emphasize win-win solutions.***   Inexperienced negotiators often assume that their gain must come at the expense of the other party. As noted with integrative bargaining, zero-sum results need not be the case. Often, win-win solutions can be found. But assuming a zero-sum game means missed opportunities for trade-offs that could benefit both sides. So if conditions are supportive, look for an integrative solution. Create additional alternatives, especially low-cost concessions you can make that have high value to the other party. Frame options in terms of your opponent's interests and look for solutions that can allow your opponent, as well as yourself, to declare a victory.

9. ***Create an open and trusting climate.***   Skilled negotiators listen well, ask questions, focus their arguments directly, are not defensive, and have learned to avoid words and phrases that can irritate an opponent. In other words, they are adept at creating the open and trusting climate necessary for reaching an integrative settlement.

10. ***Be open to accepting third-party assistance.***   When stalemates are reached, consider using a neutral third party. Mediators can help parties come to an agreement, but they do not impose a settlement. Arbitrators hear both sides of the dispute and then impose a solution. Conciliators are more informal and act as a communication conduit, passing information between the parties, interpreting messages, and clarifying misunderstandings.

What About Conflict Stimulation?

What about the other side of conflict management—situations that require managers to *stimulate* conflict? Few of us personally enjoy being in conflict situations, so the idea of purposely creating them seems to be the antithesis of good management. Yet the evidence demonstrates that in certain situations, an increase in conflict is constructive.[19] Following are some suggestions that managers might want to use to stimulate conflict.[20] Some, such as changing the organization's culture (discussed in Chapter 12) and restructuring the organization (discussed in Chapter 11), are more effective if you are a higher-level manager with position authority. The others, using communication strategies, bringing in outsiders, and appointing a devil's advocate, can be applied at any managerial level.

1. ***Communicate that conflict has a legitimate place in the organization.***   The initial step in stimulating functional conflict is for managers to convey to subordinates the message, supported by actions, that conflict is encouraged in the organization. This atmosphere entails changing the organizational culture so that individuals who beneficially challenge the status quo, suggest innovative ideas, offer divergent opinions, and

demonstrate original thinking are rewarded visibly with promotions, salary increases, and other positive reinforcers.

2. ***Send ambiguous messages about potentially threatening developments.*** Disclosing news that a plant might close, a department could be eliminated, or that a layoff is likely will reduce apathy, stimulate new ideas, and force reevaluation. The goal is to create healthy conflict in the spirit of joint problem solving to produce renewed interest and creative solutions.

3. ***Bring in outsiders.*** A widely used method for shaking up a stagnant unit or organization is to bring in—either by hiring from outside or by internal transfer—individuals whose backgrounds, values, attitudes, or managerial styles differ from those of present members. Many large organizations have used this technique over the last decade in filling vacancies on their boards of directors. Women, minority group members, consumer activists, and others whose backgrounds and interests differ significantly from those of the rest of the board have been purposely selected to add a fresh perspective.

4. ***Restructure the organization.*** Centralizing decisions, realigning work groups, increasing formalization, and increasing interdependencies between units are all structural devices that disrupt the status quo and act to increase conflict levels.

5. ***Appoint a devil's advocate.*** A devil's advocate is a person who purposely presents arguments that run counter to those proposed by the majority or against current practices. He or she plays the role of the critic, even to the point of arguing against positions with which he or she actually agrees in order to stimulate discussion. A devil's advocate acts as a check against groupthink and practices that are left in place with no better justification than "that's the way we've always done it." When thoughtfully listened to, the advocate can improve the quality of group decision making.

In contrast, others in the group often view devil's advocates as time wasters, and their appointment is almost certain to delay any decision process. Another thing to consider is rotating the person playing the devil's advocate role so that he or she does not become stereotyped as a "yes, but" type of person.

How Do You Manage Conflict Between Groups and Departments?

Groups that are able to cooperate with other groups are usually more productive than those that are not.[21] But the potential areas of conflict are many. Conflict erupted at Apple Computer in the early 1980s, for example, even though groups were in independent divisions. The newly created Macintosh division was assigned the task of developing a creative breakthrough product as quickly as possible and was receiving a disproportionate share of the company's publicity and resources. At least the Apple II division, which was bringing in most of the company's profits, viewed it that way. This situation led to jealousy, resentment, and name calling between the two divisions. The animosity only dissipated after employees were reshuffled into new task teams working together to develop new products.

Because it can have destructive organizational consequences, it is important to detect, reduce, and act to prevent the recurrence of dysfunctional intergroup conflict. On the other hand, even dysfunctional conflict is useful in that it signals needed changes.

Also, functional intergroup conflict that serves to improve the quality of decision making and stimulate creative breakthroughs should be judiciously managed to achieve the most beneficial results for the organization.[22] Consequently, the critical issue is not how to eliminate intergroup conflict but how to manage it productively to obtain positive change and avoid negative consequences. Persistent dysfunctional intergroup conflict, however, needs to be confronted.[23]

As with interpersonal conflict, attempts to manage intergroup conflict can result in win-lose (competing and accommodating), lose-lose (avoiding), win-win (collaborating), or compromise (bargaining) outcomes. Win-lose outcomes are brought about by all-or-nothing competitive strategies that encourage one group to win at the expense of the other. Because organizations consist of ongoing relationships, zero-sum strategies create destructive political environments. Instead of solving problems, avoiding strategies leave problems to fester and erupt later. At best they allow temporary productivity until the groups can address the conflict more effectively. Compromise strategies allow both groups to gain a little but neither to obtain all that its members desire. Because win-win strategies allow both groups to obtain their goals through creative integration of their concerns, the best practice is to try win-win strategies first. If they do not work, a compromise strategy can provide some benefits to both groups. Organizations with effective intergroup coordination strategies can often manage conflict effectively without it becoming destructive at all. Techniques that can prevent[24] and reduce[25] intergroup conflict are presented next.

Superordinate Goals

One of the most effective ways to reduce intergroup conflict is to determine an overriding goal that requires the cooperative effort of the conflicting groups. Such a goal must be unattainable by either group alone and of sufficient importance to supersede all their other goals. One fairly common superordinate goal is survival of the organization. Overall survival usually requires the elimination of suboptimal strategies on the part of conflicting groups. In the airline industry, for example, several unions have agreed to forgo pay increases and have even accepted temporary pay reductions when the survival of an airline was threatened.

This strategy eliminates win-lose situations as groups shift efforts toward cooperation and pull together to maximize organizational effectiveness. Setting up an appraisal system that rewards total organizational effectiveness rather than individual group accomplishments also supports these efforts by promoting cooperation rather than competition between groups.

A derivative strategy to restore alliances and increase cooperation is focusing on a common enemy. At the international level, bickering nations unite against a common adversary in times of war or natural catastrophe. Players on athletic teams that normally compete in a particular league join together to produce an all-star team and challenge another league. Nothing halts the squabbles of Democrats faster than a reminder that the Republicans are gaining strength. Like all these factions, warring groups will suppress their conflicts and join together to help their organization compete successfully against another. Sometimes, however, they must be reminded that the opposition is out there.

Increased Communication

In cases where groups are not competing for scarce resources or trying to achieve inherently conflicting goals, devising means to increase communication can do much to correct misunderstandings, reduce negative stereotypes, and develop more positive feelings among group members. Requiring groups to meet together to solve common problems can reduce stereotypical images and faulty perceptions, and contribute to mutual understanding. NCR Corp. (formerly, National Cash Register Company) began tearing down the walls between its engineering and manufacturing groups by putting people from design, purchasing, manufacturing, and field support in adjacent cubicles to allow them to communicate with one another throughout the design and manufacturing process. This process reduced assembly time from 30 minutes to five and permitted assembly without special tools. The free flow of information across groups enabled NCR to get better products to market much faster.[26]

Problem Solving

Problem solving is a more structured means of bringing together conflicting groups for a face-to-face confrontation. The purpose of a problem-solving meeting is to identify and solve conflicts through a mutual airing of differences, complaints, and negative feelings. An effort is made to work through differences and bring about a greater understanding of the opposing group's attitudes, perceptions, and position. The problem-solving approach requires considerable time and commitment but it can be effective when conflicts stem from misunderstandings or different perceptions. Specific problem-solving strategies and techniques can be found in Chapter 9.

Negotiating

As previously described, negotiating is a form of problem solving in which two groups with conflicting interests alter their positions in order to reach a mutually agreeable resolution. One of the most publicized forms of negotiating is when unions bargain for better wages, working conditions, benefits, and job security, while management bargains for lower labor costs and increased efficiency. Many informal forms of intergroup bargaining go on constantly, like when one department agrees to stay in an old office space in exchange for new computer equipment.

When choosing representatives, groups should be aware that personality, experience, training, and chosen strategy make a difference in how well a negotiator negotiates.[27] The guidelines for successful negotiating described for interpersonal negotiating also apply in an intergroup situation.

Expansion of Resources

When the major cause of intergroup conflict is limited resources, the likely outcome is a win-lose situation in which one group succeeds at the expense of another. If at all possible, the organization should eliminate this source of conflict by expanding its resource base. Additional investments may pay off handsomely in terms of increased productivity.

Third-Party Judgment

Groups may appeal to a common boss or an outside judge to serve as a mediator in resolving their conflict. The National Conference of Commissioners on Uniform State Laws has proposed an employment statute that would let most fired workers who feel their terminations were unjustified to take their cases to a neutral arbitrator. The arbitrators would decide the disputes in a few weeks, as opposed to the other common option of expensive and time-consuming lawsuits.[28]

Common superiors are often called in to recommend solutions to conflicts between departments. Arbitrators have more third-party clout in that the warring parties must agree before the fact to abide by an arbitrator's decision.

Arbitrators' most common business function is to resolve disputes between unions and management. Arbitration becomes necessary when time is of the essence or when high-ranking executives feel the decision needs to go a certain way. Often it is an easier and less expensive approach than working through every issue with time-consuming intergroup problem-solving techniques.

The advantages of arbitration can carry a hidden cost. An arbitrator usually hands down a win-lose decision that is unlikely to receive the loser's full commitment. Like a parental decision on who is "right" when two children fight over a toy, an arbitrated outcome may solve the immediate problem but increase hostility between the conflicting factions. No one is left with an enhanced understanding of what caused the basic conflict or how future clashes can be prevented. When an arbitrator hands down a compromise solution that only partially fulfills the demands of both sides, neither group is totally satisfied with the outcome. Although this solution may be slightly preferable to a win-lose decision, the sources of conflict are likely to remain.[29]

Changes in Organizational Structure

When the reasons for intergroup conflict are scarce resources, status differences, or power imbalances, changes in organizational structure may be the answer.[30] Structural changes include issues such as those in the preceding discussion about coordinating intergroup relations: rotating group members on a semipermanent basis, creating liaison or coordinator positions, and eliminating special-interest groups that exist within the organization. Marshall Industries, for example, rotates new employees through a variety of assignments in different groups to ease the competitive effects of single-group identification, enhance understanding of interaction in the whole system, and provide a total organization identification. Marshall Industries regroups people from different departments with different specialties into overlapping, cross-trained teams. This approach decreases identity with one particular department and increases understanding of the requirements and needs of other groups.[31] In other situations, conflicting groups can be relocated, task responsibilities can be redefined, and hierarchies can be decentralized. Sometimes two conflicting groups can be merged into one. If the conflict clearly centers around the personal animosities of two or more strong individuals, the key instigators can be removed.

Restructuring has produced increased quality, productivity, and cooperation for companies such as Corning Glass Works, Ford Motor, and Hewlett-Packard, which are shifting their focus from how individual departments function to how different departments work together. Companies such as Conrail, Dun & Bradstreet Europe, DuPont, and Royal Bank of Canada are creating network groups of department managers with appropriate business skills, personal motivations, resource control, and positions to shape and implement organizational strategy. The free flow of information to all network group members who need it and the emphasis on horizontal collaboration and leadership have clarified joint business goals and helped meet deadlines.[32]

Smoothing

Smoothing is a means of providing conflicting groups with some incentive to repress their conflict and avoid its open expression. The smoothing process plays down the differences between the groups and accentuates their similarities and common interests. The rationale is that eventually the groups will realize they are not as alienated from one another as they initially believed. Because this approach circumvents full confrontation of the sources of conflict, they will probably resurface in the future and possibly cause a more serious disturbance. Smoothing is at best a temporary solution.

Avoidance

Some groups may be able to ignore dysfunctional situations temporarily by looking the other way or disregarding the threatening actions of others in the hope that the situation will resolve itself. But most conflicts do not fade; usually, they worsen with time. Although avoidance is ineffective in the long run, certain controlled conditions can be established to lessen the short-term consequences of conflict. Sometimes conflicting groups can be physically separated; sometimes the amount of interaction between them can be limited. Procrastination, disregard for the demands of others, and attempts at peaceful coexistence are all variations of the avoidance process.

CONCEPT QUIZ

Complete the following true-false quiz by circling the correct answer. Answers are at the end of the quiz. After marking your answers, remember to go back and check your understanding of any answers you missed.

True or False	1. Conflicts cannot be ignored because they always hinder organizational effectiveness.
True or False	2. Most people have the ability to vary their conflict response according to the situation.
True or False	3. Every conflict does not justify a manager's attention.
True or False	4. Some conflicts are unmanageable.
True or False	5. Most conflicts are caused by lack of communication.
True or False	6. You should suppress emotions and deal with conflict logically.
True or False	7. Accommodation requires each party to give up something of value.
True or False	8. Forcing is effective for resolving important issues where unpopular actions need implementing.
True or False	9. Collaboration is an effective strategy for arriving at an expedient solution under time pressures.
True or False	10. Effective negotiators make sure they get public credit for a win and spread the word that the other party lost.

Answers.   (1) False; (2) True; (3) True; (4) True; (5) False; (6) False; (7) False; (8) True; (9) False; (10) False

BEHAVIORAL CHECKLIST

Look for these behaviors when evaluating your own and others' conflict management skills.

For Effective Conflict Resolution

- Assess the nature of the conflict.
- Be judicious in selecting conflicts to engage in.
- Determine your own conflict management style.
- Know your options.
- Evaluate and empathize with the other conflict party.
- Deal with the emotional components of the conflict.
- Determine your objective.
- Stimulate conflict when appropriate.
- Implement the optimal long-range strategy for all involved.

> **Attention!**
> Do not read the following until assigned to do so by your instructor.

MODELING EXERCISE

Instructions.   Two people volunteer to be role-players. One person is to play Lee, the supervisor. Another plays B. J., a conservative senior cost accountant. The class uses the

Observer's Rating Sheet to evaluate the skills of Lee and to prepare notes for feedback after the role-play. Everyone reads the situation, but the role-players read only their own role. The observers read both roles and review the Observer's Rating Sheet located at the end of this exercise.

Actors.

Lee Lattoni

B. J. O'Malley

Situation. Lee Lattoni supervises an eight-member cost accounting department in a large metals fabricating plant in Albuquerque, New Mexico. Lee was promoted about six months ago to this supervisory position after only a year as an accountant. It was no secret that Lee got the promotion predominantly because of education. Lee has an MBA, whereas no one else in the department has a college degree.

Lee Lattoni's Role Your transition to supervisor has gone smoothly; you have encountered little in the way of problems until now. Business has been prospering at the plant for some time, and it has become apparent that you need an additional cost accountant in the department to handle the increased workload. In fact, it has been on your mind for over a month. Department members have been complaining about the heavy workload. Overtime has become commonplace and is adversely affecting your department's efficiency statistics. You do not think you will have any trouble supporting your request for a new, full-time position with your boss.

The search for a new employee should be relatively hassle-free. The reason is that you have already spotted someone you think can fill the slot nicely. The person you have in mind is currently working in the production control department of the plant.

Unofficially, you have talked with the production control supervisor and the plant's personnel director about moving Regi Simpson, a young clerk in production, into your department. Regi has been with the company for eight months, has shown above average potential, and is only six units shy of a bachelor's degree (with a major in accounting), which Regi has been earning at night at the state university. You are aware that the department currently is made up of older male employees who have worked their way up through the ranks based on experience and longevity. None of them has a college degree, and the attitude of most members is that advanced education is just a frivolous waste of time. They are a macho, raucous group who tell a lot of chauvinistic jokes, but always get the job done well. You are aware that Regi may have a problem gaining acceptance in this group but Regi is certainly a qualified candidate and deserving of the promotion.

You met with Regi earlier in the week and discussed the possibility that cost accounting will have a vacancy. Regi was interested in the position. After further discussion over lunch—all unofficially—you said that although you could not make any promises, you were prepared to recommend Regi for the job. However, you emphasized that it would be a week to 10 days before a final decision and an official announcement were made.

You are in your office when B. J. O'Malley comes in. B. J. works for you as a cost accountant and has been at the plant for 26 years. You like B. J. but consider B. J. closed-minded and the most extreme of the chauvinistic old timers. If Regi were to join the department, you would expect B. J. to be the least receptive. Why? B. J. was raised by a conservative working class family and you have heard B. J. speak disparagingly about college kids.

B. J. O'Malley's Role You are a cost accountant in the plant, working for Lee. You are 58 years old, were raised in a conservative working class family, and have been working at the Albuquerque plant since it opened 26 years ago. You have heard rumors that Lee is planning to bring Regi Simpson, a young and inexperienced college kid into the department. You understand the need to hire another cost accountant, because the workload has gotten too heavy and the department's overtime budget has gotten out of hand. The current department is made up of older employees who have worked their way up through the ranks based on experience and longevity. None of them has a college degree and the attitude of most members is that advanced education is just a frivolous waste of time. They are a macho, raucous group who have a lot of fun and tell a lot of chauvinistic jokes, take breaks throwing darts at each month's *Playboy* centerfold, but always get the job done well. You are concerned that Regi will cause problems for your group and you believe there must be equally qualified and experienced locals around who could do the job better.

You believe that Lee should be sensitive to your feelings. You are not prejudiced; you just want to maintain the camaraderie and efficiency of your department. You want Lee to talk with all department members before making an appointment. You view the department as a close-knit, homogeneous group and you do not want to add a newcomer who will have trouble fitting in. In the back of your mind, you know that if all the department members get to vote on who joins the department, a young, inexperienced college kid who will probably need constant handholding is unlikely to be hired. However, you also know that if you do not speak up, no one else will. You are quite upset and have decided to go to Lee's office and let Lee know that you have no intention of working with a uppity, know-it-all college kid who probably does not know the first thing about cost accounting.

Time. Not to exceed 15 minutes.

OBSERVER'S RATING SHEET

Evaluate Lee Lattoni's conflict-management skills on the following scale. Write concrete examples in the space for comments below each behavior to use in explaining your feedback.

1	*2*	*3*	*4*	*5*
Unsatisfactory	*Weak*	*Adequate*	*Good*	*Outstanding*

_____ Assesses the nature of the conflict.

_____ Judicious in selecting conflicts to engage in.

_____ Determines own conflict management style.

_____ Knows options.

_____ Empathizes with other.

_____ Deals with the emotions.

_____ Determines objective.

_____ Negotiates effectively.

_____ Stimulates conflict when appropriate.

GROUP EXERCISES

The following three exercises are designed to give you a chance to practice your conflict management skills in small groups and receive feedback from others about your strengths and weaknesses. The first exercise consists of a set of short conflict cases for you to analyze and select the best approach for managing. Next is a role-play where you can practice negotiating for a used car. Last is an exercise that challenges you to resolve a values-based conflict among several group members.

Group Exercise 1: Deciding How to Manage Conflicts[33]

Directions. Form groups of three to five people. Each group member is to begin by independently ranking the five alternative courses of action in each of the following four incidents. You are to rank the responses from the most desirable or appropriate way of dealing with the conflict situation to the least desirable. Rank the most desirable course of action 1, the next most desirable 2, and so on, with the least desirable or least appropriate action as 5. Enter your rank for each item in the space next to each choice. Next, identify the conflict style being used with each of the possible courses of action (competing, accommodation, avoidance, compromise, or collaboration).

Discussion. After each person has completed the steps for all four incidents, group members are to compare their answers for each situation. Begin with Incident 1. When completed do the same for the remaining incidents. For each incident (1) defend *why* you answered as you did; (2) if you do not all agree, discuss why not; (3) reach a group consensus with some of you changing your answers as a result of the discussion; and (4) prepare to present your group's consensus answer and rationale for each incident to the rest of the class. Confine the analysis and discussion of each incident to 10 minutes or less.

Incident 1

Pete is lead operator of a production molding machine. Recently, he has noticed that one of the men from another machine has been coming over to his machine and talking to one of his men (not on break time). The efficiency of Pete's operator seems to be falling off and causing some rejects because of his inattention. Pete thinks he detects some resentment among the rest of the crew. If you were Pete, what would you do?

a. Talk to your worker and tell him to limit his conversations during on-the-job time.
b. Ask the foreman to tell the lead operator of the other machine to keep his operators in line.
c. Confront both men the next time you see them together (as well as the other lead operator, if necessary), find out what they are up to, and tell them what you expect of your operators.
d. Say nothing now; it would be silly to make a big deal out of something so insignificant.
e. Try to put the rest of the crew at ease; it is important that they all work well together.

Incident 2

Sally is the senior quality control (QC) inspector and has been appointed group leader of the QC people on her crew. On separate occasions, two of her people have come to her with different suggestions for reporting test results to the machine operators. Paul wants to send the test results to the supervisor and then to the machine operator, because the supervisor is the person ultimately responsible for production output. Jim thinks the results should go directly to the lead operator on the machine in question, because the operator is the one who must take corrective action as soon as possible. Both ideas seem good, and Sally can find no ironclad procedures in the department on how to route the reports. If you were Sally, you would

a. Decide who is right and ask the other person to go along with the decision (perhaps establish it as a written procedure).
b. Wait and see; the best solution will become apparent.
c. Tell both Paul and Jim not to get uptight about their disagreement; it is not that important.
d. Get Paul and Jim together and examine both of their ideas closely.
e. Send the report to the supervisor, with a copy to the lead operator (even though it might mean a little more copy work for QC).

Incident 3

Ralph is a module leader; his module consists of four complex and expensive machines and five crew members. The work is exacting, and inattention or improper procedures could cause a costly mistake or serious injury. Ralph suspects that one of his crew is taking drugs on the job, or at least is showing up for work under the influence of drugs. Ralph feels he has some strong indications, but he knows he does not have a "case." If you were Ralph, you would

a. Confront the man outright, tell him what you suspect and why, and that you are concerned for him and for the safety of the rest of the crew.
b. Ask that the suspected offender keep his habit off the job; what he does on the job is part of your business.
c. Not confront the individual right now; it might either "turn him off" or drive him underground.
d. Give the man the "facts of life;" tell him it is illegal and unsafe to use drugs, and that if he gets caught, you will do everything you can to see that he is fired.
e. Keep a close eye on the man to see that he is not endangering others.

Incident 4

Gene is supervisor of a production crew. From time to time in the past, the product development section tapped the production crews for operators to augment their own operator personnel to run test products on special machines. This use of personnel put little strain on the production crews because the demands were small, temporary, and infrequent. Lately, however, the demand seems almost constant for four production operators. The rest of the production crew must fill in for these missing people, usually by working harder and taking shorter breaks. If you were Gene, you would

a. Let it go for now; the "crisis" will probably be over soon.
b. Try to smooth things over with your own crew and with the development supervisor; we all have jobs to do and cannot afford a conflict.
c. Let development have two of the four operators they requested.
d. Go to the development supervisor or his or her supervisor and talk about how these demands for additional operators could best be met without placing production in a bind.
e. Go to the supervisor of production (Gene's boss) and get him or her to "call off" the development people.

Time. Not to exceed 10 minutes per incident.

Group Exercise 2: Used Car Role-Play[34]

Directions. Form groups of three. One volunteer assumes the role of the buyer and another assumes the role of the seller. The third person is the observer. Role-players read only their own role and prepare for the role play. The observer reads both roles and reviews the Observer's Rating Sheet. After the role-play discussion, the observer will provide feedback to both parties, on their performance, using the Observer's Rating Sheet as a guide.

Actors. Buyer and Seller

Situation. You are about to negotiate the purchase/sale of an automobile. Before advertising it in the local newspaper, the seller took the car to the local Volkswagen dealer for an independent assessment. The dealer's write up stated:

> 1998 VW Jetta convertible; standard shift.
>
> White with red upholstery, tinted glass.
>
> AM/FM, cassette.
>
> 30,450 miles.
>
> Steel-belted radial tires expected to last 65,000.
>
> 35 miles per gallon.
>
> No rust; dent on passenger door barely noticeable.
>
> Mechanically perfect except exhaust system, which may or may not last another 10,000 miles (costs $300 to replace).
>
> "Blue book" retail value, $5,000; wholesale, $4,400.
>
> Car has spent its entire life in the local area.

Buyer's Role   Your car was stolen and wrecked two weeks ago. You do a lot of traveling in your job, so you need a car that is economical and easy to drive. The Jetta that was advertised looks like a good deal, and you would like to buy it right away if possible. The insurance company gave you $4,000 for your old car. You have only $700 in savings that you had intended to spend on a vacation trip—a chance you really do not want to pass up.

Your credit has been stretched for some time, so that if you borrow money, it will have to be at an 18 percent interest rate. Furthermore, you need to buy a replacement car quickly, because you have been renting a car for business purposes, and it is costing you a great deal. The Jetta is the best deal you have seen, and the car is fun to drive. As an alternative, you can immediately buy a used 1999 Ford Escort for $3,800 (the whole-sale value), which gets 28 miles per gallon and will depreciate much faster than the Jetta.

The seller of the Jetta is a complete stranger to you. Before beginning this negotiation, set the following targets for yourself:

1. The price you would like to pay for the car   _____
2. The price you will initially offer the seller   _____
3. The highest price you will pay for the car   _____

Seller's Role   You have bought a used Mercedes C230 from a dealer. The down payment is $4,700 on the car, with steep monthly payments. You are stretched on credit, so if you cannot make the down payment, you will have to borrow at 18 percent. You are going to pick up the Mercedes in two hours, so you want to sell your old car, the Jetta convertible, before you go.

You advertised the car, which is in particularly good condition, in the newspaper and have had several calls. Your only really good prospect right now is the person with whom you are about to bargain—a stranger. You do not *have* to sell it to this person, but if you do not sell the car right away, you will have to pay high interest charges until you do sell it.

The Mercedes dealer will only give you $4,400 for the Jetta, because he will have to resell it to a Volkswagen dealer. The local VW dealer is not anxious to buy the car from you because he just received a shipment of new cars; in any case, he probably would not give you more than $4,400 either.

Before beginning this negotiation, set the following targets for yourself:

1. The price you would like to receive for the car   _____
2. The price you will initially request   _____
3. The lowest price you will accept for the car   _____

Time.   Not to exceed 15 minutes.

OBSERVER'S RATING SHEET

Evaluate the parties' conflict-management and negotiation skills on the following scale. Write concrete examples in the space for comments below each behavior to use in explaining your feedback.

1 Unsatisfactory	2 Weak	3 Adequate	4 Good	5 Outstanding
			Buyer	Seller

- Determines objectives.

- Plans a concrete strategy before negotiating.

- Knows options.

- Begins with a positive overture.

- Maintains a rational, goal-oriented frame of mind.

- Empathizes with other party's position.

- Addresses problems, not personalities.

- Does not take initial offers too seriously.

- Insists on objective criteria.

Group Exercise 3: The Alligator River Conflict[35]

Objectives.   To demonstrate how different perceptions, values, and attitudes lead to conflicts. To learn about your own conflict management style and practice conflict resolution skills.

Time.   50 minutes (5 minutes for set up, 30 minutes for the exercise, and 15 minutes for debriefing).

Procedure.

1. Read The Alligator River Story, which follows.
2. After reading the story, individually rank the five characters in the story beginning with the one whom you consider as the most offensive and ending with the one whom you consider the least objectionable. Briefly note your reasons.

The Alligator River Story

There once lived a woman named Abigail who was in love with a man named Gregory. Gregory lived on the shore of a river. Abigail lived on the opposite shore of the same river. The river that separated the two lovers was teeming with hungry alligators. Abigail wanted to cross the river to *be* with Gregory. Unfortunately, the bridge that had spanned the river had been washed out by a heavy flood the previous week. So, she went to ask Sinbad, a river boat captain, to take her across. He said he would be glad to if she would consent to go to bed with him prior to the voyage. She promptly refused and went to a friend named Ivan to explain her plight. Ivan did not want to get involved at all in the situation. Abigail felt her only alternative was to accept Sinbad's terms. Sinbad fulfilled his promise to Abigail and delivered her into the arms of Gregory. When Abigail told Gregory about what she did in order to cross the river, Gregory cast her aside with disdain. Heartsick and rejected, Abigail turned to Slug with her tale of woe. Slug, feeling compassion for Abigail, sought out Gregory and beat him brutally. Abigail was overjoyed at the sight of Gregory getting his due. As the sun set on the horizon, people heard Abigail laughing at Gregory.

3. Now form *groups* of five or six members. Compare rankings and share reasons for them.
4. Reach a group consensus decision on a final set of rankings, that is, talk it through until all are satisfied your agreed-upon ranking is the best you can do in your group. Do not just add up ranks or take a quick vote, talk through and explain all positions until all agree on a common set of rankings.
5. Using the Observer's Rating Sheet, give each group member feedback on the conflict management skills he or she exhibited during the group ranking.

Individual Ranking Form		
Rank	*Character*	*Reasons*
First (Worst)		
Second		
Third		
Fourth		
Fifth		

Group Consensus Ranking		
Rank	*Name*	*Reasons*
First (Worst)		
Second		
Third		
Fourth		
Fifth		

OBSERVER'S RATING SHEET

Evaluate conflict-management *es and obs*
member on the following scale. Make a chec
below each behavior to use in ex
group member at a time, until all

Names of Group Members

1	2
Unsatisfactory	*Wea*

- Assesses the nature of the conflict.

- Judicious in selecting conflicts to engage in.

- Determines own con-flict management style.

- Knows options.

- Empathizes with other party's position.

- Deals with the emotions.

- Determines objective.

- Does not take initial offers too seriously.

- Insists on objective criteria.

APPLICATION
gree? Why?

gnificant other?

REINFORCEM
d. How did your
you believe your
ion: (a) be sure to
ific situation; and
on behavior.
at was the source
t? Was it resolved
might have been

olved in a conflict.

ACTION PLA

the Reinforcement

NOTES

1. D. W. Johnso *lict," Sloan* 986): 45–51.
Effectiveness as, "Developing a
and Bacon, 1 flict Handling
2. D. Tjosvold a ent," *Educational and*
Management ummer 1997): 309–25.
York: Irving onflict Management,"
3. M. A. Rahim k *of Industrial and*
ed. (Westpor hicago: Rand McNally,
4. S. P. Robbins.
Resolution' *ensions of*
Management d. (Cincinnati: South-
Tjosvold, Wo 997) 189–90.
(Lexington, N International
5. S. P. Robbins, and Prospects," in
Nontraditiona r, eds., *Handbook for*
Prentice Hall esearch (Cambridge,
"Managing W S.
Review (July
6. C. O. Kursh, "
Psychologica

SUMMARY CHECKLIST

On the basis of your experiences and observations, assess yourself on each of the following conflict skill behaviors. Make a check (✓) next to those behaviors on which you think you need improvement.

_____ **Assessing the nature of the conflict.**

_____ **Being judicious in selecting conflicts to engage in.**
   1. Some conflicts might not be worth the effort.
   2. Others might be unmanageable.
   3. Save your efforts for conflicts that have serious consequences.

_____ **Determining my own conflict management style.**
   1. Competing.
   2. Accommodating.
   3. Avoiding.
   4. Collaborating.
   5. Compromising.

_____ **Knowing my options.**
   1. Knowing when it is appropriate to use each of the five conflict management styles.
   2. Agreeing to no deal.

_____ **Empathizing with the positions of others.**
   1. Get to know the players.
   2. What interests does each party represent?
   3. What are each player's values, personality, feelings, and resources?
   4. View the conflict situation through the eyes of the conflicting parties.

_____ **Dealing with emotions.**
   1. Treat the other person with respect.
   2. Listen and restate to the other's satisfaction.
   3. Briefly state your views, needs, and feelings.

_____ **Negotiating.**
   1. Consider the other party's situation.
   2. Have a concrete strategy.
   3. Begin with a positive overtone.
   4. Address problems, not personalities.
   5. Maintain a rational, goal-oriented frame of mind.
   6. Insist on using objective criteria.
   7. Pay little attention to initial offers.
   8. Emphasize win-win solutions.
   9. Create an open and trusting climate.
  10. Be open to accepting third-party assistance.

_____ **Stimulating conflict when appropriate.**
   1. Communicate that conflict has a legitimate place in the organization.
   2. Send ambiguous messages about potentially threatening developments.
   3. Bring in outsiders with different backgrounds, values, and attitudes.
   4. Restructure the organization to disrupt the status quo.
   5. Appoint a "devil's advocate."

APPLICATION QUESTIONS

1. Most people dislike conflict because it is dysfunctional. Do you agree or disagree? Why?
2. Is conflict inevitable in organizations? Why?
3. When is conflict likely to hinder an organization? When can it help?
4. What are the key steps in diagnosing a conflict situation?
5. What type of outcomes would you desire when resolving a conflict with a significant other? How about with a used car dealer?

REINFORCEMENT EXERCISES

1. Describe in detail three recent interpersonal conflicts you have experienced. How did your basic conflict handling style influence your actions? To what degree do you believe your conflict style is flexible? The next time you find yourself in a conflict situation: (a) be sure to recall your basic conflict style; (b) consider its appropriateness to this specific situation; and (c) if inappropriate, practice exhibiting more appropriate conflict resolution behavior.
2. Think of a recent conflict you had with a colleague, friend, or relative. What was the source of the conflict? What goals did you seek? How did you handle the conflict? Was it resolved consistently with your goals? What other ways of handling this conflict might have been more effective?
3. Take the role of a third-party consultant for an individual or a group involved in a conflict. Advise the party/parties as to their options. Note how your advice works.

ACTION PLAN

1. Which behavior do I most want to improve?
2. Why? What will be my payoff?
3. What potential obstacles stand in my way?
4. What are the specific things I will do to improve? (For examples, see the Reinforcement Exercises.)
5. When will I do them?
6. How and when will I measure my success?

NOTES

1. D. W. Johnson, *Reaching Out: Interpersonal Effectiveness and Self-Actualization* (Boston: Allyn and Bacon, 1993) 205–07.
2. D. Tjosvold and D. W. Johnson, *Productive Conflict Management: Perspectives for Organizations* (New York: Irvington Publishers, 1983) 10.
3. M. A. Rahim, *Managing Conflict in Organizations,* 2d ed. (Westport, CT: Praeger, 1992).
4. S. P. Robbins, "'Conflict Management' and 'Conflict Resolution' Are Not Synonymous Terms," *California Management Review* (Winter 1978): 67–75; D. Tjosvold, *Working Together to Get Things Done* (Lexington, MA: D.C. Heath, 1986) 111–12.
5. S. P. Robbins, *Managing Organizational Conflict: A Nontraditional Approach* (Upper Saddle River, NJ: Prentice Hall, 1974) 31–55; and Yuan-Duen Lee "Managing Workplace Conflict," *Management Review* (July 1993): 57.
6. C. O. Kursh, "The Benefits of Poor Communication," *Psychological Review* (Summer–Fall 1971): 189–208.
7. L. Greenhalgh, "Managing Conflict," *Sloan Management Review* (Summer 1986): 45–51.
8. R. H. Kilmann and K. W. Thomas, "Developing a Forced-Choice Measure of Conflict Handling Behavior: The MODE Instrument," *Educational and Psychological Measurement* (Summer 1997): 309–25.
9. K. W. Thomas, "Conflict and Conflict Management," in M. Dunnette, ed., *Handbook of Industrial and Organizational Psychology* (Chicago: Rand McNally, 1976) 889–935.
10. N. J. Adler, *International Dimensions of Organizational Behavior,* 3d ed. (Cincinnati: South-Western College Publishing, 1997) 189–90.
11. See for example, S. D. Weiss, "International Negotiations: Bricks, Mortar, and Prospects," in B. J. Punnett and O. J. Shenkar, eds., *Handbook for International Management Research* (Cambridge, MA: Blackwell, 1996) 209–65.
12. Adler, 1997, 194–95.
13. Robbins, 1974, 31–55.

14. D. Cyr, "How To Argue," *Attache* (US Airways, January 1998) 49–51.

15. S. R. Covey, *The 7 Habits of Highly Effective People* (New York: Simon & Schuster, 1990) 207–14.

16. J. A. Wall, Jr., *Negotiation: Theory and Practice* (Glenview, IL: Scott, Foresman, 1985).

17. D. J. McConville, "The Artful Negotiator," *Industry Week* (August 15, 1994): 40.

18. R. Fisher and W. Ury, *Getting to Yes: Negotiating Agreement Without Giving In* (New York: Penguin Books, 1986) 84–98.

19. See, for instance, Tjosvold and Johnson, 1983.

20. Robbins, 1974, 31–55.

21. D. G. Ancona, "Outward Bound: Strategies for Team Survival in an Organization," *Academy of Management Journal* (June 1990): 334–56.

22. R. A. Cosier and C. R. Schwenk, "Agreement and Thinking Alike: Ingredients for Poor Decisions," *Academy of Management Executive* (February 1990): 69–74.

23. W. L. Ury, J. M. Brett, and S. Goldberg, *Getting Disputes Resolved: Designing Systems to Cut the Costs of Conflict* (San Francisco: Jossey-Bass, 1988).

24. D. H. Schein, *Organizational Psychology,* 3d ed. (Upper Saddle River, NJ: Prentice Hall, 1980) 177–78.

25. M. Afzalur Rahim, ed., *Managing Conflict: An Interdisciplinary Approach* (New York: Praeger Publishers, 1989); R. Likert and J. Likert, *New Ways of Managing Conflict* (New York: McGraw-Hill, 1976).

26. "A Smarter Way to Manufacture," *Business Week,* April 30, 1990, 110–17.

27. R. J. Lewicki, J. A. Litterer, J. W. Minton, and D. M. Saunders, *Negotiation,* 2d ed. (Burr Ridge, IL: Irwin, 1994) 45–128.

28. A. Bernstein and Z. Schiller, "Tell It to the Arbitrator," *Business Week,* November 4, 1991, 109.

29. For a current prescriptive model of third-party dispute intervention, see A. R. Elangovan, "Managerial Third-Party Dispute Intervention: A Prescriptive Model of Strategy Selection," *Academy of Management Review* 20, no. 4 (1995): 800–30.

30. J. W. Galbraith, *Designing Complex Organizations* (Reading, MA: Addison-Wesley, 1973) 15.

31. C. W. Cook, R. E. Coffey, and P. L. Hunsaker, *Management and Organizational Behavior* (Chicago: Irwin, 1997) 376–77.

32. R. Charan, "How Networks Reshape Organizations for Results," *Harvard Business Review* (September–October 1991), 179; and "Theory P Stresses How Departments Interact" *Wall Street Journal*, December 13, 1991, B1.

33. Adapted from A. Zoll, *Explorations in Managing* © 1974, Addison-Wesley Publishing Company, Inc. Based on a format suggested by Allen A. Zoll, III. Reprinted with permission.

34. Adapted from a role-play developed by Prof. Leonard Greenhaigh, Dartmouth College, as presented by R. J. Lewicki, J. A. Litterer, D. M. Saunders, and J. W. Minton, *Negotiation: Readings, Exercises, and Cases,* 2d ed. (Homewood, IL: Richard D. Irwin, 1993) 573–75. Used with permission.

35. Adapted from S. B. Simon, H. Kirschenbaum, and L. Howe, *Values Clarification, The Handbook,* rev. ed. (Sunderland, MA: Values Press, 1991).

MANAGING CONFLICT

Conflicts are not negative; they are a natural feature of every organization and can never be completely eliminated. However, they can be managed to avoid hostility, lack of cooperation, and failure to meet goals. When channeled properly, conflicts can lead to creativity, innovative problem solving, and positive change.

Recall the five basic conflict resolution approaches available to managers: avoidance, accommodation, forcing, compromise, and collaboration. Each has its specific function, but in all cases, treating all parties with respect and using listening skills will go a long way towards achieving positive results.

There are two main conflicts taking place at Quicktakes in this segment. Janet and Jeff have a disagreement about the quality of Jeff's current project, which quickly escalates into an impasse over when Jeff will fix the problems, if at all. Eddie and Andrew discuss how much money Andrew spends in his London office. The two have different ideas about what level of expense is appropriate for the amount of income Andrew generates.

Each of these conflicts moves up the line to Hal Boylston's office. Eddie lets Hal know the result of his conversation with Andrew, and Janet brings her dissatisfaction with Jeff to Hal for resolution. Look for the roots of these conflicts, and the reason one escalates and the other does not. Do you agree with Eddie that his conflict with Andrew has been resolved? What do you think will happen to resolve the situation between Janet and Tom? ■

QUESTIONS

1. What conflict resolution strategy did Janet choose? Do you think she made the right choice? What other options did she have?

2. What could Jeff do differently to bring the conflict to a more positive resolution?

3. What strategies do Eddie and Andrew use in their discussion? Does anyone win, and if so, who?

4. What strategy does Hal use in the conflict between Eddie and Andrew? Why?

5. How does Hal manage the conflict between Janet and Jeff? Do you think his strategy is successful? What else does he need to do to resolve the problem to the company's benefit?

PART IV
Organizing Skills

CHAPTER 11

Designing Work

Learning Objectives

After completing this chapter, you should be able to:

- Diagnose job characteristics.
- Apply motivation theories to design satisfying jobs.
- Design jobs to maximize employee performance.

Look closely at any organization and you will see it is composed of thousands of tasks. These tasks, in turn, are grouped into jobs. When jobs are designed with consideration of both the organization's needs and technology, and the skills, abilities, and preferences of employees, they can motivate employees to achieve their productive potentials. On the other hand, if jobs just evolve by chance, productivity and satisfaction are not as likely.[1]

Jobs, like people, come in all shapes and sizes. Also like people, jobs cause different individuals to react differently. Some employees, for instance, are bored by jobs that others would find challenging. Some people favor routine tasks, others abhor any job without challenge. Some do their best work while analyzing small details, while other workers thrive only when focusing on the big picture.

A major determinant in effective job performance is appropriate job design.[2] *Job design* refers to the way tasks are combined to form complete jobs. Effective job design involves trying to shape the right jobs to conform with the right people, taking into account both the organization's goals and the employee's satisfaction. Complete the following self-assessment exercise to determine your current understanding of job design.

SELF-ASSESSMENT EXERCISE

Respond as candidly as possible to the statements seeking to explore your instincts and knowledge about job design. Describe your level of agreement with each statement by circling the number in the appropriate column.

		Strongly Agree				Strongly Disagree
1. I do not think much can be done about the fact that all jobs are essentially boring.		1	2	3	4	5
2. If I gave workers some control over their tasks I would feel diminished as a manager.		1	2	3	4	5
3. I believe employees' feelings about their jobs are central to how they perform.		5	4	3	2	1
4. I think everyone has the same desire to improve themselves as I do.		1	2	3	4	5
5. I do not pay much attention to what others say or seem to think about my job, and my coworkers do not care what others think about theirs either.		1	2	3	4	5
6. Feedback helps me and others to perform better.		5	4	3	2	1
7. I would not want my employees working from home or on the road because that would encourage them to goof off or be distracted.		1	2	3	4	5
8. I believe many workers function better when they can see a project through from beginning to end rather than being involved in just one phase of the task.		5	4	3	2	1
9. Jobs that I have held that had a substantial impact on the lives of other people were the most rewarding.		5	4	3	2	1
10. I think that a manager can help employees by reminding them how interesting and important their jobs are.		5	4	3	2	1

Scoring and Interpretation. Add the numbers you have circled to obtain your total score.

41–50   You have excellent instincts about jobs and how employees respond to them.

30–39   You show average or better awareness of the principles of motivating people through job design.

20–29   You have some sense of how the structure of jobs affects workers, but you need to increase your knowledge.

0–19   You definitely need to bolster your knowledge and scrutinize your impulses before getting involved in job design.

CONCEPTS

Why Do We Design Jobs?

In the early 1900s, cigar makers paid people to read stories to employees. During the same period, textile manufacturers allowed kittens to play on the factory floor. A century later, some modern firms permit workers to listen to music on individual headsets, play computer games, or spend time in cyberspace chatrooms. The aims of such activities, past and present, are the same: fight boredom and improve productivity.[3] Even though no universally accepted way to improve work productivity exists, several approaches to job design have evolved over the years.

The Job Specialization Approach

Historically, job design was concerned with making jobs smaller and more specialized. This approach, popularized by Frederick Taylor more than a century ago, involved fitting people to jobs as a way to achieve maximum efficiency. His assumptions were that employees will gradually adjust and adapt to any work situation and their individual attitudes are much less important than the needs of the organization. Thus, Taylor's concept of *scientific management* involved making jobs smaller, more specialized, and standardized, such as on an assembly line. Many manufacturing and production-oriented firms are still organized along those principles.

Although early results indicated that the scientific management approach did make workers more efficient and productive in the short term, research suggests that repetitive jobs also lead to dissatisfaction, poor mental health, a low sense of accomplishment, and no opportunities for personal growth.[4] Consequently, motivating employees is a real challenge. Further, the principles of scientific management are not applicable to the increasing numbers of "knowledge workers" who are required to scan the environment for new data to generate creative alternatives for jobs in areas such as advertising or investment banking. Scientific management ideas also do not fit well with the trend to empower both employees and work teams. Thus, many organizations have sought other design options.

Job Expansion Approaches

The more recent approaches to job design entail fitting jobs to people. Such methods assume that employees often are underutilized and that they desire more challenge and responsibility. The **job enlargement** approach attempts to overcome the drawbacks of specialization by horizontally expanding a job by increasing the job scope—the number of different tasks required in a job and the frequency with which these tasks are repeated. A secretary's job could be enlarged, for example, by adding to typing duties additional tasks such as sorting and delivering mail, keeping supply cabinets full, and greeting visitors.

Job enlargement has been found to provide more job satisfaction, enhance customer service, and generate fewer errors.[5] It does overcome the lack of diversity of over-specialized jobs, but job enlargement is often not sufficient to create real meaning and challenge for most employees.

Job enrichment attempts to design more meaning and challenge into jobs by adding planning and evaluating responsibilities. It increases job depth—control over one's own work. When a job in enriched, employees are responsible for planning and completing an entire activity on their own, including the assessment and correction of their own performance. So instead of requiring salespeople in a department store to call a supervisor whenever a customer has a complaint, they might be authorized to handle any complaints that would cost the store $100 or less as they see fit.

Redesigning Jobs Today

The changing nature of work is certain to challenge managers to better define work and design jobs. The jobs that people perform should not evolve by chance or from a standardized procedure that was used in the past. Managers should design jobs deliberately and thoughtfully to reflect the organization's changing needs as well as the abilities and preferences of its employees.

In some cases, redesigning a job may mean nothing more than requiring the employee to use a calculator rather than making calculations manually. In other situations, it might mean completely restructuring how the work is done, for example, by forming teams rather than having individuals do the work alone.

Increasingly, technology comes into play, allowing managers much more latitude in job design. An interesting example of large-scale work redesign occurred at Chiat/Day, a large advertising agency in California. Its headquarters has no executive suites, no permanent work cubicles, desks, filing cabinets, or other trappings of an office. Why? Because the firm has made its office into a virtual workplace where employees are free to work where they please.[6]

Half of Chiat/Day's workers telecommute either from home or on the road. The only space at headquarters that employees can call their own is the high-school style locker where each can stow personal belongings. Employees who choose to go into the office stop first in the lobby to pick up their laptop computers and portable phones. Then they pull up a desk-on-wheels, plug in their telecommunications, and go to work.

A virtual office staffed by highly mobile employees is not for every firm or every organization, but at Chiat/Day, where the mission involves free-wheeling creativity and out-of-the-box thinking, the firm has moved to meet the challenge. In this chapter, we will identify the primary dimensions of jobs and describe how these dimensions can be mixed and matched by managers to maximize both comfort and performance.

What Makes a Job?

We all know that a lifeguard's job is radically different from an accountant's or a cement mason's. But what is it that makes these jobs so dissimilar? A pragmatic answer to that question is provided by the job characteristics model (JCM). According to researchers who developed and tested the JCM, any job can be described in terms of five core job dimensions, or characteristics.[7]

1. *Skill variety.* The degree to which a job requires a variety of different activities so that the worker can employ a number of different skills and talents.
2. *Task identity.* The degree to which a job requires completion of a whole and identifiable piece of work.
3. *Task significance.* The degree to which a job has a substantial impact on the lives of other people.
4. *Autonomy.* The degree to which a job provides substantial freedom and discretion to the worker in scheduling tasks and in determining how the work will be carried out.
5. *Feedback.* The degree to which the worker gets direct and clear information about the effectiveness of his or her performance.

Exhibit 11-1 offers examples of job activities that rate high or low for each characteristic. Exhibit 11-2 presents the model.

Exhibit 11-2 shows how the first three characteristics—skill variety, task identity, and task significance—combine to create meaningful work. If a job has those three characteristics, we can predict that the employee will see his or her job as being important, valuable, and worthwhile. In addition, jobs that possess autonomy give workers a sense of responsibility for the results. Further, if a job provides feedback, the employee will know how effectively he or she is performing.[8]

Today, advances in job enrichment involve the strengthening of some or all of the five core dimensions—skill identity, task identity, task significance, autonomy, and feedback. The most effective job enrichment increases all five core dimensions, but a person's need for growth will determine how effective a job enrichment program will be. *Growth-need strength* is the degree to which individuals want personal and psychological development. Though almost all people respond positively to job enrichment, those with high growth-need strength particularly welcome it.[9]

Well-designed jobs lead to high motivation, high-quality performance, high satisfaction, and low absenteeism and turnover. These outcomes occur when workers experience three critical psychological states: (1) they believe they're doing something meaningful because their work is important to other people; (2) they feel personally responsible for how the work turns out; and (3) they learn how well they perform their jobs.[10]

When a job is well designed according to these core dimensions, people usually experience feelings of general satisfaction, internal work motivation, growth satisfaction, and work effectiveness. These intrinsic rewards—that is, rewards the person derives directly

EXHIBIT 11-1 Examples of High and Low Job Characteristics

	High	*Low*
Skill Variety	An auto-repair shop operator who does electrical repairs, rebuilds engines, does body work, and handles customer complaints	A body shop worker who spray paints 8 hours a day
Task Identity	A cabinetmaker who designs a piece of furniture, selects the wood, builds the object, and finishes it to perfection	A worker in a furniture factory who operates a lathe solely to make table legs
Task Significance	Nursing the sick in a hospital intensive care unit	Sweeping hospital floors
Autonomy	A police detective who schedules his or her own work for the day, makes contacts without supervision, and decides on the most effective techniques for solving a case	A police dispatcher who must handle calls as they come in according to a routine, highly specific procedure
Feedback	An electronics factory worker who assembles a modem and then tests it to see whether it operates properly	An electronics factory worker who assembles a modem and then routes it to a quality control inspector who tests it and makes adjustments, if necessary

SOURCE: Adapted from G. Johns, *Organizational Behavior: Understanding and Managing Life at Work,* 4th ed. (New York: HarperCollins, 1996) 204.

EXHIBIT 11-2 The Job Characteristics Model

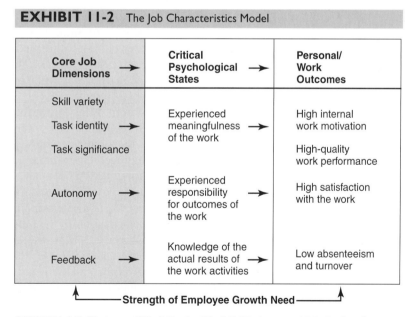

SOURCE: J. R. Hackman, "Work Design," in J. R. Hackman and J. L. Suttle, eds., *Improving Life at Work* (Glenview, IL: Scott, Foresman, 1977) 129.

from performing the job—are essential to motivation. In one study of manufacturing plants, it was found that employees initiated more patent applications, made more novel and useful suggestions, and were rated by their managers as more creative when their jobs were challenging and their managers did not control their activities closely.[11]

Many jobs today are being designed to increase motivation by offering more intrinsic rewards. For example, Opel, a German subsidiary of General Motors, operates one of the most productive plants in Europe. Opel considers employee motivation a key to its excellence and has built into its operation the characteristics of motivating tasks. As a result, employees have full responsibility over large segments of the production. In addition, workers make decisions about work procedures and can try innovative approaches to assembly, work flow, and materials. Any employee can stop the production line whenever deemed necessary. Workers seek advice and help from one another and give frank feedback to each other. Thus, tapping employee ingenuity, listening to ideas, and allowing workers some freedom and control over their work has resulted in substantial increases in productivity.[12]

Looking at the Same Job Differently

Different people work and perform differently. Too many people work in ways that are not their ways, and that almost guarantee nonperformance. According to management guru Peter Drucker, how a person performs is a given and can only be slightly modified. So, because it is unlikely that how a person performs can be completely changed, it is important to try to match people to jobs that they are good at, so they can achieve results by working in ways that they best perform.[13] Let us look at a couple of examples.

Cheri works at a fast-food restaurant—and hates it. "All day, every day, I ask people what kind of burger they want and if they also want French fries and a soda. It's not like our menu is complicated, or something. This is a job a trained monkey could do—and *should*."

Bonnie, meanwhile, has the same role and thinks it's great. "Sure, the menu is pretty limited, but the people aren't. They come in all sizes, shapes, ages, and colors and I find them endlessly fascinating. Plus, it gives me a good feeling to know I'm doing something worthwhile by serving hungry people."

Bonnie and Cheri look at exactly the same job differently. The fact that people respond to their jobs as they perceive them rather than responding objectively to the job itself greatly complicates the job design process. The central element of the *social information processing* (SIP) model says that what others tell us about our jobs is important.

The SIP model contends that employees form attitudes and behavior in response to the social cues provided by others, such as coworkers, supervisors, family members, or customers/clients.[14] Although the objective characteristics of their jobs were the same for Cheri and Bonnie in the preceding example, each may have picked up on different signals from those with whom they had contact.

Take John, who was highly motivated when he took a job selling classified ads by phone for a small newspaper. However, before his first month was over, he felt deflated and unhappy. Why? His colleagues consistently bad-mouthed both their jobs and the firm, put up derisive signs ("How can I fly with the eagles when I'm surrounded by turkeys?" and "Even a bad day on vacation is better than a good day at work!"). They also complained that the managers didn't trust them and never listened to their opinions. The objective characteristics of John's job hadn't changed, but he had reconstructed his perceived reality on the basis of messages received from his peers.

What do individual perceptions mean for the manager? In short, they mean that a manager should pay at least as much attention to the employees' perception of their jobs as to the actual characteristics of the work. The manager should listen to what employees say about their jobs and periodically ask for their opinions. You can also remind employees about the importance of the work and encourage them to apply their autonomy to making their jobs more interesting. New hires or newly transferred workers are usually more receptive to such social cues than those with greater seniority who may have fallen into a routine, which is all the more reason, however, to continually give all employees performance feedback and ask them for suggestions for improvement.

Designing Jobs for Maximum Performance

How can you design jobs to maximize your employees' performance? Using the JCM and the SIP models as a guide, the logical way to design jobs is by improving the five core dimensions: skill identity, task identity, task significance, autonomy, and feedback. As mentioned earlier, this process is often referred to as job enrichment. In addition, you should try to shape employees' perceptions by speaking positively about their work.

How can you actually enrich a job? The following suggestions, derived from the JCM, specify the types of changes in jobs that are mostly likely to lead to improvements in each of the five core dimensions.[15]

1. ***Combine tasks.*** Put existing fragmented tasks together to form a new, larger module of work and increase skill variety and task identity.

For instance, instead of having an assembly-line worker install just the coils on a toaster and have other assemblers add the other parts, a toaster might be assembled from start to finish by one operator.

2. ***Create natural work units.*** Design tasks to form an identifiable and meaningful whole to increase employee "ownership" of the work and encourage workers to view their jobs as important.

Take, for example, 10 typists in a pool who handle a random assignment of letters, reports, and other tasks. As a result, the typists do not identify with the work or with the person or department for whom it is performed. To create a natural work unit, the manager might assign continuing responsibility for a specific department's work to one or more typists. Or, one or more typists could handle the letters, another such group handle the reports, the budget, whatever. As a result, typists to whom work is assigned naturally rather than randomly have a much greater chance of performing the whole job to completion and identifying with it.

3. ***Establish client relationships.*** The client is the user of the product or the service that the employee works on. Building direct relationships between the worker and the client increases skill variety, autonomy, and feedback.

A cook who never sees the diners might be encouraged to circulate among the clientele to get direct praise or criticism. Or, the mechanic who actually repaired a transmission might meet the automobile owner and explain the procedure.

4. ***Expand jobs vertically.*** Vertical expansion—giving employees responsibilities formerly reserved for management—partially closes the gap between the "doing" and "controlling" aspects of the job and increases autonomy.

Ways to increase "vertical loading" at a packaging plant might include giving workers greater authority in setting schedules. The employees might also decide on work methods, check on quality, and advise or help to train less-experienced workers.

5. ***Open feedback channels.*** Feedback not only tells employees how well they are performing but also whether their performance is improving, deteriorating, or remaining constant. Ideally, employees should receive feedback directly as they do their jobs rather than just occasionally.[16]

For instance, quality control in many organizations often eliminates a natural source of feedback because it is done by people other than those responsible for the work. Placing quality control close to the workers—perhaps in their own hands—can dramatically increase the quantity and the quality of data that are available to them.

Working with Teams

In the modern workplace, people increasingly are working in groups and teams. For example, a group of workers might be responsible for assembling an entire automobile or an electric appliance. Can much be done about the design of group-based work? Due to the relatively recent nature of teams, we know more about the individually based job design than we do about design at the group level.[17] But researchers offer some suggestions.[18]

First, the JCM principles seem as valid for group endeavors as they are at the individual level. So managers should expect a group to perform at a high level when (1) the group task requires members to use a variety of relatively high-level skills; (2) the group task is a whole and meaningful piece of work with a visible outcome; (3) the outcomes of the group's work on the task have significant consequences for other people; (4) the task provides group members with autonomy in deciding how they do the work; and (5) work on the task generates regular, trustworthy feedback about how well the group is performing.

Second, group composition is critical to the success of the work group. Managers should try to ensure that (1) individual members have the necessary expertise to do the work, (2) the group is large enough to get the job done, (3) members possess interpersonal as well as task skills, and (4) membership is moderately diverse in terms of talents and perspectives.

Work Schedule Options

Another way to design jobs is to change the time of day set aside for work or the location at which it must be performed. Most people work an eight-hour day, five days a week, at a more or less fixed location. These are full-time employees who start and leave at fixed times. But an increasingly popular way to design work to match the employee is to use scheduling options that benefit the worker without sacrificing organizational aims. Such variation includes flextime, job sharing, and telecommuting.

Flextime is short for "flexible hours." It allows workers some discretion over when they arrive at and leave work. Employees still must work a specified number of hours per week, but they are free to vary the hours within certain limits. For example, the required core hours during which all employees must be at their jobs might be the six hours between 9 A.M. and 3 P.M., but workers would be free to add the additional two hours in the morning by coming in at 7 A.M., or in the evening by staying until 5 P.M.

Flextime has become an extremely popular option. One study of firms with more than 1,000 employees found that 53 percent offered this feature.[19] The many potential benefits include improved motivation and morale, reduced absenteeism because employees can better balance work and family responsibilities, and the ability of the organization to recruit higher-quality and more diverse employees.[20]

On the other hand, flextime cannot be used for every job. It works well with clerical tasks in which an employee's interaction with people outside his or her department is limited. It is not viable when key people must be available during standard working hours, when work flow requires tight scheduling, or when specialists are called upon to maintain coverage of all functions in a unit.[21]

Job sharing is a special sort of part-time work that allows two or more people to split a traditional 40-hour-a-week job. One person might perform the same job, say, from 8 A.M. to noon and another from 1 P.M. to 5 P.M. Or, the two could alternate full days. Job sharing, while growing, is less widespread than flextime. About 30 percent of large organizations offer this option.[22]

Job sharing allows the organization to draw upon the talents of more than one individual for a given job. It also creates the opportunity to acquire skilled workers—for instance, retirees and mothers of young children—who might not otherwise be available on a full-time basis. The major drawback from management's perspective is the difficulty of finding compatible pairs who can successfully coordinate the intricacies of one job.[23]

Telecommuting refers to employees who do their work at home or on the road using a computer linked to the office. Executives have practiced forms of telecommuting for years, and now millions of employees telecommute by doing such tasks as taking orders over the phone, filling out reports and other forms, and processing or analyzing data. In fact, telecommuting is the fastest-growing trend in work scheduling.[24] Still, it is not feasible for all workers; firefighters and police, for example, must be at their duty stations. In addition, not all employees embrace telecommuting. After the 1994 earthquake in Los Angeles, many firms there began offering telecommuting. It was popular for a week or two, but soon enthusiasm waned. Many workers complained that they were missing out on important meetings and informal interactions that led to new policies and ideas. The vast majority was willing to put up with long commutes while bridges and freeways were being rebuilt in order to maintain social contacts at work.[25]

Even among those for whom telecommuting is a possibility, other issues must be addressed: Are employees who work from home disadvantaged in office politics and in competition for salary increases and promotions? Do distractions in the home—children, neighbors, and the proximity of the television and the refrigerator—significantly reduce productivity? Will those workers for whom telecommuting is not viable feel jealousy toward those who can telecommute? In short, telecommuting is a novel, emerging issue. It is unclear yet whether telecommuting will have a long-term future in U.S. workplaces.

Job design is an ongoing, dynamic process. Obviously, what we do on the job plays a major role not only in our economic standing but also in our social, health, and psychological status. Job design attempts to identify the most important needs of both the employee and the organization, and then try to remove any obstacles that thwart those needs.

The distinguishing feature of job design in the foreseeable future is flexibility. Managers must ask: Does the job support the organization's mission? And employees must ask: Does the job meet my needs?

CONCEPT QUIZ

Complete the following true-false quiz by circling the correct answer. The answers are at the end of the quiz. After marking your answers, remember to go back and check your understanding of any answers you missed.

True or False 1. *Scientific management* refers to the idea that jobs should be made to fit people.

True or False 2. Technology is increasingly an important element of modern job design.

True or False 3. All workers want personal and psychological development to roughly the same degree.

True or False 4. Intrinsic rewards that derive directly from performing the job are essential to motivation.

True or False 5. Employees form attitudes and behavior in response to social cues provided by others.

True or False 6. The job characteristics model (JCM) is more valid for individuals than for group endeavors.

True or False	7. Flextime works best for employees whose interaction with people outside their department is limited.
True or False	8. Job sharing allows two or more people to split a traditional 40-hour-a-week job.
True or False	9. Telecommuting is not feasible for workers such as firefighters or police who must be at their duty station.
True or False	10. Jobs that possess autonomy give workers a sense of responsibility for the results.

Answers.   (1) False; (2) True; (3) False; (4) True; (5) True; (6) False; (7) True; (8) True; (9) True; (10) True

BEHAVIORAL CHECKLIST

The following behaviors are important for diagnosing job characteristics and designing jobs to maximize employee performance.

Effective Job Designers

- Study the characteristics of each job.
- Take into account the growth-strength need of the employees.
- Note what social cues workers are receiving about their jobs.
- Decide how the skill variety, task identity, task significance, autonomy, and feedback could be improved in each case.
- Seek to enrich the jobs by strengthening the five core dimensions.
- Consider work-schedule options.
- Try to improve employees' perception of their jobs.

> **Attention!**
> Do not read the following until assigned to do so by your instructor.

MODELING EXERCISE

The Job Design Process

Directions.   The entire class should read the following situation. Then three students should be assigned to play the roles of Charles, Jenny, and Rhonda. The rest of the class should observe and critique them.

Role-players should read and prepare for their assigned role but should not read the others' roles. After reading the situation, observers should read all three roles and review the Observer's Rating Sheet.

Time.   30 minutes.

Actors.

Rhonda, manager of the Acme Bakery

Charles, a college sophomore working his first summer at Acme

Jenny, a college junior in her second summer at Acme

Situation. Rhonda is manager of a busy bakery where Charles and Jenny, both college students, are working for the summer. The bakery specializes in dinner rolls and bread, most of which are sold just prior to the weekend. Most of Charles's and Jenny's work is dictated by production schedules but some time is discretionary, and Rhonda usually assigns them whatever task is a priority at that moment.

Neither Charles nor Jenny is highly skilled, but Jenny is more experienced at bakery work. Both began the summer with energy and enthusiasm. However, Charles has since lost his edge and has complained at length about the tedium of the work. His performance has fallen off, too. Jenny, on the other hand, remains ebullient and a good worker, which is why she was rehired.

The least-desirable job for an inexperienced worker is stacking trays of dinner rolls on racks as the bakers fill up the pans with dough. The employee must be quick and pay attention all the time, otherwise the bakers will be tossing the dough into already-filled pans, and the whole operation will need to come to a stop, costing money and aggravation. On the other hand, packing bread for shipment is hardly creative but is not quite so fast-paced, and a worker can take a break if he or she needs to.

Here are the tasks and schedules:

CHARLES

Schedule. Works 2:30 P.M. to 11:30 P.M. Wednesday through Sunday (with one hour for dinner break).

Tasks. Wednesday: 3 hours stacking trays of rolls on racks; 4 hours cleaning bread pans before dough is put in them; 1 hour sweeping the floor and stowing newly arrived supplies.
Thursday: 5 hours stacking trays of rolls on racks; 3 hours cleaning bread pans.
Friday: 6 hours stacking rolls on racks; 2 hours cleaning bread pans; 1 hour sweeping.
Saturday: 1 hour stacking rolls on racks; 3 hours cleaning bread pans; 2 hours sweeping; 2 hours as directed.
Sunday: 1 hour stacking rolls on racks; 4 hours cleaning bread pans; 3 hours as directed.

JENNY

Schedule. Works 1 P.M. to 10 P.M. Saturday through Wednesday (with one hour for dinner break).

Tasks. Saturday: 4 hours packing bread; 3 hours stacking roll trays on racks; 1 hour helping Rhonda with mail and clerical tasks.
Sunday: 4 hours packing bread; 2 hours stacking rolls on racks; 2 hours helping Rhonda on mail and clerical tasks.
Monday: 4 hours packing bread; 4 hours stacking rolls on racks.
Tuesday: 4 hours packing bread; 4 hours stacking rolls on racks.
Wednesday: 2 hours stacking rolls on racks; 1 hour cleaning bread pans; 3 hours packing bread; 2 hours as directed.

Rhonda's Role Making the college students happy with their work is not your highest priority. Still, it would be nice if everyone liked his or her job and performed it well. You are especially fond of Jenny. She and Charles are equals in terms of pay and status (such as it is), but you try to give her a break by assigning her mostly to the bread-packing job, which is slightly less tedious than stacking trays of rolls. You also use her as a clerical assistant whenever possible. Charles has been disappointing in that he complains a lot and his performance has fallen off after a good early start. If he quits, you're going to be in a pickle because finding someone in mid-summer to replace him won't be easy.

Jenny's Role   You like your job which is why you came back for a second year. The work is not glamorous, but it is a nice change of pace from studying and now that you have some experience, Rhonda has given you a slightly better schedule and an array of tasks. You especially enjoy helping with the mail and clerical tasks. You think you deserve the breaks she has given you because you worked so hard last summer, often stacking trays of rolls for what seemed likes days at a time.

Charles's Role   You knew this job would mean hard work, but you hoped for a more equitable division of tasks. It is not Jenny's fault, but it does trouble you that she seems to get the better schedule and assignments. Stacking trays of rolls is an especially deadening job, but one on which you cannot let your attention drift for a second. Compared to it, sweeping the floor is a pleasure. You do not know whether you can gut it out the whole summer. There has got to be a better way to make some tuition money than this!

Modeling Exercise Observations

During the dialogue, observers should note how Rhonda treats Charles and Jenny, what questions she asks, how flexible she seems, and how the two workers respond. Be prepared to suggest additional questions or alternatives and to draw conclusions about Rhonda's commitment to making a good-faith effort to redesign the jobs.

OBSERVER'S RATING SHEET

Using the following scale, rate Rhonda's application of techniques discussed in this chapter. Also write comments in the spaces below each of the behavioral criteria that will help explain your feedback.

1 Unsatisfactory	*2* Weak	*3* Adequate	*4* Good	*5* Outstanding

_____ Found out what was wrong with the present situation.

_____ Explored the employees' motivation.

_____ Examined each worker's growth-need strength.

_____ Considered the role of social cues.

_____ Analyzed what would work for the firm as well as for the employees.

_____ Showed creativity in coming up with alternatives.

_____ Involved the employees in the search for solutions.

_____ Looked at schedule options as well as changes in assignment of tasks.

GROUP EXERCISES

In the three exercises that follow, you will be asked to practice the elements of good job design. The first exercise is designed to encourage you to brainstorm about how you would redesign a job. Group Exercise 2 gives you a detailed work situation to analyze, and the third exercise allows you to "overhear" and critique a conversation between two managers who are planning a job redesign.

Group Exercise 1: Brainstorming Job Redesign[26]

Step 1: Identify a Target Job.   Class members volunteer to share the description of a job they now hold or have held. The student selected should explain the job thoroughly so that everyone becomes familiar with it. If several students volunteer, the class and/or the instructor can select a job that seems the most interesting. **(10 minutes)**

To help identify a job that will be a good candidate for job redesign, make sure it meets the following criteria.

1. ***A specific problem or exploitable opportunity is identified.***   Unless a specific organizational problem can be identified, the diagnosis should stop there.
2. ***The problem or opportunity involves employee motivation, satisfaction, or work effectiveness.***   If the issues are irrelevant to these matters, work redesign is unlikely to help.
3. ***The redesign is likely to help resolve the problems.***   Many factors affect poor performance, motivation, and satisfaction. Is the design of the work one of the reasons?
4. ***Specific aspects of the job can be pinpointed as being most troublesome.***   What deserves special attention?
5. ***The employees are ready for change.***   Check the level of employee knowledge and skill, growth-need strength, and overall satisfaction. If one or more of these factors is low, the decision might be to proceed with work redesign cautiously, if at all.
6. ***The organization is hospitable to change.***   If work design is called for, the organization must be ready to embrace it.

Step 2.   The class interviews the person who holds (or held, or knows) the target job so that everyone understands the job activities. Before proceeding, make sure the group is in agreement on the activities performed by the person holding the job. Check to see whether anyone has questions about the job. **(10 minutes)**

Step 3.   Form groups of three to seven students. Brainstorm as many possible changes in the job as you can think of. **(20 minutes)**

Rules for Brainstorming

1. Write down all ideas that are produced.
2. Praise one another's ideas, help each develop ideas, and add to others' ideas whenever possible.
3. Do *not* evaluate or criticize anyone's ideas. The creative process is a fragile one. Ideas—not criticism—are needed at this point.

After you've finished brainstorming, then you can be critical. Go over your brainstormed list and delete proposed changes that (a) will not affect core job characteristics, (b) are technologically impossible or obviously not cost effective, or (c) are too abstract and general.

Then pick a spokesperson to report your recommended changes to the rest of the class.

Step 4. Each group's representative reads off that group's list of recommendations. **(10 minutes)**

Step 5: Job Incumbent's Reactions. Ask the person who holds (or held, or knows) the job to comment on the job redesign ideas. How realistic are they? What impact would they have? Have they ever been tried there? Would they likely improve motivation, satisfaction, or performance? **(5 minutes)**

Group Exercise 2: Redesigning Assembly-Line Jobs[27]

Time. 80 minutes.

Instructions. Meet in groups of five to seven people. Take 10 minutes to read each part of the Hovey and Beard Co. case as directed. Take another 10 minutes to come to a group decision on the questions at the end of each part.

Part I. The Hovey and Beard Co. Case

The Hovey and Beard Co. manufactures wooden toys of various animals. One part of the manufacturing involves spray painting the partially assembled toys. This operation was staffed entirely by women.

The toys are cut, sanded, and partially assembled in the wood room. Then they are dipped in shellac and, finally, painted. The toys are predominantly two-colored, though a few are painted with more than two colors. Each additional color requires an extra trip through the paint room.

For a number of years, production of these toys had been entirely by hand. However, to meet tremendously increased demand, the painting operation recently has been reengineered so that the eight operators sit in a line by a seemingly endless chain of hooks. These hooks are in continuous motion, past the line of operators and into a large oven. A woman sits at her own painting booth designed to carry away fumes and to backstop excess paint. The operator takes a toy from the tray in front of her, positions it in a jig inside the painting cube, sprays on the color according to a pattern, then releases the toy and hangs it on the hook passing by. The pace at which the hooks move had been calculated by the engineers so that the women, when fully trained, should be able to hang a painted toy on each hook before it passes her reach.

The operators working in the paint room are on a group bonus plan. Because the operation was new to them, they are receiving a learning bonus that decreases by regular amounts each month. The learning bonus is scheduled to vanish in six months, by which time it was expected that they will be on their own—that is, be able to meet the standard and to earn a group bonus when they exceed that standard.

Discuss. What do you expect will happen over the next few months? Will production go up, down, or stay the same?

All the groups meet briefly as a full class. Make a tally of how many groups think production will go up, how many think it will go down, and how many think it will stay the same.

Now read Part II of the case.

Part II

By the second month of the training period, trouble had developed. The employees learned more slowly than had been anticipated, and it began to look as though their production would stabilize far below what was planned. Many of the hooks were going by empty. The women complained that they were going by too fast, and that the time-study engineer had set the rates wrong. A few women quit and had to be replaced with new operators, which further aggravated the learning problem. The team spirit that the management had expected to develop automatically through the group bonus was not in evidence except as an expression of what the engineers called "resistance." One woman whom the group regarded as its leader (and the management regarded as the ringleader) was outspoken in making various complaints of the group to the supervisor: The job was messy, the hooks moved too fast, the incentive pay was not being correctly calculated, and it was too hot working so close to the drying oven.

Discuss. If you were a consultant, what would you recommend?

Now read Part III.

Part III

A consultant who was brought into this picture worked entirely with and through the supervisor. After many conversations with the consultant, the supervisor felt that the first step should be to get the employees together for a general discussion of the working conditions. The supervisor took this step with some hesitation, but he took it on his own volition.

The first meeting, held immediately after the shift was over at 4 P.M., was attended by all eight operators. They voiced the same complaints again. The hooks went by too fast, the job was too dirty, the room was hot and poorly ventilated. For some reason, it was this last item that they complained of most. The supervisor promised to discuss the problem of ventilation and temperature with the engineers, and he scheduled a second meeting to report back to the employees. In the next few days the supervisor had several talks with the engineers. They and the superintendent felt that the complaint was trumped up and that the expense of any effective corrective measure would be prohibitively high.

The supervisor came to the second meeting with some apprehensions. The operators, however, did not seem to be much put out, perhaps because they had a proposal of their own to make. They felt that if several large fans were set up so as to circulate the air around their feet, they would be much more comfortable. After some discussion, the supervisor agreed that the idea might be tried. The supervisor and the consultant discussed the question of the fans with the superintendent, and three large propeller-type fans were purchased.

The fans were brought in. The women were jubilant. For several days the fans were moved about in various positions until they were placed to the satisfaction of the group. The operators seemed completely satisfied with the results, and the relations between them and the supervisor improved visibly.

The supervisor, after this encouraging episode, decided that further meetings might also be profitable. He asked the operators if they would like to meet and discuss other aspects of the work situation. They were eager to do so. The meeting was held, and the discussion quickly centered on the speed of the hooks. The operators maintained that the time-study engineer had set the hooks at an unreasonably fast speed and that the operators would never be able to reach the goal of filling enough of them to make a bonus.

The turning point of the discussion came when the group's leader frankly explained that the point was not that they could not work fast enough to keep up with the hooks, but that they could not work at that pace all day long. The supervisor explored the point. The employees were unanimous in their opinion that they could keep up with the belt for short periods if they wanted to, but they didn't want to because if they showed they could do this for short periods they would be expected to do it all day long. The meeting ended with an unprecedented request: "Let us adjust the speeds of the belt faster or slower depending on how we feel." The supervisor agreed to discuss this request with the superintendent and the engineers.

The reaction of the engineers to the suggestion was negative. However, after several meetings the engineers conceded that some latitude could be given within which variation in the speed of the hook would not affect the finished product. After considerable argument with the engineers, it was agreed to try out the operators' ideas.

With misgiving, the supervisor had a control with a dial marked "low, medium, fast," installed at the booth of the group leader; she could now adjust the speed of the belt anywhere between the lower and upper limits that the engineers had set.

Discuss.   What do you think the results of this action will be? Will production go up, down, or stay the same? Will satisfaction go up, down, or stay the same?

Now read Part IV.

Part IV

The operators were delighted, and spent many lunch hours deciding how the speed of the belt should be varied from hour to hour throughout the day. Within a week the pattern had settled down to one in which the first half hour of the shift was run on what the operators called a medium speed (a dial setting slightly above the point marked "medium"). The next two and one-half hours were run at high speed; the half hour before lunch and the half hour after lunch were run at low speed. The rest of the afternoon was run at high speed with the exception of the last 45 minutes of the shift, which was run at medium.

In view of the operators' reports of satisfaction and ease in their work, it is interesting to note that the constant speed at which the engineers had originally set the belt was slightly below medium on the dial of the control that had been given the women. The average speed at which the women were running the belt was on the high side of the dial. Few, if any, empty hooks entered the oven, and inspection showed no increase of rejects from the paint room.

Production increased, and within three weeks (some two months before the scheduled ending of the learning bonus), the operators were operating at 30 to 50 percent above the level that had been expected under the original arrangement. Naturally their earnings were correspondingly higher than anticipated. They were collecting their base pay, a considerable piece-rate bonus, and the learning bonus that, it will be remembered, had been set to decrease with time and not as a function of current productivity. The operators were earning more now than many skilled workers in other parts of the plant.

Discuss.   What do you think will be the final reaction of plant management? If you were part of Hovey and Beard's top management team, what would you recommend?

Group Exercise 3: Getting Ready to Redesign Work

Directions.   Split into three groups. Each group should read the situation and the dialogue that follows it, then try to answer the questions. Reconvene as a class and compare answers.

Situation.   The vice president for personnel at a large manufacturing firm has received numerous complaints from employees in the Human Resources Department that their work is undervalued and that they do not feel "a part of the company." The vice president calls Leo and Clare, the two managers in the HR department, to his office. He tells them to find out what is going on and report what changes, if any, can and should be made. His tone is less than friendly.

Leo and Clare have the following conversation:

> **LEO:** What is this problem about our employees feeling unwanted and unloved? Don't they know how good they have it compared to those who work in other parts of this outfit? If they operated a lathe or a router for a few days, they would wish they were back on the clerical side, don't you agree?
>
> **CLARE:** Of course. But our boss wants us to improve things. The question is how do we start?
>
> **LEO:** Well, how do we know that what we do will have any effect?
>
> **CLARE:** Work can always be better—it just can't be made perfect. So we have got to sort out the chronic whiners from those with legitimate gripes. I suggest we interview everybody, then compare notes. Maybe we can get a consensus about the kinds of problems we face.
>
> **LEO:** That is a lot of work.
>
> **CLARE:** I don't see any way around it if we are going to improve things.
>
> **LEO:** Okay, but then what?
>
> **CLARE:** I don't know.

A week later, Leo and Clare meet again after having talked to all the employees in the department. They were bombarded with complaints. The HR workers feel the manufacturing employees are given special treatment while the clerical workers are expected to do unrewarding jobs without the possibility of bonuses, scheduling options (the manufacturing employees can choose to work a 10-hour day, four days a week), or getting any significant feedback on their work.

> **LEO:** So what do you think now?
>
> **CLARE:** I think we have a lot of work to do. I definitely do not want to take any more heat from the VP about this. I say: Give them what they want. Where should we start?
>
> **LEO:** Well, if we think this scheduling complaint is valid, we could draw up some alternatives and present them to top management.
>
> **CLARE:** I don't care if it is valid. I just want to stop the flak. Why don't you handle that? I will find out how the bonus system works on the manufacturing side and then we can see whether we can adapt it for the white-collar rank-and-file.
>
> **LEO:** What about the feedback question?
>
> **CLARE:** What about it, Leo. Who can change that?

QUESTIONS FOR DISCUSSION

1. Should Leo and Clare have known about this situation before being called in by the vice president? Why or why not?

2. Did they go about their investigation in the right way? Why or why not?

3. What important factors did Clare not include in her rush to get the job done?

4. What is the answer to Leo's question about who can improve the feedback? Why?

SUMMARY CHECKLIST

Take a few minutes to reflect on your performance in the preceding exercises. Assess yourself as to how your analysis compared to other students (and if you were a presenter, how others rated your skill). Make a check (✓) next to those behaviors on which you may need improvement.

_____ **Understand the present situation.**
1. Know your employees' strengths and weaknesses.
2. Know who are chronic complainers and who are not.
3. Perform an analysis of each affected job.
4. Evaluate how the job stacks up on the five-element JCM model.

_____ **Show creativity in coming up with alternatives.**
1. How can jobs be combined?
2. Can natural work units be established?
3. Is it possible to have the worker interact with the client?
4. Should jobs be expanded vertically to give rank-and-file employees more authority?
5. Can feedback channels be opened?
6. Are telecommuting, job sharing, and flextime possible options?

_____ **Involve employees in the search for solutions.**
1. Elicit comments about what is wrong.
2. Encourage realistic suggestions.

_____ **Make sure your recommendations work for the organization as well as the employees.**
1. Is performance enhanced?
2. Is the job enrichment likely to cause problems with unaffected groups of employees?

APPLICATION QUESTIONS

1. *Is your work environment a healthy one?* Answer the following questions. If you reply Yes to nine or more of the questions, your work environment is likely a psychologically healthy one. If you can answer Yes to only six or fewer, your work environment probably isn't as healthy as it could be.[28]

CONTROL AND INFLUENCE
_____ Do you have influence over the pace of your work?
_____ Do you have a say in your work assignments and goals?
_____ Is there an opportunity for you to comment on your performance appraisal?

INFORMATION AND UNCERTAINTY
_____ Do you have access to all the information you need at work?
_____ Is there adequate planning for changes that affect you at work?
_____ Do you receive complete information for your work assignments?

CONFLICT AT WORK
_____ Does the organization apply policies clearly and consistently?
_____ Are job descriptions and task assignments clear and unambiguous?
_____ Are policies and procedures in place for resolution of conflicts?

JOB SCOPE AND TASK DESIGN
_____ Do your work activities and assignments provide adequate variety?
_____ Do you receive timely, constructive feedback on your work?
_____ Is your work important to the overall mission?
_____ Do you work on more than one small piece of a big project?

REINFORCEMENT EXERCISES

The following are suggested activities for reinforcing the job design techniques described in this chapter. You may want to adapt them to the Action Plan you will develop next, or try them independently.

Examine the motivating potential in your job or a job you have held. For each of the following questions, circle the number of the most accurate description of the job. Be as objective as you can in describing the job by answering these questions.[29]

1. *How much autonomy is present in this job? That is, to what extent does the job permit a person to decide on his or her own how to go about doing the work?*

1	2	3	4	5	6	7
Very little. The job gives a person almost no say about how and when the work is done.		Moderate. Many things are standardized and not under control of the jobholder, but he or she can make some decisions about the work.			Very much. The job gives the employee complete responsibility for deciding how and when the work is done.	

2. *To what extent does the job involve doing an identifiable piece of work? That is, is the job a complete piece of work with an obvious beginning and end? Or is it a small part of an overall piece of work, which is finished by other people or by machines?*

1	*2*	*3*	*4*	*5*	*6*	*7*

The job is only a tiny part in the overall piece of work. The results of this person's effort cannot be seen in the final product or service.

The job is a moderate-sized chunk of the overall piece of work. The person's contribution can be seen in the final outcome.

The job involves doing the whole piece of work from start to finish. The person's activities can be easily seen in the final product or service.

3. *How much variety is present in the job? That is, to what extent does the job require a person to do many different things at work, using a variety of his or her skills and talents?*

1	*2*	*3*	*4*	*5*	*6*	*7*

Very little. The job requires the person to do the same routine things over and over again.

Moderate variety.

Very much. The job requires the person to do many different things, using a number of different skills and talents.

4. *In general, how significant or important is the job? That is, are the results of the person's work likely to affect significantly the lives or well-being of other people?*

1	*2*	*3*	*4*	*5*	*6*	*7*

Not significant. The outcome of the work is not likely to affect anyone in any important way.

Moderately significant.

Highly significant. The outcome of the work can affect others in important ways.

5. *To what extent does doing the job itself provide the person with information about his or her work performance? That is, does the actual work itself provide clues about how well the person is doing—aside from any feedback coworkers or supervisors may provide.*

1	*2*	*3*	*4*	*5*	*6*	*7*

Very little. The job itself is set up so a person could work forever without finding out how well he or she was doing.

Moderately. Sometimes doing the job provides feedback to the person, sometimes it does not.

Very much. The job is set up so that the person gets almost constant feedback as he or she works about how well he or she is doing.

Scoring and Interpretation. To score the questionnaire, place your responses to questions 3, 2, 4, 1, and 5, respectively, in the blank spaces in the following equation:

$$\text{Motivating Potential Score (MPS)} = \frac{[\ \ \overset{Q\#3}{}\ \ ] + [\ \ \overset{Q\#2}{}\ \ ] + [\ \ \overset{Q\#4}{}\ \ ]}{3} \times [\ \ \overset{Q\#1}{}\ \ ] \times [\ \ \overset{Q\#5}{}\ \ ] = \text{_____}$$

200–343 means the job is high in motivating potential
120–199 means the job is moderate in motivating potential
  0–119 means the job is low in motivating potential

Thinking of that same job, what could be done to make it more motivating?

	Yes	*No*	*Maybe*
1. Could the skill variety be increased?	_____	_____	_____
2. Could the task identity be improved?	_____	_____	_____
3. Could the task significance be enhanced?	_____	_____	_____
4. Could more autonomy be granted?	_____	_____	_____
5. Could more feedback be given?	_____	_____	_____

ACTION PLAN

1. What are specific things I can do to improve when designing jobs?
2. What will be the benefits of these improvements?
3. What potential obstacles stand in my way?
4. When will I start these improvements?
5. How and when will I measure my success?

NOTES

1. S. Caudron, "The De-Jobbing of America," *Industry Week*, September 5, 1994, 31–36.
2. K. H. Hammonds, K. Kelly, and K. Thurston, "Rethinking Work," *Business Week*, October 12, 1994, 75–87.
3. C. Powell, "When Workers Wear Walkmans on the Job," *Wall Street Journal*, July 11, 1994, B1, B8; J. Stuller, "Games Workers Play," *Across the Board* (July–August 1997): 16–22; C. Harmon, "Goofing Off at Work: First You Log On," *International Herald Tribune*, September 23, 1997, 1, 10.
4. S. Melamed, I. Ben-Avi, J. Luz, and M. S. Green, "Objective and Subjective Work Monitoring: Effect on Job Satisfaction, Psychological Distress, and Absenteeism in Blue-Collar Workers," *Journal of Applied Psychology* (February 1995): 29–42.
5. M. A. Campion, and C. L. McClelland, "Follow-Up and Extension of the Interdisciplinary Costs and Benefits of Enlarged Jobs," *Journal of Applied Psychology* (June 1993): 339–51.
6. Description based on S. Lohr, "Hey, Who Took the Office Doors?" *New York Times*, August 11, 1997, p. C7.
7. J. R. Hackman and G. R. Oldham, "Motivation Through the Design of Work: Test of a Theory," *Organizational Behavior and Human Performance* (August 1976): 250–79; J. R. Hackman and G. R. Oldham, "Development of the Job Diagnostic Survey," *Journal of Applied Psychology* (April 1975): 159–70.
8. J. R. Hackman, "Work Design," in J. R. Hackman and J. L. Suttle, eds., *Improving Life at Work*, (Glenview, IL: Scott, Foresman, 1977) 129.
9. M. Campion and G. Sanborn, "Job Design," in G. Salvendy, ed., *Handbook of Industrial Engineering*, (New York: John Wiley, 1991).
10. J. R. Hackman, G. Oldham, R. Janson, and K. Purdy, "A New Strategy for Job Enrichment," *California Management Review* 16 (Fall 1975): 57–71.
11. G. Oldham and A. Cummings, "Employee Creativity: Personal and Contextual Factors at Work," *Academy of Management Journal* 39 (1996): 607–34.
12. A. Haasen, "Opel Eisenach GMBH—Creating a High-Productivity Workplace," *Organizational Dynamics* (Spring 1996): 80–85.
13. P. F. Drucker, "Managing Oneself," *Harvard Business Review* (March–April 1999): 67.

14. G. R. Salancik and J. Pfeffer, "A Social Information Processing Approach to Job Attitudes and Task Design," *Administrative Science Quarterly* (June 1978): 224–53.
15. Hackman, "Work Design," 129.
16. Ibid., 136–40.
17. R. W. Griffin and G. C. McMahan, "Motivation Through Job Design," in J. Greenberg, ed., *Organizational Behavior: The State of the Science* (Hillsdale, NJ: Lawrence Erlbaum Associates, 1994) 36–38.
18. J. R. Hackman, "The Design of Work Teams," in J. W. Lorsch, ed., *Handbook of Organizational Behavior* (Upper Saddle River, NJ: Prentice Hall, 1987) 324–27.
19. Cited in C. M. Solomon, "Job Sharing: One Job, Double Headache?" *Personnel Journal* (September, 1994): 90.
20. D. R. Dalton and D. J. Mesch, "The Impact of Flexible Scheduling on Employee Attendance and Turnover," *Administrative Science Quarterly* (June 1990), 370–87; and K. S. Kush and L. K. Stroh, "Flextime: Myth or Reality?" *Business Horizons* (September–October, 1994): 53.
21. Kush and Stroh, 1994, 53.
22. Solomon, 1994, 90.
23. S. Shellenbarger, "Two People, One Job: It Can Really Work," *Wall Street Journal*, December 7, 1994, B1.
24. "Portrait of a Telecommuter," *INC. Technology* (November 1994): 18.
25. S. Silverstein, "Telecommuting Boomlet Has Few Follow Up Calls," *Los Angeles Times*, May 16, 1994, A1.
26. Adapted from D. D. Bowen, R. J. Lenicki, et al., *Experiences in Management and Organizational Behavior*, 4th ed. (New York: John Wiley, 1997), 51–53.
27. Adapted from A. Bavelas and G. Strauss "The Hovey and Beard Case" in W. F. Whyte, ed., *Money and Motivation* (New York: Harper & Row, 1955).
28. Adapted from D. L. Nelson and J. C. Quick, *Organizational Behavior: Foundations, Realities, and Challenges* (Minneapolis/St. Paul: West Publishing, 1997) 431.
29. J. R. Hackman and G. R. Oldham, "The Job Diagnostic Survey: An Instrument for the Diagnosis of Jobs and the Evaluation of Job Redesign Projects," *Technical Report No. 4* (New Haven, CT: Department of Administrative Sciences, Yale University, 1974) 2–3 of the Short Form.

CHAPTER 12

Diagnosing and Modifying Organizational Culture

Learning Objectives

After completing this chapter, you should be able to:

■ Identify an organization's culture.

■ Assess how a person fits into a specific culture.

■ Instill cultural values and norms in subordinates.

■ Make appropriate changes to an organization's culture.

SELF-ASSESSMENT EXERCISE

Respond as candidly as possible to the following statements designed to assess your understanding of organizational culture. Describe your level of agreement with each statement by circling the number in the appropriate column.

	Strongly Agree				Strongly Disagree
1. If a person can do well in one organization, he or she ought to do well in any organization.	1	2	3	4	5
2. An organization's culture is whatever the current CEO says it is.	1	2	3	4	5
3. Skills and experience are all that really matter; how a job candidate will "fit in" is not an important factor in hiring.	1	2	3	4	5
4. Members of an organization explicitly tell people how to adhere to its culture.	1	2	3	4	5
5. After appropriate study, astute managers can fairly quickly change a corporate culture.	1	2	3	4	5
6. A common culture is important for unifying employees but does not necessarily affect the firm's financial health.	1	2	3	4	5
7. Conscientious workers are not really influenced by an organization's culture.	1	2	3	4	5
8. Strong organizational cultures are not necessarily associated with high organizational performance.	1	2	3	4	5
9. Members of a subculture share the common values of the subculture but not those of the dominant organizational culture.	1	2	3	4	5
10. A job candidate seeking to understand a prospective employer's culture can do so by just asking the interviewers.	1	2	3	4	5

Scoring and Interpretation.   Each of the preceding statements describes an important implication of organizational culture. The higher your score, the better you understand the organizational culture's ramifications.

Add the numbers you have circled to obtain your total score.

41–50	You have excellent instincts about organizational cultures and how people respond to them.
30–39	You show average or better awareness of the principles of organizational culture.
20–29	You have some sense of how cultures affect workers, but you need to increase your knowledge.
0–19	You definitely need to bolster your knowledge before trying to assess or modify a culture.

CONCEPTS

• Legendary industrialist David Packard, who cofounded electronics giant Hewlett-Packard, once personally ordered an engineer to halt work on a new computer monitor. "When I come back next year I do not want to see that project in the lab," Packard said. The engineer, however, decided that if the model were in production, it wouldn't be in the lab, so he pushed ahead. The monitor turned out to be a huge success and created an entirely new market. Packard then rewarded the engineer with a "Medal of Defiance" for bucking his boss. As a result, young HP employees, knowing they won't be punished for aggressively pursuing ideas, still look for ways to get their products or prototypes completed before top managers have figured out whether they even want them.[1]

• At Amy's Ice Creams, employees sometimes break-dance on the freezer tops. Or urge customers to imitate barnyard-animal sounds in return for free ice cream. Or wear pajamas to work for Sleep-Over Night. Job applicants are often given a test: Take this plain, white paper bag and do something interesting with it. Owner Amy Miller wants to differentiate her small Texas chain from all the other ice-cream shops. So at Amy's, every employee—and every customer—knows the emphasis is on *fun*.[2]

• The annual Mary Kay Cosmetics award meeting is a gala. Before a large, cheering audience, salespeople swathed in glamorous evening clothes receive flashy gifts—such as gold and diamond pins, furs, and even pink Cadillacs—for meeting their goals. The ritual sends out the message loud and strong: Reaching sales goals is important and those who work hard enough to meet them are the elite.[3]

Each of those anecdotes suggests what that organization prizes. Those shared values are the cornerstone of an organization's culture, and they greatly influence behavior at work. An organization's **culture,** or personality, refers to the key characteristics that the organization values and that distinguish it from other organizations. Managers need to be particularly aware of organizational culture because they are expected to respond to the dictates of the culture themselves and also inculcate them in their subordinates.

Most often the cultural imperatives are not written down or even discussed, but they are there, and all successful managers must learn what to do and what not to do in their organizations. In fact, the better the match between the manager's personal style and the organization's culture, the more successful he or she is likely to be.[4]

Why Culture Is So Important

When Pharmacia AB and Upjohn merged in 1995, many saw it as a perfect corporate marriage. Both firms were second-tier players fighting to survive in a world of global drug giants, and all the financial and marketing signals were positive for the merger. Pharmacia, based in Sweden, had a solid, if aging, product line but its distribution in the United States was weak. Upjohn, a U.S. firm, had some solid household name brands but suffered from stagnant sales. Thus, the merger was seen as a way to cut costs, improve global market penetration, and allow the new firm to better compete against Merck, Bristol-Myers Squibb, Pfizer, and other pharmaceutical giants.[5]

In the first few years after the merger, however, earnings plummeted, the stock fell sharply, many executives left, and company morale hit bottom. Why? Most experts point to the incompatibility between the two corporate cultures. For example:

- The hard-driving, mission-oriented American approach of Upjohn clashed with the consensus-oriented Swedish style of Pharmacia. Upjohn managers focused on ambitious cost-cutting and numerical accountability while Pharmacia managers emphasized keeping their employees informed and seeking feedback.

- The internationally experienced Pharmacia managers were surprised by the lack of global savvy and what they saw as the parochial attitudes of the Upjohn leaders. Upjohn's rules, for example, banned smoking and required all workers to take drug and alcohol tests. By contrast, at some Pharmacia sites, wine was poured freely in the company dining room and the boardrooms were well stocked with cigars.

- Pharmacia people, used to an open management system in which small teams were left largely on their own, were put off by Upjohn's tightly centralized management style. The Upjohn-based CEO required frequent reports, budgets, and staffing updates. Many of the Swedes viewed these reports as a waste of time and stopped taking them seriously.

Not surprisingly, such conflicts came to be reflected in the company's performance. Profits fell and top executives were replaced before stronger efforts were launched to blend the disparate styles. The case illustrates the importance of cultures: Even though the two firms matched up well on traditional business criteria, they stumbled in blending their corporate personalities.

What Constitutes Culture?

Research suggests seven primary dimensions that, in aggregate, express the essence of an organization's culture.[6] Each characteristic exists on a continuum from low to high. In many organizations, especially those with strong cultures, one dimension often rises above the others and shapes the organization and the way its members work.

1. *Innovation and risk taking.* The degree to which employees are encouraged to be innovative and take risks. Companies such as Microsoft and Coca-Cola pride themselves on tolerance, even encouragement, of failure. Microsoft, for instance, is known for asking potential job candidates about their failures and what they learned from them.[7]
2. *Attention to detail.* The degree to which employees are expected to exhibit precision, analysis, and attention to detail. Such organizations make quality their driving theme. A well-known example is Motorola, whose "Six Sigma" program spearheaded a dramatic decrease in manufacturing defects.
3. *Outcome orientation.* The degree to which management focuses on results rather than on the process used to produce those results. Nordstrom, for instance, stresses customer service in which the employee is to do whatever is needed to make each transaction a positive one.
4. *People orientation.* The degree to which management decisions take into account how people within the organization will be affected. Hewlett-Packard,

through its progressive personnel policies, has made its rank-and-file employees central to its culture.[8] HP workers got profit sharing as early as the 1940s and automatic stock grants in the 1950s. As one of the first firms to offer flextime, HP has also kept layoffs to a minimum by requiring that all divisions hire HP insiders before looking to the outside and by asking all workers during tough times to cut their pay and hours so none have to lose their job.

5. ***Team orientation.*** The degree to which work is organized around teams rather than individuals. An increasing number of smaller organizations and divisions of larger organizations are defining their culture around teams. For instance, Perkins Cole, the largest law firm in the Pacific Northwest, has its more than 300 lawyers operating in litigation, business, personal planning, and environmental law teams.[9]

6. ***Aggressiveness.*** The degree to which people are aggressive and competitive rather than easygoing. At General Electric, management sets demanding goals, as seen in their strategy, to have either the number one or number two market share in each of its markets, or exit those markets.[10]

7. ***Nonstability.*** The degree to which organizational activities emphasize growth as opposed to maintaining the status quo. Few firms better illustrate this than Samsung, South Korea's largest business with operations in electronics, chemicals, finance, and heavy machinery. It has ambitious plans to expand into many more industries, and it indoctrinates employees by, for example, displaying banners proclaiming the firm as "The Leader for the Twenty-First Century the World Will Notice."[11]

The more members accept the core values and the greater their commitment to them, the stronger the culture is.[12] Strong cultures have great influence on their members' behavior. Seattle-based Nordstrom is an example of one of the strongest service cultures in retailing, and it conveys that culture succinctly. Exhibit 12-1 shows the 5-by-8-inch card that is given to employees.

Evidence indicates that strong cultures are associated with high organizational performance.[13] Why? A strong culture gives everyone a clear vision. Such a culture also increases employee commitment and loyalty as well as yielding a sustainable competitive advantage that competitors cannot easily replicate.[14]

Strong cultures have their downsides, however. For example, strong cultures that do not value adaptability may actually decrease performance in changing times. When the personal-computer revolution began, for instance, IBM's strong culture may have blinded its executives to the need to change its long-time emphasis on mainframes. A

EXHIBIT 12-1   The Essence of Nordstrom's Organizational Culture

Welcome to Nordstrom

We're glad to have you with our Company.
Our number one goal is to provide outstanding customer service.
Set both your personal and professionals goals high.
We have great confidence in your ability to achieve them.
So our employee handbook is very simple.
We have only one rule …

Our only rule:

Use good judgment in all situations

Please feel free to ask your Department Manager, Store Manager, or Human Resource Manager any question at any time.

SOURCE: Used with permission of Nordstrom.

strong culture also may be a barrier to achieving workforce diversity and capitalizing on its benefits. Hiring new employees who are different in terms of race, gender, or ethnicity may fly in the face of the culture's pressure to conform.

On the other hand, employees in weak cultures are neither sure what is expected of them nor how the organization will succeed. Real change may be even more difficult in weak cultures because members may feel impotent and unable to act decisively.[15]

Where Does Culture Come From?

An organization's culture often springs from what has worked for an organization before. Thus, the vision or mission of the founders of successful organizations is frequently reflected in the culture for decades, even centuries, to come.[16] The founders, not bound by previous approaches, projected an image of what the organization should be. Further, because the new organization was small at first, the founders probably were able to stamp their vision on the members and the organization.

Founders create culture in three ways.[17] First, they hire and keep employees who think and feel the way they do. Second, founders indoctrinate and socialize these employees to their way of thinking. Third, the founder acts as a role model and his or her personality becomes central to the culture of the organization.

For example, the founder of McDonald's, Ray Kroc, died in 1984, but his philosophy of giving customers quality, service, cleanliness, and value continue to shape the fast-food chain. Other founders whose creations continue to reflect their impact include the late Akio Morita at Sony, Ted Turner at Turner Broadcasting (now part of Time Warner), Bill Gates at Microsoft, May Kay at Mary Kay Cosmetics, Steve Jobs at Apple Computer, Chung Ju Yung at Hyundai, and Richard Branson at the Virgin Group.

Once a culture is created, though, it must be transmitted to employees. Among the most effective means of doing so are stories, rituals, material symbols, and language.

Stories

Organization "stories" typically anchor the present in the past and provide explanations and legitimacy for current practices.[18] A popular tale of Nordstrom lore involves a customer who brought in a set of used tires and asked for a refund. It may sound far-fetched, but it actually happened. Of course, Nordstrom never sold tires. However, in 1975 it purchased four stores from a company that did—Northern Commercial of Alaska. The Northern Commercial Company offered an eclectic mix of goods—everything from fishing rods and lines to automotive supplies. When Nordstrom took over the locations, it narrowed the merchandise mix to essentially apparel and shoes. One day a customer brought in a set of faulty tires and asked for her money back. The salesperson on duty could have refused the return—after all, the tires obviously had been purchased from another company. But the Nordstrom employee gladly refunded the customer her money and she walked away happy.[19] Thus, the story strongly conveys the company's policy toward customer satisfaction.

Rituals

Repetitive activities express and reinforce the key values of the organization. A clear example is the process college faculty members go through in their quest for permanent employment, or tenure. Typically, a faculty member is on probation for six years, and then is granted tenure by his or her colleagues, or given a one-year terminal contract. Of course, what satisfies tenure requirements for one university, or even one department at one university, may differ from another. Teaching performance, service to the college, and scholarly activities are among the areas judged, but the key is that tenured professors pass judgment on the candidate. Candidates who are denied tenure are deemed not to have performed well in those areas the tenured faculty considers important, or in a broad sense, to not have "fit in." Thus, the tenured faculty propagates the culture by insisting that the candidates view as paramount what it considers paramount.

Material Symbols

These "perks" given to certain employees convey who is important, the degree of egalitarianism desired by top management, and the kinds of behavior (e.g., risk-taking or conservative, authoritarian or participative) that are expected. Such symbols might include size of offices, elegance of furnishings, "extras" such as country club memberships or use of the company gym, reserved parking spaces, or the existence of employee lounges or on-site dining rooms.

Language

Many organizations and units within organizations use language to identify members of a culture. By learning this language, members show they accept the culture and are helping to preserve it. When Louis Gerstner left RJR Nabisco for the top job at IBM, for example, he had to learn a whole new vocabulary, including *the Orchard* (the firm's Armonk, New York, headquarters), *big iron* (mainframe computers), *hypo* (a high-potential employee), and *a one performer* (an employee with a top performance rating).[20] Once absorbed by new employees, such a special lexicon helps unite members of an organizational culture.

The Role of Subcultures

Most large organizations have a dominant culture and numerous sets of subcultures.[21] These subcultures usually develop around departmental distinctions or around a geographical separation. The accounting department, for example, may have its own subculture. If so, those employees would share the core values of the dominant culture, plus additional values unique to the accounting department. Similarly, an office or unit of the organization that is physically separated from the main operation may take on a different personality.

How to Read an Organization's Culture

Being able to read an organization's culture is a valuable skill. Whether you are seeking to land a job, strike a business deal with a firm, or just understand the "rules" so you can perform well for your employer, accurately assessing the culture can be a big plus. It is not a simple task, though. Many organizations have given little thought to their culture and do not readily display it. Instead what they display are socially acceptable slogans or buzzwords ("Change is our only constant," "We empower our employees," or "People are our most important product") that mask the organization's true nature.

The way to get an accurate read is by observing a lot and by asking many members the same questions. For example, let's say you are a job applicant seeking to learn about the potential employer's culture. You might:

Observe the physical surroundings.   Look at signs, pictures, styles of dress, length of hair, the degree of openness among offices, and how those offices are furnished and arranged.

Ask to sit in on a team meeting.   Notice how the different ranks of employees are treated and to what degree they are encouraged to actively participate. How open is the communication?

Listen to the language.   For example, do managers use military terms, such as "take no prisoners," and "divide and conquer"? Or do they speak about "intuition," "care," and "our family"?

Note to whom you are introduced and how they act.   Do you meet just your prospective supervisor, or are you also invited to talk with potential colleagues, other managers, and senior executives? Are they formal or casual, serious or jovial?

Ask different people the same questions and compare their answers.   You might ask: What is the background of the founders and of the senior managers? How does this company define success (e.g., annual profit, market share, favorable publicity, serving customers, growth)? For what are employees most rewarded (e.g., seniority, cost-cutting, innovation, performance)? Who is on the "fast track" and what put them there? Who is considered a deviant within the organization? Why? How has the organization responded to his or her unorthodoxy?

Get the views of outsiders.   Talk with former employees, especially the job's previous incumbent. Also contact suppliers, customers, and maybe executive recruiters who have placed others in the organization.

Assessing the Individual-to-Organization Fit

The better the match between your personal values and behavioral style and the organization's culture, the better your chances of being satisfied at work and perceived as doing well. Thus, a good individual-to-organization fit can be a critical factor in your career.[22] Though variations in culture are infinite, Exhibit 12-2 presents four symbolic descriptions that are helpful for understanding and classifying cultures.

An *academy* is a culture for steady climbers who prefer to master each new job they hold. Such firms like to recruit recent college graduates, train them, and then steer them through a myriad of specialized jobs within a particular function. This traditional career path is exemplified by such firms such as IBM, General Motors, and Procter & Gamble.

A *club* culture places a high value on fitting in and on loyalty and commitment. Age, experience, and seniority count for a lot at such employers, where supervisory personnel are groomed as generalists rather than specialists. United Parcel Service, the Bell operating phone companies, government agencies, and the military are examples of clubs.

By contrast, risk takers and innovators fit best in entrepreneurially oriented cultures known as *baseball teams.* Organizations with baseball team cultures seek talented workers of all ages and experiences and reward them for what they produce, not for their seniority or loyalty. Typically, employees are given great freedom, and those who excel are paid lavishly. Thus, job-hopping is frequent. The kinds of organizations fitting this description include those in accounting, law, consulting, advertising, software, and bioresearch.

Although baseball teams value innovation, organizations with *fortress* cultures are more concerned with survival. Many of these organizations were once academies,

---

EXHIBIT 12-2   Four Types of Organizational Culture

Type	*Description*
Academy	Employees stay within a narrow specialty and are promoted after they thoroughly master a new job.
Club	Employees are trained as generalists and promoted on the basis of seniority.
Baseball team	Employees are rewarded for what they produce. Risk taking and innovation are highly valued.
Fortress	Preoccupied with survival, these cultures reward employees who can reverse the organization's sagging fortunes.

SOURCE: C. Hymowitz, "Which Culture Fits You?" *Wall Street Journal,* July 17, 1989, B1.

clubs, or baseball teams, but a turn of fortune caused them to change. Fortresses may offer little job security but can be an exciting workplace for those who are energized by the challenge of a turnaround. Large retailers, hotels, and oil and gas firms may be among fortress organizations.

Each of these four cultural types tends to attract certain personalities. A good fit between the employee and the organization affects how far and how easily an employee may move up in the ranks. A risk taker, for example, will likely thrive at a baseball team but could fare poorly at an academy.

How compatible the attitudes of the individual are with the organization also may influence job offers, performance appraisals, and promotions. Not surprisingly, job satisfaction also will be higher when an employee matches up with the employer's culture.

Sustaining a Culture

Once a culture is in place, the organization naturally tries to maintain and reinforce it. How? Much of that occurs as managers perform human resources duties, described in other chapters of this book. Examples are selecting and developing people (Chapter 13), giving performance appraisals (Chapter 8), and choosing candidates for promotion.[23] The following three managerial activities, however, play an especially important role in sustaining the culture.

1. *Selection practices.* When hiring, the manager typically finds more than one candidate who meets the job's requirements. The final choice likely will take into account the important, but intangible, factor of how the candidates will "fit in." This consideration results in the hiring of candidates with values essentially consistent with those of the organization.[24] During the hiring process, the applicants also learn about the organization. Thus, they can self-select themselves out of the pool of candidates if they sense a mismatch. Selection, therefore, is a two-way street and tends to eliminate individuals who might be at odds with the organization's core values.

2. *Top management's behavior.* The actions of senior executives have a major impact on an organization's culture.[25] By what they say and how they behave, these officials establish norms, such as how much risk taking is desirable, how much freedom managers should grant employees, and what actions will pay off in terms of pay raises and promotions.

3. *Socialization.* Organizations also help employees adapt to their cultures. The new worker, for instance, is taught what behaviors are rewarded and gradually assumes this new role, accepted by his or her peers and confident that he or she understands the "system." Though less explicitly, this socialization takes place throughout one's entire career in the organization.

At Starbuck's, for example, each of the more than 20,000 employees goes through a set of formal classes during his or her first weeks on the job.[26] These classes include a history of the firm, coffee-making techniques, coffee-tasting classes, and even how to explain Starbuck's Italian drink names to baffled customers. The firm's socialization program turns out employees who are well-versed in the company's culture and understand management's obsession with "elevating the coffee experience," as one official puts it.

Changing the Culture

A culture commonly takes a long time to form, but once established, it's tough to change.[27] Reinforced by the selection process, top management behavior, and socialization, the culture takes on a life of its own. At organizations where a given culture is judged to be no longer appropriate, management often finds there's little that can be done in the short run. Even in the most favorable conditions, changes in culture tend to be measured in years, not weeks or months.

Conditions Facilitating Cultural Change

Still, as we have all experienced, change does happen. Cultural change is most likely to occur in organizations when most, or all, of the following conditions exist:

A dramatic crisis.   A shock undermines the status quo and calls into question the relevance of the current culture; for instance, the loss of a major customer, a serious decline in market share, or a startling breakthrough by a competitor.

Turnover in leadership.   An organization in crisis may turn to one or more new top leaders who seek to provide an alternative set of key values.

Young and small organization.   The younger and smaller an organization, the easier it will be for top officials to instill new values, which is why multibillion-dollar corporations find the task especially difficult.

Weak culture.   The more widely held a culture is and the higher the agreement among its members on the core values, the more difficult it will be to change. Thus, weak cultures are more amenable to a turnaround.

Actions to Change Culture

If such factors are favorable, how can change be encouraged? Well, no single action is likely to succeed in changing a culture that is highly valued and entrenched. Thus, a comprehensive and coordinated strategy is needed.

Do a Cultural Analysis   The best place to begin is with a cultural analysis.[28] First, you would do a cultural audit to assess the current culture. Then compare the present culture with that which is desired, and finally, a gap evaluation to identify what cultural elements require changing.

Create Sense of Urgency   Management must make it clear to employees that the organization's survival is at risk if change does not occur. If employees cannot see the urgency for change, apathy is likely to win out over revolution.

Appoint Visionary Change Agent   The appointment of a new top executive may dramatize that major changes are going to take place. The new chief may offer a new role model, a new vision, and new standards of behavior. Ideally, the new executive will move promptly to introduce his or her new vision and to staff key management positions with similarly committed individuals.

Create Supporting Conditioning Components   This new leadership also will want to create new stories, symbols, rituals, and perhaps language to replace those that previously conveyed to employees the organization's dominant values. These new elements will need to be put in place rapidly so that the previous culture is not associated with the new leadership. Finally, management will need to change the selection and socialization processes and the appraisal and rewards system to support employees who share the new values.

Taking these steps does not guarantee that the change in culture will succeed. Asking employees to let go of values they understand and that have worked well in the past is, at best, a slow process. Managers will need to be on constant alert to prevent regression to the old, familiar practices.

Recent success stories, such as the change of cultures at Bankers Trust, British Airways, First Chicago, and General Electric, have several common denominators.[29] These turnarounds took from 4 to 10 years and were led by CEOs who were essentially outsiders, either brought in from outside the firms or from a division not in the corporate mainstream. In addition, all of the CEOs started their new jobs by trying to create an atmosphere of perceived crisis.

CONCEPT QUIZ

Complete the following true-false quiz by circling the correct answer. Answers are at the end of the quiz. After marking your answers, remember to go back and check your understanding of any answers you missed.

True or False   1. Usually, company stories about the founders have little validity and should be ignored.

True or False   2. Organizational culture is a system of shared meaning held by members, which distinguishes the organization from other organizations.

True or False   3. Employees learn their organization's culture through stories, rituals, material symbols, and language.

True or False   4. The words and deeds of senior executives rarely impact an organization's culture.

True or False   5. Two disadvantages of strong cultures are the pressure for conformity and resistance to change.

True or False   6. Leaders can affect an organizational culture, but they cannot unilaterally determine what that culture should be.

True or False   7. In many organizations, the nature of the culture is not something written down or even discussed.

True or False   8. The better the manager's personal style matches the organization's culture, the more successful the manager is likely to be.

True or False   9. A culture can be changed quickly if the conditions are right.

True or False   10. When subcultures develop, they usually develop around departmental lines or geographical separation.

Answers. (1) False; (2) True; (3) True; (4) False; (5) True; (6) True; (7) True; (8) True; (9) False; (10) True

BEHAVIORAL CHECKLIST

The following behaviors are important for diagnosing and meshing with an organizational culture.

An Effective Manager of Organizational Culture
- Identifies existing organizational culture.
- Assesses how people fit into specific cultures.
- Instills desirable values and norms in subordinates.
- Makes appropriate changes in organizational culture when needed.

> **Attention!**
> Do not read the following until assigned to do so by your instructor.

MODELING EXERCISE

Diagnosing Organizational Culture

Directions.   The entire class should read the following situation. Then three students should be assigned to play the roles of Phyllis, Diane, and Pete. The rest of the class should observe and critique them.

Role-players should read and prepare for their roles but should not read the others' roles. After reading the situation, observers should read all three roles and study the sections on observations and the Observer's Rating Sheet.

Time.   30 minutes.

Actors.

Phyllis, general manager of Booksco, a publishing firm

Diane, Booksco's managing editor

Pete, a job candidate

Situation.   Phyllis is general manager of Booksco, where she has spent her entire 30-year career, rising from a stock clerk to general manager. The firm publishes books for pet owners and veterinarians. Diane is the managing editor, having been with the company for 12 years. Diane has the major role in deciding which books Booksco should publish, then assigning writers and editors to produce them, and, finally, overseeing production of the books. Diane answers to Phyllis, who is a businessperson, not an editor. But Phyllis, by dint of her position and her seniority, effectively has veto power over which book manuscripts are chosen. Pete is a writer who is considering joining Booksco.

During this exercise, Pete has a job interview with Diane, who will introduce him to Phyllis for a separate interview.

Phyllis's Role   You have been here so long you sometimes think you *are* Booksco. In ways large and small, you've shaped this company to fit your values: hard-working, no-nonsense, profit-oriented, and tough but fair. As you like to say, "There are only two 'cant's' here: If you *can't* do the work, you *can't* stay." Such a hard-nosed philosophy has allowed Booksco to survive and prosper in a notoriously unstable publishing field. You would rather be respected than loved by your employees, which is probably what you are. If employees want state-of-the-art fringe benefits and/or a wimpy management that "empowers" them, they can go somewhere else. Here, what they get is hard work, decent pay, fair management, and a company that will be around when the others have gone belly up.

For example, Booksco does not give awards for writing; writers have their professional associations that can do that. Booksco does have annual awards, though, for those who come up with the best expense-cutting ideas. Those ideas and employees are what made this company strong and will keep it strong in the future.

Diane's Role   In your dozen years here, you have learned a lot about publishing, and even more about how to get along with Phyllis. She's a good, if demanding, boss who consciously and unconsciously sets the tone for the company. You wish she were more open to new ideas and more sensitive about her employees. But you cannot deny that she oversees a commercially successful line of books. Employee turnover, though, is more than it should be, and the book line has become rather predictable. Phyllis's—and thus Booksco's—approach to publishing is that if something worked well in the past, it will work in the future. So why bother with change? Thus, she has rejected your idea for a line of children's books aimed at giving kids an appreciation of their pets and another suggestion for books about non-pet animals that serve the community, like seeing-eye dogs and carriage horses. Phyllis just wants basic pet books, geared to adults, that veterinarians and bookstores will sell and animal lovers will buy.

You think intuition is at the heart of publishing: sensing what people will read and then providing it. As a result, you think a publisher's got to take some chances, allow some mistakes in hopes of making a big score. But Phyllis likes things nailed down, distrusts intuition and spontaneity. "If it ain't broke, do not fix it" is one of Phyllis's favorite aphorisms. If you had a favorite, it would be: "You can be what you imagine."

You like Pete, whom you have come to know over the years from professional association meetings. He seems bright, creative, and easy to get along with. But you know that his previous job gave him a good deal of freedom in choosing what he wanted to write about. You wonder how he will fit into this organization, and you wonder what you will say if he asks you tough questions about what kind of place this is to work at.

Pete's Role Booksco has a reputation for being a good place to work. Not on the cutting edge perhaps, but stable: a place where someone can carve out a good career niche. You think it is time for a move to a stable company. Your previous employer, a rival of Booksco, satisfied you artistically. Management was so loose nobody knew what would happen next. Every day was an adventure, if not an accident. You were encouraged to write some things there of which you are especially proud. But because of poor management, the company was also flirting with financial disaster, and that made you nervous. Though you loved the creative, off-the-wall atmosphere and made many friends there, you are in your late thirties now and need a more solid place to roost. But you wonder: Is *this* the place? You hope to decide that during your next job interview with Diane, the firm's managing editor, and Phyllis, the GM.

Instructions. After Pete has talked to both Diane and Phyllis, he should tell the other class members what he concluded about the culture from the interviews, what else he observed, and what his feeling is about how he would fit in at Booksco.

Modeling Exercise Observations

During the dialogue, observers should watch Pete's interaction with Diane and with Phyllis. What questions does he ask of each? How do the two managers respond? What signals do they send? Be prepared to suggest additional questions for Pete and different ways for Diane and Phyllis to send out messages about the culture. What conclusions should Pete draw about Booksco's culture? Would it be a good place for him to work? What would be the pluses and the minuses for Pete?

OBSERVER'S RATING SHEET

Using the following scale, rate Pete's use of techniques discussed in this chapter for assessing and deciding whether he would fit into Booksco's culture. Also write comments that will help explain your feedback in the spaces between the criteria.

1 *Unsatisfactory*	*2* *Weak*	*3* *Adequate*	*4* *Good*	*5* *Outstanding*
				Rating

- Noted the physical surroundings.   _____

- Listened to the language.   _____

- Asked different people the same questions and compared answers.   _____

- Probed meaning of legends and rites.   _____

- Deduced how he will "fit in."   _____

GROUP EXERCISES

In the following four exercises you will be asked to show an understanding of organizational cultures. The first exercise involves maintaining a culture, the second concerns assessing the culture of your college, the third entails diagnosing the culture of a workplace, and the fourth concerns how you might go about changing a culture.

Group Exercise 1: Maintaining an Organizational Culture[30]

Time. 30 minutes.

Instructions. Break into several groups of three to four persons each. Read the case study and discuss the questions within each group. The instructor will put each group's suggestions on the chalkboard and encourage further discussion by the whole class.

The Bean Queen Case

The Bean Queen, the Bean Counters, and the Human Beans can all be found at Buckeye Beans and Herbs in Spokane, Washington. Jill Smith is the Bean Queen. She's the self-proclaimed hippie artist-turned-entrepreneur who started the company in 1983 with an investment of just $1,000. From that small, inauspicious beginning, Buckeye Beans now has sales revenue approaching $8 million a year and employs 50 people (the aforementioned Human Beans).

Buckeye Beans has expanded its product lines. It began with just one product—Buckeye Bean Soup—but now includes a full line of "all-natural" soups as well as chili, bread mixes, and pasta. One innovation that Buckeye is especially fond of is special-occasion-shaped pasta: pasta molded into miniature Christmas trees, hearts, bunnies, dolphins, leaves, grapes, baseballs, and even golf balls. However, what is as unique as Buckeye's products is its organizational culture.

The firm's motto is "We Make People Smile!" Jill Smith believes that cooking should be fun, not drudgery. Because of this philosophy, the first ingredient listed on all of Buckeye's product packages is a cup of good wine for the cook. Buckeye's strategy—crafted by Jill and her accountant-husband Jim (the Bean Counter)—is that its products go beyond a simple bag of beans and become entertainment.

Likewise, the Smiths believe running the company should be fun. Casual clothes are the rule, not the exception. On Fridays, employees are encouraged to dress in bean-related garb—hats made of beans, or shirts with bean buttons, or jewelry dotted with beans instead of gems. Each Friday, the most original bean couture is awarded—*you guessed it!*—a bag of beans.

Many of the employees are family and long-time friends, but they all share the belief that not only the products but the work environment should be built on a firm foundation of fun. Buckeye's employee and customer relationships run on the basis of trust, confidence, loyalty, and working together to get things done.

Jill and Jim have never given much thought to organizational culture. They have just made the company a projection of themselves, but they do perceive that it has a special flair.

They worry, though, that as it grows (and sales are climbing at more than 20 percent each year) and more employees are added that this special flavor will be diluted and may be eventually lost. Imagine yourselves as consultants brought in to advise them about how to maintain and appropriately change Buckeye Beans' corporate culture.

QUESTIONS FOR DISCUSSION

1. How would you describe Buckeye's organizational culture? What is its dominant values? Its other values?
2. As Buckeye grows, what, specifically, can it do it perpetuate its culture?
3. How does it or could it use (a) stories, (b) rituals, (c) material symbols, and/or (d) language to transmit that culture? Give examples.
4. How difficult would it be to change this culture? Why?
5. What changes would you recommend?
6. What process would you recommend Jill use to make these changes?

Group Exercise 2: Assessing the Culture of the College

Time.   45 minutes.

Instructions.   Break into teams of four or five. Assess your college's culture using the seven primary characteristics presented earlier in this chapter. As your team attempts to categorize your college, pay particular attention to the criteria various members use in order to draw their individual conclusions.

Step 1: Individual Ratings.   Rate your college in the following categories.

1. **Innovation and risk taking:**   Low 1-2-3-4-5 High
   Remarks:

2. **Attention to detail:**   Low 1-2-3-4-5 High
   Remarks:

3. **Outcome orientation:**   Low 1-2-3-4-5 High
   Remarks:

4. **People orientation:**   Low 1-2-3-4-5 High
   Remarks:

5. **Team orientation:**   Low 1-2-3-4-5 High
   Remarks:

6. **Aggressiveness:**   Low 1-2-3-4-5 High
   Remarks:

7. **Nonstability:**   Low 1-2-3-4-5 High
   Remarks:

Step 2: Team Discussion.   Team members share their ratings and reasons for each criterion and then reach a consensus.

Step 3: Class Comparison.   Each team presents its findings to the class. Then the various teams' conclusions are compared and the class discusses the following questions:

- How much agreement was there?
- What explains the differences?
- Where were differences noted between individuals on a team? How did the group reconcile these differences?
- To what degree can the college's culture be traced to its founders?
- What rituals, stories, symbols or language reflect the culture?
- If you were charged with changing this culture, how would you begin?

Step 4: Compare and Contrast.   The instructor asks students who have attended other colleges to contrast the cultures of those schools with what the students perceive to be the culture at the present school.

Group Exercise 3: Deciding Whether You Mesh with the Culture

Directions.   Split into three groups. Each group should read the situation and the dialogue, then try to answer the questions. Reconvene as a class and compare answers.

Situation.   Charlene, a middle-aged woman, is a candidate for a job as an investment counselor at Stallion State Bank. She previously worked for a small brokerage firm specializing in online trading. She began there as a clerk, then worked her way up to account executive while going to school at night and eventually earning her MBA. But when the brokerage firm was merged with another, many of the best jobs were transferred to another city, and Charlene took a buyout and began looking for a new position. She is a single mother with two teenaged sons and does not want a job that involves a lot of travel or irregular hours. Thus, the position at a bank has appeal.

But she wonders whether she can make the transition from the frenetic, but free-wheeling, atmosphere of the small brokerage to what she suspects is the almost glacial tempo of a large, button-down branch of a staid bank. Further, she wonders whether the people at the bank will accept her. At the brokerage, most of the business was done over the computer or the phone, so account executives were encouraged to dress casually, a style to which she has become accustomed. A lot of friendly, but spirited, banter went on among the account execs and even practical jokes (a dead fish was once hidden under a pile of papers on Charlene's notoriously untidy desk on the bet that she wouldn't find it for weeks!). She thinks Stallion will probably not be like that. As a broker, she was responsible for her results (each account exec's commission totals were published in the newsletter, adding to the firm's competitive atmosphere) but yet felt a part of the team, which was a David amid the brokerage Goliaths. She is not sure the bank will be like that, either. But she wants to be fair, and being rather adaptable, she thinks she could adjust to any culture as long as performance is valued.

Charlene has her first interview with Horace, the manager of the branch to which she would be assigned. They meet in his nicely paneled office, which is off the lobby of the bank. She notices that no one could ever hide a fish under the papers on his desk; it has no papers. All such material is neatly tucked into baskets, and his pens, stapler, and other stationery items are placed in order on the desktop. Horace is a distinguished-looking man about her age. He seems quite proper yet gracious, speaking slowly and clearly with perhaps a hint of condescension.

Charlene and Horace have the following conversation:

HORACE:	Do you think you would enjoy working here? You haven't previously worked at a bank, I see from your résumé.
CHARLENE:	Well, I think I would, but I guess I need to know more about how you operate. How would you describe the work environment?
HORACE:	In a word, *professional. Very* professional. Our customers want a sense of stability in addition to good service. So we try to give them an experience that is both gracious and competent. How does that match with where you previously worked?
CHARLENE:	Well, it was a different situation there. We worked mainly over the phones or the computer, so interacting face to face with the customers was infrequent. It was probably more casual … but the bottom line was the same: We had to serve the customers and serve them well.
HORACE:	Indeed. Our founder, whose picture hangs on the wall there, used to say, "Make every customer encounter a Moment of Magic, not a Moment of Misery." This bank is built on that credo. A wonderful man, our founder.
CHARLENE:	What was he like?
HORACE:	Well, in 1897 he rode a horse 17 miles through a howling storm to return a diamond stickpin that a customer had accidentally dropped in the bank. That's how strongly he felt about winning the customers' respect and admiration.
CHARLENE:	That's good to hear. How do you encourage "Moments of Magic"?
HORACE:	In addition to our "How Was Your Service?" questionnaire available in the lobby, we include a similar form with each bank statement mailed to our customers. So, we do a lot to encourage feedback. And we share those results with our staff, in private if the report is negative and in public, at our semiannual Stallion Service Awards Ceremony if a staffer gets repeated positive feedback. Employees who are exceptionally good and diligent about service can receive all manner of rewards, from small appliances to vacation holidays. But probably the most coveted prize—next to the Maui vacation getaway perhaps—is the Golden Stallion, a statuette of the horse that our founder rode. For 12 months it sits on the desk of the employee who had the best service record during the previous calendar year. It is the object of much envy and admiration.
CHARLENE:	And I would also be eligible for prizes, including the Golden Stallion?

HORACE: Of course. Usually our new employees are on probation for the first six months, during which time they are given monthly reviews by me or by their immediate supervisor and they are not considered fully trained and eligible until that probationary period is concluded. But in your case, because of your education and experience, we would waive that probation. You would be a full-fledged, permanent employee—a member of "Team One," as we call it—from your first day here.

CHARLENE: I like what I'm hearing. This sounds like, as you say, a "very professional" operation. But I must be honest and tell you that my previous employer, while highly successful, was very different. Competitive, but casual. We probably didn't do things by the book there, but we got things done. I'm used to a fast-paced, looser style of working than what I perceive to be the norm here. Do you think that will be a problem?

HORACE: Well, we do take our professionalism seriously. *Professional* is a word you hear around here a lot. Even the janitor, I think, describes himself as "professional." What that means to me is that people take their jobs seriously and seek to project a certain decorum that customers expect from a bank. We don't dress-down on Fridays. We don't wear cutesy costumes on Valentine's Day or on Halloween. We don't post Dilbert cartoons in our workspaces. We're bankers, *professional* bankers.

Charlene nods, but says nothing.

HORACE: I like you and your credentials. I think you would fit in: You're articulate, well-dressed and, I gather, well-mannered. I'd like to offer you the job. But before you accept or reject it, I think you need to ask yourself: "Would I feel comfortable here?" In short, can you adapt? *We're* not going to change. If there is to be change, it will need to come from *you*. What do you think?

QUESTIONS FOR DISCUSSION

1. What good questions did Charlene ask? What other questions should she ask?
2. What did she learn about the bank's culture from Horace? Its stories? Its rituals? Its symbols?
3. Who else, if anyone, should she talk to inside the bank? Elsewhere?
4. How should she reply to Horace's offer? Why?

Group Exercise 4: Changing a Culture

Time. 20 minutes.

Instructions. Break into groups. Each group should study the following situation and answer the questions, then reconvene as a class and compare answers.

Situation. You are a midlevel manager at a department store chain in Cleveland when you are promoted to store manager in Chicago. Your main task, as you understand it, is to shape up the store and the staff to go head-to-head with Nordstrom's, which operates in Chicago but not in Cleveland. However, you know of Nordstrom's reputation for excellent service.

You do not know much about the new store yet, but you know the parent firm is sales conscious, sending managers like yourself weekly updates on how each store is performing. It also is fairly quick to replace managers whose sales lag. The most successful sales personnel—known as "QBs," or quota-busters—are annually feted at the headquarters in New York.

Midway through your first week, you're wandering through the housewares section when you see an item you might like to get your spouse for your anniversary. You examine it, decide to buy it, and look for a clerk. But the only clerk is at the other end of the floor helping a customer with a drapery purchase.

You approach, and the lone clerk, not recognizing you, turns from the drapery customer and says, "Look, I'm the only person up here, and I'm helping this customer right now. Why don't you come back another day when we have more help on the floor?" At that point, you realize just how big a job you face in reshaping this store.

QUESTIONS FOR DISCUSSION

1. How can the current culture be described?
2. What are its legends? Rites? Symbols? Language?
3. What can you do to begin to change the culture?
4. Do you need to promote a "crisis"? Why or why not?
5. How much time should you give yourself?

Summary Checklist

Take a few minutes to reflect on your performance in the preceding exercises. Assess yourself as to how your analysis compared to other students (and if you were a presenter, how others rated your skill). Make a check (✓) next to those behaviors on which you may need improvement.

_____ **Identify organizational cultures.**
    1. Note the physical surroundings.
    2. Listen to the language.
    3. Ask different people the same questions and compare answers.
    4. Probe meaning of legends, rites, and symbols.

_____ **Deduce how people will "fit" into the culture.**
    1. Choose candidates for hiring/promotion based in part on their organizational "fit."
    2. Determine whether they value what the organization values.
    3. See whether their personal style matches up with those who are getting ahead in the organization.

_____ **Instill desirable values and norms in subordinates.**
    1. Speak and act in a way that models the appropriate behavior.
    2. Continuously train employees.

_____ **Make appropriate changes in culture when needed.**
    1. Do a cultural audit of existing culture to see whether change is needed.
    2. Emphasize the urgency of the need for change.
    3. Put new leadership—with alternative values—in place.
    4. Create new stories, symbols, rituals, and perhaps language.

APPLICATION QUESTIONS

Analyze the culture of an organization you know well by answering the following questions and then drawing conclusions. Ideally, this place is where you work, but a church or social group also will do.[31]

1. What is the background of the founders?
2. What explains the organization's growth and survival?
3. What does the organization stand for? What is its motto?
4. What values does the organization talk about?
5. What values does it act out?
6. What does it take for a person to do well in this organization? To stay out of trouble?
7. What kinds of mistakes are not forgiven?
8. How does the organization treat those who break the "rules"?
9. How are good employees/members rewarded?
10. How does the organization respond to crises?
11. What message is conveyed by the physical setting?
12. How do things get done in this organization?
13. How does the group take in new members?
14. What kinds of stories are told about the organization?
15. Who are the heroes? Why?
16. How do the leaders exercise power?

Based on the answers to these questions, how would you describe the culture of this organization?

REINFORCEMENT EXERCISES

1. Think of a favorite television show that portrays the members of an organization—perhaps a hospital emergency room, a law office, or a police force.

   a. How would you diagnose that organization's culture?
   b. Are leaders portrayed as those who exemplify that culture's values? Why? What do they do?
   c. Do some characters not "fit in"? Why? What do they do that puts them at cross-purposes with the culture? What happens to them?

2. Compare the cultures of the various classes you are taking this semester/quarter? How do they differ? How do they match, or clash, with your personal style?
3. What was the culture at your home when you were growing up? Identify its stories, rituals, symbols, and language.

ACTION PLAN

1. On what aspects of diagnosing and modifying organizational culture do I need to most improve?
2. What benefits will I gain in my future workplace by improving my skills in this area?
3. How can I start improving in the organizations with which I am now associated?
4. When will I start?
5. How and when will I measure my success?

NOTES

1. N. K. Austin, "Managing by Parable," *Working Woman* (September 1995): 14–16.
2. J. Case, "Corporate Culture," *INC.* (November 1996): 42–52.
3. Cited in J. M. Beyer and H. M. Trice, "How an Organization's Rites Reveal Its Culture," *Organizational Dynamics* (Spring 1987): 15.

4. A. Ede, "Leadership and Decision Making: Management Styles and Culture," *Journal of Managerial Psychology* (July 1992): 28–31.
5. Based on J. Flynn and K. Naughton, "A Drug Giant's Allergic Reaction," *Business Week*, February 3, 1997, 122–25; and R. Frank and T. M. Burton, "Cross-Border Merger Results in Headaches for a

Drug Company," *Wall Street Journal*, February 4, 1997, A1.

6. C. A. Reilly III, J. Chatman, and D. F. Caldwell, "People and Organizational Culture: A Profile Comparison Approach to Assessing Person-Organization Fit," *Academy of Management Journal* (September 1991): 487–516: and J. A. Chatman and K. A. Jehn, "Assessing the Relationship Between Industry Characteristics and Organizational Culture: How Different Can You Be?" *Academy of Management Journal* (June 1994): 522–53.

7. B. Gates, "Failure Is a Part of the Game and Should Be Used," *Seattle Post-Intelligencer*, April 26, 1995, B5.

8. J. C. Collins and J. I. Porras, *Built to Last* (New York: HarperCollins, 1994) 207–08.

9. R. S. Wellins, W. C. Byham, and G. R. Dixon, *Inside Teams: How 20 World-Class Organizations Are Winning Through Teamwork* (San Francisco: Jossey-Bass, 1994) 164–78.

10. J. Castro, T. McCarroll, J. Moody, and W. McWhirter, "Jack in the Box," *Time*, October 3, 1994, 56–58.

11. S. Glain, "Korea's Samsung Plans Very Rapid Expansion into Autos, Other Lines," *Wall Street Journal*, March 3, 1995, A1.

12. Y. Wiener, "Forms of Value Systems: A Focus on Organizational Effectiveness and Cultural Change and Maintenance," *Academy of Management Review* (October 1988): 536.

13. See, for example, D. R. Denison, *Corporate Culture and Organizational Effectiveness* (New York: John Wiley, 1990); G. G. Gordon and N. DiTomaso, "Predicting Corporate Performance from Organizational Culture," *Journal of Management Studies* (November 1992): 784–98; and D. R. Denison and A. K. Misha, "Toward a Theory of Organizational Culture and Effectiveness," *Organization Science* (March–April 1995): 204–23.

14. J. P. Kotter and J. L. Heskett, *Corporate Culture and Performance* (New York: Free Press, 1992) 16; and J. Pfeffer, "Will the Organization of the Future Make the Mistakes of the Past?" in F. Hesselbein, M. Goldsmith, and R. Beckhard, eds., *The Organization of the Future* (San Francisco: Jossey-Bass, 1997) 48.

15. H. M. Rice and J. M. Beyer, "Studying Cultures Through Rites and Ceremonies," *Academy of Management Review* 9 (October 1984): 666.

16. E. H. Schein, "The Role of the Founder in Creating Organizational Culture," *Organizational Dynamics* (Summer 1983): 13–28.

17. E. H. Schein, "Leadership and Organizational Culture," in F. Hesselbein, M. Goldsmith, and R. Beckhard, eds., *The Leader of the Future* (San Francisco: Jossey-Bass, 1996) 61–62.

18. A. M. Pettigrew, "On Studying Organizational Cultures," *Administrative Science Quarterly* (December 1979): 576.

19. S. Robbins, *Managing Today* (Upper Saddle River, NJ: Prentice Hall, 1999) 347.

20. "LOB, Anyone?" *Business Week*, October 4, 1993, 94.

21. S. A. Sackmann, "Culture and Subcultures: An Analysis of Organizational Knowledge," *Administrative Science Quarterly* (March 1992): 140–61.

22. S. P. Robbins and D. DeCenzo, *Supervision Today!* 2d ed. (Upper Saddle River, NJ: Prentice Hall, 1998) 584.

23. J. R. Harrison and G. R. Carroll, "Keeping the Faith: A Model of Cultural Transmission in Formal Organizations," *Administrative Science Quarterly* (December 1991): 552–82.

24. B. Schneider, "The People Make the Place," *Personnel Psychology* (Autumn 1987): 437–53.

25. D. C. Hambrick and P. A. Mason, "Upper Echelons: The Organization as a Reflection of Its Managers," *Academy of Management Review* (April 1984): 193–206; and B. P. Niehoff, C. A. Enz, and R. A. Grover, "The Impact of Top Management Actions on Employee Attitudes and Perceptions," *Group & Organization Studies* (September 1990): 337–52.

26. Based on J. Reese, "Starbucks: Inside the Coffee Cult," *Fortune*, December 9, 1996, 190–200.

27. T. H. Fitzgerald, "Can Change in Organizational Culture Really Be Managed?" *Organizational Dynamics* (Autumn 1988): 5–15; and B. Doumaine, "Creating a New Company Culture," *Fortune*, January 15, 1990, 127–31.

28. M. Albert, "Assessing Cultural Change Needs," *Training and Development Journal* (May 1985): 94–98.

29. Kotter and Heskett, 1992, 94–106.

30. Based on *Small Business 2000, Show 203*.

31. Adapted from D. Kolb , J. Osland, and I. Rubin, *Organizational Behavior: An Experiential Approach*, 6th ed. (Upper Saddle River, NJ: Prentice Hall, 1995) 369–71.

INTERVIEWING JOB CANDIDATES

Structured interviews, with their prepared situational, willingness, and job knowledge questions, are designed to assist interviewers in reaching objective conclusions about candidates. All three types of questions are hypothetical job-oriented questions with predetermined answers that are consistently asked of all applicants. When applicants' answers are compared, the result is usually an unbiased basis for comparing their job skills, willingness and motivation to work, and quality of judgment and decision-making skills.

You may already have interview experience, on either side of the desk. Have you ever interviewed for a job and been nervous and anxious to make a good impression? You may have worried about saying too much or too little, or you may have felt unprepared for the questions you were asked.

Although you might at first identify with Quicktakes' new job applicant, Mary Byrns, you should also try to see the situation in the video from Hal's point of view. He is looking for a new producer, and in a small company, such as Quicktakes, it is difficult to invest a lot of time in training new employees who have little or no experience. Hal needs someone who can get off to a quick start and maintain a high degree of self-motivation. Try to evaluate Mary's potential as a self-starter based on her behavior in the interview.

Evaluate Hal's interviewing skills. Since there is no human resources department at Quicktakes, Hal, like managers at many small-to-medium-sized firms, has the responsibility both for screening job candidates and for making the final hiring decision. How well does he put Mary at ease? How does he react to her volunteering information about herself? Does he make any interviewing errors? ■

QUESTIONS

1. Did Hal conduct a structured interview? Explain your answer.

2. Hal has rated Mary a "strong candidate for the job." How do you think he arrived at this conclusion? Do you agree with his assessment? Why or why not?

3. What other facts about Mary's background and experience do you think Hal should have before he makes a decision about whether to hire her? (Assume that her resume provides a brief job history and basic personal data.) How should Hal go about finding this information?

4. What should Mary know about Quicktakes before she decides whether to accept any offer that Hal may make? How can she find this out?

5. How could Hal have better prepared himself for the interview? How could Mary?

CHAPTER 13

Developing People

Learning Objectives

After completing this chapter, you should be able to:

- Conduct competent job interviews.

- Adhere to antidiscriminatory regulations.

- Help employees through assistance and education.

- Develop others through delegation.

- Provide meaningful feedback for learning.

- Coach employees about performance problems at work.

- Counsel employees about personal problems and careers.

- Mentor employees for long-term development.

SELF-ASSESSMENT EXERCISE

The Best Ways to Develop Employees

For each of the following actions, indicate whether you believe it is effective for developing employees by circling the correct answer.

1. Tell employees the right way to do a job.	T	F
2. Suspend judgment and evaluation.	T	F
3. Act as a role model.	T	F
4. Provide long-term career planning.	T	F
5. Use a collaborative style.	T	F
6. Apply active listening.	T	F
7. Respect an employee's individuality.	T	F
8. Focus on getting each employee's performance up to a minimum standard.	T	F
9. Dismiss mistakes.	T	F
10. Delegate responsibility for performance outcomes to the employee.	T	F

11. If possible, assist rather than educate employees because assistance   T   F
    is much faster.

12. Save feedback for yearly performance evaluations where it can   T   F
    all be given at once.

13. Be flexible in your approach helping depending upon what   T   F
    causes the problem.

14. Exhibit warm regard for the employee as a person of   T   F
    unconditional self-worth and value no matter what the problem is.

15. Approach mistakes as opportunities to learn.   T   F

Scoring and Interpretation.   Check the following scoring key and add up the number
of answers you had correct:

(1) F; (2) T; (3) T; (4) F; (5) T; (6) T; (7) T; (8) F; (9) F; (10) F; (11) F; (12) F; (13) T;
(14) T; (15) T

Number of correct answers = _____.

12 or above: You possess a valid working knowledge about developing employees.

8–11:   You may be good at some aspects of helping but not at others.

7 or below: You need to improve on most aspects of your helping behavior.

CONCEPTS

Developing competent employees begins with hiring people who have the ability and
motivation to do the job and get along with coworkers. "All we can do is bet on the
people whom we pick," says Jack Welch, the former CEO of General Electric. "So my
job is picking the right people."[1] The happiness of employees, the morale of the workforce, the reputation of managers, and even the functioning of entire organizations rest
on the performance of people.

Developing people is also an important part of any manager's job. CEOs need to
build a viable succession or leadership by creating positive emotional energy, instilling
appropriate values, sharing their insights about how to run the business, and developing
vibrant stories that motivate.[2] For other managers, developing employees is important
for a number of reasons. First, more skilled and competent employees make a manager's job a lot easier because you can delegate more responsibilities without worrying
so much about controlling every detail of the work. Second, by helping employees
resolve their personal problems, develop their skill competencies, and build an exciting
career plan, you will motivate them to accomplish higher-quality work. Developing
employees is a three-way win for the organization, yourself, and the employees.

Methods for Selecting Employees

Once a list of candidates is obtained, the manager's task is to choose among them. This
exercise in prediction can be aided by a number of selection devises.

Application Forms   Some information on application forms—for example, rank in
high school graduating class, college grade-point average, previous jobs, skills, and
accomplishments—may help in predicting performance for some jobs.[3] However, keep
in mind that up to 30 percent of all resumes contain false information,[4] making it
imperative for you to do some checking.

Background Investigations   More than a third of job applicants exaggerate or
misrepresent dates of employment, job titles, past salaries, or reasons for leaving an

earlier position.[5] Considering the liability that potential employees may create, you will probably want to seek as much background information as possible.[6] You will also want to do references checks by contacting persons suggested by the applicant. Keep in mind that applicants normally furnish the names only of people expected to speak highly of them, and that past employers are increasingly reluctant to give candid evaluations for fear of legal repercussions.[7]

Written Tests   Written tests of intellectual ability, spatial and mechanical ability, perceptual accuracy, and motor ability are moderately valid predictors for many semiskilled and unskilled operative jobs in industrial firms. Intelligence tests are also reasonably good predictors of success for supervisory positions. However, an enduring criticism of written tests is that intelligence, for example, is not necessarily a good indicator of general performance.[8]

Performance Simulations   Exercises requiring the application of actual job behaviors to complete goals almost always produce validity scores superior to those of written aptitude, personality, or intelligence tests.[9] *Work sampling* involves giving applicants a miniature model of a job and having them perform the tasks. For example, can a candidate for a technical writing slot actually write a technical manual?

Assessment centers that measure a candidate's managerial potential are expensive to administer but they consistently predict job performance in managerial positions.[10] Managers or trained psychologists evaluate candidates as they undergo two to four days of exercises simulating real problems they might face on the job. Such activities might include interviews, in-basket problem-solving exercises, group discussions, and business-decision games.

Interviews   The interview is the only selection device that is two-way—the applicant learns facts about the job, and the manager learns things about the applicant. Unfortunately, though, many interviews are poorly conducted and may result in distorted findings.[11] This doesn't mean that interviews can't be valid and reliable devices. It's just that untrained interviewers tend to make common mistakes.

The *unstructured interview*—short, casual, and composed of random questions—has been proven to be an ineffective selection device.[12] The information gathered in such interviews is often biased and unrelated to future job performance. Specific interviewing problems can include[13]

- *Similarity error.*   This occurs when the interviewer has a bias in favor of a candidate who looks or acts like the interviewer. Interviewers often hold the stereotype that a "good" applicant is like themselves.
- *Halo error.*   A candidate's overall potential may be judged on the basis of a single positive characteristic, for example, that the candidate went to a prestigious college or dresses well.
- *Horns error.*   Negative information tends to be given unduly high weight. For example, a candidate was once fired from a job.
- *Contrast error.*   This common judgment error occurs when the interviewer rates a candidate in comparison to the preceding interviewee, as opposed to the job criteria or the entire field of candidates. In these cases, the order in which applicants are interviewed often influences evaluation.
- *Premature closure.*   Interviewers sometimes decide about a person early in the interview and then spend the rest of the time seeking information to support that decision.

- *Previous bias.* Conclusions may be skewed depending on how much prior knowledge the interviewer has about the applicant.
- *Forgetfulness.* Interviewers forget much of the content of an interview within minutes of its conclusion.

Having interviewers ask a *standardized set of questions*, use a uniform method of recording information, and standardize the rating of the applicant's qualifications enhance the validity of the interview as a selection device. Interviews are most valid in determining an applicant's intelligence, degree of motivation, and interpersonal skills.[14] Although an interview may not determine how well someone will perform, it may indicate how he or she will fit in with other members of the work group.

Interviewing Techniques

Because the interview is so essential no matter what the job, the technique of interviewing deserves amplification. Not only is the interview widely used, it also tends to wield disproportionate influence on selection. The candidate who performs poorly in the interview is likely to be cut from the pool of applicants regardless of experience, test scores, letters of recommendation, or other signs of suitability. Conversely, the candidate who performs well in the interview may well be hired even though he or she isn't the best candidate.[15]

What can managers do to make interviews more valid and reliable? Exhibit 13-1 provides some specific suggestions.

Questions make the interview, allowing you to get the information you need to make a decision. The kinds of questions you might use include[16]

Closed-Ended. These require a limited response, often just "yes" or "no," and are most appropriate in dealing with fixed aspects of the job. For example:

- "Are you over 21 years of age?"
- "Do you prefer the night shift or the day shift?"

Open-Ended. These require an unlimited response and are appropriate for determining abilities and motivation. For instance:

- "What is it about this job that interests you?"
- "What were your major achievements in your last job?"

Probing. These questions require a clarification and are used to improve understanding. Unplanned, these queries are used in a semistructured or unstructured interview. Examples might include:

- "What do you mean by 'It was tough'?"
- "Can you give me an example of how you cut costs?"

EXHIBIT 13-1 Suggestions for Interviewing[17]

1. Structure a fixed set of questions for all applicants.
2. Have detailed information about the job for which applicants are interviewing.
3. Minimize any prior knowledge of applicants' background, experience, interests, test scores, and other characteristics.
4. Ask questions that require applicants to give detailed accounts of actual job behaviors.
5. Use a standardized evaluation form.
6. Take notes during the interview.
7. Avoid short interviews that encourage premature decision making.

Hypothetical. These require the candidate to describe what he or she would do in a given situation. The answers may help assess capabilities. For instance:

- "What would you do and say if the customer swore at you?"
- "How would you respond if the machine made a screeching sound?"

Skill Guidelines for Interviewing Candidates[18]

In short, good interviewing is an art. To do it well you need to know what to do and how to do it. Once you know that, it's a matter of practice. Here are some guidelines to keep in mind as you apply your interviewing skills.

1. ***Review job description and job specifications.*** This helps remind you of the criteria on which you're going to be assessing the candidate. Reviewing the job requirements also helps to eliminate interview bias.

2. ***Prepare a structured set of questions for all applicants.*** This will ensure that you'll be able to compare all candidates' answers to a common base. It will also prevent you from forgetting some key query.

   Emphasize questions that can't be answered with a mere "yes" or "no." Inquiries beginning with a *how* or *why* tend to evoke extended answers. Avoid leading questions that telegraph the desired response (e.g., "Would you say you're ethical?") or that force the applicant to choose among your options (e.g., "Are you an extrovert or an introvert?")

   Since the best predictor of future behavior is past behavior, good questions may include those that focus on previous experience that are relevant to the current opening (e.g., "What have you done in your previous job that demonstrates your creativity?" or "What goals did you have in the last job that you accomplished? And which ones didn't you accomplish and why?").

3. ***Review the candidate's application before meeting him or her.*** This helps you create a complete picture of the candidate. You may also identify areas you wish to explore in the interview—for example, areas not defined in the resume or application but that are essential for the job.

4. ***Open the interview by putting the applicant at ease.*** Interviews are naturally stressful, and it's the rare interviewee who isn't at least a bit nervous. If you want genuine insights into what this person is really like, you'll need to put the applicant at ease. Introduce yourself. Be friendly, and begin with some small talk about, say, the traffic or the weather to give the candidate time to adjust. It's also helpful to briefly preview the topics to be discussed, so the candidate knows the purpose and range of the interview. Explain if you'll be taking notes, and encourage him or her to ask questions.

5. ***Ask your questions and listen carefully to the answers.*** Ask all the questions on your list, but also pose follow-up questions that flow from the answers given. Focus on the responses as they relate to information about the job.

   Ask situational questions. Avoid the traditional "What are your strengths and weaknesses?" query, which is likely to produce a rehearsed answer. Instead, ask candidates to describe a time when they had to carry out a decision unpopular with other workers, or perhaps a situation in which they felt their ethics were challenged, and ask them how they handled it.

   If you feel the candidate's response is superficial or inadequate, seek elaboration in a nonhostile way. "Tell me more about that issue," you might say, or "Could you amplify on that one point a bit more?"

6. ***Give the candidate a chance to ask questions.*** This not only helps the candidate learn more, but also may give the interviewer insight into the candidate's understanding and areas of concern.

7. ***Close the interviewing by explaining what happens next.*** Applicants typically are anxious about the status of the hiring decision. Be candid about others being interviewed and the steps remaining in the hiring process. Tell the applicant when you expect to make a decision and how you plan to notify him or her about your decision.

8. ***Write your evaluation of the applicant while the interview is still fresh in your mind.*** Don't wait until the end of the day or the end of the week. The sooner you record your observations, the more likely you will remember the details.

Antidiscrimination Requirements

A collection of statutes and executive orders prohibit discrimination based on race, color, religion, sex, or national origin in all employment practices. The federal Equal Employment Opportunity Commission's (EEOC) guidelines list Hispanics, Asians, Blacks, Native Americans, and Alaskan natives as minorities. Women, people over the age of 40, and disabled Vietnam veterans are also protected from employment discrimination by equal opportunity regulations.[19]

EEOC also encourages affirmative action programs, which are plans to put the principle of equal employment opportunity into practice. These programs, which may be required of organizations that do business with the federal government, require the organization to make good-faith efforts to recruit from diverse groups and set goals and timetables for hiring from protected groups.

Antidiscrimination laws and regulations also require valid testing and limit what questions can be asked on an application or during an interview. There are two rules of thumb in deciding whether a question is discriminatory: (1) Every question should be job related, and (2) every general question should be asked of *all* candidates. Exhibit 13-2 suggests the most "dangerous" questions or topics—those most likely to be viewed as potentially discriminatory.

After new employees are hired, they should be given a proper orientation. This introduces new employees to their job responsibilities, their coworkers, and the organization's policies. A job description should be given to the new hire and explained in

---

EXHIBIT 13-2 The 10 Most "Dangerous" Topics That Should Not Be Raised During an Interview[20]

1. ***Children.*** Do not ask applicants if they have children or plan to have children, or if they use child care.
2. ***Age.*** Do not ask an applicant's age.
3. ***Disabilities.*** Do not ask if the candidate has a physical or mental disability that would interfere with doing the job.
4. ***Physical characteristics.*** Don't ask for such identifying characteristics as height or weight.
5. ***Woman's name.*** Don't ask a female candidate for her maiden name.
6. ***Citizenship.*** Don't ask an applicant about citizenship. However, you may ask if the employee has a legal right to work in the United States.
7. ***Lawsuits.*** Don't ask a candidate if he or she has ever filed a suit or a claim against a former employer.
8. ***Arrest record.*** Don't ask applicants if they have an arrest record.
9. ***Smoking.*** Don't ask the applicant if he or she smokes. While smokers are not protected under the Americans with Disabilities Act (ADA), asking applicants if they smoke might lead to legal difficulties if an applicant is turned down because of fear that smoking would drive up the employer's health care costs.
10. ***AIDS or HIV.*** Don't ask if applicants have AIDS or are HIV-positive. Such queries violate the ADA and could violate state and federal civil-rights laws as well.

---

detail. Explain the organization's objectives, policies, and rules. Explain your performance expectations and encourage the new hire to ask questions.

Managers are also responsible for training and developing employees. Not only do new workers need to be trained in the job, but current employees must be retrained and their skills updated to meet rapidly changing environments and job requirements.

Developing Employees

Managers can develop employees by helping them resolve personal problems and enhance job competencies. Five ways of doing this are delegating, providing meaningful feedback, coaching about performance problems, counseling about personal problems and careers, and mentoring for long-term development.

Assistance or Education?[21]

Your goal when developing employees is to enable them to effectively accomplish tasks independently. Although you could often *assist* an employee by just doing the job yourself, that is like giving a vagrant money for a meal; it improves the immediate situation but does not improve handling of reoccurrences. Assistance may be necessary in emergencies, but in the long run the employee fails to learn how to handle similar situations independently and becomes more dependent on you, which will take more of your time.

Consequently, a better approach is to *teach* employees to solve their own problems and perform effectively independently. Education may be frustrating for employees who want immediate relief, and it may cause some short-term resentment because you don't solve the problem for them, but in the long run, most employees will be grateful for the increased competence and self-esteem your coaching, training, or counseling has provided.

Determine the Source of the Problem

Unsatisfactory performance often has multiple causes. Some are within the control of the employee and others are not. Here are some questions that managers can ask to determine what type of help would be most appropriate.[22]

1. Are employees unaware that their performance is unsatisfactory? If the answer is yes, the manager can provide feedback.
2. Does poor performance occur because employees are not really sure what is expected of them at work? If so, the manager can provide clear expectations.
3. Is employee performance hampered by obstacles that are beyond their control? If this is the case, the manager removes the obstacles.
4. Do employees know how to perform a task? If they don't, the manager provides coaching or training.
5. Is good performance followed by negative consequences? If it is, managers should eliminate the negative consequences.
6. Is poor performance being rewarded by positive consequences? If so, managers should eliminate the positive reinforcement.

If all these steps have been taken to ensure good performance, and the employee is still not able or willing to perform well, it is time to try counseling to see if it is a personal problem. Although there are differences in coaching, counseling, and mentoring, there are common steps that should be followed before, during, and after these helping sessions. These are summarized in Exhibit 13-3.

Demonstrate Positive Regard

When you coach, counsel, or mentor employees, you are engaging in helping relationships. For a helping relationship to be successful, it is important that the manager holds

| EXHIBIT 13-3 Guidelines for Conducting Effective Helping Sessions[23] |

Prior to the Helping Session

- Acquire all the facts about the situation.
- Decide what type of coaching the situation requires.
- Consider how the employee might react to the discussion.
- Think about the best way to present what you want to say to the employee.

During the Helping Session

- Discuss the purpose of the session.
- Try to make the employee comfortable.
- Establish a nondefensive climate, characterized by open communication and trust.
- Praise the employee for positive aspects of performance.
- Mutually define the problem (performance or attitude).
- Mutually determine the causes. Do not interpret or psychoanalyze the employee's behavior; instead, ask questions. "What's causing the lack of motivation you describe?"
- Help the employee establish an action plan that includes specific goals and dates.
- Make sure the employee clearly understands what is expected of him or her.
- Summarize what has been agreed upon in the session.
- Affirm your confidence in the employee's ability to make needed changes based upon his or her strengths or past history.

After the Helping Session

- Follow up to see how the employee is progressing.
- Modify the action plan if necessary.

the employee in "unconditional positive regard." This means that the manager accepts and exhibits warm regard for the employee as a person of unconditional self-worth—of value no matter what his condition, problem, or feelings. This provides a climate of warmth and safety because the employee feels liked and prized as a person. This is a necessary condition for developing the trust that is crucial in a helping relationship.[24] Assuming that employees mean well, rather than assuming the worst about them, creates a self-fulfilling prophecy when they try to live up to their boss's good opinion.

Delegation

Delegation occurs when a manager transfers authority to an employee for achieving goals and making decisions about how to do a job.[25] Delegation empowers employees by increasing their involvement in their work through greater participation in decisions that control their work and by expanding responsibility for work outcomes.[26] Consequently, delegation helps develop employees by expanding their knowledge, job capabilities, and, decision-making skills. It prepares them for future promotion opportunities.

You should expect and accept some mistakes by your employees when you delegate. Mistakes are often good learning experiences for your employees, as long as the costs of these mistakes are not excessive, and you provide effective feedback. Second, to ensure that the costs of mistakes don't exceed the value of the learning, you need to put adequate controls in place. Some of these are described in Chapter 8, Evaluating and Controlling Performance.

There are a number of things that you can do to be an effective delegator. These are summarized in the following paragraphs:[27]

1. ***Clarify the assignment.***   The place to begin is to determine *what* is to be delegated to develop the particular employee. Assuming you have a willing and able employee, it is your responsibility to provide clear information on what is being delegated, the results you expect, and any time-frame or performance expectations you hold.

Unless there is an overriding need to adhere to specific methods, you should delegate only the end results. That is, agree on what is to be done and the end results expected, but let the employee decide on the means. By focusing on goals and allowing the employee the freedom to use his or her own judgment as to how those goals are to be achieved, you increase trust between you and the employee, improve that employee's motivation, and enhance accountability for the results.

2. ***Specify the employee's range of discretion.***   Every act of delegation comes with constraints. You're delegating authority to act, but not *unlimited* authority. What you're delegating is authority to act on certain issues within certain parameters. You need to specify what those parameters are so employees know, in no uncertain terms, the range of their discretion. When this has been successfully communicated, both you and the employee will have the same idea of the limits of the latter's authority and how far he or she can go without checking further with you.

3. ***Allow the employee to participate.***   One of the best sources for determining how much authority will be necessary to accomplish a task is the employee who will be held accountable for that task. If you allow employees to participate in determining what is delegated, how much authority is needed to get the job done, and the standards by which they'll be judged, you increase employee motivation, satisfaction, and accountability for performance.

Be alert, however, that participation can present its own set of potential problems as a result of employees' self-interest and biases in evaluating their own abilities. Some employees, for example, are personally motivated to expand their authority beyond what they need and beyond what they are capable of handling. Allowing such people too much participation in deciding what tasks they should take on and how much authority they must have to complete those tasks can undermine the effectiveness of the delegation process.

4. ***Inform others that delegation has occurred.***   Delegation does not take place in a vacuum. Everyone who may be affected by the delegation needs to be informed what has been delegated and how much authority has been granted. This includes people outside the organization as well as inside it. If you fail to follow through on this step, the legitimacy of your employee's authority will probably be called into question. Failure to inform others makes conflicts likely and decreases the chances that your employee will be able to accomplish the delegated task efficiently.

5. ***Establish feedback controls.***   To delegate without instituting feedback controls is to invite problems. There is always the possibility that an employee will misuse the discretion that has been delegated. The establishment of controls to monitor the employee's progress increases the likelihood that important problems will be identified early and that the task will be completed on time and to the desired specifications.

At the time of the initial assignment, agree on a specific time for completion of the task, and set progress dates when the employee will report back on how well he or she is doing and any major problems that have surfaced. This can be supplemented with periodic spot checks to ensure that authority guidelines are not being abused, organization policies are being followed, proper procedures are being met, and the like. But too much of a good thing can be dysfunctional. If the controls are too constraining, the employee will be deprived of the opportunity to build self-confidence and much of the motivational properties of delegation will be lost. A well-designed control system permits employees to make small mistakes, but quickly alerts you when big mistakes are imminent.

6. ***When problems surface, insist on recommendations from the employee.*** Many managers fall into the trap of letting employees reverse the delegation process: The employee runs into a problem and then comes back to the manager for a solution. Avoid being sucked into reverse delegation by insisting from the beginning that when employees want to discuss a problem with you, they come prepared with a recommendation. When you delegate downward, the employee's job includes making necessary decisions. Don't allow the employee to push decisions back upward to you.

Provide Meaningful Feedback for Learning

Feedback is any communication to a person that provides information about some aspect of his or her behavior and its consequences.[28] Information about the consequences of their actions is necessary if employees are expected to learn what is working or not working and then change to become more effective. It is important to be skilled at giving feedback, because the results of effective feedback can be increased performance and positive personal development.[29] There are a number of reasons why.

First, feedback conveys to employees that you care about how they're doing. It is an indirect form of recognition that can motivate people to higher levels of performance. Second, feedback can induce a person who previously had no goals to set some, and goals act as motivators to higher performance. Third, where goals exist, feedback tells people how well they're progressing toward those goals. To the degree that the feedback is favorable, it acts as a positive reinforcement. Fourth, if the feedback indicates inadequate performance, this knowledge may result in increased effort, and can suggest ways to improve performance. Finally, feedback often induces people to raise their goal sights after attaining a previous goal.[30]

The feedback process involves four primary elements that occur in the following sequence:[31] Managers communicate to the employee what they observe, how they assess it, what consequences it has, and how to effectively address the observed behavior for improvement. Development becomes an observation in the next communication loop. For example, a manager who observes development and assesses it positively may consequently praise or promote the responsible employee. Thus, feedback facilitates growth of employees because it provides information about how to improve performance and motivates development by informing them of the contingent rewards.

This assumes, of course, that feedback is effective. We've all been the recipients of ineffective feedback that just leaves us angry, confused, and frustrated. One example is vague feedback based on fuzzy impressions, such as "you really are not performing very well," which is generally very hard to translate into the specific developmental goals that are so important to improvement. Some guidelines for providing effective feedback that can promote development are summarized in Exhibit 13-4. Other helpful hints can be found in Chapters 3 and 8 of this book that address interpersonal communication and performance appraisal.

Coaching and Counseling

Both coaching and counseling have the same objective: to improve the employee's performance, but *coaching* deals with ability issues, whereas *counseling* deals with personal problems. When an employee needs help mastering skills and figuring out how to apply instructions, coaching is required. When an employee has an attitude, emotional, drinking, or family problem, the manager needs to engage in counseling behaviors.

EXHIBIT 13-4   Eight Rules of Thumb for Giving Effective Feedback[32]

- Is descriptive rather than evaluative.
- Is specific and data based rather than general.
- Is directed toward controllable behaviors rather than personality traits or characteristics.
- Is solicited rather than imposed.
- Occurs close to the event under discussion rather than delayed for several months.
- Occurs when the receiver is most ready to accept it.
- Suggests rather than prescribes avenues for improvements.
- Is intended to help, not punish.

Both coaching and counseling also apply essentially the same problem-solving process: listening to understand, identifying the problem, clarifying alternatives, deciding on an action plan, and implementing the action plan. Both also require the same behavioral skills: establishing a supportive climate, listening actively, being nonjudgmental and understanding, solving problems jointly, and teaching the employee how to solve problems on her own rather than temporarily fixing things yourself. The following sections explain these skills more thoroughly.

Coaching to Improve Performance Problems

Coaching is the ongoing process of helping employees improve their work performance. As coaches, managers analyze performance, provide insight for improvement, and offer encouragement to help employees improve their job performance. The most effective coaching occurs without judgment and evaluation about the person—only *behaviors* should be addressed. The focus is on helping employees make continual improvements toward previously established performance goals.

Not all coaching is done by managers. In most work groups, buddy systems develop where more experienced employees informally help new members develop necessary skills and offer them guidance when they have problems. Organizations sometimes formalize buddy systems into *mentoring* programs where senior employees are assigned junior protégés to whom they lend the benefit of their experience. Mentors perform as both coaches and counselors as they guide their less experienced associates towards improved performance.

So, what can managers do to coach employees toward performance improvement? The following three general skills have been found to be essential:[33]

1. ***Continuously assessing ways to improve.***   A coach continually looks for opportunities to expand employee's performance capabilities. How? By ongoing *observation* of employee's behavior; by *asking questions* (why do you do a task this way?); by *listening* to employees to understand their perspectives; by *respecting* employee's individuality and crafting unique improvement strategies.

2. ***Creating a supportive climate.***   Effective coaches reduce barriers to development, and facilitate climates that encourage performance improvement. How? Through *active listening* to promote free and open exchange of ideas. By *empowering* employees to implement appropriate ideas they suggest. By being *available* for assistance, guidance, or advice if asked. By being *positive and upbeat* to provide encouragement. By *never using threats* of punishment for poor performance. Threats only create fear and inhibit people from trying new behaviors. By focusing on *mistakes as learning opportunities*. By *validating employees' efforts* by rewarding them when they succeed.

EXHIBIT 13-5   Teaching New Skills

The coaching process for teaching new skills consists of the following steps:[34]

1. Explain the purpose and importance of what you are trying to teach.
2. Explain the process to be used.
3. Demonstrate how it is done.
4. Observe while the person practices the process.
5. Provide immediate and specific feedback (coach again or reinforce success).
6. Express confidence in the person's ability to be successful.
7. Agree on follow-up actions.

---

3. *Influencing employees to change their behavior.*   The criterion for coaching effectiveness is whether employee's performance improves. This is not a static concept—it applies to ongoing development. How can a manager continually motivate employees to improve? One way is by recognizing and *rewarding even small improvements.* Another is by using a *collaborative decision style*—employees will be more responsive to accepting change if they participate in identifying and choosing among improvement ideas. Appropriate *empowerment* is necessary for effective implementation. *Breaking complex projects into a series of simpler tasks* can boost employees' confidence for small wins when confronting large and complex projects. Finally, *modeling* the qualities that you expect from your employees, such as openness, dedication, commitment, and responsibility will demonstrate our own commitment to these qualities. Your employees will look to you as a role model so make sure your deeds match your words. Some suggested steps for effective coaching are summarized in Exhibit 13-5.

Counseling to Resolve Personal Problems
Counseling is the discussion of an emotional problem in order to resolve it, or help the employee better cope with it. Examples of problems that might require counseling include divorce, serious illness, financial problems, coworker conflicts, drug and alcohol abuse, or frustration over a lack of career progress. Usually, employees come to managers for assistance with problems, but other times the first step is making them recognize that problems exist. Then counselors help employees gain insight into behaviors that cause problems, feelings about them, and alternatives for resolution. Most managers are not trained psychologists, but there are several reasons why they should take on a counseling role before referring the employee to employee assistant programs or a professional therapist.

Sometimes an employee just needs a sounding board for the *release of tension* and *clarification* of thoughts that can become a prelude to identifying possible solutions and taking corrective action on their own. Counseling can provide *reassurance* to employees when their problems have solutions that they have the ability to improve. If this is not the case, counseling can *identify employee problems requiring professional treatment*, such as severe depression, debilitating phobias, family problems, and substance abuse. Counseling can *circumvent the need for disciplinary actions* if troubled employees recognize and correct problems or behaviors before they become debilitating.

When dealing with emotional and personal problems, it is important to maintain *confidentiality.* To open up and share the reasons for many personal problems, employees must really feel that they can trust you and that there is no threat to their self-esteem or their reputation with coworkers. As soon as it is determined that counseling is what is called for, emphasize that everything the employee says regarding personal matters will be treated in confidence.

Mentoring

The role of a mentor is to help another person achieve his or her career goals. As a mentor, managers formally pair up with employees to help show them the ropes and provide emotional support and encouragement on an ongoing basis. In essence, it is serving as the employee's permanent coach and counselor. Some companies, such as IBM, have formal mentoring programs where pair assignments are made. Others, such as AT&T, rely on informal mentoring because they believe it's more flexible and effective.[35] Either way, helping employees achieve success is an important attribute of successful managers.

Mentors help new employees gain a better understanding of the organization, its goals, and advancement criteria. They also make employees more politically savvy and warn them of possible traps. By explaining how to do things, mentors reduce employees' stress caused by uncertainty when dealing with challenging assignments. They are also a source of comfort when newer employees need to let off a little steam or discuss career dilemmas.[36] In general, mentors strive to help employees live up to their full potential and encourage them to be more proactive in managing their careers.

CONCEPT QUIZ

Complete the following true-false quiz by circling the correct answer. Answers are at the end of the quiz. After marking your answers, remember to go back and check your understanding of any answers you missed.

True or False	1. Coaching and counseling are the same thing.
True or False	2. Counselors have to be judgmental so employees understand they need to improve.
True or False	3. Coaches should always be looking for ways to improve employee performance.
True or False	4. Coaches should focus on mistakes as learning opportunities.
True or False	5. The test of helping effectiveness is whether an employee's performance improves.
True or False	6. Threats are a good development tool for coaches to use to emphasize consequences.
True or False	7. Sometimes it is more beneficial to employee development if coaches just do the task themselves.
True or False	8. The coaching job is finished when employees have mastered a task satisfactorily.
True or False	9. Coaches need to model the behaviors they want from employees.
True or False	10. It is preferable to let employees come up with their own ways to improve performance than it is for coaches to provide solutions.

Answers. (1) False; (2) False; (3) True; (4) True; (5) True; (6) False; (7) False; (8) False; (9) True; (10) True

BEHAVIORAL CHECKLIST

The following skills are important to developing employees. Use them when evaluating your own developing skills and those of others.

To Develop Others

- Ask questions to discover sources of problems and how to improve.
- Listen actively and show genuine interest.
- Demonstrate unconditional, positive regard by suspending judgment of the person.
- Educate rather than assist.
- Delegate increased responsibilities and authority.
- Accept mistakes and use them as learning opportunities.
- Provide meaningful feedback for learning.
- Recognize and reward even small improvements.
- Model qualities expected from employees.
- Help develop action plans for continued improvements.

> **Attention!**
> Don't read this or the following exercises until assigned to do so by your instructor.

MODELING EXERCISE

Building Problems in Napa Valley

Actors. Lorin Wilcox (manager) and T. J. Corsetti (broker)

Situation. Lorin Wilcox is the supervisor of the Napa Valley office of a large mortgage brokering company that has 30 offices throughout California. Lorin supervises seven mortgage brokers, an assistant, and a secretary. The business entails helping home buyers find mortgages and acting as a link between lenders and borrowers in getting loans approved and processed.

T. J. Corsetti is one of the brokers. T. J. has been in the Napa Valley office for two and a half years. Before that, T. J. sold commercial real estate. Lorin Wilcox has been in the Napa Valley job for fourteen months, prior to supervising a smaller office for the same company.

Lorin Wilcox's Role   You have not been pleased with T. J.'s job performance, so you decided to review the personnel file. T. J.'s first six-month review stated, "Enthusiastic. A bit disorganized but willing to learn. Seems to have good potential." After a year, T. J.'s previous supervisor had written, "T. J. seems to be losing interest. Seems frequently disorganized. Often rude to clients. Did not mention these problems previously. Hope T. J. will improve. Long-term potential now much more in question."

You have not spent much time with T. J. Your offices are far apart, but probably the real reason is that T. J.'s not a person who's easy to talk to and you have little in common. When you took the Napa Valley job, you decided that you'd wait a period of time before attacking any problems to make sure you had a good grasp of the people and the situation.

T. J.'s problems have become too visible to ignore. T. J. is consistently missing quarterly sales projections. Based on mortgages processed, T. J. is your lowest performer. In addition, T. J.'s reports are constantly late. After reviewing last month's performance reports, you made an appointment yesterday to meet together today at 9:00 A.M., but T. J. wasn't in the office when you arrived for that appointment. You waited 15 minutes, then gave up. Your secretary tells you that T. J. regularly comes in late for work in the morning and takes extra-long coffee breaks.

Last week, Valerie Oletta, who has the office next to T. J.'s, complained to you that T. J.'s behavior was demoralizing her and some of the other brokers.

You don't want to fire T. J. It wouldn't be easy to find a replacement. Moreover, T. J. has a lot of contacts with new-home builders, which brings quite a few borrowers to your office. In fact, maybe 60 percent of the business generated by your entire office comes from builders who have personal ties to T. J. If T. J. were to leave your company and go to a competitor, chances are that the builders would follow.

T. J. Corsetti's Role   The mortgage brokering business has been pretty good for you. From your previous job in commercial real estate, you developed a lot of contacts with new-home builders. In fact, maybe 60 percent of the business generated by your entire office comes from builders who have personal ties with you, personally.

Although your old builder buddies supply you with plenty of business, you realized early in your first year that the brokering business required some word-processing, mathematical, and computer skills that you still haven't acquired, even though you graduated from high school. Most of the other brokers have college degrees in business administration, and one even has an MBA. You have been embarrassed to ask for help because you are older than most of the other brokers. Consequently, it takes you quite a bit longer to process the mortgages and your reports are often late because you have to type one keystroke at a time.

To try to a get up to speed, you have enrolled in an 8:00 A.M. extension course in typing and word processing at the community college, which makes you about an hour late for work three days a week, but you think it certainly is going to be worth it in the long run. You're hoping that the correspondence course in business mathematics you signed up for will have an equal payoff. You are working on it in the evenings and during your breaks at work.

All this is a bit overwhelming at the moment, and you have fallen a little behind in your work. You overheard some of the other brokers discussing your lack of involvement with them a couple of weeks ago, but you're too busy to worry about that until you complete your courses. Then you will be right up with the best of them. Besides, you're still making a contribution in a way. It's your contacts with the builders that brings in a majority of the business for your office. In fact, you are also taking a broker course on weekends so you can take them with you when you start your own company next year.

The broker in the next office mentioned that your boss, Lorin Wilcox, was at your office for an appointment that Lorin had scheduled for 9:00 A.M. yesterday. You went to your usual class and completely forgot about it. You decide to go up to Lorin's office to see what the appointment was about.

Time.   10 minutes for the role-play.

OBSERVER'S RATING SHEET

On completion of the exercise, evaluate the development skills of Lorin Wilcox from 1 to 5 using the following scale. Write in concrete examples in the space for comments below each criteria skill to use in explaining your feedback.

1 Unsatisfactory	2 Weak	3 Adequate	4 Good	5 Outstanding

_____ Asked questions to discover sources of problems and how to improve.

_____ Actively listened and showed genuine interest.

_____ Demonstrated unconditional positive regard by suspending judgment of the other person.

_____ Educated instead of assisted.

_____ Delegated increased responsibilities and authority.

_____ Accepted mistakes and used them as learning opportunities.

_____ Provided meaningful feedback for learning.

_____ Recognized and rewarded small improvements.

_____ Modeled the qualities expected.

_____ Helped develop action plans for improvement.

GROUP EXERCISES

The first group exercise provides participants a chance to experience the selection process. The second gives you a chance to get help and help a peer with a real problem. The third exercise is a role-play situation where an employee has personal problems that the manager needs to help with.

Group Exercise 1: The Selection Process[37]

1. ***Develop the job description and the position specifications*** (20 minutes).   The entire class should read the following situation, and then develop a job description (activities required to do the job) and job specifications (requirements for job holder) for the position described. When in doubt about the details, class members should use their imagination. The objective is for the class to agree that these two lists are reasonable and complete. When finished, record the job description and job specifications on the board, newsprint, or overhead projector.

2. ***Develop a set of interview questions*** (15 minutes).   In addition to the actual questions, the class also should consider other ways to determine whether a candidate would be appropriate (e.g., observing some aspects of the candidates' behavior during the interview). It should also take into consideration the goal of more closely matching the age and ethnicity of the employees to that of the clientele.

3. ***Role-play*** (15 minutes).   Four class members volunteer to act out the roles of Sam and the three candidates. Each candidate explains his or her background and why he or she would be right for the job. (Actors should feel free to add details to their descriptions.) Sam should interview each candidate for no more than five minutes.

Actors.

- Sam: the owner-manager of Sammy's Restaurant
- Candidate 1: a young, eager college student without experience
- Candidate 2: a woman who appears to be about 60 years old, with eight years of experience
- Candidate 3: a man with four years of experience as a server in five different restaurants
- Candidate 4: a middle-aged minority woman with little job experience

Situation.   Sam owns and manages Sammy's, a family-style restaurant that needs to hire a server. Although the pace is quick, the pay is minimal; because the restaurant is part of a small chain, an ambitious employee who performs well can advance within the organization.

Sam's Role   You recognize that as a result of hiring inexperienced people, the restaurant has suffered a high attrition rate, so you would like to hire a more seasoned server. However, you're also aware that the salary and benefits are not competitive with other industries in your area. The restaurant is in an older neighborhood populated by many senior citizens and minority group members. Your current servers are young and white. You think that hiring a capable, older, minority server would be a good idea.

Observer Instructions   Using the Observer's Rating Sheet, observers should note closely how Sam treats each candidate, what questions he asks, and how the candidates respond both verbally and nonverbally. Be prepared to suggest additional questions and to draw conclusions both about Sam's interviewing technique as well as who seems to be the best-qualified applicant.

OBSERVER'S RATING SHEET

Using the following scale, rate Sam's application of interview skills discussed in this chapter. Also write in comments in the spaces below each technique that will help explain your feedback.

1 Unsatisfactory	2 Weak	3 Adequate	4 Good	5 Outstanding

_____ Put the candidates at ease.

_____ Interviewed objectively.

_____ Covered all important points.

_____ Used open-ended questions.

_____ Asked the same questions of each candidate.

_____ Listened actively and showed genuine interest

_____ Gave candidates a chance to ask questions.

_____ Did not violate antidiscrimination laws.

QUESTIONS FOR DISCUSSION (Time 15 minutes)

1. How did the candidates appear? What could each have done differently?
2. By a show of hands, the class votes for which candidate it would recommend hiring. Why? List the pros and cons of each candidate.
3. How did the manager's style of questioning help or hurt the information-gathering process? Did the candidates reveal anything about their acceptability in nonverbal ways? How did the interviewing experience feel to the candidates? To Sam?

Total Time.   45–60 minutes

Group Exercise 2: Helping with a Peer Problem

Divide the class into groups of three. Each group will conduct three coaching or counseling sessions. Each participant will share a problem and receive help. Each participant will also act as a helper to help another peer resolve a problem.

If you are the person receiving help, think of a problem you are currently experiencing or have experienced in the past. Briefly share the nature of the problem and its consequences with your coach. If you do not have a problem you want to share, you can role-play someone else's problem instead.

The person who is the helper is responsible for conducting a coaching or counseling session. At the conclusion of the session the observer will provide the helper with feedback based on the following Observer's Rating Sheet.

Time.   20 minutes per helping session.

OBSERVER'S RATING SHEET

On completion of the exercise, evaluate the development skills of the person acting as the helper from 1 to 5 using the following scale. Write in concrete examples in the space for comments below each criteria skill to use in explaining your feedback.

1	2	3	4	5
Unsatisfactory	*Weak*	*Adequate*	*Good*	*Outstanding*

_____ Asked questions to help discover sources of problems and how to improve.

_____ Listened actively and showed genuine interest.

_____ Demonstrated unconditional positive regard by suspending judgment of the other person.

_____ Educated versus assisted.

_____ Delegated increased responsibilities and authority.

_____ Accepted mistakes and use them as learning opportunities.

_____ Provided meaningful feedback for learning.

_____ Recognized and rewarded small improvements.

_____ Modeled qualities expected.

_____ Helped develop action plans for improvement.

Group Exercise 3: Role-Play: Why Is the Camera Out of Focus?

Actors.   Fran Delano is a camera operator and Alex Maher, Fran's supervisor.

Situation.   Alex has supervised the 11 camera operators at KSLC-TV in Salt Lake City for more than five years. Fran has worked for Alex for more than four of those years. Two years ago, Fran Delano was the number-one-rated camera operator at KSLC. Of the 11 operators that the station employed, Fran was every producer's first choice. Fran had a choice of hours and shows. Fran was extremely competent, creative, and dependable. Fran's supervisor, Alex Maher, had even been a bit protective. As Alex said 18 months ago, "Everyone knows Fran's the best we've got. Everyone wants Fran for their shows. I've got to make sure we don't burn out our best camera operator."

Alex Maher's Role   You have become far less enthusiastic about Fran over the past four months. The problems began with Fran coming in late for assigned shifts. First it was just 10 or 15 minutes late. Then it got to be 30 minutes. Last week, Fran was over an hour late for shifts twice, and 15 to 20 minutes late each of the other three days. Yesterday, Fran called in sick just 10 minutes before the show was to go "on the air." This morning, Fran came in 40 minutes late.

In addition to the lateness, you have noticed two other disturbing signs. Fran is not nearly as talkative and outgoing as usual. And, several times last week, you are certain that you smelled alcohol on Fran's breath. Nick Randolph, another camera operator, told you two weeks ago that he was certain Fran had been drinking before coming to work, and again during the lunch break. Nick was particularly upset about the quality of Fran's work. Alex, of course, knew what he was talking about. Fran's mind seemed to be wandering during shows: missing director's instructions, and slow in getting the camera into new positions.

You don't know much about Fran's personal life. You've heard Fran lives with or is married to a graphic artist but that's about all you know.

Up to this point, you haven't said anything to Fran about this behavior, but now something has to be done. After today's work shift, you called Fran into your office. As Fran walks in, you can't help noticing the smell of alcohol.

Fran Delano's Role   Becoming the number-one-rated camera operator at KSLC paid off in giving you your choice of hours and shows. The problem is that you take every show you can possibly handle. You feel that your place on the top rung is precarious because of the multitude of other talented camera operators jockeying to get some of your shows. It's very lucrative for you right now and you feel that you had better get all you can while the getting is good. Actually, you don't have much choice if you are to maintain your house payments because your spouse has been unemployed for the past two years and the prospects don't look good because there are hundreds of others in the same situation. In fact, your spouse has quit looking altogether recently, and is quite depressed.

This is not an easy business and it requires all you've got to handle it—the intense concentration when everything depends on you during the show, the relentless hours from the early morning news broadcasts to late-night variety shows, and the constant worry that someone else will show their stuff if you miss a show for any reason. As if this wasn't enough, you constantly worry about your spouse's deteriorating state of mind.

You are so exhausted when you get off work, often close to midnight, that you just go home and have a few drinks. That's what your spouse is doing anyway. You are usually happy when your spouse is already in bed because your relative success seems to provoke hostile verbal attacks or icy silence. You can't decide which is worse, but your relationship is definitely floundering.

Lately, you noticed that it takes a whole bottle of wine or more than a six pack of beer to calm you down enough to get to sleep. You've discovered that a shot of brandy in your morning coffee seems to help the dull headaches you wake up with. Also, a couple of glasses of wine at lunch can make the stress seem much less severe, and a short nip from the flask of Wild Turkey you keep in your coat pocket helps you relax between shows.

You know you are probably drinking a little too much, but that seems to be the only way you can avoid worrying about your problems enough to focus on your work or even get a little sleep. You are sure that as soon as your spouse finds a job and you can cut back on your hours a little, you will be just fine.

Observers. Use the previous Observer's Rating Sheet.

Time. 15 minutes for role-play

SUMMARY CHECKLIST

Take a few minutes to reflect on your performance in the preceding exercises. Assess yourself on each of the following key helping behaviors. Make a check (✓) next to those behaviors on which you need improvement.

_____ **I follow appropriate guidelines when interviewing job candidates.**
1. Structure a fixed set of questions for all applicants.
2. Have detailed information about the job for which applicants are interviewing.
3. Minimize any prior knowledge of applicants' background, experience, interests, test scores, and other characteristics.
4. Ask questions that require applicants to give detailed accounts of actual job behaviors.
5. Use a standardized evaluation form.
6. Take notes during the interview.

_____ **I determine the *best approach* for developing employees.**
1. Only use assistance in emergencies.
2. Use education whenever possible so that the employee can perform independently.
3. Determine the source of the problem before trying to help the employee.
4. Demonstrate unconditional positive regard.

_____ **I empower employees by *delegating* increased responsibilities and authority.**
1. Allow greater participation in decisions that control their work.
2. Clarify expanded responsibilities for work outcomes.
3. Specify the range of discretion.
4. Inform others delegation has occurred.
5. Establish feedback controls.

_____ **I provide meaningful *feedback* for learning.**
1. Communicate to the employee what behavior you observe, how you assess it, what consequences it has, and how to effectively address the observed behavior and consequences.
2. Ensure that feedback is acceptable and effective by making it descriptive rather than evaluative, specific and data-based rather than general, directed toward controllable behaviors, and timely.

_____ **I *coach* employees about performance problems caused by ability issues.**
1. Analyze ways to improve an employee's performance and capabilities by observing daily behavior, asking questions, actively listening, showing genuine interest in the person as an individual.
2. Create a supportive climate by reducing barriers to development, empowering employees to implement appropriate ideas, offering to help, being positive and upbeat, treating mistakes as learning opportunities, and validating employees' efforts.
3. Influence employees to change their behavior by showing concern for ongoing development, rewarding improvements, using a collaborative problem solving style, breaking complex tasks into simpler ones, and modeling desired behaviors.

_____ **I counsel employees about personal problems.**
1. Build trust by maintaining confidentiality.
2. Help clarify thoughts and feelings into a more logical and coherent order.
3. Provide reassurance that problems have solutions and can be solved.
4. Identify employee problems requiring professional treatment.

_____ **I mentor employees for long-term development.**
1. Provide ongoing emotional support and encouragement.
2. Educate about the organization, its goals, and advancement criteria.
3. Coach to be more politically savvy and avoid possible traps.
4. Help live up to their full potential and encourage them to be more proactive in managing their careers.

_____ **I help develop action plans for improvement.**
1. Collaborate with participating employees to gain commitment.
2. Search for concrete and specific things to improve.
3. Establish a time schedule.
4. Determine criteria and how to get feedback to measure success.

APPLICATION QUESTIONS

1. Think of a particularly effective mentor or coach you had in high school, college, or any other situation (e.g., sport, debate, music). Describe why he or she was so effective. How do this helper's qualities match up with those in the Behavioral Checklist?
2. How have your parents served as helpers for your development? What did they do that was particularly helpful? What could they have done better?
3. How is coaching similar to counseling? How are the two different?
4. Which of the earlier skills in this book contribute to developing employees? How do they relate?
5. How can a manager tell if he or she is being effective in developing others? When and how does a manager know when the developing job is completed?
6. What are three things you should never do when developing others and why?
7. What are three things you should always do when developing others and why?

REINFORCEMENT EXERCISES

1. Ask a coach of a local sports team for permission to observe him or her at work. Spend a few hours watching the coach do the job. How do this coach's behaviors match up with those in the Behavioral Checklist?

2. Watch several episodes of a TV series. Determine incidences of people trying to develop others. Do they assist or educate, coach or counsel? How effectively do they use the skills described in this chapter?
3. Help someone develop. For example, help a less able student through a class-related problem; coach someone to develop an athletic skill; or counsel a friend who wants to improve a difficult relationship; mentor a younger or less experienced sibling or friend.
4. Visit the counseling department at your university. Talk to a counselor about what procedures are used when helping students solve problems and which are most effective.

ACTION PLAN

1. Which helping behaviors do I want to improve the most?
2. Why? What will be my payoff?
3. What potential obstacles stand in my way?
4. What are the specific things I will do to improve? (For examples, see the Reinforcement Exercises.)
5. When will I do them?
6. How and when will I measure my success?

NOTES

1. A. Fisher, "The World's Most Admired Companies," *Fortune* (October 27, 1997): 220–40.
2. Noel M. Tichy, *The Leadership Engine* (New York: HarperCollins Publishers, 1997) 199.
3. J. J. Asher, "The Biographical Item: Can It Be Improved?" *Personnel Psychology* (Summer 1972): 266.
4. According to Carl King, president of Team Building Systems of Houston, Tex., as cited in E. E. Spragins, "Screening New Hires." *INC.* (August 1992): 82.
5. E. E. Spragins, "Screening New Hires," *INC.* (August 1992): 83.
6. "Understanding the Liability of Negligent Hiring," *Security Management Supplement* (July 1990): 7A.
7. "If You Can't Say Something Nice," *Wall Street Journal* (March 4, 1988): 25.
8. E. E. Ghiselli, "The Validity of Aptitude Tests in Personnel Selection," *Personnel Psychology* (Winter 1973): 475; G. Grimsley and H. F. Jarrett, "The Relation of Managerial Achievement to Test Measures Obtained in the Employment Situation," *Personnel Psychology* (Spring 1973): 31–48; A. K. Korman, "The Prediction of Managerial Peformance: A Review," *Personnel Psychology* (Summer 1986): 295–322.
9. I. T. Robertson and R. S. Kanola, "Work Sample Test: Validity, Adverse Impact, and Applicant Reaction," *Journal of Occupational Psychology*, 55, no. 3 (1987): 171–83.
10. G. C. Thornton, *Assessment Centers in Human Resources Management* (Reading, MA: Addison-Wesley, 1992).
11. R. L. Dipboye, *Selection Interviews: Process Perspectives* (Cincinnati: South-Western, 1992), chapter 2.
12. A. I. Huffcutt and W. Arthur, Jr., "Hunter and Hunter (1984) Revisited: Interview Validity for Entry-Level Jobs," *Journal of Applied Psychology* (April 1994): 184–90; M. A. McDaniel, D. L. Whetzel, F. L. Schmidt, and S. D. Maurer, "The Validity of Employment Interviews: A Comprehensive Review and Meta-Analysis," *Journal of Applied Psychology* (August 1994): 599–616; and J. M. Conway, R. A. Jako, and D. F. Goodman, "A Meta-Analysis of Interrater and Internal Consistency Reliability of Selection Interviews," *Journal of Applied Psychology* (October 1995): 565–79.
13. See, for example, R. L. Dipboye, *Selection Interviews: Process Perspectives* (Cincinnati: South-Western, 1992) pp. 42–44; R. D. Arveny and J. E. Campion, "The Employment Interview: A Summary and Review of Recent Research," *Personnel Psychology* (Summer 1982): 281–322; M. D. Hakel, "Employment Interview," in K. M. Rowland and G. R. Ferris, eds., *Personnel Management: New Perspectives* (Boston: Allyn and Bacon, 1982), 192–255; E. C. Webster, *The Employment Interview: A Social Judgment Process* (Schomberg, Ont.: S.I.P. Publications, 1982); and M. M. Harris, "Reconsidering the Employment Interview: A Review of Recent Literature and Suggestions for Future Research, *Personnel Psychology* (Winter 1989): 691–726.
14. W. F. Cascio, *Applied Psychology in Personnel Management* (Upper Saddle River, NJ: Prentice Hall, 1991) 271.
15. T. J. Hanson and J. C. Balesteri-Spero, "An Alternative to Interviews," *Personnel Journal* (June 1985): 114.
16. Based on R. N. Lussier, *Supervision: A Skill-Building Approach* (Burr Ridge, IL: Irwin, 1994) 269–97.

17. Based on D. A. DeCenzo and S. P. Robbins, *Human Resources Management*, 4th ed. (New York: John Wiley, 1994) 208–09.

18. Adapted from various sources, including S. P. Robbins and D. A. DeCenzo, *Supervision Today* (Upper Saddle River, NJ: Prentice Hall, 1998) 249; Campbell, "Hiring Smart," Knight Ridder News Service report; W. C. Donaghy, *The Interview: Skills and Applications* (Glenview, Ill.: Scott, Foresman, 1984): 245–80; J. M. Jenkins and B. L. P. Zevnik, "ABCs of Job Interviewing," *Harvard Business Review* (July–August, 1989): 38–42.

19. L. Megginson, G. M. Franklin, and M. J. Byrd, *Human Resource Management* (Houston, TX: Dame Publications, 1995) 58–59.

20. *Nation's Business* (July 1992).

21. More on the distinction between assisting and educating can be found in D. A. Kolb, I. M. Rubin, and J. S. Osland, *Organizational Behavior: An Experiential Approach* (Upper Saddle River, NJ: Prentice Hall, 1991): 277.

22. F. Fournies, *Coaching for Improved Work Performance* (New York: Van Nostrand Reinhold, 1978).

23. For more detailed information on each of these guidelines, see D. C. Kinlaw, *Coaching for Commitment* (San Diego, CA: Pfeiffer & Company, 1993).

24. C. Rogers, *On Becoming a Person* (Boston: Houghton Mifflin, 1961) 34.

25. C. R. Leana, "Predictors and Consequences of Delegation," *Academy of Management Journal*, (December 1986): 754–74.

26. S. P. Robbins and D. A. DeCenzo, *Supervision*, 2nd ed. (Upper Saddle River, NJ: Prentice Hall, 1998): 212.

27. L. L. Steinmetz, *The Art and Skill of Delegation* (Reading, MA: Addison-Wesley, 1976) 248.

28. C. R. Mill, "Feedback: The Art of Giving and Receiving Help," in L. Porter and C. R. Mill, eds., *The Reading Book for Human Relations Training* (Bethel, ME: NTL Institute for Applied Behavioral Science, 1976): 18–19.

29. J. C. Kunich and R. I. Lester, "Leadership and the Art of Feedback: Feeding the Hands That Back Us," *Journal of Leadership Studies* 3 (1996): 3–22.

30. C. W. Cook, P. L. Hunsaker, and R. E. Coffey, *Management and Organizational Behavior*, 2nd ed. (Burr Ridge, IL: Irwin, 1997) 271–273.

31. M. Mavis, "Painless Performance Evaluations," *Training and Development* (October 1994): 40–44.

32. Adapted from D. A. Kolb, I. M. Rubin, and J. S. Osland, *Organizational Behavior: An Experiential Approach* (Upper Saddle River, NJ: Prentice Hall, 1991) 448–50, who provide an extended discussion of each of these guidelines.

33. C. D. Orth, H. E. Wilkinson, and R. C. Benfari, "The Manager's Role as Coach and Mentor," *Organizational Dynamics* (Spring 1987): 67.

34. W. C. Byham with J. Cox, *Zapp! The Lightning of Empowerment* (Pittsburg, PA: DDI Press, 1989) 129.

35. "Labor Letter," *Wall Street Journal* (March 24, 1992), p. A1.

36. K. E. Kram and D. T. Hall, "Mentoring as an Antidote to Stress During Corporate Trauma," *Human Resource Management* (Winter 1989): 493–511.

37. Adapted from S. C. Certo, *Supervision: Quality, Diversity, and Technology* (Chicago: Irwin, 1997) 500–501.

CHAPTER 14

Creating High-Performing Teams

Learning Objectives

After completing this chapter, you should be able to:

■ Identify the characteristics of effective teams.

■ Design high-performing teams.

■ Recognize the stages of team development.

■ Adapt leadership style to different stages of team development.

■ Identify obstacles to effective team performance.

■ Facilitate team processes.

■ Conduct effective meetings.

SELF-ASSESSMENT EXERCISE

Do You Have a Team Mentality?

Circle the answer that most closely resembles your attitude.

	Strongly Disagree						Strongly Agree
1. Only those who depend on themselves get ahead in life.	7	6	5	4	3	2	1
2. To be superior, a person must stand alone.	7	6	5	4	3	2	1
3. If you want something done right, you must do it yourself.	7	6	5	4	3	2	1
4. What happens to me is my own doing.	7	6	5	4	3	2	1
5. In the long run, the only person you can count on is yourself.	7	6	5	4	3	2	1
6. Winning is everything.	7	6	5	4	3	2	1
7. I feel that winning is important in both work and games.	7	6	5	4	3	2	1
8. Success is the most important thing in life.	7	6	5	4	3	2	1
9. It annoys me when other people perform better than I do.	7	6	5	4	3	2	1
10. Doing your best is not enough; it is important to win.	7	6	5	4	3	2	1

	Strongly Disagree					*Strongly Agree*	
11. I prefer to work with others in a group rather than to work alone.	1	2	3	4	5	6	7
12. Given the choice, I would rather do a job where I can work alone rather than doing a job where I have to work with others in a group.	7	6	5	4	3	2	1
13. Working with a group is better than working alone.	1	2	3	4	5	6	7
14. People should be made aware that if they are going to be part of a group then they are sometimes going to have to do things they do not want to do.	1	2	3	4	5	6	7
15. People who belong to a group should realize that they are not always going to get what they personally want.	1	2	3	4	5	6	7
16. People in a group should realize that they sometimes are going to have to make sacrifices for the sake of the group as a whole.	1	2	3	4	5	6	7
17. People in a group should be willing to make sacrifices for the sake of the group's well-being.	1	2	3	4	5	6	7
18. A group is most productive when its members do what *they* want to do rather than what the group wants to do.	7	6	5	4	3	2	1
19. A group is most efficient when its members do what *they* think is best rather than doing what the group wants them to do.	7	6	5	4	3	2	1
20. A group is most productive when its members follow their own interests and concerns.	7	6	5	4	3	2	1

SOURCE: Adapted from J. A. Wagner III, "Studies of Individualism-Collectivism: Effects on Cooperation in Groups," *Academy of Management Journal* (February 1995): 162.

Scoring and Interpretation. Add your answers to calculate your score. Your total score will be between 20 and 140.

The higher your score, the higher your collectivist orientation, so high scores are more compatible with being a team player. For comparative purposes, 492 undergraduate students enrolled in an introductory management course at a large U.S. university scored an average of approximately 89. We might speculate that scores below 69 indicate a strong individualistic ethic, which would mean that you prefer to work alone. Scores above 109 indicate a strong team mentality and preference for collaborating with others.

CONCEPTS

Successful managers are those who work with successful teams. Lee Iacocca, former CEO of the Chrysler Corporation, said in his autobiography that "all business operations can be reduced to three words: People, product, and profit. People come first. Unless you've got a good team, you cannot do much with the other two."[1]

Working with others is not easy. Nevertheless, groups constitute the basic building blocks of any organization. For many tasks, teams accomplish much more work in less time than the same number of individuals can working separately. Employees can also grow more quality conscious through group interaction as they learn about others' experiences, problems, and solutions as work-in-process flows through the organization.[2]

Groups can be defined as two or more people who meet regularly over a period of time, perceive themselves as a distinct entity distinguishable from others, share common values, and strive for common objectives.[3] Most of us are members of several different types of groups in organizations ranging from the lunch bunch that meets to enjoy each other's company, to problem-solving task forces that are charged with developing plans for major organizational change.

All teams are groups, but they are more sophisticated forms of the group. **Teams** are groups with complementary skills, who are committed to a common purpose, set of performance goals, and approach for which they hold themselves mutually accountable.[4] A team engages in collective work produced by coordinated joint efforts that result in more than the sum of the individual efforts, or *synergy*. Members are accountable for performance both as individuals and as a group.

The lunch bunch or people working independently in a radio assembly group would not be classified as a team, but their lack of team status is not a problem because they do not need coordinated joint efforts, complementary skills, and other ingredients necessary for group synergy. In other situations, such as a symphony orchestra or an emergency room hospital unit, complementary skills, coordinated joint efforts, shared and individual responsibility, and other team characteristics are necessary ingredients to produce the required synergistic output.

Effective teamwork has been found to be a key characteristic of America's 100 best companies.[5] Without proper preparation, however, quality circles, autonomous work teams, and cross-functional teams may not live up to expectations.[6] A number of findings from studies of successful teams provide insights to the essential ingredients. In this chapter, you will learn the skills to develop groups into high-energy teams and intervene when your team gets off track.

The Importance of Creating High-Performance Teams

Don Callahan and Brian Large huddled around a half-built Dodge Intrepid, trying to figure out why the warning light on the instrument panel was on even though the air conditioner was working fine. Both men were members of the LH cars' A platform at Chrysler's assembly plant at Brampton, Ontario. Don Callahan, an hourly assembly-line worker, and Brian Large, a product engineer, have worked together since the Intrepid prototype was first built. In a few hours, they managed to fix the electrical glitch and send their car down the line.

If Chrysler had developed the LH in the same way most U.S. vehicles have been developed, Callahan wouldn't have contacted Large about the problem, because the two would never have met, and the early production cars would likely have reached customers' hands with the electrical system still on the fritz. However, the workers, designers, and engineers who collaborated in developing the first test batch of cars thrashed out the final stages of a vehicle development process that sought to blur the traditional lines between people in different functional work units.

The team approach paid off in a number of ways for Chrysler. The LH team, for example, shaved a full year off Chrysler's average vehicle development cycle, which historically averaged four and a half years, and team members did it with 40 percent fewer engineers than a typical product program would use. At a price tag of just over $1 billion, the LH budget came in well under those of two other well-known team efforts, Ford's $3 billion Taurus/Sable and GM's $3.5 billion Saturn.[7]

What is it about teams that gives them the potential to contribute these types of organizational benefits? Eight things that teams can provide are described in Exhibit 14-1. You should keep in mind, however, that these are only *potential* benefits that have a better chance of being realized if the skills in this chapter are applied. For each of these success stories of outstanding team performance, however, many times work groups do not work out at all.[8] What makes the difference between high-performing teams and group failures is the subject of this chapter. Let's start by taking a look at the characteristics of high-performing teams.

EXHIBIT 14-1   Eight Ways Your Organization Can Benefit from Teams

1. ***Team output usually exceeds individual output.***   Although a single person can make a big difference in an organization, he or she rarely has the knowledge, experience, or skill equal to a team. Research is clear that major gains on quality and productivity most often result from organizations with a team culture.

2. ***Complex problems can be solved more effectively.***   Complex problems usually require diverse, in-depth technical knowledge that can be found only among several subject-matter experts. Complexity mandates teams.

3. ***Creative ideas are usually stimulated in the presence of other individuals who have the same focus, passion, and excitement.***   Creative ideas, or leaps from conventional wisdom, are usually spawned in the tension of differences, which can most easily occur in teams.

4. ***Support arises among team members.***   Process improvement and product innovation are hard work and take a long time. It would be natural for one person's energy to drop during the long effort. The synergy and optimism that come from people working together productively can sustain team member enthusiasm and support even through difficult times.

5. ***Teams infuse knowledge.***   When many people work on an organizational problem, more organization members will see the need for change and a vision of what is better. Team members become "sensors" for how the rest of the organization will view the proposed change as well as ambassadors for the proposed change.

6. ***Teams promote organizational learning in a work setting.***   The team setting naturally promotes both formal (training events and educational experiences) and informal learning because of the diverse knowledge and skills present in the group members, which then are ingested through problem identification and problem solving.

7. ***Teams promote individual self-disclosure and examination.***   Teams require flexibility in behavior and outlook from individual team members. Egos must be checked at the door in favor of passionate commitment to a common goal.

8. ***Teams both appreciate and take advantage of diversity.***   Preconceived ideas about people and things will ultimately be challenged in teams. Emotions and ideas that do not support tolerance will be challenged in teams.

SOURCE: S. F. Woodring, and D. Zigarmi, *The Team Leader's Idea-A-Day Guide* (Chicago: Dartnell, 1997) 5. Reprinted with permission. © by Dartnell, 360 Hiatt Drive, Palm Beach Gardens, FL 33418. All rights reserved. For more information on this or other products published by Dartnell, please call (800) 621-5463, ext 567.

Characteristics of High-Performing Teams

Studies of effective teams have found that they contain a small number of people with complementary skills who are equally committed to a common purpose, goals, and working approach for which they hold themselves mutually accountable.[9] Let's examine these characteristics in a little more depth.

Small Size

The best teams tend to be small. When they have more than about 10 members, it becomes difficult for them to get much done. They have trouble interacting constructively and agreeing on much. Large numbers of people usually cannot develop the common purpose, goals, approach, and mutual accountability of a real team, so in designing effective teams, keep them to 10 or less. If the natural working unit is larger, and you want a team effort, break the group into subteams. FedEx, for instance, has divided the 1,000 clerical workers at its headquarters into teams of 5 to 10 members each.

Complementary Skills

To perform effectively, a team requires three types of skills. First, it needs people with *technical expertise*. Second, it needs people with the *problem-solving and decision-making skills* to identify problems, generate alternatives, evaluate those alternatives, and make competent choices. Finally, teams need people with good *interpersonal skills*.

No team can achieve its performance potential without developing all three types of skills, but teams do not need to have all the complementary skills at the beginning. Where team members value personal growth and development, one or more members often take responsibility to learn the skills in which the group is deficient, as long as the skill potential exists. Additionally, personal compatibility among members is not critical to the team's success if the technical, decision-making, and interpersonal skills are in place.

Common Purpose

High-performing teams have a common vision and meaningful purpose that provide direction, momentum, and commitment for members. The development team at Apple Computer that designed the Macintosh, for example, was almost religiously committed to creating a user-friendly machine that would revolutionize the way people used computers. Production teams at Saturn Corporation are united by the common purpose of building an American automobile that can successfully compete in terms of quality and price with the best Japanese cars.

Members of successful teams put a tremendous amount of time and effort into discussing, shaping, and agreeing upon a purpose that belongs to them collectively and individually. This common purpose, when accepted by the team, becomes the equivalent of what celestial navigation is to a ship captain: It provides direction and guidance under any and all conditions.

Specific Goals

Successful teams translate their common purpose into specific, measurable, and realistic performance goals. Just as goals lead individuals to higher performance (see Chapter 7 for more on planning and goal setting), they also energize teams. Specific goals facilitate clear communication and help teams maintain their focus on getting results. Examples of specific team goals might be responding to all customers within 24 hours, cutting production-cycle time by 30 percent over the next six months, or maintaining equipment at a level of zero downtime every month.

Common Approach

Goals are the ends a team strives to attain. Defining and agreeing upon a common approach assures that the team is unified on the *means* for achieving those ends. Team members need to determine how to share the workload, set schedules, resolve conflicts, and make decisions. The recent implementation of work teams at Olin Chemicals' Macintosh, Alabama, plant included having teams complete questionnaires on how they would organize themselves and share specific responsibilities.[10] Integrating individual skills to further the team's performance is the essence of shaping a common approach.

Mutual Accountability

The final characteristic of high-performing teams is accountability at both the individual and group level. Successful teams make members individually and jointly accountable for the team's purpose, goals, and approach. Members understand what they are individually responsible for and what they are jointly responsible for.

When teams focus only on group-level performance targets, and ignore individual contributions and responsibilities, team members often engage in *social loafing*.[11] They reduce their inputs because their individual contributions cannot be identified and become "free riders" coasting on the team's effort. The result is that the team's overall performance suffers. This issue reaffirms the importance of measuring both individual contributions to the team as well as the team's overall performance.

Designing High-Performing Teams

It is easier to design high-performing teams when a new organization is being created than to impose them on an existing structure because appropriate applicants and technology can be selected for the new system. General Motors, for example, realized instant success when it started producing the Saturn automobile by establishing cross-functional teams with new members in an entirely new plant. The cross-functional teams were able to coordinate the entire project from the beginning, as opposed to GM's traditional method of having the design team pass its work on to the production team.

So what actions can be taken to get new teams off to a productive start like GM's Saturn division? Exhibit 14-2 summarizes a set of questions that new teams need to address in the following order until all the answers are clearly understood and agreed upon by all team members.[12] Established teams also need to develop procedures to address the issues associated with these questions.

Who Are We?

When team members share their strengths, weaknesses, work preferences, values, and beliefs with others, diversity can be dealt with before it causes unspoken conflicts. The end result is a set of common beliefs that creates a group identity, a feeling of "what we stand for." The "My Asset Base" exercise at the end of this chapter is a good way to answer this question in a structured manner. To start the team-building process, have each member answer the following questions and then share them with each other: What are my strengths that can be a resource for the team? What are my weaknesses where I may need some coaching or training? What are my work preferences where I will best fit team requirements? What are my values and beliefs?

EXHIBIT 14-2   High Energy Team Development Model

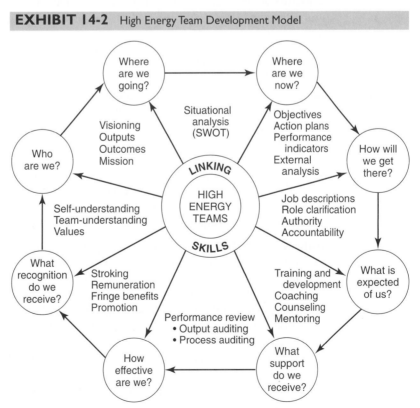

SOURCE: Adapted from C. Margerison and D. McCann, *The Team Development Manual* (Toowong, Queensland, Australia: Team Management Resources, 1990) 20.

After all have shared this personal information, the team should discuss the implications for working productively together. For example, what differences in basic values might cause conflicts? What are the common beliefs that allow for a shared identity regarding what the team "stands for"? What are the implications for working together as a team?

Where Are We Going?

Teams need to envision the pot of gold at the end of the rainbow. They need a mission, purpose, and goals, as described in Chapter 7. They need to consider what the team will be like in one, two, or five years and develop a vision they are all excited about. They need an overriding reason for existing and concrete goals to strive for.

Where Are We Now?

All teams have strengths and weaknesses, but most tend to concentrate on the things they do well and ignore those that they do not do well. Examining the team's strengths, weaknesses, opportunities, and threats (a team SWOT analysis as described in Chapter 7) can be done by having the team address each of the following questions: What strengths should we reinforce, build on, and improve? What weaknesses can we improve on, and how can we do it? What opportunities do we have for improvement, learning new skills, and undertaking new tasks? What internal threats (e.g., role ambiguity or conflict) and external threats (e.g., budget decreases or increased competition) do we face?

How Will We Get There?

Based on its mission and goals, the team needs to set specific team objectives and then integrate individual objectives. Objectives are the basis for action plans, which spell out who does what, when, and how, including external linkages with other departments and individuals who can facilitate goal attainment. Performance indicators need to be set up to measure how well the team is doing.

What Is Expected from Us?

A team cannot perform if it does not know what is expected! Therefore, team members need to understand their job description, roles on the team, responsibilities, and areas of authority and accountability. Teams will accomplish team objectives more effectively by better using the talents of all members appropriately. Roles and responsibilities should correspond with members' strengths and preferences. Questions to be considered when allocating roles and responsibilities include the following: Who is good at administering and maintaining systems? Who is good at initiating change? Who is good at whipping up enthusiasm? Who is comfortable managing details of implementation?[13] Two structured techniques that can facilitate clarifying role expectations are the role analysis technique and responsibility charting.

Role Analysis Technique The role analysis technique is designed to clarify role expectations and obligations of team members through a structured process of mutually defining and delineating role requirements. Each individual analyzes the rationale, significance, and specific duties of his or her role with the inputs of other team members until all are satisfied that the role has been completely defined. Then each individual shares his or her expectations for other roles on the team, which are discussed until the entire team is in agreement. Finally, each member writes a *role profile* to summarize the activities in his or her role, the obligations of that role to each individual on the team, and the expected contributions of other roles to the member's role. This profile is shared and agreed upon by the entire team.[14]

Responsibility Charting Responsibility charting clarifies who is responsible for which decisions and actions. The first step is to construct a grid: The types of decisions and actions the team deals with go in a vertical column on the left side, and the team members who are involved in the decisions go across the top of the grid. Then each team member is assigned one of five behavioral expectations for each of the actions: responsibility to initiate action, approving or vetoing rights, support for implementation, right to be informed (but with no influence), and noninvolvement in the decision. This process is carried out with the entire team participating and reaching a consensus.

What Support Do We Get/Need?

A review of each member's training and development needs (i.e., a personal SWOT analysis) can set the stage for individual training, counseling, and mentoring assignments that will strengthen both the individual and the team. The support given by key managers who ran interference for the LH team at Chrysler Corporation were crucial to its surviving intact throughout the initial three years. LH team "believers" helped protect the team from less enthusiastic factions in the company. Often, these executives signaled their support by simply staying out of the team's way. But even silent allies in high places were useful when company veterans began to feel threatened by a new team's deviations from the norm.[15]

How Effective Are We?

Regular performance reviews of quantity and quality outputs should be set up to ensure achievement of team goals and provide members with standards. It is equally important to set up a regular review of the team process.

What Recognition Do We Get?

As you will read in Chapter 17, Motivating Others, managers get what they reward. The same is true for teams. Types of team recognition include stroking (psychological rewards such as saying "thank you"), praise when someone on the team makes a contribution, equitable remuneration and bonuses for outstanding achievements, fringe benefits including such team fringes as celebration lunches or parties, and promotions that include preparation for more responsibility. Team members will also be more motivated if their assigned roles and responsibilities match up with their strengths and preferences.

The Five Stages of Team Development

Several research-based theories suggest that most teams progress in sequence through the five stages of forming, storming, norming, performing, and adjourning.[16] Different groups, however, remain at various stages of development for different lengths of time, and some may stall at a given stage permanently. By being aware of a team's process, the manager can facilitate members' functioning at each stage and enhance the transition to the next stage of development.

Two variables can be observed to determine team development stage: productivity and morale.[17] The model in Exhibit 14-3 illustrates how productivity and morale vary during each stage of a team's development. **Productivity,** the team's ability to work together and achieve results, steadily increases from the initial team formation throughout the life of the team. **Morale,** the team's motivation, confidence, and cohesion, starts out high initially but then decreases as members realize that initial expectations are not being met and conflicts develop. As differences are explored, expectations are aligned with reality and the team achieves positive results, raising morale again through the performance stage. If a manager can diagnose productivity and morale to determine a team's developmental stage, it will be possible to then make the necessary adjustments in leadership style to meet team needs at any specific stage, which will allow transition to the next stage.

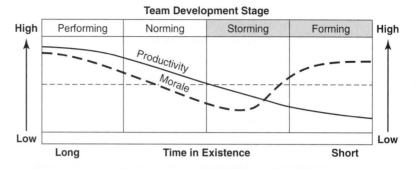

EXHIBIT 14-3   Variations in Productive and Morale During Team Development

SOURCE: Adapted from D. Carew, E. Parisi-Carew, and K. Blanchard, *Team Development and Situational Leadership II* (Escondido, CA: Blanchard Training and Development, Inc., 1998) 4.

To effectively diagnose the stage of a team's development, it is necessary to understand the characteristic behaviors at each stage. Then, to intervene to facilitate progression to the next stage of development, the manager needs to know the specific group needs at each stage and how to satisfy them. The following section will explain the characteristics and team needs at each stage of development. These are summarized in Exhibit 14-4.

Forming

In a newly formed group, many uncertainties exist about the group's purpose, structure, and leadership. Members are concerned about exploring friendship and task potentials. They do not have a strategy for addressing the group's task. They do not know yet what behaviors are acceptable as they try to determine how to satisfy needs for acceptance and personal goal satisfaction. As awareness increases, members begin to accept themselves as a group and commit to group goals.

Teams at the forming stage have a number of needs to satisfy before they can allay these concerns and move on to the next stage. A structured approach to satisfying these needs is for members to address the questions presented in the previous section for designing high-performing teams. Answers to these questions will provide the information the team needs to know about its purpose, members' resources, ground rules for working together, roles, timelines, standards, decision-making authority, accountability, and available resources. Answering these questions to everyone's satisfaction will help the team move through not only the first, but *all* of the stages of development more efficiently.

The length of this stage depends on the clarity and difficulty of the task, as well as how easily the team members become comfortable working together. With fairly simple tasks, the forming stage may be a relatively short period of the team's life, say, 5 to 10 percent. With complex tasks, however, the team may spend 30 to 60 percent of its existence at this stage.[18]

Storming

After the team has spent some time forming, difficulties accomplishing the task and working together lead to frustration and conflict. Disagreement is inevitable as members attempt to decide on task procedures, role assignments, ways of relating, and power allocations. Then emerges a growing dissatisfaction with the team's

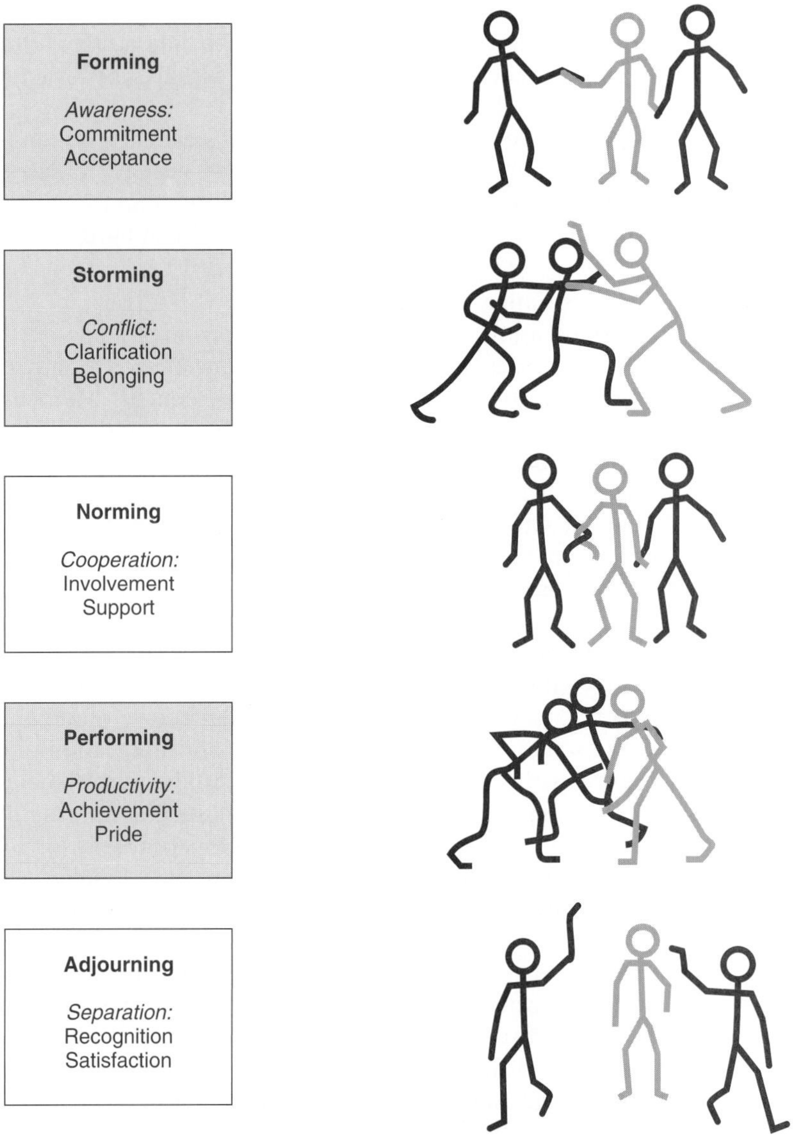

Forming *Awareness:* Commitment Acceptance	
Storming *Conflict:* Clarification Belonging	
Norming *Cooperation:* Involvement Support	
Performing *Productivity:* Achievement Pride	
Adjourning *Separation:* Recognition Satisfaction	

EXHIBIT 14-4   Five Stages of Team Development

dependence on the leader, who is blamed for a majority of the problems. Although productivity is increasing from stage one, it is still low. Communications begin to break down, which contributes to inability to problem solve and lowered trust. Negative reactions to each other develop, polarizing the team and leading to the formation of conflicting subgroups. Morale drops as team members deal with their concerns about power, control, and the discrepancy between their initial expectations and reality.

Before teams at the storming stage can move on, they need to resolve conflicts about power and task structure. They also need to work through the accompanying hostility and replace it with a sense of acceptance and belonging. Progress in these directions requires open and honest discussions of issues including emotional blocks, coalitions, and personality conflicts. Simultaneously, members need to develop productive communication processes, including active listening, the exchange of nonjudgmental feedback, and a problem-solving orientation. Team members also need to value differences, encourage and reassure each other, and recognize their accomplishments in order to clarify the big picture; redefine their purpose, roles, goals, and structure; and regain commitment to essential values and norms.

The amount of time spent in this stage depends on the degree of conflict and emotions that develop. It also depends on the team's ability to resolve the issues. Occasionally groups with significant problems can become stuck in the storming stage, which leads to continued demoralization and little if any productivity.

Norming

Cooperation is the theme of the norming stage. Resolving issues in the storming stage causes team members to value the differences among themselves and contributes to increased task accomplishment. Members agree on a structure that divides work tasks, provides leadership, and allocates other roles. This progress causes morale to rise and increases commitment to purpose, values, norms, roles, and goals. Trust and cohesion grow as communication becomes more open and task oriented. Members demonstrate a willingness to share responsibility and control as team members start thinking in terms of "we" rather than "I." On the down side, team members may avoid conflict for fear of losing the positive climate. This reluctance to deal with conflict can slow progress if remaining issues are not dealt with and less effective decisions are made.

Although productivity at this stage is moderately high and morale is improving, several needs still must be addressed before the team can move on to the performing stage. Among them are the further integration of roles, goals, norms, and structure with a focus on increasing productivity. The team members also need to continue skill development in areas such as sharing different perspectives and disagreeing in order to further develop problem-solving effectiveness and enhance their ability to learn from each experience. Finally, room still remains for continued building of trust and positive relationships through things such as the recognition and celebration of success.

This stage can be relatively short depending on the ease of resolving feelings of dissatisfaction and integrating new skills. If conflict avoidance is prolonged, the team could possibly return to the storming stage. On the other hand, if teams become too contented they can stall at this stage because they do not want to create conflict or challenge established ways of doing things.

Performing

In this stage of development, group members are no longer conflicted about acceptance and how to relate to each other. Purpose, goals, and roles are clear. Now members work interdependently to solve problems and are committed to the group's mission. The primary focus is on performance, and productivity is at its peak. Morale is high, and members experience a sense of pride and excitement in being part of a high-performing team. Communication is open, and leadership is shared. Mutual respect and trust are the norms.

The major concerns include preventing loss of enthusiasm and sustaining momentum. The challenges are how to continue meeting the high standards of productivity through refinements and growth, and how to maintain morale through recognition and celebration of both team and individual accomplishments. For permanent work groups, this stage is hopefully the final and ongoing state of development. The performing stage is likely to continue with moderate fluctuations in feelings of satisfaction throughout the life of the team.

Adjourning

With ongoing teams this stage is not really relevant because it is never reached unless a drastic reorganization occurs. Termination, however, does occur in ad hoc teams or temporary task forces, and team members need to be prepared for its outcomes. Productivity may increase or decrease as the end approaches and team members strive for perfection or begin to disassociate from the team. Morale can also be impacted either positively, as team members pride themselves on their accomplishments, or negatively, as the end of the experience draws near and they feel sadness or loss. Feelings about disbanding range from sadness and depression at the loss of friendships to happiness and fulfillment due to what has been achieved. The leader can facilitate positive closure at this stage by recognizing and rewarding group performance. Ceremonial events bring closure to the desired emotional outcome, which is a sense of satisfaction and accomplishment.

Adapting Leadership Style to Facilitate Team Development[19]

Teams that are successful and productive in the performance stage do not just automatically start out that way. By understanding and diagnosing team needs at each stage of development, managers can provide appropriate leadership to move teams along the path from forming to performing.

Effective team leadership is the ability to diagnose the needs of the team and behave in ways that meet those needs. A manager can adapt leadership behaviors toward building productivity and morale as needed to achieve success in any given situation, which will allow transition to the next stage of team development.

A leader's productivity-related behaviors provide direction toward the team's task achievement. These behaviors are critical during the early stages of a team, but as time goes on, they are needed less. Morale-oriented behaviors, on the other hand, focus on how the team is working together and provide support. These behaviors are needed less in the forming stage of team development, but become critical during the storming and performing stages. The Leadership Style and Team Development Model illustrated in Exhibit 14-5 provides a framework for identifying the leadership behaviors needed to build a high-performing team at each stage of team development.

Behaviors that *provide direction* focus on getting the job done. They include behaviors such as developing a compelling team purpose and values, clarifying team norms and ground rules, establishing roles, identifying goals and standards, agreeing on structure and strategies, and teaching team and task skills.

Behaviors that *provide support* focus on how the team is working together with the goals of developing harmony, involvement, and cohesion. These morale-related behaviors include involving others in decision making, encouraging participation, valuing differences, active listening, sharing leadership, acknowledging and praising, and building relationships.

Exhibit 14-5 illustrates how direction and support combine to form four leadership styles. These four styles—structuring, resolving, collaborating, and validating—vary in the amount of direction and support provided, which depends on the extent of leadership responsibility assumed by team members.

To determine appropriate leadership style, first diagnose the team's stage of development in relation to its goal, considering both productivity and morale. Then, locate the team's present stage of development in Exhibit 14-5 and follow a perpendicular line up to the curve. The point of intersection indicates the appropriate leadership style for the team. This model yields four matches of leadership style to stage of team development: structuring in the forming stage; resolving in the storming stage; collaborating in the norming stage; and validating in the performing stage.

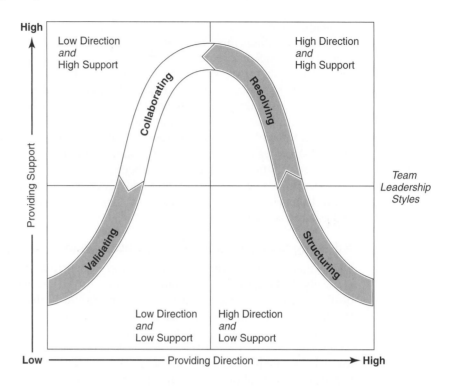

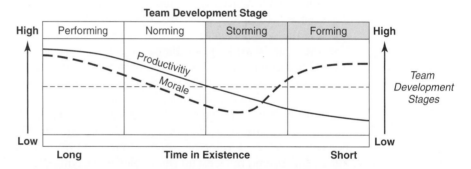

EXHIBIT 14-5 Leadership Style and Team Development

SOURCE: Adapted from D. Carew, E. Parisi-Carew, and K. Blanchard, *Team Development and Situational Leadership II* (Escondido, CA: Blanchard Training and Development, Inc., 1998) 5.

Structuring

When teams are initially formed, people usually are eager to be there and have high expectations. Therefore, morale is high at the start, but productivity is low due to lack of knowledge about the task and the resources each team member possesses. Direction is needed to provide the information and skills necessary to get the team started. Some need for support is present, but it is much less than the need for task-oriented behavior. Structuring behaviors include clarifying the team's relationship to organizational vision, purpose, and values; developing a clear and compelling team purpose; developing norms and ground rules to guide behavior; orienting team members to one another; establishing and clarifying roles; setting goals, objectives, and standards; and developing structure and boundaries.

Resolving

At the storming stage of group development, anger, frustration, confusion, and discouragement can arise due to the discrepancy between initial expectations and reality. Appropriate leader behaviors are high levels of direction and an increase in support to include more input on decision making and encouragement. Resolving behaviors include redefining purpose, roles, goals, and standards; revisiting values and norms; encouraging active listening; providing big-picture perspective and rationale; encouraging and valuing different perspectives; encouraging feedback amid self-disclosure; recognizing and addressing difficult issues; and building supportive relationships.

Collaborating

The norming stage is characterized by increasing levels of morale and harmony and task competence as team members learn to work together. Goals and strategies are becoming clearer or have been redefined. Negative feelings are being resolved. Team members are more willing and able to assume leadership functions, but continued collaboration is needed to help team members develop confidence in their ability to work together. The team needs less direction in regard to the task and more support focused on building confidence, cohesion, and involvement. Collaborating behaviors include facilitating involvement in problem solving and decision making; encouraging participation and open communication; acknowledging team accomplishments and individual contributions; encouraging interdependence and shared responsibility; integrating team purpose, norms, and structure into the team's operation; examining team functioning to reduce obstacles; and encouraging and valuing different perspectives.

Validating

In the performing stage the team is providing its own direction and support. Both productivity and morale are high. At this point the manager can confidently share leadership and encourage full participation by all members. Validating behaviors include recognizing and celebrating team accomplishments, acknowledging individual contributions, continuing to evaluate and learn from experience, creating new challenges and higher standards, and encouraging continuous improvement.

Terminating

For adjourning teams with a distinct ending point, productivity can continue to increase, or it may go down because of a rush to complete the task. The approaching end of an important experience may also cause morale to increase or drop from its previous high levels. Accepting and acknowledging the feelings that are present during this stage may be helpful. A significant downturn in productivity and morale should be met with an increase in support, as well as some direction in order to maintain high performance.

Improving Team Effectiveness

The newly created Saturn teams at GM had many benefits including new members with common goals, agreed-upon work procedures, and shared responsibilities. Their creation is quite a contrast to Chrysler, which took people from functional work groups, with different backgrounds, who had previously competed for resources, and transformed them into cooperating LH teams. It took more than three years of team-building training in areas such as trust building and consensus decision making for the LH teams to overcome their history of buck passing, negative stereotypes, and competitiveness.[20]

Managers can learn valuable lessons about improving team performance by studying how coaches develop athletic teams. To win games, a sports team must coordinate the efforts of individual players. A sports team practices hours each week for that one hour of critical playing time where its performance counts. Members review films of past games, identify mistakes, set up goals, and plan strategies for the next game. Then the team practices until weaknesses are eliminated and it is skilled at implementing its new action plans.

Work teams also must coordinate the efforts of individual members to be effective. Most work teams, however, seldom take time out to review past actions to determine what worked and what did not. They fail to spend time learning from past mistakes, nor do they consistently set goals, plan new strategies, practice new ways of behaving, or get coaching on new methods of communicating and working together. Work team members are usually intuitively aware of problems but just do not know what to do about them. So how can a manager assess problems and determine what is needed to improve team performance?

Becoming Aware of Team Problems

A team-building program usually is initiated because someone (the leader, a higher-level manager, a team member, or consultant) recognizes that the group is having problems working productively as a team.[21] Chrysler managers became aware of serious difficulties on the new LH teams when they noticed symptoms such as overt hostilities between team members, chronic lateness and absenteeism at meetings, low quantity and quality of production, negative gossip and rumors, decisions not carried out because of misunderstandings, lack of willingness to take responsibility, and lack of interest in helping each other with problems. Remember that problem awareness is the first step in the creative problem-solving process as described in Chapter 9. The rest of this section describes how to apply that process as it pertains to assessing and solving problems to team effectiveness.

Determining Symptoms of Ineffective Teams

The success of a team development program depends on the accurate identification of the group's specific needs and problems. It would make little sense, for example, to apply interventions aimed at increasing trust and openness of members of an executive staff if the primary problems it encountered centered on job ambiguity and role conflict. In becoming aware of and diagnosing ineffective team functioning, watch for the following key indicators.[22]

- *Communicating outside the group.* When team members are unwilling to get necessary information out in the open during group meetings, it usually means something is wrong in the functioning of the team. Signals that all is not well are closed-door meetings and hallway discussions to share issues and express concerns.

- *Overdependency on the leader.* Even though the leader is an important initiator of team action, members should have enough confidence to move ahead when it is clear that action is needed, even if the leader is absent.

- *Unrealized decisions.* Decisions made but not carried out indicate that people are working on matters of low concern or are not committed to the decisions that were made.

- *Hidden conflicts.* To be effective, teams need to tolerate disagreements and work them through to mutually satisfactory solutions. Pretending that differences do not exist causes increased tension, which gets in the way of productivity and satisfaction.

- *Fighting without resolution.* The continual presence of open infighting and attempts to put down, deject, or hurt others is a symptom of deep-rooted team problems.

- *Subgroups.* When subgroups put themselves before the needs of the total unit, the common interests of the team are in jeopardy.

Data Gathering

Data need to be gathered about the team situation so that the correct diagnosis can be made. Why do negative factors exist, and what can be done about them? Data gathering can take a variety of forms. Two of the most common are questioning individual team members and team process observation.

Questioning Individual Team Members   One method for getting to the core of problems is to privately *interview* each team member, assuring confidentiality. Common and significant problems can later be shared with the team, but who mentioned them should not be disclosed. Usually, this interview process can be most effectively accomplished by an outside expert who can gather and present the information in an unbiased manner.

Interviews usually start with a set of common questions such as: What do you like best and least about the team? What obstacles keep you from being as productive as you could be? What are some of the strengths and weaknesses of the leader and of each member? What changes could make you and your team more effective? As the interview progresses, however, other significant factors can be investigated as they are revealed by the interviewees, in an attempt to understand and pinpoint all significant problems.

An alternative to face-to-face interviews is to distribute *written questionnaires* to team members and ask them to complete them (anonymously or not, depending on the office climate and content of the questionnaire). The team-building checklist in Exhibit 14-6, is one example of such a questionnaire.

Process Observation   Process observation focuses on how the team is interacting (processing) rather than what (content) members are talking about to achieve their objectives. Effective team leaders pay attention to both content and process, so they can intervene when necessary in an appropriate manner. Although work teams spend most of their time on content, a failure to address process issues can prevent a team from reaching its maximum potential and accomplishing its task in a timely manner. Other chapters address skills for enhancing quality and productivity: goal setting, evaluating and controlling performance, and designing work. Here, we focus on several process issues that can help enhance team functioning: role behaviors, communication patterns, decision-making procedures, influence strategies, and emotional issues.

Team Roles.   There are three types of team-member behaviors that can be observed.[23] The first are *task* behaviors that address how the team accomplishes work. Examples are setting agendas, suggesting decision-making procedures, and determining deadlines. The second are *maintenance* behaviors that focus on meeting members' social and emotional needs. Examples are resolving conflicts, giving recognition, and dealing with difficult behaviors. The third are *personal* behaviors that only serve individual needs and usually interfere with the team's task and maintenance needs. Exhibit 14-7 describes some of the most frequently occurring roles in each area.

As teams mature, the frequency of personal role behaviors decreases, and behaviors associated with task and maintenance roles increase. Members are capable of performing a variety of task and maintenance roles in different teams, but most team members are more comfortable in particular roles. To increase team effectiveness, members should expand their role repertoire to include whatever behaviors are necessary at any given moment. By becoming proficient participant-observers, members are constantly aware of the team process, and practice role flexibility by intervening with appropriate role behavior.

Problem Identification

Content analysis of the interview, questionnaire, and process observation data identifies common and significant problems, major themes, and suggested solutions. These results can then be summarized for presentation to team members.

EXHIBIT 14-6 Team-Building Checklist

Identify to what extent you see evidence of the following problems in your work unit of either your present or a past job.

	Low		Some		High
1. Loss of production or work unit output.	1	2	3	4	5
2. Grievances within the work unit.	1	2	3	4	5
3. Conflicts or hostility between unit members.	1	2	3	4	5
4. Confusion about assignments or unclear relationships between people.	1	2	3	4	5
5. Lack of clear goals, or low commitment of goals.	1	2	3	4	5
6. Apathy or general lack of interest or involvement of unit members.	1	2	3	4	5
7. Lack of innovation, risk taking, imagination, or initiative.	1	2	3	4	5
8. Ineffective staff meetings.	1	2	3	4	5
9. Problems in working with the boss.	1	2	3	4	5
10. Poor communications; people afraid to speak up, not listening to each other, or not talking together.	1	2	3	4	5
11. The lack of trust between boss and member or between members.	1	2	3	4	5
12. Decisions made that people do not understand or agree with.	1	2	3	4	5
13. People feel that good work is not recognized or rewarded.	1	2	3	4	5
14. People are not encouraged to work together for better team effort.	1	2	3	4	5

Scoring. Add up the score for the 14 items and interpret as follows:

14–28: Few indications of a need for team building.
29–42: Some evidence of a need, but no immediate pressure unless two or three items are high.
43–56: Seriously think about a team-building program.
57–70: Make team building a top priority.

SOURCE: Excerpted from W. Dyer, R. H. Daines, and W. C. Giauque, *The Challenge of Management* (New York: Harcourt Brace & Company, 1990) 343.

If it is determined that some of the group's problems are caused by scarce resources, job ambiguity, role conflict, unrealistic workloads, and/or some other factors not directly related to how individuals function as a team, job redesign, allocation of additional resources, or better job-person matching may be called for. If outside difficulties are not the source of problems, then the manager needs to identify specific team problems.

After all the data are available, the team determines which issues are most important. Anything that will help clarify the issues already identified should be shared. Anything that keeps the group from being as effective as possible is fair game.

Communication Patterns. One of the easiest aspects of team process to observe is the pattern of communication: Who talks? For how long? How often? At whom do people look when they talk: individuals, possibly potential supporters, the team in general, or maybe nobody? Who talks after whom, or who interrupts whom? What style of communication is used: assertions, questions, tone of voice, gestures?

Observing these types of communication behaviors can provide clues about who is most influential, whether coalitions exist, and how members feel about each other and the task. More frequent participators are often more influential, especially if they are assertive, articulate, and repeat their ideas over and over. High frequency contributors, however, can have their influence diluted by blocking coalitions of two or more members. While all this is going on, more introverted members may feel safer just listening and keeping quiet. The problem is that they may be the ones with the best ideas.

EXHIBIT 14-7 Classification of Functional Team Roles

Task Roles. Behaviors directed toward accomplishing the team's objective, primarily through contributing to the problem-solving process. Most of these roles aid in defining and achieving common goals.

Role Name	Description
Initiator	Proposes tasks, goals, or actions; defines team problems; suggests a procedure
Clarifier	Interprets ideas or suggestions; defines terms; clarifies issues before the team
Summarizer/ coordinator	Pulls together related ideas; restates suggestions; offers a decision or conclusion for the team to consider.
Reality tester	Makes a critical analysis of an idea; tests an idea against some set of data to see if it will work
Procedural technician	Records suggestions; distributes materials

Building and Maintenance Roles. Behaviors aimed at helping the interpersonal functioning of the team. Like the maintenance required to keep a car in good running condition, these behaviors are necessary to keep team members feeling good about the team and interacting effectively with one another.

Role Name	Description
Harmonizer	Attempts to reconcile disagreements; reduces tension; gets people to explore differences
Gatekeeper	Helps keep communication channels open; facilitates participation of others; suggests procedures that permit sharing remarks
Encourager	Friendly, warm, and responsive to others; indicates by facial expression or remark the acceptance of others' contributions
Compromiser	Offers a personal compromise for the good of the total team cohesion and growth
Observer/commentor	Comments on and interprets team's internal process

Personal Roles. Behaviors intended to satisfy individual needs rather than contribute to goals or maintenance of the team. Personal-role behaviors are not conducive to team functioning.

Role Name	Description
Aggressor	Deflates others' status; attacks the team or its values; jokes in a barbed way
Social Loafer	Makes a display of his/her lack of involvement; "abandons" the team while remaining with it physically; seeks recognition in ways not relevant to team task
Evader	Pursues special interests not related to tasks; stays off subject to avoid commitment; prevents team from facing up to controversy
Help seeker	Uses team to gain sympathy and solve personal problems unrelated to team's goal
Recognition seeker	Calls attention to self by boasting and referring to personal achievements; acts in inappropriate ways to gain attention

SOURCE: Adapted from K. D. Benne and P. Sheats, "Functional Roles of Group Members," *Journal of Social Issues* 4, no. 2 (Spring 1948): 41–49.

Charting these behaviors and their consequences can be aided by the use of a sociogram, like the one illustrated in Exhibit 14-8.[24] To use a sociogram, make a drawing of the team seating arrangement and draw circles representing each member. Put the members' names or initials in each circle. Draw lines between circles

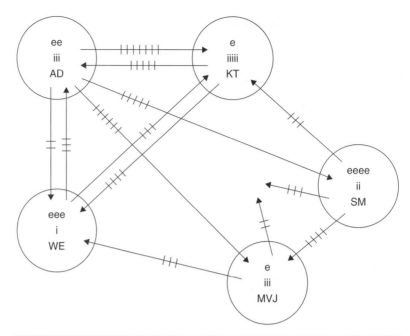

EXHIBIT 14-8 Sociogram of Team Communication Patterns

SOURCE: D. Ancona, T. Kochan, M. Scully, J. Van Maanen, and D. E. Westney, *Managing for the Future: Organizational Behavior & Process*, 2d ed. (Cincinnati: South-Western College Publishing, 1999) M-5, 10.

when members make statements to each other, and to the center of the diagram when a comment is directed to the team as a whole. Each time a member says something, make a mark on the appropriate connecting line and indicate the nature of the statement by entering the appropriate letter within the initiator's circle. Use letters that will help you understand and provide feedback about the process. For example, you could use an "i" for interrupting, an "e" for encouraging, and a "q" for asking questions.

In Exhibit 14-8, for example, AD has the highest total frequency of communications. MVJ has the fewest communications. KT interrupted another five times. WE interrupted only once. SM was the most encouraging. There is a possible coalition between WE and KT, who may or may not be supporting AD.

Decision-Making Procedures. Teams make decisions all the time but members are not always aware of how they are made. Decisions concerning team norms and operating procedures are often subconscious, as are decisions not to decide. It is important that the team uses appropriate decision-making procedures because team decisions are notoriously hard to undo. When someone says, "Well, we decided to do it, didn't we?" any budding opposition is quickly immobilized. Some common team decision procedures are summarized in Exhibit 14-9.

The effectiveness of any team decision process depends on the specific nature of the task, the individuals on the team, the existing constraints, and other situational variables. The important thing is to use the most appropriate process. A history of decisions based entirely on self-authorized agendas or handclasps, for example, may not be in the best interests of total team welfare.

EXHIBIT 14-9 Team Decision-Making Procedures

Decision Type	*Description*	*Example*
The plop	An assertive statement followed by silence.	If a statement such as "I think we need to establish our objectives" is followed by nothing but silence from group members, a nonverbal decision to reject the suggested line of action has been made.
The self-authorized agenda	An assertive statement followed by action implementing the suggestion.	"I think we ought to introduce ourselves. My name is Elena Cortez."
The handclasp	A suggestion made by one person and implemented by another.	Person A says, "I think we should introduce ourselves." Person B replies, "So do I; my name is Howard Johnson."
The minority decision (Does anyone object?)	An expressed agreement by a few that meets no resistance from the disjointed or undecided many.	"We all seem to agree with Elena's suggestion." "If no one objects to Howard's plan, let's go with it."
Voting	The typical voting system in which the majority wins.	"Let's vote and whoever has the most votes wins."
Polling	Checking with each group member individually to obtain his or her opinion or vote:	"Let's go around the table and see where everyone stands. Elena, what do you think?"
Consensus	Essential agreement by all.	The issue is explored in enough depth that all group members agree that a certain course of action is the best that can be agreed to at the present time.

SOURCE: Adapted from the *Reading Book (Revised) of the NTL Institute for Applied Behavior Science* (Washington, DC: The National Education Association, 1970) 22.

Influence Strategies. Team members influence each other through a variety of strategies. Although the most powerful member is usually the formal leader, other members of the team have varying amounts of influence, depending on differences in status, expertise, experience, and personality. Members' ability to persuade others also varies according to their choices of influence tactics and skills in applying them. Answer the questions in Exhibit 14-10 to assess your own use of some common influence tactics.

Self-Oriented Emotional Behavior.[25] The processes described so far deal with the team's attempts to solve work-related problems relating to task and maintenance, but there is a kind of emotional undercurrent in the stream of team life that can disturb team effectiveness.[26] These underlying emotional issues produce a variety of emotional behaviors, which interfere with or are destructive of effective team functioning. Unresolved emotional issues are manifest in the personal roles, such as aggressor or help seeker, described in Exhibit 14-7. They cannot be ignored or wished away, however. Rather, they must be recognized, their causes must be understood, and as the team develops, conditions must be created that permit these same emotional energies

---

EXHIBIT 14-10 A Checklist of Influence Tactics

Which of these behaviors do you use in your attempts to get others to do your bidding? Which have others used on you? Why did they succeed or fail? Check those used and make a note of the result.

	I Have Used on Others	*Others Have Used on Me*	*Results*
Assertiveness			
Point out that the rules require the person to do it.	_____	_____	_____
Repeatedly remind the person what is wanted.	_____	_____	_____
Ingratiation			
Appear polite and humble while making the request.	_____	_____	_____
Sympathize about the hardships the request causes.	_____	_____	_____
Rational appeals			
Write a detailed plan justifying a request.	_____	_____	_____
Explain the reasons for your request.	_____	_____	_____
Sanctions			
Threaten to expel the person from the group.	_____	_____	_____
Threaten to complain to a higher authority.	_____	_____	_____
Exchanges			
Propose an exchange of favors.	_____	_____	_____
Remind the person of past favors you provided.	_____	_____	_____
Upward appeals			
Appeal to higher levels to support a request.	_____	_____	_____
Send the person to see a superior.	_____	_____	_____
Blocking			
Threaten to stop working with the person.	_____	_____	_____
Ignore the person and stop being friendly.	_____	_____	_____
Coalitions			
Obtain support of coworkers to back a request.	_____	_____	_____
Make request at meeting where others will back it.	_____	_____	_____

SOURCE: Adapted from David Kipnis, Stuart M. Schmidt, and Ian Wilkinson, "Intraorganizational Influence Tactics: Explorations in Getting One's Way," *Journal of Applied Psychology* 65 (1980): 440–52.

---

to be channeled in the direction of productive team effort. The basic causes of these emotion-based roles are

1. The problem of *identity:* Who am I in this team? What role will I play?
2. The problem of *personal goals and needs:* What do I want from the team? Are team objectives consistent with my goals? What can I contribute to the team goals?
3. The problem of *power and control:* Who will control what we do? How much power and influence do I have? How much influence do I want?
4. The problem of *acceptance and intimacy:* Do the others accept me? How close will we get to each other? How personal do I want to become? How much can we trust each other?

These personal issues manifest themselves in self-oriented behaviors and are more prevalent in the forming and storming stages of new teams. Members are unfamiliar with each other and team expectations, so exploring how to satisfy personal issues needs to be addressed. Some of the disruptive behaviors that result in response to trying to resolve these emotional issues include the following:

- *Dependency.*   Waiting passively for a leader to emerge who will provide structure and solve problems
- *Counterdependency.*   Opposing or resisting anyone on the team who represents authority, especially the leader.
- *Fighting and controlling.*   Asserting personal dominance. Attempting to get own way regardless of others.
- *Withdrawing.*   Trying to remove the sources of uncomfortable feelings by psychologically leaving the team and withdrawing from conversations with others.
- *Pairing up.*   Seeking out one or two supporters and forming a kind of emotional sub-team in which the members protect and support each other.

The forgoing are only some issues that can be observed in a team. What is important to observe will vary with what the team is doing, its stage of development, its goals and needs, and many other situational factors. Improving skills in observing what is going on in the team will provide important data for understanding teams and increasing team members' effectiveness.

Intervening.   The key to effective interventions to improve team functioning is a careful analysis of problem processes and behaviors.

After process observations are fed back to team members, the next step is to decide on the most appropriate interventions. These might include structural changes such as developing an agenda, setting norms, or assigning task and maintenance roles. Power and control issues can be addressed by empowering more introverted members, forming new coalitions, breaking up existing coalitions, and appointing task leaders. Communications might be improved by assigning a moderator as gate-keeper and decisions can be improved by establishing a rational problem-solving process.

The next task is to set priorities and determine the group's agenda. It is vital that only those issues that the team can realistically do something about are included on the agenda so that the group can accomplish something positive and start to feel good about itself and its problem-solving abilities. Issues might be broken down into those that can be worked on immediately, those that are not possible for the group to influence and must be accepted, and those that should be delegated to someone else to act on. Following are critical obstacles that often prevent teams from being high performers.

- *Weak sense of direction.*   Teams perform poorly when members are not sure of their purpose, goals, and approach. Add weak leadership and you have the recipe for failure. Nothing will undermine enthusiasm for the team concept as quickly as the frustration of being an involuntary member of a team that has no focus.
- *Infighting.*   When team members are spending time bickering and undermining their colleagues, energy is being misdirected. Effective teams are not necessarily composed of people who all like each other; however, members must respect each other and be willing to put aside petty differences in order to facilitate goal achievement.
- *Shirking of responsibilities.*   A team is in trouble if members exhibit lack of commitment to the team, maneuver to have others do part of their job, or blame colleagues or management for personal or team failures.

- *Lack of trust.* When there is trust, team members believe in the integrity, character, and ability of each other. When trust is lacking, members are unable to depend on each other. Teams that lack trust tend to be short lived.

- *Critical skills gaps.* When skill gaps occur, and the team doesn't fill these gaps, the team flounders. Members have trouble communicating with each other, destructive conflicts are not resolved, decisions are never made, or technical problems overwhelm the team.

- *Lack of external support.* Teams exist within the larger organization. They rely on that larger organization for a variety of resources—money, people, equipment—and if those resources are not there, it is difficult for teams to reach their potential. For example, teams must live with the organization's employee selection process, formal rules and regulations, budgeting procedures, and compensation system. If these systems are inconsistent with the team's needs and goals, the team suffers.

Make Action Plans to Solve Problems

The task of finding solutions to problems can be assigned to subteams of concerned and qualified individuals, or the entire team can work through the prioritized agenda item by item to develop action plans. Action plans should include a statement of the problem, the recommended solution, people responsible for implementing action, and deadlines for results. Some of the things that can be done to overcome obstacles and help teams to reach their full potential are listed here:

- *Clarify goals.* Members of high-performance teams have a clear understanding of their goals and believe that their goals embody a worthwhile or important result. The importance of these goals encourages individuals to sublimate personal concerns to these team goals. In effective teams, members are committed to the team's goals, know what they are expected to accomplish, and understand how they will work together to achieve these goals.

- *Encourage teams to go for small wins.* The building of real teams takes time. New teams cannot be expected to hit homeruns, right at the beginning, every time they come to bat. Team members should begin by trying to hit singles. Small wins can be facilitated by identifying and setting attainable goals. The eventual goal of cutting overall costs by 30 percent, for instance, can be dissected into five or 10 smaller and more easily attainable goals. As the smaller goals are attained, the team's success is reinforced. Cohesiveness is increased and morale improves. Confidence builds. Success breeds success.

- *Build mutual trust.* Trust is fragile. It takes a long time to build and can be easily destroyed. Several things can be done to create a climate of mutual trust.[27] Keep team members informed by explaining upper-management decisions and policies and by providing accurate feedback. Create a climate of openness where employees are free to discuss problems without fear of retaliation. Be candid about your own problems and limitations. Make sure you are available and approachable when others need support. Be respectful and listen to team members' ideas. Develop a reputation for being fair, objective, and impartial in your treatment of team members. Show consistency in your actions, and avoid erratic and unpredictable behavior. Finally, be dependable and honest. Make sure you follow through on all explicit and implied promises.

Appraise Both Group and Individual Performance

Team members should all share in the glory when their team succeeds, and they should share in the blame when it fails. So a large measure of each member's performance appraisal should be based on the overall team performance. But members need to know that they cannot ride on the backs of others. Therefore, each member's individual contribution should also be identified and made a part of his or her overall performance appraisal.

Provide the Necessary External Support

Managers are the link between the teams and upper management. It is their responsibility to make sure that teams have the necessary organizational resources to accomplish their goals. They should be prepared to make the case to key decision makers in the organization for tools, equipment, training, personnel, physical space, or other resources that the teams may require.

Offer Team-Building Training

Teams, especially in their early stages of formation, will need training to build their skills. Typically, these skills would include problem solving, communication, negotiation, conflict resolution, and group processing. If you cannot personally provide this kind of skill training for your team members, look to specialists in your organization who can or secure the funds to bring in outside facilitators who specialize in this kind of training.

Role Negotiation Technique

When team ineffectiveness is based on problems of power and authority within the group, the role negotiation technique can be used to control negotiations between team members. The process focuses on work behaviors, not personal feelings. Members write down what they want others to do more of, do less of, stop doing, and maintain unchanged. Then members agree to change certain behaviors if others will do the same, and a written contract is established.[28]

Conducting Effective Meetings

The most important team decisions are almost always reached in meetings.[29] As a manager of teams, you are the one in charge of them. You choose who will attend. You set and control the agenda. In fact, what you do or fail to do will largely influence the meeting's effectiveness. While no magic formulas guarantee success, managers can employ a number of skills and procedures to improve the quality of their meetings.

The suggestions that follow are divided into planning activities to carry out before the meeting, leadership activities to engage in during the meeting, and management activities to follow up on after the meeting. It is essential to be skilled at all phases of meeting management: The most thorough preparation will be wasted if you are careless during the meeting. Outstanding meeting leadership rarely overcomes poor planning, and if action plans are not implemented, then even the best decisions will not achieve expected results.

Preparing for the Meeting

Perhaps the most useful way to begin is simply to sit down with a blank sheet of paper and think through what you need to accomplish and what the meeting should be like. Write down all the issues that are likely to come up, what decisions need to be made, what you want to happen after the meeting, and what things have to happen before the meeting can take place. Now that you have reviewed the big picture, you can get down to planning the meeting. Your plan should include the following activities.

Set Objectives   Most meetings are called either to exchange information or to solve team problems. Be explicit about your purposes because they have major implications for who should attend, which items belong on the agenda, when and where you hold the meeting, and what kinds of decision-making procedures you should use.

An information-exchange meeting can be an efficient mechanism if the information to be shared is complex or controversial, if it has major implications for the meeting participants, or if symbolic value comes through conveying the information personally. If none of these conditions are present, it may be more efficient, and just as effective, to write a memo, send an e-mail, or make a few telephone calls. Problem-solving meetings, however, provide an opportunity to combine the knowledge and skills of everyone on the team in an open-ended discussion, which usually produces more creative ideas than those the same people could produce working individually.

Select Participants   Invite only those people to the meeting who will either contribute to or be affected by its outcome. Select individuals who have knowledge or skills relevant to the problem, or who command organizational resources (time, budgets, other people, power, and influence) that you need access to. Do everything you can to keep the size of the group appropriate to your objectives. Although an information-exchange meeting can be almost any size, a problem-solving group should not exceed eight to 10 people if at all possible.[30]

Plan the Agenda   The agenda is the planning document that guides what you hope to accomplish at the meeting. The agenda should start by stating the meeting's purpose. It should also identify who will be in attendance; what, if any, preparation is required of each participant; a detailed list of items to be covered; the specific time and location of the meeting; and a specific finishing time.

By defining the meeting's purpose, an agenda gives the participants a sense of direction and serves as a vehicle for premeeting discussions with participants. During the meeting, the agenda will be a valuable means of controlling the discussion and placing boundaries between relevant and irrelevant topics.

Distribute the Agenda and Relevant Materials in Advance   If you want to ensure that people will attend and be prepared for the meeting, get your agenda out well in advance. Providing adequate lead time will depend on the importance of the meeting and the amount of preparation necessary, but you should circulate the agenda and relevant background papers at least two or three days before the meeting. Keep your demands on their time reasonable, however. People are more likely to read and think about brief memos than long, comprehensive reports.

Consult with Participants Before the Meeting   Few events are as frustrating as a meeting of people who are unprepared to discuss or decide the issues on the agenda. It is your responsibility to ensure that members are prepared by circulating relevant data and background materials far enough in advance that participants can prepare adequately. Encourage participants to do their homework. If all are prepared, the meeting can proceed much more quickly.

Another reason for contacting participants prior to the meeting is to collect all the relevant information you can, and to consider its implications. The more important and the more controversial the subject, the more contact you should have with other participants before the actual meeting. These contacts will help you anticipate issues and disagreements that may arise during the meeting.

Set a Time and Place   The timing and location of your meeting can have a subtle but significant impact on the quality of the discussion. When will the people you want at the meeting be available, given scheduled work constraints? Given other activities, what time of day is best for your meeting? Be sure the time is sheltered to keep interruptions at a minimum. Also, gear your starting time to the meeting's desirable length. For example, if you want the meeting to last only an hour, a good time to schedule it is at 11 A.M.

Try not to plan meetings that last more than 90 minutes. Most people's endurance—or at least their creative capacity—will not last much longer than that. If the subject is so complex or lengthy that it will take longer, be sure to build in coffee and stretching breaks at least every 90 minutes.

Where you hold the meeting can have a marked influence on its tone and content. For example, consider the difference between calling three team members to your office versus meeting them for lunch in a restaurant. A "neutral" conference room creates a different climate than someone's office. Each setting implies a particular level of formality and signals what kind of discussion you expect to have. The appropriate setting depends on your purposes.

The discussion climate will also be affected by the arrangement of the furniture in the meeting room. In your office, you can choose to stay behind your desk and thereby be more authoritative, or to use a chair that puts you on a more equal basis with the other participants. In a conference room, you can choose to sit at the head of the table to symbolize your control, or in the center to be "one of the team."

You should also be certain that you have arranged for any necessary mechanical equipment, such as an overhead or slide projector, an easel, or a blackboard. These vital aids can facilitate both information exchange and problem-solving discussions.

Conducting the Meeting

You called the meeting because you need something from the other participants, either information relevant to the problem or agreement and commitment to a decision. Your success in achieving those goals now depends not so much on what you know about the problem as on what you and the others can learn during the discussion. Thus, the primary concern as you begin the meeting should be with creating a healthy, problem-solving atmosphere in which participants openly confront their differences and work toward a joint solution. The following suggestions should help you achieve your goals.

Begin the Meeting with the Agenda   The first thing you should do at the meeting is to get participants to review the agenda and the meeting objectives. Be careful not to simply impose the agenda on the team; others may have useful suggestions that will speed up the meeting or bring the problem into sharper focus. Some may disagree with some of your plans, but you will not learn about that disagreement unless you clearly signal that you consider the agenda open to revision. Do modifications need to be made? If so, make them. Clarify the issues that you plan to discuss. After this review, get participants to approve the final agenda. The more the others participate in defining the meeting, the more committed they will be to fulfilling that definition.

Establish Specific Time Parameters   Meetings should begin on time and have a specific time for completion.[31] This way, no one has to waste their time waiting for latecomers and everyone can be sure that they will be able to attend later scheduled commitments. If you have set a specific ending time, and everyone knows you mean it, the tendency for the discussion to wander will be greatly reduced. It is your responsibility to specify these time parameters and to hold to them.

Control the Discussion   As the formal leader of the meeting, you have formal authority to influence the group's actions. You will normally want to exercise greater control when the topic generates strong, potentially disruptive feelings, when the group is moving toward a decision, or when time pressures are significant. A whole range of informal to formal control techniques is available for use if needed.

If you began the meeting with an explicit discussion of the agenda, you will find this focusing task easier to carry out. Often a simple reminder to the group, with a glance at the clock, is enough to get things back on track if the discussion wanders.

Other times a pointed look, or even just a lifted eyebrow, is all you need to indicate approval or disapproval of someone's behavior.

If you need more formal control, you can permit participants to speak only when you call on them, or if you comment on or summarize each statement, direct confrontations between other individuals will be minimized. If you use a flip chart or chalkboard to summarize ideas, you will also increase the level of formality and reduce the number of direct exchanges. In highly charged circumstances where destructive conflict is probable, you may even want to employ formal parliamentary procedures, such as requiring motions and limiting debate.

Encourage Problem Solving   As you read in Chapter 9, effective problem-solving meetings generally pass through several phases. Early in the discussion the team will be seeking to understand the nature of the problem. Understanding can be facilitated by encouraging factual, nonevaluative discussion that emphasizes describing symptoms and searching for all possible causes. As understanding is gained, the focus will shift to a search for solutions, which also is enhanced by nonevaluative suggestions. Only after all potential alternatives have been explored and the team moves toward a decision should the discussion become evaluative.

Encourage and Support Participation by All Members   Participants were not selected randomly. Each is there for a purpose. To maximize the effectiveness of problem-oriented meetings, each participant must be encouraged to contribute. Quiet or reserved personalities sometimes need to be drawn out so their ideas can be heard.

Encourage the Clash of Ideas, but Discourage the Clash of Personalities   You need to encourage different points of view, critical thinking, and constructive disagreement. Your goals should be to stimulate participants' creativity and to counter the group members' desire to reach an early consensus. An effective meeting is characterized by the critical assessment of ideas. If disagreements ever disintegrate into attacks on people, however, you should quickly intercede.

Exhibit Effective Listening Skills   Applying the listening skills you learned in Chapter 3 can contribute to encouraging participation and the expression of different ideas. Effective listening also reduces misunderstandings, improves the focus of discussion, and encourages the critical assessment of ideas. Even if other group members do not exhibit good listening skills, if you do, you can keep the discussion focused on the issues and facilitate critical thinking.

Reach a Consensus   Many teams fall into decision-making habits without thinking carefully about the consequences of those habits. The two major approaches to reaching a team decision are voting and reaching a consensus. Each strategy has its advantages and disadvantages.

Voting is often resorted to when the decision is important and the group seems deadlocked. The major benefit of taking a vote is that you are guaranteed a decision. However, voting requires public commitment to a position, and it creates a win-lose situation for the group members. Some individuals will be clearly identified as having favored a minority position. Losers on one issue often try to balance their account on the next decision, or they may withdraw their commitment to the total group. Either way, you may have won the battle but lost the war.

Reaching a team consensus, where everyone agrees that the best solution under the circumstances has been reached, is generally a much more effective decision-making procedure. It is often more difficult, however, and is almost always more time-consuming. Working toward a genuine consensus means hearing all points of view, and usually results in a better decision—a condition that is especially important when the team members will be responsible for implementing the decision. Even when individuals do not fully agree with the team decision, they are more likely to support it (or less likely to sabotage it) when they believe their positions have had a complete hearing. As a caveat, never assume that silence means agreement; more often it signals some level of difference with the dominant theme of the discussion.

End the Meeting by Clarifying What Happens Next   Close the meeting by summarizing the group's accomplishments, clarifying what actions need to follow the meeting, and allocating follow-up assignments.[32] If any decisions have been made, who will be responsible for communicating and implementing them? If the team will meet again, you can save a lot of time by scheduling your next meeting before people depart.

Follow Up After the Meeting

Depending on the discussion topic and the decisions that have been made, either you or someone else should follow up after the meeting with a brief memo summarizing the discussion, the decisions, and the follow-up commitments that each participant has made. This kind of document serves not only as a record of the meeting, but also as a next-day reminder to the participants of what they decided and what they are committed to doing.

It can be a valuable learning experience for future meetings to spend the last five minutes debriefing the meeting process. Which processes contributed and which ones detracted from the meeting's success. How can they be improved for the next meeting? The best time to share your reactions to the meeting is right after it has ended.

CONCEPT QUIZ

Complete the following true-false quiz by circling the correct answer. Answers are at the end of the quiz. After marking your answers, remember to go back and check your understanding of any answers you missed.

True or False	1. All teams are groups, but not all groups are teams.
True or False	2. When teams are measured only on group-level performance, individual members often reduce their efforts.
True or False	3. The three types of complementary skills that a team needs to succeed are technical expertise, problem solving, and common purpose.
True or False	4. The five stages of team development proceed in the following order: forming, norming, storming, performing, and adjourning.
True or False	5. When a temporary team reaches the adjourning stage, a manager no longer needs to be concerned about members' feelings, morale, or productivity.
True or False	6. Task deadlines, team composition, and leader direction and support are all contingencies that can facilitate a team's progress through the five stages of development.
True or False	7. Communicating outside the group, overdependency on the leader, and hidden conflicts are all signs that a team is ineffective.
True or False	8. Structuring is the most important team leadership style.
True or False	9. Effective meeting planning includes all of the following: setting objectives, selecting participants, planning the agenda, and consulting with participants in advance.
True or False	10. When the team is moving toward a decision, the leader should refrain from controlling the discussion.

Answers.   (1) True; (2) True; (3) False; (4) False; (5) False; (6) True; (7) True; (8) False; (9) True; (10) False

BEHAVIORAL CHECKLIST

The following skills are important to effective team building. Use them when evaluating your own team-building skills and those of others.

The Effective Team Builder

- Ensures that all members agree on a common team mission and goals.
- Establishes specific, measurable, and realistic goals for each member of the team.
- Develops agreement on a common approach for achieving goals.
- Makes sure that members are individually and jointly accountable for the team's performance.
- Facilitates the exploration of team process and structure issues before beginning on the task.
- Adapts leadership style to facilitate team development.
- Applies the rational problem-solving process to determine and overcome obstacles to team effectiveness.
- Prepares for team meetings by setting objectives and planning the agenda.
- Controls team meetings by use of an agenda and encouraging productive participation.
- Follows up after team meetings to ensure that action commitments are being carried out.

MODELING EXERCISE

Instructions. Seven volunteers form a circle in the front of the class. They will demonstrate team skills at completing an assigned task while the remainder of the class observes and rates the team's performance on the Observer's Rating Sheet. After the task has been completed, observers share their observations with the task team and each other. The last step is to draw conclusions about what helps and hinders team performance in tasks like the one observed and in general.

Team Task. Create a list of the 10 most important characteristics of high-performing teams. Then reach a consensus rank order of the importance of each characteristic.

Time. The total time for this exercise ranges from 45 to 55 minutes. Allow 30 minutes for the task team to complete the task. Allow 10 to 15 minutes for feedback to team members from the Observer's Rating Sheet. Allow 5 to 10 minutes for class generalizations and applications.

OBSERVER'S RATING SHEET

On completion of the exercise, evaluate the task group's team-building skills. Rate each skill set between 1 and 5 using the following scale. Write concrete examples in the space for comments below each criteria skill to use in explaining your feedback.

1	*2*	*3*	*4*	*5*
Unsatisfactory	*Weak*	*Adequate*	*Good*	*Outstanding*

_____ Agreed on a common team mission and goals.

_____ Established specific, measurable, and realistic goals for each member of the team.

_____ Developed agreement on a common approach for achieving goals.

_____ Made sure that members are individually and jointly accountable for the team's performance.

_____ Explored team process and structure issues before beginning on the task.

_____ Adapted leadership style to facilitate team development.

_____ Applied the rational problem-solving process.

_____ Set objectives and planned an agenda.

_____ Controlled the meeting by use of an agenda and encouraging productive participation.

_____ Followed up to ensure that action commitments are being carried out.

GROUP EXERCISES

Three different types of group exercises are presented here. First is a fishbowl exercise for you to practice your observation and diagnostic skills. Second is an opportunity to experience a technique to inventory member assets at the forming stage of team development. Third is a team meeting role-play.

Group Exercise 1: Assessing Team Process Through a Fishbowl

Purpose. To sharpen participant-observer skills of team process behaviors.

Format. Half the class will be involved in a decision-making exercise, while the other half act as observers of the team process. Observers will provide feedback first to the team as a whole and then to team members individually. Decision makers and observers will switch roles and repeat the procedure.

Procedure. Part I: Team decision making and observations (30 minutes).

1. The entire class should pair ups.

2. One member of each pair participates in the first round of decision-making exercises. These decision makers should form teams of 5 to 10 and arrange their seats in a small circle. Their partners are observers for the first round; Observers seat themselves opposite their partners around the outside of the decision-making circle. Optimal team size is 6 to 12 members. In large classes, run several exercises simultaneously.

3. The task for the decision-making team is to generate and rank the 10 factors that most influence the effectiveness of small teams. They must arrive at one set of prioritized rankings that reflects the team's consensus. Time limit is 20 to 30 minutes, depending on class length.

4. Observers view the team's process in general and their partner's behavior in particular. Questions serving as guides for observer's observations are provided in Part II, number 5, below. Observers should remain silent during the decision-making process.

Part II: Feedback and discussion (team: 10 minutes; individual: 5 minutes each).

5. When the decision-making team completes its task (or after 30 minutes, whichever comes first), the observers provide feedback on the behavior that occurred in the team. The following questions serve as guidelines:

    a. What things seemed to help the team complete its task successfully? What things seemed to inhibit or hold the team back?

    b. Did the team spend any time discussing how it was going about the task (process issues)? What were the effects?

    c. What communication patterns developed? What were the effects?

    d. What influence structure emerged? Why? With what results?

    e. What decision-making procedures were used?

6. The observers meet with the team member they observed and provide individual feedback. This is done in dyads.

Part III. With the partners exchanging roles, repeat the procedure for Part I using a different task for the decision-making exercise, such as generating and ranking the most important characteristics of effective team leaders.

Part IV. Repeat the procedure for Part II, providing feedback to the new decision-making team.

Note: If there is not time for two decision exercises, one exercise with a longer observer debriefing accomplished the goals of this exercise.

Group Exercise 2: My Asset Base[33]

Purpose. To help team members get to know each other quickly and to build cohesiveness in the team.

Introduction. Each of us has an asset base that supports our ability to accomplish the things we set out to do. We refer to our personal assets as talents, strengths, or abilities. When new teams form, one of the first items of concern is getting to know each other and what assets each member can contribute to the team.

Directions. The following steps will help you assess your own strengths and share them with others to provide an understanding of team member assets.

Step 1: Individually fill out the following T chart. On the right-hand side of the T, list four or five of your accomplishments of which you are most proud. Your accomplishments would only include those things where you can take credit for achieving them. When you have completed the right-hand side of the chart, fill in the left-hand side by listing the talents, strengths, and abilities that have enabled you to accomplish the outcomes listed on the right-hand side. Try to be specific in describing what assets you have that have enabled you to do what you have done.

Step 2: If you have already formed teams for class projects, meet with your assigned group. If not, form groups of four to six members. In a round-robin fashion, members share first their accomplishments, and then their talents, strengths, and abilities.

Step 3: As a group, discuss the following questions.

1. How did your attitudes and feelings toward other members of the team change as you pursued this activity.

2. What does your reaction tell you about the process whereby we come to get to know and care about people?

3. What strengths does your team possess?

4. What areas would you like to increase your team assets in if you had a group research project to complete?

MY ASSET BASE	*Name:* _____
Talents, Strengths, and Abilities	*Achievements and Accomplishments*

Group Exercise 3: Meeting Management[34]

This role-play can be conducted as a modeling or small group exercise. If conducted as a modeling exercise, five people volunteer to play the roles from the roster below and the audience observes. If done as a group exercise, form groups of six people: Five people volunteer to play the roles from the roster below and the sixth observes.

Directions.   Read the following description of the situation and your assigned role. Do not read the roles of the other actors.

Actors.

Fran Meltzer: Section head of the group. The engineers who report to Fran and their assistants are listed below:

Lee Clark: Senior design engineer—21 years with the company, has two technicians

Chris Manos: Senior design engineer—16 years with the company, has one technician

B. J. Pelter: Senior design engineer—15 years with the company, has two technicians

Pat Rosen: Design engineer—8 years with the company, has one technician

Sandy Solas: Design engineer—3 years with the company, has one technician

Situation.   Five electronics engineers design new products for the Alta Electronics Company, a medium-sized electronics firm. The engineers work individually on projects aided by technicians and, when needed, drafters. All of the engineers in the design group are proud of the products that they have designed, both for the technical developments they incorporate and their reliable performance in use. Fran Meltzer is in charge of the group and has called a meeting to discuss some changes in the company travel policy.

For the last several years, the company has been experiencing financial difficulties. While these have not resulted in layoffs, there has been a severe restriction on wage increases and an absolute freeze on building alterations, travel to professional meetings, magazine subscriptions, and similar expenditures. While most of these have been of a minor nature, some (such as not attending professional meetings) have made it difficult for you and other engineers to keep abreast of technical developments and to maintain your professional contacts. Recently, you have heard that the company has begun to see a modest economic upturn.

Company policy dictates that engineers are responsible for a project not only through the design phase but also to see it through production startup to the point where acceptable products are regularly being produced. On many projects the amount of time spent on handling problems in production is minor. On others, especially those with particularly difficult standards, the time spent in handling production problems can be considerable.

Fran Meltzer's Role   You are the section head of the design engineering group and have reporting to you a competent group of engineers who individually handle design products. Because of financial difficulties, the company has not allocated funds to send engineers to professional meetings for the last several years. You have just heard from your superior that enough money has been appropriated to send one engineer from each group to the national meetings of your professional society next month. He also stated that the vice president of engineering thought it would be best if the limited travel funds were allocated to engineers rather than to managerial personnel, which includes section heads like yourself.

You are quite sure that all of your engineers will want to go and know that there is the possibility of hurt feelings and resentment developing over this matter unless it is handled properly. Therefore, you have decided that rather than make the decision yourself, you will call a meeting of your group and turn the matter over to them and let them make the decision. You will tell them of the funds available for travel and that you want them to make the decision as to who will go in the manner they feel most fair. Your superior has also reminded you that these funds can only be used to send someone to the professional meetings. Do not take a position yourself as to who should be selected to go to the meetings.

Sandy Solas's Role   You feel like the low person on the totem pole in this group. A lot of your equipment is old and frequently breaks down. You don't think Fran has been particularly concerned about the inconvenience this has caused you. Further, ever since you graduated from college, you have not been able to attend a professional meeting because of the freeze the company has placed on travel. You feel that this has kept you from making the contacts you need to develop professionally. You hope that the recent upturn in the company's business will finally make some money available for you to go to professional meetings.

Chris Manos's Role   You feel strongly about attending professional meetings. Through no fault of your own, you missed attending meetings for several years before the freeze on travel was imposed. For two years there were crash projects that kept you tied to the plant. The year before that, your daughter had gotten married. An unplanned chain of events, certainly, but one that has kept you from building new professional contacts or even maintaining old ones. As a result you feel you are in serious danger of slipping professionally and getting stale.

Pat Rosen's Role   Lately, you have been swamped with a series of lengthy tests on some new equipment you have designed. The work has completely overwhelmed your technician, and so you have had to work alongside with him to keep the job moving. Even with your effort, however, it looks as if you may be on this a long time. You would like very much to get to the professional meetings next month to see if a manufacturer may have come out with an item that would ease your testing problem. You are thinking seriously of making a strong pitch for this to Fran, even though you know there has been no money for such trips for the last several years. Additional technician help would be an alternative, but you doubt there is any possibility of hiring a new technician.

B. J. Pelter's Role   The line of work you are now in is taking you in exciting new directions, not only for yourself and the company but also for your professional area. You feel a real need to talk to other engineers doing similar work, both to confirm what you have been doing and also to get ideas on some problems you have been facing. You know that several will be giving papers on topics in the new area at the professional meeting next month. Fortunately, you recently finished debugging the production problems on the last product you designed and now have more time to travel.

Lee Clark's Role   If funds become available for sending people to professional meetings, but not enough to send everyone, you feel that you should be the person to go because you have the most seniority. You feel strongly that in professional work seniority should count. In addition, you have a wide array of contacts developed over the years through which you can pick up much information useful to the company.

Time.   This meeting should not last for more than 25 minutes.

OBSERVER'S RATING SHEET

Evaluate the meeting facililtation skills of Fran Meltzer on a 1 to 5 scale (5 being highest). Use the spaces between checklist behaviors to make comments to explain your ratings.

- Prepares and distributes agenda in advance _____

- Consults with participants before meeting _____

- Establishes time parameters _____

- Maintains focused discussion _____

- Encourages participation by all _____

- Encourages clash of ideas _____

- Discourages clash of personalities _____

- Makes a proper closure _____

SUMMARY CHECKLIST

Take a few minutes to reflect on your performance and look over others' ratings of your team-building skills. Now assess yourself on each of the key learning behaviors. Make a check (✓) next to those behaviors on which you need improvement.

_____ **Ensure teams have the characteristics to make them effective.**
1. Small size—no more than about ten members.
2. Complimentary skills—technical, problem solving, interpersonal.
3. Common purpose—all agree on team mission and goals.
4. Specific goals—specific, measurable, and realistic.
5. Common approach—unified on the *means* for achieving goals.
6. Mutual accountability—individually and jointly accountable for the team's performance.

_____ **Facilitate the exploration of issues necessary to design high-performing teams.**
1. Who Are We? (strengths, weaknesses, work preferences, values, and beliefs)
2. Where Are We Now? (the team's strengths, weaknesses, opportunities, and threats)
3. Where Are We Going? (mission, purpose, and goals)
4. How Will We Get There? (action plans, which spell out who does what, when, and how)
5. What Is Expected From Us? (job description, roles, responsibilities, authority, and accountability)
6. What Support Do We Get/Need? (training, counseling, and mentoring)
7. How Effective Are We? (regular performance reviews of quantity and quality outputs)
8. What Recognition Do We Get? (praise, remuneration, fringe benefits, and promotions)

_____ **Recognize and facilitate the stages of team development.**
1. Forming—helping newly formed groups resolve uncertainties about purpose, structure, relationships, tasks, and leadership.
2. Storming—facilitating the resolution of conflicts about power and task structure.
3. Norming—integrating roles, goals, norms, and structure with a focus on increasing productivity. Continued building of trust and positive relationships.
4. Performing—preventing loss of enthusiasm and sustaining momentum.
5. Adjourning—preparing for termination of the team in temporary task forces.

_____ **Adapt leadership style to different stages of team development.**
1. Diagnose the needs of the team.
2. Use productivity-related behaviors to provide direction for task achievement.
3. Use morale-oriented behaviors to provide support and help the team work better together.
4. Structure style in the forming stage to provide needed direction.
5. Resolve style in the storming stage to provide both direction and support.
6. Collaborate style in the norming stage to provide continued support.
7. Validate style in the performing stage to reward and avoid interference with the team's demonstrated effectiveness.

_____   **Assess and solve problems to team effectiveness.**
1. Become aware of problems by determining symptoms of ineffective teams.
2. Gather data through interviews or questionnaires.
3. Analyze data.
4. Identify problems.
5. Determine action plans to solve problems.
6. Follow up to ensure effective implementation of solutions.

_____   **Prepare for team meetings** by setting objectives, selecting participants, planning the agenda, setting a time and place, distributing the agenda in advance, and consulting with participants.

_____   **Control team meetings.**
1. Begin with a review of the agenda and the meeting objectives.
2. Establish specific time parameters.
3. Encourage participation by all members in problem solving by active listening and encouraging the clash of ideas, but not personalities.
4. Reach a consensus decision and debrief the meeting process.
5. End the meeting by clarifying what happens next.

_____   **Follow up after the meeting** by distributing minutes that summarize the discussion, the decisions, and the action commitments that each participant has made.

APPLICATION QUESTIONS

1. How would you build a high-energy team out of a group of students with differing talents, goals, and levels of motivation, who were randomly put together to complete a class project?
2. Have you ever been a member of a team that has social loafers going along for a free ride? How did this condition develop? What were the consequences? Was anything done to rectify the situation? If so, what? If not, what should have been done?
3. Contrast a team you have been on where members trusted each other versus another group where members did not trust each other. How did these conditions develop? What were the consequences in terms of interaction patterns and performance?
4. One way to avoid conflicts at meetings is to avoid having the meeting in the first place. But if you do need to have a meeting, how would you suggest managing potential conflicts?
5. How did the last formal meeting you participated in compare with the guidelines for effective meetings presented in this chapter? What were the main differences and consequences?

REINFORCEMENT EXERCISES

1. Assess the skills of your friends and family. Who has the technical skills? Who has the problem-solving/decision-making abilities? Who has the interpersonal skills? If you can correctly identify them, you will be able to apply this to your team experiences.
2. Observe the interaction in a team you are on in a class or at work. Can you identify the team's strengths and weaknesses? If so, share them with the team and develop plans to make the team more effective.
3. Take a personal inventory of yourself as a team member. What are your strengths and weaknesses that would influence how you can most effectively contribute to a team?
4. Pay attention to what the leader does in meetings you attend, such as those of your sorority, fraternity, club, sports team, or work group. Make mental notes of what principles of effective planning and conducting the leader put into effect and how they contributed to the effectiveness of the meeting. Then think about what the leader could have done better.
5. The next time you get the chance, volunteer to plan or help plan a meeting. Put your new skills to work!

ACTION PLAN

1. Which team-building behavior do I want to improve the most?
2. Why? What will be my payoff?
3. What potential obstacles stand in my way?
4. What are the specific things I will do to improve? (For examples, see the Reinforcement Exercises.)
5. When will I do them?
6. How and when will I measure my success?

NOTES

1. L. Iacocca, *Iacocca: An Autobiography* (New York: Bantam Books, 1986) 74.

2. M. Gates, "The Quality Challenge: Can Managers and Workers See Eye to Eye?" *Incentive 163,* no. 8 (August 1989): 20–22.

3. M. E. Shaw, *Group Dynamics: The Psychology of Small Group Behavior,* 3d ed. (New York: McGraw-Hill, 1981) 11–12.

4. J. R. Katzenback and D. K. Smith, *The Wisdom of Teams: Creating the High-Performance Organization* (Boston: Harvard Business School Press, 1993) 45.

5. W. L. French and C. H. Bell, Jr., *Organization Development: Behavioral Science Interventions for Organization Improvement* (Upper Saddle River, NJ: Prentice Hall, 1990) 127; M. Mascowitz, "Lessons from the Best Companies to Work For," *California Management Review* (Winter 1985): 42–47; and W. G. Dyer, R. H. Daines, and W. C. Giauque, *The Challenge of Management* (New York: Harcourt Brace Jovanovich, 1990) 343.

6. R. D. Smither, "The Return of the Authoritarian Manager," *Training* (November 1991): 40.

7. A. Harmon, "TEAMWORK: Chrysler Builds a Concept as Well as a Car," *Los Angeles Times,* April 26, 1992, D1–D3.

8. J. R. Katzenback and D. K. Smith, *The Wisdom of Teams: Creating the High-Performance Organization* (Boston: Harvard Business School Press, 1993); and P. F. Drucker, "There's More Than One Kind of Team," *Wall Street Journal,* February 11, 1992, A16.

9. J. R. Katzenback and D. K. Smith, *The Wisdom of Teams: Creating the High-Performance Organization* (Boston: Harvard Business School Press, 1993) 43–64.

10. Ibid.

11. J. A. Sheppard, "Productivity Loss in Performance Groups: A Motivation Analysis," *Psychological Bulletin* (January 1993): 67–81.

12. C. Margerison and D. McCann, *Team Management Systems: The Team Development Manual* (Toowong, Queensland, Australia: Team Management Resources, 1990) 19–36.

13. T. G. Cummings and C. G. Worley, *Organizational Development and Change,* 5th ed. (St. Paul, MN: West, 1993) 226–28.

14. W. L. French and C. H. Bell, Jr., *Organization Development: Behavioral Science Interventions for Organization Improvement* (Upper Saddle River, NJ: Prentice Hall, 1990) 133–34.

15. A. Harmon, 1992, D1.

16. B. W. Tuckman and M. A. C. Jensen, "Stages of Small Group Development Revisited," *Group and Organizational Studies* 2 (1977): 419–27; M. F. Maples, "Group Development: Extending Tuckman's Theory," *Journal for Specialists in Group Work* (Fall 1988): 17–23; and C. Kormanski and A. Mozenter, "A New Model of Team Building: A Technology for Today and Tomorrow," in J. W. Pfeiffer and J. E. Jones, eds., *The 1987 Annual: Developing Human Resources* (San Diego: University Associates, 1987) 255–68.

17. D. Carew, E. Parisi-Carew, and K. Blanchard,*Team Development and Situational Leadership II* (Escondido, CA: Blanchard Training and Development, Inc., 1998) 4.

18. Information about length of duration of each stage of team development is based on R. B. Lacoursiere, *The Life Cycle of Groups: Group Development Stage Theory* (New York: Human Service Press, 1980).

19. This section is adapted from D. Carew, E. Parisi-Carew, and K. Blanchard,*Team Development and Situational Leadership II* (Escondido, CA: Blanchard Training and Development, Inc., 1998).

20. A. Harmon, 1992, D1.

21. W. G. Dyer, *Team Building: Issues and Alternatives,* 2d ed. (Menlo Park, CA: Addison-Wesley, 1987) 97–108.

22. W. G. Dyer, R. H. Daines, and W. C. Giauque, *The Challenge of Management* (New York: Harcourt Brace Jovanovich, 1990) 343.

23. K. D. Benne and P. Sheats, "Functional Roles of Team Members," *Journal of Social Issues* 4, no. 2 (Spring 1948): 41–49.

24. D. Ancona, T. Kochan, M. Scully, J. Van Maanen, and D. E. Westney, *Managing for the Future: Organizational Behavior & Process,* 2d ed. (Cincinnati: South-Western College Publishing, 1999). M-5, 9-10.

25. This section is adapted from the *Reading Book (Revised) of the NTL Institute for Applied Behavior*

Science (Washington, DC: The National Education Association, 1970) 23–24.

26. For more on emotional behavior in groups, see W. C. Schutz, "Interpersonal Underworld," *Harvard Business Review* 36, no. 4 (July–August 1958): 123–25.

27. F. Bartolome, "Teaching About Whether to Give Negative Feedback," *The Organizational Behavior Teaching Review* XI, no. 2 (1986–1987): 95–104.

28. R. Harrison, "When Power Conflicts Trigger Team Spirit," *European Business* (Spring 1972): 27–65.

29. E. A. Michaels, "Business Meetings," *Small Business Reports* (February 1989): 82–88.

30. A. S. Grove, "How (and Why) to Run a Meeting," *Fortune,* July 11, 1983, 132–39.

31. D. Stoffman, "Waking Up to Great Meetings," *Canadian Business* (November 1986): 75–79.

32. Ibid.

33. Adapted from D. D. Bowen, R. J. Lewicki, D. T. Hall, and F. S. Hall, eds., *Experiences in Management and Organizational Behavior*, 4th ed. (New York: John Wiley & Sons, 1982) 14–16.

34. Adapted from Roy J. Lewicki and Joseph A. Litterer, *Negotiation: Readings, Exercises, and Cases* (Homewood, IL: Richard D. Irwin, 1985) 423–25, 565, 568, 572, 606, 627.

PART V
Leading Skills

CHAPTER 15

Building a Power Base

Learning Objectives

After completing this chapter, you should be able to:

- Perform a political diagnostic analysis.

- Enhance your power base through impression management.

- Apply power tactics to get what you need.

- Utilize political strategies to enhance your power.

- Appropriately utilize defensive strategies to protect your power.

SELF-ASSESSMENT EXERCISE[1]

Directions. Answer true or false to indicate your beliefs about the following statements.

	True	False
1. Keeping the leader happy should take priority over other work.	_____	_____
2. The need and desire for power is universal.	_____	_____
3. Courtesy is one of the most effective tools for getting things done.	_____	_____
4. Power and politics are the foundations of most organizational results.	_____	_____
5. Managers need to be fair to subordinates.	_____	_____
6. In a fair organization, the people will succeed and get ahead.	_____	_____
7. It is necessary and effective to criticize subordinates for their mistakes.	_____	_____
8. Withholding my viewpoint and relevant facts to get along with someone with different prejudices would be a sellout of my integrity.	_____	_____
9. Being cordial to people, even if I don't like them, is as important as being good at my job.	_____	_____
10. I should not have to curry favor to get people to cooperate with me or to do the job they are paid to do.	_____	_____

Scoring.　Award yourself one point for each answer that matches the following key:

1. True	4. True	7. True	10. False
2. True	5. False	8. False	
3. True	6. False	9. True	

Interpretation.　Interpret your score according to the following directions. Keep in mind that this self-perception instrument has a wide variety of possible interpretations. The following descriptions are intended only to help you take a closer look at your own attitudes and potential behavior in political situations.

If you scored 0 to 3, your view of organizational politics is naive. People are likely to take advantage of you.

If you scored 8 to 10, you are extremely power oriented. You may actually be abrasive in your use of power and probably tolerate little pressure from others without fighting back. You may even turn an ordinary problem into an unnecessary confrontation for the pleasure of winning the point.

If you scored 4 to 7, you are in the assertive medium and tend to be cooperative or moderately competitive in your use of power, depending on how you read the situation. You do not mind confrontations, but usually will not provoke them.

CONCEPTS

In the first *Godfather* film, Marlon Brando plays the part of Don Corleone, the head, or Godfather, of a prominent Mafioso family. In one classic scene, the Godfather is told about an individual who is unwilling to comply with a family "request" to assassinate a difficult politician. The Godfather illustrates a perfect demonstration of power when he states this now-famous line: "I'm gonna make him an offer he can't refuse." The implied message was that either the person will comply or "take a swim with cement shoes"!

You may have already surmised from previous chapters how power can be used to produce positive outcomes in goal achievement, performance evaluation, career planning, problem solving, and work design. Power is a natural reality of organizational life and is not going away. Learning how power is acquired and exercised in organizations will help you manage others and your own career more effectively.

What Is Power?

Power is the capacity to influence an individual or group of individuals to behave in ways they would not on their own.[2] This definition implies a *dependency* relationship and a *potential* that need not be actualized, but only recognized, to be effective. The Godfather does not have to actually pull the trigger to obtain compliance because the person being influenced recognizes that his or her well-being is dependent upon doing what is requested.

Probably the most important aspect of power is that it is a function of dependence.[3] The more person A's well-being is dependent on person B, the more power person B has in the relationship. Dependence, in turn, is based on the alternatives that A is aware of and the importance that A places on the alternative(s) that B controls. If, for example, your boss has the authority to fire you, you desperately need your job to pay your bills, and you don't think it would be possible to find a comparable job, your boss is likely to have considerable power over you. Likewise, the Godfather could expect compliance with his requests because he knew that people value their lives.

Why Is Power Important?

Managers need power to do their jobs. Power is a means to facilitate goal attainment, solve problems, create strategy, evaluate performance, design work, motivate others, and manage teams. Also, in the real world of organizations, the "good guys" do not always win. At times, in order to get things done or to protect your interests against the maneuvering of others, you will have to play "hard ball." To play hard ball effectively, you need to have power.

How Can Power Be Acquired?

Power originates from an individual's *personal characteristics* and *position* in an organization.[4] Additional power can be acquired by creating dependency, impression management, and politicking.

Position Power

In formal organizations, managerial positions come with authority. *Authority* is the right to give orders and expect the orders to be obeyed. People accept position authority regarding legitimate activities as a part of the psychological contract of a job description. In addition, people in managerial positions typically have the discretion to allocate *rewards* and enact *punishments.* Managers can give out desirable work assignments, appoint people to interesting or important projects, provide favorable performance reviews, and recommend salary increases. They also can dish out undesirable work shifts and assignments, put people onto boring or low-profile projects, write unfavorable appraisals, recommend undesirable transfers or even demotions, and limit merit raises.

Managers need to realize, however, that position power is relative; commanding obedience is risky if the manager's performance depends on the creative action or expertise of subordinates.[5] Furthermore, if legitimate authority alone is consistently used to influence behavior, others will likely seek to gain counterbalancing power. Even the mere possession of formal authority isolates the manager from subordinates who inherently resist influence, fear possible punishment, or are simply uncomfortable with authority figures.[6] Nevertheless, formal authority is often necessary to resolve complex differences of opinion, as when a higher-level manager dictates a solution to how differences are to be resolved between two or more battling departments.

Personal Power

You don't have to be a manager with formal authority to have power. You can also influence others if you possess needed expertise, personal charisma, access to important information, and positive relationships with powerful associates.

Expertise   In today's high-tech world, expertise has become an increasingly powerful source of influence. As jobs become more specialized and complex, organizations have become dependent on experts with special skills to achieve goals. Software analysts, tax accountants, environmental engineers, and industrial psychologists are examples of individuals in organizations who influence others as a result of their expertise.

Charisma   Charisma exists when others identify with and are attracted to someone they admire.[7] If others want your acceptance because they like and admire you, you have what is known as *referent* power. When others refer to your behaviors as those they want to model themselves, you have considerable influence over what they do. Referent power explains why celebrities are paid millions of dollars to endorse products in commercials.

Access to Information   When others need information that only you have access to, you have power in the relationship because others are dependent on you for what they need to know. People in accounting, information systems, marketing, and purchasing often have access to information others seek, which gives them considerable influence. Control over the distribution of critically needed information enables people to define reality for others, which can influence how they perceive situations and how they behave. One example would be people in the accounting department who generate information about how salespeople are reimbursed for specific expenses. Another example is receptionists and secretaries who have access to information needed by others, sometimes even their bosses.

Association Power   We have all heard the saying, "It's not what you know, but who you know." In most organizations, success usually results from a combination of both. However, some people who possess no position or personal power themselves are able to influence others because they have close associations with other people who do have position and/or personal power. Family members, confidantes, and aides to public officials in powerful positions often develop friendships with office holders, which in turn gives them influence over others. Another example of people with association power are staff members with no formal organizational authority who develop close advisory relationships with the high-ranking managers.

Creating Dependency

When you alone control a resource that others want, you have power over them because they are dependent on you to provide it to them so they can meet their needs. Whether the resource you control is information, money, status, expertise, or friends in high places, the more important, scarce, and not substitutable it is, the more dependence others have on you, and the more power you possess over them.

To create dependency, the resources you control must be perceived as being important. At Intel, a technological company, engineers are clearly a powerful group because the company is extremely dependent on their knowledge to maintain its products' technical advantages and quality. At Procter & Gamble, however, marketing is the key to success, making marketers the most powerful occupational group.

A resource must also be perceived as scarce to create dependency. Scarcity explains how low-ranking organizational members who have important knowledge not available to high-ranking members can achieve power. Extreme examples of scarcity creation occur when people "lose" procedure manuals, refuse to train other people, and create specialized codes and languages.

Impression Management

Impression management is the process of shaping the image you project during interactions with others in order to favorably influence how others see and evaluate you.[8] Organization members are especially likely to use impression management tactics to affect the perception of their bosses on whom they are dependent for evaluations, raises, and promotions.[9] Nevertheless, impression management is utilized by individuals at all organizational levels as they interact with superiors, peers, and subordinates as well as with suppliers, customers, and other people outside the organization.

When using impression management to enhance your power in an organization, you want to create the image that you have the potential to alter circumstances so that others do as you request.[10] Some frequent impression management techniques are agreeing with someone else's opinion in order to gain his or her approval, making excuses to minimize the outcomes of mistakes, apologizing to get a pardon for negative actions, acclaiming desirable implications for yourself when sharing favorable events, using flattery to make yourself appear perceptive and likable, doing favors to gain a person's approval, and publicizing your associations with high-ranking managers.[11]

These techniques are often observed in the classroom when students pretend to be interested in lectures that they do not really care about. You can also probably think of several examples of impression management techniques when going on a first date with someone you are interested in.

Outright deceit can be used in impression management but is probably not that common. Ingrained moral or ethical codes prevent most people from deliberately misrepresenting themselves or lying, especially if the chances of being found out are great.[12] When applying for a job, for example, stating that you received a degree from a prestigious university when you did not graduate, or that you worked for a company when you never did, would not be perceived as honest by people and the probability is great that the truth would be found out during a reference check.

As a general guide, communications are ethical when they present accurate, relevant information. They are unethical when they prevent another person from securing information relevant to a choice. Unethical communications can produce a choice the other person would not normally make if he or she had all of the relevant information.[13]

Deception is the conscious alteration of information to significantly influence another's perceptions.[14] Deception includes lying, which is concealing or distorting truthful information, and behaviors that do not reflect our true feelings or beliefs, like smiling at people we dislike or acting busy to avoid more work.

An overt lie is a false statement made with deliberate intent to deceive. Covert lying occurs when you omit something relevant, leading others to draw incorrect inferences. Lying or hiding the truth is unethical because it prevents another person from getting complete and correct information to fully explore all possible alternatives.

Interpersonal deception is prevalent in the workplace. It is mainly used to avoid punishment,[15] but also serves to present a better image, protect others' feelings, attain personal goals, and avoid embarrassment.[16] Because honesty and trust are so important for productive long-term relationships, however, deception can be a serious flaw that can undermine your power.

It is also risky because most people can detect it by noticing behavioral changes. Common clues that indicate when people are practicing deception are vagueness, uncertainty, and reticence; messages that are less plausible; and speech that contains more errors and is less fluent.[17] Liars avoid eye contact and have a tendency to squirm more than honest people.[18]

Ethical behavior has important consequences for maintaining your power in an organization. When polled, people find honesty most important in a leader, friend, partner, or workmate. The biggest cost of lying is that you may lose the trust of other people who depend on you and on whom you depend.[19]

Given these ethical considerations, a definition of positive impression management might be an attempt to convey as positive an impression as possible without lying about one's capabilities, achievements, and experiences. Keep this definition in mind when engaging in impression management to obtain more desirable job assignments, promotions, raises, or the good opinions of others. Otherwise, your efforts could backfire and do considerable damage.

Politicking

All is not fair in organizations and you don't always win just by being a competent performer. There will be times when, to get things done or to protect your interests, you'll have to engage in politics. **Politicking** is taking actions to influence, or attempt to influence, the distribution of advantages and disadvantages within your organization.[20] It involves the use of strategies intended to tip the balance of power and influence decision outcomes in your favor.[21] By completing the following inventory you can determine your political tendencies.

How Political Are You?

It will take about 10 minutes to complete the following inventory and read the interpretation. To determine how political you are, check the answer that best represents your behavior or belief, even if that particular behavior or belief is not present all the time.

	True	*False*
1. You should make others feel important through an open appreciation of their ideas and work.	_____	_____
2. Because people tend to judge you when they first meet you, always try to make a good first impression.	_____	_____
3. Try to let others do most of the talking, be sympathetic to their problems, and resist telling people that they are wrong.	_____	_____
4. Praise the good traits of the people you meet and always give people an opportunity to save face if they are wrong or make a mistake.	_____	_____
5. Activities like spreading false rumors and planting misleading information are necessary, even though somewhat unpleasant, methods to deal with your enemies.	_____	_____
6. Sometimes it is necessary to make promises that you know you will not or cannot keep.	_____	_____
7. It is important to get along with everybody, even with those who are generally recognized as windbags, abrasive, or constant complainers.	_____	_____
8. It is vital to do favors for others so that you can call in these IOUs at times when they will do you the most good.	_____	_____
9. Be willing to compromise, particularly on issues that are minor to you, but major to others.	_____	_____
10. On controversial issues, it is important to delay or avoid your involvement if possible.	_____	_____

SOURCE: J. F. Byrnes, "Political Behavior Inventory." This all that was provided on p. 84 in S. P. Robbins, *Self-Assessment Library: Insights into Your Skills, Abilities, & Interests,* 2nd Ed. (Upper Saddle River, NJ: Pearson Education, 2002), pp 84–85. Used with permission.

Interpretation.   According to the author of this instrument, a complete organizational politician will answer "true" to all ten questions. Organizational politicians with fundamental ethical standards will answer "false" to questions 5 and 6, which deal with deliberate lies and uncharitable behavior. Individuals who regard manipulation, incomplete disclosure, and self-serving behavior as unacceptable will answer "false" to all or almost all of the questions.

Implications.   What are the implications of your scores for your political effectiveness and organizational power building in organizations? Which power tactics and political strategies are you most and least comfortable with? How might your political profile impact on your career choices? Are you happy with your results? If so, why? If not, why not? What can you do about it? Did you identify any behavior that you want to change as a result of this inventory? To help gain insights into these questions, read on about strategies for political effectiveness.

Whereas power can be a latent force (i.e., potential capability), politicking involves deliberate actions to develop and use power to advance your interests.[22] It is important to be skilled at politicking because political incompetence, political naiveté, and the inability or unwillingness to effectively perform required political tasks are all sources of management failure.[23] What are the steps to successful politicking?

Before you consider your political options you need to perform a comprehensive evaluation of the specific situation you are in. We recommend the following three-step political diagnostic analysis.

1. *Assess the organizational culture.*   Begin by assessing your organization's culture to ascertain which behaviors are deemed desirable or undesirable. One of the fastest and most effective means for tapping the power aspects of an organization's culture is to learn as much as you can about the organization's performance appraisal system and the criteria used for determining salary increases, promotions, and other rewards. Then turn your attention to the reward system. Determine who gets the raises and promotions, and who does not. These reward-allocation decisions can tell you what behaviors "pay off" in your organization and which behaviors do not.

2. *Assess the power of others.*   People are either powerful or they are not, right? Wrong! Power is differential. On some issues, a certain person may be powerful. Yet that same person may be relatively powerless on other issues. Consequently, you need to determine which individuals or groups will be most powerful in different situations. We suggest the following ideas for assessing power.

First, determine who has formal authority to affect the issues you are concerned about. Then consider what individuals, coalitions, and departments may have vested interests in the decision's outcome. This determination helps to identify the power players—those motivated to engage in politicking. It also pinpoints your likely adversaries. Next, specifically assess the power of each player or group of players. This assessment includes not only formal authority, but also the scarce resources each controls, such as key information or expert knowledge.

While you are at it, assess your boss's power status in the organization and his or her position on issues of concern to you. The support of a powerful boss can obviously benefit you. On the other hand, the support of a weak boss is likely to be of little help and can even be harmful to your cause. If your power assessment uncovers that your boss is widely perceived throughout the organization as "deadwood," you should probably attempt to create an image of distance between yourself and your boss to avoid guilt by association.

3. *Assess your own power.*   Determine where you stand relative to others who hold power. Examine your personal power with respect to each of the power bases already discussed. Does your position in the organization provide power through the authority to reassign people, approve time off, hand out salary increases, initiate suspensions, or fire employees? Are you fortunate enough to have charisma, that magnetic personality that draws others to you? Are others dependent on you for expertise or specialized information that they need? Do you have positive relationships with powerholders who support you and your position?

Also examine the dynamics between yourself and other powerholders. Determine the degree to which the other power players support or oppose you. Identify who your allies are; who your opponents are likely to be; the intensity of support or opposition each can be expected to exert; and the amount of personal, positional, and coalitional power you and your supporters can exert to counter the resistance of opponents.

Using Power to Maximize Your Managerial Effectiveness

How do you turn your conceptual understanding of power into effective influence strategies? Following are some general guides for improving your political effectiveness. Then some specific power tactics to translate your power bases into specific influence actions are explained.

What Can You Do to Improve Your Political Effectiveness?

If you want to be more politically adept in your organization, what can you do? The following strategies have been found to improve political effectiveness.[24]

1. ***Frame arguments in terms of organizational goals.*** People whose actions appear to blatantly further their own interests at the expense of the organization's are almost universally denounced. They are likely to lose influence, and may ultimately be expelled from the organization when the opportunity arises. Even if your objective is self-serving, your arguments should still emphasize the benefits that will accrue to the organization.

2. ***Develop the right image.*** Style is as important as substance for political success. Determine what your organization values and wants from its managers. Then apply impression management by dressing acceptably, associating with the "right" people, and applying the appropriate leadership style to project the desired image.[25]

3. ***Gain control of organizational resources.*** As mentioned previously, possession of needed knowledge and expertise are particularly effective in making you more valuable to the organization. Gaining control of important organizational resources that are scarce and nonsubstitutable can provide you with substantial leverage.

4. ***Make yourself appear indispensable.*** This strategy is the previous strategy applied to yourself: making yourself a valuable and nonsubstitutable resource to your organization. You do not really have to be indispensable as long as key people in the organization believe that you are. How do you make yourself appear indispensable? The most effective means is to develop expertise in areas critical to the organization's success. Maybe you already have skills that you can publicize. If not, you can plan to acquire them through experience in related work assignments, developing contacts with key information sources, or obtaining training in techniques needed by your organization. After that you can convince key decision makers through impression management that no one else possesses this expertise to the extent that you do.

5. ***Be visible.*** Because the evaluation of managerial effectiveness has a substantial subjective component, it is important that your boss and those in power in the organization be made aware of your contributions. If you are fortunate enough to have a job that brings your accomplishments to the attention of others, it may not be necessary to take direct measures to increase your visibility. Many jobs, however, require you to handle activities that are low in visibility, or your specific contributions may be indistinguishable because you are part of a team. In such cases, without creating the image of a braggart, you can call attention to yourself by giving progress reports to your boss and others, being seen at social functions, being active in your professional associations, and developing powerful allies who speak positively about your accomplishments. Another rule of thumb is to get assigned to projects that will increase your visibility.

6. ***Get a mentor.*** An important part of a manager's role is helping and developing subordinates by acting as a mentor. On the other hand, obtaining a high-ranking sponsor of your own signals to others in the organization that you have powerful resources behind you.

How do you get a mentor? The more contacts you make with higher-ups, both formally and informally, the greater chance you have of being singled out as someone's protégée. Participating in company golf tournaments, going out for drinks with colleagues after work, and taking on visible projects are examples of activities that are likely to bring you to the attention of a potential mentor.

7. ***Develop powerful allies.*** In addition to a mentor, you can cultivate contacts with other influential people at all levels in the organization. It is obviously helpful to have

friends in high places, but peer support and a strong following by subordinates also promote your influence in the organization. Any of these sources can provide you with important information that may not be available through normal channels. Also, at times decisions will be made by those with the greatest support. Strength in numbers makes the difference when decisions come down to a vote.

8. *Avoid "tainted" members.* Almost every organization has fringe members whose status is questionable. Their performance and perhaps loyalty are under close scrutiny. Carefully keep your distance from them. We all tend to judge others by the company they keep. Your own effectiveness might be called into question if you are perceived as being too closely associated with "tainted" people.

9. *Support your boss.* Your immediate future is in the hands of your current boss. Because this boss evaluates your performance, you should find out what criteria are used to assess your effectiveness and then do whatever is necessary to have your boss on your side.

Make every effort to help your boss succeed. First and foremost, never speak negatively about your boss to others. Support your boss when he or she is under siege. If your boss is moving up the organizational hierarchy, you will have increased likelihood of being pulled up as well because of your high-ranking ally.

What if your boss's performance is poor and power low? Politically, it is better to switch than fight. Your credibility will be challenged if your boss is perceived as weak. Your performance evaluations, even if highly positive, are not likely to carry much weight. You will suffer from guilt by association. It is extremely difficult to distance yourself from your immediate boss without your boss perceiving you as a traitor. The most effective solution in such a situation, and the one that carries the least risk, is to quietly lobby for a transfer, couching your request in terms of the organization's best interests (i.e., a transfer will increase your experience, prepare you to assume greater responsibilities, and allow you to make bigger contributions to the organization).

What Specific Power Tactics Can You Apply?

In this section, you will learn how to translate your power bases into specific actions to obtain the outcomes you desire. You will also learn specific strategies appropriate for different kinds of situations.[26]

1. **Reasoning** is the use of facts and data to make a logical or rational presentation of ideas. This strategy is most likely to be effective in a culture characterized by trust, openness, and logic; and where the vested interests of other parties in your request are low.
2. **Friendliness** is using flattery, creating goodwill, acting humble, and being supportive prior to making a request. It is more effective for obtaining favors than for selling ideas. Being friendly works best when you are already well liked and have a productive interpersonal relationship with the target of influence.
3. **Coalitions** exist when a number of other people in the organization support you and what you want to happen. Forming coalitions and using them effectively are complex actions and require planning and coordination. They are also most effective where the final decision relies more on the quantity than on the quality of support. Consequently, managing coalitions is usually only worth the energy when important outcomes are at stake in situations such as a committee meeting where the decision will be made by majority rule.
4. **Bargaining** involves the exchange of benefits or favors to negotiate outcomes acceptable to both parties. Bargaining is essential where two conflicting parties are interdependent and must rely on each other for goal accomplishment.

Bargaining is easier to apply where the organizational culture promotes give-and-take cooperation.

5. **Higher authority** consists of gaining the support of higher-ups in the organization to back your requests. This strategy is only effective in bureaucratic-structured organizations that have cultures with great respect for authority. It is only appropriate in less structured organizations where higher-ups have power because they are either liked or feared.

6. **Assertiveness** is being direct and forceful when indicating what you want from others. Examples of this approach are demanding compliance with requests, issuing reminders, ordering individuals to do what you need done, and pointing out that rules require compliance. This strategy is most effective when the balance of power is clearly in your favor. For example, because of your position you have considerable ability to reward and punish others, and their power over you is low. The drawback to this method is that the target is likely to feel resentful and look for later opportunities to retaliate.

7. **Sanctions** is the use of organizationally derived rewards and punishments to obtain desired outcomes. Examples include preventing or promising a salary increase, threatening to give an unsatisfactory performance appraisal, and withholding a promotion. This strategy is similar to assertiveness, except the influence here depends solely on your position. Obviously, it is not an approach for influencing superiors; and even when used with subordinates, it may be perceived as manipulative or illegitimate.

Should You Use Defensive Behaviors to Protect Your Power?

Organizational politics includes protection of self-interest as well as promotion. Individuals often engage in reactive and protective "defensive" behaviors to avoid action, blame, or change.[27] This section discusses common varieties of defensive behaviors classified by their objectives.

Avoiding Action

Sometimes the best action is no action. However, role expectations typically dictate that you at least give the *impression* of doing something. Six popular ways to avoid action while appearing supportive are overconforming to rules, passing the buck to others, pretending to be unaware of what is going on, depersonalizing requests, providing an image of being so overburdened that you have no time for additional activities, and stalling so you can avoid decisive conflicts when you are the underdog.

Avoiding Blame

Six commonly used tactics can help you avoid blame for actual or anticipated negative outcomes. One is *documenting activities* to protect yourself against others who may try to pin the blame for mistakes on you. It is like having an alibi or "covering your rear." Another is *playing it safe* by evading situations that may reflect unfavorably on you. Better to be safe than sorry. Third is *justifying actions* by developing explanations for negative outcomes that lessen your responsibility, which is called developing a "spin" or rationalization for why you are not at fault. *Scapegoating* involves redirecting the blame for a negative outcome elsewhere. Examples are "if it weren't for what he did," or "now see what you made me do." *Misrepresenting* involves leaving out, changing, or distorting facts so that behaviors and intentions are evaluated differently than they actually were. It is often accomplished through distortion, embellishment, deception, or selective presentation. *Escalating commitment* occurs when you increase time and resources to a poor decision. The hope is that these actions will signal your commitment to turning around a negative outcome, which will cause others to remain confident in you.

Avoiding Change

People avoid change if they feel that the result will be a decrease in their relative power. Two forms of defensiveness frequently used by people who feel personally threatened by change are resisting change altogether so that it never occurs, and protecting turf to defend your territory from encroachment by others.

Effects of Defensive Behavior

In the short run, the use of defensiveness may suitably promote your self-interest. But in the long run, defensiveness usually becomes a liability. First of all, ethics becomes an issue because some defensive behaviors may be viewed as unethical by the actor or others. If so, defensive behaviors can have negative consequences on the actor's self-esteem and career. You may want to review Chapter 5 on ethics to derive more potential consequences.

Another problem is that defensive behavior frequently becomes chronic or even pathological over time. People who constantly rely on defensiveness find that eventually it becomes the only way they know how to react to change. At this point, defensive people lose the trust and support of their peers, bosses, subordinates, and clients. In moderation, however, defensive behavior can be an effective device for surviving and flourishing in an organization. In fact, it is often deliberately or unwittingly encouraged by management.

Consider the Cost-Benefit Equation

Before you select a political strategy or power tactic, be sure to weigh all the potential costs of using it against its potential benefits. Some forms of power are accepted more readily than others, and in many instances, the costs of applying influence exceed the benefits derived. While the benefits of power are quite obvious, the costs are often overlooked. It has been noted, "Power is effective when held in balance. As soon as power is *used,* it gets out of balance and the person *against whom* the power is used automatically resorts to some activities designed to correct the power imbalance."[28]

Through physics, we learn that for every action there is an equal and opposite reaction. As applied to the study of management, it means that every use of power has a corollary reaction by those it is used on. Consequently, your choice of a power strategy should depend on consideration of both sides of the equation. On the one hand, is it the most effective and efficient way to achieve your short-term goals? On the other hand, what are the consequences? For example, will it minimize resentment, use up the least possible amount of future credits, and avoid other negative reactions? Such analysis usually suggests a preference for strategies emphasizing reason, friendliness, and rewards to obtain compliance, and avoidance of coercive approaches.[29] Remember, whenever you use the "do this or else" approach, you run the risk that your bluff will be called or that the future negative reactions will be worse than your immediate gains. In other words, in cost-benefit terms the results may not be desirable; you may win the battle but lose the war.

Even if you can "get away with it," ethical considerations must be weighed along with the effect they have on your self-esteem. When considering political actions, Exhibit 15-1 illustrates a decision tree containing three questions you can ask yourself to determine whether your actions are ethical.

The first question checks to see whether your actions are consistent with the organization's goals, or merely self-serving. The second ensures that your action respects the rights of other involved parties. The third relates to whether the political activity conforms to standards of equity and justice. Be careful when answering these questions to be truthful and avoid rationalizations, which may justify the behaviors that benefit you. As discussed in Chapter 5, the long-run benefits from ethical political behavior will outweigh the short-term gains from rationalizing questionable behaviors.

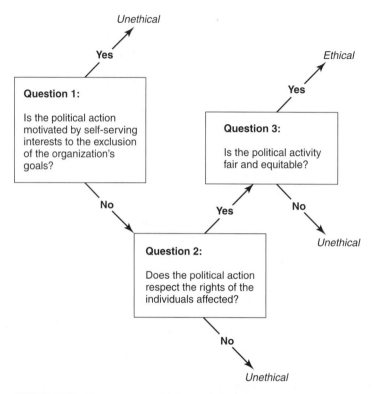

EXHIBIT 15-1   Is a Political Action Ethical?

SOURCE: Based on G. F. Cavanagh, D. J. Moberg, M. Valasquez, "The Ethics of Organizational Politics," *Academy of Management Journal* (June 1981): 363–74.

CONCEPT QUIZ

Complete the following true-false quiz by circling the correct answer. Answers are at the end of the quiz. After marking your answers, remember to go back and check your understanding of any answers you missed.

True or False   1. Most people try to conceal their influence attempts because the application of power is unethical.

True or False   2. The degree of power one person holds over another is primarily a function of dependency in the relationship.

True or False   3. It is what you know, not who you know, that determines your power in an organization.

True or False   4. Power is potential, but politics is action.

True or False   5. A manager does not have to be concerned about acquiring power in larger organizations because with enough resources the "good guys" always win.

True or False   6. You cannot have power in a large organization unless you have a position that has formal authority.

True or False   7. Defensive behaviors that protect your self-interests are effective in the long run.

True or False   8. Impression management relies on the idea that style is as important as substance.

True or False 9. Effective politicking requires covering up self-interest and framing arguments in terms of organizational goals.

True or False 10. "Winning the battle but losing the war" is an important consideration when deciding on specific power tactics.

Answers. (1) False; (2) True; (3) False; (4) True; (5) False; (6) False; (7) False; (8) True; (9) True; (10) True

BEHAVIORAL CHECKLIST

The following skills are important when building a power base. Use them when evaluating your power-building skills and those of others.

The Effective Power Builder

- Identifies where the power is in the organization.
- Attempts to make others dependent.
- Practices impression management.
- Applies formal authority sparingly.
- Constantly strives to develop personal power bases.
- Frames desires in terms of organizational benefits.
- Considers the cost-benefit equation before selecting a political strategy or power tactic.
- Uses defensive behaviors only sparingly for short-term survival.

Attention!
Do not read the following until assigned to do so by your instructor.

MODELING EXERCISE

Role-Play: Power and the Truck Trading Problem[30]

All class members should read the following situation.

Situation. A large electric appliance company has six repair technicians. It is necessary for them to drive to various locations in the city to complete their work. Each repair technician drives a small truck and takes pride in keeping it looking good. The technicians have a possessive feeling about their trucks and like to keep them in good running order. Naturally, they would prefer to have new trucks because it gives them a feeling of pride.

A new truck has just been allocated to the crew. The new truck is a Chevrolet. The supervisor has just called a meeting to determine who will get the new truck.

Here are some facts about the trucks and the repair technicians in the crew who report to Sean Marshall, the supervisor of appliance repairs. Most technicians do all of their driving in the city, but Jo and Charlie cover the jobs in the suburbs.

Jo: 17 years with the company, has a 2-year-old Ford truck
Bo: 11 years with the company, has a 5-year-old Dodge truck
Jean: 10 years with the company, has a 4-year-old Ford truck
Charlie: 5 years with the company, has a 3-year-old Ford truck
Fran: 3 years with the company, has a 5-year-old Chevrolet truck

Directions.   After the class reads the previous situation, pick one role-player to be the supervisor and five more role-players to be crew members. The role-players read the reminders for role-playing and their own role, but not the other roles, and prepare for the role-play.

The remainder of the class will be observers and provide feedback on the power dynamics in the role-play. They should be divided into five equal groups, each of which is assigned to observe one of the specific role-players. Observers should NOT read any of the roles. The observers' job is to see whether they can determine which power bases and political tactics the various role-players are applying. They also provide specific feedback to their assigned role-player on his or her effectiveness in applying power in the exercise. Observers should review the Observer's Rating Sheet to prepare for providing meaningful feedback at the end of the exercise.

Sean Marshall's Role   You are the supervisor of a crew of repair technicians, each of whom drives a small service truck to and from the various jobs. Every so often you get a new truck to exchange for an old one, and you have to decide which of your crew will receive the new truck. Even though you always try to be fair, the decision often generates hard feelings because each crew member feels entitled to the new truck. No matter what you decide, most of the crew is unsatisfied. You now have to face the issue again because a new Chevrolet truck has just been allocated to you for distribution.

Most of the crew drive in the city and make fairly short trips. The exceptions are Jo and Charlie who cover the suburbs. In order to solve the problem this time, you have decided to allow the crew to decide who gets the new truck themselves. You will tell them about the new truck and will put the problem in terms of what they think would be the most fair way to distribute the truck. You will avoid taking a position yourself because you want to do what the crew thinks is fair.

If the crew is unable to reach a consensus themselves, you can always exercise your supervisor's authority to make the final decision. You know that it is your responsibility as supervisor to guide and direct the meeting.

Jo's Role   You have to do more driving than most of the other technicians because you work in the suburbs. You have a fairly old truck and feel your large amount of driving makes you the best candidate for a reliable new truck. You were an automobile mechanic prior to becoming an appliance technician and you know that several trucks have problems that can be easily fixed to make them perfectly satisfactory for their current drivers. If any of these drivers argue for the new truck, you will explain how to make easy repairs rather than discarding them. You plan to assertively use your expertise in favor of winning the new truck for yourself.

Jean's Role   When a new Chevrolet truck becomes available, you think you should get it because you have the most seniority and do not like your present truck. Your personal car is a Chevrolet, and you prefer the Chevy truck you drove before you were allocated the current Ford. You have known Sean Marshall's boss since you both hired on as technicians more than 20 years ago. If your seniority does not work to get you the new truck, maybe a tactful bit of name dropping will do the job.

Fran's Role   You have the least desirable truck in the company. It is five years old, and before you got it, it was in a bad wreck. It never has driven well and feels unsafe, but you have put up with it for three long years and feel the next one should be yours. You have an admirable accident record. In fact, the only accident you ever had occurred when you sprung the door of Charlie's truck when he opened it as you backed out of the garage. You hope the new truck is a Ford because you prefer driving them to other brands. You are well liked by the rest of the crew because of your charismatic personality. You plan to use friendliness, flattery, and humility to really sweet talk the crew during the meeting in hopes of securing the new truck for yourself.

Charlie's Role   The heater in your present truck is inadequate. The door lets in too much cold air, and you attribute your frequent colds to this problem. You want a warm truck because you have a good deal of driving to do. As long as it has good tires, brakes, and is comfortable you don't care about its make. Although Fran never admitted it, you know that it was Fran who backed into the door of your truck, and it has never been repaired to fit right. You also know that Dodge trucks have better maintenance records than other makes, and that an allocation is currently pending for another new truck next month. You plan to use this information to bargain for the new truck for yourself.

Bo's Role   You feel you deserve a new truck. Your present truck is old, and beause the senior man has a fairly new truck, you should get the next one. You have taken excellent care of your present Dodge and have kept it looking like new. A person deserves to be rewarded for treating a company truck like a personal vehicle. You plan to use this logic to reason with the others that those who conscientiously maintain their vehicles should get their just desserts.

OBSERVER'S RATING SHEET

On completion of the exercise, rate how well the role players applied the power-building skills using the following rating scale. Write concrete examples in the space below each skill component to use when explaining your feedback. Also note examples of behaviors that demonstrate applications of power tactics and political strategies and indicate how effective they were.

1 Unsatisfactory	2 Weak	3 Adequate	4 Good	5 Outstanding

Name of Person Observed _____

- Identified where the power is in the organization.   _____

- Attempted to make others dependent.   _____

- Practiced impression management.   _____

- Applied formal authority sparingly.   _____

- Constantly worked to develop personal power bases.   _____

- Framed desires in terms of organizational benefits.   _____

- Considered the cost-benefit equation before selecting tactics.   _____

- Used defensive behaviors only sparingly for short-term survival.   _____

GROUP EXERCISES

Three different types of group exercises are presented here. First is a case for you to practice your awareness, analysis, and action planning skills. Second is an exercise for you to apply and get feedback about your personal power strategies. Third is an opportunity to solicit the help of others to analyze and plan how to better build your power base.

Group Exercise 1: Case Analysis of the Bill and Mary Show[31]

Instructions.   The following case can be discussed in small groups or by the class as a whole. It should take about 15 minutes to read and think about the questions, then another 20 to 30 minutes to discuss the case.

Case.   Mary Cunningham was a hot topic at Bendix Corporation long before September 1980, when Bill Agee stood before more than 600 employees and denied that her rapid advancement had anything to do with "a personal relationship that we have." Cunningham joined the company right after obtaining her MBA from Harvard in June of the previous year. She was hired as executive assistant to the CEO, Bill Agee, after a three-hour interview in New York at the Waldorf-Astoria. "A meeting of kindred spirits," she said. Exactly one year later, Agee gave her a promotion to vice president for corporate and public affairs. Three months after that came another promotion to vice president for strategic planning. Agee tried to confront the uproar that immediately followed by announcing to employees that his new vice president and he were "very, very good friends" but not romantically involved. The comment backfired, creating a national media furor so intense and so focused on Cunningham's youth, blonde hair, and shapely figure that in the fall of 1980 the Bendix board of directors forced her resignation.

Inside Bendix, gossip about the relationship between Cunningham and Agee escalated after her June promotion, and all sorts of additional events kept the noise level up. A television camera focusing on former President Gerald Ford at the Republican National Convention happened to find Agee and Cunningham sitting next to him. Some Bendix people suggested that Agee was less accessible than he had once been, and Cunningham's growing influence with him did not help to allay suspicions. She had called herself his "alter ego" and "most trusted confidante"; he said she was his "best friend."

Top corporate executives in the United States had been accused of almost everything imaginable except having romances with one another. But, what was one to think? Here were two attractive people working together, traveling together, even staying in the same two-bedroom suite at the Waldorf Towers. They had to be having an affair—that would explain Cunningham's sprint up the ranks. On the other hand, was Cunningham, as Gail Sheehy portrayed her in a four-part newspaper series, a brilliant, idealistic corporate missionary destroyed by jealous cynics? Barbara Seaners interviewed Cunningham, and feminist leaders like Gloria Steinem rallied to her defense asking whether her treatment meant that young, talented, attractive, ambitious, and personable female executives were permitted only slow climbs upward, lest they invite gossip.

Insisting that their relationship had been platonic until after she left Bendix, Agee and Cunningham married in June 1982. By then, Agee had converted to Catholicism and divorced his wife of 25 years. Cunningham's six-year marriage to Howard Gray, an executive with American Express, was annulled. The same year, after resurfacing as a vice president at Seagram's, Cunningham acted as Agee's unpaid adviser during Bendix's attempted takeover of the Martin Marietta Corporation. Their ambitious plan collapsed, however, when Bendix was swallowed by the Allied Corporation in a merger that cost hundreds of Bendix employees their jobs. The fiasco was blamed, in part, on the chair's young wife, the strategic planner.

In 1988, Bill Agee was named CEO of the Morrison Knudsen Corporation in Boise, Idaho. Six years later, in 1994, Morrison Knudsen posted losses of $310 million and lurched toward bankruptcy. In February 1995, Bill Agee was ousted as MK stock fell from $30 a share to $5\frac{1}{2}$; employees and retirees alike watched their futures evaporate. In February, too, Mary Agee resigned as executive director of the nonprofit Morrison Knudsen Foundation, a position critics say she used to benefit the Nurturing Network, a nonprofit women's organization that she founded in 1983.

The Boise community did not regret the Agees' demise. It was not only the shareholders' losses and the hundreds of MK workers Bill Agee fired, but the fact that the Agees rubbed Boise the wrong way almost from the start—so much so that after being excluded from the town's private clubs and most prestigious boards, the couple and their two children abruptly relocated in 1992, to a $3.4 million estate in Pebble Beach, California. From that Pacific Coast setting 600 miles away from their offices, Mary Agee managed her charity and Bill Agee ran Morrison Knudsen by phone, fax, FedEx, and from a $17 million corporate Falcon jet peeved MKers dubbed "Mary's taxi."

Now, with more than a dozen lawsuits filed by shareholders charging that Bill Agee and the Morrison Knudsen board wasted assets and managed the company recklessly, Mary Agee's role is under legal as well as public scrutiny regarding the use of MK assets to benefit the Nurturing Network. The lawyers are also eyeing the close relationship linking MK and its foundation with the Nurturing Network—a complex web of friendships, business interests, and moral commitments. In 1992, half the MK board members had wives on the Nurturing Network board, and Bill Agee served on both boards. "Once so many of the directors and their wives had joined with the Agees in … a moral crusade," the *New York Times* pointedly asked, "how likely was it that they would challenge Mr. Agee in the boardroom?"

QUESTIONS FOR DISCUSSION

1. What are the major power issues in this case?
2. What were Mary Cunningham's original power bases when she first joined Bendix? What other sources of power did she acquire? How?
3. What bases of power did Bill Agee have? Did he acquire any more?
4. How did the effectiveness of Bill Agee's power bases change? Why?
5. How did politics enter into this case? What were the consequences?
6. What could Bill and Mary have done differently to avoid the negative outcomes?

OBSERVER'S RATING SHEET

When you finish reading the case, rate how well both Bill Agee and Mary Cunningham applied power building skills, using the following rating scale. Write concrete examples in the space below for each skill component to use when discussing your ratings.

1 Unsatisfactory	2 Weak	3 Adequate	4 Good	5 Outstanding

	Bill	Mary
• Identified where the power is in the organization.	_____	_____
• Attempted to make others dependent.	_____	_____
• Practiced impression management.	_____	_____
• Applied formal authority sparingly.	_____	_____
• Constantly worked to develop personal power bases.	_____	_____
• Framed desires in terms of organizational benefits.	_____	_____
• Considered the cost-benefit equation before selecting tactics.	_____	_____
• Used defensive behaviors only sparingly for short-term survival.	_____	_____

Group Exercise 2: Role-Play: Power Plays Within Universal Care, Inc.

This role-playing exercise enables class members, working in groups of 7 to 10, to experience political behaviors when confronted with obvious differences in power. You will assume the position of a vice president who sits on the board of directors. Because a variety of crises have been plaguing the firm, the CEO just resigned and you and other company vice presidents must now elect a replacement from among your peers. When told by your instructor, your group will assemble as a board of directors to nominate, discuss, and eventually to elect the new CEO using the bylaws of UCI. Following the board meeting and election, you will then discuss what you learned.

Purpose. The exercise serves three purposes: (1) to create complex and realistic roles from sketchy data; (2) to confront issues and negotiate decisions when actors have explicit power differences; and (3) to stimulate introspection about your personal reactions to having more or less power than other group members and the behaviors you use to deal with power discrepancies.

Time. 45 to 60 minutes.

Materials. One index card per student (5 × 7 suggested) and one felt-tip marker per group.

Background on Universal Care, Inc. Universal Care, Inc., was founded 15 years ago by a physicist, a biologist, a chemist, and an engineer. The company has grown erratically into what is now a $5 billion multidivisional firm. UCI branched beyond its entrepreneurial beginnings in molecular research into diverse lines of business, all related to health care. The firm currently has products in pharmaceuticals, genetic engineering, medical instrumentation, residential nursing, and prosthetics (including a mechanical heart).

During the past year, UCI has increasingly come under a variety of pressures, even attacks. Several lawsuits against the firm for alleged product malfunctions that resulted in injury or death were won by the plaintiffs. Fortunately, no class action suits have yet been settled against the company, although two are pending—one involving a heart implant valve alleged to be associated with three patient deaths. Three suits have been filed by other biotech firms alleging infringement of patents on DNA-related products. Several of these incidents have made the front pages of major daily newspapers, each raising questions about the propriety of the firm's products and/or operations.

Management is faced with the likelihood of a significant fourth-quarter loss that is expected to result in negative earnings for the year (which ends in two months). The expected loss is due to a combination of legal judgments against UCI; reserves set aside for possible future legal losses; intensified competitive action in several product segments, causing loss of market share; and the difficulty in assimilating seven recent acquisitions (especially in the residential nursing segment). Additionally, a number of key employees in research and management have recently defected, leaving human resource gaps in some key areas. (A few of these former employees left after blowing the whistle on questionable company practices.)

Under these intense pressures, the CEO announced today a personal decision to resign and take early retirement, effective in two weeks. Because of the rapid growth of the firm in the past few years, no serious effort had been given to developing a successor. Now, however, the company faces a pressing need for a new CEO, and the corporate bylaws are explicit on the process. According to the wishes of the founders (who withdrew from active management within two years of UCI's going public six years ago), the bylaws state that a new CEO must be elected from the ranks of incumbent managers who sit on the board of directors.

You are a vice president of UCI and a member of the board of directors. You are quite concerned by the sudden resignation of the CEO and the need to quickly elect a replacement. A special board meeting has been scheduled solely for the purpose of electing a new CEO. You have a little time to prepare for that meeting and to communicate selectively with some of your peers on the board.

ROLE-PLAY PREPARATION

1. Students form "companies" of 7 to 10 members. Sit in a circle or around tables, if possible, facing one another within a company.
2. Students read "Background on Universal Care, Inc."
3. While students are reading, the instructor distributes to each group a number of 5 × 7 index cards equal to the number of team members, and one marker each.
4. After reading the background note, each person within a company selects a vice presidency, such as finance, operations, the medical instruments division, etc.
5. One person per team marks the index cards with numbers, beginning with 200 and working up in 100 unit denominations until all cards are used (equal to the number of team members). Numbers should be written so that when folded into a tent shape, a number will appear on both sides. Now, that person shuffles and deals the cards face down, one to a person.
6. The number on the card each person receives represents the number of shares of stock they own or control by proxy. Once the directors (vice presidents) move into the election phase of the board meeting, shares of stock become important in electing a new CEO. Students write the title (vice presidency) they are assuming and display their card in front of them for others to see.

Phase 1: E-Mail Communications   Because of Universal's problems, all VPs are out in the field putting out fires. Although they cannot communicate face-to-face with one another, they keep in touch by e-mail. You initiate e-mails by writing notes (on paper) and passing them to others with whom you want to communicate. As an "interested executive and board member," the instructor is concerned about the forthcoming board meeting for the specific purpose of selecting a new CEO (who must be one of the VPs).

As VPs you can communicate to whomever you want about whatever you want, but most likely you will discuss the pending election, candidates, qualifications, and so on. If you want several people to receive the same message, provide a routing by listing names. Use this phase as an opportunity to get into your role. You have about 5 minutes for this email phase.

Phase 2: Face to Face at Company Headquarters   When the instructor calls time on the e-mail phase, everyone stands up. All VPs are now back at company headquarters, waiting for the board meeting to begin. You may now caucus with whomever you choose. Join up with the person or persons you want to meet with and then back away from the table for your conversations. This time is not for a meeting of the whole—you'll get that opportunity soon enough.

Phase 3: Board Meeting   When instructed to by the facilitator, take a seat for the board meeting. The facilitator will pick a VP and introduce him or her: "The outgoing chair and CEO has asked that [person] with _____ shares of stock chair this meeting. The CEO has also provided a written reminder that the bylaws are specific on how to elect a new CEO. Discussions and nominations are in order, as are questions to the candidates and perhaps a formal statement from candidates. Once the group is ready to vote, follow these guidelines. Voting must be public by voice, beginning with the person who controls the greatest number of shares, working to the smallest in descending order. When it is your time to vote, you can split votes (shares) among the candidates, or can abstain; however, if you abstain, you cannot reenter voting for that round of voting. If an impasse (no clear winner) occurs, then on the next round of voting anyone who previously abstained can now vote. To elect a new CEO requires a vote of two-thirds of all outstanding shares. You may begin your board meetings." When finished, report your results to the instructor.

Debriefing. Discuss the following questions in your groups to bring out reactions to power differences and to methods of exerting influence or political behavior.

1. For those with low power (200–400 shares), what was your initial reaction once you realized the significance of the number you were dealt? What did this suggest to you about the possible strategy you might follow to be heard and perhaps influential? How about high power people?
2. Who received the most e-mail messages? Why? What is the significance of this phase?
3. What did people with low power do during the e-mail phase to increase their base of power? How about the high-power players?
4. Describe the nature of coalitions formed within your company and the extent to which they remained together or either broke up or consolidated?
5. What other political behaviors did you either observe or engage in? Why were political behaviors more or less effective?
6. Of those of you with high power, did anyone choose not to seek the CEO position, and if so, why?
7. What were your overall reactions to having to confront the reality of working with people where formal power was hierarchically differentiated? Did high-power or low-power people feel more comfortable with this situation, and why?

Group Exercise 3: Personal Power Strategies for Allocating Resources

In preparation for this exercise, students should review the bases of power and influence tactics described in the text. They should also be advised in advance to bring $1 to class on the day of the exercise and to be prepared to risk it if they wish to participate.

Purpose. To increase awareness of power bases and strategies participants actually use, and to provide feedback on how their political effectiveness can be enhanced.

Time. Total time is 45 minutes: 30 minutes for the exercise; 15 minutes for feedback and debriefing.

Instructions. The class is divided into groups of six to eight participants. Each group member must contribute $1 to a pot. It is possible that a participant will lose his or her $1. On the other hand, it is possible that he or she will receive more than originally contributed or even the whole pot. The money distribution will be made at the end of the exercise according to the following procedure:

Each group's task is to decide how to divide the money in the pot any way they want between two thirds of its members, i.e., two people in a group of six will not get their money back. It is not legitimate to use any sort of chance procedure like drawing straws, or to avoid the exercise like agreeing to return each person's money after the exercise regardless of what happens. The final decision is to be determined by group consensus, i.e., all must agree to the final allocation. Do not make a hasty decision. Wait until all have argued their viewpoints and are ready to decide.

The objective for each individual participant is to get as much money as possible for him or herself. The 30-minute time limit in which the group must make its consensus decision is critical. The time limit is important, because if a group cannot decide how to allocate the money in 30 minutes, the instructor gets the entire pot!

Reflection. Immediately following the end of the exercise, each participant should write down the answers to the following questions:

1. What were your feelings during this exercise?
2. What power bases did you draw upon?
3. What influence strategies did you utilize?
4. How successful were you in achieving your goals? Why?
5. What did you learn about yourself with respect to how you feel and deal with power and politics?

Debriefing. One at a time, *each participant* should (1) discuss answers to the preceding questions with others in the group; (2) receive feedback regarding the effectiveness of his or her personal power tactics; and (3) solicit suggestions about how they could be improved. After each individual has received feedback, the *total group* discusses (1) why the winners (those who received the most money) were more successful than the losers (who lost their money); (2) how the outcome might be different under different circumstances; and (3) what they learned about using power in conflict situations.

SUMMARY CHECKLIST

Take a few minutes to reflect on your performance and look over others' ratings of your power-building skills. Now assess yourself on each of the key learning behaviors. Make a check (✓) next to those behaviors on which you need improvement.

_____ **Identifying where the power is in the organization.**
1. Assess the organizational culture for desirable behaviors, the performance-appraisal system, and the criteria used for determining salary increases, promotions, and other rewards.
2. Assess your own power by examining your personal power (expertise, charisma, associations, etc.) and your position power (formal authority).
3. Assess the power of others by determining who has formal authority, discovering coalitions, and finding out who controls scarce resources.

_____ **Making others dependent.**
1. Gain control of important scarce resources.
2. Develop needed expertise.
3. Acquire needed specialized information that others need.

_____ **Practicing impression management.**
1. Agree with others' opinion in order to gain their approval.
2. Make excuses to minimize the outcomes of mistakes.
3. Apologize to get a pardon for negative actions.
4. Claim desirable implications for yourself when sharing favorable events.
5. Use flattery to make yourself appear perceptive and likable.
6. Do favors to gain a person's approval.
7. Publicize your associations with the high ranking.

_____ **Applying formal authority sparingly.**
1. Use discretion to allocate rewards and enact punishments.
2. Be on the lookout for resistance to formal authority, such as lack of upward communications, coalition formation, and decreased creativity.

_____ **Developing personal power bases.**
1. Acquire needed expertise.
2. Develop personal charisma.
3. Gain access to important information.
4. Build positive relationships with powerful associates.

_____ **Framing desires in terms of organizational benefits.**
1. Avoid actions that appear to blatantly further your own interests at the expense of the organization's.
2. Emphasize the benefits that will accrue to the organization.

_____ **Considering the cost-benefit equation before selecting a political strategy or power tactic.**
1. Weigh all potential costs of a strategy against potential benefits.
2. Consider all potential consequences, such as minimizing resentment, not using up future credits, and avoiding other negative reactions.

_____ **Using defensive behaviors only sparingly for short-term survival.**
1. Use defensive behaviors for protection of self-interest.
2. Avoid using defensive behaviors to avoid action, blame, or change.

APPLICATION QUESTIONS

1. Can you be an effective manager in a large organization and avoid politics?
2. You have just joined a large organization as a first-line supervisor. Using your power-building skills, what can you do to increase the probability of succeeding on this job?
3. How are you currently involved in power and politics on your job, in your classes, and with those you live with?
4. How do you currently practice impression management? Give examples.

REINFORCEMENT EXERCISES

The following suggestions are activities you can do to reinforce the power-building techniques in this chapter. You may want to adapt them to the Action Plan you will develop next, or try them independently.

1. Review six recent issues of _Business Week_ or _Fortune_ magazine. Look for articles on reorganizations, promotions, and departures from upper management. Do these articles suggest that power or political factors were involved in the management changes? Explain.
2. Interview three managers from three different organizations. Ask them to describe the roles that they perceive power and politics play in decision making in their organization. Ask for examples that they have participated in or been affected by.
3. Watch a movie based on organization power and politics and see what you can learn from it about how power is acquired, utilized, and what the consequences of using power are. Example movies are _The Firm, Godfather I_ and _II, Nine to Five, Disclosure, Rising Sun,_ or _Goodfellas._
4. Review newspaper, magazine, or television shows (such as _New York Times, Time,_ or "60 Minutes" 1998–1999) about the presidential impeachment of President Bill Clinton. What implications about power and politics can you draw from the cast of characters [e.g., Monica Lewinsky, Kenneth Starr] and the processes of investigation and impeachment?

ACTION PLAN

Think of a situation in which you want to increase your power. Develop a plan to do so, applying what you have learned in this chapter.

1. Why do I want to increase my power? What will be my payoff?
2. Where is the power in the organization?
3. How can I make others dependent on me and decrease my dependency on them?
4. What are the specific things I will do to increase my personal power? For example, frame desires in terms of organizational benefits, practice impression management, and use defensive behaviors only sparingly for short-term survival.
5. When will I do them?
6. How and when will I measure my success?

NOTES

1. This instrument appeared in E. Raudsepp and J. C. Yeager, "Power in the Pecking Order: Do You Act Like a Top Chicken?" *Inc.* 3, no. 3 (March 1981): 42–46.
2. See, for instance, H. Mintzberg, *Power In and Around Organizations* (Upper Saddle River, NJ: Prentice Hall, 1983); K. Pfeffer, *Managing with Power* (Boston: Harvard Business School Press, 1992); and R. I. Dilenschneider, *On Power* (New York: Harper Business, 1994).
3. R. E. Emerson, "Power-Dependence Relations," *American Sociological Review* 27 (1962): 31–41.
4. Based on J. R. P. French, Jr., and B. Raven, "The Bases of Social Power," in D. Cartwright, ed., *Studies in Social Power* (Ann Arbor: University of Michigan, Institute for Social Research, 1959), 150–67; G. E. Littlepage, J. L. Van Hein, K. M. Cohen, and L. L. Janiec, "Evaluation and Comparison of Three Instruments Designed to Measure Organizational Power and Influence Tactics," *Journal of Applied Social Psychology* (January 1993): 107–25.
5. N. W. Biggart, "The Power of Obedience," *Administrative Science Quarterly* 29 (1984): 540–49.
6. S. H. Ng, *The Social Psychology of Power* (London: Academic Press, 1980) chapter 3.
7. A. Schweitzer, *The Age of Charisma* (Chicago: Nelson-Hall, 1984).
8. B. R. Schlenker and M. F. Weigold, "Interpersonal Processes Involving Impression Regulation and Management," in M. R. Rosenzweig and L. W. Porter, eds., *Annual Review of Psychology* 43 (Palo Alto, CA: Annual Reviews Inc., 1992), 133–68.
9. M. R. Leery and R. M. Kowalski, "Impression Management: A Literature Review and Two-Component Model," *Psychological Bulletin* 107 (1990): 34–47.
10. K. K. Eastman, "In the Eyes of the Beholder: An Attributional Approach to Ingratiation and Organizational Citizenship Behavior," *Academy of Management Journal* (October 1994): 1379–91.
11. S. J. Wayne and R. C., Liden, "Effects of Impression Management on Performance Ratings: A Longitudinal Study," *Academy of Management Journal* (February 1995): 232–60; W. L. Gardner and M. J. Martinko, "Impression Management in Organizations," *Journal of Management* (June 1986): 332; and R. B. Cialdini, "Indirect Tactics of Image Management: Beyond Basking," in R. A. Giacalone and P. Rosenfeld, eds., *Impression Management in the Organization* (Hillsdale, NJ: Lawrence Erlbaum Associates, 1989) 45–71.
12. M. R. Leery, and R. M. Kowalski, "Impression Management: A Literature Review and Two-Component Model," *Psychological Bulletin* 107 (1990): 34–47.
13. J. A. DeVito, *The Interpersonal Communication Book,* 6th ed. (New York: Harper Collins Publishers, 1992) 77.
14. M. Knapp and M. Comadena, "Telling It Like It Isn't: A Review of Theory and Research on Deceptive Communication," *Human Communication Research* 5 (1979): 270–85.
15. D. McLellan, "That's a Lie," *Los Angeles Times,* February 9, 1993, E3.
16. B. Goss and D. O'Hair, *Communicating in Interpersonal Relationships* (New York: Macmillan, 1988), 258–66.
17. M. Cody, P. Marston, and M. Foster, "Deception: Paralinguistic and Verbal Leakage," in R. Bostrom, ed., *Communication Yearbook* 8 (Beverly Hills, CA: Sage Publications, 1978).
18. R. Kraut, "Verbal and Nonverbal Cues in the Perception of Lying," *Journal of Personality and Social Psychology* 36 (1978): 380–91.
19. D. McLellan, 1993, E3.
20. D. Farrell and J. C. Petersen, "Patterns of Political Behavior in Organizations," *Academy of Management Review* (July 1982): 430–42.
21. A. Drory and T. Romm, "The Definition of Organizational Politics: A Review," *Human Relations* (November 1990): 1133–54.

22. J. Pfeffer, *Managing with Power: Politics and Influence in Organizations* (Boston: Harvard Business School Press, 1992) 7.

23. S. Young, "Developing Managerial Political Skills: Some Issues and Problems," paper presented at the National Academy of Management Conference, Chicago, August 1986; K. E. Lauterbach and B. J. Weiner, "Dynamics of Upward Influence: How Male and Female Managers Get Their Way," *Leadership Quarterly* (Spring 1996): 87–107; K. R. Xin and A. S. Tsui, "Different Strokes for Different Folks? Influence Tactics by Asian-American and Caucasian-American Managers," *Leadership Quarterly* (Spring 1996): 109–32.

24. S. P. Robbins and P. L. Hunsaker, *Training in Interpersonal Skills,* 2d ed. (Upper Saddle River, NJ: Prentice Hall, 1996) 131–34.

25. C. K. Stevens and A. L. Kristof, "Making the Right Impression: A Field Study of Applicant Impression Management During Job Interviews," *Journal of Applied Psychology* (October 1995): 587–606.

26. This section is adapted from D. Kipnis, S. M. Schmidt, C. Swaffin-Smith, and I. Wilkinson, "Patterns of Managerial Influence: Shotgun Managers, Tacticians, and Bystanders," *Organizational Dynamics* (Winter 1984): 58–67; B. Keys and T. Case, "How to Become an Influential Manager," *Academy of Management Executive* (November 1990): 38–51; G. Yukl, H. Kim, and C. M. Falbe, "Antecedents of Influence Outcomes," *Journal of Applied Psychology* (June 1996): 309–17.

27. This section is based on B. E. Ashforth and R. T. Lee, "Defensive Behavior in Organizations: A Preliminary Model," *Human Relations* (July 1990): 621–48.

28. D. J. Lawless, *Effective Management* (Upper Saddle River, NJ: Prentice Hall, 1972) 243.

29. P. A. Wilson, "The Effects of Politics and Power on the Organizational Commitment of Federal Executives," *Journal of Management* (Spring 1995): 101–18.

30. Adapted from N. R. F. Maier, *Problem Solving and Creativity in Individuals and Groups* (Belmont, CA: Brooks/Cole Publishing Company, 1970) 298–302.

31. Based on L. Berman, "The Gospel According to Mary," *Working Woman* (August 1995): 47–49, 68–72; and P. W. Bernstein, "Things the B-School Never Taught," *Fortune,* November 3, 1980, 53–56.

CHAPTER 16

Leading

Learning Objectives

After completing this chapter, you should be able to:

- Differentiate between management and leadership opportunities.

- Know how and when to act as a transactional or transformational leader.

- Adapt your leadership style to follower needs.

- Facilitate followers in finding paths to goals.

- Use charisma to influence others.

- Act as a servant leader.

SELF-ASSESSMENT EXERCISE

Are You Ready for Leadership?[1]

For each statement, circle the number on the scale that best describes you.

	Strongly Agree				Strongly Disagree
1. I like to stand out from the crowd.	5	4	3	2	1
2. I feel proud and satisfied when I influence others to do things my way.	5	4	3	2	1
3. I enjoy doing things as part of a group rather than achieving results on my own.	5	4	3	2	1
4. I have a history of becoming an officer or captain in clubs or organized sports.	5	4	3	2	1
5. I try to be the one who is most influential in task groups at school or work.	5	4	3	2	1
6. In groups, I care most about good relationships.	5	4	3	2	1
7. In groups, I most want to achieve task goals.	5	4	3	2	1
8. In groups, I always show consideration for the feelings and needs of others.	5	4	3	2	1
9. In groups, I always structure activities and assignments to help get the job done.	5	4	3	2	1
10. In groups, I shift between being supportive of others' needs and pushing task accomplishment.	5	4	3	2	1

Scoring.

> ***Leadership Readiness Score:***   Add the scale values you circled on items 1 through 5: _____
>
> ***Leadership Style Score:***
>> ***Task Emphasis Score:***   Add the scale values you circled on items 7 and 9: _____
>>
>> ***Relationship Emphasis Score:***   Add the scale values you circled on items 6 and 8: _____
>>> Difference between task and relationship scores: _____
>>> Check the higher score: task _____ relationship _____.
>
> ***Adaptability Score:***   Your score on item 10: _____

Interpretation.   *Leadership readiness.* If your total score on items 1 through 5 is 20 or more, you are likely to enjoy being a leader. If 10 or less, at this time in your life you are likely more interested in personal achievement. If you score in the middle range, your leadership potential could go either direction, depending on events.

Leadership style. Your leadership style is suggested by your responses to items 6 through 10. Check the following totals to determine whether you prefer a task-oriented, relationship-oriented, or flexible leadership style.

Your *leadership style preference* is indicated by which is the highest of your task emphasis or relationship emphasis scores. The difference between these scores indicates how strong this preference is.

Your *leadership style adaptability* is indicated by your adaptability score. A score of 4 or 5 on item 10 suggests you may adapt to circumstances as you see the need.

CONCEPTS

Fortune magazine proclaimed Larry Bossidy "the most sought-after CEO in America."[2] Bossidy left the number two position at General Electric in 1991 to take the helm at ailing Allied-Signal, and has since been courted by IBM, Kodak, Westinghouse, and others. Brutally demanding and seldom satisfied, Bossidy sets challenging growth targets for his managers, helps them lay out strategies, provides resources, then grills them to make sure they follow through.

Bossidy is not a leader who isolates himself in his executive suite, making only the big, global decisions. Instead, he immerses himself in the operating details of Allied-Signal's 20 businesses and guides unit managers in crafting business strategies. He claims, "A strategist divorced from operations is an incomplete person. You make far better judgments doing both."

Leaders such as Larry Bossidy are the people who create, grow, and transform organizations. They lead change processes and redirect people's energies toward transformation of products, technologies, and organizational practices to produce growth. At the same time, they manage to preserve order and achieve productivity. They have to manage costs and timetables and coordinate tasks across departments so that quality and efficiency are achieved.

As a manager, Bossidy is able to excel at driving down costs and developing innovative processes for getting work done more efficiently. He is also a visionary leader who provides a clear sense of direction for transforming ideas into commercial successes, and he energizes others by challenging them to help make possibilities come true. Larry Bossidy is both an accomplished manager and a superlative leader.

What Distinguishes Leaders from Managers?

Managers exist at all levels of organizations, with titles such as supervisors, managers, directors, administrators, or executives. They typically devote most of their day to managing resources, projects, and deadlines to achieve stated organizational objectives. *Leaders*, on the other hand, excite people about visions of opportunities and empower them to innovate and excel. Like managers, leaders can be found at all organizational levels. Unlike managers, leaders do not necessarily need a title to effectively guide and control—in fact, the leader may not be a manager at all. Managers can be leaders, but leaders do not have to be managers.

Managers Have *Authority* to Be in Charge, Leaders *Influence* Others to Follow

Because of the position they hold, managers are people granted the formal authority to be in charge of an organization or one of its subunits. They are responsible for controlling activities to achieve organizational goals. *Authority* is the right to make decisions and commit organizational resources based on one's position within the organizational hierarchy. Managers draw on their position of authority to make decisions and initiate action.

Leadership is the process of providing direction, energizing others, and obtaining their voluntary commitment to the leader's vision.[3] A leader creates a vision and influences others to share that vision and work toward the goals. It is easy to think of world leaders, such as presidents of countries or successful organizations, who are *formal leaders* because they hold a stated, defined position. You may work, or associate with, people who are always stirring up new ideas, championing new causes, and inspiring others to pursue different directions. Such *informal leaders* do not have the advantage of formal authority, but they emerge in leaderless teams to provide direction and enthusiasm for goal attainment.

Managers Do Things Right, Leaders Do the Right Things

Managers are concerned with doing things right: mastering routines and maintaining control to achieve their assigned goals in the most efficient manner. Sometimes, unfortunately, managers are efficient at doing things that are no longer appropriate because the environment has changed. Leaders, on the other hand, are more concerned with being effective: doing the right things to accomplish the organization's mission, which often entails changes to match environmental developments.[4]

Jack Welsh, former CEO of General Electric, provided an outstanding example of how a leader can promote change in an organization that is efficient in doing the wrong things. In 1981 when Welsh became CEO, one-half of GE's $27.2 billion in revenue came from aging slow-growth businesses. Welsh decided that the company was wasting capital by staying in businesses that weren't going to be champions, so he divested more than $16.2 billion of marginal businesses, and spent $53 billion on acquisitions of growth companies. Welsh's shorthand slogan was that the company must be "No. 1, or No. 2, in every business that GE is in, or we fix, close, or sell it."[5]

All organizations need both managers and leaders. Although one person, like Larry Bossidy, might fill the roles of both manager and leader, those roles exhibit distinct differences. Management involves controlling complexity, while leadership involves initiating change.[6]

Transactional Versus Transformational Leadership

Transactional leaders perform the functions of management such as planning, directing, controlling, budgeting, and measuring results. They generally focus on keeping an organization running smoothly and efficiently. Transactional leaders determine and then meet follower needs, and in exchange, followers perform required tasks and meet specified objectives. Transactional leaders build followers' confidence and help them succeed by clarifying expectations. Because they focus on commitment to "follow the rules," and "do things right," transactional leaders usually maintain stability within the organization.

To lead an entire organization through major changes, *transformational leaders* are required. They tend to be more visionary and concerned about charting a mission and direction. These pathfinders are entrepreneurs and charismatic leaders who are more concerned about where the organization ought to try to go than in keeping it on a steady course.[7] Both types of leadership behaviors are necessary and effective leaders, like Larry Bossidy in this chapter's opening vignette, exhibit both transactional and transformational leadership patterns. This chapter focuses primarily on transactional leadership skills, and Chapter 18 looks at how transformational leaders bring about change.

Leader Traits

Successful leaders do stand out from other people, but traits such as drive and self-confidence are by themselves not sufficient to predict leadership success. They are only preconditions or enablers from which leaders must initiate actions such as clarifying a vision, setting goals, and role modeling.[8] So what is the right stuff that leaders are made of?

Recent research has found that, above all, followers look most for credibility in their leaders.[9] Credibility means being honest, competent, forward looking, and inspiring. Another stream of recent research concludes that six traits distinguish leaders from nonleaders: drive, leadership motivation, honesty and integrity, self-confidence, cognitive ability, and knowledge of the business.[10] Exhibit 16-1 summarizes these qualities. When followers look to leaders for direction and inspiration, they expect to find embodied in them certain characteristics. Leaders "need to have the 'right stuff' and this stuff is not equally present in all people."[11] Personal characteristics are important; however, they are merely a precondition for jump-starting leadership. The leader's behavior and cognitive skills make the real difference in leadership success.

EXHIBIT 16-1　Traits That Distinguish Leaders

As you read the following descriptions of these six traits, try to create an image of a leader at work. Does this describe you?

- *Drive.* Has the need for achievement through challenging assignments, the desire to get ahead, high energy to work long hours with enthusiasm, tenacity to overcome obstacles, and initiative to make choices and take action that leads to change.
- *Leadership motivation.* Exemplifies a strong desire to lead, the willingness to accept responsibility, the desire to influence others, and a strong socialized desire for power—the desire to exercise power for the good of the organization.
- *Honesty and integrity.* Demonstrates truthfulness, honesty, and consistency between word and deed, is predictable, follows ethical principles, is discreet, and makes competent decisions.
- *Self-confidence.* Gains the trust of others by being sure of own actions and not being defensive about making mistakes. Being assertive and decisive, maintaining emotional stability (not losing one's cool), and remaining calm and confident in times of crisis.
- *Cognitive ability.* Has a keen mind and thinks strategically, reasons analytically, and exercises good judgment in decisions and actions; has the ability to reason deductively and inductively.
- *Knowledge of the business.* Beyond formal education, develops technical expertise to understand the concerns of followers, comprehends the economics of the industry, and knows the organization's culture and behavior.

SOURCE: S. A. Kirkpatrick and E. A. Locke, "Leadership: Do Traits Matter?" *Academy of Management Executive* 5 (May 1991); 48–60.

Leader Behaviors

Ultimately, people decide whether they want to follow a leader based on his or her behavior. More than 50 years of research have determined only two overriding types of leader behaviors.[12] *Task-oriented behavior* focuses on careful supervision of group members to obtain consistent work methods and accomplishment of the job. It centers on *initiating structure* to establish reporting relationships, channels of communication, and methods of procedure. *Employee-oriented behavior* aims at satisfying the social and emotional needs of group members. It focuses on *showing consideration* to develop friendship, mutual trust, respect, and warmth among the leader and staff members.[13]

Neither behavior alone ensures maximum work-group performance and satisfaction.[14] In general, leaders high in *both* initiating structure and showing consideration tend to have better follower performance and satisfaction than leaders low in either or both. However, these outcomes often are conditional on other variables so trying to predict group performance solely on the basis of a consistent leader behavior is usually a futile endeavor.

Other research has focused on leader decision-making behaviors and its impact on productivity and satisfaction. Four principal *leader decision styles* are identified in Exhibit 16-2, according to the degrees of task and relationship behavior exhibited.[15] The first is *autocratic*, characterized by unilaterally taking charge and giving assignments to others. The *democratic* style is easy-going, using suggestions and encouragement to reach a group consensus. With the *laissez-faire* style the leader is passive and noncommittal, allowing others to make their own decisions independently. The fourth decision style is *participative*, emphasizing consultation with those who are involved to gather data and opinions before making a decision.[16]

Although there have been proponents of each decision style, the most appropriate use of these different leader behaviors depends on a number of organizational contingencies including the task complexity, the leader's formal power, and the time frame available, and follower characteristics such as competency, motivation, goals, and attitude toward the leader. Chapter 9 provides the Vroom and Yetton framework for deciding which decision style to apply, considering these contingencies. Other leader skills needed to deal with these contingencies include adapting to follower needs, explaining and motivating others to follow paths to goals, applying charisma to obtain follower commitment, and acting as a servant leader.

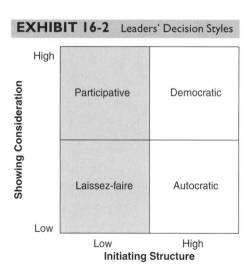

EXHIBIT 16-2 Leaders' Decision Styles

The Situational Leadership Model

In Paul Hersey and Kenneth Blanchard's situational leadership model, combinations of task and relationship behaviors are prescribed relative to the maturity of followers. *Task behaviors* include things such as organizing and defining roles, explaining what activities need to be done, establishing organization structure, channels of communication, and methods of getting jobs accomplished. *Relationship behaviors* include maintaining personal relationships with followers by opening channels of communication, providing socioemotional support (psychological strokes), and facilitating behaviors.[17]

Followers' have two types of maturity: job maturity, or their ability to do required tasks, and psychological maturity, or their degree of willingness to complete required tasks on their own. Job maturity depends on the degree to which followers have the skills, education, and experience to accomplish required tasks. Psychological maturity depends on followers' motivation to take responsibility for achieving goals."[18] Follower maturity varies with the task. For example, a salesperson may be particularly responsible in securing new sales but very casual about completing the paperwork necessary to close on a sale. As a result, it is appropriate for her manager to leave her alone in terms of closing on sales, but to supervise her closely in terms of her paperwork until she can start to do well in that area, too.[19]

Effective leader behaviors in relation to follower maturity are presented in Exhibit 16-3. To determine the appropriate leadership style, select one of the four boxes indicating your estimate of a follower's maturity. Draw a line straight upward; where it

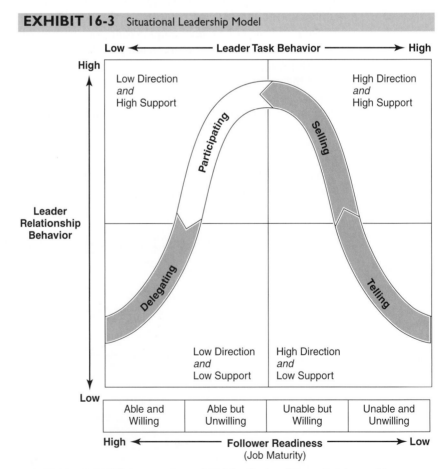

EXHIBIT 16-3 Situational Leadership Model

SOURCE: Based on Paul Hersey, Kenneth H. Blanchard and Dewey E. Johnson, *Management of Organizational Behavior*, 8th ed. (Upper Saddle River, NJ.: Prentice Hall 2001) 182.

intersects the normal curve indicates the appropriate leader behavior. As a follower's job maturity changes, the leader's behavior toward that person should also change.

For example, an assistant grocery store manager hires a new cashier who has never worked in that environment. The manager begins the socialization by emphasizing responsibilities and training in how tasks should be performed (high task behavior—"telling" style). As the cashier begins to demonstrate that she can handle basic jobs, the leader shifts to providing reassurance and praise to make the cashier feel valued (high relationship behavior—"selling" style). Over time, the leader's task guidance diminishes as performance becomes self-sustaining. Once the cashier reaches a high level of competence, the leader grants greater autonomy (for example, the ability to cash checks without the manager's approval). Interaction then occurs on an as-needed, or participating, basis.

Path-Goal Theory

The major concern of path-goal theory is how a leader can increase employees' motivation to attain organizational goals. As illustrated in Exhibit 16-4, a leader can increase follower motivation by clarifying followers' pathways to obtaining organizational goals and by providing meaningful personal rewards.[20] When clarifying paths to goals, leaders help employees identify and learn the behaviors that will enable them to successfully accomplish tasks. Second, leaders consult with employees to determine which rewards are important to them. Then the leader increases personal payoffs to employees for goal attainment.

Like situational leadership, the path-goal approach indicates that leaders engage in instrumental (task) behaviors and supportive (relationship) behaviors that combine to form four leadership styles.[21] *Directive leadership* (highly task oriented) lets followers know what is expected of them, provides guidance as to what is to be done and how, clarifies performance standards and time schedules, and calls attention to work procedures and policies. *Achievement-oriented leadership* (highly task and relationship oriented)

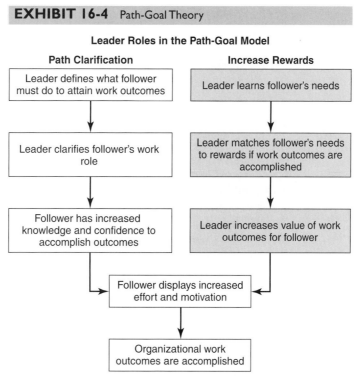

EXHIBIT 16-4 Path-Goal Theory

Leader Roles in the Path-Goal Model

Path Clarification	Increase Rewards
Leader defines what follower must do to attain work outcomes	Leader learns follower's needs
Leader clarifies follower's work role	Leader matches follower's needs to rewards if work outcomes are accomplished
Follower has increased knowledge and confidence to accomplish outcomes	Leader increases value of work outcomes for follower

Follower displays increased effort and motivation

Organizational work outcomes are accomplished

SOURCE: Based on B. M. Bass, "Leadership: Good, Better, Best," *Organizational Dynamics* 13 (Winter 1985): 26–40.

establishes challenging goals, seeks performance improvement, and displays confidence that people will exert high levels of effort. *Participative leadership* (moderately task and highly relationship oriented) involves consulting with and soliciting the ideas of others in decision making and action taking. *Supportive leadership* (highly relationship oriented) shows concern for the needs and goals of others and strives to make the work situation pleasant and equitable.

Two important contingencies determine which leadership style will be most effective for motivating employees in different situations. The first one, like situational leadership, concerns the personal maturity level of employees: ability, skills, needs, and motivations. The second contingency factor concerns three environmental conditions: the degree of task structure, the leader's formal authority, and the quality of interpersonal relationships among group members.

Task-focused instrumental leader behavior helps followers clarify ambiguous roles. Under conditions of low task structure (complex and/or ambiguous jobs), instrumental leaders have higher follower job satisfaction and goal attainment, but in highly structured tasks, such as purchasing or accounts payable, group members view instrumental leader behavior as an attempt to exert added, unnecessary structure and control over their lives—too much management. In well-defined and routine situations, supportive relationship behavior from the leader is more appropriate.[22]

Charismatic Leadership

Charismatic leaders have the ability to inspire and motivate people to do more than they would normally do, despite obstacles and personal sacrifice. They have an emotional impact on people because they appeal to both their hearts and minds. Charismatic leaders can raise people's consciousness about new possibilities and motivate them to transcend their own interests for the sake of the team, or organization.[23]

Herb Kelleher, CEO of Southwest Airlines, and Mary Kay Ash, CLO of Mary Kay Cosmetics, have been examples of charismatic leaders. They used special relationships with their followers and elicited high levels of performance, loyalty, sacrifice, and enthusiasm. They developed visions to which they were strongly committed that touched the emotions of their followers. Such leaders are very self-confident, good at communicating, take risks, and act in unconventional ways.[24]

Kelleher and Ash represent examples of *ethical charismatic leaders* who use power to serve others, align their vision with their followers' needs and aspirations, accept and learn from criticism, encourage followers to think independently, work to develop followers into leaders, and rely on internal moral standards. Unfortunately, there is also a dark side to charisma, as exemplified by Hitler.[25] *Unethical charismatic leaders* are motivated by personalized power, pursue their own vision and goals, censure critical or opposing views, encourage blind obedience, dependency, and submission in their followers, and lack an internal moral compass.[26]

Charismatic leaders excel in managing the four areas of attention, meaning, trust, and self. They manage attention by being highly committed to a compelling vision or outcome. They manage meaning by making ideas seem real and tangible for others. They manage trust by being reliable and congruent so that people know what they stand for. And they manage self by knowing and using their skills effectively, learning from mistakes, and focusing on success rather than failure.[27] Exhibit 16-5 presents a short inventory to help you assess your own potential for charismatic leadership.

Charismatic leaders apply five practices to accomplish extraordinary achievements in their organizations. They are

1. *Challenging the process.*   Questioning the status quo, seeking new opportunities to improve and grow, and taking risks.
2. *Inspiring a shared vision.*   Envisioning an uplifting and ennobling future.

EXHIBIT 16-5 Have You Got Charisma?

This short quiz will help you determine whether you have characteristics that are associated with charismatic leaders. Circle the answer that best describes you.

1. I am most comfortable thinking in
   a. Generalities
   b. Specifics
2. I worry most about
   a. Current competition
   b. Future competition
3. I tend to focus on
   a. The opportunities I've missed
   b. The opportunities I've seized
4. I tend to
   a. Promote traditions and procedures that have led to success in the past
   b. Suggest new and unique ways of doing things
5. I tend to ask
   a. How can we do this better?
   b. Why are we doing this?
6. I believe
   a. There's always a way to minimize risk.
   b. Some risks are too high.
7. I tend to persuade people by using
   a. Emotion
   b. Logic
8. I prefer to
   a. Honor traditional values and ways of thinking
   b. Promote unconventional beliefs and values
9. I would prefer to communicate via
   a. A written report
   b. A one-page chart
10. I think this quiz is
    a. Ridiculous
    b. Fascinating

Scoring and Interpretation. The following answers are associated with charismatic leadership: 1. a; 2. b; 3. a; 4. b; 5 b; 6. a; 7. a; 8. b; 9. b; 10. b

If you responded in this way to seven or more questions, you have a high charisma quotient and may have the potential to be a charismatic leader. If you answered this way to four or fewer questions, your charisma level is considered low. Do you believe a person can develop charisma?

SOURCE: Based on "Have You Got It?" a quiz that appeared in Patricia Sellers, "What Exactly Is Charisma?" *Fortune*, January 15, 1996, 68–75.

3. ***Enabling others to act.*** Fostering collaboration and empowerment
4. ***Modeling the way.*** Setting a good example and planning small wins.
5. ***Encouraging the heart.*** Recognizing individual contributions and celebrating team accomplishments.[28]

Servant Leadership

In the United States, the growing interest in spirituality has brought with it the notion that leaders should be stewards who choose service over self-interest.[29]

Leaders subscribing to stewardship are willing to be accountable for the well-being of the larger organization by operating to serve rather than to control those around them. Servant leaders accept the duty to be a servant to those responsible to them.[30]

Servant leadership turns the traditional authority upside-down. Servant leaders transcend self-interest to serve the needs of others, help others grow and develop, and provide opportunity for others to gain materially and emotionally. The fulfillment of others is the servant leader's principal aim. Jesus Christ has been described as the epitome of the servant leader. Of course, it is doubtful whether normal human beings can ever achieve this level of pure selflessness in service to others, but it's a vision to aspire to.[31]

Some companies have shown, however, that they can operate from the basic precepts of servant leadership. Shell Oil Company, for example, encourages servant leadership among its managers and defines a servant leader as one who

- recognizes that, as an individual, one does not have all the answers.
- is able to demonstrate a sense of humility and vulnerability.
- advances the transformation of him- or herself, others, and the organization
- builds the capability of the organization and the people in it.[32]

In addition to the principles of stewardship, servant leaders act in the following four ways:[33]

1. ***Put service before self-interest.***   Servant leaders use their power and influence to help individuals and the organization grow, versus advancing their own well-being. They view the organization as existing as much to provide meaningful work to people as the people existing to perform work for the organization. Servant leadership means doing what is right for others even if it does not pay off financially.
2. ***Listen first to affirm others.***   The servant leader knows that he or she does not have all the answers. Consequently, servant leaders know they need to listen to others. By careful listening, they can better understand the problems others are dealing with and take actions that will further their desires.
3. ***Inspire trust by being trustworthy.***   Servant leaders build trust by doing what they say they will do, being totally honest with others, giving up control, and focusing on the well-being of others. They share all information, good and bad, and they make decisions to further the good of the group rather than their own interests. In addition, trust grows from trusting others to make their own decisions. Servant leaders gain trust because they give *everything* away—power, control, rewards, information, and recognition. Trust allows others to flourish.
4. ***Nourish others and help them develop.***   Servant leaders help others accept their responsibilities and self-actualize, that is, become all they are capable of becoming. This requires an openness and willingness to share in the pain and difficulties of others. Being close to people also means leaders make themselves vulnerable to others and are willing to show their own pain and humanity.

CONCEPT QUIZ

Complete the following true-false quiz by circling the correct answer. The answers are at the end of the quiz. After marking your answers, remember to go back and check your understanding of any answers you missed.

True or False   1. Path-goal leadership is most effective when applied in highly structured and routine job situations.

True or False   2. Transformational leaders are much like managers—concerned with controlling resources and tasks in an organization.

True or False	3. Transactional leaders can be a resisting force to change because of their concern with maintaining stability in the organization.
True or False	4. Transformational leaders bring about change by creating a vision and empowering followers to work toward it.
True or False	5. Managers do things right; leaders do the right things.
True or False	6. Six traits can predict leadership success.
True or False	7. The major concern of path-goal leaders is how to increase employees' motivation to attain organizational goals
True or False	8. Charismatic leaders encourage the hearts of followers.
True or False	9. Servant leaders turn traditional authority upside-down.
True or False	10. Servant leaders gain trust because they give *everything* away.

Answers. (1) False; (2) False; (3) True; (4) True; (5) True; (6) False; (7) True; (8) True; (9) True; (10) True

BEHAVIORAL CHECKLIST

The following skills are important to effectively leading others. Use them when evaluating your own leadership skills and those of others.

Effective Leaders

- Promote changes to match environmental developments.
- Create an inspiring vision.
- Maintain control to achieve goals efficiently.
- Adapt leadership style to follower maturity.
- Empower others to act by clarifying pathways to goals.
- Provide meaningful rewards for goal attainment.
- Model desired behaviors.
- Put service to stakeholders before self-interest.
- Listen to learn and affirm others.
- Inspire trust by being trustworthy.
- Help others develop.

> **Attention!**
> Do not read this or the following exercises until assigned to do so by your instructor.

MODELING EXERCISE

What Does the Leader Do Now?

Purpose. What would you do as a leader as you encounter changing situations? This role-play gives several members of the class the opportunity to test their approach.

Time. 20 minutes.

Directions. Two people volunteer to be leaders, one for situation A, the other for B. Next, everyone reads the background for situation A. Then, leader A conducts a meeting for 7 to 8 minutes to review the issues generated by the grand opening of your computer store. After concluding situation A, everyone reads the background for situation B. Then leader B will conduct a group discussion for 7 to 8 minutes pertaining to situation B issues.

Situation A   You are the newly appointed manager of a new computer store, the 21st in a fast-growing regional chain. The grand opening just concluded, which turned in a better-than-expected sales performance, but it was a week scarred by confusion and numerous customer service problems. With two exceptions, the full-time sales service staff you hired has no previous computer sales experience. You personally did all the hiring two to three weeks before the store opened, looking for people experienced in working with computers. The glitches during the last week were a combination of the staff not knowing the technical specifications of inventory items they had not personally used, and so at times faking their recommendations to customers, and staff acting with indifference toward customers. You decide to meet with your entire staff before the store opens on Monday morning to share with them the sales success of opening week, and to begin correcting the types of customer-related problems that caused you to be less than pleased with their overall performance during the opening.

Situation B   Your store is now into its second quarter of operation. You have hired four more staff. With a couple of exceptions, the staff has settled into their roles quite nicely. People have learned the technical side of the business and have generally become versatile across several brands of equipment. They demonstrate a basic knowledge of most software products. Paul, however, continues to generate two to four customer complaints per week, usually about his impatient, condescending attitude in working with customers who lack technical expertise. Samantha has proven to be a capable technician, especially in configuring hardware and installing software, but she is often hesitant to make specific recommendations when serving customers. You have decided to hold your first staff meeting of the quarter to review progress to date and engage your people in a quest for continuous improvement.

Debriefing   Select a third volunteer to conduct a class discussion of the following questions:

1. What did leader A do that seemed effective? What was not as effective?
2. Which leadership theories seem to have relevance for the way leader A handled the group? What is your assessment of the job maturity of group members in situation A? Did the leader's behavior seem to take this factor into account? How?
3. What did leader B do that was effective? What was not as effective?
4. What leadership theories have relevance for leader B's handling of the situation? To what degree has employee job maturity changed in situation B? Did the leader seem to take this change into account? How?

OBSERVER'S RATING SHEET

After completing the two role-plays and the debriefing, rate the leadership skills of each of the leader volunteers using the following scale. First rate and provide feedback for the volunteer in situation A. Then do the same for the leader volunteer in situation B. Finally, complete the process for the third volunteer who led the debriefing. Write concrete examples to use in explaining your feedback in the spaces following each behavior.

1	*2*	*3*	*4*	*5*
Unsatisfactory	*Weak*	*Adequate*	*Good*	*Outstanding*

_____ Promoting changes to match environmental developments.

_____ Creating an inspiring vision.

_____ Maintaining control to achieve goals efficiently.

_____ Adapting leadership style to follower maturity.

_____ Empowering others to act by clarifying pathways to goals.

_____ Providing meaningful rewards for goal attainment.

_____ Modeling desired behaviors.

_____ Putting service to stakeholders before self-interest.

_____ Listening to learn and to affirm others.

_____ Inspiring trust by being trustworthy.

_____ Helping others develop.

GROUP EXERCISES

Three different types of group exercises are presented here. First is a short case for you to apply your conceptual leadership skills. Second is a nonverbal exercise to use your emergent leadership skills to solve a unique task. Third is a card tower exercise to practice your transactional leadership skills in a competitive task situation.

Group Exercise 1: Case Study: The Caring Navy Commander[34]

Under the leadership of Commander Michael Abrashoff, the USS *Benfold*, one of the U.S. Navy's most modern warships, has become a model of performance. In 1999, the *Benfold* was ranked as having the best combat readiness in the Pacific fleet; for two years in a row, it achieved the highest gunnery score and lowest rate of key equipment failures. The ship's crew has completed several of its training missions in record time, and fully 100 percent of its career sailors have signed on for an additional tour of duty, as opposed to the 54 percent average rate for the rest of the navy. The *Benfold* has returned $600,000 of its $2.4 million maintenance budget and continues to reduce its spending every year. Morale is excellent, and Commander Abrashoff's future promotion is guaranteed.

Much of the ship's and crew's outstanding performance can be attributed to Abrashoff's leadership. His focus is on his crew. He states, "When you shift your organizing principle from obedience to performance, the highest boss is no longer the guy with the most stripes—it's the sailor who does the work. . . . My job was to listen, . . . to see the ship from the eyes of the crew." One of the commander's first steps after joining the ship was to interview all crew members and ask them what they liked about their ship and what they wanted to change. He then identified non-value-added tasks that caused the most dissatisfaction and proceeded to tackle them.

Several steps were taken to address problems. The metal parts of the ship were replaced with stainless-steel bolts and a specially coated metal that required no constant painting; the youngest sailors, who dreaded the constant chipping and painting, were delighted. An agreement with an SAT administrator allowed sailors who wanted to go to college to take the SATs while they were stationed in Bahrain. Because the crew spends months at a time away from their families, Abrashoff set up a special account through America On-Line to allow his sailors to stay more easily in touch with their families. He disregarded strict navy rules for shore leave and rented minivans to allow his sailors more freedom, under the supervision of senior petty officers. Another sore spot for the crew was the quality of the food. The commander rejected naval provisions, switched to purchasing lower-cost brand names, and used the savings to send his ship's cooks to culinary school. Other special touches include pumpkins during Halloween, and music videos projected on the side of the ship. The chief navigator is even known for his Elvis impersonations during social events!

Abrashoff knows every one of his crew by name. He wants to help them "chart a course through life. . . . I consider my job to improve my little 300-person piece of society." Interestingly, although the *Benfold* and its commander do not focus on strict discipline, there is no lack of respect or cohesion on the ship. The crew willingly salutes its commanding officer, and there is a strong sense of duty and cooperation. One indicator of the positive culture is the results of the ship surveys that indicate that only 3 percent of minorities report prejudice and only 3 percent of the female sailors report any sexual harassment.

Abrashoff states; "I have to prepare higher-level people to step into leadership roles. If all you do is give orders, then all you'll get are order takers. Removing many of the nonreadiness aspects of the job—from chipping paint to cleaning—lets us spend more time on learning." Abrashoff's caring for his crew, his ability to listen to them, his relative disregard for rules while focusing on performance and problem solving, and his commitment to improving the quality of life have created enviable results.

QUESTIONS FOR DISCUSSION

1. What is Commander Abrashoff leadership style? What specific clues led to your conclusions?
2. What are the elements of Abrashoff's leadership style that contribute to his effectiveness?
3. Is transformational leadership taking place? In what ways? What are its effects?
4. Is transactional leadership taking place? In what ways? What are its effects?

Group Exercise 2: The Perfect Square[35]

Objectives. The purpose of this exercise is to provide an opportunity to observe different types of leadership and followership.

Time. 80–90 minutes.

Instructions. Instructions for conducting the exercise are spelled out in the steps below. Observer and facilitator instructions follow.

Step 1: Form a circle with 8 to 18 people in a large area of empty space where you can spread out without running into chairs or walls.

Step 2: Ask for a volunteer(s) to be an observer. If your group is small, one observer will do. If your group has 18 people, you can have up to three observers. The observers should withdraw from the circle. The observer instructions are found at the end of this exercise.

Step 3: The members of the circle should blindfold themselves or keep their eyes closed. If you wear glasses, place them in your pocket or give them to an observer to hold.

Step 4: The facilitator will read the instructions for the exercise found at the end of the chapter. The blindfolded group has 20 minutes to complete the assigned task (25 minutes).

Step 5: Take time for individual reflection. Answer the following questions by yourself (10 minutes).

    a. What different types of leadership emerged in this exercise? In your opinion, who were the leaders and why? What leader behaviors did they exhibit?

    b. What occurred in the group to help you solve the problem?

    c. What occurred in the group that hindered you from solving the problem or from solving it quickly?

    d. What did you learn about leadership from this exercise?

    e. What did you learn about yourself as a leader in this exercise?

Step 6: Discuss these questions with your group. Ask the observers what they noticed. Choose a representative to report to the entire class a summary of your answers to these questions (20–30 minutes).

Step 7: Debriefing session (20 minutes).

    a. Have an observer from each group briefly and objectively describe what happened when his or her group did the blindfolded exercise. Next, the group representative presents his or her report.

    b. Can you see any relationships between this exercise and experiences you have had at work or in other organizational settings?

434   PART V   Leading Skills

   c. What are the important contingencies in this particular situation? What type of leadership works best in a situation such as this? What leader behaviors are needed?

   d. There are no leaders without followers. In this exercise, what were the characteristics of a good follower?

   e. What did you learn about yourself as a leader in this exercise?

   f. If you were to repeat this exercise, what would you do differently to be a better leader?

Observer Instructions

Please do not talk, laugh, or make any noises at all during the exercise so you do not disturb the group. Do keep an eye out for their safety; move any items that could trip them, and warn them if they are approaching anything dangerous. Otherwise, do not talk to them or to the other observers.

Answer the following questions based on your observations.

1. Look for leadership behavior in the group. Who emerged as leaders and what exactly did they do to become leaders?
2. Observe and describe the group's communication patterns and nonverbal language.
3. How did the group make decisions?
4. Be prepared to share these observations in your group discussion period.
5. Be prepared to give a very brief description of your group's strategy for resolving this problem and ifs degree of success during the plenary debriefing session.

Attention!
For the facilitator only: Do not read unless you are a facilitator.

Facilitator Instructions

Have the groups form into a circle in a large, empty area away from a wall or sidewalk they could use as a guide. Ask for the number of volunteers your instructor has set and have them stand outside the circle.

Pass out the blindfolds, or explain that participants are to keep their eyes closed at all times during the exercise. When the participants are blindfolded and cannot see, read them the instructions below and pass out the rope. Do not let them see the rope beforehand—they shouldn't know how long it is.

The last person to receive the rope should be the quietest person—take the slack (leftover rope) and lay it on the ground behind the last person so he or she has to search for the end. This is a test to see whether the group listens to quiet people. Identify the quietest person and give the first end of the rope to the person on his or her side and hand out the rope in that direction around the circle so you end with the quiet person. Don't tell the group there is leftover rope.

Watch their group process as they work, but don't intervene unless someone is in danger of falling or hurting themselves. Don't talk at all during the exercise except to read them the instructions and give them a five-minute warning.

Note what time they start; when 15 minutes have passed, tell them they have five minutes left. When the 20 minutes are up, have them take off their blindfolds and answer individually the questions in step 5. If they finish earlier, ask if they are satisfied with their square. If so, let them take off their blindfolds. Collect the blindfolds and the rope while they work on step 5.

Participant Instructions

Please form a circle. Who would like to observe this exercise? Everyone else should put on a blindfold or close your eyes so you cannot see. I'll give you the rest of the instructions once everyone is blindfolded or have your eyes closed.

Your task is to form a perfect square utilizing all the rope that I am passing out. Here are the rules:

1. Use all the rope so that your square is taut, with no slack.
2. You must keep both your hands on the rope at all times.
3. You have 20 minutes to form a perfect square.

I can repeat these rules if you like, but after that I cannot answer any question. Shall I repeat the rules?

Reminders. Notification of 5-minute warning (after 15 minutes have passed). Call time when 20 minutes are up and refer them to Step 5.

Group Exercise 3: Do Not Topple the Tower[36]

Purpose. This action exercise helps to examine leader-member relationships that affect team performance on a tangible production project. In teams of three or four people, the objective is to see how many folded index cards can be stacked up, two cards per tier, with each tier at a 90° angle to the tier below, to form a multitiered tower of up to 20 cards. You say it sounds easy? Wait until you are a worker and try to do it blindfolded!

Primary attention is paid to the thoughts and interaction behaviors of the leader. During each production debriefing, other situational factors are examined: skill differences among workers; worker needs, expectations, and perceptions; physical factors; and so on.

Time. 35 to 65 minutes.

Materials Needed. Large index cards (5×7 recommended), 20 per team, and strips of cloth suitable for blindfolds, two per team.

Procedures.

1. Assign participants to teams of three or four persons. If the available time is limited to about 45 minutes, three-person teams allow sufficient time for each member to serve in a leadership role during one five-minute building period. If time is not so limited, four-person teams provide more comparison data.

2. The production exercise will be repeated (in five-minute intervals, timed by the instructor) as many times as there are persons per team. Roles are to be rotated following each action cycle. The roles are

- Leader or supervisor (one person)
- Employees, builders (two people)
- Process observer (one person, but only if using four-person teams)

3. Once teams are assembled, each team receives its 20 index cards and two blindfolds. Fold cards lengthwise in the middle to form "tents." If 5×7 cards are used, each tent will be 2-1/2 × 7, flared about an inch at the bottom.

4. After teams and materials are assembled, develop whatever procedures you believe will be necessary to ensure good performance, as long as they are consistent with the instructions. During the planning and preparation time, it will be the leader's responsibility to establish a team output goal (expressed as number of cards stacked without toppling the tower). Blindfold the two initial builders, and designate them as

worker A and worker B. If you have time, practice until the instructor is ready to start all teams on the first five-minute production period.

Production Instructions

1. Using the nondominant hand for stacking cards, blindfolded worker A will place the first card tent in the middle of a desk or table. Blindfolded worker B places the second card, parallel to the first, as close or far apart as directed by the leader. These cards form the base tier. Worker A then places the third card at right angles to the base; worker B places the fourth card parallel to the third. Work continues in this manner, with workers alternating the stacking of each card, with two parallel cards per tier.

2. Because workers are blindfolded, the leader/supervisor must guide the work through verbal instructions to the work team. The supervisor cannot touch either the workers or the cards at any time during the five-minute timed production period.

3. The round is terminated for a work team when (a) the goal is achieved, i.e., the tower is 10 tiers high; (b) a card that was previously stacked on the tower is knocked off; (c) the entire tower topples; (d) the instructor calls time at the end of five minutes. If a worker is placing a card that slips off without knocking off another card, the leader may direct the worker to retrieve the card and resume building.

4. After each round, the instructor records on the board each team's goal and actual results. This record can be made in matrix form with numbers inserted as each round is completed.

5. At the end of each round, each team privately debriefs the factors that contributed to productivity or problems, satisfaction, and developmental learning. The observer (if one is used) should lead this discussion using notes of observed behaviors. Questions can be asked of workers and leader about their experience: Did they feel anxiety, tension, or frustration? What were their thoughts, motives, and suggestions for improving performance? Following a few minutes for team debriefing and planning, the instructor may debrief the class with one or more focusing questions. If time is scarce, the debriefing can be held until after the final round. The objective of the debriefing phase is to move beyond having fun and help focus learning from this direct experience.

SUMMARY CHECKLIST

Take a few minutes to reflect on your performance and look over others' ratings of your leadership skills. Now assess yourself on each of the key learning behaviors. Make a check next to those behaviors on which you need improvement when leading change.

_____ **Promoting changes to match environmental developments.**
1. Scan environment, looking for relevant changes.
2. Create mission and strategic plans.
3. Motivate followers to commit to change.

_____ **Creating an inspiring vision**
1. Influence others to share a common vision.
2. Appeal to both hearts and minds.

_____ **Maintaining controls to achieve goals efficiently.**
1. Motivate others by providing opportunities for growth and development.
2. Provide appropriate rewards and punishments.

_____ **Adapting leadership style to follower maturity.**
1. Engage in *task-oriented behavior* when appropriate—provide structure and control.
2. Engage in *relationship-oriented behavior* when appropriate—provide respect, warmth, conflict resolution.
3. Adapt to relevant *contingencies*, such as differences in followers skill and motivation, task structure, formal authority, and work group cohesiveness.

_____ **Empowering others to act by clarifying pathways to goals.**
1. Help employees identify and learn behaviors to successfully accomplish tasks.
2. Apply appropriate decision styles: directive, achievement, participative, or supportive.

_____ **Providing meaningful rewards for goal attainment.**
1. Consult with followers to determine which rewards are important to them.
2. Increase desired personal payoffs to employees for goal attainment.

_____ **Modeling desired behaviors.**
1. Walk your talk.
2. Set a good example.
3. Celebrate small wins.

_____ **Putting service to stakeholders before self-interest.**
1. Demonstrate a sense of humility and vulnerability.
2. Do what is right for others even if it does not pay off financially.

_____ **Listening to learn and affirm others.**
1. Recognize that, as an individual, you don't have all the answers.
2. Demonstrate that you understand others by paraphrasing.

_____ **Inspiring trust by being trustworthy.**
1. Honor your commitments—do what you say you will do.
2. Be totally honest with others.
3. Give up control.
4. Focus on the well being of others.

_____ **Helping others develop.**
1. Share all information.
2. Make yourself vulnerable to others by showing your own pain and humanity.
3. Share in the pain and difficulties of others.
4. Provide opportunities for growth by sharing power, offering training and education, and delegating responsibilities.

APPLICATION QUESTIONS

1. Describe the best leader you have known. What were his or her particular leadership qualities and strengths or weaknesses? How did this leader acquire his or her capability?
2. What do you consider your own strengths and weaknesses for leadership? What activities should you undertake to improve your leadership capability in areas where you are weak?
3. Why do you think so few people succeed at both management and leadership?
4. In what specific situations is it necessary to have transactional rather than transformational leaders? What about the reverse?
5. Are there differences in the leadership styles of men and women? Why do you think so?

REINFORCEMENT EXERCISES

1. Interview several managers about how they make decisions. Compare the answers you receive to the steps in the rational problem-solving model. Also, check the degree of participation that these managers used against those recommended by the participation decision tree.
2. Think of a situation when you were a successful leader, whether in a club, school, or at work. Identify what you did that made you successful. Were you acting as a transactional or transformational leader?
3. Interview several managers about their leadership style. Find out what it is and why they think it is effective.
4. Interview several people who work for the same manager about their manager's leadership style. Find out what it is and why they think it is or is not effective. It is preferable, but not necessary, that the interviewees work for the same manager that you interviewed in question three so that perceptions can be compared.

ACTION PLAN

1. Which leadership behavior do I most want to improve?
2. Why? What will be my payoff?
3. What potential obstacles stand in my way?
4. What are the specific things I will do to improve?

(For examples, see the Reinforcement Exercises.)

5. When will I do them?
6. How and when will I measure my success?

NOTES

1. Adapted from C. W. Cook, P. L. Hunsaker, and R. E. Coffey, *Management and Organizational Behavior*, 2d ed. (Homewood, IL: Irwin, 1997) 465.
2. S. Tully, "So, Mr. Bossidy, We Know You Can Cut. Now Show Us How to Grow," *Fortune*, August 21, 1995, 70–80.
3. W. Bennis and B. Nanus, *Leaders: The Strategies for Taking Charge* (New York: Harper & Row, 1985) 20.
4. Ibid, 21.
5. N. M. Tichy, *The Leadership Engine* (New York: HarperCollins, 1997) 36–37.
6. J. P. Kotter, "What Leaders Really Do," *Harvard Business Review* 68 (May–June 1990): 103–11. For a more expansive distinction, see Kotter's *A Force for Change: How Leadership Differs from Management* (New York: Free Press, 1990).
7. H. J. Leavitt, *Corporate Pathfinders* (New York: Penguin, 1987) 3.
8. S. A. Kirkpatrick and E. A. Locke, "Leadership: Do Traits Matter?" *Academy of Management Executive* 5 (May 1991): 48–60.
9. W. H. Schmidt and B. Z. Posner, *Managerial Values and Expectations: The Silent Power of Personal and Organizational Life* (New York: American Management Association, 1982).
10. Kirkpatrick and Locke, 1991, 48–60.
11. Ibid, 59.
12. For comprehensive reviews of this early research see R. Likert, *New Patterns of Management* (New York:

McGraw-Hill, 1961) 36; and R. M. Stodgill and A. E. Coons, *Leader Behavior: Its Description and Measurement* (Columbus, OH: Ohio State University, Bureau of Business Research, 1957) 75.
13. A. W. Halpin, *The Leadership Behavior of School Superintendents* (Chicago: Midwest Administration Center, University of Chicago, 1959) 4.
14. A. K. Korman, "Consideration, Initiating Structure, and Organizational Criteria—A Review," *Personnel Psychology* (Winter 1966): 349–61.
15. K. Lewin and R. Lippitt, "An Experimental Approach to the Study of Autocracy and Democracy: A Preliminary Note," *Sociometry* 1 (1938): 292–300.
16. L. Berkowitz, "Group Standards, Cohesiveness, and Productivity," *Human Relations* 7 (1954): 509–14; and S. E. Seashore, *Group Cohesiveness in the Industrial Work Group* (Ann Arbor: University of Michigan Survey Research Center, 1954).
17. P. Hersey and K. H. Blanchard, *Management of Organizational Behavior: Utilizing Human Resources*, 7th ed. (Upper Saddle River, NJ: Prentice Hall, 1996) chapter 8.
18. Ibid, 161.
19. Ibid.
20. R. J. House and T. R. Mitchell, "Path-Goal Theory of Leadership," *Journal of Contemporary Business* 3 (Autumn 1974): 81–97.
21. Ibid, 81–97.

22. C. Schriesheim and M. A. Von Glinow, "The Path-Goal Theory of Leadership: A Theoretical and Empirical Analysis," *Academy of Management Journal* 20 (September 1977): 398–405.

23. P. Sellers, "What Exactly Is Charisma?" *Fortune*, January 15, 1996, 68–75.

24. B. Bass, "Evolving Perspectives on Charismatic Leadership," J. Conger and R. N. Kanungo, eds., *Charismatic Leadership* (San Francisco: Jossey-Bass, 1988), 40–77.

25. J. Conger, "The Dark Side of Leadership," *Organizational Dynamics* (Autumn 1990): 44–55.

26. J. Howell, "Two Faces of Charisma: Socialized and Personalized Leadership in Organizations, in J. Conger and R. Kanungo, eds., *Charismatic Leadership* (San Francisco: Jossey-Bass, 1988) 213–36.

27. W. Bennis and B. Nanus, *Leaders* (New York: Harper & Row, 1985).

28. J. M. Kouzes and B. Z. Posner, *The Leadership Challenge: How to Get Extraordinary Things Done In Organizations* (San Francisco: Jossey-Bass, 1995) 14.

29. P. Block, *Stewardship: Choosing Service Over Self-Interest* (San Francisco: Berrett-Koehler, 1993).

30. Lawrence G. Foster, *Robert Wood Johnson—The Gentleman Rebel* (Lemont, PA: Lillian Press, 1999).

31. K. Blanchard, B. Hybels, and P. Hodges, *Leadership by the Book* (New York: William Morrow, 1999).

32. W. B. Brenneman, J. B. Keys, and R. M. Fulmer, "Learning Across a Living Company: The Shell Companies' Experience," *Organizational Dynamics* 27, no. 2 (1998): 61–71.

33. W. Kiechel III, "The Leader as Servant," *Fortune*, May 4, 1992, 121–122.

34. Adapted from P. LaBarre, "Grassroots Leadership," *Fast Company* (April 1999): 115–126.

35. Adapted from J. S. Osland, D. A. Kolb, and I. M. Rubin, *Organizational Behavior: An Experiential Approach* (Upper Saddle River, NJ: Prentice Hall, 2001) 293–99.

36. Adapted from C. W. Cook, "Debriefing with Serialized Theory Development for Task-Team Development," *Exploring Experiential Learning: Simulations and Experiential Exercises* (Tempe, AZ: Bureau of Business and Economic Research, Arizona State University, 1978) 7–8.

CHAPTER 17

Motivating Others

Learning Objectives

After completing this chapter, you should be able to:

- Determine motivational factors to keep employees on the job.

- Identify the factors that motivate people to perform.

- Diagnose sources of performance problems.

- Apply appropriate methods to motivate employees to perform better.

SELF-ASSESSMENT EXERCISE

How Do I Motivate Others?

For each statement, enter the number from the rating scale that best describes what you do when another person needs to be motivated:

All of the time 6	Most of the time 5	More than half the time 4	Less than half of the time 3	Not much of the time 2	Almost Never 1

_____ 1. I assume that performance problems are caused by lack of motivation.

_____ 2. I always establish a clear standard of expected performance.

_____ 3. I always offer to provide training and information, without offering to do tasks myself.

_____ 4. I am honest and straightforward in providing feedback on performance and assessing advancement opportunities.

_____ 5. I use a variety of rewards to reinforce exceptional performances.

_____ 6. When discipline is required, I give specific suggestions for improvement.

_____ 7. I design task assignments to make them interesting and challenging.

_____ 8. I strive to provide the rewards that each person values.

_____ 9. I make sure that people feel fairly and equitably treated.

_____ 10. I make sure that people get timely feedback from those affected by task performance.

_____ 11. I carefully diagnose the causes of poor performance before taking any action.

_____ 12. I always help people establish performance goals that are challenging, specific, and time bound.

All of the time 6	Most of the time 5	More than half the time 4	Less than half of the time 3	Not much of the time 2	Almost Never 1

_____ 13. Only as a last resort do I attempt to reassign or release a poorly performing individual.

_____ 14. Whenever possible I make sure valued rewards are linked to high performance.

_____ 15. I consistently intervene when performance is below expectations and below capabilities.

_____ 16. I try to combine or rotate assignments so that people can use a variety of skills.

_____ 17. I try to arrange for an individual to work with others in a team, for the mutual support of all.

_____ 18. I make sure that people use realistic standards for measuring fairness.

_____ 19. I provide immediate compliments and other forms of recognition for meaningful accomplishments.

_____ 20. I always determine whether a person has the necessary resources and support to succeed in a task.

Scoring and Interpretation.[1]   Add up your point ratings for the 20 questions to obtain your total score for how you motivate others. You can determine how well you motivate others by comparing your scores to three standards:

1. The maximum score possible is 120 points.
2. The scores of your classmates.
3. A norm group of 500 business school students. In comparison to the norm group, if you scored:

101 or above	You are in the top quartile
94–100	You are in the second quartile
85–93	You are in the third quartile
84 or below	You are in the bottom quartile

CONCEPTS

People make at least two decisions about motivation every day when they come to work. One is whether to stay in the organization or look for another source of work. The other is how much effort to put into performance on the job. Consequently, managers need to be concerned about two corresponding aspects of motivation: motivating workers to stay on the job and motivating them to perform at their best.

Motivation consists of a conscious decision to direct effort in an activity to achieve a goal that will satisfy a predominate need. This definition of motivation contains three elements: (1) some need, motive, or goal that triggers action; (2) a selection process that directs the choice of action; and (3) the intensity of effort that is applied to the chosen action. In essence, motivation governs behavior selection, direction, and level of effort.[2]

From mastering the previous chapters, you already have a number of skills necessary to motivate others. The chapters on leading and building power explained how to motivate others by showing them how to achieve goals that will provide rewards they desire. The chapters on planning, goal setting, and evaluating performance demonstrated how to set challenging goals, provide feedback to encourage sustained efforts for success, and reinforce motivation by making desired rewards contingent on performance. Finally, the chapters on creating high-performing teams and interpersonal communication provided guidelines for eliminating barriers to exchanging required information and developing supportive interpersonal relationships to sustain high motivation levels.

This chapter will build on these previous skills and provide more specific methods for motivating employees to stay on the job and to perform at their best. First what motivates workers to stay in an organization will be discussed. Then the discussion will shift to the determinants of job performance, followed by what we know about the needs that motivate people to perform. Finally, methods you can apply to motivate employees will be described.

What Motivates Workers to Stay on the Job?

In a recent survey of nearly 1,300 U.S. managers and employees, Kepner-Tregoe, a New Jersey human resources consulting firm, found that nearly two-thirds said their companies have suffered increased worker turnover since 1996. They said the loss of high-performing employees has "dulled their companies' competitive edge and led to a decline in quality and in customer service."[3] These consequences are serious, and because it is the high-performing employees who usually leave for more desirable surroundings and rewards, it is important to determine what causes them to leave.

In a survey of 500,000 employees at more than 300 U.S. firms, the Hay Group, a large human resources consulting firm, discovered that among 50 factors affecting employee staying power, pay ranked the lowest. If pay is not the motivator, what is? In its study, the Hay Group found that giving employees the opportunity to learn new skills ranked highest. Coaching and feedback from superiors was another top factor. The employees perceived a problem here because top performers receive less of both, because managers think the "stars" do not need their help. Yet ironically they value feedback the most, which points to the third major factor causing employee retention problems: a "bad boss." Even if organizations have all other programs right, if managers do not treat their direct reports equitably and with respect, then none of the other stuff matters.[4]

One of the greatest mistakes managers make in implementing a reward system that will retain and motivate employees is assuming that they know precisely what employees want in return for doing their jobs. Two of the main reasons for these mistakes is that managers assume that all workers want the same outcomes, which are the same ones that the managers think workers prefer. Several studies have indicated a low correlation between workers' actual priorities for work rewards and the priorities attributed the same rewards by their bosses.[5] In general, managers most often believe that what workers want most from their jobs are things such as good wages, job security, promotions, and good working conditions. The workers themselves, however, usually rank aspects such as challenging work, recognition for good work, participation in decisions that affect them, and sympathetic understanding of personal problems higher than job security and good wages.[6]

If managers do not provide workers with opportunities to obtain the rewards they desire in the organization, the workers will go somewhere else where they can get what they want. It is important to be aware that the things employees want most are, for the most part, easily provided by their immediate managers. Consequently, a manager should always take advantage of opportunities to provide more challenging work, recognition for good work, participation in decisions that affect employees, and sympathetic understanding of personal problems. These efforts are free, and they pay great motivational dividends.

What Motivates People to Perform Well on the Job?

The desire to perform well isn't always enough to ensure good performance. It is also necessary to have the ability to perform. The determinants of task performance can be summarized in the model in Exhibit 17-1.[7]

EXHIBIT 17-1	Determinants of Task Performance

Performance = Ability × Motivation
  Ability = Aptitude × Training × Resources
 Motivation = Desire × Commitment

Performance is the product of a person's ability multiplied by his or her motivation. Ability is the product of aptitude multiplied by training and resources. Motivation is the product of desire and commitment. All elements in these equations are necessary for high performance levels. For example, a worker could have 100 percent motivation, but if he or she only has 10 percent of the required ability, performance will not be satisfactory, no matter how hard the worker tries.

Given these multiple determinants of task performance, the first question a manager should ask when below-par performance is observed, is whether it is caused from lack of ability or lack of motivation. If the manager determines that the problem is lack of ability, rather than motivation, no amount of pressure or encouragement will help. What the person needs is training, additional resources, or a redesign of the job. Chapter 13 discussed how to develop employee's ability. In this chapter, the focus is on increasing motivation by enhancing desire and commitment.

Motivation was earlier defined as a conscious decision to direct effort in an activity to achieve a goal that will satisfy a predominate need. Therefore, it is needs that drive, or motivate, behavior to satisfy the tension they create. An unsatisfied need creates tension, which sets off a drive to satisfy that need. In order to motivate employees, a good place to start is to determine what types of needs exist and what is required to satisfy them.

Basic Needs

Perhaps the best known theory of motivation is Abraham Maslow's hierarchy of needs.[8] Maslow proposed that every individual has a five-level hierarchy of needs that they attempt to satisfy beginning with physical well-being, and progressing successively through safety, belonging, esteem, and self-actualization (see Exhibit 17-2). According to Maslow, once a lower-level need has been largely satisfied, its impact on behavior diminishes. The individual then is freed up to progress to the next higher-level need, and it becomes a major determinant of behavior. Each of these needs is described, followed by an example.

Physiological Needs   Physiological needs refer to our physical survival. These basic needs include hunger, thirst, and shelter. They can be satisfied at work by receiving enough pay to purchase the basics for survival such as groceries, clothing, and housing.

Safety Needs   When physiological needs are reasonably satisfied, the safety needs become aroused. For example, if you are having an asthma attack and cannot breathe, all you care about is getting a breath of fresh air. Once your attack has subsided, however, you become concerned with safety, security, and protection from another life-threatening event. At that point you might be motivated to find a prescription inhaler or other drug that you could keep on hand to feel more secure in case you have another asthma attack. Safety needs can be satisfied at work by receiving job security, medical benefits, and safe working conditions.

Social Needs   Once you feel reasonably secure and have had enough to eat and drink, social needs begin to drive your behavior. They are the needs people have for affiliation, for giving and receiving affection, and for friendship. Social needs can be satisfied at work by having good relationships with coworkers and participating in social functions such as company picnics.

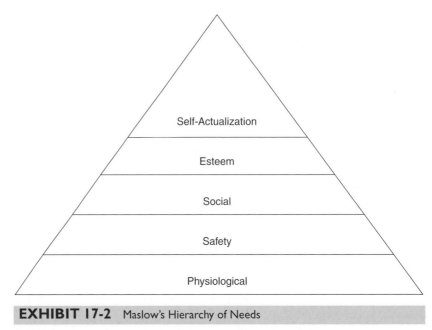

EXHIBIT 17-2 Maslow's Hierarchy of Needs

SOURCE: A. H. Maslow. "A Theory of Human Motivation," *Psychological Review* 50 (1943): 370–96.

Esteem Needs   Two types of esteem needs motivate us after we have fairly well satisfied our physiological, safety, and social needs. One type is those needs that relate to one's *self-esteem*, including needs for self-confidence, independence, achievement, competence, and knowledge. The second type of esteem needs concern esteem from others. They include things that affect your reputation, such as needs for recognition, status, appreciation, and respect. Esteem needs can be satisfied at work by being recognized for accomplishments and receiving promotions.

Self-Actualization Needs   These highest-level needs only begin to really affect our behavior after all lower-level needs have been reasonably satisfied. They are the needs for fulfillment by becoming the person we feel we have the potential for becoming. Self-actualization motivates us to continue self-development and learning. Self-actualization needs can be satisfied at work by receiving tuition reimbursement for continuing education, attending training sessions, and having opportunities to exercise your creativity in endeavors that fully utilize your skills and abilities.

So how does the need hierarchy work in a real situation? Imagine that Theresa, a technical writer and single parent, has been earning a good salary and benefits that enable her to provide for her family's physical well-being—ample food, comfortable housing and clothing, good medical care. Then her company announces it is downsizing (reducing the number of employees), and she fears being laid off (which triggers a safety need). She is unlikely to be overly concerned about the higher-order need of belonging to a group or her own self-esteem need to perform creative and technically accurate work. Rather, she is likely to be motivated to do whatever she believes will enable her to keep her job and/or to begin looking discreetly for other employment. Once the layoffs have been announced and Theresa realizes she is not on the list, she breathes a sigh of relief, and focuses back on her work with a higher-order need energizing her behavior.

As the preceding example demonstrates, current circumstances automatically determine which level of inherent basic needs will be aroused and acted on. Another category of needs, however, is learned or socially acquired. Depending on your personal experience, you may have one or two strong socially learned needs. These needs are learned through repeated positive reinforcement in previous experiences, and they motivate our behavior whenever we perceive an opportunity to satisfy them.

Learned Needs

David McClelland and his colleagues have studied three learned motives that he believes are especially important for motivating people at work.[9] They are the needs for achievement, power, and affiliation. These higher-level needs are associated with Maslow's social, esteem, and self-actualization categories. But, since most of the employees that a manager supervises have their basic physiological and safety needs satisfied by the organization, the higher, learned motives are the ones that hold the most potential for motivating others. Because individuals have learned to value these acquired needs differently, the manager's job is to determine which ones specific individuals are most concerned about, and then provide opportunities for them to satisfy these needs in the organization.

The Achievement Motive   Because achievement is highly valued in most Western societies, most of us like to think of ourselves as being achievement oriented. However, people's achievement motives vary in intensity, as do all motives. People who really have a high need to achieve are self-motivated; they seek tasks that will provide them with a sense of accomplishment. For example, they will choose an opportunity to confront a challenging but doable task rather than attend the company's Friday afternoon pizza social.

The achievement motive can be measured by what people say, do, or write. Several behavioral characteristics distinguish the achievement-motivated person.[10]

1. Achievers prefer a moderate level of difficulty or challenge. Just as they avoid tasks that are too easy, they also shy away from those that are extremely difficult. Being realistic, they know their limitations. The most desired task is one that requires a high level of exertion but carries a reasonable probability of success.
2. High achievers also like to feel that they are in reasonable control of an outcome. If the element of chance or luck is a primary factor in success, or if others over whom they have little influence are involved, they experience a reduced incentive to try.
3. Achievement-motivated people also like to receive frequent and specific feedback about how well they are doing. This preference does not mean they need constant praise from their supervisors. Ideally the task itself should provide enough feedback so they can evaluate themselves; self-approval is a strong motivator for an achiever.

The Power Motive   As you learned in Chapter 15, power is the ability to influence others to behave as you want. People who have a high need for power, or power motive, find satisfaction from being in charge and controlling and influencing others. Although it is important to have high achievers in an organization, it is also necessary to have some take-charge types for whom power is the dominant motive. These people are willing to specify organizational goals and influence others to achieve them. It is difficult to be a successful manager without a need for power, especially in large organizations. Managers must learn to take satisfaction in acquiring and exercising the means for influencing others.

Managers with strong power needs can be classified into two types, depending upon how they exhibit their needs.[11] Managers with high personal power needs exemplify the stereotypical self-serving, exploitative, dominating boss. Such a need for power reflects the aim of personal gain through manipulation and control of others without exhibiting self-control and inhibition. A personal-power boss may coerce and even threaten subordinates in a forceful attempt to get them to carry out commands. Such a manager then takes credit for their successes. Contrary to what is presented in soap operas, these managers usually don't make it to the top of an organization because people they have stepped on earlier find ways to sabotage their careers.[12]

Managers with high institutional power needs, on the other hand, temper their influence over others with inhibition and self-control. They are altruistic and believe power should be used more for the good of the organization than for personal advantage. Satisfaction is obtained more from the process of influencing others to carry out their work in pursuit of organizational goals than from their own personal success. Research indicates that higher-level managers in large organizations are more likely to be successful if they possess a high need for power that is institutionalized combined with low affiliation needs.[13]

The Affiliation Motive   People with a high need for affiliation find satisfaction in the quality of their social and interpersonal relationships. Affiliators avoid isolation (whereas achievers often welcome it), because interaction with others is so important for them. Such people easily develop wide circles of friends both in and out of the workplace. They are likely to show concern for the feelings of others and to be sympathetic to opposing views. Given the opportunity, they often try to help others work through problems.

People who are high affiliators most often make weak bosses. One study found that only 20 percent of the "above-average" sales departments in a research sample were supervised by managers whose affiliation needs were more dominant than their power needs. Of the "below-average" departments in their sample, 90 percent were run by affiliation-motivated managers. By contrast, power-motivated managers ran 80 percent of the best and only 10 percent of the worst departments. The researchers concluded that because of their need to be liked, affiliation-motivated managers made "wishy-washy decisions." They bent company rules to make particular individuals happy, and in the process they were seen as unfair.[14]

Diagnosing and Using Learned Motives to Motivate Others   Correctly recognizing another's motive patterns helps a manager motivate others by selecting assignments that energize them. For example, the achiever is excited by his assignment to a challenging project. The power-motivated person enjoys representing her group in a negotiating session. Be cautious in making attributions about another's motives. However, the better you know another person, the better you will be able to identify the motivation patterns underlying his or her behavior.

How Do People Decide How to Behave to Satisfy Their Needs on the Job?

Need-based theories of motivation are useful to managers because they provide a general answer to the question of what needs or motives drive human behavior. They are often referred to as the *content* theories of motivation. If you are going to motivate people to behave in ways that will accomplish organizational objectives as well as satisfy their own needs, however, you should understand how and why workers select specific behaviors to satisfy these needs. *Process* theories of motivation explain how and why workers select behaviors and how they determine whether their choices were successful. Because people are creatures of perception, thought, and a certain degree of rationality, they are capable of making informed choices about where and how to channel energy. In making choices, the human tendency is to embrace the most advantageous option or at least avoid functioning at a disadvantage. With this tendency in mind, the process considerations for understanding how people decide what to do to satisfy their needs include goals, expectations, reinforcements, and perceptions of equity.

How Do Goals Enhance Motivation?

A **goal** is the desired outcome of an action. Chapter 7 explains a great deal about using goals to motivate behavior selections that will enhance performance and satisfaction. You can revisit Chapter 7 to review the characteristics of effective goals, how to set goals, how to obtain commitment to goals, and how to apply goal setting through the management by objectives process. This section will summarize what we know about using goals to motivate others to strive for organizational objectives.

Participation in Goal Setting Goals become motivational when an individual desires them and strives to achieve them. It is critical, therefore, that goals are understood and accepted by those striving to achieve them. Subordinates are more likely to "buy into" goals if they have a part in determining what they will be and how they will be accomplished.[15] Ironically, however, while participation often produces greater commitment to goals and perceptions of self-control and fairness,[16] participation does not necessarily lead to higher performance than manager-assigned goals. One workable combination is for managers to assign goals, hold people responsible for results, grant people the autonomy to plan their actions and exercise control over how they do their work, then measure results. People who have the capability to do the task and are committed to achieving it generally will perform well regardless of their degree of participation in setting the goal itself.[17]

Characteristics of Effective Goals To activate energetic, task-focused behavior, a person needs clear, specific, and challenging goals. Especially when delegating tasks, managers should describe clearly what is wanted and provide specific feedback as to the appropriateness of work being done.[18] Suggestions on how to write goals that satisfy the clear, specific, challenging criteria are offered in Chapter 7. An example of how these skills might work follows.

Rose Vasquez, vice president of human resources for a large insurance company, was concerned that Ed Tran, her director of training and development, has been using too many contract training programs from outside consultants, programs that were not central to company needs. During a performance review with Tran 18 months ago, Vasquez stated, "Next year your staff needs to develop and deliver more in-company training for sales agents and cut back on off-the-shelf contract programs."

During the next review, Vasquez expressed disappointment that training originated by the training staff was only 30 percent of the total, although she acknowledged it was up almost 5 percent. She decided to be more explicit: "Ed, for this next year I want you to target 60 percent of your training days for staff-delivered programs and only 40 percent for outside vendors. You develop a plan for achieving it, and let's review it and then meet monthly to review progress toward that plan and the milestones you set." Six months later, Tran was ahead of plan and close to a 50–50 milestone. Participant satisfaction ratings were up nearly 25 percent, a major improvement in the quality of sales training. Vasquez celebrated the progress by taking Tran and his group to a celebration luncheon.

The incident between Vasquez and Tran demonstrates the complex impact of participation in goal setting. When initially given freedom to set his own goals, Tran failed to make the shift Vasquez apparently desired. Tran was then assigned a specific goal and timelines by his boss, but he was responsible for planning how to achieve the target, and did so.

Even though goal achievement is intrinsically rewarding, motivation is usually increased when people believe that increased efforts will produce desired results that will lead to fair rewards they value. To get the best from their people, managers should clarify the links between effort-performance and fair rewards. This premise underlies the motivational process theories based on expectancy and equity that we will discuss next.

How Do Expectancies About Effort, Performance, and Rewards Affect Work Motivation?

Motivation based on expectancy theory focuses on a person's beliefs about the relationships among effort, performance, and rewards for doing a job. The basics of expectancy theory for managers can be converted into a series of three questions that people often ask themselves about their work situation.[19]

1. ***Does how hard I try really affect my performance?*** To be motivated, you must have a positive answer to this *expectancy* question. You must believe that your personal efforts have the potential to make a positive performance difference. You must also have the capacity for internal attribution, or a willingness to take personal credit or blame for your performance. Positive task motivation begins when you see a link between personal effort and task performance.

2. ***Are personal consequences linked to my performance?*** In some jobs or roles little association exists between effort and rewards or punishments. To answer this *instrumentality* question, you must believe that task performance results will enable you to obtain personal consequences or payoffs. Increased motivation is possible when you perceive a positive personal consequence arising from satisfactory task performance.

3. ***Do I value the consequences that occur?*** Answers to this *valence* question depend on how much you value a particular expected personal outcome or payoff. If you really do not care about the potential payoff, it provides little if any incentive value. Suppose you want recognition, but your boss simply gives you another assignment and sends you off on another trip to the boondocks. You thus discount the value of possible payoffs, and your expectation of being rewarded in a meaningful way diminishes. A person must value the payoff if the expectancy loop is to be positive and motivational.

Motivation is enhanced when a person answers yes to all three of the preceding questions. Conversely, when one or more answers are negative, motivation potential diminishes.[20]

It is important for managers to realize that not all people value the available outcomes or rewards in the same way. One of the first things managers who want to motivate by expectancies must weigh is whether employees place a greater value on extrinsic or intrinsic rewards.

How Does the Nature of Rewards Affect Motivation?

Two basic sources provide rewards or payoffs. Many people depend on and highly value **extrinsic rewards**—rewards that are externally bestowed, such as praise from a supervisor, a promotion or pay raise, or the grade received on a term paper. Others place a high value on **intrinsic rewards**—their own personal feelings about how well they performed the task or simply the satisfaction they derived from doing it. Managers need to realize the distinction between the two and how their employees view them. For example, in work conditions where employees seek extrinsic rewards but believe their degree of effort is not clearly visible to supervisors, "social loafing" or low effort is likely to occur. However, where intrinsic involvement in the task is high, social loafing will be low even when effort is not visible to the manager.[21]

Although most people look for some mix of intrinsic and extrinsic rewards, people clearly differ as to which is the more compelling motivational force.[22] If a manager always praises an achievement-motivated professional who excels largely for the feelings of intrinsic satisfaction, this person will probably begin to view the manager as shallow or phony. The professional may think, "I know I did a superb job on this project. Why does my manager keep stating the obvious and acting so condescending?"

Even within the extrinsic rewards arena, people look for different types of rewards. Praise may be perfectly acceptable to the person motivated by relatedness needs or affiliation, but may do nothing for the person expecting a more tangible payoff. Typical extrinsic rewards are favorable assignments, trips to desirable destinations, tuition reimbursement for courses in which a good grade is earned, pay raises, bonuses, and promotions.

How Do Perceptions of Equity Affect Motivation to Work?

Along the path to expectancy motivation, things can go wrong. One of the most disruptive situations is when the payoffs or personal outcomes are perceived to be inequitable or unfair. Managers need to be aware of inequity perceptions and reduce gaps where possible.

Perceptions of equity moderate motivation. If expectancy motivation is to work, people must perceive an underlying fairness among effort-performance-reward relationships. **Equity theory** suggests that motivation is moderated by the perceived fairness or discrepancy between personal contributions and rewards relative to others. Two basic dimensions define the equity process.[23]

Ratio of Personal Outcomes to Inputs   People often think in terms of the ratio of their personal outcomes to work inputs. That is, their perceptions of equity depend on how they answer the question, What is the payoff to me (in terms of status, benefits, recognition, money, promotion, and job assignments) relative to my inputs of effort exerted, skills, job knowledge, and actual task performance?

External Comparisons   People also compare their own outcomes/input ratio to those they perceive for other people doing comparable work. These comparisons may be made on three levels.

1. *Comparisons to specific individuals.*   For example, Bev might conclude, "I guess Kerri really has been outperforming me." Bev would expect Kerri to be getting more in the way of rewards and recognition.
2. *Comparisons to another reference group.*   Workers might think, "Our department is getting much better treatment than the shipping department." This comparison recognizes differences in payoffs and concludes that "our group" is getting a better deal.
3. *Comparisons to general occupational classifications.*   At times, people compare themselves to people in similar positions in other organizations. A physical therapist at a private hospital might observe, "According to the national salary survey data, my pay is at only the 20th percentile, way below what someone with my experience should be earning." Another common comparison is across gender within the same occupation, where women often experience discrepancies and earn 20 percent to 40 percent less pay than men.

Adjusting for Equity Gaps   You might think that equity concerns would be activated only when a person believed he or she was being taken advantage of, or was undercompensated relative to others. Not necessarily. Although it may be the more common experience, people sometimes conclude that they are *over*compensated. This conclusion might have been the case in the second comparison previously listed if the workers thought, "Our group is receiving better treatment but performing no better than the group in shipping."

The equity concept affects motivation whenever a person perceives a meaningful difference in personal or group outcomes and then adjusts behavior or perceptions to reduce the gap.[24] In a research experiment, those who survived a job layoff and thought their coworkers' dismissals were random worked harder than when they believed those caught in the layoff had produced less.[25] Similarly, if Bernice believes she is inequitably overcompensated, she might intensify her efforts to produce more to be worthy of the superior benefits she receives, or she may simply change her frame of reference to reduce the perceived equity gap, say, by comparing her pay with national rather than company data. Conversely, when people perceive that they are undercompensated relative to the frame of reference, they will likely reduce or redirect their efforts in an attempt to beat the system so they end up with a fair deal. These adverse consequences are more pronounced with extrinsic inequities (especially monetary rewards) than intrinsic inequities.[26]

Methods of Motivating Employees

Enhance Commitment to Goals

We know that organizational goals become motivational only when individuals also desire them and strive to achieve them. We also know that to motivate energetic, task-focused behavior, people need clear, specific, and challenging goals. Therefore, it is important to make sure that goals are understood and accepted by those striving to achieve them. One way to get this understanding and "buy in" is to ensure that subordinates participate in setting goals and how they will be accomplished. Then managers should make sure to provide specific feedback as work toward goals is being completed.

Another way to apply goal setting to enhance motivation is to apply the more formal management by objectives (MBO) process described in Chapter 7. To apply MBO, specific performance objectives are jointly determined by subordinates and their supervisors. Progress toward objectives is periodically reviewed and rewards are allocated on the basis of this progress. MBO provides specific personal performance objectives and thus each person has an identified specific contribution. The four elements common to MBO programs are goal specificity, participative decision making, explicit time periods, and performance feedback.

Strengthen Effort–Performance–Reward Expectancies

A manager does not need to be a psychologist to benefit from applying expectancy theory. First, the theory is most applicable to those jobs in which an individual has discretion as to how and when work is performed. For example, it would have somewhat greater applicability for airline reservation agents (who can either be thorough and helpful or abrupt and indifferent) than for operators on a machine-paced assembly line. But it likely has even greater relevance for professionals such as accountants, market researchers, stockbrokers, and systems analysts.

To get the best from their people, managers should emphasize anticipated reward value, whether extrinsic or intrinsic.[27] The manager's job is to strengthen effort–performance–reward expectancies. For employees who have difficulty attributing outcomes to their performance, managers must make sure they realize performance-reward connections and then provide performance feedback.

Clarify Performance–Reward Linkages   Not all employees know about or understand how extrinsic organizational rewards link to performance. The managerial challenge is to clarify rewards available to employees and relate them to personal and team performance.[28] Even though many organizations provide little performance-based pay differentiation among people of the same salary grade, a manager can bestow other extrinsic rewards. For example, a manager can allocate more favorable job assignments to those who meet or surpass performance expectations. The key is to make obvious in advance the payoffs people can expect for certain levels of performance, then follow up on satisfactory performance with feedback and appropriate rewards.[29]

Provide Performance Feedback Managers need to provide feedback both to demonstrate that they know what others are doing and to acknowledge improved performance or a job well done. Especially for employees who seem unsure of themselves or tend to externally attribute success, a manager should point out ways in which the employee is improving.[30] Praising specific accomplishments or improvements helps bolster employee esteem and promote internal attribution. It helps forge the link between focused effort, performance improvement, and the personal outcome of recognition from powerful others and personal feelings of pride.

Provide Salient Rewards

We learned from expectance theory that it does little good to try to motivate someone to put forth extra effort in performance if they do not desire the reward you offer as a consequence. The important question for a manager to ask is, "Do subordinates feel that the rewards they can obtain for high performance are worth the effort?" We know that all employees do not value the same rewards equally, and that managers are not the best judges of what employees prefer. Therefore, perhaps the best way to make sure that employees are offered salient rewards is to ask the employees themselves what they prefer. Of course, we also know a wide diversity of answers will result.

One method for adapting to the diversity in preference for work rewards is to offer cafeteria-style benefits.[31] This increasingly popular practice is to let people select from among a portfolio or menu of benefits. One way to implement such a plan is to allocate performance-based credits that employees can cash in on a variety of benefits including bonuses, increased insurance or health benefits, extended vacations, or tuition reimbursements for education.

For example, Arthur has a wife who stays at home with their three children. He may be quite concerned that he has comprehensive family medical coverage with minimum deductibles. Felicia, on the other hand, is single and in her early twenties. She might prefer increased vacation allowances and educational reimbursement benefits in exchange for a higher deductible in her medical insurance plan. Such flexibility in selecting benefits, while not necessarily related to employee output, helps promote a positive answer to the expectancy question: Do I value the rewards available to me?

Reinforce the Right Behavior

Quite often what managers say they want, what they reward, and what they get from employees are not the same.[32] If innovation is espoused, but doing things by the book is what is rewarded, it does not take a psychologist to figure out what the manager actually values. Here are some other familiar examples of rewarding A while hoping for B. One is universities that typically say they emphasize teaching, but most of the rewards they grant are linked to research, and faculty quickly learn where to channel their energy for maximum payoff. Another is businesses that say they want to take care of their customers, then reward managers for cutting costs in ways that negatively impact customers. The lesson is that often, without thinking, managers reinforce the wrong behavior. Such errors in judgment suggest that the selective use of rewards should be a key tactic in managers' efforts to motivate employees. One approach that can help avoid such errors is to apply reinforcement theory through behavior modification.

Behavior modification is a technique of changing behavior through the use of contingent rewards or punishments. Behaviors that lead to positive consequences (rewards) tend to be repeated, whereas behaviors that lead to negative consequences (punishments), or are not reinforced, tend not to be repeated. Consequently, if behaviors are not reinforced, or are punished, they will be extinguished. Also, by providing valued rewards at the right times, a person is more likely to change his or her behavior in a desired direction.[33] Several types of reinforcement and their consequences are described next.

Positive reinforcement occurs when a reward, such as praise or a bonus is given after a desired behavior occurs. Jack Welch, former CEO of General Electric, applied the power of positive reinforcement to motivate employee achievement on an ongoing basis. When he was a group executive in charge of purchasing agents, whenever he learned that an agent obtained a price concession or other win, he would immediately call or write out a note to congratulate the agent.[34]

To eliminate an undesired behavior, *negative reinforcement* can be applied. For example, a manager could punish a late employee in hopes that the behavior would not be repeated. *Punishment* usually is effective in stopping a specific undesired behavior, but it does not reinforce desired behaviors and often causes negative feelings with associated detrimental consequences. It is usually better to try and decrease the frequency of the undesired behavior by withholding any reward when it occurs.

This process of *extinction* can be especially useful when someone is inadvertently being rewarded for doing the wrong thing, as in the preceding examples of rewarding A while hoping for B. Therefore, in the case of the managers who say they want employees to do whatever is necessary to take care of their customers, but then reward people for cutting costs in ways that negatively impact customers, those rewards for any activities, including cost cutting, that negatively impact customers need to be stopped. Now employees no longer have any incentive for cutting costs in ways that negatively impact customers, so this behavior will probably be extinguished over time. The employees still have no incentive to take the desired actions, so to get exactly what you want in terms of changed behavior—in this case, of customer service—positive reinforcement is preferred.

Even highly valued rewards, however, lose their motivating potential unless they are given at the correct times. It is the timing of reinforcements that lets employees know which behaviors are being encouraged. As we saw in the cases of rewarding A while hoping for B, giving rewards at the wrong times can inadvertently increase an undesirable behavior. For example, if an employee comes into a manager's office and complains that a fully warranted raise is long overdue, and the manager grants the raise as a result, the employee may learn to complain more rather than to work harder. In addition, not giving a reward when a desired behavior occurs may extinguish it, as in the case of a professor who quit doing research because she received the same cost of living increase as all other professors at the end of the year, regardless of her superior publication record. Let's look at what the behavioral science research suggests about the timing of rewards.

Reward in a Timely Manner

We know that to motivate a behavior change, we need to reward desirable behaviors. Unfortunately, most organizations have established reward systems that postpone rewards for months, for example, until annual performance reviews are scheduled. These delays dilute the motivational potential of rewards because it is difficult to tie them to specific performance. As you learned in Chapter 8, annual performance reviews can be valuable opportunities to provide feedback on past performance and set new goals, which may cause employees to leave with a new set of commitments.

However, like New Year's resolutions, this high soon wears off because the employee has little to look forward to until next year. To motivate employees to perform at their best throughout the year, more frequent reinforcement is required.

So, how frequently should positive behaviors be rewarded? The schedule you utilize to reward positive behaviors can make a big difference. Is it better to reward employees every time they do well, or only periodically?

The fastest way to establish a desirable behavior is through *continuous reinforcement:* reinforce the desired behavior continuously each and every time it occurs. The drawback is that the desired behavior also diminishes quickly once you stop reinforcing it. Say, for example, that you consistently praise an employee for arriving at work on time. What will happen if you must be away from work for an extended training program? The employee may slip back in being late because without the reinforcement of the expected rewards, behavior is extinguished.

An alternative is *intermittent reinforcement* where the reward is not provided every time it is warranted, but on a random basis that is frequent enough to hook the person to continue trying the desired behavior. Although it may take longer to get someone to change their behavior, intermittent reinforcement is the most powerful way to get sustained changes in behavior. With this schedule, people will continue producing the desired behavior for a long time even without reinforcement, because they are always expecting to "hit the jackpot" on the next try. Have you ever experienced the addictive nature of playing a slot machine, which only pays off infrequently and intermittently?

Administer Rewards Equitably

Once appropriate rewards have been determined for each employee, linkages have been clarified to performance, and the best reinforcement schedule determined, managers still need to consider how workers feel about the equity of the distribution. Motivation is moderated by the perceived fairness or discrepancy between personal contributions and rewards relative to others.

The important question is "Do subordinates feel that work-related benefits are distributed fairly?" If they don't, and especially if they believe that they are on the short end of the distribution, people will make their own adjustments to compensate. Remember the earlier example of the professor who did more research than her colleagues but received the same cost-of-living pay increase each year as everyone else? The result was that the professor quit doing the research because it was not an activity that was being rewarded equitably. If any of the motivation-enhancement skills are going to work, people must perceive an underlying fairness among effort–performance–reward relationships.

An important thing to remember about fairness is that it concerns perceptions about equity that may or may not be valid. Nevertheless, whether they are accurate or distorted, they are accurate in the mind of the beholder. Consequently, managers need to closely monitor employees' perceptions of equity by gathering data and asking clarifying questions. It is possible that this monitoring may uncover false assumptions about how the organization values various behaviors, or faulty comparisons regarding the performance of others. If misperceptions are discovered, they can be clarified, which may reinstate employees' acceptance of the fairness in the reward system. On the other hand, such monitoring may uncover overlooked inequities that management needs to correct.

Tie Pay to Performance

It seems intuitively obvious that if you want to motivate people to perform that you would tie their level of pay to the quantity and/or quality of work that they produce. It is a fact, however, that since the 1950s, most employees have been paid on the basis of nonperformance factors, such as their job classification, pay grade, hours worked, or seniority. Uniform systems of pay may seem equitable, but from a motivational perspective, such nonperformance payments do not necessarily encourage stellar performance.

By the mid-1990s, nearly 60 percent of firms participating in a national compensation survey were offering "results-sharing" programs that did tie pay with performance.[35] Walt Disney Company began offering an annual bonus program for animators, directors, and producers who work on its profitable animated movies. A majority of its employees receive bonuses based on division profitability. In the executive suite, after years of defending shareholder charges of excessive pay, corporations are finally linking executive pay to performance. A major performance benchmark for CEOs is the firm's stock performance. When Quaker Oats Co. stock fell by 13 percent, CEO William D. Smithburg received an 11 percent cut in salary and bonus to $1.4 million.[36] Such a scenario, with fluctuating rewards, is becoming more commonplace.

Performance-based compensation schemes are consistent with the expectancy theory of motivation. Employees compare rewards received for performance with what they expect to receive. They also compare what they receive with what others receive (the equity factor). Overall satisfaction is likely a composite of how the employee perceives both the extrinsic and intrinsic rewards from the job.[37] In the following paragraphs, some methods of administering performance-based compensation are explained.

Piecework or Standard-Hour Systems   The classic performance-based reward system is based on *piecework,* or payment for the amount produced consistent with specified quality standards. Piecework systems do motivate workers when a person can directly affect his or her rate of output, and the output (quality and quantity) can easily be measured or verified. Some programmers' pay depends on how many lines of code they write; magazine writers are often paid by the number of words in their articles. Shirt makers in El Salvador are paid a few cents (typically about 7 cents) for each shirt they sew.

A pay-for-performance variation is to use a *standard-hour plan.* Such plans specify the normal time required to complete a task, coupled with a standard rate of pay. For example, the standard for a dental hygienist to clean a patient's teeth may be 45 minutes at a rate of $40. The more skillful technician may be able to serve more patients per day, receiving pay for each at the standard rate.

Two difficult issues plague any piece- or standard-rate plan.[38] One is evaluating work methods to arrive at an equitable standard and rate. Because managers like to periodically adjust one or both compensation factors, the issue of equity can be controversial. The second concern is the quality-quantity trade-off. Without appropriate quality controls, quality may be sacrificed to reach quantity targets. As previously noted, behavior tends to focus on what is measured.

Merit Pay   Rather than tie pay only to output, an alternative is to provide a base salary or hourly wage and then an incentive or bonus based on output. Where the base plus merit incentive system is used, the performance-based portion depends on some measurable level of output over which the employee has control. Output could be measured by volume, defect rate (or quality), or cost savings. Sales representatives often earn a base salary plus commissions based on the level of sales above a set base figure.

Bonus and Profit-Sharing Plans   Many compensation plans are based on the overall performance of the enterprise rather than the individual's contribution. Profit sharing has become common in many firms including Domino's Pizza, where everyone owns stock and profits are distributed back to members.[39] In merit-based pay plans, a pool of money is divided among eligible employees based on some performance evaluation or rating system. The objective of profit-sharing plans such as bonuses and stock options is to link everyone's fate to overall organization performance, reinforcing corporate cultures that emphasize group results over individual performance.

For Wal-Mart, corporate profit growth is a primary goal, and the profit-sharing plan is keyed to it.[40] Every employee who works at least 1,000 hours per year is eligible for profit sharing. The firm contributes a percentage of every eligible employee's wages or salary (an average of 6 percent over the last 10 years) into a fund, from which the employee can withdraw cash when leaving the company. This plan helps employees commit to long-term corporate and personal financial growth.

Gainsharing Plans Gainsharing is an umbrella for approaches to encourage employees at all levels to be responsible for improving organizational efficiency. Gainsharing plans link financial rewards for all employees to improvements in performance of the entire business unit.[41]

Houston-based Panhandle Eastern Corp. introduced gainsharing following deregulation of the natural gas industry in an effort to make employees more cost and profit conscious. In their plan, if the company achieves earnings per share of $2.00, all Panhandle employees receive a bonus of 2 percent of their salary at year-end. For earnings of $2.10 or more per share, the bonus climbs to 3 percent. Panhandle's gainsharing expectancies apply at all organizational levels.

Empower Employees to Achieve

Empowerment describes conditions that enable people to feel competent and in control, energized to take the initiative and persist at meaningful tasks.[42] Empowerment aspires to bring about positive self-perceptions (self-concept, self-esteem, and self-efficacy) and task-directed behaviors. A manager can empower employees by giving them the authority, tools, and information they need to do their jobs with greater autonomy. As a result, employees' feelings of self-efficacy are enhanced and they are enabled to more fully use their potential, which satisfies their higher-level needs for achievement, recognition, and self-actualization.

As a management practice, empowerment also means managers open communications, delegate power, share information, and cut away at the debilitating tangles of corporate bureaucracy. The manager who deliberately works to empower his or her employees gives them the license to pursue their visions, to champion projects, and to improve practices consistent with organizational missions and goals. The manager who shares responsibilities with subordinates and treats them as partners is likely to get the best from them.[43]

Empowered people usually intensify their task focus and are energized to become more committed to a cause or goal. They experience self-efficacy, which stimulates motivation by enabling people to see themselves as competent and capable of high performance.[44]

Empowerment also is manifested in active problem-solving behaviors that concentrate energy on a goal. The empowered person is more flexible in behavior, tries alternative paths when one is blocked, and eagerly initiates new tasks or adds complexity to current ones.[45] Behavior becomes self-motivated when the individual seeks to carve out greater personal autonomy in undertaking tasks without the manager's help.

Empowerment success stories abound. At Sun Microsystems, CEO Scott G. McNealy has built an empowering corporate culture around his motto, "Kick butt and have fun."[46] At Saturn Corporation, self-managing work teams are responsible for resolving their own conflicts, planning their own work schedule, determining their own job assignments, making selection decisions about new members, performing within their own budgets, and obtaining their own supplies. At Scandinavian Air Systems, ticket agents have the authority to reticket a passenger or move the passenger up a class, if they feel the situation warrants it. At a Marriott chain subsidiary, every hotel employee is empowered to offer guests a free night's stay if they believe that the hotel has been lax in serving the guest.[47]

Redesign Jobs

Chapter 11 describes how well-designed jobs lead to high motivation, high-quality performance, high satisfaction, and low absenteeism and turnover. For these outcomes to occur, managers need to ensure that workers experience challenging work, believe they are doing something meaningful because their work is important to other people, feel personally responsible for how the work turns out, and receive feedback on how well they perform their jobs.[48] If these conditions exist, employees can experience high-level motivators such as increased responsibility, achievement, recognition, growth, and learning. Additional benefits of jobs rating high in motivational design are lower boredom and absenteeism.

A manager can do several things to enrich oversimplified jobs that lack motivational incentives. Job enhancement strategies need to empower employees by providing control over the resources needed to perform well and the authority to make decisions about how to do the tasks. The five following strategies can be used to enrich jobs.[49]

1. ***Combine tasks.*** To improve skill variety, task identity, and interdependence, jobs can be enlarged by combining tasks that are overly specialized and fragmented. Tasks may be combined by having one individual complete a larger module of work or by establishing teams in which members periodically switch tasks.
2. ***Load jobs vertically.*** To improve autonomy, you can empower employees by combining responsibilities for planning, executing, and adjusting work activities. For this type of loading, you can authorize employees to schedule their own work, decide on work methods, troubleshoot problems, train others, and monitor quality.
3. ***Open feedback channels.*** To improve interaction with others and clarify task significance, managers should develop systems where employees directly receive all possible feedback about factors that affect their work. The best feedback sources are the job itself, peers, and access to computerized databases, not the manager's perceptions and judgmental comments.
4. ***Establish client relationships.*** To improve skill variety, autonomy, interaction with others, and feedback, employees whose actions impact on customers should periodically interact directly with customers. To enable this interaction a manager can (a) identify a relevant client or customer contact for employees, (b) structure the most direct contact possible, such as on-site visits for commercial customers, and (c) have the work group set up criteria by which the customer can evaluate work quality and channel any remarks directly to the employee or work team.
5. ***Form natural work teams.*** To improve skill variety, task significance, friendship, and interdependence, link people together when the job performed by one person affects others. Bringing people together as a team enhances identification with the whole task and creates a sense of shared responsibility. Some Hewlett-Packard divisions, for example, have moved design engineers into the middle of the production area to provide a team project focus. They interact with assemblers and manufacturing operators and obtain clues to improving manufacturing processes.[50] Such experiences are expanding the use of teams to engage nonmanagers in wide-ranging problem solving and quality improvement.

Make Available Opportunities to Learn

Making available opportunities to learn is motivational because it enables employees to grow and develop, which provides a route to fulfilling their potential. As employees learn new skills, they become competent to complete more complex tasks. This competency satisfies their needs for achievement, enhances their sense of self-efficacy, and helps them progress towards self-actualization. An outstanding example of learning motivation in action has been provided by Chevron USA, which survived dramatic industry changes by training and redeploying employees cut during downsizing so they could assume new jobs. Not only were employees grateful to Chevron for avoiding threats to their basic survival needs, but Chevron's help in upgrading their skills has made them highly motivated by the recognition that they are valued by the firm.[51]

Some companies, recognizing the payoff to the organization that has multiskilled, committed employees, have added incentives to continue learning by basing salaries on the number and quality of skills employees possess.[52] This pay basis provides satisfaction for basic needs and esteem needs. When increased education and skills lead to promotions to higher positions in the company, learning also satisfies needs for growth and self-actualization.

Managers can provide some forms of learning personally through helping, mentoring, and coaching subordinates. Information was provided about these methods in Chapter 13. A large variety of companywide programs can also be set up to provide incentives to learn, including on-the-job training, in-house seminars, tuition reimbursement for courses and degree programs, and sponsorship for attending continuing education certification programs, workshops, conferences, or correspondence courses.

CONCEPT QUIZ

Complete the following true-false quiz by circling the correct answer. Answers are at the end of the quiz. After marking your answers, remember to go back and check your understanding of any answers you missed.

True or False   1. Motivation consists of a conscious decision to direct effort in an activity to achieve a goal that will satisfy a predominate need.

True or False   2. All workers want the same outcomes, so managers can effectively motivate people by providing rewards that managers think workers prefer.

True or False   3. People will always do their best on a job if they have the necessary training, skills, and abilities.

True or False   4. Because most employees have their basic physiological and safety needs satisfied, the higher, learned needs are the ones that hold the most potential for motivation.

True or False   5. It is not good to promote people with high institutional power needs to management positions because they become self-serving, exploitative, and dominating bosses.

True or False   6. Subordinates are more likely to "buy into" goals if they have a part in determining what they will be and how they will be accomplished.

True or False   7. The most important question in expectance theory is: does how hard I try really affect my performance?

True or False   8. Most people prefer intrinsic rather than extrinsic rewards.

True or False   9. Motivation is moderated by the perceived fairness or discrepancy between personal contributions and rewards relative to others.

True or False   10. Even highly valued rewards lose their motivating potential unless they are given at the correct times.

Answers.   (1) True; (2) False; (3) False; (4) True; (5) False; (6) True; (7) False; (8) False; (9) True; (10) True

BEHAVIORAL CHECKLIST

The following skills are important to motivating others. Use them when evaluating your own motivation skills and those of others.

The Effective Motivator

- Enhances commitment to goals through clarification and participation.
- Strengthens effort–performance–reward expectancies.
- Provides salient rewards.
- Utilizes positive reinforcement.
- Rewards in a timely manner.
- Administers rewards equitably.
- Ties pay to performance.
- Empowers employees to achieve.
- Redesigns jobs to motivate employees.
- Makes available opportunities to learn.

> **Attention!**
> Do not read the following until assigned to do so by your instructor.

MODELING EXERCISE

Reshaping Unacceptable Behaviors[53]

One of the most challenging aspects of management is transforming inappropriate behaviors into appropriate behaviors. Managers commonly take insufficient action to transform negative actions into positive ones. Some of these insufficient responses include assuming that ignoring an employee's shortcomings will make them go away; praising positive aspects of an individual's performance in hopes that the praise will encourage him or her to rechannel unproductive energies; discussing problems in vague, general terms in a group meeting, in hopes that the unproductive person will take the "hint" and change; and getting upset with an individual and demanding that he or she shape up.

Directions.   One volunteer assumes the role of the manager Andre Tate, and another assumes the role of a staff member Shaheen Matombo. Role-players read only their own role, and prepare for the role-play. Other class members read both roles and review the Observer's Rating Sheet. After the role-play discussion, observers will provide feedback to the person playing the manager, Andre Tate, on his or her performance, using the Observer's Rating Sheet as a guide. Then, the class discusses other options to resolve this problem.

Andre Tate's Role   Shaheen has been a member of your staff for only three months. You don't know much about her other than that she is a single parent who has recently entered the workforce after a difficult divorce. She is often 10 to 20 minutes late for work in the morning. You are the manager of a hectic customer relations office for a utility company. The phones start ringing promptly at 8:00. When she is late for work, you have to answer her phone, which interrupts your own work schedule. This morning, you are particularly annoyed. She is 25 minutes late, and the phones are ringing like crazy. Because you have been forced to answer them, it will be difficult for you to complete an important assignment by its noon deadline. You are getting more upset by the minute.

While you are in the middle of a particularly unpleasant phone conversation with an irate customer, you look out your window and see Shaheen bounding up the steps to the building. You think to yourself, "This is ridiculous, I've got to put a stop to her tardiness. Maybe I should just threaten to fire her unless she shapes up." Upon further reflection, you realize this action would be impractical, especially during this period of retrenchment after a rate hike was turned down. Given the rumors about a possible hiring freeze, you know it may be difficult to refill any vacancies.

Also, Shaheen is actually a pretty good worker when she is there. She is conscientious and has a real knack with cranky callers. Unfortunately, it has taken her much longer than expected to learn the computer program for retrieving information on customer accounts. She frequently has to put callers on hold while she asks for help. These interruptions have tended to increase an already tense relationship with the rest of the office staff. She has had some difficulty fitting in socially; the others are much younger and have worked together for several years. Shaheen is the first new hire in a long time, so the others are not used to breaking someone in. Three of your staff have complained to you about Shaheen's constant interruptions. They feel their productivity is going down as a result. Besides, she seems to expect them to drop whatever they are doing every time she has a question. They had expected their workload to be lighter when a new person was hired, but now they are having second thoughts. (In the past, you have had enough time to train new hires, but your boss has had you tied up on a major project for almost a year.)

Shaheen enters the office obviously flustered and disheveled. She has "I'm sorry" written all over her face. You motion for her to pick up the blinking phone line and then scribble a note on a tablet while you complete your call: "See me in my office at 12:00 sharp!" It is time you got to the bottom of Shaheen's disruptive influence on an otherwise smooth-flowing operation.

Shaheen Matombo's Role   Boy, what a morning! Your babysitter's father died during the night, and she called you from the airport at 6:30 A.M. saying she would be out of town for three or four days. You tried three usually available backups before you finally found someone who could take Keen, your three-year-old. Then Shayla, your seventh-grader, went through five outfits before she was satisfied that she had just the right look for her first yearbook picture. It is a miracle that Buddy, your oldest, was able to pull himself out of bed after getting only five hours of sleep. On top of football and drama, he has now joined the chess team, and they had their first tournament last night. Why did it have to fall on the night before his final in physics? This morning you wished you had his knack for juggling so many activities. By the time you got the kids delivered, you were already 10 minutes behind schedule. Then an incredible accident on the expressway slowed traffic to a crawl.

As you finally pull off the downtown exit ramp, you notice you are almost 20 minutes late for work. "My kingdom for a cell phone with a charged battery!" you groan. As you desperately scan the side streets for a parking space, you begin to panic. "How am I going to explain this to Andre? He will be furious. I'm sure he is upset about my chronic lateness. On top of that, he is obviously disappointed with my lack of computer skills, and I am sure the others complain to him about having to train a newcomer." You are sure that one of the reasons you got the job was that you had completed a computer class at the local community college. Unfortunately, the carryover to the incredibly complex computer program you use at work had been minimal. (It seems to defy every convention of logic.)

"What am I going to tell him about my being late for work so often?" Unfortunately, you have no easy answer. "Maybe it will get better as the kids and I get used to this new routine. It's just very difficult to get the kids to the bus stop and the sitter, commute 20 minutes, and arrive precisely at 8:00. I wonder if he would allow me to come in at 8:30 and only take a half-hour lunch. Staying late wouldn't work because they close down the computers at 5:00, unless I could do some paperwork for half an hour."

Then what about the problems with the computer and the other staff members? "Sooner or later he's going to get on my case about those things. Is it my fault I don't think like a computer? Some people might be able to sit down and figure this program out in a couple of hours, but not me. So is that my fault or should someone be giving me more training? I wish the others weren't so cliquish and unwilling to help me out. I wonder why that's the case. It is as if they are afraid I will become as good as they are if they share their experience with me. I wish Andre had more time to help me learn the ropes, but he seems to always be in meetings."

"Well, I'm probably going to catch it this morning. I've never been this late. Maybe I'll be back home full-time sooner than I expected."

OBSERVER'S RATING SHEET

On completion of the exercise, evaluate Andre's motivation skills. Rate the motivation skills between 1 and 5 using the following scale. Write in concrete examples in the space for comments below each criteria skill to use in explaining your feedback.

1	*2*	*3*	*4*	*5*
Unsatisfactory	*Weak*	*Adequate*	*Good*	*Outstanding*

_____ Enhanced commitment to goals through clarification and participation.

_____ Strengthened effort–performance–reward expectancies.

_____ Provided salient rewards.

_____ Utilized positive reinforcement.

_____ Rewarded in a timely manner.

_____ Administered rewards equitably.

_____ Tied pay to performance.

_____ Empowered employees to achieve.

_____ Redesigned jobs to motivate employees.

_____ Made available opportunities to learn.

GROUP EXERCISES

Three different types of group exercises are presented here. First is a short case for you to practice diagnosing motivational problems. Second is an interview role-play to determine what motivates a team member. Third is a team problem-solving exercise for improving motivation.

Group Exercise 1: Case Study: Ralph Henry's Motivational Crisis

Ralph Henry had worked as a production chemist at Systems Diagnostics Corporation (SDC) for seven years. The last four of those years were with the MED group, during which he received two promotions to become the group's senior chemist. Conscientious and thorough in his work, Ralph was a stickler for details in the lab yet always willing to help others. Coworkers liked Ralph's pleasant, friendly manner and his lively conversations about sports and running (his major avocations). However, beyond the immediate group, Ralph was rather private. He interacted with few people outside the MED group and rarely attended social functions and company parties.

Ralph had always enjoyed his career as a chemist. He was particularly pleased with the laboratory environment, which allowed him to work freely and independently, pursuing whatever challenge or idea that came along. It was no big surprise, then, when Ken Chang asked Ralph to become supervisor of the MED group and take over the role Chang had held for three years.

The Reorganization. Systems Diagnostics Corporation makes diagnostic reagent kits and pharmaceutical instrumentation for hospitals, clinical laboratories, and some government agencies. The firm was having difficulties containing costs and had recently announced the third consecutive decline in quarterly profits. Although sales were steady, with the latest announcement of profit erosion, senior management also announced a reorganization to consolidate product lines. As a result of the reorganization, Ken Chang was promoted to production manager of a newly created division, leaving vacant his former position as supervisor of the MED group. While a supervisor, Ken spent much of his time outside the group and, in doing so, granted considerable autonomy to his chemists.

When offered the supervisor's position, Ralph initially balked. He explained to Ken his reluctance to leave the lab bench and his feelings of uneasiness about supervising a group of longtime peers. All of his education was in pure science; he had no management training or experience. Ken promised that Ralph could participate in management training seminars and expressed his confidence that Ralph would quickly master the art of management.

The Promotion. After a week of contemplation, Ralph accepted. When his appointment was announced, members of the MED group were delighted and hosted a congratulatory luncheon for Ralph.

Six months into the supervisory job, Ralph's attitude was as conscientious and upbeat as ever. Much of his time was spent thoroughly checking each group member's work. Unlike Ken in the role of supervisor, Ralph required that all product tests be documented in detail and often requested that routine lab testings be repeated to confirm accuracy. Rather than delegate difficult problems to group members, Ralph took on most of these complex lab tasks himself and often worked late into the evening.

The Crisis. In mid-December a major crisis required Ralph's immediate attention. The deadline on a large naval contract assigned to the MED group was moved from mid-February to mid-January. Management wanted very much to make good on this contract because the Navy was a potential major customer. However, because of technical difficulties and because SDC had a tradition of shutting down during the holidays, Ralph did not believe MED would meet the deadline. To respond to the pressure, Ralph called a meeting of all group members, something he rarely did. He spelled out the situation:

"As you are all aware, we are having a big technical problem with the Navy contract. To compound our troubles, I just got word from management that the deadline has been moved up one month to mid-January. This change really puts us in a jam because the plant is scheduled to be shut down for 10 days over the holidays.

"Personally, I know the project is more important than my holiday plans, so I'm canceling them. What I'd like to know is who will be willing to work with me, say, a few of the 10 days. Of course you will get comp time or overtime pay, if you prefer. How many of you will be willing to work with me?"

The group was silent. Not one of the 10 members raised a hand or spoke up.

QUESTIONS FOR DISCUSSION

1. What motivates Ralph Henry? How do these forces impact on his behavior as a chemist? As a supervisor?
2. What likely motivates the other chemists in the MED group? How well does Ralph understand these motivational forces and adjust his supervisory behavior to bring out their best? Compare the motivational impact on the chemists of Ken Chang's approach to supervision with that of Ralph Henry.
3. Why the "no hands" response to Ralph's request for help? What does it indicate about Ralph's development as a supervisor? Given no volunteers, what does Ralph do now?

Group Exercise 2: Role-Play: Uncovering Motivational Valences[54]

Purpose.   To provide an opportunity to practice determining the motivational factors that keep employees on the job and motivate them to perform.

Directions.   The class divides into pairs of students. In each pair, one student plays the role of a team leader who is developing a plan to highly motivate the team member being interviewed. The other student plays the role of the team member being interviewed. The twist to this role play is that the team member reflects on his or her actual motivators (rewards that he or she would like to attain).

The team leader might ask several questions while conducting an interview for approximately 3 minutes. In addition, when the team member reveals an important piece of information, the team leader will dig for more details. Suggested interview questions are as follows:

1. Why are you working on this team?
2. What can the company do to make you really happy?
3. What would be a fair reward for performing up to your capacity? On a scale of 1 to 10, how badly do you want this reward?
4. What would be an outstanding reward for you for performing up to your capacity?
5. What would be a fantasy reward for you for performing up to your capacity? On a scale of 1 to 10, how badly do you want this reward?
6. What do you hope to get out of this job?

Debriefing.   A brief class discussion might follow the completion of the interviews. A key issue to address in the discussion is the extent to which each interview appeared helpful in motivating the team member. For example, were the interviews an effective method of uncovering the valences the team members attached to specific rewards?

Group Exercise 3: Improving Motivation at Lightning Rod Steel

Purpose.　This team-based exercise is designed to (1) analyze the motivational implications of data generated by a group of engineers working for Lightning Rod Steel (LRS), (2) develop and present to the class a theory-supported action plan for improving motivation of the engineers, and (3) use the same criteria developed by the engineers to assess motivational factors affecting you in a work situation.

Time.　35 to 45 minutes.

Directions.　Perform the following five tasks:

1. Assemble the class into teams of five to seven students each.
2. As a team, read the background material, including Exhibit 17-3 (**about 3 to 4 minutes**).
3. Have each team first analyze the Lightning Rod situation to determine the presumed lack of motivation among engineers. Then, use one established theory of motivation as the basis for developing an action plan of recommendations to "improve the motivation" of the steel company engineers. What specific actions should the managers take? Make sure your plan is feasible and reasonable for the managers to accept (**10 to 15 minutes**).
4. Have each team member score the 19 motivational factors listed by the engineers in Exhibit 17-3. Determine how much each factor contributes to *your* motivation in an ideal work situation. Assign points from 0 to 5, where 5 means "extremely desirable" and 0 indicates "unimportant." Record your points in the Your Ideal Scores section of the exhibit. Then think of any factors important to you that are missing from the list. Compare your responses to those of the engineers and your team members. Plan to comment to the class on why your team scores were similar to or different from the engineers' scores (**10 minutes**).
5. Present your recommendations and observations to the class. Debrief the activity to look for insights into how motivational expectations and motives differ among your peers (**15 minutes**).

Background of Lightning Rod Steel (LRS)

Lightning Rod produces a number of rolled, bar, and tubular steel products from a single mill fueled by two electric hearth furnaces that melt recycled scrap metal. Kent Olsen, the director of manufacturing services, and his two engineering managers are concerned that, given a recession-induced soft market for steel and the constant need to cut costs by improving efficiencies, "we aren't getting 100 percent from our engineering staff." Engineers number about three dozen and are of two types. Design engineers work on special projects for plant modernization. Industrial engineers update work standards, work method improvements, compensation incentives, and similar projects.

Olsen approaches your consulting group with a couple of questions: "One of the issues we have been unable to resolve among ourselves is how to determine the productivity of engineering professionals, and then how to improve it. Second, why aren't more of our engineers being pirated away by our seven operating general managers for higher paying managerial jobs?" He hands you a page (Exhibit 17-3) developed by the engineers during a recent training session. The data were developed in response to the question "Brainstorm a list of what you would like to experience more often or have more of in your work situation, then evaluate ideal and actual conditions on a 0-to-5-point scale." Olsen continues, "Maybe this gives you some clues as to what we could do better to motivate engineers."

EXHIBIT 17-3 What LRS Engineers Expect at Work

Note: Scores reflect the group mean, with 5 points maximum.

| | Engineers' Scores | | |
Work Factors	Ideal Conditions	Actual Experience	Your Ideal Scores
1. Open and honest communication	4.8	2.2	_____
2. A sense of fairness and justice	4.3	2.0	_____
3. Seeing the results of my work	4.3	2.7	_____
4. The opportunity to get my job done	4.2	2.5	_____
5. Feedback about how I am doing	4.0	2.0	_____
6. Interesting work assignments	4.0	2.2	_____
7. Opportunity for advancement	4.0	0.5	_____
8. Being compensated for performance	4.0	1.5	_____
9. Upward and/or lateral job mobility	4.0	0.8	_____
10. Recognition for work accomplishments	3.8	1.8	_____
11. A say in things that affect me	3.8	1.8	_____
12. A sense of involvement in the company	3.7	2.0	_____
13. Being informed of policies/job openings	3.5	0.7	_____
14. Working for a winning/successful team	3.2	1.7	_____
15. Even work distribution (no peaks/valleys)	3.0	2.0	_____
16. Equitable access to benefits	3.0	2.8	_____
17. A variety of tasks (job rotation)	2.8	1.8	_____
18. Security of not working myself out of job	2.5	1.5	_____
19. Good physical working environment	2.0	1.3	_____

SUMMARY CHECKLIST

Take a few minutes to reflect on your performance and look over others' ratings of your motivation skills. Now assess yourself on each of the key learning behaviors. Make a check (✓) next to those behaviors on which you need improvement.

_____ **Enhancing commitment to goals.**
    1. Encourage participation.
    2. Clarify.
    3. Make specific goals.
    4. Ensure that goals are challenging.

_____ **Strengthening effort–performance–reward expectancies.**
    1. Emphasize anticipated reward value.
    2. Clarify performance–reward linkages.
    3. Provide performance feedback.

_____ **Providing salient rewards.**
    1. Do not assume that all people want the same thing.
    2. Do not assume that you know what people want for rewards.

3. Ask the employees themselves what rewards they prefer.
4. Offer cafeteria-style benefits.

_____ **Utilizing positive reinforcement.**
1. Beware of rewarding A while hoping for B—you get what you actually reward.
2. Provide rewards after desired behaviors occur to positively reinforce their reoccurrence.
3. Punish, or do not reinforce, undesired behaviors so that they will be extinguished.

_____ **Rewarding in a timely manner.**
1. To get the fastest change in behavior, reinforce the desired behavior continuously each and every time it occurs.
2. Use intermittent reinforcement where the reward is provided on a random basis to get sustained changes in behavior.

_____ **Administering rewards equitably.**
1. Determine whether subordinates feel that work-related benefits are distributed fairly.
2. Clarify misperceptions.
3. Correct inequities.

_____ **Tying pay to performance.**
1. Use piecework to pay for the amount produced when workers can directly affect their rate and quality of output.
2. Use merit pay where a salary plus merit incentive system is based on some measurable level of output over which the employee has control.
3. Use profit sharing, bonuses, and stock options to link everyone's fate to overall organization performance and reinforce corporate cultures emphasizing group results over individual performance.
4. Use gainsharing to link financial rewards for all employees to improvements in performance of the entire business.

_____ **Empowering employees to achieve.**
1. Give employees the authority, tools, and information they need to do their jobs with greater autonomy.
2. Open communications, delegate power, share information, and cut away debilitating corporate bureaucracy.
3. Give employees license to pursue their visions, to champion projects, and to improve practices consistent with organizational mission and goals.
4. Share responsibilities with subordinates and treat them as partners.

_____ **Redesigning jobs to motivate employees.**
1. Combine tasks to improve skill variety, task identity, and interdependence.
2. Load jobs vertically to improve autonomy by combining responsibilities for planning, executing, and adjusting work activities.
3. Develop systems where employees directly receive all possible feedback about factors that affect their work.
4. Establish worker-client relationships.
5. Form natural work teams to enhance identification with the whole task and create a sense of shared responsibility.

_____ **Making available opportunities to learn.**
1. Help, mentor, and coach subordinates yourself.
2. Provide opportunities for on-the-job training, in-house seminars, and tuition reimbursement for courses, degree programs, and sponsorship for workshops and conferences.

APPLICATION QUESTIONS

1. Think of a coach, teacher, or supervisor who really motivated you to enhance your performance in a specific task. What did this person do that motivated you so?
2. What are the predominate needs that you want to satisfy in task situations? Are you more concerned about compensation, status, achieving something worthwhile, being in charge of others, socializing with members of a team, learning something new, or what?
3. Have you ever had a mentor at work or school? What was it about this person that was valuable to you? If you have not had a mentor, what characteristics would you like to have in one?
4. What motivates you to stay on a job, or in a degree program versus look for another, better alternative?
5. As long as you are receiving the job benefits you agreed to when you started a job, does it matter to you that others are receiving better or worse deals? Why or why not?

REINFORCEMENT EXERCISES

1. Interview several professors about what motivates them in their jobs. Compare the answers and determine whether professors are intrinsically or extrinsically motivated, what needs they seek to satisfy on the job, and how they decide where to invest their efforts. Repeat these interviews with people in different occupations and see if you can determine any differences.
2. Practice behavioral modification. Choose a friend, a small child, or a pet. Decide on a behavior that you want to modify. Provide rewards after the desired behavior occurs to positively reinforce its reoccurrence. Punish with a negative reaction on your part, or do not reinforce, undesired behaviors so that they will be extinguished. After a week of reinforcement, how successful were you in modifying the behavior? Share your experiences with your class or a group of classmates. What were the common lessons you learned?
3. Interview a human resources director in any type of organization (company, school, hospital, etc.) about the compensation packages available for hourly employees, skilled workers, and managers. What did you learn about how the organization uses pay to motivate employees? Did you find differences in the compensation for different types of employees? If so, what motivational assumptions do you think these differences were based on?
4. Talk to five or six of your friends about their career plans and why they are choosing particular careers. What can you determine from your conversations about what motivates different people to choose different careers?

ACTION PLAN

1. Which motivation behavior do I most want to improve?
2. Why? What will be my payoff?
3. What potential obstacles stand in my way?
4. What are the specific things I will do to improve? (For examples, see the Reinforcement Exercises.)
5. When will I do them?
6. How and when will I measure my success?

NOTES

1. Adapted from D. A. Whetten and K. S. Cameron, *Developing Management Skills,* 4th ed. (Reading, MA: Addison-Wesley, 1998) 276–277.
2. C. W. Cook, P. L. Hunsaker, and R. E. Coffey, *Management and Organizational Behavior,* 2d ed. (Homewood, IL: Irwin, 1997) 185.
3. *Manpower Argus* no. 375 (December 1999), 11.
4. Ibid.
5. See for example, K. A. Kovach, "What Motivates Employees? Workers and Supervisors Give Different Answers," *Business Horizons* (September–October 1987): 60–66.
6. D. A. Whetten and K. S. Cameron, 1998.
7. For elaboration, see V. Vroom, *Work and Motivation* (New York: Wiley, 1964); R. M. Steers, L. W. Porter, and G. A. Begley, *Motivation and Leadership at Work* (New York: McGraw-Hill, 1996).
8. A. Maslow, *Motivation and Personality* (New York: Harper & Row, 1954).
9. D. C. McClelland, *The Achieving Society* (New York: Van Nostrand Reinhold, 1961).
10. D. C. McClelland, "Achievement Motivation Can Be Developed," *Harvard Business Review* 43 (November–December 1965), 6–8.
11. D. C. McClelland and D. H. Burnham, "Power Is the Great Motivator"; D. C. McClelland, *Power: The Inner Experience* (New York: Irvington, 1975).
12. C. M. Kelly, "The Interrelationship of Ethics and Power in Today's Organizations," *Organizational Dynamics* 5 (Summer 1987).
13. Ibid.
14. D. C. McClelland and D. H. Burnham, "Power Is the Great Motivator," *Harvard Business Review* 73 (January–February 1995): 126–39.
15. P. C. Earley and R. Kanfer, "The Influence of Component Participation and Role Models on Goal Acceptance, Goal Satisfaction and Performance," *Organizational Behavior and Human Decision Processes* 36 (1985): 378–90.
16. M. Erez, P. C. Earley, and C. L. Hulin, "The Impact of Participation on Goal Acceptance and Performance: A Two-Step Model," *Academy of Management Journal* 28 (February 1985): 50–66.
17. G. P. Latham and H. A. Marshal, "The Effects of Self-Set, Participatively Set and Assigned Goals on the Performance of Government Employees," *Personnel Psychology* 35 (1982): 399–404.
18. G. Dangot-Simpkin, "Getting Your Staff to Do What You Want," *Supervisory Management* 36 (January 1991): 4–5.
19. J. P. Wanous, T. L. Keon, and J. C. Latack, "Expectancy Theory and Occupational/Organizational Choices: A Review and Test," *Organizational Behavior and Human Performance* (August 1983): 66–86.
20. L. W. Porter and E. E. Lawler III, *Managerial Attitudes and Performance* (Homewood, IL: Irwin, 1968); and E. E. Lawler III, *Motivation in Work Organizations* (Monterey, CA: Brooks/Cole, 1973).
21. J. M. George, "Extrinsic and Intrinsic Origins of Perceived Social Loafing in Organizations," *Academy of Management Journal* 35 (March 1992): 191–202.
22. R. M. Steers and L. W. Porter, *Motivation and Work Behavior,* 4th ed. (New York: McGraw-Hill, 1987).
23. R. T. Mowday, "Equity Theory Predictions of Behavior in Organizations," in R. M. Steers and L. W. Porter, eds., *Motivation and Work Behavior,* 4th ed. (New York: McGraw-Hill, 1987) 91–113.
24. Ibid.
25. J. Brockner et al., "Layoffs, Equity Theory, and Work Performance: Further Evidence of the Impact of Survivor Guilt," *Academy of Management Journal* 29 (June 1986): 373–84.
26. P. K. Tyagi, "Inequities in Organizations, Salesperson Motivation and Job Satisfaction," *International Journal of Research in Marketing* 7 (December 1990): 135–48.
27. J. A. Bradt, "Pay for Impact," *Personnel Journal* 70 (May 1991): 76–79.
28. T. L. Quick, "Simple Is Hard, Complex Is Easy, Simplistic Is Impossible," *Training and Development Journal* 44 (May 1990): 94–99.
29. J. T. Knippen and T. B. Green, "Boost Performance Through Appraisals," *Business Credit* 92 (November–December 1990): 27.
30. M. F. Villere and S. J. Hartman, "The Key to Motivation Is in the Process: An Examination of Practical Implications of Expectancy Theory," *Leadership and Organization Development Journal* 11, no. 4 (1990): 1–3.
31. "More Benefits Bend with Workers' Needs," *Wall Street Journal,* January 9, 1990, B1.
32. S. Kerr, "On the Folly of Rewarding A, While Hoping for B," in B. M. Staw, ed., *Psychological Dimensions of Organizational Behavior* (New York: Macmillan, 1991) 65–75, originally published in *Academy of Management Journal* 18 (1975): 769–83.
33. W. C. Hamner, "Reinforcement Theory in Management and Organizational Settings," in H. Tosi and W. C. Hamner, *Organizational Behavior and Management: A Contingency Approach* (Chicago: Saint Claire, 1974), 86–112.
34. T. Peters and N. Austin, *A Passion for Excellence: The Leadership Difference* (New York: Random House, 1985) 267.
35. "Employers Spice Up Their Compensation Packages with Special Bonuses," *Wall Street Journal,* October 24, 1995, A-1.

36. "Deliver—or Else: Pay for Performance Is Making an Impact on CEO Paychecks," *Business Week,* March 27, 1995, 36.

37. E. E. Lawler III, *Pay and Organizational Development* (Reading, MA: Addison-Wesley, 1981).

38. C. W. Hamner, "How to Ruin Motivation with Pay," *Compensation Review* 21 (1975): 88–89.

39. "When Are Employees Not Employees? When They're Associates, Stakeholders . . . ," *Wall Street Journal,* November 9, 1988, B1.

40. S. Walton with J. Huey, *Sam Walton: Made in America* (New York: Doubleday, 1992) 132–33.

41. T. M. Welbourne and L. R. Gomez-Mejia, "Gainsharing: A Critical Review and a Future Research Agenda," *Journal of Management* 21 (September 1995): 559+.

42. J. A. Conger and R. N. Kanungo, "The Empowerment Process: Integrating Theory and Practice," *Academy of Management Review* 13 (July 1988): 471–82.

43. A. R. Cohen and D. L. Bradford, *Managing for Excellence: The Guide to High Performance in Contemporary Organizations* (New York: John Wiley & Sons, 1984).

44. L. A. Kappelman and V. R. Prybutok, "A Small Amount of Empowerment Pays Off Big in a Regional Bank," *National Productivity Review* 14 (September 1995): 39–42.

45. K. W. Thomas and B. A. Velthouse, "Cognitive Elements of Empowerment: An 'Interpretative' Model of Intrinsic Task Motivation," *Academy of Management Review* 15 (October 1990): 673.

46. R. D. Hof, "Scott McNealy's Rising Sun," *Business Week,* January 22, 1996, 66–73.

47. A. J. H. Thorlackson and R. P. Murray, "An Empirical Study of Empowerment in the Workplace," *Group and Organization Management* 21, no. 1 (March 1996): 670–83.

48. J. R. Hackman, G. Oldham, R. Janson, and K. Purdy, "A New Strategy for Job Enrichment," *California Management Review* 16 (Fall 1975): 57–71.

49. R. Blackburn and B. Rosen, "Total Quality and Human Resources Management: Lessons Learned from Baldrige Award-Winning Companies," *Academy of Management Executive* 7 (August 1993), 49–66.

50. Ibid.

51. G. Flynn, "New Skills Equals New Opportunities," *Personnel Journal* (June 1996): 77–79.

52. T. L. Prior, "If I Were President," *Inc.,* April 1995, 56–61.

53. Adapted from Whetten & Cameron, 1998, pp. 312–14.

54. A. J. DuBrin, *Applying Psychology: Individual & Organizational Effectiveness,* 5th ed. (Upper Saddle River, NJ: Prentice Hall, 2000) 136.

CHAPTER 18

Managing Organization Change

Learning Objectives

After completing this chapter, you should be able to:

■ Appreciate the necessity of managing change.

■ Recognize what causes change.

■ Identify targets for change.

■ Plan and implement change.

■ Recognize and overcome resistance to change.

■ Lead the planned change process.

SELF-ASSESSMENT EXERCISE

Are You Ready for Change?[1]

People vary in their comfort with change. By answering the following questions, you can gain insight into one aspect of your readiness for change.

Instructions. Circle the number after each question that represents your response. Key: 7 = strongly agree; 6 = moderately agree; 5 = slightly agree; 4 = neither agree nor disagree; 3 = slightly disagree; 2 = moderately disagree; 1 = strongly disagree.

	Strongly Agree						*Strongly Disagree*
1. An expert who doesn't come up with a definite answer probably doesn't know too much.	7	6	5	4	3	2	1
2. I would like to live in a foreign country for a while.	7	6	5	4	3	2	1
3. There is really no such thing as a problem that can't be solved.	7	6	5	4	3	2	1
4. People who fit their lives to a schedule probably miss most of the joy of living.	7	6	5	4	3	2	1
5. A good job is one where what is to be done and how it is to be done are always clear.	7	6	5	4	3	2	1
6. It is more fun to tackle a complicated problem than to solve a simple one.	7	6	5	4	3	2	1

	Strongly Agree						*Strongly Disagree*
7. In the long run, it is possible to get more done by tackling small, simple problems rather than large and complicated ones.	7	6	5	4	3	2	1
8. Often, the most interesting and stimulating people are those who don't mind being different and original.	7	6	5	4	3	2	1
9. What we are used to is always preferable to what is unfamiliar.	7	6	5	4	3	2	1
10. People who insist on a yes or no answer just don't know how complicated things really are.	7	6	5	4	3	2	1
11. A person who leads an even, regular life in which few surprises or unexpected happenings arise really has a lot to be grateful for.	7	6	5	4	3	2	1
12. Many of our most important decisions are based on insufficient information.	7	6	5	4	3	2	1
13. I like parties where I know most of the people more than ones where all or most of the people are complete strangers.	7	6	5	4	3	2	1
14. Teachers or supervisors who hand out vague assignments give one a chance to show initiative and originality.	7	6	5	4	3	2	1
15. The sooner we all acquire similar values and ideals the better.	7	6	5	4	3	2	1
16. A good teacher is one who makes you wonder about your way of looking at things.	7	6	5	4	3	2	1

Scoring Instructions.

1. Reverse the scores for even-numbered items. This means for the even-numbered items only: $7 = 1, 6 = 2, 5 = 3, 4 = 4, 3 = 5, 2 = 6$, and $1 = 7$.
2. Sum the scores for all 16 items (using the reverse scores from step 1) to get your **total score** = _____.
3. Compute your subscores using the following:

   (N) Novelty score $(2 + 9 + 11 + 13)$ = _____.
   (C) Complexity score $(4 + 5 + 6 + 7 + 8 + 10 + 14 = 15)$ = _____.
   (I) Insolubility score $(1 + 3 + 12)$ = _____.

Interpretation. The form you have just completed assesses your tolerance of ambiguity, which is the ability to cope with uncertain, conflicting, or complex situations. People who feel comfortable with sudden change, novelty, and uncertainty have a high tolerance for ambiguity, and those who feel uncomfortable have a low tolerance for ambiguity. The average total score range is 46. Scores *below* 44 indicate high tolerance for ambiguity. Scores *above* 48 indicate high intolerance for ambiguity.

Tolerance for ambiguity is made up of three dimensions. One is your tolerance for novelty—new and unexpected situations. The second is your tolerance for complexity—lots of information that may not all be relevant and organized, and which may be conflicting or incomplete. The third dimension is your tolerance of problem-solving situations in which answers are not readily discovered.

People with a high tolerance of ambiguity are better able to cope with unstructured and dynamic situations characterized by uncertainty. It is not surprising that effective managers usually have a high tolerance for ambiguity. The level of an individual's tolerance for ambiguity is a fairly fixed personality trait, but it can be modified and changed with conscious effort by those who are motivated to do so. Becoming more accepting of ambiguity as a natural condition in the world today helps us cope with the change and uncertainty that inevitably faces each of us.

CONCEPTS

Why is managing change important? The most basic reason is that entities, whether they be individuals, managers, teams, or organizations, that do not adapt to change in timely ways are unlikely to survive. *Fortune* magazine first published its list of America's top 500 companies in 1956. Sadly, from the top 100 on the original list only 29 companies remain today. The other 71 have disappeared through dissolution, merger, or downsizing. Survival, even for the most successful companies, cannot be taken for granted. Remaining giants such as General Motors, Ford, and Chrysler (now Daimler-Chrysler) know that, to survive, they must adapt to accelerating and increasingly complex environmental dynamics. Today's norm of pervasive change brings not only problems and challenges, but also opportunities. Those individuals, managers, and organizations that recognize the inevitability of change, learn to adapt to it, and attempt to manage it, will be the most successful.

What Is Change?

Change is the coping process of moving a present state to a more desired state in response to dynamic internal and external factors. Essentially, change means that we have to do things differently in the future. In general, most people dislike change because of the uncertainty between what is and what might be. To successfully implement changes, managers need to possess the skills to convince others of the need for change, identify gaps between the current situations and desired conditions, create visions of desirable outcomes, design appropriate interventions, and implement them so that desired outcomes will be obtained.

There are two major types of change. The first is *unplanned* change, which is forced on an organization by the external environment. This type of change is dealt with as it happens through emergency measures, a practice often called *firefighting*. Sources of unplanned change include technology, economic conditions, global competition, world politics, social and demographic changes, and internal challenges. Examples are genetic engineering, recession or expansion, the European Union, wars, environmental concerns, and organizational politics.

The second type of change is *planned*. It results from deliberate attempts by managers to improve organizational operations. One example of this type of program is total quality management, with a focus on continuous process improvement. All too often, busy managers introduce short-run, expedient change programs aimed solely at cost savings. Such programs usually have unintended dysfunctional effects on participant satisfaction and the long-term goals of the organization. Change programs that are aimed at improving long-term effectiveness, efficiency, and participant well-being are usually more successful.

The Three Phases of Planned Change

There are three general phases of planned change illustrated in Exhibit 18-1. They include unfreezing, changing, and refreezing.[2]

Unfreezing

In the first phase, a manager needs to help people accept that change is needed because the existing situation is not adequate. Existing attitudes and behaviors need to be altered during this phase so that resistance to change is minimized. Unfreezing requires some event to upset current work norms and relationships. Sometimes these

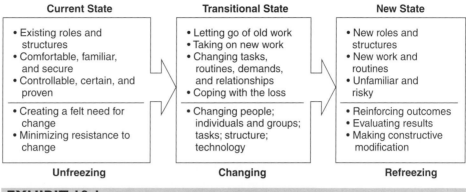

Current State	Transitional State	New State
• Existing roles and structures • Comfortable, familiar, and secure • Controllable, certain, and proven	• Letting go of old work • Taking on new work • Changing tasks, routines, demands, and relationships • Coping with the loss	• New roles and structures • New work and routines • Unfamiliar and risky
• Creating a felt need for change • Minimizing resistance to change	• Changing people; individuals and groups; tasks; structure; technology	• Reinforcing outcomes • Evaluating results • Making constructive modification
Unfreezing	**Changing**	**Refreezing**

EXHIBIT 18-1 Three Phases of Planned Change

SOURCE: Adapted from K. Lewin, *Field Theory in Social Science* (New York: Harper & Row, 1951).

occur naturally, as they do with changes in the economy or technology. More often, however, managers need to provide the impetus to let go of old ways of doing things. It helps to explain how the change can increase productivity for the organization, but it is also necessary to demonstrate the consequences of not changing on the participants. They need to understand that the cost of making the change will be worth some other gain they care about. Managers' goals are to help the participants see the need for change and to increase their willingness to help make the change a success.

Changing

The second phase involves rearranging current work norms and relationships to meet new needs. It requires participants to let go of old ways of doing things and develop new ones. This phase is difficult because of the anxiety involved in letting go of the comfortable and familiar to learn new ways of behaving, with new people, doing different tasks with perhaps more complex technology. In more complex changes, several targets of change may need to be changed simultaneously.

Refreezing

The third phase reinforces the changes made so that the new ways of behaving become stabilized. New norms and relationships need to be cemented in place to keep them from drifting back to the status quo. Refreezing may be achieved through social reinforcement, management control systems, or technical arrangements. If people perceive the change to be working in their favor, positive results will serve as reinforcement. If they perceive the change as not working in their favor, it may be necessary for the manager to use positive or negative external reinforcers.[3] For example, a manager might encourage the employees to keep working at the change with small rewards, such as a lunch or an afternoon off when benchmarks have been completed. The goal of this phase of the change process is to cause the desired attitudes and behaviors to become a natural, self-reinforcing pattern.

Managing the Planned Change Process

Planned changes attempt to accomplish two general types of outcomes. The first is improving the organization's ability to cope with unplanned changes that are thrust on it. For example, improving information gathering and forecasting systems could help an organization adapt in advance to competitors' new products, changes in governmental regulations, or forthcoming supply limitations. The second type of planned change consists of modifying employees' attitudes and behaviors to make them more effective contributors to the organization's goals. Examples are motivational seminars, values clarification exercises, skill training, and incentive systems.

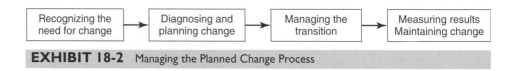

EXHIBIT 18-2   Managing the Planned Change Process

Building on the three phases of planned change discussed in the previous section, Exhibit 18-2 shows in more detail the steps required in planning and implementing change. These steps are not always followed in sequence, but effective change normally includes each of them.

Recognize the Need for Change

The need for change is sometimes obvious, as when results are not in line with expectations, things clearly are not working well, or dissatisfaction is apparent. As the "pain" in such situations increases, so does the incentive to change. Sometimes the need for change is less obvious. If all appears to be going well for the individual, team, or organization, the obvious incentives to change are not present. For example, companies may miss signals in changing markets because they are performing successfully and assume all is well. This occurred in the 1980s when IBM executives failed to appreciate the impact of personal computers on its mainframe business.

Managers need to monitor their environments to anticipate and recognize changes that might affect them. These changes can occur in any area, including knowledge, skills, technology, customers, regulators, competitors, and suppliers.

Diagnose and Plan Change

Once the need for change has been recognized, managers need to plan what to do. Several questions need to be addressed:

- What are our performance gaps between actual and desired states?
- What are the reasons for these gaps?
- What do we want to achieve to close these gaps?
- What are our specific goals?
- Who are the involved stakeholders?
- What targets do we want to change?
- What process will we apply to change them?
- What consequences do we anticipate from the change?
- Who will be the change agents responsible for making the change?
- What interventions will we use?
- How will we measure success?

Formulate Goals

The first step is to determine how to close the performance gaps between actual and desired states. So the question is, What has to be done to close these gaps? The accomplishment of these actions can be assigned to responsible individuals and formulated as their specific goals. Differentiating between means and ends, and between short-term and long-term goals, can help a manager choose the appropriate alternative.

Take, for example, production managers who need to achieve greater output. They may assume the way to accomplish this goal is to add more machines. If they mistakenly define their goal as adding more machines without evaluating other options, they decrease the chances of making the best decision. Another option may be to add people and operate a second shift. A third may be to reengineer existing processes to achieve greater output with existing machines and people. Both of the latter options offer more flexibility in case the need for increased output is temporary.

Determine Stakeholders' Needs

Stakeholders include employees, managers, stockholders, suppliers, customers, and even regulators. When planning a change, all groups of people who might be affected by the change should be considered. Why? Let us say, for example, that management decides to increase employees' pay to encourage motivation. Choosing this particular action, however, might irritate stockholders, who may view the increase as an unnecessary expense that cuts into earnings.

Examine Driving and Restraining Forces

An existing situation can be envisioned as an interaction of multiple opposing forces tending toward a state of equilibrium.[4] For change to occur, it is necessary to tip the balance of forces so that the system (be it an individual, group, or organization) can move toward a more desirable equilibrium. The following force-field model promotes a comprehensive analysis of factors to consider when evaluating alternative ways to promote positive changes. The force-field model is diagrammed in Exhibit 18-3.

Force-field analysis is the process of analyzing the forces that drive change and the forces that restrain it. *Driving forces* are factors that push toward the new, more desirable and away from the status quo. *Restraining forces* are factors that exert pressure to continue past behaviors or to resist new actions. If these opposing forces are approximately equal, the organization will make not move from the status quo. For change to occur the driving forces need to be increased (in number or intensity) and/or the restraining forces need to be reduced (in number or intensity).

An example of force-field analysis application occurred when the general manager of a hospital employing 300 workers discovered a 6 percent daily absentee rate.[5] Since a 3 percent daily absentee rate was the desired state, the manager wanted to close this performance gap. The manager and work team supervisors met and conducted a force-field analysis to diagnose the problem. Exhibit 18-4 shows how they listed the restraining forces that tended to hold back decreases in absenteeism and the driving forces that tended to decrease absenteeism.

To illustrate the impacts of the various driving and restraining factors, the managers made the lengths of the arrows proportional to the strength of the forces. Now

---

EXHIBIT 18-3 Force-Field Analysis Model

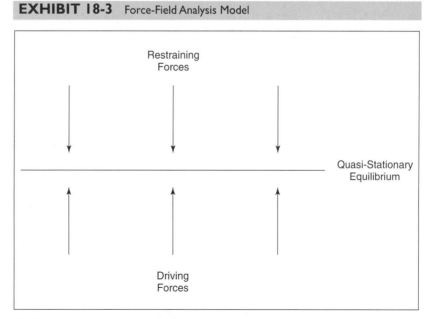

SOURCE: Don Harvey and Donald R. Brown, *An Experiential Approach to Organization Development*, 6th ed. (Upper Saddle River, NJ: Prentice Hall, 2001) 140.

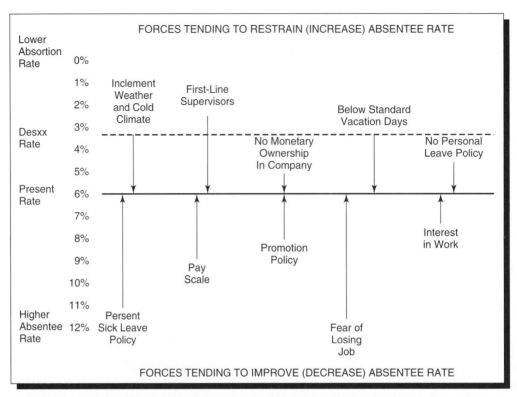

FORCES TENDING TO RESTRAIN (INCREASE) ABSENTEE RATE

Lower Absorption Rate — 0%

Desxx Rate — 3%, 4%

Present Rate — 6%

Higher Absentee Rate — 12%

Inclement Weather and Cold Climate

First-Line Supervisors

Below Standard Vacation Days

No Monetary Ownership In Company

No Personal Leave Policy

Interest in Work

Promotion Policy

Pay Scale

Persent Sick Leave Policy

Fear of Losing Job

FORCES TENDING TO IMPROVE (DECREASE) ABSENTEE RATE

EXHIBIT 18-4   Example of the Use of Force-Field Analysis

SOURCE: Don Harvey and Donald R. Brown, *An Experiential Approach to Organization Development*, 6th ed. (Upper Saddle River, NJ: Prentice Hall, 2001) 140.

that the impact of all contributing factors was clear, the managers debated several strategies to reduce the performance gap. They could decrease the strength of the restraining forces, increase the strength of the driving forces, or a combination of both. Increasing forces that put pressure on people (such as fear of losing their job) can also increase resistance and unpredictability in behavior. It is preferable to increase forces that do not put pressure on people (for instance, promotion policy) to reduce restraining forces, or to add new driving forces.

Consider Contingencies to Determine the Best Interventions

The best way to change a given situation depends on various contingencies. Key factors to consider include time; importance; anticipated resistance; power positions; ability, knowledge, and resources required; and source of relevant data.[6] If a change needs to be made quickly, is not critically important, and resistance is not anticipated, using direct authority may be appropriate. However, if the change is important, resistance is anticipated, and the power position of those who must change is relatively high, a participative approach might be more suitable.

Manage the Transition[7]

Introducing a change seldom leads immediately to the desired results because people require time to learn how to behave differently. Individual performance usually declines during the learning period, inducing fear and anxiety among participants. During this period, many participants may experience a strong desire to return to more familiar and proven behaviors. This doubt and fear may be reinforced if individuals share their concerns and complaints with one another.

Managers can help people get through the transition period by anticipating sub-par performance and attitudinal problems and by being ready with increased support, education, encouragement, and resources to help employees adapt. When people begin to experience positive results, the new behaviors will become internalized and the external supports given by the manager can be reduced.

Measure Results and Maintain Change[8]

In order to ascertain whether the change is accomplishing desired results, information needs to be gathered and compared to benchmark goals. If feedback from surveys, sensing groups, or interviews indicate that initial enthusiasm has faded as people encounter operating problems, managers need to intervene to sustain the momentum. Sometimes, additional training or resources are called for. Other times, emotional support is needed. This can be provided through support groups, off-site retreats, and personal reinforcement through praise, bonuses, or award dinners.

Identifying Targets for Change

Exhibit 18-5 illustrates the primary factors that a manager can target for change. They are strategy, structure, people, technology, processes, management, and products and services.[9] Because change targets are interdependent parts of the organizational system, a change in one will usually affect others. For example, a new strategic plan may lead to new products, which in turn stretch goals for people and require changes in technology. Changes in people and culture may also be necessary to overcome resistance to change.

Although managers do have a responsibility to identify areas of improvement, they should also always be open to "bottom-up" ideas. Employees at lower levels have the most expertise to propose meaningful changes in the jobs they perform. Two workers at Dana Corporation's Elizabethtown, Kentucky, plant, for example, had an idea for automatically loading steel sheets into a forming press. This technology change saved the auto parts maker $250,000 a year.[10]

Recognizing Resistance to Change

Resistance to change is obvious when actions such as strikes, slow downs, and complaints occur. It is more difficult to detect resistance that is implicit, such as decreased motivation or loyalty. Resistance to change is sometimes beneficial because it promotes functional conflict and debates, which can promote more thorough analyses of alternatives and their consequences. On the other hand, excessive or irrational resistance can hinder progress and even survival. Why is change often resisted even when its benefits clearly outweigh its costs? The following paragraphs describe the main reasons change is resisted. Some are based in human nature,[11] and others are created from organizational dynamics.[12]

EXHIBIT 18-5   Targets for Organizational Change

Targets	*Examples*
Strategy	• Develop new visions, missions, strategic plans.
Structure	• Add a new department or division, or consolidate two existing ones.
People	• Replace a person new, or change knowledge, skills, attitudes, or behaviors.
Technology	• Upgrade a data-processing system.
Processes	• Change the pay system from hourly wages to salaries.
Management	• Encourage participation by those involved in solution of problems.
Product & service	• Marketing people pass customer complaints to research to use in the design of new products.

Selective Perception   People often perceive the same things differently. Individuals tend to focus on how they will be personally affected by change rather than seeing the big picture for the entire organization. For example, if it is decided that productions will henceforth be paid on a piecework rather than an hourly basis, Irma, who is fast and highly skilled, may eagerly embrace the change as an opportunity to increase her pay. Angelo, a new employee, may object for fear of falling behind the others. Individuals may also perceive changes as incompatible with their personal beliefs and values.

Lack of Information   People resist change if they do not understand what is expected or why the change is important. Many people take the attitude "If it's not broken, don't fix it." If the reasons for change are not clearly presented, the worst is often assumed in terms of initiator intentions and personal impact. In addition, if people do not have enough information about how to change, they won't know what to do and will not try.

Fear of the Unknown   Individuals resist change when they are uncertain about how it will affect their well-being. They ask themselves, for example, "How will downsizing or new automation affect my job security?"[13] Other fears include not being able to perform as well as before the change; losing position, income, status, or power; having to perform less convenient or more difficult work; and losing desirable social interactions.

Habit   Organizational processes that appear to be working satisfactorily are not usually improved upon, even though environmental conditions may have changed in ways that indicate changes are desired.[14] People prefer familiar actions and events, even if they are not optimal. Have you ever tried to break a bad habit like smoking, drinking too much coffee, or not exercising? Breaking a habit is difficult because it takes hard work and involves giving up benefits the habit provided, even if the new behavior has more desirable consequences.

Resentment Toward the Initiator   People usually react negatively to changes that seem arbitrary and unreasonable. They get angry when timing and implementation of changes lack consideration of their concerns. When their thoughts and feelings about changes that affect them are not considered, people feel controlled and fear that they are losing autonomy over their work lives. These types of actions decrease trust in the initiators' intentions, breed resentment, and promote resistance to change.

Suboptimization   Changes that are beneficial to one group can be dysfunctional for another. People usually think of themselves first when evaluating potential changes. They support those changes that enhance their own welfare, but resist the ones that reduce it. People benefiting from changes in decision-making authority, control of resource allocations, or job assignments will endorse change, but those losing benefits will resist.

Structural Stability   Organizations create hierarchies, subgroups, rules, procedures, values, and norms to promote order and guide behavior. Organizational changes usually alter this structural stability, so they are resisted.

Overcoming Resistance to Change

Exhibit 18-6 illustrates six general strategies for overcoming resistance to change, the kinds of situations in which each approach is most appropriate, and their advantages and disadvantages.[15] Promoting positive attitudes toward change can also help. Several of the following strategies can apply simultaneously.

Education and Communication

Even if the consequences of a change are generally perceived as positive, extensive communication will help reduce anxiety and ensure that people understand what is

EXHIBIT 18-6	Methods for Dealing with Resistance to Change		
Approach	*Commonly Used*	*Advantages*	*Drawbacks*
Education and communication	Where there is a lack of information or inaccurate information and analysis.	Once persuaded, people will often help with the implementation of the change.	Can be very time-consuming if lots of people are involved.
Participation and involvement	Where the initiators do not have all the information they need to design the change, and where others have considerable power to resist.	People who participate will be committed to implementing change, and any relevant information they have will be integrated into the change plan.	Can be very time-consuming if participants design an inappropriate change.
Facilitation and support	Where people are resisting because of adjustment problems.	No other approach works as well with adjustment problems.	Can be time-consuming, expensive, and still fail.
Negotiation and agreement	Where someone or some group will clearly lose out in a change, and where that group has considerable power to resist.	Sometimes it is a relatively easy way to avoid major resistance.	Can be too expensive in many cases if it alerts others to negotiate for compliance.
Manipulation and co-optation	Where other tactics will not work, or are too expensive.	It can be a relatively quick and inexpensive solution to resistance problems.	Can lead to future problems if people feel manipulated.
Explicit and implicit coercion	Where speed is essential, and the change initiators possess considerable power.	It is speedy, and can overcome any kind of resistance.	Can be risky if it leaves people mad at the initiators.

SOURCE: Excerpt from John P. Kotter and Leonard A. Schlesinger, "Choosing Strategies for Change," *Harvard Business Review* 57 (March–April 1979): 111.

happening, what will be expected of them, and how they will be supported in adapting to change.[16] The objective is to help people learn beforehand the reasons for the change, how it will take form, and what the likely consequences will be.

Participation and Involvement

Participation increases understanding, enhances feelings of control, reduces uncertainty, and promotes a feeling of ownership when change directly affects people. Encourage those involved to help design and implement the changes in order to draw out their ideas and to foster commitment. It is difficult for people to resist changes that they themselves have helped bring about.

Facilitation and Support

By accepting peoples' anxiety as legitimate and helping them cope with change, managers have a better chance of gaining respect and the commitment to make it work. Provide encouragement and support, training, counseling, and resources to help those affected by the change adapt to new requirements.

Negotiation and Agreement

This tactic is often necessary when dealing with powerful resisters, such as collective bargaining units. Bargain to offer incentives in return for agreement to change. Sometimes specific things can be exchanged in return for help in bringing about a change. Other times, general perks can be widely distributed to help make the change easier to undertake.

Manipulation and Co-Optation

Manipulation is framing and selectively using information and implied incentives to maximize likelihood of acceptance. An example would be if management tells employees that accepting pay cuts is necessary to avoid a plant shutdown, when it is possible that plant closure would not really have to occur. Co-optation is influencing resistant parties to endorse the change effort by providing them with benefits they desire and opportunities to fill desired roles in the process.

Explicit and Implicit Coercion

At certain times, managers may have to use authority and the threat of negative incentives to force acceptance of the proposed change. For example, if employees do not accept proposed changes, it may be necessary to shut the plant down, decrease salaries, or lay people off.

Promote Positive Attitudes Toward Change[17]

How a person reacts to change depends on his or her attitude. Some people act like victims. Their negative emotions cause them to become depressed or angry and resist the change. Others view change as a challenge and focus on the opportunities and benefits that change can bring.

Change often means loss, and loss can be difficult to deal with. Potential losses from change include job security, power, self-confidence, and important relationships. Healthy coping involves dealing with loss realistically and letting go of what must be given up in order to move on.

Exhibit 18-7 shows the typical attitude curve in response to changes that involve loss. The sequence progresses from the negative attitudes of denial, resistance, and attitude trough, through the positive attitudes of exploration, responsibility, and commitment.

EXHIBIT 18-7   Attitude Curve in Response to Change

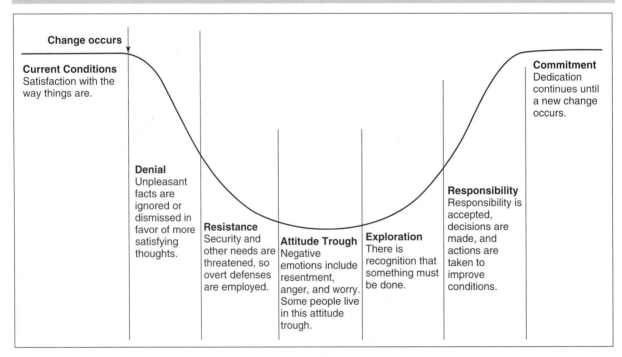

SOURCE: Cynthia D. Scott and Dennis T. Jaffe, *Managing Personal Change: Self-Management Skills for Work and Life Transitions* (Los Altos, CA: Crisp Publications, 1989).

EXHIBIT 18-8 Strategies for Promoting Positive Attitudes to Change		
	What the Individual Can Do	*What Others Can Do*
Denial	Don't put your head in the sand like an ostrich. Remember the adage "He who drinks from the cup of denial will sleep in the inn of defeat." Live by the principle "Know the truth and it will set you free."	Provide information. Answer questions. Communicate, communicate, communicate, ideally in person.
Resistance	State how you feel. Get it off your chest.	Listen and acknowledge feelings. Show understanding. Listening shows respect for others and may yield and otherwise unknown information.
Attitude trough	Say this is intolerable—enough is enough. Resolve to improve. Say good-bye to the past. Be willing to alter techniques.	Model and reinforce positive actions. Be patient.
Exploration	Have an open mind. Consider all possibilities. Coping includes fact finding and visioning an ideal future.	Focus on priorities. Channel energy in a helpful way. Brainstorm ideas and alternatives. Provide helpful training. Set short-term goals.
Responsibility	Have courage. Take action. Accept the consequences.	Encourage and expect the best. Help with planning and goal setting. Show support when decisions are made.
Commitment	Learn from the past. Enjoy the present. Plan for the future.	Acknowledge and celebrate accomplishments. Help prepare for future challenges.

SOURCE: Cynthia D. Scott and Dennis T. Jaffe, *Managing Personal Change: Self-Management Skills for Work and Life Transitions* (Los Altos, CA: Crisp Publications, 1989).

Exhibit 18-8 suggests strategies that can be taken by both individuals and managers at each phase of the attitude curve to help successful adjustments to change. The overall strategy is to get through the negative attitudes of denial, resistance, and attitude trough as quickly as possible so that people can focus on the positive attitudes of exploration, personal responsibility, and commitment. These positive reactions are most likely to happen when people:

- Believe the change is the right thing to do.
- Have influence on the nature and process of the change.
- Respect the person who is championing the change.
- Expect the change will result in personal gain.
- Believe this is the right time for change.[18]

Leading Organizational Change

Major organizational change does not happen easily. As we have seen, the change process goes through stages, each of which is important, and requires a significant amount of time. Exhibit 18-9 presents an eight-stage sequence of skills that managers need to apply to successfully bring about planned change in organizations.[19] Stages in

1. **Establishing a Sense of Urgency**
   - Examining the market and competitive realities
   - Identifying and discussing crises, potential crises, or major opportunities

2. **Creating the Guiding Coalition**
   - Putting together a group with enough power to lead the change
   - Getting the group to work together like a team

3. **Developing a Vision and Strategy**
   - Creating a vision to help direct the change effort
   - Developing strategies for achieving that vision

4. **Communicating the Change Vision**
   - Using every vehicle possible to constantly communicate the new vision and strategies
   - Having the guiding coalition role-model the behavior expected of employees

5. **Empowering Broad-Based Action**
   - Getting rid of obstacles
   - Changing systems or structures that undermine the change vision
   - Encouraging risk taking and nontraditional ideas, activities, and actions

6. **Generating Short-Term Wins**
   - Planning for visible improvements in performance, or "wins"
   - Creating those wins
   - Visibly recognizing and rewarding people who made the wins possible

7. **Consolidating Gains and Producing More Change**
   - Using increased credibility to change all systems, structures, and policies that don't fit together and don't fit the transformation vision
   - Hiring, promoting, and developing people who can implement the change vision
   - Reinvigorating the process with new projects, themes, and change agents

8. **Anchoring New Approaches in the Culture**
   - Creating better performance through customer—and productivity—oriented behavior, more and better leadership and more effective management
   - Articulating the connections between new behaviors and organizational success
   - Developing means to ensure leadership development and succession management

EXHIBIT 18-9   Eight-Stage Sequence of Skills for Planned Change

Reprinted by permission of Harvard Business School Press from *Change* by John P. Kotter, Boston, MA 1996, p. 21. Copyright © 1996 by John P. Kotter, all rights reserved.

the change process generally overlap, but skipping stages or making critical mistakes at any stage can cause the change process to fail.

Establish a Sense of Urgency

Establishing a sense of urgency that change is really needed is often necessary to unfreeze people from traditional ways of behaving. Obvious threats to organizational survival provide a sense of urgency for all stakeholders. At other times, no current crisis may be obvious, but managers identify potential problems by scanning the external environment, looking at such things as competitive conditions, market position, and social, technological, and demographic trends. In these cases, managers need to find ways to communicate the information broadly and dramatically to make others aware of the need for change.

Form a Powerful Guiding Coalition

A critical variable in successful changes is the development of a shared commitment to the need and direction of organizational change. One way to do this is to establish a team of opinion leaders with enough power to guide the change process. All levels of management should be included in this coalition to ensure support from the top and enthusiastic implementation from middle and lower managers. Mechanisms such as off-site retreats can get people together and help them develop a shared assessment of problems and how to approach them.

Develop a Compelling Vision and Strategy

People need a vision that will guide the change effort. When Jack Sparks was CEO of Whirlpool he developed a vision that transformed Whirlpool from a conservative company with some marketing skills into a marketing organization with some manufacturing and engineering skills, thus making it stronger in the face of new competition.[20]

Communicate Widely

Leaders need to use every means possible to communicate the vision and strategy to all stakeholders. Transformation is impossible unless the majority of people in the organization are involved and willing to help. Managers in the change coalition should start this process by modeling the new behaviors themselves, sometimes referred to as "walking your talk."

Empower Others to Act on the Vision

People can be empowered to make things happen with knowledge, resources, and discretion. Risk taking in the forms of nontraditional ideas and actions should be encouraged and rewarded. Systems, structures, and procedures that hinder or undermine the change effort need to be revised. For example, with the survival of the company at stake, labor and management at Rolls-Royce Motor Company took hundreds of precise job descriptions that were undermining the change and revised them into a new contract specifying that all employees will do anything within their capabilities to support the company.[21]

Generate Short-Term Wins

Major change takes time, and a transformation effort loses momentum if no short-term goal achievements are recognized and celebrated by employees. Consequently, managers should plan for visible performance improvements, provide the means for them to happen, and celebrate employees who were involved in the improvements. These successes can boost the credibility of the change process and renew the commitment and enthusiasm of employees.[22]

Consolidate Gains and Create Greater Change

The credibility achieved by short-term wins can help motivate all concerned to tackle bigger problems and create greater change. This is an opportunity to change systems, structures, and policies that have not yet been confronted, and to hire, promote, and develop employees who can implement the vision and perhaps work to implement further changes. For example, when Rolls-Royce was at this stage of change, "change teams" were established to communicate and develop new ideas together. Members of the team were horizontally cross-trained so they could perform one another's jobs, and vertically integrated from executives to shop floor workers.[23]

Institutionalize Changes in the Organizational Culture

At this refreezing stage, new values and beliefs are instilled in the culture so that employees view the changes not as something new but as a normal and integral part of how the organization operates. This is achieved by rewarding new behaviors so that old habits, values, traditions, and mindsets are permanently replaced.

CONCEPT QUIZ

Complete the following true-false quiz by circling the correct answer. The answers are at the end of the quiz. After marking your answers, go back and check your understanding of any answers you missed.

True or False	1. Planned change involves proactively trying to make things different.
True or False	2. Firefighting is a common reaction to unplanned change.
True or False	3. Increasing driving forces is the best way to move to a desired state.
True or False	4. The three phases of planned change are recognizing, unfreezing, and refreezing.
True or False	5. Ideas for product and service changes usually come from top management.
True or False	6. If everything is going well management need not worry about change.
True or False	7. Resistance to change is sometimes beneficial.
True or False	8. Resistance to change can be overcome through participation of involved parties.
True or False	9. Change happens when driving forces and restraining forces are unequal.
True or False	10. How a person reacts to change depends on his or her attitude.

Answers. (1) True; (2) True; (3) False; (4) False; (5) False; (6) False; (7) True; (8) True; (9) True; (10) True

BEHAVIORAL CHECKLIST

The following skills are important for managing change. Use them when evaluating your own change management skills and those of others.

Effective Change Managers

- Develop goals, vision, and strategy for change.
- Perform force-field analysis.

- Identify targets of change.
- Form a guiding coalition.
- Create a sense of urgency.
- Overcome resistance to change.
- Communicate widely.
- Empower others.
- Generate short-term wins.
- Institutionalize changes through reinforcement.

Attention!
Don't read the following until assigned to do so by your instructor.

MODELING EXERCISE

Changing the Grading System

Objectives.   Plan a change.
Practice stakeholder analysis.
Practice force-field analysis.

Total Time Required.   60 minutes.

Background.   Assume that several students have petitioned your instructor to grade your current course on a pass-fail basis. Your instructor has reservations about doing this, but is willing to ask the dean if there is a possibility of changing the grading in this course from an A through F basis to pass-fail. The dean expresses willingness to consider the question but has asked for a more detailed proposal, including the pros and cons of the scheme and how such a plan might be implemented. Your instructor, in turn, has asked your group to develop a preliminary analysis of how such a change might be made.

Specific Instructions

Step 1:   Join a group of four to seven students to do the following:

1. Identify all stakeholders and their interests and concerns (10 minutes).
2. Prepare a force-field analysis. Identify the driving and restraining forces and estimate the intensity and importance of each (15 minutes).
3. Prepare a preliminary plan for introducing and implementing the change. Identify who will do what and when. Be specific about the order and priority of actions (15 minutes).

Step 2:   Entire class reconvenes.

1. Each group reports its recommendation.
2. Compare the analyses.
3. Provide feedback to each group using the Observer's Rating Sheet (20 minutes).

OBSERVER'S RATING SHEET

After the groups have reported their strategy for change, check the degree that their presentations covered all of the steps for managing change on the following scale. Write concrete examples to use in explaining your feedback in the spaces following each behavior.

1 *Unsatisfactory*	*2* *Weak*	*3* *Adequate*	*4* *Good*	*5* *Outstanding*

_____ Developed goals, vision, and strategy for change.

_____ Performed force-field analysis.

_____ Identified targets of change.

_____ Formed a guiding coalition.

_____ Created a sense of urgency.

_____ Overcame resistance to change.

_____ Communicated widely.

_____ Empowered others.

_____ Generated short-term wins.

_____ Institutionalized changes through reinforcement.

GROUP EXERCISES

Three different types of group exercises are presented here. The first deals with overcoming resistance to change. The second is a personal force-field analysis. The third requires change managers to communicate accurately with implementers.

Group Exercise 1: Changing to Total Quality Management[24]

Purpose.   Develop skills for managing and overcoming employee resistance to change.

Procedure

1. Form groups of three to five students.
2. Read the following scenario, Changing to Total Quality Management, and develop an action plan for dealing with resistance to change.
3. Answer the discussion questions.

Changing to Total Quality Management

Meritron Corporation is a major provider of wireless communication services based in Palo Alto, California. It employs about 2,000 workers at its world headquarters and another 1,200 workers at various regional offices around the United States. Owing to concerns regarding inefficiencies and ineffectiveness (e.g., poor quality) in administrative processes at the corporate office (e.g., customer service, order processing), senior management has decided to implement a total quality management (TQM) program. This new initiative will entail the implementation of fundamentally new ways of thinking and doing things, including (1) a process orientation, (2) identifying and tracking critical measures at success, (3) benchmarking, and (4) using data-based decision making.

When senior management sent a brief memo outlining the new TQM program, employees responded with skepticism and frustration. Many felt that this was just another management fad that would quickly pass. Others felt that TQM was applicable only to manufacturing settings. One employee even commented that he thought TQM was a Japanese management method and therefore it could not work in a very different culture such as that of the United States.

Group Task.   Develop an action plan for dealing with the employees' resistance to change. Be sure to base your plan on the strategies for dealing with resistance to change discussed in this chapter.

CLASS DISCUSSION QUESTIONS

1. What were the causes of the resistance to change?
2. Which strategies did you propose to use to handle the resistance to change? Why do you feel that they will be effective?
3. What barriers to success would your action plan face? What could you do to overcome them?
4. What are the implications for you as a future change manager?

Group Exercise 2: Personal Force-Field Analysis

Purpose.   Develop an action plan to change an undesirable situation.

Time Required.   25 minutes for developing the personal force field. 30 minutes for team feedback.

Directions. Individually complete the force-field problem-solving module below for a current personal problem. This could range from a habit you are trying to break (e.g., drinking coffee, smoking, procrastination) to something you want to improve but are having trouble with (e.g., public speaking skills, learning a foreign language, mastering a new computer program), or any other type of problem you are putting off for some reason (e.g., looking for a new job, breaking off a dysfunctional relationship, starting a diet or exercise program to get in shape) (25 minutes).

1. ***Describe the current situation that you want to change.*** What exactly is the problem? Describe the current situation as accurately and briefly as possible.
2. ***Describe the desired situation.*** This is not necessarily the ideal situation, which is often unrealistic. Indicate the direction and realistic change you desire.
3. ***List the opposing or restraining (negative) forces that resist improvement.***
4. ***List the driving or pushing (positive) forces that are motivating you to change.***
5. ***Number the driving and restraining forces according to their impact on the situation*** (1 is most important, 2 is second in impact, 3 is third, etc.).

Force-Field Analysis		
Less Desirable Situation	***Current Situation***	***Desired Situation***
Driving Forces	⟶|⟵	Restraining Forces
	⟶|⟵	
	⟶|⟵	
	⟶|⟵	
	⟶|⟵	
	⟶|⟵	
	⟶|⟵	

6. ***Action steps.*** How can you change the driving and restraining forces that maintain the current problem situation so that it shifts to the more desired direction? Your options are to (1) increase the strength of or add driving forces, or (2) decrease the strength of or take away restraining forces. The most influential forces diagnosed in step 5, will have the most impact. List as many *action steps* as possible.

   - Add driving forces.
   - Increase the strength of driving forces.
   - Eliminate restraining forces.
   - Reduce the strength of restraining forces.

7. ***Prioritize action steps.*** Arrange the top five action steps you created in step 6 according to their impact and ease of implementation in the action step diagram below.
8. ***Organize resources.*** List the materials, people, and other resources available to help you achieve the five top priority action steps in the following table:

Action Step Analysis	
Action Step	***Resources***
1. _____	_____
2. _____	_____
3. _____	_____
4. _____	_____
5. _____	_____

9. *Agenda.* Complete the four implementation steps for each of your five action steps:

- *What is going to be done?*
- *Who is going to do it?*
- *When is it going to be done?*
- *How will you evaluate results?*

10. *Team feedback.* When you complete all the nine steps in your force-field analysis, pick a partner who is also finished, and share your work. Your partner's job is to ask for clarification, provide you with feedback about additional information you may want to add, and reality-test your plans so that you can make sure that you have the best possible chance of success for implementation. After the first partner is finished, the second partner shares the force-field analysis and gets feedback (15 minutes each).

Group Exercise 3: Innovation and Change[25]

When managing change within an organization, it is important to assess the appropriateness of specific actions that you might take as a manager. Less effective managers spend too much time, energy, and resources on activities that are not likely to facilitate change and ultimate acceptance by others.

Purpose. This exercise allows you to practice the skill of assessing the appropriateness of alternative actions available to a manager who wants to introduce needed change.

Procedure

Step 1: Individually read the Computer Soft Corporation case. The information will familiarize you with the company, its history, and why changes are being considered (10 minutes).

Step 2: Individually rate the 16 action alternatives for bringing about change in terms of their desirability for improving the Computer Soft situation. Use the four-point rating scale provided on the Available Action Alternatives Sheet that is presented on page 491 (approximately 10 minutes).

Step 3: Form groups of four to six people and establish a consensus on the ratings for each action alternative. Each group should articulate a rationale for each rating (approximately 40 minutes).

Step 4: Assemble the whole class and discuss the group results and recommendations for change.

Computer Soft Corporation

Computer Soft Corporation's success is owed to the massive growth in customer demand for tailor-made computer software. Computer Soft began as a small unit within a larger university in the Northeast. It was created to take advantage of the excess capacity within the computer and business departments of the university. In addition, it was hoped that this venture would generate funds to offset the increasing shortfall of government funding for universities. Within three years, Computer Soft grew from an idea into a thriving business employing 250 workers and generating $65 million in gross sales.

Key to the success of any software company is its ability to service its clients and work the bugs out of the software packages. Since it started operations, Computer Soft has stratified its service to customers. For example, questions received over the telephone are handled first by the least-experienced group of programmers. If the first level of programmers cannot solve the customer's question, it is then referred to a second level of more talented and experienced programmers. Finally, if the second level of programmers cannot solve the client's problem, it is redirected to Computer Soft's most experienced group of programmers. If the problem still cannot be solved over the telephone, the senior programmer can make a personal trip to the customer and, if necessary, rewrite the program. The logic behind this system is that experienced and highly paid programmers should not waste their time solving simple problems. At the same time, the procedure will help less-experienced programmers develop their skills.

Computer Soft's stratified system is initiated by a client's service call, which is randomly directed to the first level of programmers. The same randomized process is used each time a problem is referred to a higher level within the service sequence. Consequently, customers are unlikely to talk to the same programmer more than once. To ensure that programmers in the service sequence are not disturbed while talking to customers, they are required to work in cubicles separated by movable partitions. Finally, programmers for each level are grouped together to facilitate interaction between individuals with the same level of expertise. Given the numbers involved, the company has been forced to locate each level of programmers on a different floor within the company building.

Programmers have become accustomed to the system and have expressed satisfaction with the level of personal independence, control, and ability to interact with other programmers at the same level of expertise. Unfortunately, the disadvantage of the customer service department's physical layout is that little interaction takes place *between* levels. Indeed, when the programmers are in their cubicles, there is little interaction between them at any level.

At first, Computer Soft's service system worked smoothly with few customer complaints. However, as sales grew, the complexity of the company's software packages increased. Competing firms responded with better service levels. The result was an increase in the number of customer complaints at Computer Soft. The following represent some of the complaints directed toward Computer Soft and the services they provide:

- Service is impersonal with no consistency among programmers.
- Customers are often put on hold for long periods of time when referred to a higher level.
- Customers are often referred to several programmers before they find one who can help with their problem.
- If for some reason customers are disconnected or hang up while on hold and call back later, they have to start the entire process over again.
- Because individual programmers are evaluated on the number of calls they handle on a given day. They appear to be in a hurry either to solve the problem or to refer the customer to another programmer. This often results in a software program recommendation that does not work and the customer is forced to call back a second or even a third time.
- Complex problems that should be referred to the third level of expertise at once, often bog down at lower levels as junior programmers try to handle them and make recommendations that do not work.

In response to these complaints, and pressure from top management to streamline the system, Tim Crafton, manager of the customer service department, changed the structure of the department. The old system was scrapped and in its place a system of work teams capable of solving customer problems was introduced. Each team consisted of one representative from each of the three programming levels. The company was also able to relocate all programmer teams on one floor, a move that required relocating some other departments. However, after the change, programmers continued to work in their own cubicles. Finally, to ensure ownership, customer identification, and equitable work distribution, top management assigned customers to specific service teams after contracts had been signed. The plan was introduced at a general meeting to all the programmers, who appeared to be in broad agreement that the change would address their most pressing problems.

Unfortunately, when the change was initiated, results were less than stellar. Customer complaints remained high, team identities did not develop, and interaction remained within levels and did not grow between levels. In response to this apparent failure, Tim constructed a list of 16 possible actions that might make the new system work.

Available Action Alternatives for Computer Soft Corporation

Rating scale.

1 = Best choice. Implement immediately.
2 = Desirable, but will take time and planning.
3 = Appropriateness likely to be determined by manager's alternative actions.
4 = Worst choice. Likely to make matters worse.

_____ **1.** Network with other similar organizations that have successfully implemented a team-based service department.

_____ **2.** Determine how affected employees' attitudes must change to facilitate a changeover to a team-based system.

_____ **3.** Establish a bonus system to reward programmers who process more than the set number of calls each day.

_____ **4.** Ask affected programmers to articulate problems they have encountered since the changeover.

_____ **5.** Determine the personal losses likely to be experienced by each programmer.

_____ **6.** Change individual cubicles to areas large enough to accommodate programmers and all their necessary equipment.

_____ **7.** Ask the group to brainstorm a workable solution.

_____ **8.** Assign coordination responsibilities to one manager to ensure that the change is carried out correctly.

_____ **9.** Determine the losses and threats that programmers associate with the change.

_____ **10.** Threaten to take disciplinary action if programmers do not support the change.

_____ **11.** Use your best people to establish one, or two, model teams to demonstrate how well teams can work together when given the chance.

_____ **12.** Ask programmers to contact dissatisfied customers and personally assess their complaints.

_____ **13.** Create a pay-for-performance system that will reward team performance rather than individual performance.

_____ **14.** Hold daily meetings among the three group members to build an inclusive feeling.

_____ **15.** Bring programmers together and give them a pep talk about teams and the importance of making the change work.

_____ **16.** Bring the three groups of programmers together and sell the changes that have been introduced.

SUMMARY CHECKLIST

Take a few minutes to reflect on your performance and look over others' ratings of your change management skills. Now assess yourself on each of the key learning behaviors. Make a check next to those behaviors on which you need improvement when managing change.

_____   **Planning for change.**
1. Recognize the need for change: Determine performance gaps between actual and desired states.
2. Diagnose: Explore what causes the gaps.
3. Decide on goals.
4. Formulate actions to obtain change.
5. Examine all consequences of the change.

_____   **Attending to all three phases of change.**
1. Unfreezing: Creating awareness and sense of urgency.
2. Changing: Training, coaching, and modeling.
3. Refreezing: Measuring results and reinforcing change.

_____   **Performing force-field analysis.**
1. Identify and increase driving forces.
2. Identify and decrease restraining forces.

_____   **Identifying targets for change.**
1. Strategy
2. Structure.
3. People.
4. Technology
5. Processes
6. Management.
7. Product and service

_____   **Recognizing resistance to change.**
1. Assess individual reasons: selective perception, lack of information, fear of the unknown, habit, resentment toward the initiator.
2. Assess organizational reasons: power maintenance, structural stability, suboptimization, culture, norms.

_____   **Overcoming resistance to change.**
1. Education and communication.
2. Participation and involvement.
3. Facilitation and support.
4. Negotiation and agreement.
5. Manipulation and co-optation.
6. Explicit and implicit coercion.
7. Promote positive attitudes.

_____   **Leading change.**
1. Create a sense of urgency.
2. Form a guiding coalition.
3. Develop a vision and a strategy.
4. Communicate widely.

5. Empower others.
6. Generate short-term, achievable goals.
7. Consolidate gains and produce more change.
8. Institutionalize changes.

APPLICATION QUESTIONS

1. What are some ways to recognize trends that signal needs to change?
2. Are you successful in getting other people to change? Why or why not?
3. When and why have you resisted change? What were the consequences?
4. Have you ever experienced a change that caused you to lose something you valued? How did you feel and react?
5. Have you ever tried to change a bad habit like procrastination, smoking, or not exercising enough? What happened? Why were you successful or unsuccessful?

REINFORCEMENT EXERCISES

1. Assess the campaign strategies of challengers attempting to replace existing office holders in local, state, or national government positions. Information is available from newspapers, magazines, and television. How do the challengers attempt to unfreeze voters from the current incumbent's regime and convince them to change to their new plan?
2. Think of a situation when you were involved in change, whether in a club, at school, in a sports team, or at work. Identify the leaders who made it happen and describe what they did successfully to implement the change. What did they do that hindered the change?
3. Identify an area in your work, school, or club situation where you see a need for change. Then formulate a strategy and vision of how you would motivate those involved to accept the change and how you would implement the results of the change. What resistance do you anticipate? How do you plan to overcome this resistance?

ACTION PLAN

1. Which change management behavior do I most want to improve?
2. Why? What will be my payoff?
3. What potential obstacles stand in my way?
4. What are the specific things I will do to improve? (For examples, see the Reinforcement Exercises.)
5. When will I do them?
6. How and when will I measure my success?

NOTES

1. Adapted from S. Budner, "Intolerance of Ambiguity as a Personality Variable," *Journal of Personality* 30 (March 1962): 29–50.
2. K. Lewin, *Field Theory in Social Science* (New York: Harper & Row, 1951).
3. T. G. Cummings and C. G. Worley, *Organization Development and Change*, 5th ed. (St. Paul, MN: West Publishing Company, 1993) 63.
4. Lewin, 1951.
5. D. Harvey and D. R. Brown, *An Experiential Approach to Organization Development*, 6th ed. (Upper Saddle River, NJ: Prentice Hall, 2001) 139.
6. J. P. Kotter and L. A. Schlesinger, "Choosing Strategies for Change," *Harvard Business Review* 57 (March–April 1979): 106–14.
7. J. M. Groves, "Leaders of Corporate Change," *Fortune*, December 14, 1992, 104–14.
8. Cummings and Worley, 1993, 155.
9. H. J. Levitt, *Corporate Pathfinders* (Homewood, IL.; Dow Jones–Irwin, 1986).
10. R. Teitelbaum, "How to Harness Gray Matter," *Fortune*, June 9, 1997, 168.
11. R. Likert, *The Human Organization* (New York: McGraw-Hill, 1967).

12. R. M. Kanter, *When Giants Learn to Dance: Mastering the Challenges of Strategy* (New York: Simon & Schuster, 1989).

13. C. Argyris, *Personality and Organization* (New York: Harper & Row, 1957).

14. R. H. Hall, *Organizations: Structures, Processes, and Outcomes*, 4th ed. (Upper Saddle River, NJ: Prentice Hall, 1987) 29.

15. J. P. Kotter and L. A. Schlesinger, "Choosing Strategies for Change," *Harvard Business Review* 57 (March–April 1979): 106–14.

16. J. B. Keffeler, "Managing Changing Organizations: Don't Stop Communicating," *Vital Speeches*, November 15, 1991, 92–96.

17. This section is summarized from C. D. Scott and D. T. Jaffe, *Managing Personal Change: Self-Management Skills for Work and life Transitions* (Los Altos, CA: Crisp Publications, 1989).

18. Brian L. Davis, *Successful Manager's Handbook: Development Suggestions for Today's Managers* (Minneapolis, MN: Personnel Decisions International, 1996), 426–427.

19. J. P. Kotter, "Leading Change: Why Transformation Efforts Fail," *Harvard Business Review* (March–April 1995): 59–67.

20. C. Matthews, "How We Changed Gear to Ride the Winds of Change," *Professional Manager* (January 1995): 6–8.

21. Ibid.

22. J. P. Kotter, 1995.

23. Matthews, 1995.

24. Adapted from R. J. Aldag and L. W. Kuzuhara, *Organizational Behavior and Management* (Cincinnati: South-Western, 2002), 468–489.

25. Adapted from W. Bridges, *Managing Transitions: Making the Most of Change* (Reading, MA: Addison-Wesley, 1991), 7–16.

APPENDIX A

Oral Presentation Skills[1]

Most adults fear speaking in public. Nevertheless, a study conducted by AT&T and Stanford University revealed that it is the top predictor of success and upward mobility in organizations.[2] Unfortunately, this skill is often lacking in new managers and college graduates.[3] This appendix will provide ideas on three skills necessary for making effective oral presentations: managing anxiety, planning and preparing, and delivery of the presentation.

MANAGING ANXIETY

Stage fright is a normal reaction. Almost every speaker, actor, musician, or performer experiences some degree of stage fright. Although anxiety never goes away entirely, you can learn to manage your fear so that it can actually help you perform better.[4] Exhibit A-1 provides 10 tips for overcoming stage fright.

EXHIBIT A-1   Tips for Overcoming Stage Fright

- *Know your material well.*   Being the expert gives you confidence because you know more than the audience does.
- *Practice.*   Practice your presentation and, if possible, videotape yourself so that you know how you look to others.
- *Get audience participation.*   It shifts attention from you to the audience and generates more of an easy-going conversational atmosphere.
- *Use names and eye contact.*   These establish rapport. It is easier to talk to friends than strangers.
- *Check the facilities and audiovisual equipment in advance.*   Beforehand checking eliminates worry about whether the equipment works, and you avoid having to figure things out in front of the audience if it does not work.
- *Research your audience.*   Being familiar with your audience gives you confidence because you know their needs. You might even discover that you have friends in the audience who will support you.
- *Relax.*   Take time out right before your presentation to relax. Different things will relax different people. Some concentrate on breathing deeply. Others visualize themselves successfully presenting. Some do progressive muscle relaxation (i.e., focus on relaxing specific muscle groups one at a time: neck, shoulders, arms, legs).
- *Dress comfortably and appropriately.*   The way you dress can help you avoid anxiety about your image.
- *Use your own style.*   You do not need the stress of trying to imitate someone else.
- *Use audiovisual aids.*   They can reduce anxiety by providing prompts and taking the visual impact off you personally for a while.

SOURCE: D. A. Level and W. P. Galle, Jr., *Managerial Communications* (San Diego, CA: Business Publications, Inc., 1988) 44.

PLANNING AND PREPARING

Once you have your stage fright under control, the success of your public speaking is determined primarily by the time you spend preparing before you step in front of your audience. You want to avoid speeches that are too long, too detailed, confusing, vague, boring, or off-track. The following steps will help you prepare an effective presentation.

Identify the Purpose

The first and most critical step in preparation is understanding the "what" and the "why" of your presentation. Your *purpose* is the broad general outcome you want the presentation to achieve. Ask yourself three questions to clarify the objective of your presentation:

- *Why* am I giving this presentation: to persuade, to explain, to instruct, to report on something?
- *What* do I want the audience to know or do at the end of the presentation?
- *How* do I want the audience to feel?

Analyze Your Audience

After you are clear on what you want to accomplish, mold your presentation to fit the specific characteristics of the audience. You can acquire information about your audience by

- *Asking the presentation host* about the audience.
- *Talking to people who will be in the audience.*
- *Talking to other speakers* who have spoken to the same group.

Organize the Presentation

Once you know your audience and are clear about your purpose and objectives, you are ready to start organizing your presentation. The first step is to find your focus or the "big idea" of your material. The second is to develop an outline so that you can visualize the flow of your presentation.

The Big Idea

What is the power punch of your presentation—the one thing you want your audience to walk away with? Say, for example, that you are going to explain a new marketing plan to your company's board of directors. It probably has several sections that are supported by reams of documented research and facts, but you only have 20 to 30 minutes to summarize the plan in a way that will gain the board's approval. What is it about the plan that will capture their imagination? A new theme? A new program? A high payoff possibility?

How well you translate your message into benefits for the audience determines its effectiveness. You need to structure your presentation so that it supports your one big idea. Of course, your message will contain more than one idea but they should all reinforce the primary focus.

Develop an Outline

One way to make sure you are clear on your focus is to develop a basic outline for your presentation. Begin by listing no more than five independent ideas that the audience must understand for the objectives to be accomplished. Then outline your plan for presenting the detail and persuasive material needed to allow your audience to understand those points. For the most effective delivery, break your presentation down into its three main parts: the introduction, body, and conclusion.

The Introduction   It is important to write out your introduction completely, word-for-word. This part of your presentation is too important to leave to chance, hoping you have the right words when you get there. It also acts as a security blanket. If you can get through those first few minutes, the butterflies will settle down and the rest of the presentation will flow more easily. The introduction should take 5 to 15 percent of the allowed speaking time, and it should prepare the audience for the main points of the presentation.[5]

- *Start the introduction with a bang.*   At this point you need to get the audience's attention and convince them to listen to you. Grab the audience with something vitally interesting to them. Give them an interesting story or example that ties into your focus. Or you might use a strong, meaningful quotation, a startling statistic, or appropriate humor that makes a relevant point.

- *Increase your credibility.*   Relate something about your background and experience that makes you an expert on the topic you are speaking about. This point, of course, is one of the purposes of having someone share your credentials when they introduce you before the talk. But, referring to a time when you successfully applied your expertise provides a relevant example and further amplifies your credibility.

- *Present your agenda.*   Keep in mind the familiar slogan "Tell them what you are going to tell them, tell them, and then tell them what you just told them."

- *Share what you expect of the audience.*   At the beginning of your presentation, tell listeners about the question-and-answer session at the end, or the ensuing reception, or the cards you want them to fill out before they leave.

- *Use icebreakers if appropriate.*   In some presentations it is helpful to do an opening icebreaker to set an emotional climate for the presentation. The most common icebreaker is having people introduce themselves and explain their reason for attending the presentation. Make sure your icebreakers are short, appropriate, and participative.[6] They should last no longer than 5 to 10 minutes, have something to do with the topic, and be something that each person can, and wants to, get involved with.

The Main Message   Once you have gotten the audience's attention, you need to deliver what you promised in the shortest, most interesting way possible. Keep two things in mind as you structure your message: the attention cycle of your audience and pace of your speech.[7]

Material at the beginning and end of a presentation will be remembered more than the material in the middle.[8] Our attention span lasts only for a short time and then it tapers off. When we sense the end of a message, we pull our attention back in time to catch the last material. Fluctuation of the attention cycle is one of the main reasons we put such emphasis on the introduction and conclusion.

You can also change the pace every 10 to 15 minutes to break up your talk and keep attention riveted. You can create this change by including appropriate humor, stories, exercises requiring people to move their bodies (even if it is just raising their hands), or calls for a verbal response.

Other things you do can help retention. First, use repetition. Your main ideas need to be communicated several times to make sure they get through accurately and are remembered. Second, use stories and analogies to associate and connect your ideas to something the listeners already understand. Third, change the intensity in the pitch, tone, and loudness of your voice to focus audience attention. Fourth, use audience involvement. Use visual aids, questions, hand gestures, and sound effects, anything that gets the audience involved with the message.

The Conclusion Your conclusion should repeat your main ideas to reinforce your objectives and expectations for the audience. It should be strong, succinct, and persuasive. Many speakers consider this section almost as important as the introduction and they write it out word-for-word.

Practice and Visualize Success[9]

You know your audience. You know your material. You have written a dynamite speech. The last step is to practice delivering it. The following guidelines may assist you in the process.

Rehearse

Rehearse aloud at least four or five times in order to check your timing (you read out loud slower than you read in your mind), and to make sure your presentation flows and sounds the way you want it to. You should feel comfortable explaining all of your ideas. Do not try to memorize your speech. You may end up sounding stale, as if you are reciting or reading.

Rehearse in the actual location of the presentation, if possible. It is better to work out the technicalities of visual aids, sound equipment, outlets, and positioning during a rehearsal, rather than be surprised on the day of your presentation.

You can get used to public speaking through rehearsing with family or friends. Ask them to explain what they heard. This feedback will give you a chance to make sure your message is clear. Ask them whether your visual aids are effective and whether they make your message more understandable. Ask them what you can do better.

Visualize

Once you have rehearsed your presentation and feel comfortable with the material, visualize yourself presenting it successfully. Olympic athletes use visualization to reach their peak performance. Studies have shown that visualized practice has a similar effect to actual practice. Visualizing a successful conclusion to any activity gives you a chance to experience success and become more confident in your delivery.

DELIVERY OF THE PRESENTATION

Planning and rehearsing are necessary, but not sufficient to ensure a successful presentation. No matter how well organized, logical, and supported with visual aids, if a presentation is poorly delivered it is doomed to failure. Following are some guidelines for using delivery to enhance your presentation.[10]

Be Enthusiastic

Students usually forgive a teacher's lack of platform skills if he or she appears devoted to the subject and is trying to share that appreciation with them. Similarly, an audience can become oblivious to similar speaker deficiencies if his or her gestures, vocal intonations, and attitude convey enthusiasm for the message. Your interest in your topic tends to be contagious. An enthusiastic introduction will perk audience interest to learn why you are so enthusiastic. Speak as if you are in a lively conversation with friends, but avoid shouting or preaching.

Maintain Eye Contact

Eye contact enhances audience involvement. It makes the audience feel that they are being spoken to personally and that you are sincere. It is most effective to rotate looking at audience members one at a time on a random basis.

Use Proxemics

The arrangement and use of physical space can enhance or detract from your presentation. It is better not to hide behind a podium. Eliminate distracting items from the area such as unnecessary equipment, furniture, papers, writings on the board, and irrelevant signs. You want to keep the audience's attention on you.

Body movement keeps the audience's attention. It can emphasize key points, build rapport, and signal transitions. Variety is the key, so keep alternating standing, moving, sitting, speaking, listening, and gesturing. Move closer to the audience to build rapport with particular members and make points. Back off when you are awaiting responses or addressing the entire group.

Use Appropriate Gestures

You should obviously avoid alienating or distracting gestures such as jingling keys, twisting hair, or adjusting notes. Appropriate gestures appear to be spontaneous and accentuate your verbal message. Small audiences can pick up minor variances in facial expression and hand movements, but with large audiences, your gestures need to be more accentuated and dramatic.

Never Apologize

Do not apologize for the way you look or sound, do not apologize for not being the best speaker in the world, do not apologize because your slides are upside down . . . do not apologize for anything! The minute you apologize, your ability to influence your audience is decreased. Start your speech with power. Make your audience think they are going to be informed, entertained, or enlightened. . . . Do not let them think they are getting anything except your best.

CONCEPT QUIZ

Complete the following true-false quiz by circling the correct answer. Answers are at the end of the quiz. After marking your answers, remember to go back and check your understanding of any answers you missed.

True or False	1. The three main sections of an oral presentation are the big idea, the introduction, and the conclusion.
True or False	2. Because you are the expert, it is not a good idea to involve the audience in your presentation.
True or False	3. You should never apologize during oral presentations.
True or False	4. You can minimize anxiety by dressing comfortably and appropriately.
True or False	5. An army colonel should avoid using technical military jargon when addressing the general public.
True or False	6. You should never use gestures because they are confusing.
True or False	7. Being enthusiastic about your topic can discredit your presentation.
True or False	8. Proxemics is the use of body language to convey messages.
True or False	9. You should not check on the technological capabilities of the place where you are speaking because they are your host's responsibility.
True or False	10. Preparing by practicing out loud can be detrimental and throw you off during the actual presentation.

Answers. (1) False; (2) False; (3) True; (4) True; (5) True; (6) False; (7) False; (8) True; (9) False; (10) False

BEHAVIORAL CHECKLIST

The following skills are important to effective formal oral and written communication. Use them when evaluating your communication skills and those of others.

The Effective Oral Presenter

- Includes content appropriate for the audience.
- Determines the presentation's purpose and behavioral objectives.
- Productively manages anxiety.
- Includes an introduction, body, and conclusion.
- Speaks clearly and enthusiastically.
- Effectively uses visual aids.
- Utilizes space for maximum impact.
- Maintains eye contact and uses appropriate gestures.

GROUP EXERCISE

Oral Presentations

Many students steer clear of classes and situations requiring oral presentations. The problem is that most management jobs require them. By choosing to avoid earlier discomfort in the classroom where they are expected to make oral presentation gaffes and where others can help them improve, these individuals miss opportunities that might help them avoid making gaffes in front of co-workers, clients, or bosses where career goals could be jeopardized.

Nothing substitutes for experience in honing your oral presentation skills. Consequently, this group exercise consists of everyone making and evaluating oral presentations in order to gain confidence and feedback to become better presenters.

Directions. Each class member is to prepare and deliver a three- to five-minute oral presentation to other class members. Use the following Observer's Rating Sheet as a guide for preparing and delivering your presentation. The topic can be anything relevant to this class. Some suggestions are:

- Ideas about how to make grading more fair in this class.
- Strategies for reducing stage fright.
- My most embarrassing moment.
- A sales presentation on some service or product you can provide.
- Why the CEO should serve as an ethical example for others.
- The most interesting person I ever met.
- The advantages of your chosen career.
- Let me tell you a funny story.

Time. Take 10 to 15 minutes for the class members to prepare their presentations. Each presenter will be timed by the next presenter. The timer will signal after four minutes to help the presenter conclude on time. The class may need to be divided into subgroups in order to finish within schedule time constraints.

OBSERVER'S RATING SHEET

On completion of each presentation, observers rate the presenter's application of oral presentation skills. Use the following rating scale. Write concrete examples in the space for comments below each criterion to use when explaining your feedback.

1 *Unsatisfactory*	*2* *Weak*	*3* *Adequate*	*4* *Good*	*5* *Outstanding*

Name of Presenter:	*Rating*

- Includes content appropriate for the audience. _____

- Determined the purpose and behavioral objectives. _____

- Productively managed anxiety. _____

- Included an introduction, body, and conclusion. _____

- Spoke clearly and enthusiastically. _____

- Effectively used visual aids. _____

- Utilized space for maximum impact. _____

- Used appropriate eye contact and gestures. _____

APPLICATION QUESTIONS

1. Evaluate your professor's presentation style. How does he or she rate on the Behavioral Checklist?
2. Think of a speaker who really is connected with the audience. What did the speaker do to establish and maintain the connection, e.g., tell an appropriate joke, use vivid examples, maintain eye contact, and so on?
3. Think of a situation in which you saw a speaker do a poor job presenting. What did he or she do that contributed to this failure?
4. What are some of the best visual aids you have seen? What are some of the worst? What makes the difference?
5. Have you ever been nervous before making a presentation? If so, how did you get through it? What could you do to be more relaxed? If not, what do you do to retain your cool?

REINFORCEMENT EXERCISES

The following suggestions are activities you can do to reinforce the oral skills presented in this chapter. You may want to adapt them to the Action Plan you will develop next, or try them independently.

1. Attend a local meeting of Toastmasters. Watch how others make oral presentations and learn from the feedback that is given to the presenters. Try participating yourself if you have the time and inclination.
2. Take a class in college that requires public speaking and presentations. As with anything else, you will become more comfortable the more you practice.
3. Volunteer to speak in front of a group, no matter how large or small. It can vary from reading during Sunday church to giving an impromptu speech to your group of friends. Ask family and friends for reinforcement on your appearance in front of the group.
4. Join a campus club or organization. Make a focused effort to contribute your ideas and opinions about the club's activities and issues. By speaking up more in an informal and supportive environment, you will gain confidence speaking in front of others.

NOTES

1. The conceptual outline for this appendix is adapted from J. S. Hunsaker and P. L. Hunsaker, "Effective Presentation Skills," *Industrial Management* (March 1985): 13–17.
2. T. Alessandra and P. Hunsaker, *Communicating at Work* (New York: Simon & Shuster, 1993) 169.
3. Hunsaker and Hunsaker, 1985.
4. D. A. Level, Jr., and W. P. Galle, Jr. *Managerial Communications* (San Diego, CA: Business Publications, Inc., 1988) 34.
5. Alessandra and Hunsaker, 1993, 177.
6. Alessandra and Hunsaker, 1993, 178.
7. Alessandra and Hunsaker, 1993, 179.
8. Alessandra and Hunsaker, 1993, 179.
9. Alessandra and Hunsaker, 1993, 181–82.
10. D. A. Peoples, *Presentations Plus* (New York: QED/John Wiley and Sons, 1992).

APPENDIX B

Written Communication Skills[1]

> As soon as you move one step up from the bottom, your effectiveness depends on your ability to reach others through the spoken or written word.
>
> —PETER DRUCKER

You may be bright, ambitious, and hardworking and yet have a serious handicap that will stall your career climb on the lower rungs of the management ladder: poor writing skills. Writing abilities are as visible as a person's wardrobe, but the impressions you leave through your written work last even longer. Memos, reports, and letters are read, often reread, and can be kept forever. By developing your writing skills, you will be better equipped to persuade, direct, and influence the course of your organization and the direction of your career.

Poor writing smothers even the most important messages. The reader may spend more time interpreting the message than acting on it. Writing well takes practice, effort, and a bit of talent. In the end, you want your writing to be organized and coherent, not open to multiple interpretations. You want your reader to understand your message, not point at it and exclaim, "What does *this* mean?"

The ingredients of effective writing are content, style, technique, and format. The first section of this appendix will help you understand how to powerfully focus your content and to use each of the most common business formats (memos, letters, and reports) effectively. The second section will give you guidelines on style and techniques to avoid some of the most common writing mistakes.

CONTENT

> Grasp the subject, the words will follow.
>
> —CATO THE ELDER

Good business writing is more about clear thinking than it is about writing style. Writing can only be as good as the thinking that precedes it. You must know what you want to say, what your objective is in saying it, and why it is important for your audience to read it.

Getting Organized

Organizing a writing project is similar to organizing a presentation. The good writer is just as aware of the intended audience as a good public speaker is.

One technique that can help you organize your thoughts and content is *mindmapping*. This whole-brain, visually interesting version of outlining helps you pull together all your ideas, memories, associations, and connections in a quick *mind dump*. It has none of the constraints that make the Roman numeral form of outlining so stale and dry. Instead, mindmapping allows information to flow more freely from mind to page, streaming off naturally into organized branches. According to recent brain/mind research, the mind's attention span is extremely short—between five to seven minutes depending on subject matter and level of interest. The mind works best in these short bursts of activity. Mindmapping takes advantage of the mind's tendency to work in short, intense *mind bursts* by allowing you to *dump* your ideas and thoughts onto paper in just a few minutes. Mindmapping is like a personal brainstorming session. It gives you a chance to make new connections with the information and organize it into its primary pieces or branches and the appropriate subtopics and details. It helps you quickly explore your topic creatively.

Mindmapping is extremely easy to use. The basic process includes the following flow of steps:

- *Focus.*   Print the central idea in a circle or box in the center of the page.
- *Free association.*   Allow your ideas to flow freely without judgment.
- *Connect ideas.*   Print key ideas or thoughts on lines connected to the center focus.
- *Branches.*   First branches are key ideas; related ideas are connected as subbranches.
- *Key words.*   Print key words only: mindmapping is a form of brain shorthand and needs only a few key words to capture an idea.
- *Symbols/images.*   Use any symbols or images that make sense to you.
- *Color.*   Use color to stimulate your thought processes and to help you organize the material.

Mindmapping allows you to get information down on paper the way your mind handles it rather than in a rigid outline form. Each mindmap is a unique product of the person who produces it. Mindmaps are not right or wrong and take no rigid outline forms.[2] Exhibit B-1 illustrates a mindmap.

Focus on Your Purpose

After you have mindmapped the subject of your memo, report, or letter, you should have a clear idea of your main focus. *Focus* in your business report or memo refers to

EXHIBIT B-I   Mindmapping Example

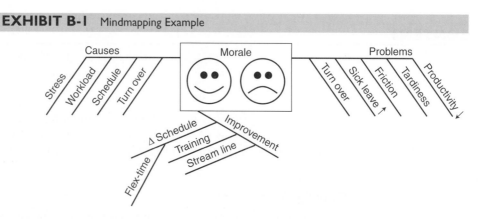

SOURCE: T. Allesandra and P. Hunsaker, *Communicating at Work* (New York: Simon & Schuster, 1993) 225.

your objective. It is the "why" of why you are bothering to write at all. A lot of business writing has its purpose buried. It has no focus: no goal, no call for action, no desired end result. If you do not provide the focus, your readers may be confused about why they are reading your document. You should have answered this question for yourself before sitting down at your word processor. Ask yourself:

- Who is my audience?
- What do I want them to do?
- What reasons will they have for not wanting to do what I want them to do?
- What might stop the reader from doing what I suggest?
- Will someone other than the reader make the decision?
- What are the politics involved?

You are not ready to start writing until you can complete this sentence: I want (WHO) to do (WHAT) because (REASON). If you can fill in that sentence, you are ready to proceed with the writing.

Analyze Your Audience

Knowing your audience will help you to organize your material so that it has the best chance of being read and understood. Put yourself in your reader's shoes, listen, and you will be better received. Do not be condescending. Phrases such as, "As you can clearly see" and "I am sure you will agree" only serve to turn your audience off.

Choosing the Appropriate Format

The format of what you are writing should fit its function. If you receive a memo and your response is a short note or decision, you may want to just jot your response on the memo and send it back. If you are responsible for presenting an analysis of a new market, however, you will need a formal report complete with charts, graphs, and documentation.

Making the format fit the function of your writing seems simple, but all too often a brief request triggers a three-page memo. Review the following hierarchy of communication formats so that you are sure your situation fits the requirements.

- *Verbal:* informal conversations where no documentation is required.
- *Handwritten:* informal communication requiring a minimum of documentation.
- *Memos:* broad communication (to more than three people) where formal documentation is required.
- *Reports:* broad communication involving complex issues that require supporting documentation, and decisions that need to be documented.
- *Business letters:* written communication generally to people outside your organization, serves several different functions and provides documentation.

Memos: Use and Abuse

Memos are most often boring, confusing, unnecessary, or all of the above. The first thing you should ask yourself is whether you really need to write it at all. Can you phone the people involved and *talk* to them? ATI Medical, Inc., (150 employees, $14 million sales) abolished memos and only occasionally writes PAPCOEs (reverse acronym for "enunciations of corporate policies and procedures"). President Paul Stevenson states, "Everyone has learned to talk to each other." Talking to people has wonderful advantages over writing: You get immediate feedback; you strengthen your social contacts; and you save trees.

Eliminating written communication probably is not practical or even desirable for most organizations. Whenever possible, however, talk to people and save your written communications for complex issues requiring extensive explanation or documentation.

When you do decide to write a memo, it should facilitate, simplify, and accelerate internal communication. When used effectively, memos provide a simple method to communicate an identical message to several people. In effect, memos are kind of a meeting on paper. Use them to give instructions, to ask for information or action, to announce or clarify a new policy or procedure, to announce changes or personnel transfers, or as "covers" for lengthier material such as reports.

Memos are an appropriate method of giving instructions to a number of people. Putting directions in writing, when done clearly, prevents misunderstandings about what is to be done, whose responsibility it is, and the date it is due.

Memos should be short (one page for most). Use every possible trick for quick communication including: headlines, short paragraphs, bullets, bolding of important points, and a modified outline format. A common heading for memos is illustrated in Exhibit B-2.

TO should include all intended recipients of the memo. The form of address depends on the culture of your organizations. Some companies use Mr./Mrs./Ms. and titles; others use only first names. *FROM* includes your name and phone number.

The *SUBJECT* of your memo should be specific. Clarify it, including only the relevant information: who, what, when, where, how, and why. This line should instantly give the reader enough information to know how to deal with it. A memo with the subject *New Marketing Plan Review Meeting* will receive a much different response than one with the subject *Salary Freeze Policy*.

The *ACTION REQUIRED* line makes it clear to the reader that the writer expects an action. It also helps the writer consider the purpose of the memo. If you are writing too many *Info Only* memos, it is time to rethink your communication policy. If you refer to an earlier memo, include it, preventing inconvenience for the receiver.

Keep your message brief, informal, and simple. Keep the specific readers' needs and circumstances in mind. Clarify the purpose and be specific about the actions the reader should take and when. Avoid words with double meanings, hidden agendas, jokes, or jargon. Artificial embellishments, fancy words, and wasteful sentences have no place in the office memo. Short and informal, a memo should never be written so hastily that it is ambiguous. Write it well and avoid misunderstandings, hurt feelings, and time spent correcting errors.

Reports: More Than Long Memos

Many people get anxious at the thought of writing a business report. Reports are generally long and deal with complex, often controversial, subjects. They require a

---

EXHIBIT B-2 Example Memo Format

Date:

TO:
FROM:
SUBJECT:
ACTION REQUIRED:

---

great deal of research and critical thought. Perhaps even more anxiety-producing is the realization that business reports generally influence major company decisions. The people who determine your future in the organization will read it, and a well-written report can enhance your opportunity for advancement. Conversely, a poorly thought-out and written report leaves a black mark that may be difficult to overcome.

The business report is a highly organized, fact-oriented document. You should use headings, subheadings, bulleted points, and details to support any conclusions. Use a variety of graphs and charts to help the reader understand the data you are presenting.

Before You Start Writing   Know the purpose of your report before you begin writing. Is it a white paper for information only? Will it recommend a specific solution?

As with every other form of communication, you should also know your intended audience. Make sure you do not insult their intelligence by presenting in detail information they already know, or confuse them with terms they may not be familiar with. Here are some excellent questions to ask yourself before you proceed with your report.

- What is the familiarity of the reader with the problem?
- What expertise does the reader have in this area?
- What conclusions are of importance to the reader?
- What are the preconceived notions of the reader?
- Why was the report requested?
- What does the reader need to know to make a decision?

Strategies for Presenting Information in a Report   You should also be thoroughly familiar with the ramifications of your suggestion and any drawbacks to it. Few solutions are perfect, so make sure you understand the limitations of yours. The purpose of the report, the proposed solution, and the intended audience will all affect the strategy you choose for your report. You should understand your strategy before you begin to write. Here are three typical strategies:

1. *Most important to least important.*   Works well when the decision or action is logical and not highly political, and the readers are objective.
2. *Least controversial to most controversial.*   Builds support gradually and is best used when the decision is expensive, controversial, politically sensitive, or when the readers are emotionally attached to a different solution than the one proposed.
3. *Negative to positive.*   Works well when readers are familiar with the problems involved with the situation and the proposed solution. It establishes a common ground and puts the positive argument last in a place of strength.

Business reports are fact-oriented and should not include opinion. If you want to add your personal opinions, they can be included in the cover letter. Opinions in the body of your report will make it seem less factual and objective.

Organization of Business Reports   Informal business reports have a fairly standard organization. This organization is outlined here.

- *Introduction.*   The introduction is similar to the opening of a presentation. It is where you grab the reader, introduce the key issues, and give the reader a sense of who, what, where, when, why, and how. It should give the reader the background of the problem, state the problem clearly and indicate why its solution is important to the reader, and define the scope and limitations of the proposed solution.
- *Table of contents.*   This table makes it easy for the reader to find key information. In a 10-page report, it is not critical, but in a 100-page report, a great deal of time

can be wasted looking for information. Reports are often reviewed in meetings, and it can be frustrating trying to find a key point.

- *Main body.* The body is where the writer presents the findings from the research, analyzes the data, evaluates the possible solutions, and develops a rationale for selecting the proposed solution. This section is often broken down into the following subsections:

  - *Background material and facts.* The two functions of this section are to give readers essential background material they may lack, and to clarify the report writer's understanding of the situation, which may well differ from the perceptions of others.
  - *Statement of problem.* This section explicitly defines the problem (as opposed to the symptoms) to be solved.
  - *Analysis.* This section contains the logical thought processes used to develop the solution; it is designed to persuade the reader regarding the advantages of the solution and thoroughness of the writer's analysis. This section could be further divided into such topics as alternatives considered, objectives for solution, evaluation of alternatives, alternatives rejected, or assumptions.
  - *Solutions and implementation.* This final section details solutions to the problem.
  - *Conclusions and recommendations.* The entire report leads up to this point. No new information is presented but the key ideas are recapped and summarized in a way that reinforces the validity of the recommendation.

- *Appendixes.* Data that is too lengthy or complex should be in this section. The body of the text can reference data in a particular appendix without bogging the reader down with the entire set of data. It is not unusual to have the body of a report be a few pages of text backed up by hundreds of pages of detailed data.

Business Letters: Your Messengers to the Outside World

Malcolm Forbes once said, "Most business letters don't make it." In his typical, direct style, he continued, "It's totally asinine to blow your chances of getting whatever you want with a business letter that turns people off instead of turning them on." He said that most business letters fall into three categories: stultifying if not stupid; mundane (most of them); and first rate (rare). His primary recommendation for reaching the first rate level is to know what you want and to be able to write it down in one sentence.

Business letters are your written contact with people outside the organization. Unlike telephone conversations, letters document your communication, providing a long-lasting record that can be referred to whenever necessary. Writing a business letter is done for many different reasons. Each purpose dictates a slightly different style and tone. Some common reasons are

- To request specific information or action from someone outside the company.
- To provide information to someone who requests it.
- For ceremonial purposes (congratulations, thank-yous, commendations).
- To exchange ideas, handle arguments, present a point of view, or explain why an action was taken or why a requested action was rejected.
- To sell goods or services or to provide information about the company.

You are representing your company when you write a business letter. Get to the point quickly. Be clear, courteous, and concise.

Your first paragraph is where you hook your reader's attention and get the reader involved with your purpose. It is not the time for mumbling, stuttering, or vagueness. It is where you persuade the reader to consider your ideas. Give a clear idea of the benefits your proposal brings to the reader or why you need the information the reader has.

Write so that the reader enjoys reading it. Write the entire letter from the reader's point of view. Answer questions and objections the reader might have. Be positive. Be nice. Be natural.

Conclude by urging the reader to act on your solution. You should get your message across in one or two pages. If not, add an appendix of materials. Read your letter out loud to see whether it sounds natural and pleasant, and clearly addresses your purpose.

Good business writing is a combination of clear thinking, good organization, and effective presentation. The previous sections have given you a technique—mindmapping—to help you think through your writing project and organize it effectively. They have also given you a guide to using the three most common formats in business writing: memos, reports, and business letters. The next few sections will help you improve your style and avoid some of the most common pitfalls in writing.

STYLE

> Colors fade, temples crumble, empires fall, but wise words endure.
> —EDWARD THORNDIKE

What exactly is style? Hemingway had style. Stephen King has style. Does that mean you have to be a professional writer to have style? No. In fiction, *style* is used to describe a distinctive voice in writing . . . a certain grace with words that sets the truly great writer apart from the rest. In business writing, we are talking about something much more basic. In business writing, we are looking for clarity, conciseness, and readability more than eloquence.

Think about the memos that you absolutely dread reading. Those with sentences so long you get lost along the way. Those that strangle you with confusing phrases, technical terms, acronyms, and words that only a dictionary could love. Those that ramble for pages without a break or even a sense of where they are going.

You have probably seen them all . . . and maybe worse. These are the memos, letters, and reports that you want to pass along to someone else to read, no matter how important the information inside may seem to be. The overwhelming temptation is to set it aside in the "To Read" file, or, better yet, the circular file. Style is what makes the difference.

The Big Three: Clear, Concise, Readable

By now you are well aware of the importance of clarity in your thinking before you begin writing. To write clearly demands a high level of preparation. If you lack confidence when you write, it shows up in the use of passive voice, jargon, indirect expressions, and lengthy, unfocused writing. To be clear, you need to say what you want to say directly rather than tiptoeing gently around the topic. Most readers are not likely to tiptoe with you, which makes you, the writer, seem to be hiding something.

To write concisely, you should use short words, sentences, and paragraphs, to grab the attention of the reader. Finally, to make your business document readable, you should consider the words you use, the voice you choose, and your level of formality.

Do Not Muddy the Water

Once you are confident about what you want to say and have it well organized and structured, three actions will help you to improve the clarity of your writing: Use active voice, avoid jargon, avoid indirectness.

Use Active Voice   Active voice is open and up-front. Business writing is about action. It requests action, suggests action, encourages action. If you want people to act, use active rather than passive voice. For example:

Passive: It is suggested that you have a meeting called at your earliest convenience.

Active: Please call a meeting ASAP.

We get into passive voice primarily in two ways: delaying the subject and using a *be* verb or past participle of an active verb. Here are two examples. The subject of the sentence is in italics and the verb is underlined:

Passive: There <u>seems</u> to be a need to review our health plan.

Active: We <u>will review</u> our health plan Friday.

Note that the first sentence is so passive, the subject fails to even make an appearance.

Passive: A new phone system <u>was chosen</u> by the committee.

Active: The committee <u>chose</u> a new phone system.

Notice that it is the same basic verb—chose—but the passive voice uses the past participle form. The active sentence is clean, clear, and simple. Active voice is much closer to the way we talk. As a writer you are talking with your reader through the written word. If you were talking to a coworker, you would say "I suggest" and not "it is suggested." The active voice not only adds vitality to your writing, but it is more direct, forceful, and personal.

Active voice depends on action verbs. Decide. Talk. Meet. Sell. Start. Buy. Merge. Choose. Hire. Fire. Plan. Negotiate. Make. Build. Ask. These action words of business telegraph meaning when not surrounded by muddy, indirect phrases.

Passive voice is a shield to hide behind. It is flat and dull, and you should only resort to it when you want to soften bad news, you want to avoid responsibility for some occurrence or remain detached, or you do not know who the main "actor" is in a sentence.

Avoid Jargon   Every profession has its terminology, acronyms, and jargon. When everyone understands the terms, it provides a quick and efficient shorthand. When everyone does not understand the terms, it creates miscommunication and misunderstandings. It is almost impossible to avoid jargon and acronyms, and when you are writing for people within your organization, you are probably safe. If you have any doubt that your readers will understand a term or acronym, define the term the first time it is used, or find a different way of expressing your idea. For example:

Jargon: The LOE required to respond to the RFP is too high.

Translation: The level of effort required to respond to the request for proposal is too high.

Plain English: We cannot afford to bid on this project.

Be Direct   Say what you mean. If you try to hide behind indirect expressions, either people will not understand what you are saying or they will figure it out anyway and just think you are a poor writer. Examples:

Indirect: It is suggested that you have a meeting called at your earliest convenience regarding the possibility of determining the feasibility of implementing a new marketing plan.

Direct: Please call a meeting ASAP to discuss a new marketing plan.

People generally go into indirect mode when they are hedging. Common hedging words are *seems, appears, might possibly be,* and *could be.* These words and phrases indicate a lack of confidence and a fuzziness of thinking. They do not inspire confidence and action in your reader.

Writing is an act of communication. We are trying to pass a message from one mind to another. It is our job as writers to make the message as clear as possible to the reader. The more active, jargon-free, and direct our writing is, the more the reader will understand what our message is.

Short Is Best

The second goal of business writing is conciseness. We are not writing the great American novel; we are transmitting information or requesting action from people who have little time or inclination to read what we are writing. If we are asking someone to take action and we can clearly convey that request in one paragraph, great! Business writing is not a college term paper with a fixed page requirement. We want to state our business in the clearest and shortest way possible. Cut out all the fluff and improve your chances of having your memos and reports read and acted on.

Short Words Start with short words. Big words are no substitute for clear thinking and often they are not as powerful as short, punchy, crisp, lean, exact, sharp, tight, and to-the-point small words. Here are a few examples of big words that have smaller alternatives. You may want to use the big word but consider the little one:

Viable = workable, useful

Interface with = meet with, work with

Optimize = make the most of

Sufficient = enough

Utilize = Use

Short Phrases Just as we often opt for a long word when a short one would do, we have developed a lot of wordy phrases that need to be trimmed back. Here are some examples:

With reference to = about, regarding

On the grounds that = because

In accordance with = by, following

To tell the truth = (avoid this one, it sounds like a lie is coming)

To the best of my ability = (eliminate)

Hold a discussion = discuss

Take action = act

At this point in time = now

Short Sentences Short sentences are active. They have punch. They telegraph. Although not all sentences can be short, watch out for these three tiny words: and, but, or. They often lead into long sentences full of dependent clauses and twists and turns that may lose the reader. The most interesting writing uses a variety of sentence lengths with the short sentence being used as the power punch. Look at a recent memo or report and count the words in three or four sentences. A common guideline is 17 words. It is okay to go over that limit occasionally, but if all your sentences are more than 17 words, your readers are going to go brain-dead. (This last sentence contained 26 words. It could have been broken into two: It is okay to go over that limit occasionally. However, if all your sentences are more than 17 words, your readers are going to go brain-dead.)

Short Paragraphs Two reasons support the use of short paragraphs: one idea and white space. Powerful paragraphs transmit one idea. Each sentence in the paragraph develops the idea. When that idea is complete, go to the next idea in the next paragraph.

Take a lesson from the advertising folks. White space sells. The space between paragraphs gives the reader time to process information and makes it easier to transition to the next idea. Short paragraphs broken by white space please the eye more than an unbroken mass of words on a page.

Short Writing   If you can say it in one page, do not take two. Brief is better. Short has more chance of being read. However, short is not easier. It is much harder to write a one-page memo than to ramble on for two. It requires clear thinking and clear writing. But, it is worth the effort.

Business is about productivity and efficiency. Business writing that is clear and concise promotes those ideals. Business writing is almost never about entertaining the reader. Reading memos is not a leisure activity. Respect your reader's time by saying what you need to say as clearly and concisely as possible.

Telegraph Your Message Through Readability

Once your message is clear and concise, make your memo readable and telegraph it to your reader's mind with a powerful format. Make it as easy to read as possible. When considering format, always keep these business principles in mind:

> *First and foremost: No one wants to read it!*
>
> *Second and important: Almost no one will read all of it!*
>
> *Third and critical: Almost everyone will misunderstand some part of it!*

No one exclaims, "Oh wow! A new report for me to read!"—except with sarcasm. In the business world, a written message is usually a call to do something, to make decisions, to add to an already overcrowded schedule. Too often we blow it from the first line. *Per your request, please find enclosed the report on the possible involvement of management in a*... Yawn. Z-Z-Z-Z.

You are competing for the time of busy people. Unless you are the chairman of the board or president, you probably have about 30 seconds to grab the interest of your reader. Just as we buy magazines based on the front-page headline or picture, we are more likely to read a memo that captures our attention. Otherwise, the magazine stays on the stand and the memo ends up in the "To Read" cemetery.

Borrowing from the journalism and advertising trade, energize your writing with the main tools for improving readability: headlines, subheads, visuals, highlighting and bullets, the use of white space, and dynamic delivery. Telegraph your message. Grab the reader's attention.

Headlines Are Golden

They must never be boring. Do not waste a headline with *Summary of Benefits* when you could have stated: *Three Million in Savings*. When writing a report, proceed in this order: Start with the headlines, then plan the graphics and subheads and, perfecting those, add the main body. This way is best to maintain focus and flow in your writing.

Visuals Sell Your Message

Pictures, graphs, or illustrations will help you get an idea across quickly or emphasize a particular point. Keep these suggestions in mind when incorporating graphics:

- Graphs and charts have more impact than tables.
- Each graph, chart, or picture should make only one point. Better to have several graphs, each making one point, than one confusing graph with little impact.
- Add color if at all possible.
- Keep the graph or picture as close to the related text as possible.

Highlighting   Use boldface and italics to highlight key ideas and introduce new topics, and bullets to emphasize list items. For example:

Boldface and *Italics*   key ideas and new topics
Bullets •   emphasize list items

Even though they can be extremely useful at the appropriate times, you should use these tools sparingly. When you are speaking in public, you can use your voice to emphasize certain ideas. When you are writing, you are using these highlighting mechanisms in the same way you would use your voice. Just as you would not try to emphasize every word to your audience, you do not emphasize every word on the page. For example, the exclamation point should be used infrequently in business writing! *Also*, if you *try* to **emphasize** *too* many words, **it** becomes *visually* **chaotic** and *makes* the **reader** want to **quit** *reading*. Did the previous sentence make the point?

White Space   Again, white space makes a page more readable. Use it to produce a page that is clean and attractive. Use wide margins and a break between paragraphs. It is much easier to read narrow columns than wide lines. Wide margins also make it easy for the reader to make notes while reading. It makes the page look clean and professional.

Additional Readability Tips   These housekeeping tips help to make your memos and reports more readable.

- *Limit upper case.*   Although uppercase may be used OCCASIONALLY for emphasis, long blocks of text in uppercase are difficult to read. It is almost always better to use boldface and italics for emphasis and save uppercase for titles and headings.
- *Numbers.*   Numbers should be written in a way that makes them easier to read. $4 million is easier to read than $4,000,000.
- *Page numbers.*   For reports of more than three pages, page numbers are mandatory. Trying to discuss unnumbered pages has ruined many meetings.
- *Hyphens.*   Before we had word processing, we seldom thought about breaking a word at the end of a line. The only purpose for hyphenation is to even out spacing. Hyphens do not improve readability. Avoid them if you can and if you cannot, review them carefully to make sure they do not break the flow of words.
- *Right justification.*   This technique is popular because magazines and newspapers use it. It makes the page look "professional." However, they use it because it packs more words into a smaller space and saves paper. The uneven spaces created by right justification make reading more difficult and should be avoided when possible.

If you use these guidelines to help you write clearly and concisely in a readable format, your writing will become far more powerful and effective. And, as your memos and reports become more powerful, you will begin to have more of an impact on your organization. The following paragraphs will give you a few more tips to help your writing style.

Avoid Sexism

A recent study of 500 college students (50 percent male and 50 percent female) showed that when they read a story using he, him, or his where the subject could be male or female, 65 percent of the study group assumed the subject was male. Recently, people have been sensitized to sexism in writing; therefore, you should avoid sexism whenever possible. However, using awkward constructions such as he/she or (s)he can break the flow of your writing and lessen readability.

Here are some ways to avoid sexism without sacrificing readability:

- Specify the person you are discussing.
- Use plurals. For example:

  A manager should listen to his staff.
  Managers should listen to their staffs.

- Alternate he and she.

  A manager should listen to her staff.

- Substitute less offensive words: person for man; synthetic for man-made; representative for spokesman; worker for workman; labor hours for man-hours.

Humor

Humor can be effective in informal writing. However, unless you are positive that the humor will not give offense, it is better not to use it. If you are a boss writing to your staff, humor directed at yourself can establish a warm, human tone. If you are an underling, humor directed at yourself might be perceived as a lack of self-confidence or weakness.

Even if you are extremely good at humor, you should limit it in your business writing. People will come to expect it and your serious communications will be more difficult.

Punctuation

Punctuation is another way we approximate in writing what we can do with our voice in speaking. Punctuation creates pauses, clarifies meaning, and adds rhythm to our writing. Reading is like listening: the more fluent and lyrical the words, the more willing the reader is to read on. Writers use punctuation to control the timing and pace of their work.

- The period stops the sentence. The semicolon creates a pause between two halves. And, the comma is a brief rest before going on.
- Dashes separate an important aspect of a larger idea—such as our discussion of punctuation—and draw attention to it.
- The colon is a pause longer than a semicolon but not as long as a period. Colons are most commonly used for two purposes: to introduce a list or serve as a link between an introductory statement and an important point.
- Parentheses tell the reader that the enclosed information is useful but not vital.

Two punctuation marks affect the tone of a paper: the question mark and quotation marks. Questions are unassuming and can add a warm, easygoing tone to your writing. Questions also facilitate transitions. For example, after explaining a change in procedure you might interject, "How are we going to do it?" Then you could explain the implementation procedure. Quotation marks not only enclose direct quotes, but also set off and denote words or phrases used in a special sense.

Editing

You have not finished your report until you have edited it thoroughly for typos, misspellings, and errors in numbers or dates. Whether you write one memo a month or 40, you should have a minimum of three reference books: a good dictionary, a thesaurus, and a style guide. Keep these by your desk and do not hesitate to refer to them. The time you take now to double-check a spelling or find the right word will make all the difference later.

HERE ARE A FEW OF THE BASICS:

- *The Elements of Style* by William Strunk, Jr. and E. B. White (New York: Macmillan, 1979).
- *The Chicago Manual of Manual of Style* 15th ed., (Chicago: University of Chicago Press, 2003).
- *The American Heritage Dictionary of the English Language*, 4th ed. (Boston: American Heritage and Houghton Mifflin, 2001).
- *The Synonym Finder* by J. I. Rodale (Emmaus, PA: Rodale Press, Inc., 1978). Lists more than 1 million synonyms.

Common Errors

We make many word errors—words with the wrong meaning, imprecise words, redundant words, out-of-date words. Know your words and, when in doubt, check a dictionary. Certain words are confused with others over and over again, which in turn confuses the reader. Here are a few of the culprits:

- *It's* vs. *Its: It's* is a contraction of "it is." *Its* is the possessive form of "it."
- *Imply* vs. *Infer: Imply* means to suggest indirectly. *Infer* means to draw meaning out of something.

  He implied that he wanted to go.

  I inferred from his actions that he wanted to go.
- *I.e.* vs. *e.g.: I.e.* (*id est*) means "that is." *E.g.* (*exampli gratia*) means "for example."
- *Appraise* vs. *Apprise: Appraise* means to measure, to assess the value or nature of something. *Apprise* means to inform in detail.

Style Strategies

Once you thoroughly understand style, you can select the style that fits your reader and the type of writing situation you face. These situations generally fall into the following four categories:

1. ***Positive situations.***   Where you are saying yes or relating good news.
   Style: Personal, at times Colorful
2. ***Situations where you are asking something of the reader.***   Where you are giving instructions or persuading someone to do as requested.
   Style: Active, at times Personal and Colorful
3. ***Information-conveying situations.***   Where you are passing along factual, detailed information.
   Style: Impersonal
4. ***Negative situations.***   Where you are delivering information that the reader would prefer not to know.
   Style: Passive, Impersonal

Here is a list of the highlights of each style:

ACTIVE STYLE

- Helps you be forceful, confident, and sure as in action requests or when you are saying no firmly but politely to an employee.
- Depends on active verbs.
- Uses short sentences.
- Makes direct statements that start with the subject.
- Speaks in first person—*I want, We need*.

PASSIVE STYLE

- Is useful when you are in a negative situation or are in a lower position than the reader.
- Avoids the imperative—never gives an order.
- Subordinates the subject to the end of the sentence or buries it completely.
- Attributes responsibility for negative statements to nameless, faceless, impersonal "others."
- Uses long sentences or dense paragraphs to slow down the reader's attention to sensitive or negative information.

PERSONAL STYLE

- Is useful when you are relating good news or a persuasive action-request.
- Refers to people by name (first name, when appropriate) instead of by title.
- Uses personal pronouns (especially "you" and "I" when you have positive things to say).
- Incorporates short, informal, and conversational sentences, with contractions if necessary.
- Asks the reader direct questions.
- Includes personal notes and references.

IMPERSONAL STYLE

- Is useful in negative and information-conveying situations, and especially in technical and scientific writing.
- Refers to people by title or job description if necessary, not by name (particularly first name).
- Avoids using personal pronouns, although a faceless "we" may be appropriate.
- Uses passive verbs.
- Uses longer sentences including complex sentences and long paragraphs.

COLORFUL STYLE

- Is useful for highly persuasive writing such as sales letters or for good-news situations.
- Includes more descriptive adjectives and adverbs.
- Incorporates metaphor and simile when appropriate.
- Allows unusual words or slang.

Memos, reports, and business letters are a critical part of an organization's communication environment. As you develop your ability to write in a clear, concise, forceful style, you will improve your personal effectiveness and the productivity of your organization. "Style," as it applies to business writing, is not as mysterious as it sounds. It is more a matter of common sense: understanding the needs of your reader, as well as your own objectives, and then presenting your message clearly and concisely in a readable format.

CONCEPT QUIZ

Complete the following true-false quiz by circling the correct answer. Answers are at the end of the quiz. After marking your answers, remember to go back and check your understanding of any answers you missed.

True or False   1. If you are bright, ambitious, or successful, poor business writing will not have a negative effect on your career.

True or False   2. Mindmapping is a powerful technique to get all your ideas and associations with a certain topic out on paper in a short, intense mind-burst.

True or False   3. You are ready to write when you can complete this sentence: I want (WHO) to do (WHAT) because (REASON).

True or False   4. Tables have more of an impact than charts and graphs.

True or False   5. In a business report, it is acceptable and appropriate to place lengthy data in appendixes.

True or False   6. Three ways to improve clarity of style are by using the active voice, avoiding jargon, and being direct.

True or False   7. Business writing is often about complex issues, so long words or sentences are necessary.

True or False   8. To improve readability, one should use all capital letters and right justification.

True or False   9. Highlighting, bullets, and headlines are unprofessional and have no place in business writing.

True or False   10. In positive situations, your style should be personal and perhaps colorful, and using active voice.

Answers.   (1) False; (2) True; (3) True; (4) False; (5) True; (6) True; (7) False; (8) False; (9) False; (10) True

BEHAVIORAL CHECKLIST

The following skills are important to effective business writing. Use them when evaluating your writing skills and those of others.

The Effective Business Writer

- Organizes thoughts before writing, so that the document flows naturally.
- Considers the audience when writing.
- Uses graphs, charts, headlines, and bullets to enhance memos and reports.
- Indicates the need for action, if there is one.
- Uses short words, sentences, and paragraphs.
- Avoids sexism, inappropriate humor, jargon, and indirectness.
- Knows what style strategy is appropriate for each type of business situation.
- Lives by the Big Three—clear, concise, and readable.

GROUP EXERCISE

Written Presentations

Many students agonize over writing papers for class. However, once you enter the business world, effective business writing is expected in virtually every type of position. Just like public speaking, good business writing requires practice. Although the prospect of writing papers may seem daunting, students are getting valuable practice toward successful careers. Consequently, the group exercise for this module consists of students preparing two different types of business documents in order to practice and receive feedback on their writing.

Directions. The students should form groups of three or four. Each member will prepare a memo and an outline for a business report based on a business scenario of mutual interest.

Step 1: Group members should describe interesting business situations they have been involved in or have heard about. Then they agree on one to write about. Examples of situations might be:

- New Marketing Plan
  —The memo might announce the introduction of the marketing plan.
  —The outline might reflect how a report on the new marketing plan should be structured.
- CEO announces hiring freeze based on low profits
  —The memo should announce the news to the employees.
  —The outline should reflect the business report stating the findings and making the recommendations for a hiring freeze.

Step 2: Students individually write their own memo and report outline.

Step 3: Students read and critique the others' work based on the effective business writer Behavioral Checklist.

Step 4: Students discuss what they have learned from their experience and make recommendations based on the exercise.

Time. Each group will have 10 minutes to brainstorm a scenario that they want to work on. Next, students will have 10 minutes to write their own memo, and another 15 minutes to write the outline. After every member has finished, the other group members will have 20 minutes to look over and critique the others' work. Finally, in the time remaining, students will discuss what they learned from their experience and make recommendations based on the exercise.

APPLICATION QUESTIONS

1. Evaluate your professor's writing. Does the syllabus follow the guidelines outlined in this section?
2. Think of a paper or a memo that you had to read that was exceptionally well written. What tactics did the writer use to capture your attention?
   Conversely, think of a paper or memo that you considered poorly written and boring. What mistakes do you remember that the writer made?
   Based on what you have just learned, how could he or she have avoided those errors?
3. Do you feel that you have noticed a distinct writing "style" in your writing or the writings of your classmates? What distinguishes different styles in your mind?
4. Name some instances when you or others have used humor in business writing. What was the effect on you? What was the ultimate outcome of using humor?

REINFORCEMENT EXERCISES

The following suggestions are activities you can do to reinforce the skills in this chapter. You may want to incorporate them into an Action Plan, or try them independently.

1. Practice your writing. Pretend that each paper, no matter how small, will be viewed by the CEO of your company, and put appropriate effort into it.
2. Take a seminar on business writing. It can enhance the basic lessons taught in this section, and you can keep reinforcing these guidelines so they become a routine in your writing.
3. Visit your school's writing center, and ask them to review your written work. Ask for feedback and suggestions.

4. Play around with your style and effective writing. When sending e-mail to friends or writing letters, structure them as you would a business document. Again, this practice will help embed the lessons in your writing.
5. Volunteer to contribute to the company newsletter or that of an organization that interests you.
6. When reading business documents written by others, try to identify all the errors and broken rules of effective business writing. Once you see it from the other side, you will be less likely to make the same mistakes yourself.

NOTES

1. The material in this appendix is adapted from T. Alessandra and P. Hunsaker, *Communicating at Work* (New York: Simon & Schuster, 1993) chapters 16 and 17.

2. If you would like more information on how to use this powerful technique, see J. Wycoff, *Mindmapping: Your Personal Guide to Exploring Creativity and Problem Solving* (New York: Berkeley Books, 1991).

APPENDIX C

E-Mail Etiquette[1]

It is amazing to find that, in this day and age, some managers have still not realized how important their e-mail communications are. Many managers send e-mail replies late or not at all, or send replies that do not actually answer the questions that have been asked. Dealing professionally with e-mail will make you a better manager and give your company a competitive edge. Moreover, by educating employees about what can and cannot be said in an e-mail, you can avoid liability issues. This appendix discusses why e-mail etiquette is necessary, outlines the main etiquette rules, and provides advice on how managers can ensure that they are implemented.

WHY DO YOU NEED E-MAIL ETIQUETTE?

It is important to implement etiquette rules for the following three reasons:

1. *Professionalism.* By using proper e-mail language you will convey a professional image.
2. *Efficiency.* E-mail that gets to the point is much more effective than poorly worded e-mail.
3. *Protection from liability.* Awareness of e-mail risks will protect you from costly lawsuits.

WHAT ARE THE ETIQUETTE RULES?

There are many etiquette guides and many different etiquette rules. Some rules will differ according to the nature of your business and the corporate culture. The 32 most important e-mail etiquette rules that apply to nearly all companies are listed in Exhibit C-1.

1. *Be concise and to the point.* Do not make an e-mail any longer than it needs to be. Remember that reading an e-mail is harder than reading printed communications and a long e-mail can be very discouraging to read.

2. *Answer all questions, and preempt further questions.* An e-mail reply must answer all questions, and preempt further questions. If you do not answer all the questions in the original e-mail, you will receive further e-mails regarding the unanswered questions, which will not only waste time but also cause considerable frustration. Moreover, if you are able to preempt irrelevant questions, others will be grateful and impressed with your efficiency and thoughtfulness.

3. *Use proper spelling, grammar, and punctuation.* This is important not only because improper spelling, grammar, and punctuation give a bad impression of you, it

EXHIBIT C-1   The Thirty-Two Most Important E-Mail Etiquette Tips

1. Be concise and to the point.
2. Answer all questions, and preempt further questions.
3. Use proper spelling, grammar, and punctuation.
4. Make it personal.
5. Use templates for frequently used responses.
6. Answer swiftly.
7. Do not attach unnecessary files.
8. Use proper structure and layout.
9. Do not overuse the high priority option.
10. Do not write in CAPITALS.
11. Don't leave out the message thread.
12. Add disclaimers to your e-mail.
13. Read the e-mail before you send it.
14. Do not overuse "Reply to All."
15. Bulk mailings—use the bcc: field or do a mail merge.
16. Take care with abbreviations and emoticons.
17. Be careful with formatting.
18. Take care with rich text and HTML messages.
19. Do not forward chain letters.
20. Do not request delivery and read receipts.
21. Do not ask to recall a message.
22. Do not copy a message or attachment without permission.
23. Do not use e-mail to discuss confidential information.
24. Use a meaningful subject.
25. Use active instead of passive voice.
26. Avoid using URGENT and IMPORTANT.
27. Avoid long sentences.
28. Don't send or forward e-mail containing libelous, defamatory, offensive, racist, or obscene remarks.
29. Don't forward virus hoaxes.
30. Keep your language gender neutral.
31. Don't reply to spam.
32. Use cc: field sparingly.

is also important for conveying the message properly. E-mails with no full stops or commas are difficult to read and can sometimes even change the meaning of the text. If your program has a spell checking option, why not use it?

4. ***Make it personal.***   Not only should the e-mail be personally addressed, it should also include personal or customized content. For this reason, auto replies are usually not very effective. However, templates can be used effectively in this way (see number 5).

5. ***Use templates for frequently used responses.***   Some questions you receive over and over again, such as directions to your office or how to complete an assignment. Save these texts as response templates and paste these into your message when you need them. You can save your templates in a Word document, or use preformatted e-mail. Even better is a tool such as ReplyMate for Outlook *(http://www.replymate.com)* that allows you to use 10 templates for free.

6. ***Answer swiftly.***   People send an e-mail because they wish to receive a quick response. If they did not want a quick response, they would have sent a letter or a fax. Therefore, each e-mail should be replied to within at least 24 hours of receipt, and preferably within the same working day. If the e-mail is complicated, just send an e-mail back saying that you have received it and that you will get back to them. This will put the person's mind at rest.

7. ***Do not attach unnecessary files.*** By sending large attachments you can annoy people and even cause their e-mail system to crash. Wherever possible, try to compress attachments and only send attachments when they are productive. Moreover, you need to have a good virus scanner in place since people will not be very happy if the documents you send contain viruses!

8. ***Use proper structure and layout.*** Since reading from a screen is more difficult than reading from the page, e-mail structure and layout is very important. Use short paragraphs, and add blank lines between each paragraph. When making points, number them or mark each point as separate to keep the overview.

9. ***Do not overuse the high priority option.*** We all know the story of the boy who cried wolf. If you overuse the high priority option, it will lose its function when you really need it. Moreover, even if an e-mail has high priority, your message will come across as slightly aggressive if you flag it as "high priority."

10. ***Do not write in CAPITALS.*** IF YOU WRITE IN CAPITALS IT SEEMS AS IF YOU ARE SHOUTING. This can be very annoying and might trigger an unwanted response in the form of a "flame" mail. Therefore, try not to send ANY e-mail text in capitals.

11. ***Don't leave out the message thread.*** When you reply to an e-mail, you must include the original mail in your reply; in other words, click "Reply," instead of "New Mail." If you receive many e-mails, you obviously cannot remember each individual e-mail. This means that a threadless e-mail will not provide enough information and you will have to spend a frustratingly long time to find out the context of the e-mail in order to deal with it. Leaving the thread might take a fraction longer in download time, but it will save the recipient much more time and frustration in looking for the related e-mail in their inbox!

12. ***Add disclaimers to your e-mail.*** It is important to add disclaimers to your internal and external mails, since this can help protect you from liability. Consider the following scenario: An employee accidentally forwards a virus to a customer by e-mail. The customer decides to sue your company for damages. If you add a disclaimer at the bottom of every external mail, saying that the recipient must check each e-mail for viruses and that the company cannot be held liable for any transmitted viruses, this will surely be of help to you in court. Another example is an employee who sues the company for allowing a racist e-mail to circulate the office. If your company has an e-mail policy in place and adds an e-mail disclaimer to every mail, stating that employees are expressly required not to make defamatory statements, you have a good case of proving that the company did everything it could to prevent offensive e-mail.

13. ***Read the e-mail before you send it.*** A lot of people don't bother to read an e-mail before they send it out, as the many spelling and grammar mistakes contained in e-mail attest. Apart from this, reading your e-mail through the eyes of the recipient will help you send a more effective message and avoid misunderstandings and inappropriate comments.

14. ***Do not overuse "Reply to All."*** Only use "Reply to All" if you really need your message to be seen by each person who received the original message.

15. ***Bulk mailings—use the Bcc: field or do a mail merge.*** When sending an e-mail bulk mailing, some people place all the e-mail addresses in the To: field. There are two drawbacks to this practice: (a) the recipient knows that you have sent the same message to a large number of recipients, and (b) you are publicizing someone else's e-mail address without their permission. One way to get around this is to place all addresses in the Bcc: field. However, the recipient would see only the address from the To: field in

their e-mail, so if this were empty, the To: field would be blank and this message may be misconstrued as spam. You could include the mailing list e-mail address in the To: field, or even better, if you have Microsoft Outlook and Word you can do a mail merge and create one message for each recipient. A mail merge also allows you to use fields in the message so that, for instance, you can address each recipient personally. For more information on how to do a Word mail merge, consult Help in Word.

16. ***Take care with abbreviations and emoticons.***   In business e-mail, try not to use abbreviations such as BTW (by the way) and LOL (laugh out loud). The recipient might not be aware of the meanings of the abbreviations and in business e-mail these are generally not appropriate. The same goes for emoticons, such as the smiley :-). If you are not sure whether your recipient knows what it means, it is better not to use it.

17. ***Be careful with formatting.***   Remember that when you use formatting in your e-mail, the sender might not be able to view such formatting, or might see different fonts from those you had intended. When using colors, use one that is easy to read on the background screen color.

18. ***Take care with rich text and HTML messages.***   Be aware that when you send an e-mail in rich text or HTML format, the sender might only be able to receive plain text e-mail. If this is the case, the recipient will receive your message as a .txt attachment. Most e-mail clients, however, including those with Microsoft Outlook, are able to receive HTML and rich text messages.

19. ***Do not forward chain letters.***   Do not forward chain letters. You can safely assume that all of them are hoaxes. If you receive them, just delete them.

20. ***Do not request delivery and read receipts.***   This will almost always annoy your recipient before he or she has even read your message. Besides, it usually does not work anyway, since the recipient may have blocked that function, or his or her software might not support it, so what is the use of using it? If you want to know whether an e-mail was received, it is better to ask the recipient to let you know if it was received.

21. ***Do not ask to recall a message.***   After an e-mail has been sent, in all likelihood it has already been delivered and read. A recall request would look very silly in that case, wouldn't it? It is better to send an e-mail to say that you have made a mistake. This will be much more honest than trying to recall a message.

22. ***Do not copy a message or attachment without permission.***   Do not copy a message or attachment belonging to another user without permission of the originator. If you do not ask permission first, you might be infringing on copyright laws.

23. ***Do not use e-mail to discuss confidential information.***   Sending an e-mail is like sending a postcard. If you don't want your e-mail to be displayed on a bulletin board, don't send it. Moreover, never make any libelous, sexist, or racially discriminating comments in e-mail, even if they are meant as a joke.

24. ***Use a meaningful subject.***   Try to use a subject that is meaningful to the recipient as well as yourself. For instance, when you send an e-mail to a company requesting information about a product, it is better to mention the actual name of the product, e.g., "Product A information" than to put a vague "product information" or the company's name in the subject.

25. ***Use active instead of passive voice.***   Try to use the active voice of a verb wherever possible. For instance, "I will set up the meeting today," sounds better than "Your request for a meeting will be processed today." The first sounds more personal, whereas the latter, especially when used frequently, sounds unnecessarily formal.

26. ***Avoid using URGENT and IMPORTANT.*** Even more so than the high-priority option, you must at all times try to avoid these kinds of words in an e-mail or subject line. Only use this if it is a really, really urgent or important message.

27. ***Avoid long sentences.*** Try to keep your sentences to a maximum of 15 to 20 words. E-mail is meant to be a quick medium and requires a different kind of writing than do letters. Also take care not to send e-mails that are too long. If a person receives an e-mail that looks like a dissertation, chances are that the e-mail will not be read!

28. ***Don't send or forward e-mail containing libelous, defamatory, offensive, racist, or obscene remarks.*** By sending or even just forwarding one libelous or offensive remark in an e-mail, you and your company can face court cases resulting in multimillion-dollar penalties.

29. ***Don't forward virus hoaxes.*** If you receive an e-mail message warning you of a new unstoppable virus that will immediately delete everything from your computer, this is most probably a hoax. By forwarding hoaxes, you use valuable bandwidth, and sometimes virus hoaxes contain viruses themselves, by attaching a "file" claiming to stop the dangerous virus. Even if the content seems to be bona fide, the senders are usually not. Since it is impossible to find out whether a virus warning is real or not, the best place for it is the delete bin until you can check it out with an expert.

30. ***Keep your language gender neutral.*** Avoid using sexist language such as "The user should add a signature by configuring *his* e-mail program." Apart from using he/she, you can also use the neutral gender: "The user should add a signature by configuring the e-mail program."

31. ***Don't reply to spam.*** By replying to spam or by unsubscribing, you are confirming that your e-mail address is "live." Confirming this will only generate even more spam. Therefore, just hit the delete button or use e-mail software to remove spam automatically or block it.

32. ***Use cc: field sparingly.*** Try not to use the cc: field unless the recipient in the cc: field knows why he or she is receiving a copy of the message. Using the cc: field can be confusing, since the recipients might not know who is supposed to act on the message. Also, when responding to a cc: message, should you include the other recipient in the cc: field as well? This will depend on the situation. In general, do not include the person in the cc: field unless you have a particular reason for wanting this person to see your response. Again, make sure that this person will know why he or she is receiving a copy.

HOW DO YOU ENFORCE E-MAIL ETIQUETTE?

The first step is to create a written e-mail policy, which should include all the do's and don'ts concerning the use of the company's e-mail system and should be distributed among all employees. Second, employees must be fully trained to understand the importance of e-mail etiquette. Finally, implementation of the rules can be monitored by using e-mail management software and e-mail response tools.

NOTES

1. Adapted from "E-Mail Etiquette,"
   http://www.emailreplies.com (September 30, 2003).

Glossary

ABC system a prioritizing approach developed by time management guru Alan Lakein in which tasks are given a value of A, B, or C, depending upon their urgency and importance.

Academy a type of organizational culture in which employees stay within a narrow specialty and are promoted after they thoroughly master a job.

Accommodation a conflict resolution approach of placing another's needs and concerns first in order to maintain a harmonious relationship.

Achievement motive the desire to perform tasks that will provide a sense of accomplishment.

Achievement-oriented leadership a highly task- and relationship-oriented leadership style that establishes challenging goals, seeks performance improvement, and displays confidence that people will exert high levels of effort.

Active listening the process of listening in which the listener refrains from evaluating other people's words, tries to see things from their point of view, and demonstrates a sincere effort to understand.

Adjourning the last of the five stages of team development in which the group goals have been met and the team is disbanded.

Affiliation motive the desire to perform tasks that provide satisfaction through quality social and interpersonal relationships.

Attending the ability of an active listener to send verbal, vocal, and visual messages to the speaker to indicate the listener's full attention.

Authority the right to give orders and expect the orders to be obeyed; the right to make decisions and commit organizational resources.

Avoidance a conflict resolution approach of withdrawing from or postponing the conflict.

Bargaining a process in which two or more parties exchange goods or services and attempt to agree upon the exchange rate for them; also known as negotiating.

Baseball team a type of organizational culture in which employees are rewarded for what they produce, and where risk taking and innovation are highly valued.

Behavior modification a technique of changing behavior through the use of contingent rewards or punishments.

Behaviors a set of criteria used in appraising performance in which individual actions are the basis of measurement.

Benchmark a specific level of performance against which actual results are measured and compared.

Bias occurs when managers develop feelings—positive, negative, or neutral—about employees based on work-related interactions that have little to do with worker performance.

Brainstorming a highly participative group decision-making process in which group members generate as many ideas as possible without criticism or evaluation of the ideas in order to accumulate a large number of solution alternatives that can be evaluated later for feasibility.

Cause-and-effect diagram a construction that represents the relationship between some effect and all possible causes influencing it; also known as a fishbone chart.

Central tendency the grouping of employee evaluation ratings at average or just above average on the performance scale even though employees do not perform the same all the time on specific tasks.

Certainty a situation in which the exact results of implementing a problem solution are known in advance.

Changing a phase of planned change that involves moving or actually altering the way things are done.

Closed-loop system the problem-solving process in that if performance fails to match the success criteria, the problem needs to be identified by again applying the problem-solving process.

Club a type of organizational culture in which employees are trained as generalists and promoted on the basis of seniority.

Coaching a problem-solving process that helps an employee in mastering skills and figuring out how to apply instructions.

Collaboration a conflict resolution approach in which all parties to the conflict seek to satisfy their interest through a solution that is advantageous to all parties.

Combined comparison an approach to evaluating an individual's performance by blending two or more of the comparison methods of evaluation.

Communication the process that occurs when one person sends a message to another with the intent of evoking a response.

Competitive strategy plans that provide a distinct advantage by capitalizing on the strengths of the organization and the industry it is in.

Compromise a conflict resolution approach that requires each party to give up something of value.

Conceptual skills the mental ability to analyze and diagnose complex situations.

Conflict a disagreement between two or more parties who perceive that they have incompatible concerns.

Continuous reinforcement to reward a desired behavior continuously each and every time it occurs.

Control the process of monitoring activities to ensure that they are accomplishing planned goals and of correcting any significant deviations.

Controlling the management function of monitoring performance, evaluating performance against organizational goals, and detecting and correcting any deviations.

Control process a system in which (1) actual performance is measured; (2) actual performance is compared against a standard; and (3) managerial actions are taken to correct any deviations or inadequate standards.

Co-optation influencing resistant parties to endorse the change effort by providing them with benefits they desire.

Cost leadership a competitive strategy in which the organization strives to be the low-cost producer in the industry.

Counseling a problem-solving process that helps employees deal with personal issues and attitudes.

Credibility others' perceptions of the degree to which an individual is honest, competent, forward looking, and inspiring.

Criteria specific, measurable, attainable, complementary, and ethical statements of objectives that need to be met for a problem to be solved.

Culture the key characteristics that the organization values and that distinguish it from other organizations.

Decision making the process of selecting the best solution from among feasible alternatives.

Decode the process of perceiving a communication and interpreting its meaning.

Delegation the transfer of authority from a manager to a subordinate for achieving goals and making decisions about how to do a job.

Delphi technique an independent group decision-making process in which participants at their own individual locations write and then pool a variety of ideas that they may comment on and eventually vote to give a specific solution priority.

Differentiation a competitive strategy in which the organization seeks to be unique in its industry in ways that are widely valued by buyers.

Directive leadership a highly task-oriented leadership style that lets followers know what is expected of them, provides guidance as to what is to be done and how, clarifies performance standards and schedules, and calls attention to work procedures and policies.

Distinctive competence unique skills or resources that give an organization a competitive edge.

Distributive bargaining a negotiation process that operates under a zero-sum condition, that is, any party's gain comes at the expense of the other party.

Diversity the individual variations in the values, needs, interests, and expectations of a group of people.

Emotion-focused strategies a category of stress management techniques that deal with stressors by modifying negative reactions to stressful situations, and that allow individuals to feel more optimistic and self-confident.

Employee-oriented behavior a pattern of organizational actions that aims to satisfy social and emotional needs of group members.

Empower the process of encouraging and providing tools to another to complete a task.

Encode the process of putting a message in a format that the receiver will understand.

Environmental scanning the process in which managers look outside their organization to ensure that their goals align well with current and future environments.

Environmental stressors economic, political, and technological factors that affect a person's well-being but are outside of that person's control, potentially causing worry and concern.

Equity theory a theory suggesting that motivation is moderated by the perceived fairness or discrepancy between personal contributions and rewards relative to others.

Ethical guideposts company policies on ethics that describe what the organization perceives as ethical behavior and what it expects its stakeholders, specifically its workers, to do.

Ethics the rules or principles that define right and wrong conduct.

Experiential learning model a theory stating that the development of behavioral skills comes from observation and practice.

Extinction a process of not rewarding or acknowledging undesired behavior so that it will cease to occur.

Extrinsic rewards rewards that are externally bestowed, such as praise, monetary compensation, or promotion.

Extrovert a person characterized by an interest in the outer world, a responsiveness to external events, a desire to influence and be influenced by events, and a strong association with image.

Feedback a primary tool for determining how clearly a message was understood and what effect it had on the receiver.

Filtering selectively omitting certain information from messages that are sent.

Flextime a work schedule that allows workers some discretion over when they arrive at and leave work; short for "flexible hours."

Flowchart a pictorial representation of all the steps of a process.

Focus a competitive strategy in which an organization seeks uniqueness in a narrow market segment, or niche.

Focusing on activities occurs when a manager rates employees on how busy they appear versus how well they perform in achieving results.

Forcing a conflict resolution approach that attempts to satisfy personal needs at the expense of the other party; used when quick resolutions on important issues are needed or where unpopular actions must be taken.

Formal leaders individuals who hold positions of authority through office or title.

Forming the first of five stages of team development in which a group of people comes together to answer questions as to a team's purpose, its resources, its ground rules, roles, timelines, and accountability, and its authority.

Fortress a type of organizational culture in which employees who can reverse the organization's sagging fortunes are rewarded.

Gantt chart a graphic planning and control method that breaks down a project into separate tasks and estimates the time needed for their completion.

Goal the specific desired outcome of individual, group, or organizational action.

Group two or more people who meet regularly over a period of time, who perceive themselves as a distinct entity, who share common values, and who strive for common objectives.

Group decision support systems electronic and computer-supported data processing tools that can facilitate group decision making in certain situations.

Group order ranking an evaluation of an individual's performance by comparing it against all employees' performances and then placing it in a particular hierarchical classification.

Groupthink a phenomenon that occurs when group members' desire to agree is so great that it tends to override the concern for realistic appraisal of alternative courses of action.

Habit a familiar action or event that is continued because it is familiar even when it may not be optimal.

Halo effect occurs when a manager's positive feelings about an employee influence the performance ratings for that employee more positively in all areas because of outstanding performance in a single area.

Horizontal scheduling the determination of what an individual will be doing over the longer term, as in the next month or the next week.

Horns effect occurs when a manager's negative feelings about an employee influence the performance ratings for that employee more negatively in all areas because of unfavorable performance in a single area.

Human resources management (HRM) the title or department under which much of an organization's staffing activities are grouped.

Impression management an individual's process of shaping the image projected during interactions with others in order to favorably influence how others see and evaluate that individual.

Individual ranking an approach to evaluating an individual's performance by placing that employee in a rank-order from best to worst.

Individual task outcomes a set of criteria used in appraising performance in which ends rather than means are the basis for measurement.

Informal leaders individuals who inspire new ideas or champion causes without the benefit of formal authority.

Integrative bargaining a negotiation process that operates under the assumption that at least one settlement exists that can create a win-win solution.

Intermediate goals the steps that are required in order to accomplish long-term lifetime goals.

Intermittent reinforcement the reward for a desired behavior on a random basis that is frequent enough to encourage the person to continue performing the desired behavior.

Interpersonal skills the ability to work with, understand, and motivate other people, both individually and in groups.

Intrinsic rewards an individual's personal feelings about how well a task was performed or simply the satisfaction of completing the task.

Introvert a person who is introspective and preoccupied with personal thoughts and reflections.

Job burnout a feeling of exhaustion that develops when an individual simultaneously experiences too much pressure and too few sources of satisfaction.

Job characteristics model (JCM) the description of a job according to its skill variety, task identity, task significance, autonomy, and feedback.

Job description a listing of activities to be performed by an employee, how they are done, and why they are done.

Job design the way tasks are combined to form complete jobs.

Job enlargement an approach that attempts to overcome the drawbacks of specialization by horizontally expanding a job and increasing job scope, or the number of different tasks required within the job.

Job enrichment an approach that attempts to design more meaning and challenge into jobs by adding planning and evaluation responsibilities, thereby increasing job depth and employees' control over their own work.

Job sharing a work arrangement that allows two or more people to split a traditional 40-hour-a-week job.

Job specification a listing of the minimal acceptable qualifications that an employee must have to successfully perform the job.

Known risk the probability that a given alternative will produce specific outcomes as predicted.

Leading the management function of directing people and coordinating their efforts through motivating them, resolving their conflicts, and selecting effective communication channels.

Leniency the grouping of employee evaluation ratings at the positive end of the performance scale in which employees are rated higher than actual performance warrants.

Lifetime goals achievements a person wishes to bring about in the areas of career, family, religion, recreation, and relationships during the person's life.

Management by objectives (MBO) a management system in which subordinates and supervisors apply goal-setting skills in jointly determining specific performance objectives, which are then periodically reviewed and rewarded according to progress toward those goals.

Management function the activities of planning, organizing, leading, and controlling that are typically performed by organizational leaders in order to meet the organization's goals.

Management skills the abilities or behaviors that are crucial to success in a managerial position, including planning, organizing, leading, controlling, and evaluating.

Managers organizational members who oversee the activities of other people with the purpose of accomplishing organizational goals.

Manipulation framing and selectively using information and implied incentives to maximize the likelihood of acceptance.

Maslow's hierarchy of needs Maslow's proposal that all individuals have a five-level hierarchy of needs that they attempt to satisfy, beginning with physical well-being, and progressing successively through safety, belonging, esteem, and self-actualization.

Mentoring guiding a less experienced associate toward improved performance.

Merit pay compensation that is tied to output over which the employee has control.

Mission statement an articulation that defines an organization's purpose and answers the questions: Why do we exist? What do we do? What business are we in?

Morale the team's motivation, confidence, and cohesion.

Motivation the conscious decision to direct effort in an activity to achieve a goal that will satisfy a predominate need.

Negative reinforcement occurs when a punishment is applied in order to eliminate an undesired behavior.

Negotiation a process in which two or more parties exchange goods or services and attempt to agree upon the exchange rate for them; also known as bargaining.

Niche a unique set of opportunities that provide an organization with a competitive advantage.

Noise anything that interferes, at any stage, with the communication process.

Nominal group technique a highly structured group decision-making process in which participants write ideas independently; the ideas are then evaluated and ranked, with the alternative with the highest ranking being the solution of choice.

Norming the third of five stages of team development in which members agree on a structure, experience increased morale and commitment, and communicate more openly as they work toward the team's goals.

Objectives the desired outcomes for individuals, groups, or entire organizations.

Operational plans plans, usually short term in nature, that specify the details of how the overall objectives in the strategic plan are to be achieved.

Opportunities situations that an organization can take advantage of in working to meet its goals.

Organizing the management function that involves designing an organization's structure: determining what tasks are to be done, who is to do them, how tasks are to be grouped, who reports to whom, and where decisions are made in the organization.

Overload the experience of a person who is expected to accomplish more than ability or time permits.

Paired comparison an approach to evaluating an individual's performance by comparing that person with every other employee and rating the employee as either superior or weaker in comparison.

Participative leadership a moderately task-oriented and highly relationship-oriented leadership style that involves consulting with and soliciting the ideas of others in decision making and action taking.

Path-goal theory an approach to leadership in which leaders motivate through clarification of employees' pathways to meet organizational goals and through providing meaningful rewards.

Perceiving becoming aware of ideas, facts, and occurrences.

Performance appraisal a managerial assessment of a worker's actions and productivity and the worker's effectiveness in meeting specific goals of the organization.

Performing the fourth of five stages of team development in which team members work to solve problems and are committed to the group's mission.

Piecework system a reward system based on payment for the amount produced consistent with specified quality standards.

Planning the management function that encompasses defining an organization's goals, establishing an overall strategy for achieving those goals, and developing a comprehensive hierarchy of plans to integrate and coordinate activities.

Politicking taking actions to influence, or attempt to influence, the distribution of advantages and disadvantages within an organization.

Positive reinforcement occurs when a reward is given after a desired behavior.

Power motive the desire to perform tasks that will provide satisfaction from being in charge and controlling and influencing others.

Problem-focused strategies a category of stress management techniques that deals directly with stressors by either removing or changing them.

Problem solving the process of eliminating the discrepancy between actual and desired outcomes.

Productivity a team's ability to work together and achieve results.

Punishments an organization's negative response to employees' undesirable behavior, which employees generally try to avoid.

Recency emphasis performance evaluations that are based on the most recent work performance rather than the performance of the entire evaluation period.

Referent power the influence of a person's image over others' behavior or values.

Reflecting summarizing and giving feedback to the speaker about the content and feeling of the speaker's message.

Reframing changing personal perception from being helpless to being in control of altering the situation to cope with life stressors.

Refreezing a phase of planned change in which changes that have been made are reinforced, causing desired attitudes and behaviors to become a natural, self-reinforcing pattern.

Relationship behaviors aspects of the situational leadership model that include maintaining personal relationships through opening channels of communication, providing socio-emotional support, and facilitating productive behaviors.

Reliability the extent to which a selection device measures the same thing consistently.

Restraining forces the factors that exert pressure on an organization to continue past behaviors or to resist new actions.

Rewards organizational behavior or recognition that employees value and that may motivate performance.

Role ambiguity occurs when a worker is expected to work without a clear understanding of job definition, performance expectations, or consequences of behavior.

Role analysis technique a definition of a group member's role based on the individual's analysis of the rationale, significance, and specific duties of the role.

Role conflict a situation that occurs when an individual's duties or responsibilities conflict with one another.

Role profile a summary of a group member's activities and obligations to the group.

Rushing occurs when a manager hurries through the appraisal process because of insufficient time or a heavy workload.

Satisficing choosing the first satisfactory alternative that meets minimal requirements.

Selective perception a person's interpretation of an idea or event based on how the individual is personally affected.

Semantics the meanings and uses of words.

Sensing the ability to recognize the silent messages that the speaker is sending.

Short-term goals the steps that are compatible and contribute to the next longer-term goal.

Small-wins strategy a method of breaking a large, perhaps overwhelming situation into smaller parts that are more likely to be attained and provide visible success on the way to accomplishing the larger task.

Smoothing a means of providing conflicting groups with some incentive to repress their conflict and avoid its open expression.

Social audits an evaluation of the organization's decisions and practices according to a code of ethics.

Social information processing model (SIP) the description of a job based on the attitudes and behaviors of employees in response to social feedback provided by others.

Social loafing a reduction in a group member's input to the group based on the reasoning that individual contributions, or lack of, cannot be identified.

Stakeholders an organization's employees, managers, stockholders, suppliers, customers, and regulators.

Standard-hour plan a pay-for-performance system in which the normal time required to complete the task is associated with a standard rate of pay.

Storming the second of five stages of team development in which the team needs to resolve conflicts about power and task structure.

Strategic plans overall objectives determined by top-level managers, which set out the long-term focus and direction of the entire organization.

Strengths an organization's available internal resources or things that an organization does well.

Stress the body's psychological, emotional, and physiological response to any demand perceived as threatening to a person's well-being.

Suboptimization a lower than desired performance level caused by differences in functional orientation, goals, and resources dependencies among organizational units that may influence acceptance or rejection of changes based on perceptions of self-preservation.

Superordinate goal an overriding goal that requires the cooperative effort of conflicting groups.

Supportive leadership a highly relationship-oriented leadership style that shows concern for the needs and goals of others and strives to make the work situation pleasant and equitable.

SWOT analysis an examination of the fit between an organization's strengths and weaknesses, and the environmental opportunities and threats.

Synergy coordinated joint efforts that result in more than the sum of the individual efforts.

Task behaviors aspects of the situational leadership model that include organizing and defining roles, explaining activities, and establishing structure, channels of communication, and methods of getting jobs done.

Team a group with complementary skills, who are committed to a common purpose, a set of performance goals, and an approach for which they hold themselves mutually accountable.

Technical skills the ability to apply specialized knowledge or expertise.

Telecommuting a work arrangement in which employees do their tasks at home or on the road using a computer linked to the office.

Threats environmental situations that may endanger an organization's ability to meet its goals.

Training in management skills (TIMS) a 10-step training program for acquiring managerial skills, based on the experiential learning model.

Traits a set of criteria used in appraising performance in which individual characteristics are the basis of measurement.

Transactional leaders leaders who perform the management functions of planning, directing, controlling, budgeting, and measuring results.

Transformational leaders leaders with the ability to lead changes in the organization's vision, strategy, and culture as well as promote innovation in products and technologies.

Transmit the process of sending a message to a receiver, whether in oral, nonverbal, written, or electronic format.

Turbulence the irregularity of a rapidly changing environment in which decision makers are not clear about relevant variables, available solution options, or potential consequences of decisions.

Uncertainty a situation in which decision makers are unable to assign any probabilities to the consequences associated with an alternative.

Underutilization occurs when an organization requires less of a person's time or abilities than the person is able to and wants to give or perform.

Unfreezing a phase of planned change in which leaders help people to see that change is needed and motivate employees to make those needed changes.

Validity the characteristic of a selection device that demonstrates a proven relationship between the device and some relevant criterion.

Value judgments an evaluation based on a message hearer's own experience or culture.

Values enduring personal beliefs about what is worthwhile.

Vertical scheduling an individually developed daily plan for what the person will do and when it will be done.

Weaknesses activities that an organization does not do well or resources it needs but does not possess.

Index